The Tree of Life
EXPANDED EDITION

*The life and teachings of
the Lord Jesus Christ,
as recorded in the Gospels of
the King James Version of
the Holy Bible.*

*Merged into one story and
arranged for ease of reading.*

Gregory J. Madsen

2020
Penny Farthing Publishing

Copyright © 2020 Penny Farthing Publishing

All rights reserved. No part of this publication may be reproduced, distributed, stored in any retrieval system or transmitted in any form or by any means, whether electronically or mechanically, including photocopying, recording, or otherwise, without the prior written consent from the copyright holder, except in the case of brief quotations in a book review and certain other noncommercial uses permitted by copyright law. For permission requests, contact the publisher at PennyFarthing.pub. The Penny Farthing logo is a trademark of Penny Farthing Publishing.

www.PennyFarthing.pub

ISBN: 978-1-9525-2700-5 (Paperback Edition)
ISBN: 978-1-9525-2701-2 (Digital Edition)
ISBN: 978-1-9525-2702-9 (Paperback - Expanded Edition)
ISBN: 978-1-9525-2703-6 (Digital - Expanded Edition)

Printed in the United States of America.

Cover Photo by Sumner Mahaffey on Unsplash
Cover and Map Design by Gregory J. Madsen

Publisher's Note: The views and opinions expressed herein are those of the author and do not necessarily reflect the views of the publisher. Every effort has been made to ensure the faithfulness of the information presented in this book. The publisher will not assume liability for damages caused by the use of, or reliance upon, any of the information contained herein and makes no warranty whatsoever, whether express or implied. Comments and corrections from readers will be considered for incorporation in future editions. Every effort has been made to trace copyright holders and seek permission to use illustrative and other material.

THE TREE OF LIFE

Table of Contents

Foreword	i
Map of the Holy Land	vii
Epigraph	1
Prologue	3
Chapter One	5
Chapter Two	19
Chapter Three	23
Chapter Four	29
Chapter Five	33
Chapter Six	37
Chapter Seven	39
Chapter Eight	41
Chapter Nine	45
Chapter Ten	47
Chapter Eleven	53
Chapter Twelve	57
Chapter Thirteen	59
Chapter Fourteen	61
Chapter Fifteen	65
Chapter Sixteen	89
Chapter Seventeen	93
Chapter Eighteen	95
Chapter Nineteen	97
Chapter Twenty	103
Chapter Twenty One	107
Chapter Twenty Two	109
Chapter Twenty Three	115
Chapter Twenty Four	119
Chapter Twenty Five	121
Chapter Twenty Six	127
Chapter Twenty Seven	133
Chapter Twenty Eight	135
Chapter Twenty Nine	143
Chapter Thirty	145
Chapter Thirty One	147
Chapter Thirty Two	151
Chapter Thirty Three	153
Chapter Thirty Four	155
Chapter Thirty Five	157
Chapter Thirty Six	161
Chapter Thirty Seven	163
Chapter Thirty Eight	171
Chapter Thirty Nine	175
Chapter Forty	177
Chapter Forty One	179
Chapter Forty Two	181
Chapter Forty Three	185
Chapter Forty Four	189
Chapter Forty Five	193
Chapter Forty Six	195
Chapter Forty Seven	207
Chapter Forty Eight	209
Chapter Forty Nine	215
Chapter Fifty	219
Chapter Fifty One	225
Chapter Fifty Two	231
Chapter Fifty Three	235
Chapter Fifty Four	239
Chapter Fifty Five	241
Chapter Fifty Six	243
Chapter Fifty Seven	245
Chapter Fifty Eight	247
Chapter Fifty Nine	251
Chapter Sixty	255
Chapter Sixty One	259
Chapter Sixty Two	263
Chapter Sixty Three	271
Chapter Sixty Four	275
Chapter Sixty Five	279
Chapter Sixty Six	283
Chapter Sixty Seven	285
Chapter Sixty Eight	287
Chapter Sixty Nine	295
Chapter Seventy	297
Chapter Seventy One	299
Chapter Seventy Two	301
Chapter Seventy Three	319
Chapter Seventy Four	335
Chapter Seventy Five	337
Chapter Seventy Six	339
Chapter Seventy Seven	349
Chapter Seventy Eight	355
Chapter Seventy Nine	357
Chapter Eighty	363
Chapter Eighty One	367
Chapter Eighty Two	369
Chapter Eighty Three	375
Chapter Eighty Four	377
Chapter Eighty Five	379
Chapter Eighty Six	385
Chapter Eighty Seven	389
Chapter Eighty Eight	391
Chapter Eighty Nine	395
Chapter Ninety	399
Epilogue	407
Appendix	409
Afterword	413

Foreword

Roughly two millennia ago, the life and teachings of Jesus of Nazareth were documented in the form we recognize today as the four Gospels of the New Testament of the Holy Bible. While much has been written since then about this unique teacher, and countless sects have branched from this common source, the common language shared by all true disciples is, of necessity, the direct teachings of the Master. These predate the many councils and creeds honestly striving to understand and codify such profound wisdom, so contrary to the baser instinctual mind.

This book is an attempt at a consolidation of the four gospels from a layman's perspective. My goal is to be able to present the story of Jesus in a format more familiar to the modern reader, in the flow of events and ideas from one to the next in some form of logical succession, with the objective of its reading more like a novel. While the expert will no doubt find it wanting, to the average reader my hope is that it will clarify and magnify their understanding of this, as it has been called, the greatest story ever told. There is a rich contextual background in the earlier Jewish traditions and knowledge found in the books of the Old Testament and the Apocrypha. I am given to understand that the books of the Apocrypha were included between the Old and New Testaments in some early editions of the King James Bible and this, among other reasons, is why I chose this version. Additionally, since Jesus quotes directly the Apocrypha, and states in Luke 16:16 that "the law and the prophets were until John [the baptist]" as opposed to "the law and the prophets were until Malachi," I therefore view the KJV deuterocanonical books as authoritatively scriptural on a par with the Old Testament. However, as the timing or authenticity of the Apocrypha is questionable to some, quotes from Apocryphal books appear in the footnotes with their book names being italicized to segregate them from the Old Testament verses.

My goal in this book was to use as references only those scriptures which appeared previous to the Gospels in the expanded KJV Bible as source material, with one exception in Chapter 19 wherein a small section of Luke's Gospel is quoted. I have attempted to include every relevant and related Old Testament and Apocrypha scripture of which I am aware. I am sure it is by no means fully inclusive. I have also included duplicate references where the context requires to eliminate the reader's need to look for the last time it was quoted.

For the sake of transparency, in the Afterword is presented every one of the 3,779 verses from the four Gospels used in the construction of this book in the order in which I have rearranged them. Other than their arrangement, each verse in the Afterword is otherwise untouched. My text and the originals are therefore easily comparable to the interested reader.

While great liberty has been taken in order to attempt a logical progression using the available chronological or contextual indicators given to the events referenced throughout the story, the reader should otherwise find great consistency and internal continuity. Of necessity judgment calls must be made in any such attempt, and certainly others would arrange the verses differently. But this is not meant to be a perfect and exact stitching together, such a thing is impossible in the absence of additional verified and authoritative ancient texts becoming available. The goal of this imperfect work is simply to be *good enough*; to attempt to bring these four versions of the same story into some form of harmony, that the reader may be profited thereby.

In organizing, I prioritized teachings over semantics. For example, Matthew's Sermon on the Mount and Luke's Sermon on the Plain are valuable because of what they say, and far less due to where they might have occurred.

While taking great care to leave the actual text as close to its original reading as possible, once arranged, I did take the liberty of merging repetitive sayings, along with standardizing punctuation and capitalization, and inserting very minimal clarifying contextual additions. Also, as the authors of the Gospels used the Greek version of the Old Testament (the Septuagint) for their quotes therefrom, some of the actual wording varies greatly from the more familiar Hebrew sourced versions present in the footnotes citing Old Testament passages.

Another consequence of the New Testament being translated from the Greek is that the spelling of proper names found in the Gospels follows the Greek. Therefore, to ensure consistency, I have standardized the majority of the proper names to those found in the Old Testament, which have a Hebrew linguistic origin. For example, the very common Elias becomes Elijah, Noe becomes Noah, Jeremy becomes Jeremiah, and so on. The exceptions to this are the genealogies contained in the Appendix, which retain the original Greek leaning proper names; and for obvious reasons, Jesus and the apostles' names retain their more familiar New Testament spellings.

While some parts of the story were rather difficult to assemble without clear contradiction from the various sources, for the most part, I used the 'majority rules' method wherever it was available. For instance, the story of the transfiguration has three versions regarding its timing, Matthew 17:1 and Mark 9:2 both say "after six days" later while Luke 9:28 says it was "about an eight days" later; in which case, I use the more sure footed six days figure.

The Map of the Holy Land is included for study and informational purposes only, and while every reasonable effort towards accuracy was taken in its creation, everything within it should be viewed as approximations only.

I am releasing two versions of this book. In comparison to this expanded version, the other version contains only the story as I have arranged it, with all footnotes and the Afterword removed for the sake of simplicity.

Finally, it should be emphasized that I am a layman. I have no formal clerical training and, as referenced above, the outcome of this attempt would be very different if undertaken by one with such an education. As with many similar projects, I started this one purely as a learning tool for myself, but as it reaches its final form, I feel it important to share it.

I hope this book will be of some value to the reader, it certainly has been to me.

— G. J. Madsen
January 1, 2020

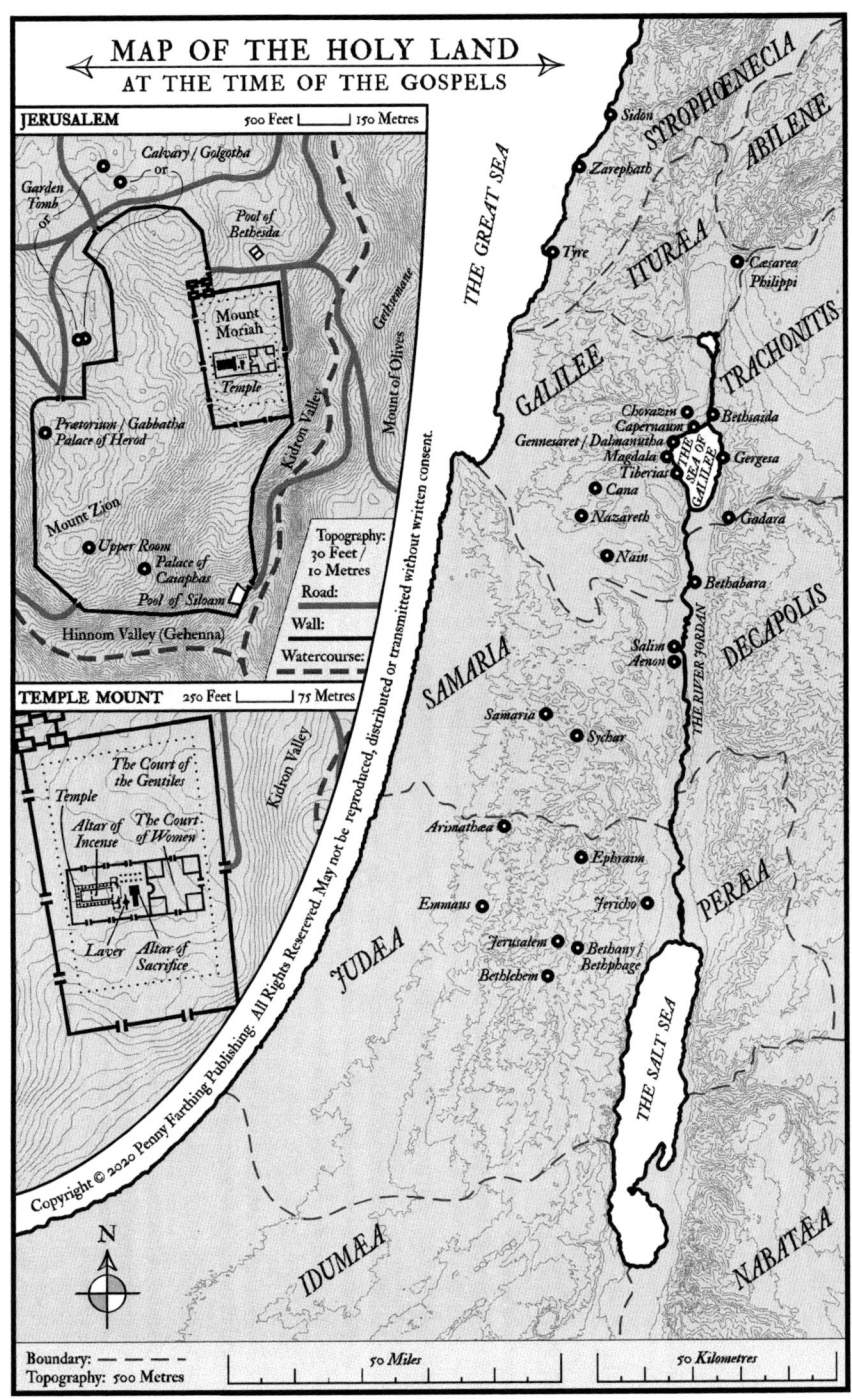

THE TREE OF LIFE

Epigraph

*In the beginning[1] was the Word,
and the Word was with God,
and the Word was God.
The same was in the beginning with God.
All things were made by him, and without him
was not any thing made that was made.[2]
In him was life, and the life was the light of men.[3]
And the light shineth in darkness, and the
darkness comprehended it not.[4]*

---

[1] Compare <u>Genesis 1:1</u>: "In the beginning God created the heaven and the earth."

[2] Compare <u>Psalms 33:6,9</u>: "By the word of the LORD were the heavens made; and all the host of them by the breath of his mouth. For he spake, and it was done; he commanded, and it stood fast."
<u>Nehemiah 9:6</u>: "Thou, even thou, art LORD alone; thou hast made heaven, the heaven of heavens, with all their host, the earth, and all things that are therein, the seas, and all that is therein, and thou preservest them all; and the host of heaven worshippeth thee."
<u>Wisdom 9:1</u>: "O God of my fathers, and Lord of mercy, who hast made all things with thy word,"

[3] Compare <u>Proverbs 20:27</u>: "The spirit of man is the candle of the LORD, searching all the inward parts of the belly."

[4] Compare <u>Isaiah 9:2</u>: "The people that walked in darkness have seen a great light; they that dwell in the land of the shadow of death, upon them hath the light shined."
<u>Exodus 10:21</u>: "And the LORD said unto Moses, 'Stretch out thine hand toward heaven, that there may be darkness over the land of Egypt, even darkness which may be felt.' And Moses stretched forth his hand toward heaven; and there was a thick darkness in all the land of Egypt three days. They saw not one another, neither rose any from his place for three days; but all the children of Israel had light in their dwellings."
<u>Exodus 14:19</u>: "And the angel of God, which went before the camp of Israel, removed and went behind them; and the pillar of the cloud went from before their face, and stood behind them. And it came between the camp of the Egyptians and the camp of Israel; and it was a cloud and darkness to [the Egyptians], but it gave light by night to [the Israelites]; so that the one came not near the other all the night."

THE TREE OF LIFE

Prologue

The beginning of the gospel of Jesus Christ, the Son of God: Forasmuch as many have taken in hand to set forth in order a declaration of those things which are most surely believed among us, even as they delivered them unto us, which from the beginning were eyewitnesses and ministers of the word, it seemed good to me also, having had perfect understanding of all things from the very first, to write unto thee in order that thou mightest know the certainty of those things wherein thou hast been instructed.

THE TREE OF LIFE

THE TREE OF LIFE

Chapter One

There was in the days of Herod, the king of Judaea, a certain priest named Zacharias, of the course of Abijah,[5] and his wife was of the daughters of Aaron, and her name was Elisabeth. And they were both righteous before God, walking in all the commandments and ordinances of the Lord blameless. And they had no child, because that Elisabeth was barren, and they both were now well stricken in years.

And it came to pass, that while he executed the priest's office before God in the order of his course, according to the custom of the priest's office, his lot was to burn incense[6] when he went into the temple of the Lord. And the whole multitude of the people were praying without at the time of incense. And there appeared unto him an angel of the Lord standing on the right side of the altar of incense. And when Zacharias saw him, he was troubled, and fear fell upon him. But the angel said unto him, "Fear not, Zacharias, for thy

---

[5] See 1 Chronicles 24:7-10,19: "Now the first lot came forth to Jehoiarib, the second to Jedaiah, the third to Harim, the fourth to Seorim, the fifth to Malchijah, the sixth to Mijamin, the seventh to Hakkoz, the eighth to Abijah. These were the orderings of them in their service to come into the house of the LORD, according to their manner, under Aaron their father, as the LORD God of Israel had commanded him."

[6] See Exodus 30:7-8: "And Aaron shall burn thereon sweet incense every morning; when he dresseth the lamps, he shall burn incense upon it. And when Aaron lighteth the lamps at even, he shall burn incense upon it, a perpetual incense before the LORD throughout your generations."

THE TREE OF LIFE

prayer is heard,[7] and thy wife Elisabeth shall bear thee a son, and thou shalt call his name John.[8] And thou shalt have joy and gladness, and many shall rejoice at his birth, for he shall be great in the sight of the Lord, and shall drink neither wine nor strong drink,[9] and he shall be filled with the Holy Ghost, even from his mother's womb.

---

[7] Compare 1 Samuel 1:9-11,17,20,24,26-28: "So Hannah rose up after they had eaten in Shiloh, and after they had drunk. Now Eli the priest sat upon a seat by a post of the temple of the LORD. And she was in bitterness of soul, and prayed unto the LORD, and wept sore. And she vowed a vow, and said, 'O LORD of hosts, if thou wilt indeed look on the affliction of thine handmaid, and remember me, and not forget thine handmaid, but wilt give unto thine handmaid a man child, then I will give him unto the LORD all the days of his life, and there shall no razor come upon his head.' Then Eli answered and said, 'Go in peace; and the God of Israel grant thee thy petition that thou hast asked of him.' Wherefore it came to pass, when the time was come about after Hannah had conceived, that she bare a son, and called his name Samuel, saying, 'Because I have asked him of the LORD.' And when she had weaned him, she took him up with her, with three bullocks, and one ephah of flour, and a bottle of wine, and brought him unto the house of the LORD in Shiloh; and the child was young. And she said, 'Oh my lord, as thy soul liveth, my lord, I am the woman that stood by thee here, praying unto the LORD. For this child I prayed; and the LORD hath given me my petition which I asked of him. Therefore also I have lent him to the LORD; as long as he liveth he shall be lent to the LORD. And he worshipped the LORD there.'"

[8] Compare Genesis 16:11: "And the angel of the LORD said unto her, 'Behold, thou art with child, and shalt bear a son, and shalt call his name Ishmael; because the LORD hath heard thy affliction.'"

[9] Compare Judges 13:2-5: "And there was a certain man of Zorah, of the family of the Danites, whose name was Manoah; and his wife was barren, and bare not. And the angel of the LORD appeared unto the woman, and said unto her, 'Behold now, thou art barren, and bearest not; but thou shalt conceive, and bear a son. Now therefore beware, I pray thee, and drink not wine nor strong drink, and eat not any unclean thing. For, lo, thou shalt conceive, and bear a son; and no razor shall come on his head; for the child shall be a Nazarite unto God from the womb; and he shall begin to deliver Israel out of the hand of the Philistines.'"
Numbers 6:1-3,5: "And the LORD spake unto Moses, saying, 'Speak unto the children of Israel, and say unto them, "When either man or woman shall separate themselves to vow a vow of a Nazarite, to separate themselves unto the LORD; he shall separate himself from wine and strong drink, and shall drink no vinegar of wine, or vinegar of strong drink, neither shall he drink any liquor of grapes, nor eat moist grapes, or dried. All the days of the vow of his separation there shall no razor come upon his head; until the days be fulfilled, in the which he separateth himself unto the LORD, he shall be holy, and shall let the locks of the hair of his head grow."'"
See also Numbers 6:1-21.

And many of the children of Israel shall he turn to the Lord their God. And he shall go before him in the spirit and power of Elijah, *to turn the hearts of the fathers to the children*,[10] and the disobedient to the wisdom of the just, to make ready a people prepared for the Lord." And Zacharias said unto the angel, "Whereby shall I know this, for I am an old man, and my wife well stricken in years?"[11] And the angel answering said unto him, "I am Gabriel, that stand in the presence of God, and am sent to speak unto thee, and to shew thee these glad tidings. And, behold, thou shalt be dumb,[12] and not able to speak, until the day that these things shall be performed, because thou believest not my words, which shall be fulfilled in their season."

And the people waited for Zacharias, and marvelled that he tarried so long in the temple. And when he came out, he could not speak unto them, and they perceived that he had seen a vision in the temple, for he beckoned unto them, and remained speechless.

And it came to pass, that, as soon as the days of his ministration were accomplished, he departed to his own house. And after those days his wife Elisabeth conceived, and hid herself five months, saying, "Thus hath the Lord dealt with me in the days wherein he looked on me, to take away my reproach among men."[13]

---

[10] See Malachi 4:5-6: "Behold, I will send you Elijah the prophet before the coming of the great and dreadful day of the LORD. And he shall turn the heart of the fathers to the children, and the heart of the children to their fathers, lest I come and smite the earth with a curse."
[11] Compare Genesis 18:10-12: "And he said, 'I will certainly return unto thee according to the time of life; and, lo, Sarah thy wife shall have a son.' And Sarah heard it in the tent door, which was behind him. Now Abraham and Sarah were old and well stricken in age; and it ceased to be with Sarah after the manner of women. Therefore Sarah laughed within herself, saying, 'After I am waxed old shall I have pleasure, my lord being old also?'"
[12] Compare Ezekiel 3:26: "And I will make thy tongue cleave to the roof of thy mouth, that thou shalt be dumb, and shalt not be to them a reprove; for they are a rebellious house."
[13] Compare Genesis 29:31, 30:22-23: "And when the LORD saw that Leah was hated, he opened her womb; but Rachel was barren. And God remembered Rachel,

THE TREE OF LIFE

And in the sixth month the angel Gabriel was sent from God unto a city of Galilee, named Nazareth, to a virgin espoused to a man whose name was Joseph, of the house of David, and the virgin's name was Mary. And the angel came in unto her, and said, "Hail, thou that art highly favoured, the Lord is with thee,[14] blessed art thou among women." And when she saw him, she was troubled at his saying, and cast in her mind what manner of salutation this should be. And the angel said unto her, "Fear not, Mary, for thou hast found favour with God. And, behold, thou shalt conceive in thy womb, and bring forth a son, and shalt call his name JESUS.[15] He shall be great, and shall be called the Son of the Highest, and the Lord God shall give unto him the throne of his father David, and he shall reign over the house of Jacob for ever, and of his kingdom there shall be no end."[16] Then said Mary unto the angel, "How shall this be, seeing I know not a man?" And the angel answered and said unto her, "The Holy Ghost shall come upon thee, and the power of the Highest shall overshadow thee,[17] therefore also that holy thing

---

and God hearkened to her, and opened her womb. And she conceived, and bare a son; and said, 'God hath taken away my reproach.'"
See also Genesis 11:29-30, 17:15-22, 18:1,9-15, 21:1-7 (Sarah/Isaac); Genesis 25:21 (Rebekah/Jacob); Genesis 30:22-24 (Rachel/Joseph); Judges 13:2-24 (Samson); 1 Samuel 1:1-28 (Samuel).
[14] Compare Judges 6:12: "And the angel of the LORD appeared unto him, and said unto him, 'The LORD is with thee, thou mighty man of valour.'"
[15] Compare Genesis 17:19: "And God said, 'Sarah thy wife shall bear thee a son indeed; and thou shalt call his name Isaac; and I will establish my covenant with him for an everlasting covenant, and with his seed after him.'"
2 Esdras 7:28: "For my son Jesus shall be revealed with those that be with him, and they that remain shall rejoice within four hundred years."
[16] Compare Isaiah 9:6-7: "For unto us a child is born, unto us a son is given; and the government shall be upon his shoulder; and his name shall be called Wonderful, Counsellor, The mighty God, The everlasting Father, The Prince of Peace. Of the increase of his government and peace there shall be no end, upon the throne of David, and upon his kingdom, to order it, and to establish it with judgment and with justice from henceforth even for ever. The zeal of the LORD of hosts will perform this."
[17] Compare Exodus 40:34: "Then a cloud covered the tent of the congregation, and the glory of the LORD filled the tabernacle."

which shall be born of thee shall be called the Son of God."[18] And, behold, thy cousin Elisabeth, she hath also conceived a son in her old age, and this is the sixth month with her, who was called barren. For with God nothing shall be impossible."[19] And Mary said, "Behold the handmaid of the Lord, be it unto me according to thy word." And the angel departed from her.

And Mary arose in those days, and went into the hill country with haste, into a city of Judah, and entered into the house of Zacharias, and saluted Elisabeth. And it came to pass, that, when Elisabeth heard the salutation of Mary, the babe leaped in her womb, and Elisabeth was filled with the Holy Ghost, and she spake out with a loud voice, and said, "Blessed art thou among women, and blessed is the fruit of thy womb. And whence is this to me, that the mother of my Lord should come to me? For, lo, as soon as the voice of thy salutation sounded in mine ears, the babe leaped in my womb for joy. And blessed is she that believed, for there shall be a performance of those things which were told her from the Lord." And Mary said,[20] "My soul doth magnify the Lord, and my spirit hath rejoiced in God my Saviour. For he hath regarded the low estate of his handmaiden, for, behold, from henceforth all generations shall call me blessed.[21] For he that is mighty hath done to me great

---

[18] See 2 Esdras 13:29,32: "Behold, the days come, when the most High will begin to deliver them that are upon the earth. And the time shall be when these things shall come to pass, and the signs shall happen which I shewed thee before, and then shall my Son be declared, whom thou sawest as a man ascending."
Psalms 89:26-27: "He shall cry unto me, 'Thou art my father, my God, and the rock of my salvation.' Also I will make him my firstborn, higher than the kings of the earth."
[19] Compare Genesis 18:14: "Is any thing too hard for the LORD? At the time appointed I will return unto thee, according to the time of life, and Sarah shall have a son."
[20] Compare 1 Samuel 2:1-10 (Hannah); Judges 5:1-31 (Deborah); Exodus 15:20-21 (Miriam); Judith 16:1-17 (Judith).
[21] Compare Genesis 30:13: "And Leah said, 'Happy am I, for the daughters will call me blessed;' and she called his name Asher."

things,²² and holy is his name.²³ And his mercy is on them that fear him²⁴ from generation to generation.²⁵ He hath shewed strength with his arm,²⁶ he hath scattered the proud in the imagination of their hearts.²⁷ He hath put down the mighty from their seats, and exalted them of low degree. He hath filled the hungry with good things, and the rich he hath sent empty away.²⁸ He hath holpen his

---

²² Compare Psalms 126:2: "'Then was our mouth filled with laughter, and our tongue with singing; then said they among the heathen, 'The LORD hath done great things for them.'"
²³ See Psalms 111:9: "He sent redemption unto his people; he hath commanded his covenant for ever; holy and reverend is his name."
Isaiah 57:15: "For thus saith the high and lofty One that inhabiteth eternity, whose name is Holy; I dwell in the high and holy place, with him also that is of a contrite and humble spirit, to revive the spirit of the humble, and to revive the heart of the contrite ones."
²⁴ Compare Exodus 20:6: "And shewing mercy unto thousands of them that love me, and keep my commandments."
²⁵ Compare Isaiah 51:8: "For the moth shall eat them up like a garment, and the worm shall eat them like wool; but my righteousness shall be for ever, and my salvation from generation to generation."
²⁶ Compare Isaiah 51:9: "Awake, awake, put on strength, O arm of the LORD; awake, as in the ancient days, in the generations of old. Art thou not it that hath cut Rahab, and wounded the dragon?"
Isaiah 40:10: "Behold, the Lord GOD will come with strong hand, and his arm shall rule for him; behold, his reward is with him, and his work before him."
²⁷ See Numbers 10:35: "And it came to pass, when the ark set forward, that Moses said, 'Rise up, LORD, and let thine enemies be scattered; and let them that hate thee flee before thee.'"
Proverbs 16:5: "Every one that is proud in heart is an abomination to the LORD; though hand join in hand, he shall not be unpunished."
²⁸ Compare Isaiah 11:4: "But with righteousness shall he judge the poor, and reprove with equity for the meek of the earth; and he shall smite the earth with the rod of his mouth, and with the breath of his lips shall he slay the wicked."
Psalms 138:6: "Though the LORD be high, yet hath he respect unto the lowly; but the proud he knoweth afar off."
Proverbs 3:34: "Surely he scorneth the scorners; but he giveth grace unto the lowly."
Isaiah 2:12: "For the day of the LORD of hosts shall be upon every one that is proud and lofty, and upon every one that is lifted up; and he shall be brought low."
Psalms 107:8-9: "Oh that men would praise the LORD for his goodness, and for his wonderful works to the children of men! For he satisfieth the longing soul, and filleth the hungry soul with goodness."

servant Israel, in remembrance of his mercy, as he spake to our fathers, to Abraham, and to his seed for ever."²⁹

And Mary abode with her about three months, and returned to her own house.

Now the birth of Jesus Christ was on this wise: when as his mother Mary was espoused to Joseph, before they came together, she was found with child of the Holy Ghost. Then Joseph her husband, being a just man, and not willing to make her a publick example, was minded to put her away privily. But while he thought on these things, behold, the angel of the LORD appeared unto him in a dream, saying, "Joseph, thou son of David, fear not to take unto thee Mary thy wife, for that which is conceived in her is of the Holy Ghost. And she shall bring forth a son, and thou shalt call his name JESUS, for he shall save his people from their sins." Now all this was done, that it might be fulfilled which was spoken of the Lord by the prophet, saying, *"Behold, a virgin shall be with child, and shall bring forth a son, and they shall call his name Immanuel,"*³⁰ (which being interpreted is, God with us). Then Joseph being raised from sleep did as the angel of the Lord had bidden him, and took unto him his wife, and knew her not till she had brought forth her firstborn son.

Now Elisabeth's full time came that she should be delivered, and she brought forth a son. And her neighbours and her cousins heard how the Lord had shewed great mercy upon her, and they rejoiced with her. And it came to pass, that on the eighth day they

---

Job 27:19: "The rich man shall lie down, but he shall not be gathered; he openeth his eyes, and he is not."
²⁹ Compare Psalms 98:3: "He hath remembered his mercy and his truth toward the house of Israel; all the ends of the earth have seen the salvation of our God."
Genesis 17:7: "And I will establish my covenant between me and thee and thy seed after thee in their generations for an everlasting covenant, to be a God unto thee, and to thy seed after thee."
³⁰ "Therefore the Lord himself shall give you a sign; Behold, a virgin shall conceive, and bear a son, and shall call his name Immanuel." – Isaiah 7:14

THE TREE OF LIFE

came to circumcise the child,[31] and they called him Zacharias, after the name of his father. And his mother answered and said, "Not so, but he shall be called John." And they said unto her, "There is none of thy kindred that is called by this name." And they made signs to his father, how he would have him called. And he asked for a writing table, and wrote, saying, "His name is John." And they marvelled all. And his mouth was opened immediately, and his tongue loosed, and he spake, and praised God. And fear came on all that dwelt round about them, and all these sayings were noised abroad throughout all the hill country of Judaea. And all they that heard them laid them up in their hearts, saying, "What manner of child shall this be!" And the hand of the Lord was with him.

And his father Zacharias was filled with the Holy Ghost, and prophesied, saying, "Blessed be the Lord God of Israel,[32] for he hath visited and redeemed his people,[33] and hath raised up an horn of salvation for us in the house of his servant David,[34] as he spake by the mouth of his holy prophets, which have been since the world began, that we should be saved from our enemies, and from the hand of all that hate us,[35] to perform the mercy promised to our fathers, and to remember his holy covenant, the oath which he

---

[31] See Genesis 17:12: "And he that is eight days old shall be circumcised among you, every man child in your generations, he that is born in the house, or bought with money of any stranger, which is not of thy seed."
[32] Compare 1 Kings 1:48: "And also thus said the king, 'Blessed be the LORD God of Israel, which hath given one to sit on my throne this day, mine eyes even seeing it.'"
[33] See Psalms 136:24: "And hath redeemed us from our enemies; for his mercy endureth for ever."
Nehemiah 1:10: "Now these are thy servants and thy people, whom thou hast redeemed by thy great power, and by thy strong hand."
[34] Compare Psalms 18:2: "The LORD is my rock, and my fortress, and my deliverer; my God, my strength, in whom I will trust; my buckler, and the horn of my salvation, and my high tower."
1 Samuel 2:10: "The adversaries of the LORD shall be broken to pieces; out of heaven shall he thunder upon them; the LORD shall judge the ends of the earth; and he shall give strength unto his king, and exalt the horn of his anointed."
[35] See Psalms 106:10: "And he saved them from the hand of him that hated them, and redeemed them from the hand of the enemy."

THE TREE OF LIFE

sware to our father Abraham, that he would grant unto us,[36] that we being delivered out of the hand of our enemies might serve him without fear, in holiness and righteousness before him, all the days of our life.[37] And thou, child, shalt be called the prophet of the Highest, for thou shalt go before the face of the Lord *to prepare his ways*,[38] to give knowledge of salvation unto his people by the remission of their sins, through the tender mercy of our God,[39] whereby the dayspring from on high hath visited us, to give light to them that sit in darkness and in the shadow of death, to guide our feet into the way of peace."[40]

---

[36] See Micah 7:20: "Thou wilt perform the truth to Jacob, and the mercy to Abraham, which thou hast sworn unto our fathers from the days of old."
[37] See Genesis 22:16-18: "And said, 'By myself have I sworn, saith the LORD, for because thou hast done this thing, and hast not withheld thy son, thine only son. That in blessing I will bless thee, and in multiplying I will multiply thy seed as the stars of the heaven, and as the sand which is upon the sea shore; and thy seed shall possess the gate of his enemies; and in thy seed shall all the nations of the earth be blessed; because thou hast obeyed my voice.'"
Genesis 17:7-8: "And I will establish my covenant between me and thee and thy seed after thee in their generations for an everlasting covenant, to be a God unto thee, and to thy seed after thee. And I will give unto thee, and to thy seed after thee, the land wherein thou art a stranger, all the land of Canaan, for an everlasting possession; and I will be their God."
Psalms 105:8: "He hath remembered his covenant for ever, the word which he commanded to a thousand generations."
[38] See Malachi 3:1: "Behold, I will send my messenger, and he shall prepare the way before me; and the Lord, whom ye seek, shall suddenly come to his temple, even the messenger of the covenant, whom ye delight in; behold, he shall come, saith the LORD of hosts."
[39] Compare Psalms 51:1-3: "Have mercy upon me, O God, according to thy lovingkindness; according unto the multitude of thy tender mercies blot out my transgressions. Wash me throughly from mine iniquity, and cleanse me from my sin. For I acknowledge my transgressions; and my sin is ever before me."
[40] See Malachi 4:2: "But unto you that fear my name shall the Sun of righteousness arise with healing in his wings; and ye shall go forth, and grow up as calves of the stall."
Numbers 24:17: "I shall see him, but not now; I shall behold him, but not nigh; there shall come a Star out of Jacob, and a Sceptre shall rise out of Israel, and shall smite the corners of Moab, and destroy all the children of Sheth."
Isaiah 9:2: "The people that walked in darkness have seen a great light; they that dwell in the land of the shadow of death, upon them hath the light shined."

THE TREE OF LIFE

And the child grew, and waxed strong in spirit, and was in the deserts till the day of his shewing unto Israel.

And it came to pass in those days, that there went out a decree from Caesar Augustus, that all the world should be taxed. (And this taxing was first made when Cyrenius was governor of Syria.) And all went to be taxed, every one into his own city. And Joseph also went up from Galilee, out of the city of Nazareth, into Judaea, unto the city of David, which is called Bethlehem, because he was of the house and lineage of David, to be taxed with Mary his espoused wife, being great with child. And so it was, that, while they were there, the days were accomplished that she should be delivered. And she brought forth her firstborn son, and wrapped him in swaddling clothes, and laid him in a manger, because there was no room for them in the inn.

And there were in the same country shepherds abiding in the field, keeping watch over their flock by night. And, lo, the angel of the Lord came upon them, and the glory of the Lord[41] shone round about them, and they were sore afraid. And the angel said unto them, "Fear not, for, behold, I bring you good tidings of great joy, which shall be to all people. For unto you is born this day in the city of David a Saviour, which is Christ the Lord.[42] And this shall be a sign unto you: ye shall find the babe wrapped in swaddling clothes, lying in a manger." And suddenly there was with the angel a

---

Isaiah 42:16: "And I will bring the blind by a way that they knew not; I will lead them in paths that they have not known; I will make darkness light before them, and crooked things straight. These things will I do unto them, and not forsake them."
Baruch 3:13: "For if thou hadst walked in the way of God, thou shouldest have dwelled in peace for ever."
[41] See Exodus 24:17: "And the sight of the glory of the LORD was like devouring fire on the top of the mount in the eyes of the children of Israel."
[42] Compare Jeremiah 23:5-6: "Behold, the days come, saith the LORD, that I will raise unto David a righteous Branch, and a King shall reign and prosper, and shall execute judgment and justice in the earth. In his days Judah shall be saved, and Israel shall dwell safely; and this is his name whereby he shall be called, THE LORD OUR RIGHTEOUSNESS."

multitude of the heavenly host[43] praising God, and saying, "Glory to God in the highest, and on earth peace, good will toward men."

And it came to pass, as the angels were gone away from them into heaven, the shepherds said one to another, "Let us now go even unto Bethlehem, and see this thing which is come to pass, which the Lord hath made known unto us."

And they came with haste, and found Mary, and Joseph, and the babe lying in a manger. And when they had seen it, they made known abroad the saying which was told them concerning this child. And all they that heard it wondered at those things which were told them by the shepherds. But Mary kept all these things, and pondered them in her heart. And the shepherds returned, glorifying and praising God for all the things that they had heard and seen, as it was told unto them.

And when eight days were accomplished for the circumcising of the child,[44] his name was called JESUS, which was so named of the angel before he was conceived in the womb. And when the days of her purification according to the law of Moses[45] were accomplished, they brought him to Jerusalem, to present him to the Lord,[46] (as it is written in the law of the LORD, "*Every male that openeth the womb shall be called holy to the Lord*"),[47] and to offer a sacrifice according

---

[43] See 1 Kings 22:19: "And he said, 'Hear thou therefore the word of the LORD; I saw the LORD sitting on his throne, and all the host of heaven standing by him on his right hand and on his left."
[44] See Genesis 17:12: "And he that is eight days old shall be circumcised among you, every man child in your generations, he that is born in the house, or bought with money of any stranger, which is not of thy seed."
[45] See Leviticus 12:1-8.
[46] See Nehemiah 10:35-36: "And to bring the firstfruits of our ground, and the firstfruits of all fruit of all trees, year by year, unto the house of the LORD; also the firstborn of our sons, and of our cattle, as it is written in the law, and the firstlings of our herds and of our flocks, to bring to the house of our God, unto the priests that minister in the house of our God."
[47] "Sanctify unto me all the firstborn, whatsoever openeth the womb among the children of Israel, both of man and of beast: it is mine." – Exodus 13:2
See also Exodus 13:12, 22:29, 34:19; Numbers 18:15.

THE TREE OF LIFE

to that which is said in the law of the Lord, "*A pair of turtledoves, or two young pigeons.*"[48] And, behold, there was a man in Jerusalem, whose name was Simeon, and the same man was just and devout, waiting for the consolation of Israel, and the Holy Ghost was upon him. And it was revealed unto him by the Holy Ghost, that he should not see death, before he had seen the Lord's Christ. And he came by the Spirit into the temple, and when the parents brought in the child Jesus, to do for him after the custom of the law, then took he him up in his arms, and blessed God, and said, "Lord, now lettest thou thy servant depart in peace, according to thy word. For mine eyes have seen thy salvation,[49] which thou hast prepared before the face of all people, a *light to lighten the Gentiles*,[50] and the glory of thy people Israel." And Joseph and his mother marvelled at those things which were spoken of him. And Simeon blessed them,[51] and said unto

---

[48] "And when the days of her purifying are fulfilled, for a son, or for a daughter, she shall bring a lamb of the first year for a burnt offering, and a young pigeon, or a turtledove, for a sin offering, unto the door of the tabernacle of the congregation, unto the priest. And if she be not able to bring a lamb, then she shall bring two turtles, or two young pigeons; the one for the burnt offering, and the other for a sin offering; and the priest shall make an atonement for her, and she shall be clean." - Leviticus 12:6-8

[49] Compare Lamentations 3:26: "It is good that a man should both hope and quietly wait for the salvation of the LORD." See also Genesis 49:18; Isaiah 62:1; Micah 7:7.

[50] Compare Isaiah 49:6: "And he said, 'It is a light thing that thou shouldest be my servant to raise up the tribes of Jacob, and to restore the preserved of Israel; I will also give thee for a light to the Gentiles, that thou mayest be my salvation unto the end of the earth.'"

Isaiah 60:1-3: "Arise, shine; for thy light is come, and the glory of the LORD is risen upon thee. For, behold, the darkness shall cover the earth, and gross darkness the people; but the LORD shall arise upon thee, and his glory shall be seen upon thee. And the Gentiles shall come to thy light, and kings to the brightness of thy rising."

Isaiah 11:10: "And in that day there shall be a root of Jesse, which shall stand for an ensign of the people; to it shall the Gentiles seek; and his rest shall be glorious."

[51] See Numbers 6:23-26: "Speak unto Aaron and unto his sons, saying, 'On this wise ye shall bless the children of Israel, saying unto them, "The LORD bless thee, and keep thee. The LORD make his face shine upon thee, and be gracious unto thee. The LORD lift up his countenance upon thee, and give thee peace.""'"

Mary his mother, "Behold, this child is set for the fall[52] and rising again[53] of many in Israel, and for a sign which shall be spoken against, (yea, a sword shall pierce through thy own soul also,) that the thoughts of many hearts may be revealed."[54]

And there was one Anna, a prophetess,[55] the daughter of Phanuel, of the tribe of Asher. She was of a great age, and had lived with an husband seven years from her virginity, and she was a widow of about fourscore and four years, which departed not from the temple, but served God with fastings and prayers night and day. And she coming in that instant gave thanks likewise unto the Lord, and spake of him to all them that looked for redemption in Jerusalem.

---

[52] Compare Isaiah 8:14-15: "And he shall be for a sanctuary; but for a stone of stumbling and for a rock of offence to both the houses of Israel, for a gin and for a snare to the inhabitants of Jerusalem. And many among them shall stumble, and fall, and be broken, and be snared, and be taken."
[53] Compare Isaiah 28:16: "Therefore thus saith the Lord GOD, Behold, I lay in Zion for a foundation a stone, a tried stone, a precious corner stone, a sure foundation; he that believeth shall not make haste."
Psalms 18:2: "The LORD is my rock, and my fortress, and my deliverer; my God, my strength, in whom I will trust; my buckler, and the horn of my salvation, and my high tower."
[54] Compare Jeremiah 17:10: "I the LORD search the heart, I try the reins, even to give every man according to his ways, and according to the fruit of his doings."
2 Esdras 16:53-54,63-64: "Let not the sinner say that he hath not sinned; for God shall burn coals of fire upon his head, which saith before the Lord God and his glory, 'I have not sinned.' Behold, the Lord knoweth all the works of men, their imaginations, their thoughts, and their hearts. Surely he knoweth your inventions, and what ye think in your hearts, even them that sin, and would hide their sin. Therefore hath the Lord exactly searched out all your works, and he will put you all to shame."
[55] See also Exodus 15:20 (Miriam); Judges 4:4 (Deborah); 2 Kings 22:14 & 2 Chronicles 34:22 (Huldah); Isaiah 8:3 (Unnamed prophetess).

THE TREE OF LIFE

Chapter Two

And when they had performed all things according to the law of the Lord, they returned to Bethlehem of Judaea. And in the days of Herod the king, behold, there came wise men from the east to Jerusalem, saying, "Where is he that is born King of the Jews? For we have seen his star[56] in the east, and are come to worship him."[57] When Herod the king had heard these things, he was troubled, and all Jerusalem with him. And when he had gathered all the chief priests and scribes of the people together, he demanded of them where Christ should be born. And they said unto him, "In Bethlehem of Judaea, for thus it is written by the prophet, *'And thou Bethlehem, in the land of Judah, art not the least among the princes of Judah, for out of thee shall come a Governor, that shall rule my people Israel.'*"[58]

---

[56] See Numbers 24:17: "I shall see him, but not now; I shall behold him, but not nigh; there shall come a Star out of Jacob, and a Sceptre shall rise out of Israel, and shall smite the corners of Moab, and destroy all the children of Sheth."
[57] Compare Isaiah 60:5-6: "Then thou shalt see, and flow together, and thine heart shall fear, and be enlarged; because the abundance of the sea shall be converted unto thee, the forces of the Gentiles shall come unto thee. The multitude of camels shall cover thee, the dromedaries of Midian and Ephah; all they from Sheba shall come; they shall bring gold and incense; and they shall shew forth the praises of the LORD."
[58] "But thou, Beth-lehem Ephratah, though thou be little among the thousands of Judah, yet out of thee shall he come forth unto me that is to be ruler in Israel; whose goings forth have been from of old, from everlasting." – Micah 5:2

THE TREE OF LIFE

Then Herod, when he had privily called the wise men, enquired of them diligently what time the star appeared. And he sent them to Bethlehem, and said, "Go and search diligently for the young child, and when ye have found him, bring me word again, that I may come and worship him also." When they had heard the king, they departed, and, lo, the star, which they saw in the east, went before them, till it came and stood over where the young child was. When they saw the star, they rejoiced with exceeding great joy. And when they were come into the house, they saw the young child with Mary his mother, and fell down, and worshipped him, and when they had opened their treasures, they presented unto him gifts: gold, and frankincense, and myrrh.[59]

And being warned of God in a dream[60] that they should not return to Herod, they departed into their own country another way. And when they were departed, behold, the angel of the Lord appeareth to Joseph in a dream, saying, "Arise, and take the young child and his mother, and flee into Egypt, and be thou there until I bring thee word, for Herod will seek the young child to destroy him." When he arose, he took the young child and his mother by night, and departed into Egypt, and was there until the death of Herod, that it might be fulfilled which was spoken of the Lord by the prophet, saying, "*Out of Egypt have I called my son.*"[61]

---

[59] Compare <u>Tobit 13:11:</u> "Many nations shall come from far to the name of the Lord God with gifts in their hands, even gifts to the King of heaven; all generations shall praise thee with great joy."
[60] Compare <u>Genesis 20:3,7:</u> "But God came to Abimelech in a dream by night, and said to him, 'Behold, thou art but a dead man, for the woman which thou hast taken; for she is a man's wife. Now therefore restore the man his wife; for he is a prophet, and he shall pray for thee, and thou shalt live; and if thou restore her not, know thou that thou shalt surely die, thou, and all that are thine.'"
<u>Genesis 31:24:</u> "And God came to Laban the Syrian in a dream by night, and said unto him, 'Take heed that thou speak not to Jacob either good or bad.'"
[61] "When Israel was a child, then I loved him, and called my son out of Egypt." - <u>Hosea 11:1</u>

Then Herod, when he saw that he was mocked of the wise men, was exceeding wroth, and sent forth, and slew all the children[62] that were in Bethlehem, and in all the coasts thereof, from two years old and under, according to the time which he had diligently enquired of the wise men. Then was fulfilled that which was spoken by Jeremiah the prophet, saying, "*In Ramah was there a voice heard, lamentation, and weeping, and great mourning, Rachel weeping for her children, and would not be comforted, because they are not.*"[63]

But when Herod was dead, behold, an angel of the Lord appeareth in a dream to Joseph in Egypt, saying, "Arise, and take the young child and his mother, and go into the land of Israel, for they are dead which sought the young child's life."[64] And he arose, and took the young child and his mother, and came into the land of Israel. But when he heard that Archelaus did reign in Judaea in the room of his father Herod, he was afraid to go thither Notwithstanding, being warned of God in a dream, he turned aside into the parts of Galilee, and he came and dwelt in a city called Nazareth, that it might be fulfilled which was spoken by the prophets, "He shall be called a Nazarene."[65]

And the child grew, and waxed strong in spirit, filled with wisdom, and the grace of God was upon him.

Now his parents went to Jerusalem every year at the feast of the passover.[66] And when he was twelve years old, they went up to Jerusalem after the custom of the feast. And when they had fulfilled

---

[62] Compare Exodus 1:22: "And Pharaoh charged all his people, saying, 'Every son that is born ye shall cast into the river, and every daughter ye shall save alive.'"
[63] "Thus saith the LORD; 'A voice was heard in Ramah, lamentation, and bitter weeping; Rahel weeping for her children refused to be comforted for her children, because they were not.'" – Jeremiah 31:15
[64] Compare Exodus 4:19: "And the LORD said unto Moses in Midian, 'Go, return into Egypt; for all the men are dead which sought thy life.'"
[65] Source unknown.
[66] See Exodus 12:1-51; Leviticus 23:5-8; Numbers 28:16-25; Deuteronomy 16:1-8.

the days, as they returned, the child Jesus tarried behind in Jerusalem, and Joseph and his mother knew not of it. But they, supposing him to have been in the company, went a day's journey, and they sought him among their kinsfolk and acquaintance. And when they found him not, they turned back again to Jerusalem, seeking him. And it came to pass, that after three days they found him in the temple, sitting in the midst of the doctors, both hearing them, and asking them questions. And all that heard him were astonished at his understanding and answers. And when they saw him, they were amazed, and his mother said unto him, "Son, why hast thou thus dealt with us? Behold, thy father and I have sought thee sorrowing." And he said unto them, "How is it that ye sought me? Wist ye not that I must be about my Father's business?" And they understood not the saying which he spake unto them. And he went down with them, and came to Nazareth, and was subject unto them, but his mother kept all these sayings in her heart.[67] And Jesus increased in wisdom and stature, and in *favour with God and man*.[68]

---

[67] Compare Deuteronomy 6:6: "And these words, which I command thee this day, shall be in thine heart."
[68] Compare Proverbs 3:1-4: "My son, forget not my law; but let thine heart keep my commandments; for length of days, and long life, and peace, shall they add to thee. Let not mercy and truth forsake thee; bind them about thy neck; write them upon the table of thine heart. So shalt thou find favour and good understanding in the sight of God and man."

THE TREE OF LIFE

Chapter Three

Now in the fifteenth year of the reign of Tiberius Caesar, Pontius Pilate being governor of Judaea, and Herod being tetrarch of Galilee, and his brother Philip tetrarch of Ituraea and of the region of Trachonitis, and Lysanias the tetrarch of Abilene, Annas and Caiaphas being the high priests; the word of God came unto a man sent from God in the wilderness of Judaea, whose name was John the son of Zacharias. And he came into all the country about Jordan, preaching the baptism of repentance for the remission of sins.[69]

And John came for a witness, to bear witness of the Light,[70] that all men through him might believe. He was not that Light, but

---

[69] Compare Isaiah 1:16-18: "Wash you, make you clean; put away the evil of your doings from before mine eyes; cease to do evil; learn to do well; seek judgment, relieve the oppressed, judge the fatherless, plead for the widow. Come now, and let us reason together, saith the LORD; though your sins be as scarlet, they shall be as white as snow; though they be red like crimson, they shall be as wool."
Psalms 51:1-3: "Have mercy upon me, O God, according to thy lovingkindness; according unto the multitude of thy tender mercies blot out my transgressions. Wash me throughly from mine iniquity, and cleanse me from my sin. For I acknowledge my transgressions; and my sin is ever before me."
Jeremiah 4:14: "O Jerusalem, wash thine heart from wickedness, that thou mayest be saved. How long shall thy vain thoughts lodge within thee?"
See also 2 Kings 5:1-19.
[70] Compare Isaiah 60:1-3: "Arise, shine; for thy light is come, and the glory of the LORD is risen upon thee. For, behold, the darkness shall cover the earth, and gross darkness the people; but the LORD shall arise upon thee, and his glory shall be seen

THE TREE OF LIFE

was sent to bear witness of that Light, that was the true Light, which lighteth every man that cometh into the world.[71] He was in the world, and the world was made by him, and the world knew him not. He came unto his own, and his own received him not.[72] But as many as received him, to them gave he power to become the sons of God,[73] even to them that believe on his name, which were born, not of blood, nor of the will of the flesh, nor of the will of man, but of God. And the Word was made flesh, and dwelt among us,[74] and we beheld his glory, the glory as of the only begotten of the Father, full of grace and truth. And of his fulness have all we received, and grace

---

upon thee. And the Gentiles shall come to thy light, and kings to the brightness of thy rising."
[71] Compare <u>Proverbs 20:27</u>: "The spirit of man is the candle of the LORD, searching all the inward parts of the belly."
[72] Compare <u>1 Samuel 10:18-19</u>: "And ye have this day rejected your God, who himself saved you out of all your adversities and your tribulations; and ye have said unto him, 'Nay, but set a king over us.' Now therefore present yourselves before the LORD by your tribes, and by your thousands."
[73] Compare <u>Wisdom 18:13</u>: "For whereas they would not believe any thing by reason of the enchantments; upon the destruction of the firstborn, they [the Egyptians] acknowledged this people to be the sons of God."
<u>Sirach</u> 4:1-10: "My son, defraud not the poor of his living, and make not the needy eyes to wait long. Make not an hungry soul sorrowful; neither provoke a man in his distress. Add not more trouble to an heart that is vexed; and defer not to give to him that is in need. Reject not the supplication of the afflicted; neither turn away thy face from a poor man. Turn not away thine eye from the needy, and give him none occasion to curse thee. For if he curse thee in the bitterness of his soul, his prayer shall be heard of him that made him. Get thyself the love of the congregation, and bow thy head to a great man. Let it not grieve thee to bow down thine ear to the poor, and give him a friendly answer with meekness. Deliver him that suffereth wrong from the hand of the oppressor; and be not fainthearted when thou sittest in judgment. Be as a father unto the fatherless, and instead of an husband unto their mother; so shalt thou be as the son of the most High, and he shall love thee more than thy mother doth."
<u>Psalms 2:7</u>: "I will declare the decree; the LORD hath said unto me, 'Thou art my Son; this day have I begotten thee.'"
[74] Compare <u>Leviticus 26:11-12</u>: "And I will set my tabernacle among you; and my soul shall not abhor you. And I will walk among you, and will be your God, and ye shall be my people."
<u>1 Samuel 3:7,21</u>: "Now Samuel did not yet know the LORD, neither was the word of the LORD yet revealed unto him. And the LORD appeared again in Shiloh; for the LORD revealed himself to Samuel in Shiloh by the word of the LORD."

for grace. For the law was given by Moses, but grace and truth came by Jesus Christ.

And the same John did baptize in the wilderness, and had his raiment of camel's hair, and a leathern girdle about his loins,[75] and he did eat locusts and wild honey.[76]

And there went out unto John all the land of Judaea, and they of Jerusalem, and were all baptized of him in the river Jordan, confessing their sins. But when he saw many of the Pharisees and Sadducees come to be baptized of him, he said unto them, "O generation of vipers, who hath warned you to flee from the wrath to come?[77] Bring forth therefore fruits worthy of repentance, and begin not to say within yourselves, 'We have Abraham to our father,'[78] for I say unto you, that God is able of these stones to raise

---

[75] Compare 2 Kings 1:7-8: "And he said unto them, 'What manner of man was he which came up to meet you, and told you these words?' And they answered him, 'He was an hairy man, and girt with a girdle of leather about his loins.' And he said, 'It is Elijah the Tishbite.'"

[76] Compare 1 Kings 17:2-4: "And the word of the LORD came unto [Elijah], saying, 'Get thee hence, and turn thee eastward, and hide thyself by the brook Cherith, that is before Jordan. And it shall be, that thou shalt drink of the brook; and I have commanded the ravens to feed thee there.'"

[77] Compare Malachi 3:2-3, 4:1: "But who may abide the day of his coming? And who shall stand when he appeareth? for he is like a refiner's fire, and like fullers' soap. And he shall sit as a refiner and purifier of silver; and he shall purify the sons of Levi, and purge them as gold and silver, that they may offer unto the LORD an offering in righteousness. For, behold, the day cometh, that shall burn as an oven; and all the proud, yea, and all that do wickedly, shall be stubble; and the day that cometh shall burn them up, saith the LORD of hosts, that it shall leave them neither root nor branch."

[78] See Genesis 17:1-8: "And when Abram was ninety years old and nine, the LORD appeared to Abram, and said unto him, 'I am the Almighty God; walk before me, and be thou perfect. And I will make my covenant between me and thee, and will multiply thee exceedingly.' And Abram fell on his face. And God talked with him, saying, 'As for me, behold, my covenant is with thee, and thou shalt be a father of many nations. Neither shall thy name any more be called Abram, but thy name shall be Abraham; for a father of many nations have I made thee. And I will make thee exceeding fruitful, and I will make nations of thee, and kings shall come out of thee. And I will establish my covenant between me and thee and thy seed after thee in their generations for an everlasting covenant, to be a God unto thee, and to thy seed after thee. And I will give unto thee, and to thy seed after thee, the land wherein

up children unto Abraham. And now also the axe is laid unto the root of the trees, every tree therefore which bringeth not forth good fruit is hewn down, and cast into the fire. Therefore repent ye, for the kingdom of heaven is at hand."

And the people asked him, saying, "What shall we do then?" He answereth and saith unto them, "He that hath two coats, let him impart to him that hath none, and he that hath meat, let him do likewise."

Then came also publicans to be baptized, and said unto him, "Master, what shall we do?" And he said unto them, "Exact no more than that which is appointed you."

And the soldiers likewise demanded of him, saying, "And what shall we do?" And he said unto them, "Do violence to no man, neither accuse any falsely, and be content with your wages."

And the Jews sent priests and Levites from Jerusalem to ask him, "Who art thou?" And as the people were in expectation, and all men mused in their hearts of John, whether he were the Christ,[79] or not, he confessed, and denied not, but confessed, "I am not the Christ." And they asked him, "What then? Art thou Elijah?"[80] And he saith, "I am not." "Art thou that prophet?"[81] And he answered, "No." Then said they unto him, "Who art thou, that we may give an answer to them that sent us? What sayest thou of thyself?" And he saith, "As it is written in the prophets, *'Behold, I send my messenger before thy*

---

thou art a stranger, all the land of Canaan, for an everlasting possession; and I will be their God.'"
[79] See <u>Genesis 49:10</u>: "The sceptre shall not depart from Judah, nor a lawgiver from between his feet, until Shiloh come; and unto him shall the gathering of the people be."
[80] See <u>Malachi 4:5</u>: "Behold, I will send you Elijah the prophet before the coming of the great and dreadful day of the LORD."
[81] See <u>Deuteronomy 18:15</u>: "The LORD thy God will raise up unto thee a Prophet from the midst of thee, of thy brethren, like unto me; unto him ye shall hearken."

face, which shall prepare thy way before thee.'[82] I am 'the voice of one crying in the wilderness, "Prepare ye the way of the Lord, make his paths straight. Every valley shall be filled, and every mountain and hill shall be brought low, and the crooked shall be made straight, and the rough ways shall be made smooth, and all flesh shall see the salvation of God,"'[83] as said the prophet Isaiah." (For this is he that was spoken of by the prophet Isaiah.)

And they which were sent were of the Pharisees. And they asked him, and said unto him, "Why baptizest thou then, if thou be not that Christ, nor Elijah, neither that prophet?" John answered, saying unto them all, "I indeed baptize you with water unto repentance, but there standeth one among you, whom ye know not, he it is that cometh after me, and is mightier than I, the latchet of whose shoes I am not worthy to stoop down and unloose, whose fan is in his hand, and he will thoroughly purge his floor,[84] and will gather his wheat into the garner, but he will burn up the chaff with

---

[82] "Behold, I will send my messenger, and he shall prepare the way before me; and the Lord, whom ye seek, shall suddenly come to his temple, even the messenger of the covenant, whom ye delight in; behold, he shall come, saith the LORD of hosts." - Malachi 3:1
[83] "The voice of him that crieth in the wilderness, 'Prepare ye the way of the LORD, make straight in the desert a highway for our God. Every valley shall be exalted, and every mountain and hill shall be made low; and the crooked shall be made straight, and the rough places plain; And the glory of the LORD shall be revealed, and all flesh shall see it together; for the mouth of the LORD hath spoken it.'" - Isaiah 40:3-5
[84] Compare Psalms 1:4: "The ungodly are not so; but are like the chaff which the wind driveth away."
Hosea 13:3: "Therefore they shall be as the morning cloud, and as the early dew that passeth away, as the chaff that is driven with the whirlwind out of the floor, and as the smoke out of the chimney."
Isaiah 41:16: "Thou shalt fan them, and the wind shall carry them away, and the whirlwind shall scatter them; and thou shalt rejoice in the LORD, and shalt glory in the Holy One of Israel."

unquenchable fire, and he shall baptize you with the Holy Ghost and with fire."[85]

And many other things in his exhortation preached he unto the people. These things were done in Bethabara beyond Jordan, where John was baptizing.

---

[85] Compare Isaiah 66:15-16: "For, behold, the LORD will come with fire, and with his chariots like a whirlwind, to render his anger with fury, and his rebuke with flames of fire. For by fire and by his sword will the LORD plead with all flesh; and the slain of the LORD shall be many."
Isaiah 5:24: "Therefore as the fire devoureth the stubble, and the flame consumeth the chaff, so their root shall be as rottenness, and their blossom shall go up as dust; because they have cast away the law of the LORD of hosts, and despised the word of the Holy One of Israel."
Jeremiah 23:29: "Is not my word like as a fire? saith the LORD; and like a hammer that breaketh the rock in pieces?"
Isaiah 11:4: "But with righteousness shall he judge the poor, and reprove with equity for the meek of the earth; and he shall smite the earth with the rod of his mouth, and with the breath of his lips shall he slay the wicked."
2 Esdras 13:10-11,20,37-38: "But only I saw that he sent out of his mouth as it had been a blast of fire, and out of his lips a flaming breath, and out of his tongue he cast out sparks and tempests. And they were all mixed together; the blast of fire, the flaming breath, and the great tempest; and fell with violence upon the multitude which was prepared to fight, and burned them up every one, so that upon a sudden of an innumerable multitude nothing was to be perceived, but only dust and smell of smoke. When I saw this I was afraid. And he said unto me, 'And this my Son shall rebuke the wicked inventions of those nations, which for their wicked life are fallen into the tempest; And shall lay before them their evil thoughts, and the torments wherewith they shall begin to be tormented, which are like unto a flame; and he shall destroy them without labour by the law which is like unto me.'"
Deuteronomy 33:2: "And he said, 'The LORD came from Sinai, and rose up from Seir unto them; he shined forth from mount Paran, and he came with ten thousands of saints; from his right hand went a fiery law for them.'"

THE TREE OF LIFE

Chapter Four

The next day John seeth Jesus coming from Nazareth of Galilee to Jordan, to be baptized of him, and John bare witness of him, and cried, saying, "Behold the Lamb of God,[86] which taketh away the sin of the world. This is he of whom I said, 'After me cometh a man which is preferred before me,' for he was before me. And I knew him not, but that he should be made manifest to Israel, therefore am I come baptizing with water."

But John forbad him, saying, "I have need to be baptized of thee, and comest thou to me?" And Jesus answering said unto him, "Suffer it to be so now, for thus it becometh us to fulfil all righteousness." Then he suffered him.

Now it came to pass that Jesus, when he was baptized, and praying, went up straightway out of the water, and, lo, the heavens were opened unto him,[87] and he saw the Spirit of God descending

---

[86] See Exodus 12:21-23: "Then Moses called for all the elders of Israel, and said unto them, 'Draw out and take you a lamb according to your families, and kill the passover. And ye shall take a bunch of hyssop, and dip it in the blood that is in the bason, and strike the lintel and the two side posts with the blood that is in the bason; and none of you shall go out at the door of his house until the morning. For the LORD will pass through to smite the Egyptians; and when he seeth the blood upon the lintel, and on the two side posts, the LORD will pass over the door, and will not suffer the destroyer to come in unto your houses to smite you.'"

[87] Compare Ezekiel 1:1: "Now it came to pass in the thirtieth year, in the fourth month, in the fifth day of the month, as I was among the captives by the river of Chebar, that the heavens were opened, and I saw visions of God."

like a dove, and lighting upon him.[88] And there came a voice from heaven,[89] saying, "This is my beloved Son,[90] in whom I am well pleased."

And John bare record, saying, "I saw the Spirit descending from heaven like a dove, and it abode upon him. And I knew him not, but he that sent me to baptize with water, the same said unto me, 'Upon whom thou shalt see the Spirit descending, and remaining on him, the same is he which baptizeth with the Holy Ghost.' And John saw, and bare record that this is the Son of God,[91]

---

[88] Compare Isaiah 11:1-2: "And there shall come forth a rod out of the stem of Jesse, and a Branch shall grow out of his roots; and the spirit of the LORD shall rest upon him, the spirit of wisdom and understanding, the spirit of counsel and might, the spirit of knowledge and of the fear of the LORD."
Isaiah 42:1: "Behold my servant, whom I uphold; mine elect, in whom my soul delighteth; I have put my spirit upon him; he shall bring forth judgment to the Gentiles."
Isaiah 61:1: "The Spirit of the Lord GOD is upon me; because the LORD hath anointed me to preach good tidings unto the meek; he hath sent me to bind up the brokenhearted, to proclaim liberty to the captives, and the opening of the prison to them that are bound."
1 Samuel 16:13: "Then Samuel took the horn of oil, and anointed him in the midst of his brethren; and the Spirit of the LORD came upon David from that day forward. So Samuel rose up, and went to Ramah."
1 Samuel 10:6: "And the Spirit of the LORD will come upon thee, and thou shalt prophesy with them, and shalt be turned into another man."
[89] See 2 Samuel 22:14: "The LORD thundered from heaven, and the most High uttered his voice."
Psalms 50:6: "And the heavens shall declare his righteousness; for God is judge himself. Selah."
Daniel 4:31-32: "While the word was in the king's mouth, there fell a voice from heaven, saying, 'O king Nebuchadnezzar, to thee it is spoken; The kingdom is departed from thee. And they shall drive thee from men, and thy dwelling shall be with the beasts of the field; they shall make thee to eat grass as oxen, and seven times shall pass over thee, until thou know that the most High ruleth in the kingdom of men, and giveth it to whomsoever he will.'"
[90] Compare Psalms 2:7: "I will declare the decree; the LORD hath said unto me, 'Thou art my Son; this day have I begotten thee.'"
[91] See 2 Esdras 13:29,32: "Behold, the days come, when the most High will begin to deliver them that are upon the earth. And the time shall be when these things shall come to pass, and the signs shall happen which I shewed thee before, and then shall my Son be declared, whom thou sawest as a man ascending."

THE TREE OF LIFE

and the Holy Ghost descended in a bodily shape like a dove upon him, and a voice came from heaven, which said, 'Thou art my beloved Son, in thee I am well pleased.'"

THE TREE OF LIFE

Chapter Five

And Jesus being full of the Holy Ghost returned from Jordan, and immediately was led by the Spirit into the wilderness to be tempted forty days of the devil.[92] And he was there in the wilderness forty days, tempted of Satan, and was with the wild beasts.

And in those days he did eat nothing, and had fasted forty days and forty nights,[93] and when they were ended, he was

---

[92] Compare Deuteronomy 8:2: "And thou shalt remember all the way which the LORD thy God led thee these forty years in the wilderness, to humble thee, and to prove thee, to know what was in thine heart, whether thou wouldest keep his commandments, or no."
Job 1:6-8: "Now there was a day when the sons of God came to present themselves before the LORD, and Satan came also among them. And the LORD said unto Satan, 'Whence comest thou?' Then Satan answered the LORD, and said, 'From going to and fro in the earth, and from walking up and down in it.' And the LORD said unto Satan, 'Hast thou considered my servant Job, that there is none like him in the earth, a perfect and an upright man, one that feareth God, and escheweth evil?'"
1 Chronicles 21:1: "And Satan stood up against Israel, and provoked David to number Israel."
[93] Compare Exodus 24:18: "And Moses went into the midst of the cloud, and gat him up into the mount; and Moses was in the mount forty days and forty nights."
Exodus 34:28: "And [Moses] was there with the LORD forty days and forty nights; he did neither eat bread, nor drink water. And he wrote upon the tables the words of the covenant, the ten commandments."
1 Kings 19:4-8: "But [Elijah] went a day's journey into the wilderness, and came and sat down under a juniper tree; and he requested for himself that he might die; and said, 'It is enough; now, O LORD, take away my life; for I am not better than my fathers.' And as he lay and slept under a juniper tree, behold, then an angel touched

THE TREE OF LIFE

afterward an hungered. And when the tempter came to him, he said, "If thou be the Son of God, command that these stones be made bread." But Jesus answered him and said, "It is written, *'Man shall not live by bread alone, but by every word that proceedeth out of the mouth of God.'*"⁹⁴

Then the devil taketh him up into the holy city Jerusalem, and setteth him on a pinnacle of the temple, and said unto him, "If thou be the Son of God, cast thyself down from hence, for it is written, *'He shall give his angels charge over thee, to keep thee, and in their hands they shall bear thee up, lest at any time thou dash thy foot against a stone.'*"⁹⁵ Jesus said unto him, "It is written again, *'Thou shalt not tempt the Lord thy God.'*"⁹⁶

Again, the devil taketh him up into an exceedingly high mountain, and sheweth him all the kingdoms of the world in a moment of time, and the glory of them, and saith unto him, "All this power will I give thee, and the glory of them, for that is delivered unto me, and to whomsoever I will I give it. If thou therefore wilt

---

him, and said unto him, 'Arise and eat.' And he looked, and, behold, there was a cake baken on the coals, and a cruse of water at his head. And he did eat and drink, and laid him down again. And the angel of the LORD came again the second time, and touched him, and said, 'Arise and eat; because the journey is too great for thee.' And he arose, and did eat and drink, and went in the strength of that meat forty days and forty nights unto Horeb the mount of God."
See also Deuteronomy 9:9,18.
⁹⁴ "And he humbled thee, and suffered thee to hunger, and fed thee with manna, which thou knewest not, neither did thy fathers know; that he might make thee know that man doth not live by bread only, but by every word that proceedeth out of the mouth of the LORD doth man live." – Deuteronomy 8:3
Compare Job 23:12: "Neither have I gone back from the commandment of his lips; I have esteemed the words of his mouth more than my necessary food."
Wisdom 16:26: "That thy children, O Lord, whom thou lovest, might know, that it is not the growing of fruits that nourisheth man; but that it is thy word, which preserveth them that put their trust in thee."
⁹⁵ "For he shall give his angels charge over thee, to keep thee in all thy ways. They shall bear thee up in their hands, lest thou dash thy foot against a stone." – Psalms 91:11-12
⁹⁶ "Ye shall not tempt the LORD your God, as ye tempted him in Massah." – Deuteronomy 6:16

worship me, all shall be thine." And Jesus answered and said unto him, "Get thee hence, Satan,[97] for it is written, 'Thou shalt worship the Lord thy God, and him only shalt thou serve.'"[98]

And when the devil had ended all the temptation, he departed from him for a season, and, behold, angels came and ministered unto him.

---

[97] Compare Isaiah 30:20-22: "And though the Lord give you the bread of adversity, and the water of affliction, yet shall not thy teachers be removed into a corner any more, but thine eyes shall see thy teachers. And thine ears shall hear a word behind thee, saying, 'This is the way, walk ye in it, when ye turn to the right hand, and when ye turn to the left.' Ye shall defile also the covering of thy graven images of silver, and the ornament of thy molten images of gold; thou shalt cast them away as a menstruous cloth; thou shalt say unto it, 'Get thee hence.'"
[98] "Thou shalt fear the LORD thy God; him shalt thou serve, and to him shalt thou cleave, and swear by his name." – Deuteronomy 10:20
"Thou shalt fear the LORD thy God, and serve him, and shalt swear by his name." – Deuteronomy 6:13

THE TREE OF LIFE

THE TREE OF LIFE

Chapter Six

Again the next day after, John stood, and two of his disciples. And looking upon Jesus as he walked, he saith, "Behold the Lamb of God!" And the two disciples heard him speak, and they followed Jesus. Then Jesus turned, and saw them following, and saith unto them, "What seek ye?" They said unto him, "Rabbi, (which is to say, being interpreted, Master,) where dwellest thou?" He saith unto them, "Come and see."

They came and saw where he dwelt, and abode with him that day, for it was about the tenth hour. One of the two which heard John speak, and followed him, was Andrew, Simon Peter's brother. He first findeth his own brother Simon, and saith unto him, "We have found the Messias," (which is, being interpreted, the Christ).[99] And he brought him to Jesus. And when Jesus beheld him, he said, "Thou art Simon the son of Jonah, thou shalt be called Cephas," (which is by interpretation, a stone).

The day following Jesus would go forth into Galilee, and findeth Philip, and saith unto him, "Follow me." Now Philip was of Bethsaida, the city of Andrew and Peter. Philip findeth Nathanael, and saith unto him, "We have found him, of whom Moses in the law,

---

[99] See Jeremiah 23:5: "Behold, the days come, saith the LORD, that I will raise unto David a righteous Branch, and a King shall reign and prosper, and shall execute judgment and justice in the earth."

and the prophets, did write,[100] Jesus of Nazareth, the son of Joseph." And Nathanael said unto him, "Can there any good thing come out of Nazareth?" Philip saith unto him, "Come and see." Jesus saw Nathanael coming to him, and saith of him, "Behold an Israelite indeed, in whom is no guile!" Nathanael saith unto him, "Whence knowest thou me?" Jesus answered and said unto him, "Before that Philip called thee, when thou wast under the fig tree, I saw thee." Nathanael answered and saith unto him, "Rabbi, thou art the Son of God,[101] thou art the King of Israel."[102] Jesus answered and said unto him, "Because I said unto thee, 'I saw thee under the fig tree,' believest thou? Thou shalt see greater things than these." And he saith unto him, "Verily, verily, I say unto you, hereafter ye shall see heaven open, and the angels of God ascending and descending upon the Son of man."[103]

---

[100] See Genesis 3:15: "And I will put enmity between thee and the woman, and between thy seed and her seed; it shall bruise thy head, and thou shalt bruise his heel."
Genesis 49:10: "The sceptre shall not depart from Judah, nor a lawgiver from between his feet, until Shiloh come; and unto him shall the gathering of the people be."
Deuteronomy 18:15: "The LORD thy God will raise up unto thee a Prophet from the midst of thee, of thy brethren, like unto me; unto him ye shall hearken."
[101] See 2 Esdras 13:29,32: "Behold, the days come, when the most High will begin to deliver them that are upon the earth. And the time shall be when these things shall come to pass, and the signs shall happen which I shewed thee before, and then shall my Son be declared, whom thou sawest as a man ascending."
[102] See Jeremiah 23:5: "Behold, the days come, saith the LORD, that I will raise unto David a righteous Branch, and a King shall reign and prosper, and shall execute judgment and justice in the earth. In his days Judah shall be saved, and Israel shall dwell safely; and this is his name whereby he shall be called, THE LORD OUR RIGHTEOUSNESS."
[103] Compare Genesis 28:10-12: "And Jacob went out from Beer-sheba, and went toward Haran. And he lighted upon a certain place, and tarried there all night, because the sun was set; and he took of the stones of that place, and put them for his pillows, and lay down in that place to sleep. And he dreamed, and behold a ladder set up on the earth, and the top of it reached to heaven; and behold the angels of God ascending and descending on it."

Chapter Seven

And the third day there was a marriage in Cana of Galilee, and the mother of Jesus was there, and both Jesus was called, and his disciples, to the marriage. And when they wanted wine, the mother of Jesus saith unto him, "They have no wine." Jesus saith unto her, "Woman, what have I to do with thee? Mine hour is not yet come." His mother saith unto the servants, "Whatsoever he saith unto you, do it." And there were set there six waterpots of stone, after the manner of the purifying of the Jews, containing two or three firkins apiece. Jesus saith unto them, "Fill the waterpots with water." And they filled them up to the brim. And he saith unto them, "Draw out now, and bear unto the governor of the feast." And they bare it. When the ruler of the feast had tasted the water that was made wine, and knew not whence it was, (but the servants which drew the water knew), the governor of the feast called the bridegroom, and saith unto him, "Every man at the beginning doth set forth good wine, and when men have well drunk, then that which is worse, but thou hast kept the good wine until now." For no man also having drunk old wine straightway desireth new, for he saith, "The old is better."

This beginning of miracles did Jesus in Cana of Galilee, and manifested forth his glory, and his disciples believed on him.

THE TREE OF LIFE

Chapter Eight

After this he went down to Capernaum, he, and his mother, and his brethren, and his disciples, and they continued there not many days. And the Jews' passover[104] was at hand, and Jesus went up to Jerusalem, and found in the temple those that sold oxen and sheep and doves, and the changers of money sitting, and when he had made a scourge of small cords, he drove them all out of the temple, and the sheep, and the oxen, and poured out the changers' money, and overthrew the tables, and said unto them that sold doves, "Take these things hence, make not my Father's house an house of merchandise." And his disciples remembered that it was written, "*The zeal of thine house hath eaten me up.*"[105]

Then answered the Jews and said unto him, "What sign shewest thou unto us, seeing that thou doest these things?" Jesus answered and said unto them, "Destroy this temple, and in three days I will raise it up."[106] Then said the Jews, "Forty and six years was this temple in building, and wilt thou rear it up in three days?"

---

[104] See Exodus 12:1-51; Leviticus 23:5-8; Numbers 28:16-25; Deuteronomy 16:1-8.
[105] "For the zeal of thine house hath eaten me up; and the reproaches of them that reproached thee are fallen upon me." – Psalms 69:9
[106] Compare Hosea 6:1-2: "Come, and let us return unto the LORD; for he hath torn, and he will heal us; he hath smitten, and he will bind us up. After two days will he revive us; in the third day he will raise us up, and we shall live in his sight."
Jonah 1:17: "Now the LORD had prepared a great fish to swallow up Jonah. And Jonah was in the belly of the fish three days and three nights."

THE TREE OF LIFE

But he spake of the temple of his body. When therefore he was risen from the dead, his disciples remembered that he had said this unto them, and they believed the scripture, and the word which Jesus had said.

Now when he was in Jerusalem at the passover, in the feast day, many believed in his name, when they saw the miracles which he did. But Jesus did not commit himself unto them, because he knew all men, and needed not that any should testify of man, for he knew what was in man.[107]

And there was a man of the Pharisees, named Nicodemus, a ruler of the Jews, the same came to Jesus by night, and said unto him, "Rabbi, we know that thou art a teacher come from God, for no man can do these miracles that thou doest, except God be with him." Jesus answered and said unto him, "Verily, verily, I say unto thee, except a man be born again, he cannot see the kingdom of God." Nicodemus saith unto him, "How can a man be born when he is old? Can he enter the second time into his mother's womb, and be born?" Jesus answered, "Verily, verily, I say unto thee, except a man be born of water and of the Spirit, he cannot enter into the kingdom of God. That which is born of the flesh is flesh, and that which is born of the Spirit is spirit.[108] Marvel not that I said unto thee, 'Ye must be born

---

[107] Compare <u>Psalms 139:1-2</u>: "O LORD, thou hast searched me, and known me. Thou knowest my downsitting and mine uprising, thou understandest my thought afar off."
<u>Jeremiah 17:10</u>: "I the LORD search the heart, I try the reins, even to give every man according to his ways, and according to the fruit of his doings."
[108] Compare <u>Ezekiel 36:25-27</u>: "Then will I sprinkle clean water upon you, and ye shall be clean; from all your filthiness, and from all your idols, will I cleanse you. A new heart also will I give you, and a new spirit will I put within you; and I will take away the stony heart out of your flesh, and I will give you an heart of flesh. And I will put my spirit within you, and cause you to walk in my statutes, and ye shall keep my judgments, and do them."
<u>1 Samuel 10:6</u>: "And the Spirit of the LORD will come upon thee, and thou shalt prophesy with them, and shalt be turned into another man."
<u>Job 33:4</u>: "The Spirit of God hath made me, and the breath of the Almighty hath given me life."

again.' The wind bloweth where it listeth, and thou hearest the sound thereof, but canst not tell whence it cometh, and whither it goeth, so is every one that is born of the Spirit." Nicodemus answered and said unto him, "How can these things be?" Jesus answered and said unto him, "Art thou a master of Israel, and knowest not these things? Verily, verily, I say unto thee, we speak that which we do know, and testify that which we have seen, and ye receive not our witness. If I have told you earthly things, and ye believe not, how shall ye believe, if I tell you of heavenly things?[109] And no man hath ascended up to heaven, but he that came down from heaven, even the Son of man[110] which is in heaven. And as Moses lifted up the serpent in the wilderness,[111] even so must the

---

[109] See <u>2 Esdras 4:1-11:</u> "And the angel that was sent unto me, whose name was Uriel, gave me an answer, and said, 'Thy heart hath gone too far in this world, and thinkest thou to comprehend the way of the most High?' Then said I, 'Yea, my lord.' And he answered me, and said, 'I am sent to shew thee three ways, and to set forth three similitudes before thee. Whereof if thou canst declare me one, I will shew thee also the way that thou desirest to see, and I shall shew thee from whence the wicked heart cometh.' And I said, 'Tell on, my lord.' Then said he unto me, 'Go thy way, weigh me the weight of the fire, or measure me the blast of the wind, or call me again the day that is past.' Then answered I and said, 'What man is able to do that, that thou shouldest ask such things of me?' And he said unto me, 'If I should ask thee how great dwellings are in the midst of the sea, or how many springs are in the beginning of the deep, or how many springs are above the firmament, or which are the outgoings of paradise. Peradventure thou wouldest say unto me, "I never went down into the deep, nor as yet into hell, neither did I ever climb up into heaven." Nevertheless now have I asked thee but only of the fire and wind, and of the day wherethrough thou hast passed, and of things from which thou canst not be separated, and yet canst thou give me no answer of them.' He said moreover unto me, 'Thine own things, and such as are grown up with thee, canst thou not know; How should thy vessel then be able to comprehend the way of the Highest, and, the world being now outwardly corrupted to understand the corruption that is evident in my sight?'"
[110] See <u>Daniel 7:13:</u> "I saw in the night visions, and, behold, one like the Son of man came with the clouds of heaven, and came to the Ancient of days, and they brought him near before him."
[111] Compare <u>Numbers 21:8-9:</u> "And the LORD said unto Moses, 'Make thee a fiery serpent, and set it upon a pole; and it shall come to pass, that every one that is bitten, when he looketh upon it, shall live.' And Moses made a serpent of brass, and put it upon a pole, and it came to pass, that if a serpent had bitten any man, when he beheld the serpent of brass, he lived."

Son of man be lifted up,[112] that whosoever believeth in him should not perish, but have eternal life. For God so loved the world, that he gave his only begotten Son, that whosoever believeth in him should not perish, but have everlasting life. For God sent not his Son into the world to condemn the world, but that the world through him might be saved. He that believeth on him is not condemned, but he that believeth not is condemned already, because he hath not believed in the name of the only begotten Son of God. And this is the condemnation, that light is come into the world,[113] and men loved darkness rather than light, because their deeds were evil. For every one that doeth evil hateth the light, neither cometh to the light, lest his deeds should be reproved. But he that doeth truth cometh to the light, that his deeds may be made manifest, that they are wrought in God."

<u>Wisdom 16:5-7:</u> "For when the horrible fierceness of beasts came upon these, and they perished with the stings of crooked serpents, thy wrath endured not for ever; but they were troubled for a small season, that they might be admonished, having a sign of salvation, to put them in remembrance of the commandment of thy law. For he that turned himself toward it was not saved by the thing that he saw, but by thee, that art the Saviour of all."

[112] See <u>Isaiah 5:26:</u> "And he will lift up an ensign to the nations from far, and will hiss unto them from the end of the earth; and, behold, they shall come with speed swiftly."

<u>Isaiah 11:10:</u> "And in that day there shall be a root of Jesse, which shall stand for an ensign of the people; to it shall the Gentiles seek; and his rest shall be glorious."

<u>Isaiah 18:3:</u> "All ye inhabitants of the world, and dwellers on the earth, see ye, when he lifteth up an ensign on the mountains; and when he bloweth a trumpet, hear ye."

[113] Compare <u>Isaiah 60:1-2:</u> "Arise, shine; for thy light is come, and the glory of the LORD is risen upon thee. For, behold, the darkness shall cover the earth, and gross darkness the people; but the LORD shall arise upon thee, and his glory shall be seen upon thee."

<u>Psalms 112:4:</u> "Unto the upright there ariseth light in the darkness; he is gracious, and full of compassion, and righteous."

Chapter Nine

After these things came Jesus and his disciples into the land of Judaea, and there he tarried with them, and baptized, (though Jesus himself baptized not, but his disciples). And John also was baptizing in Aenon near to Salim, because there was much water there, and they came, and were baptized. (For John was not yet cast into prison). Then there arose a question between some of John's disciples and the Jews about purifying. And they came unto John, and said unto him, "Rabbi, he that was with thee beyond Jordan, to whom thou barest witness, behold, the same baptizeth, and all men come to him."

John answered and said, "A man can receive nothing, except it be given him from heaven. Ye yourselves bear me witness, that I said, 'I am not the Christ, but that I am sent before him.' He that hath the bride is the bridegroom, but the friend of the bridegroom, which standeth and heareth him, rejoiceth greatly because of the bridegroom's voice, this my joy therefore is fulfilled. He must increase, but I must decrease. He that cometh from above is above all, he that is of the earth is earthly, and speaketh of the earth, he that cometh from heaven is above all.[114] And what he hath seen and

---

[114] Compare *2 Esdras* 4:21: "For like as the ground is given unto the wood, and the sea to his floods; even so they that dwell upon the earth may understand nothing but that which is upon the earth; and he that dwelleth above the heavens may only understand the things that are above the height of the heavens."

heard, that he testifieth, and no man receiveth his testimony. He that hath received his testimony hath set to his seal that God is true. For he whom God hath sent speaketh the words of God, for God giveth not the Spirit by measure unto him. The Father loveth the Son, and hath given all things into his hand. He that believeth on the Son hath everlasting life, and he that believeth not the Son shall not see life, but the wrath of God abideth on him."

Chapter Ten

When therefore the LORD knew how the Pharisees had heard that Jesus made and baptized more disciples than John, he left Judaea, and departed again into Galilee. And he must needs go through Samaria.

Then cometh he to a city of Samaria, which is called Sychar, near to the parcel of ground that Jacob gave to his son Joseph. Now Jacob's well was there. Jesus therefore, being wearied with his journey, sat thus on the well, and it was about the sixth hour.

There cometh a woman of Samaria to draw water. Jesus saith unto her, "Give me to drink," (for his disciples were gone away unto the city to buy meat). Then saith the woman of Samaria unto him, "How is it that thou, being a Jew, askest drink of me, which am a woman of Samaria, for the Jews have no dealings with the Samaritans?" Jesus answered and said unto her, "If thou knewest the gift of God, and who it is that saith to thee, 'Give me to drink,' thou wouldest have asked of him, and he would have given thee living water."[115] The woman saith unto him, "Sir, thou hast nothing

---

[115] Compare <u>Zechariah 13:1:</u> "In that day there shall be a fountain opened to the house of David and to the inhabitants of Jerusalem for sin and for uncleanness."
<u>Jeremiah 2:13:</u> "For my people have committed two evils; they have forsaken me the fountain of living waters, and hewed them out cisterns, broken cisterns, that can hold no water."
<u>Proverbs 10:11:</u> "The mouth of a righteous man is a well of life; but violence covereth the mouth of the wicked."

THE TREE OF LIFE

to draw with, and the well is deep, from whence then hast thou that living water? Art thou greater than our father Jacob, which gave us the well, and drank thereof himself, and his children, and his cattle?" Jesus answered and said unto her, "Whosoever drinketh of this water shall thirst again, but whosoever drinketh of the water that I shall give him shall never thirst, but the water that I shall give him shall be in him a well of water springing up into everlasting life."[116] The woman saith unto him, "Sir, give me this water, that I thirst not, neither come hither to draw."

Jesus saith unto her, "Go, call thy husband, and come hither." The woman answered and said, "I have no husband." Jesus said unto her, "Thou hast well said, 'I have no husband,' for thou hast had five husbands, and he whom thou now hast is not thy husband, in that saidst thou truly."

The woman saith unto him, "Sir, I perceive that thou art a prophet. Our fathers worshipped in this mountain, and ye say, that in Jerusalem is the place where men ought to worship." Jesus saith unto her, "Woman, believe me, the hour cometh, when ye shall neither in this mountain, nor yet at Jerusalem, worship the Father. Ye worship ye know not what, we know what we worship, for salvation is of the Jews.[117] But the hour cometh, and now is, when

---

[116] Compare Psalms 36:9: "For with thee is the fountain of life; in thy light shall we see light."
Isaiah 58:11: "And the LORD shall guide thee continually, and satisfy thy soul in drought, and make fat thy bones; and thou shalt be like a watered garden, and like a spring of water, whose waters fail not."
Proverbs 14:27: "The fear of the LORD is a fountain of life, to depart from the snares of death."
2 Esdras 14:47: "For in [the wise] is the spring of understanding, the fountain of wisdom, and the stream of knowledge."
Sirach 21:13: "The knowledge of a wise man shall abound like a flood; and his counsel is like a pure fountain of life."
[117] Compare Genesis 12:1-3: "Now the LORD had said unto Abram, 'Get thee out of thy country, and from thy kindred, and from thy father's house, unto a land that I will shew thee. And I will make of thee a great nation, and I will bless thee, and make thy name great; and thou shalt be a blessing. And I will bless them that bless

THE TREE OF LIFE

the true worshippers shall worship the Father in spirit and in truth, for the Father seeketh such to worship him. God is a Spirit,[118] and they that worship him must worship him in spirit and in truth."[119]

---

thee, and curse him that curseth thee; and in thee shall all families of the earth be blessed.'"
Deuteronomy 7:6-8: "For thou art an holy people unto the LORD thy God; the LORD thy God hath chosen thee to be a special people unto himself, above all people that are upon the face of the earth. The LORD did not set his love upon you, nor choose you, because ye were more in number than any people; for ye were the fewest of all people. But because the LORD loved you, and because he would keep the oath which he had sworn unto your fathers, hath the LORD brought you out with a mighty hand, and redeemed you out of the house of bondmen, from the hand of Pharaoh king of Egypt."
Deuteronomy 9:5: "Not for thy righteousness, or for the uprightness of thine heart, dost thou go to possess their land; but for the wickedness of these nations the LORD thy God doth drive them out from before thee, and that he may perform the word which the LORD sware unto thy fathers, Abraham, Isaac, and Jacob. Understand therefore, that the LORD thy God giveth thee not this good land to possess it for thy righteousness; for thou art a stiffnecked people."
Deuteronomy 28:9: "The LORD shall establish thee an holy people unto himself, as he hath sworn unto thee, if thou shalt keep the commandments of the LORD thy God, and walk in his ways."
Ezekiel 36:27-28: "And I will put my spirit within you, and cause you to walk in my statutes, and ye shall keep my judgments, and do them. And ye shall dwell in the land that I gave to your fathers; and ye shall be my people, and I will be your God."
Psalms 86:9: "All nations whom thou hast made shall come and worship before thee, O Lord; and shall glorify thy name."
Isaiah 2:3 (and Micah 4:2): "And many people shall go and say, 'Come ye, and let us go up to the mountain of the LORD, to the house of the God of Jacob; and he will teach us of his ways, and we will walk in his paths;' for out of Zion shall go forth the law, and the word of the LORD from Jerusalem."
Jeremiah 3:17: "At that time they shall call Jerusalem the throne of the LORD; and all the nations shall be gathered unto it, to the name of the LORD, to Jerusalem; neither shall they walk any more after the imagination of their evil heart."
See also Genesis 22:15-18; Exodus 6:7-8; Leviticus 20:24; Deuteronomy 7:6-8, 9:5-6, 12:11, 14:2, 26:12-18, 27:9-10; 2 Chronicles 6:5; Jeremiah 13:11; et cetera.
[118] Compare Isaiah 31:3: "Now the Egyptians are men, and not God; and their horses flesh, and not spirit. When the LORD shall stretch out his hand, both he that helpeth shall fall, and he that is holpen shall fall down, and they all shall fail together."
[119] Compare Isaiah 58:2-11: "Yet they seek me daily, and delight to know my ways, as a nation that did righteousness, and forsook not the ordinance of their God; they ask of me the ordinances of justice; they take delight in approaching to God. 'Wherefore have we fasted,' say they, 'and thou seest not? Wherefore have we

THE TREE OF LIFE

The woman saith unto him, "I know that Messias cometh, which is called Christ. When he is come, he will tell us all things." Jesus saith unto her, "I that speak unto thee am he." And upon this came his disciples, and marvelled that he talked with the woman, yet no man said, "What seekest thou?" or, "Why talkest thou with her?"

The woman then left her waterpot, and went her way into the city, and saith to the men, "Come, see a man, which told me all things that ever I did, is not this the Christ?" Then they went out of the city, and came unto him.

In the mean while his disciples prayed him, saying, "Master, eat." But he said unto them, "I have meat to eat that ye know not of." Therefore said the disciples one to another, "Hath any man brought him ought to eat?" Jesus saith unto them, "My meat is to do the will of him that sent me,[120] and to finish his work.[121] Say not ye, 'There

---

afflicted our soul, and thou takest no knowledge?' Behold, in the day of your fast ye find pleasure, and exact all your labours. Behold, ye fast for strife and debate, and to smite with the fist of wickedness; ye shall not fast as ye do this day, to make your voice to be heard on high. Is it such a fast that I have chosen? A day for a man to afflict his soul? Is it to bow down his head as a bulrush, and to spread sackcloth and ashes under him? Wilt thou call this a fast, and an acceptable day to the LORD? Is not this the fast that I have chosen? To loose the bands of wickedness, to undo the heavy burdens, and to let the oppressed go free, and that ye break every yoke? Is it not to deal thy bread to the hungry, and that thou bring the poor that are cast out to thy house? When thou seest the naked, that thou cover him; and that thou hide not thyself from thine own flesh? Then shall thy light break forth as the morning, and thine health shall spring forth speedily; and thy righteousness shall go before thee; the glory of the LORD shall be thy rearward. Then shalt thou call, and the LORD shall answer; thou shalt cry, and he shall say, 'Here I am.' If thou take away from the midst of thee the yoke, the putting forth of the finger, and speaking vanity. And if thou draw out thy soul to the hungry, and satisfy the afflicted soul; then shall thy light rise in obscurity, and thy darkness be as the noonday. And the LORD shall guide thee continually, and satisfy thy soul in drought, and make fat thy bones; and thou shalt be like a watered garden, and like a spring of water, whose waters fail not."
[120] Compare Job 23:12: "Neither have I gone back from the commandment of his lips; I have esteemed the words of his mouth more than my necessary food."
Numbers 16:28: "And Moses said, 'Hereby ye shall know that the LORD hath sent me to do all these works; for I have not done them of mine own mind.'"

are yet four months, and then cometh harvest?' Behold, I say unto you, 'Lift up your eyes, and look on the fields, for they are white already to harvest. And he that reapeth receiveth wages, and gathereth fruit unto life eternal, that both he that soweth and he that reapeth may rejoice together.' And herein is that saying true, one soweth, and another reapeth. I sent you to reap that whereon ye bestowed no labour, other men laboured, and ye are entered into their labours."

And many of the Samaritans of that city believed on him for the saying of the woman, which testified, "He told me all that ever I did." So when the Samaritans were come unto him, they besought him that he would tarry with them, and he abode there two days. And many more believed because of his own word, and said unto the woman, "Now we believe, not because of thy saying, for we have heard him ourselves, and know that this is indeed the Christ, the Saviour of the world."[122]

Proverbs 3:5-8: "Trust in the LORD with all thine heart; and lean not unto thine own understanding. In all thy ways acknowledge him, and he shall direct thy paths. Be not wise in thine own eyes; fear the LORD, and depart from evil. It shall be health to thy navel, and marrow to thy bones."
[121] See Psalms 146:5-10: "Happy is he that hath the God of Jacob for his help, whose hope is in the LORD his God; which made heaven, and earth, the sea, and all that therein is; which keepeth truth for ever; which executeth judgment for the oppressed; which giveth food to the hungry. The LORD looseth the prisoners; the LORD openeth the eyes of the blind; the LORD raiseth them that are bowed down; the LORD loveth the righteous; the LORD preserveth the strangers; he relieveth the fatherless and widow; but the way of the wicked he turneth upside down. The LORD shall reign for ever, even thy God, O Zion, unto all generations. Praise ye the LORD."
[122] See Jeremiah 3:17: "At that time they shall call Jerusalem the throne of the LORD; and all the nations shall be gathered unto it, to the name of the LORD, to Jerusalem; neither shall they walk any more after the imagination of their evil heart."

THE TREE OF LIFE

Chapter Eleven

Now after two days Jesus had heard that John was cast into prison, and he departed thence, and returned in the power of the Spirit into Galilee, preaching the gospel of the kingdom of God, and saying, "The time is fulfilled, and the kingdom of God is at hand, repent ye, and believe the gospel." And there went out a fame of him through all the region round about.

Then when he was come into Galilee, the Galilaeans received him, having seen all the things that he did at Jerusalem at the feast, for they also went unto the feast. And he taught in their synagogues, being glorified of all.

And leaving Nazareth, he came and dwelt in Capernaum, which is upon the sea coast, in the borders of Zebulun and Naphtali, that it might be fulfilled which was spoken by Isaiah the prophet, saying, *"The land of Zebulun, and the land of Naphtali, by the way of the sea, beyond Jordan, Galilee of the Gentiles, the people which sat in darkness saw great light, and to them which sat in the region and shadow of death, light is sprung up."*[123]

---

[123] "Nevertheless the dimness shall not be such as was in her vexation, when at the first he lightly afflicted the land of Zebulun and the land of Naphtali, and afterward did more grievously afflict her by the way of the sea, beyond Jordan, in Galilee of the nations. The people that walked in darkness have seen a great light; they that dwell in the land of the shadow of death, upon them hath the light shined." – Isaiah 9:1-2

THE TREE OF LIFE

From that time Jesus began to preach, and to say, "Repent, for the kingdom of heaven is at hand." And it came to pass, that, as the people pressed upon him to hear the word of God, he stood by the lake of Gennesaret, and saw two brethren, Simon called Peter, and Andrew his brother, casting a net into the sea, for they were fishers.

Now as he walked by the sea of Galilee, he saw their two ships standing by the lake, but the fishermen were gone out of them, and were washing their nets. And he entered into one of the ships, which was Simon's, and prayed him that he would thrust out a little from the land. And he sat down, and taught the people out of the ship.

Now when he had left speaking, he said unto Simon, "Launch out into the deep, and let down your nets for a draught." And Simon answering said unto him, "Master, we have toiled all the night, and have taken nothing, nevertheless at thy word I will let down the net." And when they had this done, they inclosed a great multitude of fishes, and their net brake. And they beckoned unto their partners, which were in the other ship, that they should come and help them. And they came, and filled both the ships, so that they began to sink. When Simon Peter saw it, he fell down at Jesus' knees, saying, "Depart from me, for I am a sinful man, O Lord," for he was astonished, and all that were with him, at the draught of the fishes which they had taken, and so was also James, and John, the sons of Zebedee, which were partners with Simon. And Jesus said unto Simon, "Fear not, come follow me, and I will make you fishers of men."[124]

---

[124] See Jeremiah 16:16: "Behold, I will send for many fishers, saith the LORD, and they shall fish them; and after will I send for many hunters, and they shall hunt them from every mountain, and from every hill, and out of the holes of the rocks."
Compare 1 Kings 19:19-21: "So [Elijah] departed thence, and found Elisha the son of Shaphat, who was plowing with twelve yoke of oxen before him, and he with the twelfth; and Elijah passed by him, and cast his mantle upon him. And he left the oxen, and ran after Elijah, and said, 'Let me, I pray thee, kiss my father and my mother, and then I will follow thee.' And he said unto him, 'Go back again; for what have I done to thee?' And he returned back from him, and took a yoke of oxen, and

THE TREE OF LIFE

And when they had brought their ships to land, they straightway forsook all, and followed him. And when he had gone a little farther thence, he saw James the son of Zebedee, and John his brother, who also were in the ship mending their nets with Zebedee their father. And straightway he called them, and they immediately left their father Zebedee in the ship with the hired servants, and went after him.

slew them, and boiled their flesh with the instruments of the oxen, and gave unto the people, and they did eat. Then he arose, and went after Elijah, and ministered unto him."

THE TREE OF LIFE

Chapter Twelve

So Jesus came again into Cana of Galilee, where he made the water wine. And there was a certain nobleman, whose son was sick at Capernaum. When he heard that Jesus was come out of Judaea into Galilee, he went unto him, and besought him that he would come down, and heal his son, for he was at the point of death. Then said Jesus unto him, "Except ye see signs and wonders, ye will not believe." The nobleman saith unto him, "Sir, come down ere my child die." Jesus saith unto him, "Go thy way, thy son liveth." And the man believed the word that Jesus had spoken unto him, and he went his way. And as he was now going down, his servants met him, and told him, saying, "Thy son liveth." Then enquired he of them the hour when he began to amend. And they said unto him, "Yesterday at the seventh hour the fever left him." So the father knew that it was at the same hour, in the which Jesus said unto him, "Thy son liveth," and himself believed, and his whole house. This is again the second miracle that Jesus did, when he was come out of Judaea into Galilee.

THE TREE OF LIFE

THE TREE OF LIFE

Chapter Thirteen

And he came to Nazareth, where he had been brought up, and, as his custom was, he went into the synagogue on the sabbath day, and stood up for to read. And there was delivered unto him the book of the prophet Isaiah. And when he had opened the book, he found the place where it was written, *"The Spirit of the Lord is upon me, because he hath anointed me to preach the gospel to the poor, he hath sent me to heal the brokenhearted, to preach deliverance to the captives, and recovering of sight to the blind, to set at liberty them that are bruised, to preach the acceptable year of the Lord."*[125] And he closed the book, and he gave it again to the minister, and sat down. And the eyes of all them that were in the synagogue were fastened on him. And he began to say unto them, "This day is this scripture fulfilled in your ears." And all bare him witness, and wondered at the gracious words which proceeded out of his mouth. And they said, "Is not this Joseph's son?"[126] And he said

---

[125] "The Spirit of the Lord GOD is upon me; because the LORD hath anointed me to preach good tidings unto the meek; he hath sent me to bind up the brokenhearted, to proclaim liberty to the captives, and the opening of the prison to them that are bound; to proclaim the acceptable year of the LORD, and the day of vengeance of our God; to comfort all that mourn; to appoint unto them that mourn in Zion, to give unto them beauty for ashes, the oil of joy for mourning, the garment of praise for the spirit of heaviness; that they might be called trees of righteousness, the planting of the LORD, that he might be glorified." – Isaiah 61:1-3

[126] See Isaiah 53:1-2: "Who hath believed our report? And to whom is the arm of the LORD revealed? For he shall grow up before him as a tender plant, and as a root

unto them, "Ye will surely say unto me this proverb, 'Physician, heal thyself,' whatsoever we have heard done in Capernaum, do also here in thy country." And he said, "Verily I say unto you, no prophet is accepted in his own country. But I tell you of a truth, many widows were in Israel in the days of Elijah, when the heaven was shut up three years and six months, when great famine was throughout all the land, but unto none of them was Elijah sent, save unto Zarephath, a city of Zidon, unto a woman that was a widow.[127] And many lepers were in Israel in the time of Elisha the prophet, and none of them was cleansed, saving Naaman the Syrian."[128]

And all they in the synagogue, when they heard these things, were filled with wrath, and rose up, and thrust him out of the city, and led him unto the brow of the hill whereon their city was built, that they might cast him down headlong.

---

out of a dry ground; he hath no form nor comeliness; and when we shall see him, there is no beauty that we should desire him."
[127] See 1 Kings 17:8-16.
[128] See 2 Kings 5:1-19.

THE TREE OF LIFE

Chapter Fourteen

But he passing through the midst of them went his way, and came down to Capernaum, a city of Galilee. And they went into Capernaum, and straightway on the sabbath day he entered into the synagogue, and taught. And they were astonished at his doctrine, and he taught them as one that had authority,[129] and not as the scribes, for his word was with power.

And in the synagogue there was a man with an unclean spirit, and he cried out with a loud voice, saying, "Let us alone, what have we to do with thee, thou Jesus of Nazareth? Art thou come to destroy us?[130] I know thee who thou art: the Holy One of God."[131] And Jesus rebuked him,[132] saying, "Hold thy peace, and come out of

---

[129] Compare <u>1 Maccabees 4:44-46:</u> "And when as they consulted what to do with the altar of burnt offerings, which was profaned; they thought it best to pull it down, lest it should be a reproach to them, because the heathen had defiled it. Wherefore they pulled it down, and laid up the stones in the mountain of the temple in a convenient place, until there should come a prophet to shew what should be done with them."

[130] Compare <u>1 Kings 17:18:</u> "And she said unto Elijah, 'What have I to do with thee, O thou man of God? Art thou come unto me to call my sin to remembrance, and to slay my son?'"

[131] Compare <u>Psalms 89:18:</u> "For the LORD is our defence; and the Holy One of Israel is our king."
<u>Isaiah 10:17:</u> "And the light of Israel shall be for a fire, and his Holy One for a flame; and it shall burn and devour his thorns and his briers in one day."

[132] Compare <u>Zechariah 3:2:</u> "And the LORD said unto Satan, 'The LORD rebuke thee, O Satan; even the LORD that hath chosen Jerusalem rebuke thee; is not this a brand plucked out of the fire?'"

him." And when the devil had thrown him in the midst, and cried with a loud voice, he came out of him, and hurt him not. And they were all amazed, insomuch that they questioned among themselves, saying, "What thing is this? What new doctrine is this? For with authority and power he commandeth even the unclean spirits, and they do obey him and come out." And immediately his fame spread abroad throughout all the region round about Galilee.

And he arose out of the synagogue, and forthwith, when they were come out of the synagogue, they entered into the house of Simon and Andrew, with James and John. And when Jesus was come into Peter's house, he saw Simon's wife's mother was taken with a great fever, and they besought him for her. And he stood over her, and rebuked the fever, and he took her by the hand lifted her up, and immediately the fever left her, and she arose, and ministered unto them.

When the even was come, when the sun was setting, they brought unto him all that were diseased, all they that had any sick with divers diseases, and many that were possessed with devils. And all the city was gathered together at the door. And he laid his hands on every one of them, and healed them that were sick. That it might be fulfilled which was spoken by Isaiah the prophet, saying, "*Himself took our infirmities, and bare our sicknesses.*"[133] And he cast out the spirits with his word, and he rebuking them, suffered not the devils to speak, because they knew him, crying out, and saying, "Thou art Christ[134] the Son of God."[135]

---

[133] "Surely he hath borne our griefs, and carried our sorrows; yet we did esteem him stricken, smitten of God, and afflicted." – Isaiah 53:4
[134] See Jeremiah 23:5: "Behold, the days come, saith the LORD, that I will raise unto David a righteous Branch, and a King shall reign and prosper, and shall execute judgment and justice in the earth."
[135] See 2 Esdras 13:29,32: "Behold, the days come, when the most High will begin to deliver them that are upon the earth. And the time shall be when these things shall come to pass, and the signs shall happen which I shewed thee before, and then shall my Son be declared, whom thou sawest as a man ascending."

And in the morning, rising up a great while before day, he went out, and departed into a desert and solitary place, and there prayed. And Peter and they that were with him followed after him. And when they had found him, they said unto him, "All men seek for thee."

And he said unto them, "Let us go into the next towns, that I may preach there also, for therefore came I forth." And the people sought him, and came unto him, and stayed him, that he should not depart from them. And he said unto them, "I must preach the kingdom of God to other cities also, for therefore am I sent."

And Jesus went throughout all Galilee, teaching in their synagogues, and preaching the gospel of the kingdom, and healing all manner of sickness and all manner of diseases and torments among the people, and those which were possessed with devils, and those which were lunatick, and those that had the palsy, and he healed them. And his fame went throughout all Syria.

And there followed him great multitudes of people from Galilee, and from Decapolis, and from Jerusalem, and from Judaea, and from beyond Jordan. And he came down with them, and stood in the plain, and the company of his disciples, and a great multitude of people out of all Judaea and Jerusalem, and from the sea coast of Tyre and Zidon, which came to hear him, and to be healed of their diseases, and they that were vexed with unclean spirits, and they were healed. And the whole multitude sought to touch him, for there went virtue out of him, and healed them all.

THE TREE OF LIFE

THE TREE OF LIFE

Chapter Fifteen

And seeing the multitudes, he went up into a mountain, and when he was set, his disciples came unto him, and he lifted up his eyes on his disciples, and he opened his mouth, and taught them,[136] saying,

"Blessed are the poor in spirit, for theirs is the kingdom of heaven.[137] Blessed are they that mourn, for they shall be comforted.[138] Blessed are the meek, for they shall inherit the

---

[136] Compare Isaiah 61:1-3: "The Spirit of the Lord GOD is upon me; because the LORD hath anointed me to preach good tidings unto the meek; he hath sent me to bind up the brokenhearted, to proclaim liberty to the captives, and the opening of the prison to them that are bound; to proclaim the acceptable year of the LORD, and the day of vengeance of our God; to comfort all that mourn; to appoint unto them that mourn in Zion, to give unto them beauty for ashes, the oil of joy for mourning, the garment of praise for the spirit of heaviness; that they might be called trees of righteousness, the planting of the LORD, that he might be glorified."
[137] Compare Isaiah 57:15: "For thus saith the high and lofty One that inhabiteth eternity, whose name is Holy; I dwell in the high and holy place, with him also that is of a contrite and humble spirit, to revive the spirit of the humble, and to revive the heart of the contrite ones."
Isaiah 66:2: "For all those things hath mine hand made, and all those things have been, saith the LORD; but to this man will I look, even to him that is poor and of a contrite spirit, and trembleth at my word."
Psalms 34:18: "The LORD is nigh unto them that are of a broken heart; and saveth such as be of a contrite spirit."
[138] Compare Isaiah 61:2-3: "To proclaim liberty to the captives, and the opening of the prison to them that are bound; to proclaim the acceptable year of the LORD, and the day of vengeance of our God; to comfort all that mourn; to appoint unto them that mourn in Zion, to give unto them beauty for ashes, the oil of joy for

earth.¹³⁹ Blessed are they which do hunger and thirst after righteousness, for they shall be filled.¹⁴⁰ Blessed are they that hunger now, for they shall be filled.¹⁴¹ Blessed are they that weep now, for they shall laugh.¹⁴² Blessed are the merciful, for they shall

---

mourning, the garment of praise for the spirit of heaviness; that they might be called trees of righteousness, the planting of the LORD, that he might be glorified."
Isaiah 35:10: "And the ransomed of the LORD shall return, and come to Zion with songs and everlasting joy upon their heads; they shall obtain joy and gladness, and sorrow and sighing shall flee away."
Isaiah 49:13: "Sing, O heavens; and be joyful, O earth; and break forth into singing, O mountains; for the LORD hath comforted his people, and will have mercy upon his afflicted."
¹³⁹ Compare Psalms 37:11: "But the meek shall inherit the earth; and shall delight themselves in the abundance of peace."
Isaiah 29:19: "The meek also shall increase their joy in the LORD, and the poor among men shall rejoice in the Holy One of Israel."
Isaiah 57:13: "When thou criest, let thy companies deliver thee; but the wind shall carry them all away; vanity shall take them; but he that putteth his trust in me shall possess the land, and shall inherit my holy mountain."
¹⁴⁰ Compare Psalms 107:8-9: "Oh that men would praise the LORD for his goodness, and for his wonderful works to the children of men! For he satisfieth the longing soul, and filleth the hungry soul with goodness."
Psalms 42:1-2: "As the hart panteth after the water brooks, so panteth my soul after thee, O God. My soul thirsteth for God, for the living God; when shall I come and appear before God?"
Psalms 63:1,5: "O God, thou art my God; early will I seek thee; my soul thirsteth for thee, my flesh longeth for thee in a dry and thirsty land, where no water is. My soul shall be satisfied as with marrow and fatness; and my mouth shall praise thee with joyful lips."
¹⁴¹ Compare Psalms 37:3: "Trust in the LORD, and do good; so shalt thou dwell in the land, and verily thou shalt be fed."
Psalms 37:25: "I have been young, and now am old; yet have I not seen the righteous forsaken, nor his seed begging bread."
Leviticus 26:4: "Then I will give you rain in due season, and the land shall yield her increase, and the trees of the field shall yield their fruit."
Psalms 78:27-29: "He rained flesh also upon them as dust, and feathered fowls like as the sand of the sea. And he let it fall in the midst of their camp, round about their habitations. So they did eat, and were well filled; for he gave them their own desire;"
¹⁴² Compare Isaiah 25:8: "He will swallow up death in victory; and the Lord GOD will wipe away tears from off all faces; and the rebuke of his people shall he take away from off all the earth; for the LORD hath spoken it."
Genesis 18:9-12, 21:6-7: "And they said unto him, 'Where is Sarah thy wife?' And he said, 'Behold, in the tent.' And he said, 'I will certainly return unto thee according to

THE TREE OF LIFE

obtain mercy.[143] Blessed are the pure in heart, for they shall see God.[144] Blessed are the peacemakers, for they shall be called the children of God.[145] Blessed are they which are persecuted for

the time of life; and, lo, Sarah thy wife shall have a son.' And Sarah heard it in the tent door, which was behind him. Now Abraham and Sarah were old and well stricken in age; and it ceased to be with Sarah after the manner of women. Therefore Sarah laughed within herself, saying, 'After I am waxed old shall I have pleasure, my lord being old also?' And Sarah said, 'God hath made me to laugh, so that all that hear will laugh with me.' And she said, 'Who would have said unto Abraham, that Sarah should have given children suck? For I have born him a son in his old age.'"

[143] Compare Psalms 18:25 (and 2 Samuel 22:26): "With the merciful thou wilt shew thyself merciful; with an upright man thou wilt shew thyself upright."
Proverbs 11:17: "The merciful man doeth good to his own soul; but he that is cruel troubleth his own flesh."
2 Samuel 10:2: "Then said David, 'I will shew kindness unto Hanun the son of Nahash, as his father shewed kindness unto me.' And David sent to comfort him by the hand of his servants for his father. And David's servants came into the land of the children of Ammon."

[144] Compare Psalms 24:3-5: "Who shall ascend into the hill of the LORD? Or who shall stand in his holy place? He that hath clean hands, and a pure heart; who hath not lifted up his soul unto vanity, nor sworn deceitfully. He shall receive the blessing from the LORD, and righteousness from the God of his salvation."
Psalms 17:15: "As for me, I will behold thy face in righteousness; I shall be satisfied, when I awake, with thy likeness."
Psalms 27:8-9: "When thou saidst, 'Seek ye my face;' my heart said unto thee, 'Thy face, LORD, will I seek.' Hide not thy face far from me; put not thy servant away in anger; thou hast been my help; leave me not, neither forsake me, O God of my salvation."
Job 33:26: "He shall pray unto God, and he will be favourable unto him; and he shall see his face with joy; for he will render unto man his righteousness."
Psalms 63:2: "O God, thou art my God; early will I seek thee; my soul thirsteth for thee, my flesh longeth for thee in a dry and thirsty land, where no water is; to see thy power and thy glory, so as I have seen thee in the sanctuary."

[145] Compare Proverbs 16:7: "When a man's ways please the LORD, he maketh even his enemies to be at peace with him."
Psalms 37:37: "Mark the perfect man, and behold the upright; for the end of that man is peace."
Hosea 1:10: "Yet the number of the children of Israel shall be as the sand of the sea, which cannot be measured nor numbered; and it shall come to pass, that in the place where it was said unto them, 'Ye are not my people,' there it shall be said unto them, 'Ye are the sons of the living God.'"
Psalms 2:7: "I will declare the decree; the LORD hath said unto me, 'Thou art my Son; this day have I begotten thee.'"
See also Psalms 34:14; Joshua 9:15.

righteousness' sake, for theirs is the kingdom of heaven.[146] Blessed are ye, when men shall hate you, and revile you, and persecute you, and shall say all manner of evil against you falsely, for my sake, and when they shall separate you from their company, and shall reproach you, and cast out your name as evil, for the Son of man's sake.[147] Rejoice ye in that day, and leap for joy, and be exceeding glad, for behold, great is your reward in heaven, for so persecuted they the prophets which were before you, and in the like manner did their fathers unto the prophets.[148]

"But woe unto you that are rich, for ye have received your consolation. Woe unto you that are full, for ye shall hunger. Woe unto you that laugh now, for ye shall mourn and weep. Woe unto you, when all men shall speak well of you, for so did their fathers to the false prophets."

---

[146] Compare Psalms 69:7-9: "Because for thy sake I have borne reproach; shame hath covered my face. I am become a stranger unto my brethren, and an alien unto my mother's children. For the zeal of thine house hath eaten me up; and the reproaches of them that reproached thee are fallen upon me."
Jeremiah 15:15: "O LORD, thou knowest; remember me, and visit me, and revenge me of my persecutors; take me not away in thy longsuffering; know that for thy sake I have suffered rebuke."
[147] Compare Isaiah 51:7: "Hearken unto me, ye that know righteousness, the people in whose heart is my law; fear ye not the reproach of men, neither be ye afraid of their revilings."
Isaiah 66:5: "Hear the word of the LORD, ye that tremble at his word; your brethren that hated you, that cast you out for my name's sake, said, 'Let the LORD be glorified;' but he shall appear to your joy, and they shall be ashamed."
Sirach 2:1-5: "My son, if thou come to serve the Lord, prepare thy soul for temptation. Set thy heart aright, and constantly endure, and make not haste in time of trouble. Cleave unto him, and depart not away, that thou mayest be increased at thy last end. Whatsoever is brought upon thee take cheerfully, and be patient when thou art changed to a low estate. For gold is tried in the fire, and acceptable men in the furnace of adversity."
[148] See 1 Kings 18:13; 2 Chronicles 24:20-21, 16:10; Isaiah 66:5,13-14; Jeremiah 11:21, 20:2, 37:13-15; Daniel 6:13-16; Amos 7:10-13; et cetera.

THE TREE OF LIFE

"For every one shall be salted with fire, and every sacrifice shall be salted with salt.[149] Ye are the salt of the earth, and salt is good, but if the salt have lost his savour, wherewith shall it be seasoned? It is thenceforth good for nothing, neither fit for the land, nor yet for the dunghill, but to be cast out, and to be trodden under foot of men. Have salt in yourselves,[150] and have peace one with another. *He that hath ears to hear, let him hear.*[151]

"Ye are the light of the world.[152] A city that is set on an hill cannot be hid. No man, when he hath lighted a candle, putteth it in a secret place, neither under a bushel, but on a candlestick, that they which come in may see the light, and it giveth light unto all that are in the house.[153] Let your light so shine before men, that they may see your good works,[154] and glorify your Father which is in heaven.

---

[149] See Leviticus 2:13: "And every oblation of thy meat offering shalt thou season with salt; neither shalt thou suffer the salt of the covenant of thy God to be lacking from thy meat offering; with all thine offerings thou shalt offer salt."
[150] Compare 2 Kings 2:19-22: "And the men of the city said unto Elisha, 'Behold, I pray thee, the situation of this city is pleasant, as my lord seeth; but the water is naught, and the ground barren.' And he said, 'Bring me a new cruse, and put salt therein.' And they brought it to him. And he went forth unto the spring of the waters, and cast the salt in there, and said, 'Thus saith the LORD, I have healed these waters; there shall not be from thence any more death or barren land.' So the waters were healed unto this day, according to the saying of Elisha which he spake."
[151] See Ezekiel 3:27: "But when I speak with thee, I will open thy mouth, and thou shalt say unto them, 'Thus saith the Lord GOD; He that heareth, let him hear; and he that forbeareth, let him forbear;' for they are a rebellious house."
[152] Compare Isaiah 42:6: "I the LORD have called thee in righteousness, and will hold thine hand, and will keep thee, and give thee for a covenant of the people, for a light of the Gentiles."
Daniel 12:3: "And they that be wise shall shine as the brightness of the firmament; and they that turn many to righteousness as the stars for ever and ever."
[153] Compare Psalms 18:28: "For thou wilt light my candle; the LORD my God will enlighten my darkness."
Isaiah 51:4-5: "Hearken unto me, my people; and give ear unto me, O my nation; for a law shall proceed from me, and I will make my judgment to rest for a light of the people. My righteousness is near; my salvation is gone forth, and mine arms shall judge the people; the isles shall wait upon me, and on mine arm shall they trust."
[154] See Psalms 146:5-10: "Happy is he that hath the God of Jacob for his help, whose hope is in the LORD his God; which made heaven, and earth, the sea, and all that

"Think not that I am come to destroy the law, or the prophets. I am not come to destroy, but to fulfil.[155] For verily I say unto you, till heaven and earth pass, one jot or one tittle shall in no wise pass from the law, till all be fulfilled.[156] Whosoever therefore shall break one of these least commandments, and shall teach men so, he shall be called the least in the kingdom of heaven, but whosoever shall do and teach them, the same shall be called great in the kingdom of heaven. For I say unto you, that except your righteousness shall

---

therein is; which keepeth truth for ever; which executeth judgment for the oppressed; which giveth food to the hungry. The LORD looseth the prisoners; the LORD openeth the eyes of the blind; the LORD raiseth them that are bowed down; the LORD loveth the righteous; the LORD preserveth the strangers; he relieveth the fatherless and widow; but the way of the wicked he turneth upside down. The LORD shall reign for ever, even thy God, O Zion, unto all generations. Praise ye the LORD."
[155] See Genesis 49:10: "The sceptre shall not depart from Judah, nor a lawgiver from between his feet, until Shiloh come; and unto him shall the gathering of the people be."
Deuteronomy 18:15: "The LORD thy God will raise up unto thee a Prophet from the midst of thee, of thy brethren, like unto me; unto him ye shall hearken."
[156] Compare Isaiah 40:8: "The grass withereth, the flower fadeth; but the word of our God shall stand for ever."
Isaiah 51:6-8: "Lift up your eyes to the heavens, and look upon the earth beneath; for the heavens shall vanish away like smoke, and the earth shall wax old like a garment, and they that dwell therein shall die in like manner; but my salvation shall be for ever, and my righteousness shall not be abolished. Hearken unto me, ye that know righteousness, the people in whose heart is my law; fear ye not the reproach of men, neither be ye afraid of their revilings. For the moth shall eat them up like a garment, and the worm shall eat them like wool; but my righteousness shall be for ever, and my salvation from generation to generation."
Psalms 102:24-27: "I said, O my God, take me not away in the midst of my days; thy years are throughout all generations. Of old hast thou laid the foundation of the earth; and the heavens are the work of thy hands. They shall perish, but thou shalt endure; yea, all of them shall wax old like a garment; as a vesture shalt thou change them, and they shall be changed. But thou art the same, and thy years shall have no end."
2 Esdras 9:36-37: "For we that have received the law perish by sin, and our heart also which received it. Notwithstanding the law perisheth not, but remaineth in his force."
Baruch 4:1: "This is the book of the commandments of God, and the law that endureth for ever; all they that keep it shall come to life; but such as leave it shall die."

exceed the righteousness of the scribes and Pharisees, ye shall in no case enter into the kingdom of heaven.

"Ye have heard that it was said by them of old time, 'Thou shalt not kill,'[157] and 'whosoever shall kill shall be in danger of the judgment.'[158] But I say unto you, that whosoever is angry with his brother without a cause shall be in danger of the judgment. And 'whosoever shall say to his brother, "Raca," shall be in danger of the council,'[159] but I say, whosoever shall say, 'Thou fool,' shall be in danger of hell fire.[160] Therefore if thou bring thy gift to the altar, and there rememberest that thy brother hath ought against thee, leave there thy gift before the altar, and go thy way, first be reconciled to thy brother, and then come and offer thy gift. Agree with thine adversary quickly, while thou art in the way with him, lest at any time the adversary deliver thee to the judge, and the judge deliver thee to the officer, and thou be cast into prison. Verily I say unto

---

[157] "Thou shalt not kill." – Exodus 20:13 (and Deuteronomy 5:17).
[158] Compare Genesis 9:6: "Whoso sheddeth man's blood, by man shall his blood be shed; for in the image of God made he man."
Exodus 21:12: "He that smiteth a man, so that he die, shall be surely put to death."
Leviticus 24:17: "And he that killeth any man shall surely be put to death."
Deuteronomy 16:18: "Judges and officers shalt thou make thee in all thy gates, which the LORD thy God giveth thee, throughout thy tribes; and they shall judge the people with just judgment."
Numbers 35:24,30: "Then the congregation shall judge between the slayer and the revenger of blood according to these judgments. Whoso killeth any person, the murderer shall be put to death by the mouth of witnesses; but one witness shall not testify against any person to cause him to die."
[159] See Psalms 101:5: "Whoso privily slandereth his neighbour, him will I cut off; him that hath an high look and a proud heart will not I suffer."
Proverbs 19:29: "Judgments are prepared for scorners, and stripes for the back of fools."
Leviticus 19:17: "Thou shalt not hate thy brother in thine heart; thou shalt in any wise rebuke thy neighbour, and not suffer sin upon him."
[160] Compare Deuteronomy 32:21-22: "They have moved me to jealousy with that which is not God; they have provoked me to anger with their vanities; and I will move them to jealousy with those which are not a people; I will provoke them to anger with a foolish nation. For a fire is kindled in mine anger, and shall burn unto the lowest hell, and shall consume the earth with her increase, and set on fire the foundations of the mountains."

thee, thou shalt by no means come out thence, till thou hast paid the uttermost farthing.[161]

"Ye have heard that it was said by them of old time, *'Thou shalt not commit adultery.'*[162] But I say unto you, that whosoever looketh on a woman to lust after her hath committed adultery with her already in his heart.[163] And if thy right eye offend thee, pluck it out, and cast it from thee, for it is profitable for thee that one of thy members should perish, and not that thy whole body should be cast into hell.[164] And if thy right hand offend thee, cut it off, and cast it from thee, for it is profitable for thee that one of thy members should perish, and not that thy whole body should be cast into hell. It hath been said, *'Whosoever shall put away his wife, let him give her a writing of divorcement.'*[165] But I say unto you, that whosoever shall put away his wife, saving for the cause of fornication, causeth her to commit adultery, and whosoever shall marry her that is divorced committeth adultery.[166]

---

[161] Compare Proverbs 6:1-5: "My son, if thou be surety for thy friend, if thou hast stricken thy hand with a stranger, thou art snared with the words of thy mouth, thou art taken with the words of thy mouth. Do this now, my son, and deliver thyself, when thou art come into the hand of thy friend; go, humble thyself, and make sure thy friend. Give not sleep to thine eyes, nor slumber to thine eyelids. Deliver thyself as a roe from the hand of the hunter, and as a bird from the hand of the fowler."
[162] "Thou shalt not commit adultery." – Exodus 20:14 (and Deuteronomy 5:18).
[163] Compare Job 31:1: "I made a covenant with mine eyes; why then should I think upon a maid?
Sirach 9:8: "Turn away thine eye from a beautiful woman, and look not upon another's beauty; for many have been deceived by the beauty of a woman; for herewith love is kindled as a fire."
[164] See Psalms 9:17: "The wicked shall be turned into hell, and all the nations that forget God."
[165] "When a man hath taken a wife, and married her, and it come to pass that she find no favour in his eyes, because he hath found some uncleanness in her; then let him write her a bill of divorcement, and give it in her hand, and send her out of his house." – Deuteronomy 24:1
[166] Compare Leviticus 21:13-14: "And [a priest] shall take a wife in her virginity. A widow, or a divorced woman, or profane, or an harlot, these shall he not take; but he shall take a virgin of his own people to wife."

"Again, ye have heard that it hath been said by them of old time, *'Thou shalt not forswear thyself, but shalt perform unto the Lord thine oaths.'*[167] But I say unto you, swear not at all, neither by heaven, for it is God's throne, nor by the earth, for it is his footstool,[168] neither by Jerusalem, for it is the city of the great King.[169] Neither shalt thou swear by thy head, because thou canst not make one hair white or black. But let your communication be, 'Yea, yea,' 'Nay, nay,' for whatsoever is more than these cometh of evil.[170]

"Ye have heard that it hath been said, *'An eye for an eye, and a tooth for a tooth.'*[171] But I say unto you, that ye resist not evil,[172] but

---

Ezekiel 44:22: "Neither shall [the priests] take for their wives a widow, nor her that is put away; but they shall take maidens of the seed of the house of Israel, or a widow that had a priest before."

Exodus 19:5-6: "'Now therefore, if ye will obey my voice indeed, and keep my covenant, then ye shall be a peculiar treasure unto me above all people; for all the earth is mine. And ye shall be unto me a kingdom of priests, and an holy nation.' These are the words which thou shalt speak unto the children of Israel."

[167] "If a man vow a vow unto the LORD, or swear an oath to bind his soul with a bond; he shall not break his word, he shall do according to all that proceedeth out of his mouth." – Numbers 30:2
"When thou shalt vow a vow unto the LORD thy God, thou shalt not slack to pay it; for the LORD thy God will surely require it of thee; and it would be sin in thee." – Deuteronomy 23:21

[168] See Isaiah 66:1: "Thus saith the LORD, The heaven is my throne, and the earth is my footstool; where is the house that ye build unto me? And where is the place of my rest?"

[169] See Psalms 48:2: "Beautiful for situation, the joy of the whole earth, is mount Zion, on the sides of the north, the city of the great King."

[170] Compare Ecclesiastes 5:4-5: "When thou vowest a vow unto God, defer not to pay it; for he hath no pleasure in fools; pay that which thou hast vowed. Better is it that thou shouldest not vow, than that thou shouldest vow and not pay."

[171] "And if a man cause a blemish in his neighbour; as he hath done, so shall it be done to him; Breach for breach, eye for eye, tooth for tooth; as he hath caused a blemish in a man, so shall it be done to him again." – Leviticus 24:19-20
"And thine eye shall not pity; but life shall go for life, eye for eye, tooth for tooth, hand for hand, foot for foot." – Deuteronomy 19:21
See also Exodus 21:23-25; Leviticus 24:19-20.

[172] Compare Proverbs 24:19-20: "Fret not thyself because of evil men, neither be thou envious at the wicked; for there shall be no reward to the evil man; the candle of the wicked shall be put out."

THE TREE OF LIFE

whosoever shall smite thee on the one cheek, offer him the other also.[173] And if any man will sue thee at the law, and take away thy coat, let him have thy cloak also. And whosoever shall compel thee to go a mile, go with him twain. Give to every man that asketh thee, and from him that would borrow of thee turn not thou away, and of him that taketh away thy goods ask them not again.[174]

"Ye have heard that it hath been said, *'Thou shalt love thy neighbour,'*[175] and hate thine enemy.[176] But I say unto you, love your

---

[173] Compare <u>Lamentations 3:26,28,30:</u> "It is good that a man should both hope and quietly wait for the salvation of the LORD. He sitteth alone and keepeth silence, because he hath borne it upon him. He giveth his cheek to him that smiteth him; he is filled full with reproach."
[174] Compare <u>Deuteronomy 15:7-8:</u> "If there be among you a poor man of one of thy brethren within any of thy gates in thy land which the LORD thy God giveth thee, thou shalt not harden thine heart, nor shut thine hand from thy poor brother; but thou shalt open thine hand wide unto him, and shalt surely lend him sufficient for his need, in that which he wanteth."
<u>Sirach 29:8-13:</u> "Yet have thou patience with a man in poor estate, and delay not to shew him mercy. Help the poor for the commandment's sake, and turn him not away because of his poverty. Lose thy money for thy brother and thy friend, and let it not rust under a stone to be lost. Lay up thy treasure according to the commandments of the most High, and it shall bring thee more profit than gold. Shut up alms in thy storehouses; and it shall deliver thee from all affliction. It shall fight for thee against thine enemies better than a mighty shield and strong spear."
[175] "Thou shalt not avenge, nor bear any grudge against the children of thy people, but thou shalt love thy neighbour as thyself: I am the LORD." – <u>Leviticus 19:18</u>
[176] Compare <u>Psalms 139:21-22:</u> "Do not I hate them, O LORD, that hate thee? And am not I grieved with those that rise up against thee? I hate them with perfect hatred; I count them mine enemies."
<u>2 Samuel 22:35-43:</u> "He teacheth my hands to war; so that a bow of steel is broken by mine arms. Thou hast also given me the shield of thy salvation; and thy gentleness hath made me great. Thou hast enlarged my steps under me; so that my feet did not slip. I have pursued mine enemies, and destroyed them; and turned not again until I had consumed them. And I have consumed them, and wounded them, that they could not arise; yea, they are fallen under my feet. For thou hast girded me with strength to battle; them that rose up against me hast thou subdued under me. Thou hast also given me the necks of mine enemies, that I might destroy them that hate me. They looked, but there was none to save; even unto the LORD, but he answered them not. Then did I beat them as small as the dust of the earth, I did stamp them as the mire of the street, and did spread them abroad."
<u>Sirach 6:13:</u> "Separate thyself from thine enemies, and take heed of thy friends."

THE TREE OF LIFE

enemies, bless them that curse you, do good to them that hate you, and pray for them which despitefully use you, and persecute you.[177]

"And as ye would that men should do to you, do ye also to them likewise. Therefore all things whatsoever ye would that men should do to you, do ye even so to them, for this is the law and the prophets.[178] Enter ye in at the strait gate, for wide is the gate, and broad is the way, that leadeth to destruction, and many there be which go in thereat, because strait is the gate, and narrow is the way, which leadeth unto life, and few there be that find it;[179] that ye

---

[177] Compare Proverbs 16:7: "When a man's ways please the LORD, he maketh even his enemies to be at peace with him."
Proverbs 24:17-20: "Rejoice not when thine enemy falleth, and let not thine heart be glad when he stumbleth; lest the LORD see it, and it displease him, and he turn away his wrath from him. Fret not thyself because of evil men, neither be thou envious at the wicked, for there shall be no reward to the evil man; the candle of the wicked shall be put out."
Proverbs 25:21-22: "If thine enemy be hungry, give him bread to eat; and if he be thirsty, give him water to drink; for thou shalt heap coals of fire upon his head, and the LORD shall reward thee."
Exodus 23:4-5: "If thou meet thine enemy's ox or his ass going astray, thou shalt surely bring it back to him again. If thou see the ass of him that hateth thee lying under his burden, and wouldest forbear to help him, thou shalt surely help with him."
Isaiah 51:7: "Hearken unto me, ye that know righteousness, the people in whose heart is my law; fear ye not the reproach of men, neither be ye afraid of their revilings."
2 Esdras 7:36-41: "Then said I, 'Abraham prayed first for the Sodomites, and Moses for the fathers that sinned in the wilderness; and Joshua after him for Israel in the time of Achan; and Samuel and David for the destruction; and Solomon for them that should come to the sanctuary; and Elijah for those that received rain; and for the dead, that he might live; and Hezekiah for the people in the time of Sennacherib; and many for many. Even so now, seeing corruption is grown up, and wickedness increased, and the righteous have prayed for the ungodly, wherefore shall it not be so now also?"
[178] Compare Leviticus 19:18: "Thou shalt not avenge, nor bear any grudge against the children of thy people, but thou shalt love thy neighbour as thyself: I am the LORD."
Tobit 4:15: "Do that to no man which thou hatest. Drink not wine to make thee drunken; neither let drunkenness go with thee in thy journey."
[179] See Deuteronomy 30:15-19: "See, I have set before thee this day life and good, and death and evil; in that I command thee this day to love the LORD thy God, to walk in his ways, and to keep his commandments and his statutes and his

may be the children of your Father which is in heaven, for he maketh his sun to rise on the evil and on the good, and sendeth rain on the just and on the unjust. For if ye love them which love you, what reward have ye? For sinners also love those that love them. And if ye do good to them which do good to you, what thank have ye? For sinners also do even the same. And if ye lend to them of whom ye hope to receive, what thank have ye? For sinners also lend to sinners, to receive as much again. And if ye salute your brethren only, what do ye more than others? Do not even the publicans so? But love ye your enemies, and do good, and lend, hoping for nothing again, and your reward shall be great, and ye shall be the children of the Highest, for he is kind unto the unthankful and to the evil. Be ye therefore merciful, as your Father also is merciful. The disciple is not above his master, but every one that is perfect shall be as his master. Be ye therefore perfect, even as your Father which is in heaven is perfect.[180]

---

judgments, that thou mayest live and multiply; and the LORD thy God shall bless thee in the land whither thou goest to possess it. But if thine heart turn away, so that thou wilt not hear, but shalt be drawn away, and worship other gods, and serve them; I denounce unto you this day, that ye shall surely perish, and that ye shall not prolong your days upon the land, whither thou passest over Jordan to go to possess it. I call heaven and earth to record this day against you, that I have set before you life and death, blessing and cursing; therefore choose life, that both thou and thy seed may live."
[180] Compare Leviticus 19:2: "Speak unto all the congregation of the children of Israel, and say unto them, 'Ye shall be holy; for I the LORD your God am holy.'"
Deuteronomy 18:13: "Thou shalt be perfect with the LORD thy God."
Genesis 17:1: "And when Abram was ninety years old and nine, the LORD appeared to Abram, and said unto him, 'I am the Almighty God; walk before me, and be thou perfect.'"
1 Kings 8:61: "Let your heart therefore be perfect with the LORD our God, to walk in his statutes, and to keep his commandments, as at this day."
Job 1:1: "There was a man in the land of Uz, whose name was Job; and that man was perfect and upright, and one that feared God, and eschewed evil."
Job 9:21-22: "Though I were perfect, yet would I not know my soul; I would despise my life. This is one thing, therefore I said it: He destroyeth the perfect and the wicked."

"And why call ye me, 'Lord, Lord,' and do not the things which I say? Not every one that saith unto me, 'Lord, Lord,' shall enter into the kingdom of heaven, but he that doeth the will of my Father which is in heaven.[181] Many will say to me in that day, 'Lord, Lord, have we not prophesied in thy name? And in thy name have cast out devils? And in thy name done many wonderful works?' And then will I profess unto them, 'I never knew you. *Depart from me, ye that work iniquity.*'"[182]

"Judge not, and ye shall not be judged. For with what judgment ye judge, ye shall be judged, and with what measure ye mete, it shall be measured to you again.[183] Condemn not, and ye shall not be condemned, forgive, and ye shall be forgiven. For if ye forgive men their trespasses, your heavenly Father will also forgive you. But if ye forgive not men their trespasses, neither will your Father forgive your trespasses.[184]

Micah 6:8: "He hath shewed thee, O man, what is good; and what doth the LORD require of thee, but to do justly, and to love mercy, and to walk humbly with thy God?"

[181] See Psalms 146:5-10: "Happy is he that hath the God of Jacob for his help, whose hope is in the LORD his God; which made heaven, and earth, the sea, and all that therein is; which keepeth truth for ever; which executeth judgment for the oppressed; which giveth food to the hungry. The LORD looseth the prisoners; the LORD openeth the eyes of the blind; the LORD raiseth them that are bowed down; the LORD loveth the righteous; the LORD preserveth the strangers; he relieveth the fatherless and widow; but the way of the wicked he turneth upside down. The LORD shall reign for ever, even thy God, O Zion, unto all generations. Praise ye the LORD."

[182] See Psalms 6:8: "Depart from me, all ye workers of iniquity; for the LORD hath heard the voice of my weeping."

[183] Compare Psalms 18:25-26 (and 2 Samuel 22:26-27): "With the merciful thou wilt shew thyself merciful; with an upright man thou wilt shew thyself upright. With the pure thou wilt shew thyself pure; and with the froward thou wilt shew thyself froward."

2 Esdras 16:65: "And when your sins are brought forth, ye shall be ashamed before men, and your own sins shall be your accusers in that day."

Wisdom 6:10: "For they that keep holiness holily shall be judged holy; and they that have learned such things shall find what to answer."

[184] Compare *Sirach* 28:2: "Forgive thy neighbour the hurt that he hath done unto thee, so shall thy sins also be forgiven when thou prayest."

"Ask, and it shall be given you. Seek, and ye shall find. Knock, and it shall be opened unto you. For every one that asketh receiveth, and he that seeketh findeth, and to him that knocketh it shall be opened. What man is there of you, whom if his son ask bread, will he give him a stone? Or if he ask a fish, will he give him a serpent? If ye then, being evil, know how to give good gifts unto your children, how much more shall your Father which is in heaven give good things to them that ask him?[185]

"Give not that which is holy unto the dogs, neither cast ye your pearls before swine, lest they trample them under their feet, and turn again and rend you.[186]

"Take heed that ye do not your alms before men, to be seen of them, otherwise ye have no reward of your Father which is in heaven. Therefore when thou doest thine alms, do not sound a trumpet before thee, as the hypocrites[187] do in the synagogues and in the streets, that they may have glory of men. Verily I say unto you, they have their reward. But when thou doest alms, let not thy left hand know what thy right hand doeth, that thine alms may be in

---

[185] Compare Psalms 37:4: "Delight thyself also in the LORD; and he shall give thee the desires of thine heart."
[186] Compare Ezekiel 44:23: "And [the priests] shall teach my people the difference between the holy and profane, and cause them to discern between the unclean and the clean."
[187] Compare Job 13:16: "He also shall be my salvation; for an hypocrite shall not come before him."
Job 27:8: "For what is the hope of the hypocrite, though he hath gained, when God taketh away his soul?"

secret, and thy Father which seeth in secret[188] himself shall reward thee openly.[189]

"And when thou prayest, thou shalt not be as the hypocrites are, for they love to pray standing in the synagogues and in the corners of the streets, that they may be seen of men. Verily I say unto you, they have their reward. But thou, when thou prayest, enter into thy closet,[190] and when thou hast shut thy door, pray to thy Father which is in secret, and thy Father which seeth in secret shall reward thee openly. And when ye pray, use not vain repetitions, as the heathen do, for they think that they shall be heard for their much speaking.[191] Be not ye therefore like unto them, for your Father knoweth what things ye have need of, before ye ask him. After this manner therefore pray ye:

'Our Father which art in heaven,[192] hallowed be thy name.[193] Thy kingdom come.[194] Thy will be done

---

[188] Compare 1 Samuel 16:7: "But the LORD said unto Samuel, 'Look not on his countenance, or on the height of his stature; because I have refused him; for the LORD seeth not as man seeth; for man looketh on the outward appearance, but the LORD looketh on the heart.'"
Proverbs 15:3: "The eyes of the LORD are in every place, beholding the evil and the good."
[189] Compare Deuteronomy 15:10: "Thou shalt surely give him, and thine heart shall not be grieved when thou givest unto him; because that for this thing the LORD thy God shall bless thee in all thy works, and in all that thou puttest thine hand unto."
2 Samuel 12:11-12: "Thus saith the LORD, 'Behold, I will raise up evil against thee out of thine own house, and I will take thy wives before thine eyes, and give them unto thy neighbour, and he shall lie with thy wives in the sight of this sun. For thou didst it secretly; but I will do this thing before all Israel, and before the sun.'"
[190] Compare Daniel 6:10: "Now when Daniel knew that the writing was signed, he went into his house; and his windows being open in his chamber toward Jerusalem, he kneeled upon his knees three times a day, and prayed, and gave thanks before his God, as he did aforetime."
[191] Compare Sirach 7:14: "Use not many words in a multitude of elders, and make not much babbling when thou prayest."
[192] Compare Malachi 2:10: "Have we not all one father? Hath not one God created us? Why do we deal treacherously every man against his brother, by profaning the covenant of our fathers?"
2 Esdras 1:28-29: "Thus saith the Almighty Lord, Have I not prayed you as a father his sons, as a mother her daughters, and a nurse her young babes, that ye would be

THE TREE OF LIFE

in earth, as it is in heaven.[195] Give us this day our daily bread.[196] And forgive us our debts, as we forgive our debtors.[197] And lead us not into

my people, and I should be your God; that ye would be my children, and I should be your father?"
Deuteronomy 32:18: "Of the Rock that begat thee thou art unmindful, and hast forgotten God that formed thee."
Tobit 13:4: "There declare his greatness, and extol him before all the living; for he is our Lord, and he is the God our Father for ever."
[193] Compare Leviticus 22:31-33: "Therefore shall ye keep my commandments, and do them. I am the LORD. Neither shall ye profane my holy name; but I will be hallowed among the children of Israel. I am the LORD which hallow you, that brought you out of the land of Egypt, to be your God. I am the LORD."
Isaiah 57:15: "For thus saith the high and lofty One that inhabiteth eternity, whose name is Holy; I dwell in the high and holy place, with him also that is of a contrite and humble spirit, to revive the spirit of the humble, and to revive the heart of the contrite ones."
1 Kings 8:17: "And it was in the heart of David my father to build an house for the name of the LORD God of Israel."
Psalms 148:13: "Let them praise the name of the LORD; for his name alone is excellent; his glory is above the earth and heaven."
[194] Compare Daniel 2:44: "And in the days of these kings shall the God of heaven set up a kingdom, which shall never be destroyed. And the kingdom shall not be left to other people, but it shall break in pieces and consume all these kingdoms, and it shall stand for ever."
Numbers 14:21: "But as truly as I live, all the earth shall be filled with the glory of the LORD."
Joel 2:28-29: "And it shall come to pass afterward, that I will pour out my spirit upon all flesh; and your sons and your daughters shall prophesy, your old men shall dream dreams, your young men shall see visions; and also upon the servants and upon the handmaids in those days will I pour out my spirit."
[195] Compare Psalms 103:19-20: "The LORD hath prepared his throne in the heavens; and his kingdom ruleth over all. Bless the LORD, ye his angels, that excel in strength, that do his commandments, hearkening unto the voice of his word."
Prayer of Manasses 1:15: "Therefore I will praise thee for ever all the days of my life; for all the powers of the heavens do praise thee, and thine is the glory for ever and ever. Amen."
[196] Compare Exodus 16:4: "Then said the LORD unto Moses, 'Behold, I will rain bread from heaven for you; and the people shall go out and gather a certain rate every day, that I may prove them, whether they will walk in my law, or no.'"
[197] Compare Sirach 28:2: "Forgive thy neighbour the hurt that he hath done unto thee, so shall thy sins also be forgiven when thou prayest."

temptation, but deliver us from evil.[198] For thine is the kingdom, and the power, and the glory, for ever.[199] Amen.'

"Moreover when ye fast, be not as the hypocrites, of a sad countenance, for they disfigure their faces, that they may appear unto men to fast. Verily I say unto you, they have their reward. But thou, when thou fastest, anoint thine head, and wash thy face, that thou appear not unto men to fast, but unto thy Father which is in secret;[200] and thy Father, which seeth in secret, shall reward thee openly.

"Beware of false prophets, which come to you in sheep's clothing, but inwardly they are ravening wolves.[201] Ye shall know

---

[198] Compare Psalms 140:1: "Deliver me, O LORD, from the evil man; preserve me from the violent man."
[199] Compare 1 Chronicles 29:10-13: "Wherefore David blessed the LORD before all the congregation; and David said, 'Blessed be thou, LORD God of Israel our father, for ever and ever. Thine, O LORD, is the greatness, and the power, and the glory, and the victory, and the majesty; for all that is in the heaven and in the earth is thine; thine is the kingdom, O LORD, and thou art exalted as head above all. Both riches and honour come of thee, and thou reignest over all; and in thine hand is power and might; and in thine hand it is to make great, and to give strength unto all. Now therefore, our God, we thank thee, and praise thy glorious name.'"
1 Esdras 4:59-60: "And said, 'From thee cometh victory, from thee cometh wisdom, and thine is the glory, and I am thy servant. Blessed art thou, who hast given me wisdom; for to thee I give thanks, O Lord of our fathers.'"
[200] Compare Joel 2:12-13: "Therefore also now, saith the LORD, turn ye even to me with all your heart, and with fasting, and with weeping, and with mourning. And rend your heart, and not your garments, and turn unto the LORD your God; for he is gracious and merciful, slow to anger, and of great kindness, and repenteth him of the evil."
Judith 8:5: "And she made her a tent upon the top of her house, and put on sackcloth upon her loins and ware her widow's apparel."
Rest of Esther 14:16: "Thou knowest my necessity; for I abhor the sign of my high estate, which is upon mine head in the days wherein I shew myself, and that I abhor it as a menstruous rag, and that I wear it not when I am private by myself."
[201] Compare 1 Kings 22:19-23: "And he said, 'Hear thou therefore the word of the LORD: I saw the LORD sitting on his throne, and all the host of heaven standing by him on his right hand and on his left. And the LORD said, "Who shall persuade Ahab, that he may go up and fall at Ramoth-gilead?" And one said on this manner, and another said on that manner. And there came forth a spirit, and stood before

them by their fruits. Do men gather grapes of thorns, or figs of thistles? Even so, every good tree bringeth forth good fruit, but a corrupt tree bringeth forth evil fruit. For a good tree cannot bring forth evil fruit, neither can a corrupt tree bring forth good fruit. Every tree is known by his own fruit. Every tree that bringeth not forth good fruit is hewn down, and cast into the fire. A good man out of the good treasure of his heart bringeth forth that which is good,[202] and an evil man out of the evil treasure of his heart bringeth forth that which is evil, for of the abundance of the heart his mouth speaketh. Wherefore by their fruits ye shall know them.

"Lay not up for yourselves treasures upon earth, where moth and rust doth corrupt, and where thieves break through and steal.[203] But lay up for yourselves treasures in heaven,[204] where

---

the LORD, and said, "I will persuade him." And the LORD said unto him, "Wherewith?" And he said, "I will go forth, and I will be a lying spirit in the mouth of all his prophets." And he said, "Thou shalt persuade him, and prevail also; go forth, and do so." Now therefore, behold, the LORD hath put a lying spirit in the mouth of all these thy prophets, and the LORD hath spoken evil concerning thee.'"
Deuteronomy 13:1-3: "If there arise among you a prophet, or a dreamer of dreams, and giveth thee a sign or a wonder, and the sign or the wonder come to pass, whereof he spake unto thee, saying, 'Let us go after other gods, which thou hast not known, and let us serve them;' Thou shalt not hearken unto the words of that prophet, or that dreamer of dreams; for the LORD your God proveth you, to know whether ye love the LORD your God with all your heart and with all your soul."
[202] See Deuteronomy 6:5-7: "And thou shalt love the LORD thy God with all thine heart, and with all thy soul, and with all thy might. And these words, which I command thee this day, shall be in thine heart. And thou shalt teach them diligently unto thy children, and shalt talk of them when thou sittest in thine house, and when thou walkest by the way, and when thou liest down, and when thou risest up."
Joshua 1:8: "This book of the law shall not depart out of thy mouth; but thou shalt meditate therein day and night, that thou mayest observe to do according to all that is written therein; for then thou shalt make thy way prosperous, and then thou shalt have good success."
Psalms 40:8: "I delight to do thy will, O my God; yea, thy law is within my heart."
Ezra 7:10: "For Ezra had prepared his heart to seek the law of the LORD, and to do it, and to teach in Israel statutes and judgments."
[203] Compare Proverbs 11:4: "Riches profit not in the day of wrath; but righteousness delivereth from death."
Ezekiel 7:19: "They shall cast their silver in the streets, and their gold shall be removed; their silver and their gold shall not be able to deliver them in the day of

neither moth nor rust doth corrupt, and where thieves do not break through nor steal.²⁰⁵ Give, and it shall be given unto you, good measure, pressed down, and shaken together, and running over, shall men give into your bosom.²⁰⁶ For with the same measure that

---

the wrath of the LORD; they shall not satisfy their souls, neither fill their bowels; because it is the stumblingblock of their iniquity."
Isaiah 51:7-8: "Hearken unto me, ye that know righteousness, the people in whose heart is my law; fear ye not the reproach of men, neither be ye afraid of their revilings. For the moth shall eat them up like a garment, and the worm shall eat them like wool; but my righteousness shall be for ever, and my salvation from generation to generation."
Baruch 6:12-15: "Yet cannot these gods [idols] save themselves from rust and moth, though they be covered with purple raiment. They wipe their faces because of the dust of the temple, when there is much upon them. And he that cannot put to death one that offendeth him holdeth a sceptre, as though he were a judge of the country. He hath also in his right hand a dagger and an ax; but cannot deliver himself from war and thieves."
²⁰⁴ Compare *Tobit 4:8-9:* "If thou hast abundance give alms accordingly; if thou have but a little, be not afraid to give according to that little. For thou layest up a good treasure for thyself against the day of necessity."
²⁰⁵ See *Sirach 29:8-13:* "Yet have thou patience with a man in poor estate, and delay not to shew him mercy. Help the poor for the commandment's sake, and turn him not away because of his poverty. Lose thy money for thy brother and thy friend, and let it not rust under a stone to be lost. Lay up thy treasure according to the commandments of the most High, and it shall bring thee more profit than gold. Shut up alms in thy storehouses; and it shall deliver thee from all affliction. It shall fight for thee against thine enemies better than a mighty shield and strong spear."
Tobit 12:8-13: "Prayer is good with fasting and alms and righteousness. A little with righteousness is better than much with unrighteousness. It is better to give alms than to lay up gold. Help the poor for the commandment's sake, and turn him not away because of his poverty. Lose thy money for thy brother and thy friend, and let it not rust under a stone to be lost. Lay up thy treasure according to the commandments of the most High, and it shall bring thee more profit than gold. Shut up alms in thy storehouses, and it shall deliver thee from all affliction. It shall fight for thee against thine enemies better than a mighty shield and strong spear."
²⁰⁶ See Deuteronomy 15:7-10: "If there be among you a poor man of one of thy brethren within any of thy gates in thy land which the LORD thy God giveth thee, thou shalt not harden thine heart, nor shut thine hand from thy poor brother. But thou shalt open thine hand wide unto him, and shalt surely lend him sufficient for his need, in that which he wanteth. Beware that there be not a thought in thy wicked heart, saying, 'The seventh year, the year of release, is at hand;' and thine eye be evil against thy poor brother, and thou givest him nought; and he cry unto the LORD against thee, and it be sin unto thee. Thou shalt surely give him, and thine heart shall not be grieved when thou givest unto him; because that for this thing

THE TREE OF LIFE

ye mete withal it shall be measured to you again.[207] For where your treasure is, there will your heart be also.[208]

"And why beholdest thou the mote that is in thy brother's eye, but considerest not the beam that is in thine own eye? Then how canst thou say to thy brother, 'Brother, let me pull out the mote that is in thine eye,' when thou thyself beholdest not the beam that is in thine own eye? Thou hypocrite, first cast out the beam out of thine own eye, and then shalt thou see clearly to pull out the mote that is in thy brother's eye."

---

the LORD thy God shall bless thee in all thy works, and in all that thou puttest thine hand unto."
Deuteronomy 28:1-6: "And it shall come to pass, if thou shalt hearken diligently unto the voice of the LORD thy God, to observe and to do all his commandments which I command thee this day, that the LORD thy God will set thee on high above all nations of the earth. And all these blessings shall come on thee, and overtake thee, if thou shalt hearken unto the voice of the LORD thy God. Blessed shalt thou be in the city, and blessed shalt thou be in the field. Blessed shall be the fruit of thy body, and the fruit of thy ground, and the fruit of thy cattle, the increase of thy kine, and the flocks of thy sheep. Blessed shall be thy basket and thy store. Blessed shalt thou be when thou comest in, and blessed shalt thou be when thou goest out."
Proverbs 3:9-10: "Honour the LORD with thy substance, and with the firstfruits of all thine increase. So shall thy barns be filled with plenty, and thy presses shall burst out with new wine."
Sirach 35:10-11: "Give unto the most High according as he hath enriched thee; and as thou hast gotten, give with a cheerful eye. For the Lord recompenseth, and will give thee seven times as much."
Tobit 12:8-13: "Prayer is good with fasting and alms and righteousness. A little with righteousness is better than much with unrighteousness. It is better to give alms than to lay up gold. Help the poor for the commandment's sake, and turn him not away because of his poverty. Lose thy money for thy brother and thy friend, and let it not rust under a stone to be lost. Lay up thy treasure according to the commandments of the most High, and it shall bring thee more profit than gold. Shut up alms in thy storehouses, and it shall deliver thee from all affliction. It shall fight for thee against thine enemies better than a mighty shield and strong spear."
[207] Compare Psalms 18:25-26 (and 2 Samuel 22:26-27): "With the merciful thou wilt shew thyself merciful; with an upright man thou wilt shew thyself upright. With the pure thou wilt shew thyself pure; and with the froward thou wilt shew thyself froward."
[208] Compare Proverbs 23:7: "For as he thinketh in his heart, so is he. 'Eat and drink,' saith he to thee; but his heart is not with thee."

And he spake a parable unto them, "Can the blind lead the blind? Shall they not both fall into the ditch? The light of the body is the eye, therefore when thine eye is single, thy whole body also is full of light. If thy whole body therefore be full of light, having no part dark, the whole shall be full of light, as when the bright shining of a candle doth give thee light. But when thine eye is evil, thy whole body shall be full of darkness. If therefore the light that is in thee be darkness, how great is that darkness! Take heed therefore that the light which is in thee be not darkness."[209]

And he said also unto his disciples, "There was a certain rich man, which had a steward, and the same was accused unto him that he had wasted his goods. And he called him, and said unto him, 'How is it that I hear this of thee? Give an account of thy stewardship, for thou mayest be no longer steward.' Then the steward said within himself, 'What shall I do, for my lord taketh away from me the stewardship? I cannot dig, to beg I am ashamed. I am resolved what to do, that, when I am put out of the stewardship, they may receive me into their houses.' So he called every one of his lord's debtors unto him, and said unto the first, 'How much owest thou unto my lord?' And he said, 'An hundred measures of oil.' And he said unto him, 'Take thy bill, and sit down quickly, and write fifty.' Then said he to another, 'And how much owest thou?' And he said, 'An hundred measures of wheat.' And he said unto him, 'Take thy bill, and write fourscore.' And the lord commended the unjust steward, because he had done wisely. For the children of this world are in their generation wiser than the children of light. And I say unto you, make to yourselves friends of the mammon of unrighteousness, that, when ye fail, they may receive you into everlasting habitations.

---

[209] Compare Ecclesiastes 2:13-14: "Then I saw that wisdom excelleth folly, as far as light excelleth darkness. The wise man's eyes are in his head; but the fool walketh in darkness; and I myself perceived also that one event happeneth to them all."

"He that is faithful in that which is least is faithful also in much, and he that is unjust in the least is unjust also in much. If therefore ye have not been faithful in the unrighteous mammon, who will commit to your trust the true riches?[210] And if ye have not been faithful in that which is another man's, who shall give you that which is your own? No servant can serve two masters, for either he will hate the one, and love the other, or else he will hold to the one, and despise the other. Ye cannot serve God and mammon.

"Therefore I say unto you, take no thought for your life, what ye shall eat, or what ye shall drink, nor yet for your body, what ye shall put on. Is not the life more than meat, and the body than raiment? Behold the fowls of the air, for they sow not, neither do they reap, nor gather into barns, yet your heavenly Father feedeth them.[211] Are ye not much better than they? Which of you by taking thought can add one cubit unto his stature? And why take ye thought for raiment? Consider the lilies of the field, how they grow, they toil not, neither do they spin, and yet I say unto you, that even Solomon in all his glory[212] was not arrayed like one of these. Wherefore, if God so clothe the grass of the field, which to day is, and to morrow is cast into the oven, shall he not much more clothe you, O ye of little faith? Therefore take no thought, saying, 'What shall we eat?' or, 'What shall we drink?' or, 'Wherewithal shall we be clothed?' For after all these things do the Gentiles seek, and your heavenly Father knoweth that ye have need of all these things. But

---

[210] Compare Proverbs 8:10-12,17-20: "Receive my instruction, and not silver; and knowledge rather than choice gold. For wisdom is better than rubies; and all the things that may be desired are not to be compared to it. I wisdom dwell with prudence, and find out knowledge of witty inventions. I love them that love me; and those that seek me early shall find me. Riches and honour are with me; yea, durable riches and righteousness. My fruit is better than gold, yea, than fine gold; and my revenue than choice silver. I lead in the way of righteousness, in the midst of the paths of judgment."
[211] Compare Psalms 104:21: "The young lions roar after their prey, and seek their meat from God."
[212] See 1 Kings 10:1-29; 2 Chronicles 9:1-31.

THE TREE OF LIFE

seek ye first the kingdom of God, and his righteousness, and all these things shall be added unto you.[213] Take therefore no thought for the morrow, for the morrow shall take thought for the things of itself. Sufficient unto the day is the evil thereof.

"Whosoever cometh to me, and heareth these sayings of mine, and doeth them, I will liken him unto a wise man which built an house, and digged deep, and laid the foundation on a rock, and when the rain descended, and the flood arose, and the winds blew, and the stream beat vehemently upon that house, and could not shake it, for it was founded upon a rock. And every one that heareth these sayings of mine, and doeth them not, shall be likened unto a foolish man, which built his house without a foundation upon the sand, and the rain descended, and the floods came, and the winds blew, and the stream did beat vehemently upon that house, and immediately it fell, and the fall of that house was great."

And it came to pass, when Jesus had ended these sayings, the people were astonished at his doctrine, for he taught them as one having authority, and not as the scribes.[214]

---

[213] See *Sirach 40:26:* "Riches and strength lift up the heart; but the fear of the Lord is above them both; there is no want in the fear of the Lord, and it needeth not to seek help."
Deuteronomy 15:10: "Thou shalt surely give him, and thine heart shall not be grieved when thou givest unto him; because that for this thing the LORD thy God shall bless thee in all thy works, and in all that thou puttest thine hand unto."
Sirach 29:11-13: "Lay up thy treasure according to the commandments of the most High, and it shall bring thee more profit than gold. Shut up alms in thy storehouses; and it shall deliver thee from all affliction. It shall fight for thee against thine enemies better than a mighty shield and strong spear."
[214] Compare *1 Maccabees 4:44-46:* "And when as they consulted what to do with the altar of burnt offerings, which was profaned; they thought it best to pull it down, lest it should be a reproach to them, because the heathen had defiled it. Wherefore they pulled it down, and laid up the stones in the mountain of the temple in a convenient place, until there should come a prophet to shew what should be done with them."

THE TREE OF LIFE

Chapter Sixteen

When he was come down from the mountain, great multitudes followed him. And it came to pass, when he was in a certain city, behold a man full of leprosy, who, seeing Jesus, fell on his face and worshipped him and besought him, saying, "Lord, if thou wilt, thou canst make me clean." And Jesus, moved with compassion, put forth his hand, and touched him, saying, "I will, be thou clean."[215] And as soon as he had spoken, immediately the leprosy departed from him, and he was cleansed.[216] And he straitly charged him, and saith unto him, "See thou tell no man, but go thy way, shew thyself to the priest, and offer the gift for

---

[215] Compare Exodus 4:6-7: "And the LORD said furthermore unto [Moses], 'Put now thine hand into thy bosom.' And he put his hand into his bosom; and when he took it out, behold, his hand was leprous as snow. And he said, 'Put thine hand into thy bosom again.' And he put his hand into his bosom again; and plucked it out of his bosom, and, behold, it was turned again as his other flesh."

[216] Compare 2 Kings 5:6-10: "And he brought the letter to the king of Israel, saying, 'Now when this letter is come unto thee, behold, I have therewith sent Naaman my servant to thee, that thou mayest recover him of his leprosy.' And it came to pass, when the king of Israel had read the letter, that he rent his clothes, and said, 'Am I God, to kill and to make alive, that this man doth send unto me to recover a man of his leprosy? Wherefore consider, I pray you, and see how he seeketh a quarrel against me.' And it was so, when Elisha the man of God had heard that the king of Israel had rent his clothes, that he sent to the king, saying, 'Wherefore hast thou rent thy clothes? Let him come now to me, and he shall know that there is a prophet in Israel.' So Naaman came with his horses and with his chariot, and stood at the door of the house of Elisha. And Elisha sent a messenger unto him, saying, 'Go and wash in the Jordan seven times, and thy flesh shall come again to thee, and thou shalt be clean.'"

thy cleansing according as Moses commanded,[217] for a testimony unto them." But he went out, and began to publish it much, and so much the more went there a fame abroad of him, and great multitudes came together to hear, and to be healed by him of their infirmities, insomuch that Jesus could no more openly enter into the city, but was without in desert places. And he withdrew himself into the wilderness, and prayed, and they came to him from every quarter.

Now when Jesus saw great multitudes about him, he gave commandment to depart unto the other side of the sea. And it came to pass, that, as they went in the way, a certain scribe came, and said unto him, "Master, I will follow thee whithersoever thou goest." And Jesus saith unto him, "The foxes have holes, and the birds of the air have nests, but the Son of man hath not where to lay his head."

And he said unto another of his disciples, "Follow me." But he said, "Lord, suffer me first to go and bury my father." Jesus said unto him, "Follow me, and let the dead bury their dead,[218] but go thou and preach the kingdom of God." And another also said, "Lord, I will follow thee, but let me first go bid them farewell, which are at home at my house." And Jesus said unto him, "No man, having put his hand to the plough, and looking back, is fit for the kingdom of God."

And he entered into a ship, and passed over, and came into his own city. And it came to pass on a certain day, as he was teaching, that there were Pharisees and doctors of the law sitting by, which

---

[217] See Leviticus 14:1-57.
[218] Compare Jeremiah 15:1-2: "Then said the LORD unto me, 'Though Moses and Samuel stood before me, yet my mind could not be toward this people; cast them out of my sight, and let them go forth. And it shall come to pass, if they say unto thee, "Whither shall we go forth?" then thou shalt tell them, "Thus saith the LORD; Such as are for death, to death; and such as are for the sword, to the sword; and such as are for the famine, to the famine; and such as are for the captivity, to the captivity."'"
Zechariah 11:9: "Then said I, 'I will not feed you; that that dieth, let it die; and that that is to be cut off, let it be cut off; and let the rest eat every one the flesh of another.'"

were come out of every town of Galilee, and Judaea, and Jerusalem, and the power of the Lord was present to heal them.

And again he entered into Capernaum after some days, and it was noised that he was in the house. And straightway many were gathered together, insomuch that there was no room to receive them, no, not so much as about the door, and he preached the word unto them.

And, behold, four men brought in a bed a man which was sick of the palsy, and they sought means to bring him in, and to lay him before him. And when they could not find by what way they might bring him in because of the multitude, they went upon the housetop, and they uncovered the roof where he was, and when they had broken it up, they let down the bed wherein the sick of the palsy lay through the tiling into the midst before Jesus. When Jesus saw their faith, he said unto the sick of the palsy, "Son, be of good cheer, thy sins are forgiven thee." But there were certain of the scribes and Pharisees sitting there, which began to reason in their hearts, saying within themselves, "This man blasphemeth. Why doth this man thus speak blasphemies? Who can forgive sins but God only?" And Jesus knew their thoughts,[219] and immediately when Jesus perceived in his spirit that they so reasoned within themselves, he said unto them, "Why reason ye these evil things in your hearts? For whether is it easier to say to the sick of the palsy, 'Thy sins be forgiven thee,' or to say, 'Arise, and take up thy bed, and walk?' But that ye may know that the Son of man hath power on earth to forgive sins,[220]

---

[219] Compare Psalms 139:1-2: "O LORD, thou hast searched me, and known me. Thou knowest my downsitting and mine uprising, thou understandest my thought afar off."
Jeremiah 17:10: "I the LORD search the heart, I try the reins, even to give every man according to his ways, and according to the fruit of his doings."
2 Esdras 16:54,63: "Behold, the Lord knoweth all the works of men, their imaginations, their thoughts, and their hearts. Surely he knoweth your inventions, and what ye think in your hearts, even them that sin, and would hide their sin."
[220] Compare Isaiah 43:25, 44:22: "I, even I, am he that blotteth out thy transgressions for mine own sake, and will not remember thy sins. I have blotted

(then saith he to the sick of the palsy,) arise, take up thy bed, and go thy way unto thine house." And immediately he arose, took up the bed, and departed to his own house, glorifying God. But when the multitudes saw it, they were all amazed and marvelled, and glorified God, which had given such power unto men, saying, "We never saw it on this fashion," and were filled with fear, saying, "We have seen strange things to day."

---

out, as a thick cloud, thy transgressions, and, as a cloud, thy sins. Return unto me; for I have redeemed thee."

Chapter Seventeen

And after these things he went forth again by the sea side, and all the multitude resorted unto him, and he taught them. And as Jesus passed forth from thence, he saw a publican, named Levi (Matthew) the son of Alphaeus, sitting at the receipt of custom, and said unto him, "Follow me." And he left all, and rose up, and followed him.[221]

And Levi made him a great feast in his own house, and there was a great company of publicans and sinners that sat down with Jesus and his disciples, for there were many that followed him. And when the scribes and Pharisees saw him eat with publicans and sinners, they said unto his disciples, "How is it that your Master eateth and drinketh with publicans and sinners?" But when Jesus heard that, he answering said unto them, "They that be whole need not a physician, but they that are sick. I came not to call the

---

[221] Compare <u>1 Kings 19:19-21:</u> "So [Elijah] departed thence, and found Elisha the son of Shaphat, who was plowing with twelve yoke of oxen before him, and he with the twelfth; and Elijah passed by him, and cast his mantle upon him. And he left the oxen, and ran after Elijah, and said, 'Let me, I pray thee, kiss my father and my mother, and then I will follow thee.' And he said unto him, 'Go back again; for what have I done to thee?' And he returned back from him, and took a yoke of oxen, and slew them, and boiled their flesh with the instruments of the oxen, and gave unto the people, and they did eat. Then he arose, and went after Elijah, and ministered unto him."

righteous, but sinners to repentance. But go ye and learn what that meaneth, and *I will have mercy, and not sacrifice.*"[222]

---

[222] See Hosea 6:6: "For I desired mercy, and not sacrifice; and the knowledge of God more than burnt offerings."

Chapter Eighteen

Then came to him the disciples of John, saying, "Why do we and the Pharisees fast often, and make prayers, but thy disciples fast not, and eat and drink?" And Jesus said unto them, "Can ye make the children of the bridechamber mourn, while the bridegroom is with them?[223] As long as they have the bridegroom with them, they cannot fast. But the days will come,[224] when the bridegroom shall be taken away from them, and then shall they fast in those days."

And he spake also a parable unto them, "No man seweth a piece of new cloth on an old garment, else the new piece that filled it up taketh away from the old, and the rent is made worse. And no man putteth new wine into old bottles, else the new wine will burst the bottles, and the wine runneth out and be spilled, and the bottles shall perish. But new wine must be put into new bottles, and both are preserved."

---

[223] Compare Isaiah 62:5: "For as a young man marrieth a virgin, so shall thy sons marry thee; and as the bridegroom rejoiceth over the bride, so shall thy God rejoice over thee."

[224] Compare Jeremiah 7:34: "Then will I cause to cease from the cities of Judah, and from the streets of Jerusalem, the voice of mirth, and the voice of gladness, the voice of the bridegroom, and the voice of the bride; for the land shall be desolate."

THE TREE OF LIFE

Chapter Nineteen

After this there was a feast of the Jews, and Jesus went up to Jerusalem. Now there is at Jerusalem by the sheep market a pool, which is called in the Hebrew tongue Bethesda, having five porches. In these lay a great multitude of impotent folk, of blind, halt, and withered, waiting for the moving of the water. For an angel went down at a certain season into the pool, and troubled the water. Whosoever then first after the troubling of the water stepped in was made whole of whatsoever disease he had.

And a certain man was there, which had an infirmity thirty and eight years. When Jesus saw him lie, and knew that he had been now a long time in that case, he saith unto him, "Wilt thou be made whole?" The impotent man answered him, "Sir, I have no man, when the water is troubled, to put me into the pool, but while I am coming, another steppeth down before me." Jesus saith unto him, "Rise, take up thy bed, and walk." And immediately the man was made whole, and took up his bed, and walked, and on the same day was the sabbath. The Jews therefore said unto him that was cured, "It is the sabbath day, it is not lawful for thee to carry thy bed."[225] He answered them, "He that made me whole, the same said unto me,

---

[225] See Jeremiah 17:21-22: "Thus saith the LORD; 'Take heed to yourselves, and bear no burden on the sabbath day, nor bring it in by the gates of Jerusalem; neither carry forth a burden out of your houses on the sabbath day, neither do ye any work, but hallow ye the sabbath day, as I commanded your fathers.'"

'Take up thy bed, and walk.'" Then asked they him, "What man is that which said unto thee, 'Take up thy bed, and walk?'" And he that was healed wist not who it was, for Jesus had conveyed himself away, a multitude being in that place.

Afterward Jesus findeth him in the temple, and said unto him, "Behold, thou art made whole, sin no more, lest a worse thing come unto thee."[226]

The man departed, and told the Jews that it was Jesus, which had made him whole. And therefore did the Jews persecute Jesus, and sought to slay him, because he had done these things on the sabbath day. But Jesus answered them, "My Father worketh hitherto, and I work. Verily, verily, I say unto you, the Son can do nothing of himself, but what he seeth the Father do, for what things soever he doeth, these also doeth the Son likewise. For the Father loveth the Son, and sheweth him all things that himself doeth, and he will shew him greater works than these, that ye may marvel. For

---

[226] Compare Luke 11:24-26: "When the unclean spirit is gone out of a man, he walketh through dry places, seeking rest; and finding none, he saith, 'I will return unto my house whence I came out.' And when he cometh, he findeth it swept and garnished. Then goeth he, and taketh to him seven other spirits more wicked than himself; and they enter in, and dwell there; and the last state of that man is worse than the first."
Wisdom 12:23: "Wherefore, whereas men have lived dissolutely and unrighteously, thou hast tormented them with their own abominations."
Leviticus 26:13-14,16-18: "I am the LORD your God, which brought you forth out of the land of Egypt, that ye should not be their bondmen; and I have broken the bands of your yoke, and made you go upright. But if ye will not hearken unto me, and will not do all these commandments; I also will do this unto you; I will even appoint over you terror, consumption, and the burning ague, that shall consume the eyes, and cause sorrow of heart; and ye shall sow your seed in vain, for your enemies shall eat it. And I will set my face against you, and ye shall be slain before your enemies; they that hate you shall reign over you; and ye shall flee when none pursueth you. And if ye will not yet for all this hearken unto me, then I will punish you seven times more for your sins."
Psalms 103:2-4: "Bless the LORD, O my soul, and forget not all his benefits; who forgiveth all thine iniquities; who healeth all thy diseases; who redeemeth thy life from destruction; who crowneth thee with lovingkindness and tender mercies."

as the Father raiseth up the dead, and quickeneth them,[227] even so the Son quickeneth whom he will. For the Father judgeth no man, but hath committed all judgment unto the Son, that all men should honour the Son, even as they honour the Father. He that honoureth not the Son honoureth not the Father which hath sent him. Verily, verily, I say unto you, he that heareth my word, and believeth on him that sent me, hath everlasting life, and shall not come into condemnation, but is passed from death unto life. Verily, verily, I say unto you, the hour is coming, and now is, when the dead shall hear the voice of the Son of God, and they that hear shall live. For as the Father hath life in himself, so hath he given to the Son to have life in himself, and hath given him authority to execute judgment also, because he is the Son of man.[228] Marvel not at this, for the hour is coming, in the which all that are in the graves shall hear his voice, and shall come forth.[229] They that have done good, unto the resurrection of life, and they that have done evil, unto the resurrection of damnation.[230]

"I can of mine own self do nothing, as I hear, I judge, and my judgment is just, because I seek not mine own will, but the will of

---

[227] See Ezekiel 37:5-6: "Thus saith the Lord GOD unto these bones; 'Behold, I will cause breath to enter into you, and ye shall live. And I will lay sinews upon you, and will bring up flesh upon you, and cover you with skin, and put breath in you, and ye shall live; and ye shall know that I am the LORD.'"
[228] See Daniel 7:13-14: "I saw in the night visions, and, behold, one like the Son of man came with the clouds of heaven, and came to the Ancient of days, and they brought him near before him. And there was given him dominion, and glory, and a kingdom, that all people, nations, and languages, should serve him; his dominion is an everlasting dominion, which shall not pass away, and his kingdom that which shall not be destroyed."
Psalms 80:17: "Let thy hand be upon the man of thy right hand, upon the son of man whom thou madest strong for thyself."
[229] See Hosea 13:14: "I will ransom them from the power of the grave; I will redeem them from death. O death, I will be thy plagues. O grave, I will be thy destruction; repentance shall be hid from mine eyes."
[230] See Daniel 12:2-3: "And many of them that sleep in the dust of the earth shall awake, some to everlasting life, and some to shame and everlasting contempt. And they that be wise shall shine as the brightness of the firmament; and they that turn many to righteousness as the stars for ever and ever."

the Father which hath sent me.[231] If I bear witness of myself, my witness is not true.[232] There is another that beareth witness of me, and I know that the witness which he witnesseth of me is true.

"Ye sent unto John, and he bare witness unto the truth. But I receive not testimony from man, but these things I say, that ye might be saved. John was a burning and a shining light, and ye were willing for a season to rejoice in his light. But I have greater witness than that of John, for the works which the Father hath given me to finish, the same works that I do,[233] bear witness of me, that the Father hath sent me. And the Father himself, which hath sent me, hath borne witness of me. Ye have neither heard his voice at any time, nor seen his shape.[234] And ye have not his word abiding in you, for whom he hath sent, him ye believe not.

"Search the scriptures, for in them ye think ye have eternal life, and they are they which testify of me.[235] And ye will not come to

---

[231] Compare Numbers 16:28: "And Moses said, 'Hereby ye shall know that the LORD hath sent me to do all these works; for I have not done them of mine own mind.'"
[232] Compare Proverbs 27:2: "Let another man praise thee, and not thine own mouth; a stranger, and not thine own lips."
[233] See Psalms 146:5-10: "Happy is he that hath the God of Jacob for his help, whose hope is in the LORD his God; which made heaven, and earth, the sea, and all that therein is; which keepeth truth for ever; which executeth judgment for the oppressed; which giveth food to the hungry. The LORD looseth the prisoners; the LORD openeth the eyes of the blind; the LORD raiseth them that are bowed down; the LORD loveth the righteous; the LORD preserveth the strangers; he relieveth the fatherless and widow; but the way of the wicked he turneth upside down. The LORD shall reign for ever, even thy God, O Zion, unto all generations. Praise ye the LORD."
[234] See Deuteronomy 4:29: "But if from thence thou shalt seek the LORD thy God, thou shalt find him, if thou seek him with all thy heart and with all thy soul."
1 Chronicles 28:9: "And thou, Solomon my son, know thou the God of thy father, and serve him with a perfect heart and with a willing mind; for the LORD searcheth all hearts, and understandeth all the imaginations of the thoughts; if thou seek him, he will be found of thee; but if thou forsake him, he will cast thee off for ever."
[235] See Genesis 3:13-15, 49:10-12; Deuteronomy 18:15-19; Job 19:23-27; Psalms 22:1-19, 34:19-20, 69:1-36, 110:1-7, 112:1-10, 118:20-26; Isaiah 8:13-15, 9:1-8, 11:1-12:6, 25:6-8, 28:16-21, 34:1-35:10, 40:1-11, 42:1-7, 49:13-16, 50:4-9, 52:13-53:12, 59:20-63:5, 66:15-16; Jeremiah 23:1-8; Ezekiel 34:1-31; Daniel 2:44-45,

me, that ye might have life.²³⁶ I receive not honour from men.²³⁷ But I know you, that ye have not the love of God in you. I am come in my Father's name, and ye receive me not, if another shall come in his own name, him ye will receive. How can ye believe, which receive honour one of another, and seek not the honour that cometh from God only? Do not think that I will accuse you to the Father, there is one that accuseth you, even Moses, in whom ye trust. For had ye believed Moses, ye would have believed me, for he wrote of me.²³⁸ But if ye believe not his writings, how shall ye believe my words?"

Therefore the Jews sought the more to kill him, because he not only had broken the sabbath, but said also that God was his Father, making himself equal with God.

7:13-14, 9:24-27; Hosea 13:14; Micah 5:2-4; Zechariah 12:9-14:21; Malachi 4:1-6; 2 Maccabees 7:1-42; et cetera.

²³⁶ Compare Isaiah 55:1-3: "Ho, every one that thirsteth, come ye to the waters, and he that hath no money; come ye, buy, and eat; yea, come, buy wine and milk without money and without price. Wherefore do ye spend money for that which is not bread? And your labour for that which satisfieth not? Hearken diligently unto me, and eat ye that which is good, and let your soul delight itself in fatness. Incline your ear, and come unto me; hear, and your soul shall live; and I will make an everlasting covenant with you, even the sure mercies of David."

Psalms 16:11: "Thou wilt shew me the path of life; in thy presence is fulness of joy; at thy right hand there are pleasures for evermore."

Proverbs 12:28: "In the way of righteousness is life; and in the pathway thereof there is no death."

Proverbs 13:14: "The law of the wise is a fountain of life, to depart from the snares of death."

²³⁷ See Wisdom 6:7: "For he which is Lord over all shall fear no man's person, neither shall he stand in awe of any man's greatness; for he hath made the small and great, and careth for all alike."

Deuteronomy 16:19: "Thou shalt not wrest judgment; thou shalt not respect persons, neither take a gift; for a gift doth blind the eyes of the wise, and pervert the words of the righteous."

²³⁸ See Genesis 3:15: "And I will put enmity between thee and the woman, and between thy seed and her seed; it shall bruise thy head, and thou shalt bruise his heel."

Genesis 49:10: "The sceptre shall not depart from Judah, nor a lawgiver from between his feet, until Shiloh come; and unto him shall the gathering of the people be."

Deuteronomy 18:15: "The LORD thy God will raise up unto thee a Prophet from the midst of thee, of thy brethren, like unto me; unto him ye shall hearken."

THE TREE OF LIFE

Chapter Twenty

After these things Jesus went over the sea of Galilee, which is the sea of Tiberias. And a great multitude followed him, because they saw his miracles which he did on them that were diseased. And it came to pass on the sabbath, that Jesus went through the corn fields, and his disciples were an hungered, and began, as they went, to pluck the ears of corn, and to eat, rubbing them in their hands.[239] But when the Pharisees saw it, they said unto him, "Behold, thy disciples do that which is not lawful to do upon the sabbath day. Why do ye that which is not lawful to do on the sabbath days?" And Jesus answering them said, "Have ye never read what David did, when himself was an hungered, and they which were with him, how he went into the house of God in the days of Ahimelech the high priest, and did take and eat the shewbread, which is not lawful to eat but for the priests alone, and gave also to them which were with him?[240] Or have ye not read in the law, how

---

[239] See Deuteronomy 23:25: "When thou comest into the standing corn of thy neighbour, then thou mayest pluck the ears with thine hand; but thou shalt not move a sickle unto thy neighbour's standing corn."

[240] See 1 Samuel 21:1-6: "Then came David to Nob to Ahimelech the priest; and Ahimelech was afraid at the meeting of David, and said unto him, 'Why art thou alone, and no man with thee?' And David said unto Ahimelech the priest, 'The king hath commanded me a business, and hath said unto me, "Let no man know any thing of the business whereabout I send thee, and what I have commanded thee; and I have appointed my servants to such and such a place." Now therefore what is under thine hand? Give me five loaves of bread in mine hand, or what there is

that on the sabbath days the priests in the temple profane the sabbath, and are blameless?[241] But I say unto you, that in this place is one greater than the temple.[242] But if ye had known what this meaneth, *I will have mercy, and not sacrifice*,[243] ye would not have condemned the guiltless."[244] And he said unto them, "The sabbath was made for man,[245] and not man for the sabbath. Therefore the Son of man is Lord also of the sabbath day."

---

present.' And the priest answered David, and said, 'There is no common bread under mine hand, but there is hallowed bread; if the young men have kept themselves at least from women.' And David answered the priest, and said unto him, 'Of a truth women have been kept from us about these three days, since I came out, and the vessels of the young men are holy, and the bread is in a manner common, yea, though it were sanctified this day in the vessel.' So the priest gave him hallowed bread; for there was no bread there but the shewbread, that was taken from before the LORD, to put hot bread in the day when it was taken away."

[241] See <u>Numbers 28:9-10:</u> "And on the sabbath day two lambs of the first year without spot, and two tenth deals of flour for a meat offering, mingled with oil, and the drink offering thereof; This is the burnt offering of every sabbath, beside the continual burnt offering, and his drink offering."

[242] See <u>Isaiah 8:13-15:</u> "Sanctify the LORD of hosts himself; and let him be your fear, and let him be your dread. And he shall be for a sanctuary; but for a stone of stumbling and for a rock of offence to both the houses of Israel, for a gin and for a snare to the inhabitants of Jerusalem. And many among them shall stumble, and fall, and be broken, and be snared, and be taken."

[243] See <u>Hosea 6:6:</u> "For I desired mercy, and not sacrifice; and the knowledge of God more than burnt offerings."

[244] Compare <u>Exodus 23:1-2:</u> "Thou shalt not raise a false report; put not thine hand with the wicked to be an unrighteous witness. Thou shalt not follow a multitude to do evil; neither shalt thou speak in a cause to decline after many to wrest judgment."
<u>Psalms 94:20-21:</u> "Shall the throne of iniquity have fellowship with thee, which frameth mischief by a law? They gather themselves together against the soul of the righteous, and condemn the innocent blood."

[245] See <u>Exodus 20:9-10:</u> "Six days shalt thou labour, and do all thy work. But the seventh day is the sabbath of the LORD thy God; in it thou shalt not do any work, thou, nor thy son, nor thy daughter, thy manservant, nor thy maidservant, nor thy cattle, nor thy stranger that is within thy gates."
<u>Isaiah 58:13-14:</u> "If thou turn away thy foot from the sabbath, from doing thy pleasure on my holy day; and call the sabbath a delight, the holy of the LORD, honourable; and shalt honour him, not doing thine own ways, nor finding thine own pleasure, nor speaking thine own words; then shalt thou delight thyself in the LORD; and I will cause thee to ride upon the high places of the earth, and feed thee with the heritage of Jacob thy father; for the mouth of the LORD hath spoken it."

And when he was departed thence, he went into their synagogue on another sabbath, and taught. And there was a man whose right hand was withered. And the scribes and Pharisees watched him, whether he would heal on the sabbath day, that they might accuse him. But he knew their thoughts, and said to the man which had the withered hand, "Rise up, and stand forth in the midst." And he arose and stood forth. And they asked him, (that they might accuse him,) saying, "Is it lawful to heal on the sabbath days?" Then said Jesus unto them, "I will ask you one thing: is it lawful on the sabbath days to do good, or to do evil? To save life, or to kill?" But they held their peace. And he said unto them, "What man shall there be among you, that shall have one sheep, and if it fall into a pit on the sabbath day, will he not lay hold on it, and lift it out? How much then is a man better than a sheep? Wherefore it is lawful to do well on the sabbath days." And when he had looked round about on them all with anger, being grieved for the hardness of their hearts, he saith unto the man, "Stretch forth thine hand." And he stretched it out, and his hand was restored whole, like as the other. And they were filled with madness, and communed one with another what they might do to Jesus.

Then the Pharisees went out, and straightway took counsel with the Herodians against him, how they might destroy him. But when Jesus knew it, he withdrew himself from thence, and great multitudes followed him, and he healed them all. And Jesus withdrew himself with his disciples to the sea, and a great multitude came unto him and followed him from Galilee, and from Judaea, and from Jerusalem, and from Idumaea, and from beyond Jordan, and they about Tyre and Zidon.

And he spake to his disciples, that a small ship should wait on him because of the multitude, lest they should throng him. For he had healed many, insomuch that they pressed upon him for to touch him, as many as had plagues. And unclean spirits, when they saw him, fell down before him, and cried, saying, "Thou art the Son of

God." And he straitly charged them that they should not make him known. That it might be fulfilled which was spoken by Isaiah the prophet, saying, "*Behold my servant, whom I have chosen, my beloved, in whom my soul is well pleased, I will put my spirit upon him, and he shall shew judgment to the Gentiles. He shall not strive, nor cry, neither shall any man hear his voice in the streets. A bruised reed shall he not break, and smoking flax shall he not quench, till he send forth judgment unto victory. And in his name shall the Gentiles trust.*"[246]

---

[246] "Behold my servant, whom I uphold; mine elect, in whom my soul delighteth; I have put my spirit upon him; he shall bring forth judgment to the Gentiles. He shall not cry, nor lift up, nor cause his voice to be heard in the street. A bruised reed shall he not break, and the smoking flax shall he not quench; he shall bring forth judgment unto truth. He shall not fail nor be discouraged, till he have set judgment in the earth; and the isles shall wait for his law. Thus saith God the LORD, he that created the heavens, and stretched them out; he that spread forth the earth, and that which cometh out of it; he that giveth breath unto the people upon it, and spirit to them that walk therein; I the LORD have called thee in righteousness, and will hold thine hand, and will keep thee, and give thee for a covenant of the people, for a light of the Gentiles; To open the blind eyes, to bring out the prisoners from the prison, and them that sit in darkness out of the prison house." – Isaiah 42:1-7

Chapter Twenty One

And one of the Pharisees desired him that he would eat with him. And he went into the Pharisee's house, and sat down to meat. And, behold, a woman in the city, called Mary, which was a sinner, when she knew that Jesus sat at meat in the Pharisee's house, brought in an alabaster box, a pound of ointment of spikenard, and stood behind him, at the feet of Jesus weeping, and began to wash his feet with tears, and did wipe them with the hairs of her head, and kissed his feet, and anointed them with the ointment, and the house was filled with the odour of the ointment.

Now when the Pharisee which had bidden him saw it, he spake within himself, saying, "This man, if he were a prophet, would have known who and what manner of woman this is that toucheth him, for she is a sinner." And Jesus answering said unto him, "Simon, I have somewhat to say unto thee." And he saith, "Master, say on." "There was a certain creditor which had two debtors, the one owed five hundred pence, and the other fifty. And when they had nothing to pay, he frankly forgave them both. Tell me therefore, which of them will love him most?" Simon answered and said, "I suppose that he, to whom he forgave most." And he said unto him, "Thou hast rightly judged."

And he turned to the woman, and said unto Simon, "Seest thou this woman? I entered into thine house, thou gavest me no water for my feet,[247] but she hath washed my feet with tears, and wiped them with the hairs of her head. Thou gavest me no kiss, but this woman since the time I came in hath not ceased to kiss my feet. My head with oil thou didst not anoint, but this woman hath anointed my feet with ointment. Wherefore I say unto thee, her sins, which are many, are forgiven, for she loved much. But to whom little is forgiven, the same loveth little." And he said unto her, "Thy sins are forgiven." And they that sat at meat with him began to say within themselves, "Who is this that forgiveth sins also?" And he said to the woman, "Thy faith hath saved thee, go in peace."

And it came to pass afterward, that he went throughout every city and village, preaching and shewing the glad tidings of the kingdom of God, and the twelve were with him, and certain women, which had been healed of evil spirits and infirmities, Mary called Magdalene, out of whom went seven devils, and Joanna the wife of Chuza, Herod's steward, and Susanna, and many others, which ministered unto him of their substance.

---

[247] Compare Genesis 18:1-5: "And the LORD appeared unto [Abraham] in the plains of Mamre; and he sat in the tent door in the heat of the day; and he lift up his eyes and looked, and, lo, three men stood by him; and when he saw them, he ran to meet them from the tent door, and bowed himself toward the ground, and said, 'My Lord, if now I have found favour in thy sight, pass not away, I pray thee, from thy servant. Let a little water, I pray you, be fetched, and wash your feet, and rest yourselves under the tree. And I will fetch a morsel of bread, and comfort ye your hearts; after that ye shall pass on; for therefore are ye come to your servant.' And they said, 'So do, as thou hast said.'"

Chapter Twenty Two

And Jesus went about all the cities and villages, teaching in their synagogues, and preaching the gospel of the kingdom, and healing every sickness and every disease among the people. But when he saw the multitudes, he was moved with compassion on them, because they fainted, and were scattered abroad, *as sheep having no shepherd*.[248] Then saith he unto his disciples, "The harvest truly is plenteous, but the labourers are few. Pray ye therefore the Lord of the harvest, that he will send forth labourers into his harvest."

And it came to pass in those days, when it was day, that he went up into a mountain to pray, and continued all night in prayer to God. And when it was day, he called unto him his disciples, and of them he chose and ordained twelve, whom also he named apostles, that they should be with him, and that he might send them forth to preach. Then he called them together, and gave them power and

---

[248] See Numbers 27:16-17: "Let the LORD, the God of the spirits of all flesh, set a man over the congregation, which may go out before them, and which may go in before them, and which may lead them out, and which may bring them in; that the congregation of the LORD be not as sheep which have no shepherd."
1 Kings 22:17: "And he said, 'I saw all Israel scattered upon the hills, as sheep that have not a shepherd;' and the LORD said, 'These have no master; let them return every man to his house in peace.'"

authority over all devils, to cast them out, and to heal all manner of sickness and all manner of disease.[249]

Now the names of the twelve apostles are these: the first, Simon, who Jesus surnamed Peter; and Andrew his brother; James the son of Zebedee; and John his brother, whom Jesus surnamed Boanerges, (which is, the sons of thunder); Philip; and Bartholomew; Matthew (Levi) the publican; and Thomas; James the son of Alphaeus; and Simon the Canaanite called Zelotes; Lebbaeus (Judas the brother of James), whose surname was Thaddaeus; and Judas Iscariot, who was the traitor which also betrayed him.

And he called unto him the twelve, and began to send them forth by two and two, to preach the kingdom of God, and to heal the sick, and commanded them, saying, "Go not into the way of the Gentiles, and into any city of the Samaritans enter ye not, but go rather to the lost sheep of the house of Israel. And as ye go, preach, saying, 'The kingdom of heaven is at hand.' Heal the sick, cleanse the lepers, raise the dead, cast out devils. Freely ye have received, freely give.

And he said unto them, "Take nothing for your journey, neither shoes, nor yet staves, nor scrip, neither bread, neither gold, nor silver, nor brass in your purses, neither have two coats apiece, for the workman is worthy of his meat. And into whatsoever city or town ye shall enter, enquire who in it is worthy. And when ye come into an house, salute it. And if the house be worthy, let your peace come upon it,[250] but if it be not worthy, let your peace return to you. And whatsoever house ye enter into, there abide till ye depart from

---

[249] Compare Numbers 11:25: "And the LORD came down in a cloud, and spake unto him, and took of the spirit that was upon him, and gave it unto the seventy elders; and it came to pass, that, when the spirit rested upon them, they prophesied, and did not cease."

[250] Compare 1 Samuel 25:5-6: "And David sent out ten young men, and David said unto the young men, 'Get you up to Carmel, and go to Nabal, and greet him in my name. And thus shall ye say to him that liveth in prosperity, "Peace be both to thee, and peace be to thine house, and peace be unto all that thou hast."'"

that place. And whosoever shall not receive you, nor hear your words, when ye depart out of that house or city, shake off the very dust from under your feet for a testimony against them. Verily I say unto you, it shall be more tolerable for Sodom and Gomorrah in the day of judgment, than for that city.[251]

"Behold, I send you forth as sheep in the midst of wolves, be ye therefore wise as serpents, and harmless as doves. But beware of men, for they will deliver you up to the councils, and they will scourge you in their synagogues, and ye shall be brought before governors and kings for my sake, for a testimony against them and the Gentiles.[252] But when they deliver you up, take no thought how or what ye shall speak, for it shall be given you in that same hour what ye shall speak. For it is not ye that speak, but the Spirit of your Father which speaketh in you.[253] And the brother shall deliver up the brother to death, and the father the child, and the children shall rise up against their parents, and cause them to be put to death. And ye shall be hated of all men for my name's sake, but he that

---

[251] Compare Ezekiel 16:48-50: "As I live, saith the Lord GOD, Sodom thy sister hath not done, she nor her daughters, as thou hast done, thou and thy daughters. Behold, this was the iniquity of thy sister Sodom: pride, fulness of bread, and abundance of idleness was in her and in her daughters, neither did she strengthen the hand of the poor and needy. And they were haughty, and committed abomination before me; therefore I took them away as I saw good."
Lamentations 4:6: "For the punishment of the iniquity of the daughter of my people is greater than the punishment of the sin of Sodom, that was overthrown as in a moment, and no hands stayed on her."
Genesis 19:24-25: "Then the LORD rained upon Sodom and upon Gomorrah brimstone and fire from the LORD out of heaven; and he overthrew those cities, and all the plain, and all the inhabitants of the cities, and that which grew upon the ground."
[252] Compare Jeremiah 15:15: "O LORD, thou knowest; remember me, and visit me, and revenge me of my persecutors; take me not away in thy longsuffering; know that for thy sake I have suffered rebuke."
[253] Compare Jeremiah 1:9: "Then the LORD put forth his hand, and touched my mouth. And the LORD said unto me, 'Behold, I have put my words in thy mouth.'"
Exodus 4:11-12: "And the LORD said unto him, 'Who hath made man's mouth? Or who maketh the dumb, or deaf, or the seeing, or the blind? Have not I the LORD? Now therefore go, and I will be with thy mouth, and teach thee what thou shalt say.'"

endureth to the end shall be saved. But when they persecute you in this city, flee ye into another, for verily I say unto you, ye shall not have gone over the cities of Israel, till the Son of man be come.

"The disciple is not above his master, nor the servant above his lord. It is enough for the disciple that he be as his master, and the servant as his lord. If they have called the master of the house Beelzebub, how much more shall they call them of his household? Fear them not therefore,[254] for there is nothing covered, that shall not be revealed, and hid, that shall not be known.[255] What I tell you in darkness, that speak ye in light, and what ye hear in the ear, that preach ye upon the housetops.[256] And fear not them which kill the body, but are not able to kill the soul, but rather, fear him which is able to destroy both soul and body in hell.[257]

---

[254] Compare Joshua 10:8: "And the LORD said unto Joshua, 'Fear them not; for I have delivered them into thine hand; there shall not a man of them stand before thee.'"
Proverbs 29:25: "The fear of man bringeth a snare; but whoso putteth his trust in the LORD shall be safe."
[255] Compare Ecclesiastes 12:14: "For God shall bring every work into judgment, with every secret thing, whether it be good, or whether it be evil."
Wisdom 1:8,11: "Therefore he that speaketh unrighteous things cannot be hid; neither shall vengeance, when it punisheth, pass by him. Therefore beware of murmuring, which is unprofitable; and refrain your tongue from backbiting; for there is no word so secret, that shall go for nought; and the mouth that belieth slayeth the soul."
Sirach 42:18-20: "He seeketh out the deep, and the heart, and considereth their crafty devices; for the Lord knoweth all that may be known, and he beholdeth the signs of the world. He declareth the things that are past, and for to come, and revealeth the steps of hidden things. No thought escapeth him, neither any word is hidden from him."
[256] Compare Tobit 12:7: "It is good to keep close the secret of a king, but it is honourable to reveal the works of God. Do that which is good, and no evil shall touch you."
Deuteronomy 29:29: "The secret things belong unto the LORD our God; but those things which are revealed belong unto us and to our children for ever, that we may do all the words of this law."
[257] Compare Isaiah 45:5,7: "I am the LORD, and there is none else, there is no God beside me. I girded thee, though thou hast not known me. I form the light, and create darkness. I make peace, and create evil. I the LORD do all these things."

THE TREE OF LIFE

"Are not two sparrows sold for a farthing? And one of them shall not fall on the ground without your Father's knowledge. Fear ye not therefore, ye are of more value than many sparrows. And the very hairs of your head are all numbered.²⁵⁸ Whosoever therefore shall confess me before men, him will I confess also before my Father which is in heaven.²⁵⁹ But whosoever shall deny me before men, him will I also deny before my Father which is in heaven.

"Think not that I am come to send peace on earth. I came not to send peace, but *a sword*.²⁶⁰ For I am come to set a man *at variance against his father, and the daughter against her mother, and the daughter in law against her mother in law. And a man's foes shall be they of his own household*.²⁶¹ He that loveth father or mother more than me is not worthy of me, and he that loveth son or daughter more than me is not worthy of me.²⁶² And he that taketh not his

---

Ecclesiastes 12:13: "Let us hear the conclusion of the whole matter: Fear God, and keep his commandments; for this is the whole duty of man."
Psalms 9:17: "The wicked shall be turned into hell, and all the nations that forget God."
²⁵⁸ Compare Wisdom 3:1: "But the souls of the righteous are in the hand of God, and there shall no torment touch them."
²⁵⁹ See 2 Esdras 2:46-47: "Then said I unto the angel, 'What young person is it that crowneth them, and giveth them palms in their hands?' So he answered and said unto me, 'It is the Son of God, whom they have confessed in the world.' Then began I greatly to commend them that stood so stiffly for the name of the Lord."
²⁶⁰ See Ezekiel 38:21: "And I will call for a sword against him throughout all my mountains, saith the Lord GOD; every man's sword shall be against his brother."
²⁶¹ See Micah 7:5-6: "Trust ye not in a friend, put ye not confidence in a guide, keep the doors of thy mouth from her that lieth in thy bosom. For the son dishonoureth the father, the daughter riseth up against her mother, the daughter in law against her mother in law; a man's enemies are the men of his own house."
²⁶² Compare Genesis 22:1-2,9-12,15-17: "And it came to pass after these things, that God did tempt Abraham, and said unto him, 'Abraham;' and he said, 'Behold, here I am.' And he said, 'Take now thy son, thine only son Isaac, whom thou lovest, and get thee into the land of Moriah; and offer him there for a burnt offering upon one of the mountains which I will tell thee of.' And they came to the place which God had told him of; and Abraham built an altar there, and laid the wood in order, and bound Isaac his son, and laid him on the altar upon the wood. And Abraham stretched forth his hand, and took the knife to slay his son. And the angel of the LORD called unto him out of heaven, and said, 'Abraham, Abraham;' and he said, 'Here am I.' And he said, 'Lay not thine hand upon the lad, neither do thou any thing

cross, and followeth after me, is not worthy of me. He that findeth his life shall lose it, and he that loseth his life for my sake shall find it.

"Verily, verily, I say unto you, he that receiveth you receiveth me, and he that receiveth me receiveth him that sent me. He that receiveth a prophet in the name of a prophet shall receive a prophet's reward, and he that receiveth a righteous man in the name of a righteous man shall receive a righteous man's reward. And whosoever shall give to drink unto one of these little ones a cup of cold water only in the name of a disciple, verily I say unto you, he shall in no wise lose his reward."

And the twelve departed, and went out through the towns, preaching the gospel, and healing every where, and preached that men should repent. And they cast out many devils, and anointed with oil many that were sick, and healed them.

---

unto him; for now I know that thou fearest God, seeing thou hast not withheld thy son, thine only son from me.' And the angel of the LORD called unto Abraham out of heaven the second time, and said, 'By myself have I sworn, saith the LORD, for because thou hast done this thing, and hast not withheld thy son, thine only son; that in blessing I will bless thee, and in multiplying I will multiply thy seed as the stars of the heaven, and as the sand which is upon the sea shore; and thy seed shall possess the gate of his enemies.'"

Chapter Twenty Three

And it came to pass, when Jesus had made an end of commanding his twelve disciples, he departed thence to teach and to preach in their cities. Now when he had ended all his sayings in the audience of the people, he entered into Capernaum. And when Jesus was entered into Capernaum, there came unto him a centurion, beseeching him, whose servant, who was dear unto him, was sick, and ready to die. And when he heard of Jesus, he sent unto him the elders of the Jews, beseeching him that he would come and heal his servant, saying, "Lord, my servant lieth at home sick of the palsy, grievously tormented." And when they came to Jesus, they besought him instantly, saying "He is worthy for whom ye should do this, for he loveth our nation, and he hath built us a synagogue." And Jesus saith unto him, "I will come and heal him."

Then Jesus went with them. And when he was now not far from the house, the centurion sent friends to him, saying unto him, "Lord, trouble not thyself, for I am not worthy that thou shouldest enter under my roof. Wherefore neither thought I myself worthy to come unto thee, but speak the word only, and my servant shall be healed. For I also am a man set under authority, having soldiers under me, and I say unto one, 'Go,' and he goeth, and to another, 'Come,' and he cometh, and to my servant, 'Do this,' and he doeth it."

When Jesus heard it, he marvelled at him, and turned about, and said to them that followed, "Verily I say unto you, I have not found so great faith, no, not in Israel, and I say unto you, that many shall come from the east and west,[263] and shall sit down[264] with Abraham, and Isaac, and Jacob, in the kingdom of heaven. But the children of the kingdom shall be cast out into outer darkness, there shall be weeping and *gnashing of teeth*."[265]

---

[263] See Psalms 107:1-3: "O give thanks unto the LORD, for he is good; for his mercy endureth for ever. Let the redeemed of the LORD say so, whom he hath redeemed from the hand of the enemy; and gathered them out of the lands, from the east, and from the west, from the north, and from the south."
Baruch 5:5: "Arise, O Jerusalem, and stand on high, and look about toward the east, and behold thy children gathered from the west unto the east by the word of the Holy One, rejoicing in the remembrance of God."
[264] See Isaiah 25:6-8: "And in this mountain shall the LORD of hosts make unto all people a feast of fat things, a feast of wines on the lees, of fat things full of marrow, of wines on the lees well refined. And he will destroy in this mountain the face of the covering cast over all people, and the vail that is spread over all nations. He will swallow up death in victory; and the Lord GOD will wipe away tears from off all faces; and the rebuke of his people shall he take away from off all the earth; for the LORD hath spoken it."
[265] See Psalms 112:4,10: "Unto the upright there ariseth light in the darkness; he is gracious, and full of compassion, and righteous. The wicked shall see it, and be grieved; he shall gnash with his teeth, and melt away; the desire of the wicked shall perish."
Malachi 1:6-11: "A son honoureth his father, and a servant his master; if then I be a father, where is mine honour? And if I be a master, where is my fear? saith the LORD of hosts unto you, O priests, that despise my name. And ye say, 'Wherein have we despised thy name?' Ye offer polluted bread upon mine altar; and ye say, 'Wherein have we polluted thee?' In that ye say, 'The table of the LORD is contemptible.' Who is there even among you that would shut the doors for nought? neither do ye kindle fire on mine altar for nought. I have no pleasure in you, saith the LORD of hosts, neither will I accept an offering at your hand. For from the rising of the sun even unto the going down of the same my name shall be great among the Gentiles; and in every place incense shall be offered unto my name, and a pure offering; for my name shall be great among the heathen, saith the LORD of hosts."
2 Esdras 1:35-40: "Your houses will I give to a people that shall come; which not having heard of me yet shall believe me; to whom I have shewed no signs, yet they shall do that I have commanded them. They have seen no prophets, yet they shall call their sins to remembrance, and acknowledge them. I take to witness the grace of the people to come, whose little ones rejoice in gladness; and though they have not seen me with bodily eyes, yet in spirit they believe the thing that I say. And now, brother, behold what glory; and see the people that come from the east; unto

And Jesus said unto the centurion, "Go thy way, and as thou hast believed, so be it done unto thee." And his servant was healed in the selfsame hour. And they that were sent, returning to the house, found the servant whole that had been sick.

---

whom I will give for leaders, Abraham, Isaac, and Jacob, Hosea, Amos, and Micah, Joel, Obadiah, and Jonah, Nahum, and Habakkuk, Zephaniah, Haggai, Zechariah, and Malachi, which is called also an angel of the Lord."

Isaiah 60:3-5: "And the Gentiles shall come to thy light, and kings to the brightness of thy rising. Lift up thine eyes round about, and see; all they gather themselves together, they come to thee; thy sons shall come from far, and thy daughters shall be nursed at thy side. Then thou shalt see, and flow together, and thine heart shall fear, and be enlarged; because the abundance of the sea shall be converted unto thee, the forces of the Gentiles shall come unto thee."

THE TREE OF LIFE

THE TREE OF LIFE

Chapter Twenty Four

And it came to pass the day after, that he went into a city called Nain, and many of his disciples went with him, and much people. Now when he came nigh to the gate of the city, behold, there was a dead man carried out, the only son of his mother, and she was a widow, and much people of the city were with her. And when the Lord saw her, he had compassion on her, and said unto her, "Weep not." And he came and touched the bier, and they that bare him stood still. And he said, "Young man, I say unto thee, arise." And he that was dead sat up, and began to speak. And he delivered him to his mother.[266] And there came a fear on all, and they glorified God, saying, "A great prophet is risen up among us," and, "God hath visited his people." And this rumour of him went forth throughout all Judaea, and throughout all the region round about.

---

[266] Compare 1 Kings 17:1-24 (Elijah); 2 Kings 4:8-37 (Elisha).

THE TREE OF LIFE

THE TREE OF LIFE

Chapter Twenty Five

And the disciples of John came and shewed him in the prison of all the works of Christ. And he called unto him two of his disciples and sent them to Jesus, saying, "Art thou he that should come,[267] or look we for another?" When the men were come unto him, they said, "John Baptist hath sent us unto thee, saying, 'Art thou he that should come, or do we look for another?'"

And in that same hour he cured many of their infirmities and plagues, and of evil spirits, and unto many that were blind he gave sight. Jesus answered and said unto them, "Go your way, and tell John what things which ye have seen and heard, how that the blind receive their sight, the lame walk, the lepers are cleansed, the deaf hear, the dead are raised up, and the poor have the gospel preached

---

[267] See Deuteronomy 18:15: "The LORD thy God will raise up unto thee a Prophet from the midst of thee, of thy brethren, like unto me; unto him ye shall hearken."
Isaiah 11:1-4: "And there shall come forth a rod out of the stem of Jesse, and a Branch shall grow out of his roots. And the spirit of the LORD shall rest upon him, the spirit of wisdom and understanding, the spirit of counsel and might, the spirit of knowledge and of the fear of the LORD; And shall make him of quick understanding in the fear of the LORD; and he shall not judge after the sight of his eyes, neither reprove after the hearing of his ears. But with righteousness shall he judge the poor, and reprove with equity for the meek of the earth; and he shall smite the earth with the rod of his mouth, and with the breath of his lips shall he slay the wicked."

to them.[268] And blessed is he, whosoever shall not be offended in me."[269]

And as they were departed, Jesus began to speak unto the multitudes concerning John, "What went ye out into the wilderness for to see? A reed shaken with the wind? But what went ye out for to see? A man clothed in soft raiment? Behold, they that wear soft clothing, and live delicately, are in kings' courts. But what went ye out for to see? A prophet?[270] Yea, I say unto you, and much more than a prophet. For this is he, of whom it is written, *'Behold, I send my messenger before thy face, which shall prepare thy way before thee.'*[271] Verily I say unto you, among those that are born of women there hath not risen a greater prophet than John the Baptist, notwithstanding he that is least in the kingdom of heaven is greater than he. And from the days of John the Baptist until now the kingdom of heaven suffereth violence, and the violent take it by force. For all the prophets and the law prophesied until John. And if

---

[268] See Isaiah 35:5-6: "Then [in the days of Messiah] the eyes of the blind shall be opened, and the ears of the deaf shall be unstopped. Then shall the lame man leap as an hart, and the tongue of the dumb sing; for in the wilderness shall waters break out, and streams in the desert."
[269] See Isaiah 8:14-15: "And he shall be for a sanctuary; but for a stone of stumbling and for a rock of offence to both the houses of Israel, for a gin and for a snare to the inhabitants of Jerusalem. And many among them shall stumble, and fall, and be broken, and be snared, and be taken."
[270] See Zechariah 13:4: "And it shall come to pass in that day, that the prophets shall be ashamed every one of his vision, when he hath prophesied; neither shall they wear a rough garment to deceive."
[271] "Behold, I will send my messenger, and he shall prepare the way before me; and the Lord, whom ye seek, shall suddenly come to his temple, even the messenger of the covenant, whom ye delight in; behold, he shall come, saith the LORD of hosts." - Malachi 3:1

ye will receive it, this is Elijah,[272] which was for to come. *He that hath ears to hear, let him hear.*"[273]

And all the people that heard him, and the publicans, justified God, being baptized with the baptism of John. But the Pharisees and lawyers rejected the counsel of God against themselves, being not baptized of him. And the Lord said, "Whereunto then shall I liken the men of this generation? And to what are they like? They are like unto children sitting in the marketplace, and calling one to another, and saying, 'We have piped unto you, and ye have not danced. We have mourned to you, and ye have not wept.' For John the Baptist came neither eating bread nor drinking wine, and ye say, 'He hath a devil.' The Son of man came eating and drinking, and ye say, 'Behold a *gluttonous man, and a winebibber*,[274] a friend of publicans and sinners!' But wisdom is justified of all her children."[275]

Then began he to upbraid the cities wherein most of his mighty works were done, because they repented not: "Woe unto thee, Chorazin! Woe unto thee, Bethsaida! For if the mighty works, which have been done in you, had been done in Tyre and Zidon, they would have repented long ago, sitting in sackcloth and ashes.[276] But

---

[272] See Malachi 4:5: "Behold, I will send you Elijah the prophet before the coming of the great and dreadful day of the LORD."
[273] See Ezekiel 3:27: "But when I speak with thee, I will open thy mouth, and thou shalt say unto them, 'Thus saith the Lord GOD; He that heareth, let him hear; and he that forbeareth, let him forbear;' for they are a rebellious house."
[274] Compare Deuteronomy 21:20: "And they shall say unto the elders of his city, 'This our son is stubborn and rebellious, he will not obey our voice; he is a glutton, and a drunkard.'"
See also Genesis 49:10-12: "The sceptre shall not depart from Judah, nor a lawgiver from between his feet, until Shiloh come; and unto him shall the gathering of the people be. Binding his foal unto the vine, and his ass's colt unto the choice vine; he washed his garments in wine, and his clothes in the blood of grapes. His eyes shall be red with wine, and his teeth white with milk."
[275] Compare Sirach 4:11: "Wisdom exalteth her children, and layeth hold of them that seek her."
[276] Compare Jonah 3:4-10: "And Jonah began to enter into the city a day's journey, and he cried, and said, 'Yet forty days, and Nineveh shall be overthrown.' So the people of Nineveh believed God, and proclaimed a fast, and put on sackcloth, from

I say unto you, it shall be more tolerable for Tyre and Zidon[277] at the day of judgment, than for you. And thou, Capernaum, which art exalted to heaven, shalt be thrust down to hell,[278] for if the mighty works, which have been done in thee, had been done in Sodom, it would have remained until this day. But I say unto you, that it shall be more tolerable for the land of Sodom[279] in the day of judgment, than for thee."[280]

---

the greatest of them even to the least of them. For word came unto the king of Nineveh, and he arose from his throne, and he laid his robe from him, and covered him with sackcloth, and sat in ashes. And he caused it to be proclaimed and published through Nineveh by the decree of the king and his nobles, saying, 'Let neither man nor beast, herd nor flock, taste any thing; let them not feed, nor drink water; but let man and beast be covered with sackcloth, and cry mightily unto God; yea, let them turn every one from his evil way, and from the violence that is in their hands. Who can tell if God will turn and repent, and turn away from his fierce anger, that we perish not?' And God saw their works, that they turned from their evil way; and God repented of the evil, that he had said that he would do unto them; and he did it not."

[277] Compare Isaiah 23:1-2,4-5,8-9: "The burden of Tyre. Howl, ye ships of Tarshish; for it is laid waste, so that there is no house, no entering in; from the land of Chittim it is revealed to them. Be still, ye inhabitants of the isle; thou whom the merchants of Zidon, that pass over the sea, have replenished. Be thou ashamed, O Zidon; for the sea hath spoken, even the strength of the sea, saying, 'I travail not, nor bring forth children, neither do I nourish up young men, nor bring up virgins.' As at the report concerning Egypt, so shall they be sorely pained at the report of Tyre. Who hath taken this counsel against Tyre, the crowning city, whose merchants are princes, whose traffickers are the honourable of the earth? The LORD of hosts hath purposed it, to stain the pride of all glory, and to bring into contempt all the honourable of the earth."

[278] Compare Isaiah 5:14-15: "Therefore hell hath enlarged herself, and opened her mouth without measure; and their glory, and their multitude, and their pomp, and he that rejoiceth, shall descend into it. And the mean man shall be brought down, and the mighty man shall be humbled, and the eyes of the lofty shall be humbled."

[279] See Genesis 19:24-25: "Then the LORD rained upon Sodom and upon Gomorrah brimstone and fire from the LORD out of heaven; and he overthrew those cities, and all the plain, and all the inhabitants of the cities, and that which grew upon the ground."

[280] Compare Ezekiel 16:48-50,52: "As I live, saith the Lord GOD, Sodom thy sister hath not done, she nor her daughters, as thou hast done, thou and thy daughters. Behold, this was the iniquity of thy sister Sodom: pride, fulness of bread, and abundance of idleness was in her and in her daughters, neither did she strengthen the hand of the poor and needy. And they were haughty, and committed abomination before me; therefore I took them away as I saw good. Thou also, which

At that time Jesus said, "I thank thee, O Father, Lord of heaven and earth, because thou hast hid these things from the wise and prudent, and hast revealed them unto babes.[281] Even so, Father, for so it seemed good in thy sight.

"All things are delivered unto me of my Father, and no man knoweth the Son, but the Father, neither knoweth any man the Father, save the Son, which is in the bosom of the Father, and he to whomsoever the Son will reveal him.

"Come unto me, all ye that labour and are heavy laden, and I will give you rest. Take my yoke upon you,[282] and learn of me, for I am meek and lowly in heart, and ye shall find rest unto your souls. For my yoke is easy, and my burden is light."

---

hast judged thy sisters, bear thine own shame for thy sins that thou hast committed more abominable than they; they are more righteous than thou; yea, be thou confounded also, and bear thy shame, in that thou hast justified thy sisters."
Lamentations 4:6: "For the punishment of the iniquity of the daughter of my people is greater than the punishment of the sin of Sodom, that was overthrown as in a moment, and no hands stayed on her."
[281] Compare <u>Sirach 3:19:</u> "Many are in high place, and of renown; but mysteries are revealed unto the meek."
[282] Compare <u>Sirach 51:23,25-26:</u> "Draw near unto me, ye unlearned, and dwell in the house of learning. I opened my mouth, and said, 'Buy her [wisdom] for yourselves without money. Put your neck under the yoke, and let your soul receive instruction; she [wisdom] is hard at hand to find.'"
<u>Jeremiah 5:4-5:</u> "Therefore I said, 'Surely these are poor; they are foolish; for they know not the way of the LORD, nor the judgment of their God. I will get me unto the great men, and will speak unto them; for they have known the way of the LORD, and the judgment of their God; but these have altogether broken the yoke, and burst the bonds.'"

THE TREE OF LIFE

Chapter Twenty Six

And the multitude cometh together again, so that they could not so much as eat bread. And when his friends heard of it, they went out to lay hold on him, for they said, "He is beside himself." Then was brought unto him one possessed with a devil, blind, and dumb. And he healed him, insomuch that the blind and dumb both spake and saw. And it came to pass, when the devil was gone out, the people wondered and were amazed, and said, "Is not this the son of David?"[283]

But when the scribes and Pharisees which came down from Jerusalem heard it, they said, "This fellow casteth out devils through Beelzebub[284] the chief of the devils." And Jesus knew their thoughts, and said unto them, "Every kingdom divided against itself is brought to desolation, and every city or house divided against itself falleth and shall not stand." And he called them unto him, and said unto them in parables, "How can Satan cast out Satan? And if Satan cast out Satan, he is divided against himself, and if Satan rise up against himself, and be divided, he cannot stand, but hath an end. How then shall his kingdom stand? Because ye say that I cast out devils

---

[283] Compare Isaiah 35:5-6: "Then [in the days of Messiah] the eyes of the blind shall be opened, and the ears of the deaf shall be unstopped. Then shall the lame man leap as an hart, and the tongue of the dumb sing; for in the wilderness shall waters break out, and streams in the desert."
[284] See 2 Kings 1:2-4.

through Beelzebub. And if I by Beelzebub cast out devils, by whom do your children cast them out? Therefore they shall be your judges. But if I with the finger of God[285] cast out devils, then no doubt the kingdom of God is come unto you.

"When a strong man armed keepeth his palace, his goods are in peace. But when a stronger than he shall come upon him, and overcome him, he taketh from him all his armour wherein he trusted, and divideth his spoils. Or else how can one enter into a strong man's house, and spoil his goods, except he first bind the strong man? And then he will spoil his house. When the unclean spirit is gone out of a man, he walketh through dry places, seeking rest, and finding none, he saith, 'I will return unto my house whence I came out,' and when he is come, he findeth it empty, swept, and garnished. Then goeth he, and taketh with himself seven other spirits more wicked than himself, and they enter in and dwell there, and the last state of that man is worse than the first. Even so shall it be also unto this wicked generation.[286] He that is not with me is against me, and he that gathereth not with me scattereth abroad. Also I say unto you, whosoever shall confess me before men, him

---

[285] Compare <u>Exodus 8:16-19:</u> "And the LORD said unto Moses, 'Say unto Aaron, "Stretch out thy rod, and smite the dust of the land, that it may become lice throughout all the land of Egypt."' And they did so; for Aaron stretched out his hand with his rod, and smote the dust of the earth, and it became lice in man, and in beast; all the dust of the land became lice throughout all the land of Egypt. And the magicians did so with their enchantments to bring forth lice, but they could not; so there were lice upon man, and upon beast. Then the magicians said unto Pharaoh, 'This is the finger of God;' and Pharaoh's heart was hardened, and he hearkened not unto them; as the LORD had said."
[286] Compare <u>Numbers 14:26-27:</u> "And the LORD spake unto Moses and unto Aaron, saying, 'How long shall I bear with this evil congregation, which murmur against me? I have heard the murmurings of the children of Israel, which they murmur against me.'"
<u>Numbers 14:11:</u> "And the LORD said unto Moses, 'How long will this people provoke me? And how long will it be ere they believe me, for all the signs which I have shewed among them?'"

THE TREE OF LIFE

shall the Son of man also confess before the angels of God.[287] But he that denieth me before men shall be denied before the angels of God. Verily I say unto you, all manner of sin and blasphemy shall be forgiven unto the sons of men, and whosoever shall speak a word against the Son of man, it shall be forgiven him, but unto him that blasphemeth against the Holy Ghost, it shall not be forgiven him, neither in this world, nor in the world to come."

And they said, "He hath an unclean spirit." And Jesus said unto them, "Either make the tree good, and his fruit good, or else make the tree corrupt, and his fruit corrupt, for the tree is known by his fruit. O generation of vipers, how can ye, being evil, speak good things? For out of the abundance of the heart the mouth speaketh. A good man out of the good treasure of the heart bringeth forth good things, and an evil man out of the evil treasure bringeth forth evil things. But I say unto you, that every idle word that men shall speak, they shall give account thereof in the day of judgment.[288] For by thy words thou shalt be justified, and by thy words thou shalt be condemned."[289]

---

[287] See <u>2 Esdras</u> 2:46-47: "Then said I unto the angel, 'What young person is it that crowneth them, and giveth them palms in their hands?' So he answered and said unto me, 'It is the Son of God, whom they have confessed in the world.' Then began I greatly to commend them that stood so stiffly for the name of the Lord."
[288] Compare <u>Job 16:1-5</u>: "Then Job answered and said, 'I have heard many such things; miserable comforters are ye all. Shall vain words have an end? Or what emboldeneth thee that thou answerest? I also could speak as ye do; if your soul were in my soul's stead, I could heap up words against you, and shake mine head at you. But I would strengthen you with my mouth, and the moving of my lips should assuage your grief.'"
<u>Psalms 12:2-3</u>: "They speak vanity every one with his neighbor; with flattering lips and with a double heart do they speak. The LORD shall cut off all flattering lips, and the tongue that speaketh proud things."
[289] Compare <u>Proverbs 18:21</u>: "Death and life are in the power of the tongue; and they that love it shall eat the fruit thereof."
<u>Proverbs 15:4</u>: "A wholesome tongue is a tree of life; but perverseness therein is a breach in the spirit."
<u>Sirach</u> 5:13: "Honour and shame is in talk; and the tongue of man is his fall."

And it came to pass, as he spake these things, a certain woman of the company lifted up her voice, and said unto him, "Blessed is the womb that bare thee, and the paps which thou hast sucked." But he said, "Yea rather, blessed are they that hear the word of God, and keep it."

Then certain of the scribes and of the Pharisees answered, saying, "Master, we would see a sign from thee." And others, tempting him, also sought of him a sign from heaven. But he answered and said unto them, *"An evil*[290] *and adulterous generation*[291] seeketh after a sign, and there shall no sign be given to it, but the sign of the prophet Jonah. For as Jonah was a sign unto the Ninevites, so shall also the Son of man be to this generation.[292] For

---

Psalms 15:1-3: "LORD, who shall abide in thy tabernacle? Who shall dwell in thy holy hill? He that walketh uprightly, and worketh righteousness, and speaketh the truth in his heart. He that backbiteth not with his tongue, nor doeth evil to his neighbour, nor taketh up a reproach against his neighbour."
[290] See Deuteronomy 1:35: "Surely there shall not one of these men of this evil generation see that good land, which I sware to give unto your fathers."
Deuteronomy 32:5: "They have corrupted themselves, their spot is not the spot of his children; they are a perverse and crooked generation."
[291] See Jeremiah 3:20: "Surely as a wife treacherously departeth from her husband, so have ye dealt treacherously with me, O house of Israel, saith the LORD."
Hosea 1:2: "The beginning of the word of the LORD by Hosea. And the LORD said to Hosea, 'Go, take unto thee a wife of whoredoms and children of whoredoms; for the land hath committed great whoredom, departing from the LORD.'"
Hosea 9:1: "Rejoice not, O Israel, for joy, as other people; for thou hast gone a whoring from thy God, thou hast loved a reward upon every cornfloor."
[292] See Jonah 2:1-10: "Then Jonah prayed unto the LORD his God out of the fish's belly, and said, 'I cried by reason of mine affliction unto the LORD, and he heard me; out of the belly of hell cried I, and thou heardest my voice. For thou hadst cast me into the deep, in the midst of the seas; and the floods compassed me about; all thy billows and thy waves passed over me.' Then I said, 'I am cast out of thy sight; yet I will look again toward thy holy temple. The waters compassed me about, even to the soul; the depth closed me round about, the weeds were wrapped about my head. I went down to the bottoms of the mountains; the earth with her bars was about me for ever; yet hast thou brought up my life from corruption, O LORD my God. When my soul fainted within me I remembered the LORD; and my prayer came in unto thee, into thine holy temple. They that observe lying vanities forsake their own mercy. But I will sacrifice unto thee with the voice of thanksgiving; I will

as *Jonah was three days and three nights in the whale's belly,*[293] so shall the Son of man be three days and three nights in the heart of the earth. The men of Nineveh shall rise up in the judgment with this generation, and shall condemn it, for they repented at the preaching of Jonah,[294] and, behold, a greater than Jonah is here. And the queen of the south shall rise up in the judgment with the men of this generation, and shall condemn them, for she came from the uttermost parts of the earth to hear the wisdom of Solomon,[295] and, behold, a greater than Solomon is here."

---

pay that that I have vowed. Salvation is of the LORD.' And the LORD spake unto the fish, and it vomited out Jonah upon the dry land."
Psalms 16:10: "For thou wilt not leave my soul in hell; neither wilt thou suffer thine Holy One to see corruption."
[293] See Jonah 1:17: "Now the LORD had prepared a great fish to swallow up Jonah. And Jonah was in the belly of the fish three days and three nights."
[294] See Jonah 3:4-10: "And Jonah began to enter into the city a day's journey, and he cried, and said, 'Yet forty days, and Nineveh shall be overthrown.' So the people of Nineveh believed God, and proclaimed a fast, and put on sackcloth, from the greatest of them even to the least of them. For word came unto the king of Nineveh, and he arose from his throne, and he laid his robe from him, and covered him with sackcloth, and sat in ashes. And he caused it to be proclaimed and published through Nineveh by the decree of the king and his nobles, saying, 'Let neither man nor beast, herd nor flock, taste any thing; let them not feed, nor drink water; but let man and beast be covered with sackcloth, and cry mightily unto God; yea, let them turn every one from his evil way, and from the violence that is in their hands. Who can tell if God will turn and repent, and turn away from his fierce anger, that we perish not?' And God saw their works, that they turned from their evil way; and God repented of the evil, that he had said that he would do unto them; and he did it not."
[295] See 1 Kings 10:1: "And when the queen of Sheba heard of the fame of Solomon concerning the name of the LORD, she came to prove him with hard questions."
2 Chronicles 9:1: "And when the queen of Sheba heard of the fame of Solomon, she came to prove Solomon with hard questions at Jerusalem, with a very great company, and camels that bare spices, and gold in abundance, and precious stones; and when she was come to Solomon, she communed with him of all that was in her heart."

THE TREE OF LIFE

Chapter Twenty Seven

While he yet talked to the people, behold, his mother and his brethren stood without, desiring to speak with him, but could they not come at him for the press, and they sent unto him, calling him. And the multitude sat about him, and it was told him by certain which said, "Behold, thy mother and thy brethren stand without, desiring to speak with thee."

And he answered and said unto him that told him, "Who is my mother?" And "Who are my brethren?" And he looked round about on them which sat about him, and he stretched forth his hand toward his disciples, and answered and said, "Behold my mother and my brethren! My mother and my brethren are these which hear the word of God, and do it.[296] For whosoever shall do the will of my Father which is in heaven, the same is my brother, and sister, and mother."

---

[296] Compare <u>Deuteronomy 33:8-9:</u> "And of Levi he said, 'Let thy Thummim and thy Urim be with thy holy one, whom thou didst prove at Massah, and with whom thou didst strive at the waters of Meribah; who said unto his father and to his mother, "I have not seen him;" neither did he acknowledge his brethren, nor knew his own children; for they have observed thy word, and kept thy covenant.'"
<u>Deuteronomy 6:5-6:</u> "And thou shalt love the LORD thy God with all thine heart, and with all thy soul, and with all thy might. And these words, which I command thee this day, shall be in thine heart."

THE TREE OF LIFE

Chapter Twenty Eight

The same day went Jesus out of the house, and sat by the sea side, and he began again to teach. And there was gathered unto him great multitudes out of every city, so that he entered into a ship, and sat in the sea, and the whole multitude stood on the shore.

And he taught them many things by parables, and in his doctrine, saying, "Behold, a sower went forth to sow his seed, and it came to pass, as he sowed, some seeds fell by the way side, and were trodden down, and the fowls of the air came and devoured them up. And some fell on stony ground, where they had not much earth, and immediately they sprang up, because they had no deepness of earth. And when the sun was up, they were scorched, and because they had no root, and lacked moisture, they withered away. And some fell among thorns, and the thorns sprung up with them, and choked them, and they yielded no fruit. But other fell into good ground, and sprang up, and increased, and brought forth fruit, some an hundredfold, some sixtyfold, some thirtyfold." And when he had said these things, he cried, "*He that hath ears to hear, let him hear.*"[297]

---

[297] See Ezekiel 3:27: "But when I speak with thee, I will open thy mouth, and thou shalt say unto them, 'Thus saith the Lord GOD; He that heareth, let him hear; and he that forbeareth, let him forbear;' for they are a rebellious house."

And when he was alone, his disciples that were about him with the twelve asked of him the parable, saying, "What might this parable be?" And he said unto them, "Know ye not this parable? And how then will ye know all parables?

"Hear ye therefore the parable of the sower. Now the parable is this: The seed is the word of God.[298] The sower soweth the word. And these are they which received seed by the way side, where the word is sown, but, when they heareth the word of the kingdom, and understandeth it not, then cometh the wicked one immediately, and taketh away the word which was sown in their hearts, lest they should believe and be saved.

"And these are they likewise which are sown on stony ground, who, when they have heard the word, immediately receive it with joy, yet these have no root in themselves, which for a while believe and so endure for a time, and in time of temptation fall away, for when tribulation or persecution ariseth for the word's sake, immediately they are offended.[299]

---

[298] Compare 2 Esdras 9:30-31: "And thou spakest saying, 'Hear me, O Israel; and mark my words, thou seed of Jacob. For, behold, I sow my law in you, and it shall bring fruit in you, and ye shall be honoured in it for ever.'"
Deuteronomy 6:5-7: "And thou shalt love the LORD thy God with all thine heart, and with all thy soul, and with all thy might. And these words, which I command thee this day, shall be in thine heart. And thou shalt teach them diligently unto thy children, and shalt talk of them when thou sittest in thine house, and when thou walkest by the way, and when thou liest down, and when thou risest up."
Joshua 1:8: "This book of the law shall not depart out of thy mouth; but thou shalt meditate therein day and night, that thou mayest observe to do according to all that is written therein; for then thou shalt make thy way prosperous, and then thou shalt have good success."
Psalms 40:8: "I delight to do thy will, O my God; yea, thy law is within my heart."
Ezra 7:10: "For Ezra had prepared his heart to seek the law of the LORD, and to do it, and to teach in Israel statutes and judgments."
[299] Compare Isaiah 8:14-15: "And he shall be for a sanctuary; but for a stone of stumbling and for a rock of offence to both the houses of Israel, for a gin and for a snare to the inhabitants of Jerusalem. And many among them shall stumble, and fall, and be broken, and be snared, and be taken."

"And these are they which are sown among thorns, which, when they have heard the word, go forth, and are choked with the cares of this world and the deceitfulness of riches, and pleasures of this life, and the lusts of other things entering in, and they bringeth forth no fruit to perfection.

"But he that received seed into the good ground are they, which, in an honest and good heart, hear the word, and understand it, and receive it, and keep it, which also bring forth fruit with patience, some an hundredfold, some sixty, some thirty."

And the disciples came, and said unto him, "Why speakest thou unto them in parables?" He answered and said unto them, "Because it is given unto you to know the mysteries of the kingdom of heaven, but to them that are without it is not given, therefore speak I to them in parables.[300] For whosoever hath, to him shall be given, and he shall have more abundance, but whosoever hath not, from him shall be taken away even that he hath. And in them is fulfilled the prophecy of Isaiah, which saith, *'By hearing ye shall hear, and shall not understand, and seeing ye shall see, and shall not perceive. For this people's heart is waxed gross, and their ears are dull of hearing, and their eyes they have closed, lest at any time they should see with their eyes and hear with their ears, and should understand with their heart, and should be converted, and I should heal them.'*[301] But blessed are your eyes, for they see, and your ears, for they hear. For verily I say unto you, that many prophets and righteous men have desired to see those things which ye see, and

---

[300] Compare <u>Sirach 1:25:</u> "The parables of knowledge are in the treasures of wisdom; but godliness is an abomination to a sinner."
[301] "And he said, 'Go, and tell this people, "Hear ye indeed, but understand not; and see ye indeed, but perceive not." Make the heart of this people fat, and make their ears heavy, and shut their eyes; lest they see with their eyes, and hear with their ears, and understand with their heart, and convert, and be healed.'" – <u>Isaiah 6:9-10</u>

THE TREE OF LIFE

have not seen them, and to hear those things which ye hear, and have not heard them."[302]

And he said unto them, "Is a candle brought to be put under a bushel, or under a bed, and not to be set on a candlestick? No man, when he hath lighted a candle, covereth it with a vessel, or putteth it under a bed, but setteth it on a candlestick, that they which enter in may see the light. For nothing is secret, that shall not be made manifest, neither any thing hid, that shall not be known and come abroad.[303] *If any man have ears to hear, let him hear.*"[304]

And he said unto them, "Take heed therefore how ye hear, for whosoever hath, to him shall be given, and whosoever hath not, from him shall be taken even that which he seemeth to have."

And he said, "So is the kingdom of God, as if a man should cast seed into the ground, and should sleep, and rise night and day, and the seed should spring and grow up, he knoweth not how. For the earth bringeth forth fruit of herself, first the blade, then the ear,

---

[302] Compare Job 19:25: "For I know that my redeemer liveth, and that he shall stand at the latter day upon the earth."
Numbers 24:14,16-19: "And now, behold, I go unto my people; come therefore, and I will advertise thee what this people shall do to thy people in the latter days. He hath said, which heard the words of God, and knew the knowledge of the most High, which saw the vision of the Almighty, falling into a trance, but having his eyes open; 'I shall see him, but not now; I shall behold him, but not nigh; there shall come a Star out of Jacob, and a Sceptre shall rise out of Israel, and shall smite the corners of Moab, and destroy all the children of Sheth. And Edom shall be a possession, Seir also shall be a possession for his enemies; and Israel shall do valiantly. Out of Jacob shall come he that shall have dominion, and shall destroy him that remaineth of the city.'"
See also Daniel 2:1-45.
[303] Compare Proverbs 20:27: "The spirit of man is the candle of the LORD, searching all the inward parts of the belly."
Ecclesiastes 12:14: "For God shall bring every work into judgment, with every secret thing, whether it be good, or whether it be evil."
[304] See Ezekiel 3:27: "But when I speak with thee, I will open thy mouth, and thou shalt say unto them, 'Thus saith the Lord GOD; He that heareth, let him hear; and he that forbeareth, let him forbear;' for they are a rebellious house."

after that the full corn in the ear. But when the fruit is brought forth, immediately he putteth in the sickle, because the harvest is come."

Then said he, "Unto what is the kingdom of God like? And whereunto shall I resemble it? The kingdom of heaven is likened unto a man which sowed good seed in his field, but while men slept, his enemy came and sowed tares among the wheat, and went his way. But when the blade was sprung up, and brought forth fruit, then appeared the tares also. So the servants of the householder came and said unto him, 'Sir, didst not thou sow good seed in thy field? From whence then hath it tares?' He said unto them, 'An enemy hath done this.' The servants said unto him, 'Wilt thou then that we go and gather them up?' But he said, 'Nay, lest while ye gather up the tares, ye root up also the wheat with them.[305] Let both grow together until the harvest, and in the time of harvest I will say to the reapers, "Gather ye together first the tares, and bind them in bundles to burn them, but gather the wheat into my barn."'"

And he said, "Whereunto shall I liken the kingdom of God? Or with what comparison shall I compare it?" Another parable put he forth unto them, saying, "The kingdom of heaven is like to a grain of mustard seed, which a man took, and sowed in his field, which indeed is the least of all the seeds that be in the earth, but when it is grown, it is the greatest among herbs, and shooteth out great branches, and becometh a tree, so that the birds of the air come and lodge under the shadow thereof."

And again he said, "Whereunto shall I liken the kingdom of God?" Another parable spake he unto them, "The kingdom of heaven

---

[305] Compare *2 Esdras* 4:28-30: "But as concerning the things whereof thou askest me, I will tell thee; for the evil is sown, but the destruction thereof is not yet come. If therefore that which is sown be not turned upside down, and if the place where the evil is sown pass not away, then cannot it come that is sown with good. For the grain of evil seed hath been sown in the heart of Adam from the beginning, and how much ungodliness hath it brought up unto this time? And how much shall it yet bring forth until the time of threshing come?"

is like unto leaven, which a woman took, and hid in three measures of meal, till the whole was leavened."

"Again, the kingdom of heaven is like unto treasure hid in a field, the which when a man hath found, he hideth, and for joy thereof goeth and selleth all that he hath, and buyeth that field.

"Again, the kingdom of heaven is like unto a merchant man, seeking goodly pearls, who, when he had found one pearl of great price, went and sold all that he had, and bought it.

"Again, the kingdom of heaven is like unto a net, that was cast into the sea, and gathered of every kind, which, when it was full, they drew to shore, and sat down, and gathered the good into vessels, but cast the bad away. So shall it be at the end of the world, the angels shall come forth, and sever the wicked from among the just, and shall cast them into the furnace of fire, there shall be wailing and *gnashing of teeth*."[306]

All these things spake Jesus unto the multitude in parables, and with many such parables spake he the word unto them, as they were able to hear it, that it might be fulfilled which was spoken by the prophet, saying, "*I will open my mouth in parables, I will utter things which have been kept secret from the foundation of the world.*"[307] But without a parable spake he not unto the multitude, and when they were alone, he expounded all things to his disciples.

Then Jesus sent the multitude away, and went into the house, and his disciples came unto him, saying, "Declare unto us the parable of the tares of the field." He answered and said unto them, "He that soweth the good seed is the Son of man, the field is the

---

[306] See Psalms 112:4,10: "Unto the upright there ariseth light in the darkness; he is gracious, and full of compassion, and righteous. The wicked shall see it, and be grieved; he shall gnash with his teeth, and melt away; the desire of the wicked shall perish."
[307] "I will open my mouth in a parable; I will utter dark sayings of old." – Psalms 78:2

world, the good seed are the children of the kingdom, but the tares are the children of the wicked one, the enemy that sowed them is the devil, the harvest is the end of the world,[308] and the reapers are the angels. As therefore the tares are gathered and burned in the fire, so shall it be in the end of this world. The Son of man shall send forth his angels, and they shall gather out of his kingdom all things that offend, and them which do iniquity, and shall cast them into a furnace of fire, there shall be wailing and *gnashing of teeth*.[309] Then shall the righteous shine forth as the sun[310] in the kingdom of their Father. *Who hath ears to hear, let him hear.*[311]

Jesus saith unto them, "Have ye understood all these things?" They say unto him, "Yea, Lord." Then said he unto them, "Therefore every scribe which is instructed unto the kingdom of heaven is like unto a man that is an householder, which bringeth forth out of his treasure things new and old."

---

[308] Compare Joel 3:13-14: "Put ye in the sickle, for the harvest is ripe; come, get you down; for the press is full, the fats overflow; for their wickedness is great. Multitudes, multitudes in the valley of decision; for the day of the LORD is near in the valley of decision."
[309] See Psalms 112:4,10: "Unto the upright there ariseth light in the darkness; he is gracious, and full of compassion, and righteous. The wicked shall see it, and be grieved; he shall gnash with his teeth, and melt away; the desire of the wicked shall perish."
[310] Compare Daniel 12:2-3: "And many of them that sleep in the dust of the earth shall awake, some to everlasting life, and some to shame and everlasting contempt. And they that be wise shall shine as the brightness of the firmament; and they that turn many to righteousness as the stars for ever and ever."
[311] See Ezekiel 3:27: "But when I speak with thee, I will open thy mouth, and thou shalt say unto them, 'Thus saith the Lord GOD; He that heareth, let him hear; and he that forbeareth, let him forbear;' for they are a rebellious house."

THE TREE OF LIFE

Chapter Twenty Nine

And it came to pass, that when Jesus had finished these parables, when the even was come, and when they had sent away the multitude, he went into a ship with his disciples, and he said unto them, "Let us go over unto the other side of the lake." And they launched forth. And there were also with him other little ships.

But as they sailed he fell asleep, and there arose a great tempest of wind in the sea, and the waves beat into the ship, insomuch that the ship was covered with the waves, so that it was now full, and they were in jeopardy. And he was in the hinder part of the ship, asleep on a pillow,[312] and his disciples came to him, and awoke him, saying, "Master, carest thou not that we perish? Save us."

Then he arose, and rebuked the wind and the raging of the water, and said unto the sea, "Peace. Be still." And the wind

---

[312] Compare Jonah 1:5: "Then the mariners were afraid, and cried every man unto his god, and cast forth the wares that were in the ship into the sea, to lighten it of them. But Jonah was gone down into the sides of the ship; and he lay, and was fast asleep."
Proverbs 3:21,24: "My son, let not them depart from thine eyes; keep sound wisdom and discretion. When thou liest down, thou shalt not be afraid; yea, thou shalt lie down, and thy sleep shall be sweet."

ceased,³¹³ and there was a great calm. And he said unto them, "Why are ye so fearful? How is it that ye have no faith?" And they feared exceedingly, and said one to another, "What manner of man is this? For he commandeth even the winds and water, and they obey him!"

---

³¹³ Compare Psalms 107:23-30: "They that go down to the sea in ships, that do business in great waters; these see the works of the LORD, and his wonders in the deep. For he commandeth, and raiseth the stormy wind, which lifteth up the waves thereof. They mount up to the heaven, they go down again to the depths; their soul is melted because of trouble. They reel to and fro, and stagger like a drunken man, and are at their wit's end. Then they cry unto the LORD in their trouble, and he bringeth them out of their distresses. He maketh the storm a calm, so that the waves thereof are still. Then are they glad because they be quiet; so he bringeth them unto their desired haven."

THE TREE OF LIFE

Chapter Thirty

And they came over unto the other side of the sea, into the country of the Gadarenes, which is over against Galilee. And when he was come out of the ship into the country of the Gergesenes, immediately there met him a man possessed with devils a long time, coming out of the tombs, exceeding fierce, so that no man might pass by that way. And he ware no clothes, neither abode in any house, but had his dwelling among the tombs, and no man could bind him, no, not with chains, because that he had been often bound with fetters and chains, and the chains had been plucked asunder by him, and the fetters broken in pieces, neither could any man tame him. And was driven of the devil into the wilderness, and always, night and day, he was in the mountains, and in the tombs, crying, and cutting himself with stones.

But when he saw Jesus afar off, he ran and worshipped him, and with a loud voice said, "What have we to do with thee, Jesus, thou Son of the most high God? Art thou come hither to torment us before the time?"[314] I adjure thee by God, that thou torment me not." For he had commanded, saying, "Come out of the man, thou unclean spirit." And Jesus asked him, saying, "What is thy name?" And he

---

[314] Compare 1 Kings 17:18: "And she said unto Elijah, 'What have I to do with thee, O thou man of God? Art thou come unto me to call my sin to remembrance, and to slay my son?'"

answered, saying, "My name is Legion, for we are many." And they besought him much that he would not send them out into the deep.

And there was a good way off from them, nigh unto the mountains, a great herd of swine feeding. So all the devils besought him, saying, "If thou cast us out, suffer us to go into the swine, that we may enter into them." And he suffered them, and said unto them, "Go."

Then went the devils out of the man, and entered into the swine, and the whole herd of swine ran violently down a steep place into the lake, (and they were about two thousand,) and were choked, and perished in the waters. And they that fed the swine went out to see what it was that was done, and they came to Jesus, and found the man, out of whom the devils were departed, sitting at the feet of Jesus, clothed, and in his right mind, and they were afraid. And they that saw it told them how it befell to him that was possessed with the devil, and also concerning the swine, and by what means he that was possessed of the devils was healed.

And they that kept the swine fled, and went their ways into the city and in the country, and told every thing, and what was befallen to the possessed of the devils. And, behold, the whole city and the whole multitude of the country of the Gadarenes round about came out to meet Jesus, and when they saw him, they besought him that he would depart out of their coasts, for they were taken with great fear.

And he went up into the ship, and returned back again. And when he was come into the ship, he that had been possessed with the devil prayed him that he might be with him, but Jesus sent him away, saying, "Go home to thy friends, and tell them how great things the Lord hath done for thee, and hath had compassion on thee." And he went his way, and began to publish throughout the whole city of Decapolis how great things Jesus had done for him, and all men did marvel.

Chapter Thirty One

And when Jesus was returned again by ship unto the other side, the people gladly received him, for they were all waiting for him, and he was nigh unto the sea.

And, behold, there cometh one of the rulers of the synagogue, Jairus by name, and when he saw Jesus, he fell at his feet, and besought him greatly that he would come into his house, saying, "My little daughter lieth at the point of death, but come and lay thy hand upon her, that she may be healed, and she shall live." For he had one only daughter, about twelve years of age, and she lay a dying. And Jesus arose, and followed him, and so did his disciples. But as he went, much people followed him, and thronged him.

And a certain woman, which was diseased with an issue of blood twelve years, and had spent all her living upon physicians, neither could be healed of any, and was nothing bettered, but rather grew worse, when she had heard of Jesus, came in the press behind him, and touched the hem of his garment,[315] for she said within herself, "If I may but touch his garment, I shall be whole." And

---

[315] See Numbers 15:37-39: "And the LORD spake unto Moses, saying, 'Speak unto the children of Israel, and bid them that they make them fringes in the borders of their garments throughout their generations, and that they put upon the fringe of the borders a ribband of blue. And it shall be unto you for a fringe, that ye may look upon it, and remember all the commandments of the LORD, and do them; and that ye seek not after your own heart and your own eyes, after which ye use to go a whoring."

straightway the fountain of her blood was dried up, and she felt in her body that she was healed of that plague, and was made whole from that hour.

And Jesus, immediately knowing in himself that virtue had gone out of him, turned him about in the press, and said, "Who touched my clothes?" When all denied, Peter and they that were with him said, "Master, the multitude throng thee and press thee, and sayest thou, 'Who touched me?'" And Jesus said, "Somebody hath touched me, for I perceive that virtue is gone out of me." And he looked round about to see her that had done this thing. And when the woman saw that she was not hid, she came fearing and trembling, knowing what was done in her, and falling down before him, she declared unto him before all the people all the truth, and for what cause she had touched him, and how she was healed immediately. And Jesus said, "Daughter, be of good comfort, thy faith hath made thee whole, go in peace, and be whole of thy plague."

While he yet spake, there came one from the ruler of the synagogue's house, saying to him, "Thy daughter is dead, trouble not the Master any further." As soon as Jesus heard the word that was spoken, he saith unto the ruler of the synagogue, "Be not afraid, only believe, and she shall be made whole."

And Jesus came to the ruler's house, and saw the minstrels and the tumult, and them that wept and wailed greatly. And when he came into the house, he suffered no man to go in, save Peter, and James, and John, and the father and the mother of the maiden. And all wept, and bewailed her, but he said, "Why make ye this ado, and weep?[316] Give place, for the damsel is not dead, but sleepeth." And

---

[316] Compare 2 Samuel 12:21-23: "Then said his servants unto him, 'What thing is this that thou hast done? Thou didst fast and weep for the child, while it was alive; but when the child was dead, thou didst rise and eat bread.' And [David] said, 'While the child was yet alive, I fasted and wept; for I said, "Who can tell whether GOD will be gracious to me, that the child may live?" But now he is dead, wherefore

they laughed him to scorn, knowing that she was dead. But when he had put them all out, he taketh the father and the mother of the damsel, and them that were with him, and entereth in where the damsel was lying, and he took the damsel by the hand, and said unto her, "Talitha cumi," (which is, being interpreted, "Damsel, I say unto thee, arise.") And her spirit came again, and she arose straightway,[317] and walked, and he commanded that something should be given her to eat. And her parents were astonished with a great astonishment, but he charged them straitly that they should tell no man what was done. And the fame thereof went abroad into all that land.

---

should I fast? Can I bring him back again? I shall go to him, but he shall not return to me.'"
[317] Compare 1 Kings 17:1-24 (Elijah); 2 Kings 4:8-37 (Elisha).

THE TREE OF LIFE

Chapter Thirty Two

And when Jesus departed thence, two blind men came to him, crying, and saying, "Thou son of David,[318] have mercy on us." And when he was come into the house, the blind men followed him, and Jesus saith unto them, "Believe ye that I am able to do this?" They said unto him, "Yea, Lord." Then touched he their eyes, saying, "According to your faith be it unto you." And their eyes were opened, and Jesus straitly charged them, saying, "See that no man know it." But they, when they were departed, spread abroad his fame in all that country.

As they went out, behold, they brought to him a dumb man possessed with a devil. And when the devil was cast out, the dumb spake, and the multitudes marvelled, saying, "It was never so seen in Israel."

But the Pharisees said, "He casteth out devils through the prince of the devils."

---

[318] See Isaiah 35:5-6: "Then [in the days of Messiah] the eyes of the blind shall be opened, and the ears of the deaf shall be unstopped. Then shall the lame man leap as an hart, and the tongue of the dumb sing; for in the wilderness shall waters break out, and streams in the desert."

THE TREE OF LIFE

THE TREE OF LIFE

Chapter Thirty Three

And he went out from thence, and his disciples followed him. And when he was come into his own country, when the sabbath day was come, he began to teach in their synagogue, insomuch that they were astonished, and said, "What wisdom is this which is given unto him, that even such mighty works are wrought by his hands? Is not this the carpenter's son? Is not his mother called Mary? And his brethren, James, and Joses, and Simon, and Judas? And his sisters, are they not all with us? Whence then hath this man all these things?"[319] And they were offended at him.[320]

But Jesus said unto them, "A prophet is not without honour, save in his own country, and in his own house, and among his own kin." And he did not many mighty works there because of their unbelief, save that he laid his hands upon a few sick folk, and healed them. And he marvelled because of their unbelief. And he went round about the villages, teaching.

---

[319] See Isaiah 53:1-2: "Who hath believed our report? And to whom is the arm of the LORD revealed? For he shall grow up before him as a tender plant, and as a root out of a dry ground; he hath no form nor comeliness; and when we shall see him, there is no beauty that we should desire him."
[320] See Isaiah 8:14-15: "And he shall be for a sanctuary; but for a stone of stumbling and for a rock of offence to both the houses of Israel, for a gin and for a snare to the inhabitants of Jerusalem. And many among them shall stumble, and fall, and be broken, and be snared, and be taken."

THE TREE OF LIFE

Chapter Thirty Four

At that time, king Herod the tetrarch heard of the fame of Jesus and of all that was done by him. And he said, "Who is this, of whom I hear such things?" And he desired to see him. But he was perplexed, because it was said of some, that John was risen from the dead. Others said, "it is Elijah." And others said, "One of the old prophets is risen again."

And when Herod heard thereof, he said, "It is John the Baptist, whom I beheaded, he is risen from the dead, and therefore mighty works do shew forth themselves in him." For Herod feared John, knowing that he was a just man and an holy, and observed him, and when he heard him, he did many things, and heard him gladly.

But Herod had sent forth and laid hold on John, and bound him, and put him in prison for Herodias' sake, his brother Philip's wife, for he had married her. And John said unto him, "It is not lawful for thee to have thy brother's wife,"[321] and reproved him also for all the evils which he had done. Therefore Herodias had a quarrel against him, and would have killed him, but she could not. And Herod added yet this above all the evils which he had done, that he shut up John in prison. And when he would have put him to

---

[321] See Leviticus 18:16: "Thou shalt not uncover the nakedness of thy brother's wife; it is thy brother's nakedness."
Leviticus 20:21: "And if a man shall take his brother's wife, it is an unclean thing; he hath uncovered his brother's nakedness; they shall be childless."

death, he feared the multitude, because they counted him as a prophet.

And when a convenient day was come, Herod on his birthday made a supper to his lords, high captains, and chief estates of Galilee. And when Herod's birthday was kept, the daughter of Herodias came in, and danced before them, and pleased Herod and them that sat with him. And the king said unto the damsel, "Ask of me whatsoever thou wilt, and I will give it thee, unto the half of my kingdom."[322] Whereupon he promised with an oath to give her whatsoever she would ask.

And she went forth, and said unto her mother, "What shall I ask?" And she said, "The head of John the Baptist." And she, being instructed of her mother, came in straightway with haste unto the king, and asked, saying, "I will that thou give me here John Baptist's head in a charger." And the king was exceeding sorry, nevertheless for the oath's sake, and for their sakes which sat with him at meat, he would not reject her. And immediately the king sent an executioner, and commanded his head to be brought, and he went and beheaded John in the prison. And his head was brought in a charger, and given to the damsel, and she brought it to her mother.

And when John's disciples heard of it, they came and took up his corpse, and laid it in a tomb, and went and told Jesus.

And the apostles, when they also were returned, gathered themselves together also unto Jesus, and told him all things, both what they had done, and what they had taught.

And when Jesus had heard all, he took them, and said unto them, "Come ye yourselves apart into a desert place, and rest a while," for there were many coming and going, and they had no leisure so much as to eat.

---

[322] Compare Esther 5:3: "Then said the king unto her, 'What wilt thou, queen Esther? And what is thy request? It shall be even given thee to the half of the kingdom.'"

Chapter Thirty Five

And they went aside privately to depart by ship, and when the people had heard thereof, and saw them departing, they ran thither on foot out of all cities, and outwent them, and came together unto him. And Jesus went forth, and he saw a great multitude, and was moved with compassion toward them, because they were as sheep not having a shepherd,[323] and he received them, and spake unto them of the kingdom of God, and healed them that had need of healing, and he began to teach them many things.

And when the day was now far spent, and it was evening, then came the twelve, and said unto him, "This is a desert place, and the time is now far past. Send the multitude away, that they may go into the towns and country round about, and lodge, and buy themselves victuals, for they have nothing to eat."

And the passover,[324] a feast of the Jews, was nigh. But Jesus said unto them, "They need not depart, give ye them to eat." And he saith unto Philip, "Whence shall we buy bread, that these may eat?"

---

[323] Compare Numbers 27:16-17: "Let the LORD, the God of the spirits of all flesh, set a man over the congregation, which may go out before them, and which may go in before them, and which may lead them out, and which may bring them in; that the congregation of the LORD be not as sheep which have no shepherd."
1 Kings 22:17: "And he said, 'I saw all Israel scattered upon the hills, as sheep that have not a shepherd;' and the LORD said, 'These have no master; let them return every man to his house in peace.'"
[324] See Exodus 12:1-51; Leviticus 23:5-8; Numbers 28:16-25; Deuteronomy 16:1-8.

And this he said to prove him, for he himself knew what he would do. Philip answered him, "Two hundred pennyworth of bread is not sufficient for them, that every one of them may take a little." He saith unto them, "How many loaves have ye? Go and see." One of his disciples, Andrew, Simon Peter's brother, saith unto him, "There is a lad here, which hath five barley loaves, and two small fishes, but what are they among so many?" And they say unto him, "Shall we go and buy two hundred pennyworth of bread, and give them to eat?" He said, "Bring them hither to me."

And he commanded them to make all sit down by companies upon the green grass, (for there was much grass in the place). And he said to his disciples, "Make them sit down by fifties in a company." And they did so, and made the men sit down in ranks, by hundreds, and by fifties, in number about five thousand. And he said unto them, "*Give ye them to eat,*"[325] and he took the five loaves, and the two fishes, and looking up to heaven, he blessed, and brake, and he distributed to the disciples, and the disciples to the multitude that were set down, as much as they would. And they did all eat, and were all filled.[326] And when they were filled, he said unto his

---

[325] Compare 2 Kings 4:42-44: "And there came a man from Baal-shalisha, and brought the man of God [Elisha] bread of the firstfruits, twenty loaves of barley, and full ears of corn in the husk thereof. And he said, 'Give unto the people, that they may eat.' And his servitor said, 'What, should I set this before an hundred men?' He said again, 'Give the people that they may eat, for thus saith the LORD, They shall eat, and shall leave thereof.' So he set it before them, and they did eat, and left thereof, according to the word of the LORD."
[326] Compare 1 Kings 17:14-16: "For thus saith the LORD God of Israel, 'The barrel of meal shall not waste, neither shall the cruse of oil fail, until the day that the LORD sendeth rain upon the earth.' And she went and did according to the saying of Elijah; and she, and he, and her house, did eat many days. And the barrel of meal wasted not, neither did the cruse of oil fail, according to the word of the LORD, which he spake by Elijah."
Isaiah 40:11: "He shall feed his flock like a shepherd; he shall gather the lambs with his arm, and carry them in his bosom, and shall gently lead those that are with young."
2 Kings 4:1-7: "Now there cried a certain woman of the wives of the sons of the prophets unto Elisha, saying, 'Thy servant my husband is dead; and thou knowest that thy servant did fear the LORD; and the creditor is come to take unto him my

disciples, "Gather up the fragments that remain, that nothing be lost." Therefore they gathered them together, and they took up of the fragments that remained twelve baskets full. And they that had eaten were about five thousand men, beside women and children.

And straightway Jesus constrained his disciples to get into a ship, and to go before him unto the other side before unto Bethsaida, while he sent the multitudes away. Then those men, when they had seen the miracle that Jesus did, said, "This is of a truth that prophet that should come into the world."[327] When Jesus therefore perceived that they would come and take him by force, to make him a king, he sent the multitudes away, and departed again into a mountain himself to pray, and when the evening was come, he was there alone.

---

two sons to be bondmen.' And Elisha said unto her, 'What shall I do for thee? Tell me, what hast thou in the house?' And she said, 'Thine handmaid hath not any thing in the house, save a pot of oil.' Then he said, 'Go, borrow thee vessels abroad of all thy neighbours, even empty vessels; borrow not a few. And when thou art come in, thou shalt shut the door upon thee and upon thy sons, and shalt pour out into all those vessels, and thou shalt set aside that which is full.' So she went from him, and shut the door upon her and upon her sons, who brought the vessels to her; and she poured out. And it came to pass, when the vessels were full, that she said unto her son, 'Bring me yet a vessel.' And he said unto her, 'There is not a vessel more.' And the oil stayed. Then she came and told the man of God. And he said, 'Go, sell the oil, and pay thy debt, and live thou and thy children of the rest.'"
Exodus 16:15-16: "And when the children of Israel saw it, they said one to another, 'It is manna;' for they wist not what it was. And Moses said unto them, 'This is the bread which the LORD hath given you to eat. This is the thing which the LORD hath commanded, gather of it every man according to his eating, an omer for every man, according to the number of your persons; take ye every man for them which are in his tents.'"
[327] See Deuteronomy 18:15: "The LORD thy God will raise up unto thee a Prophet from the midst of thee, of thy brethren, like unto me; unto him ye shall hearken."

THE TREE OF LIFE

Chapter Thirty Six

And when even was now come, his disciples went down unto the sea, and entered into a ship, and went over the sea toward Capernaum. And it was now dark, and Jesus was not come to them. But the ship was now in the midst of the sea, tossed with waves, and he saw them toiling in rowing, for the wind was contrary unto them. And the sea arose by reason of the great wind that blew.

So when they had rowed about five and twenty or thirty furlongs, and about the fourth watch of the night, they see Jesus walking on the sea,[328] and drawing nigh unto the ship, and he would have passed by them. And when the disciples saw him walking on the sea, they supposed it had been a spirit, and cried out for fear, saying, "It is a spirit," for they all saw him, and were troubled. And immediately Jesus spake unto them, saying, "Be of good cheer, it is I, be not afraid." And Peter answered him and said, "Lord, if it be thou, bid me come unto thee on the water." And he said, "Come." And

---

[328] Compare Psalms 77:19: "Thy way is in the sea, and thy path in the great waters, and thy footsteps are not known."
2 Kings 6:4-7: "So [Elisha] went with them. And when they came to Jordan, they cut down wood. But as one was felling a beam, the axe head fell into the water; and he cried, and said, 'Alas, master! For it was borrowed.' And the man of God said, 'Where fell it?' And he shewed him the place. And he cut down a stick, and cast it in thither; and the iron did swim. Therefore said he, 'Take it up to thee.' And he put out his hand, and took it."
See also Job 9:2-8.

when Peter was come down out of the ship, he walked on the water, to go to Jesus. But when he saw the wind boisterous, he was afraid, and beginning to sink, he cried, saying, "Lord, save me." And immediately Jesus stretched forth his hand, and caught him, and said unto him, "O thou of little faith, wherefore didst thou doubt?"

Then they that were in the ship willingly received him into the ship, and came and worshipped him, saying, "Of a truth thou art the Son of God."[329] And when they were come into the ship, the wind ceased,[330] and they were sore amazed in themselves beyond measure, and wondered. For they considered not the miracle of the loaves, for their heart was hardened.[331] And immediately the ship was at the land whither they went.

---

[329] See *2 Esdras* 13:29,32: "Behold, the days come, when the most High will begin to deliver them that are upon the earth. And the time shall be when these things shall come to pass, and the signs shall happen which I shewed thee before, and then shall my Son be declared, whom thou sawest as a man ascending."

[330] Compare Psalms 107:29-30: "He maketh the storm a calm, so that the waves thereof are still. Then are they glad because they be quiet; so he bringeth them unto their desired haven."

[331] Compare 1 Samuel 6:6: "Wherefore then do ye harden your hearts, as the Egyptians and Pharaoh hardened their hearts? When he had wrought wonderfully among them, did they not let the people go, and they departed?"
Nehemiah 9:15-17: "And gavest them bread from heaven for their hunger, and broughtest forth water for them out of the rock for their thirst, and promisedst them that they should go in to possess the land which thou hadst sworn to give them. But they and our fathers dealt proudly, and hardened their necks, and hearkened not to thy commandments, and refused to obey, neither were mindful of thy wonders that thou didst among them; but hardened their necks, and in their rebellion appointed a captain to return to their bondage; but thou art a God ready to pardon, gracious and merciful, slow to anger, and of great kindness, and forsookest them not."

Chapter Thirty Seven

And when they had passed over, they came into the land of Gennesaret, and drew to the shore. And when they were come out of the ship, straightway the people knew him. And when the men of that place had knowledge of him, they sent out into all that whole country round about, and brought unto him all that were diseased, and began to carry about in beds those that were sick, where they heard he was.

And whithersoever he entered, into villages, or cities, or country, they laid the sick in the streets, and besought him that they might only touch if it were but the hem of his garment,[332] and as many as touched him were made perfectly whole.

The day following, the people which stood on the other side of the sea saw that there was none other boat there, save that one whereinto his disciples were entered, (howbeit there came other boats from Tiberias), and that Jesus went not with his disciples into the boat, but that his disciples were gone away alone. And when the

---

[332] See <u>Numbers 15:37-39:</u> "And the LORD spake unto Moses, saying, 'Speak unto the children of Israel, and bid them that they make them fringes in the borders of their garments throughout their generations, and that they put upon the fringe of the borders a ribband of blue. And it shall be unto you for a fringe, that ye may look upon it, and remember all the commandments of the LORD, and do them; and that ye seek not after your own heart and your own eyes, after which ye use to go a whoring.'"

people therefore saw that Jesus was not there, neither his disciples, they also took shipping, and came to Capernaum, seeking for Jesus.

And when they had found him on the other side of the sea, they said unto him, "Rabbi, when camest thou hither?" Jesus answered them and said, "Verily, verily, I say unto you, ye seek me, not because ye saw the miracles, but because ye did eat of the loaves, and were filled. Labour not for the meat which perisheth, but for that meat which endureth unto everlasting life, which the Son of man shall give unto you, for him hath God the Father sealed."

Then said they unto him, "What shall we do, that we might work the works of God?" Jesus answered and said unto them, "This is the work of God, that ye believe on him whom he hath sent." They said therefore unto him, "What sign shewest thou then, that we may see, and believe thee? What dost thou work? Our fathers did eat manna in the desert, as it is written, 'He gave them bread from heaven to eat.'"[333] Then Jesus said unto them, "Verily, verily, I say unto you, Moses gave you not that bread from heaven, but my Father giveth you the true bread from heaven. For the bread of God is he which cometh down from heaven, and giveth life unto the world." Then said they unto him, "Lord, evermore give us this bread." And Jesus said unto them, "I am the bread of life, he that cometh to me shall never hunger, and he that believeth on me shall never thirst.[334] But I said unto you, that ye also have seen me, and

---

[333] "Then said the LORD unto Moses, 'Behold, I will rain bread from heaven for you; and the people shall go out and gather a certain rate every day, that I may prove them, whether they will walk in my law, or no.'" – Exodus 16:4
"And gavest them bread from heaven for their hunger, and broughtest forth water for them out of the rock for their thirst, and promisedst them that they should go in to possess the land which thou hadst sworn to give them." – Nehemiah 9:15
"The people asked, and he brought quails, and satisfied them with the bread of heaven." – Psalms 105:40
See also Psalms 78:25: "Man did eat angels' food; he sent them meat to the full."
[334] Compare Jeremiah 15:16: "Thy words were found, and I did eat them; and thy word was unto me the joy and rejoicing of mine heart; for I am called by thy name, O LORD God of hosts."

THE TREE OF LIFE

believe not. All that the Father giveth me shall come to me, and him that cometh to me I will in no wise cast out. For I came down from heaven, not to do mine own will, but the will of him that sent me.[335] And this is the Father's will which hath sent me, that of all which he hath given me I should lose nothing, that every one which seeth the Son, and believeth on him, may have everlasting life, and I will raise him up at the last day."[336] The Jews then murmured at him, because he said, "I am the bread which came down from heaven." And they said, "Is not this Jesus, the son of Joseph, whose father and mother we know? how is it then that he saith, 'I came down from heaven?'"[337]

Jesus therefore answered and said unto them, "Murmur not among yourselves. No man can come to me, except the Father which hath sent me draw him, and I will raise him up at the last day. It is

---

Isaiah 55:1-3: "Ho, every one that thirsteth, come ye to the waters, and he that hath no money; come ye, buy, and eat; yea, come, buy wine and milk without money and without price. Wherefore do ye spend money for that which is not bread? And your labour for that which satisfieth not? Hearken diligently unto me, and eat ye that which is good, and let your soul delight itself in fatness. Incline your ear, and come unto me; hear, and your soul shall live; and I will make an everlasting covenant with you, even the sure mercies of David."
Deuteronomy 2:7: "For the LORD thy God hath blessed thee in all the works of thy hand; he knoweth thy walking through this great wilderness; these forty years the LORD thy God hath been with thee; thou hast lacked nothing."
[335] Compare Numbers 16:28: "And Moses said, 'Hereby ye shall know that the LORD hath sent me to do all these works; for I have not done them of mine own mind.'"
Proverbs 3:5-7: "Trust in the LORD with all thine heart; and lean not unto thine own understanding. In all thy ways acknowledge him, and he shall direct thy paths. Be not wise in thine own eyes; fear the LORD, and depart from evil."
[336] Compare Job 19:25-26: "For I know that my redeemer liveth, and that he shall stand at the latter day upon the earth. And though after my skin worms destroy this body, yet in my flesh shall I see God."
2 Maccabees 7:9: "And when he was at the last gasp, he said, 'Thou like a fury takest us out of this present life, but the King of the world shall raise us up, who have died for his laws, unto everlasting life.'"
[337] See Isaiah 53:1-2: "Who hath believed our report? And to whom is the arm of the LORD revealed? For he shall grow up before him as a tender plant, and as a root out of a dry ground; he hath no form nor comeliness; and when we shall see him, there is no beauty that we should desire him."

THE TREE OF LIFE

written in the prophets, *'And they shall be all taught of God.'*[338] Every man therefore that hath heard, and hath learned of the Father, cometh unto me. Not that any man hath seen the Father, save he which is of God, he hath seen the Father.[339] Verily, verily, I say unto

---

[338] "And all thy children shall be taught of the LORD; and great shall be the peace of thy children." – Isaiah 54:13
See also Jeremiah 31:33-34: "But this shall be the covenant that I will make with the house of Israel: After those days, saith the LORD, I will put my law in their inward parts, and write it in their hearts; and will be their God, and they shall be my people. And they shall teach no more every man his neighbour, and every man his brother, saying, 'Know the LORD;' for they shall all know me, from the least of them unto the greatest of them, saith the LORD; for I will forgive their iniquity, and I will remember their sin no more."
[339] See Genesis 18:1-2: "And the LORD appeared unto [Abraham] in the plains of Mamre; and he sat in the tent door in the heat of the day; and he lift up his eyes and looked, and, lo, three men stood by him. And when he saw them, he ran to meet them from the tent door, and bowed himself toward the ground,"
Genesis 26:24: "And the LORD appeared unto [Isaac] the same night, and said, 'I am the God of Abraham thy father; fear not, for I am with thee, and will bless thee, and multiply thy seed for my servant Abraham's sake.'"
Genesis 28:12-13: "And [Jacob] dreamed, and behold a ladder set up on the earth, and the top of it reached to heaven; and behold the angels of God ascending and descending on it. And, behold, the LORD stood above it, and said, 'I am the LORD God of Abraham thy father, and the God of Isaac; the land whereon thou liest, to thee will I give it, and to thy seed.'"
Genesis 32:24,29-30: "And Jacob was left alone; and there wrestled a man with him until the breaking of the day. And Jacob asked him, and said, 'Tell me, I pray thee, thy name.' And he said, 'Wherefore is it that thou dost ask after my name?' And he blessed him there. And Jacob called the name of the place Peniel; 'for I have seen God face to face, and my life is preserved.'"
Exodus 33:11: "And the LORD spake unto Moses face to face, as a man speaketh unto his friend."
Exodus 34:10: "And there arose not a prophet since in Israel like unto Moses, whom the LORD knew face to face."
Exodus 24:9-11: "Then went up Moses, and Aaron, Nadab, and Abihu, and seventy of the elders of Israel. And they saw the God of Israel; and there was under his feet as it were a paved work of a sapphire stone, and as it were the body of heaven in his clearness. And upon the nobles of the children of Israel he laid not his hand; also they saw God, and did eat and drink."
Job 42:1-2,5-6: "Then Job answered the LORD, and said, 'I know that thou canst do every thing, and that no thought can be withholden from thee. I have heard of thee by the hearing of the ear; but now mine eye seeth thee. Wherefore I abhor myself, and repent in dust and ashes.'"

you, he that believeth on me hath everlasting life. I am that bread of life.[340] Your fathers did eat manna in the wilderness, and are dead. I am the living bread which came down from heaven. If any man eat of this bread, he shall live for ever, and the bread that I will give is my flesh, which I will give for the life of the world." The Jews therefore strove among themselves, saying, "How can this man give us his flesh to eat?"

Then Jesus said unto them, "Verily, verily, I say unto you, Except ye eat the flesh of the Son of man, and drink his blood, ye have no life in you. Whoso eateth my flesh, and drinketh my blood, hath eternal life, and I will raise him up at the last day. For my flesh is meat indeed, and my blood is drink indeed. He that eateth my flesh, and drinketh my blood, dwelleth in me, and I in him. As the living Father hath sent me, and I live by the Father, so he that eateth me, even he shall live by me. This is that bread which came down from heaven, not as your fathers did eat manna, and are dead, he that eateth of this bread shall live for ever."

Isaiah 6:1-5: "In the year that king Uzziah died I saw also the Lord sitting upon a throne, high and lifted up, and his train filled the temple. Above it stood the seraphims; each one had six wings; with twain he covered his face, and with twain he covered his feet, and with twain he did fly. And one cried unto another, and said, 'Holy, holy, holy, is the LORD of hosts; the whole earth is full of his glory.' And the posts of the door moved at the voice of him that cried, and the house was filled with smoke. Then said I, 'Woe is me! For I am undone; because I am a man of unclean lips, and I dwell in the midst of a people of unclean lips; for mine eyes have seen the King, the LORD of hosts.'"

Judges 13:17-22: "And Manoah said unto the angel of the LORD, 'What is thy name, that when thy sayings come to pass we may do thee honour?' And the angel of the LORD said unto him, 'Why askest thou thus after my name, seeing it is secret?' So Manoah took a kid with a meat offering, and offered it upon a rock unto the LORD. And the angel did wondrously; and Manoah and his wife looked on. For it came to pass, when the flame went up toward heaven from off the altar, that the angel of the LORD ascended in the flame of the altar. And Manoah and his wife looked on it, and fell on their faces to the ground. But the angel of the LORD did no more appear to Manoah and to his wife. Then Manoah knew that he was an angel of the LORD. And Manoah said unto his wife, 'We shall surely die, because we have seen God.'"

[340] Compare *Sirach* 19:19: "The knowledge of the commandments of the Lord is the doctrine of life; and they that do things that please him shall receive the fruit of the tree of immortality."

THE TREE OF LIFE

These things said he in the synagogue, as he taught in Capernaum. Many therefore of his disciples, when they had heard this, said, "This is an hard saying, who can hear it?" When Jesus knew in himself that his disciples murmured at it, he said unto them, "Doth this offend you? What if ye shall see the Son of man ascend up where he was before? It is the spirit that quickeneth, the flesh profiteth nothing, the words that I speak unto you, they are spirit, and they are life.[341] But there are some of you that believe not." For Jesus knew from the beginning who they were that believed not, and who should betray him. And he said, "Therefore said I unto you, that no man can come unto me, except it were given unto him of my Father."

From that time many of his disciples went back, and walked no more with him. Then said Jesus unto the twelve, "Will ye also go away?" Then Simon Peter answered him, "Lord, to whom shall we go? Thou hast the words of eternal life. And we believe and are sure that thou art that Christ,[342] the Son of the living God."[343] Jesus

---

[341] Compare Jeremiah 15:16: "Thy words were found, and I did eat them; and thy word was unto me the joy and rejoicing of mine heart; for I am called by thy name, O LORD God of hosts."
Proverbs 12:28: "In the way of righteousness is life; and in the pathway thereof there is no death."
Isaiah 55:1-3: "Ho, every one that thirsteth, come ye to the waters, and he that hath no money; come ye, buy, and eat; yea, come, buy wine and milk without money and without price. Wherefore do ye spend money for that which is not bread? And your labour for that which satisfieth not? Hearken diligently unto me, and eat ye that which is good, and let your soul delight itself in fatness. Incline your ear, and come unto me; hear, and your soul shall live; and I will make an everlasting covenant with you, even the sure mercies of David."
Sirach 42:15: "I will now remember the works of the Lord, and declare the things that I have seen: In the words of the Lord are his works."
[342] See Jeremiah 23:5: "Behold, the days come, saith the LORD, that I will raise unto David a righteous Branch, and a King shall reign and prosper, and shall execute judgment and justice in the earth."
[343] See 2 Esdras 13:29,32: "Behold, the days come, when the most High will begin to deliver them that are upon the earth. And the time shall be when these things shall come to pass, and the signs shall happen which I shewed thee before, and then shall my Son be declared, whom thou sawest as a man ascending."

THE TREE OF LIFE

answered them, "Have not I chosen you twelve, and one of you is a devil?" He spake of Judas Iscariot the son of Simon, for he it was that should betray him, being one of the twelve. After these things Jesus walked in Galilee, for he would not walk in Jewry, because the Jews sought to kill him.

THE TREE OF LIFE

Chapter Thirty Eight

Then came together unto him the Pharisees, and certain of the scribes, which came from Jerusalem. And when they saw some of his disciples eat bread with defiled, that is to say, with unwashen, hands, they found fault. For the Pharisees, and all the Jews, except they wash their hands oft, eat not, holding the tradition of the elders. And when they come from the market, except they wash, they eat not. And many other things there be, which they have received to hold, as the washing of cups, and pots, brasen vessels, and of tables.

Then the Pharisees and scribes asked him, saying, "Why do thy disciples transgress the tradition of the elders? For they wash not their hands when they eat bread." But he answered and said unto them, "Why do ye also transgress the commandment of God by your tradition?" And he said unto them, "Full well ye reject the commandment of God, that ye may keep your own tradition. For God commanded, saying, 'Honour thy father and mother,'[344] and, 'He that curseth father or mother, let him die the death.'[345] But ye say,

---

[344] "Honour thy father and thy mother; that thy days may be long upon the land which the LORD thy God giveth thee." – Exodus 20:12
"Honour thy father and thy mother, as the LORD thy God hath commanded thee; that thy days may be prolonged, and that it may go well with thee, in the land which the LORD thy God giveth thee." – Deuteronomy 5:16
[345] "And he that curseth his father, or his mother, shall surely be put to death." – Exodus 21:17

THE TREE OF LIFE

'Whosoever shall say to his father or his mother, "That which thou mightest be profited by me, it is Corban, (that is to say, a gift,)"[346] he shall be free.' And ye suffer him no more to do ought for his father or his mother and honour them not. Thus have ye made the word of God of none effect through your tradition, which ye have delivered." And he answered and said unto them, "Well hath Isaiah prophesied of you hypocrites,[347] as it is written, *'This people draweth nigh unto me with their mouth, and honoureth me with their lips, but their heart is far from me. But in vain they do worship me, teaching for doctrines the commandments of men.'*[348] For laying aside the commandment of God, ye hold the tradition of men, as the washing of pots and cups, and many other such like things ye do."

"For every one that curseth his father or his mother shall be surely put to death; he hath cursed his father or his mother; his blood shall be upon him." – Leviticus 20:9

[346] See Numbers 7:5: "Take it of them, that they may be to do the service of the tabernacle of the congregation; and thou shalt give them unto the Levites, to every man according to his service."

[347] Compare Sirach 32:15: "He that seeketh the law shall be filled therewith; but the hypocrite will be offended thereat."
Job 13:16: "He also shall be my salvation; for an hypocrite shall not come before him."
Job 27:8: "For what is the hope of the hypocrite, though he hath gained, when God taketh away his soul?"

[348] "Wherefore the Lord said, 'Forasmuch as this people draw near me with their mouth, and with their lips do honour me, but have removed their heart far from me, and their fear toward me is taught by the precept of men.'" – Isaiah 29:13
Compare Ezekiel 33:30-32: "Also, thou son of man, the children of thy people still are talking against thee by the walls and in the doors of the houses, and speak one to another, every one to his brother, saying, 'Come, I pray you, and hear what is the word that cometh forth from the LORD.' And they come unto thee as the people cometh, and they sit before thee as my people, and they hear thy words, but they will not do them; for with their mouth they shew much love, but their heart goeth after their covetousness. And, lo, thou art unto them as a very lovely song of one that hath a pleasant voice, and can play well on an instrument; for they hear thy words, but they do them not."
Sirach 12:16-17: "An enemy speaketh sweetly with his lips, but in his heart he imagineth how to throw thee into a pit; he will weep with his eyes, but if he find opportunity, he will not be satisfied with blood. If adversity come upon thee, thou shalt find him there first; and though he pretend to help thee, yet shall he undermine thee."

And when he had called all the people unto him, he said unto them, "Hearken unto me every one of you, and understand, there is nothing from without a man, that entering into the mouth can defile him, but the things which come out of the mouth, those are they that defile the man. *If any man have ears to hear, let him hear.*"[349]

Then came his disciples, and said unto him, "Knowest thou that the Pharisees were offended, after they heard this saying?" But he answered and said, "Every plant, which my heavenly Father hath not planted, shall be rooted up.[350] Let them alone, they be blind leaders of the blind. And if the blind lead the blind, both shall fall into the ditch."[351]

And when he was entered into the house from the people, his disciples asked him concerning the parable. Peter said unto him, "Declare unto us this parable." And Jesus said, "Are ye so without understanding also? Do ye not perceive, that whatsoever thing from without entereth in at the mouth goeth into the belly, and is cast out into the draught? Because it entereth not into his heart, but into the belly, and goeth out into the draught, purging all meats. But those things which proceed out of the mouth come forth from the heart.

---

[349] See Ezekiel 3:27: "But when I speak with thee, I will open thy mouth, and thou shalt say unto them, 'Thus saith the Lord GOD; He that heareth, let him hear; and he that forbeareth, let him forbear;' for they are a rebellious house."
[350] See Isaiah 60:21: "Thy people also shall be all righteous; they shall inherit the land for ever, the branch of my planting, the work of my hands, that I may be glorified."
Jeremiah 15:1-2: "Then said the LORD unto me, 'Though Moses and Samuel stood before me, yet my mind could not be toward this people; cast them out of my sight, and let them go forth. And it shall come to pass, if they say unto thee, "Whither shall we go forth?" then thou shalt tell them, "Thus saith the LORD; Such as are for death, to death; and such as are for the sword, to the sword; and such as are for the famine, to the famine; and such as are for the captivity, to the captivity."'"
[351] Compare Deuteronomy 29:4: "Yet the LORD hath not given you an heart to perceive, and eyes to see, and ears to hear, unto this day."
Isaiah 44:18: "They have not known nor understood; for he hath shut their eyes, that they cannot see; and their hearts, that they cannot understand."
Isaiah 29:10: "For the LORD hath poured out upon you the spirit of deep sleep, and hath closed your eyes; the prophets and your rulers, the seers hath he covered."

THE TREE OF LIFE

For from within, out of the heart of men, proceed evil thoughts, murders, adulteries, fornications, thefts, covetousness, false witness, blasphemies, wickedness, deceit, lasciviousness, an evil eye, pride, foolishness. All these evil things come from within, and defile the man, but to eat with unwashen hands defileth not a man."

Chapter Thirty Nine

Then Jesus arose and went from thence, and departed into the borders of Tyre and Zidon, and entered into an house, and would have no man know it, but he could not be hid.

For a certain woman of Canaan, whose young daughter had an unclean spirit, heard of him, and came and fell at his feet. She was a Greek, a Syrophoenician by nation, and she besought him that he would cast forth the devil out of her daughter, saying, "Have mercy on me, O Lord, thou son of David, my daughter is grievously vexed with a devil." But he answered her not a word. And his disciples came and besought him, saying, "Send her away, for she crieth after us." But he answered and said, "I am not sent but unto the lost sheep of the house of Israel."[352] Then came she and worshipped him, saying, "Lord, help me." But he answered and said, "Let the children

---

[352] Compare Ezekiel 34:6,11-13,16: "My sheep wandered through all the mountains, and upon every high hill; yea, my flock was scattered upon all the face of the earth, and none did search or seek after them. For thus saith the Lord GOD; Behold, I, even I, will both search my sheep, and seek them out. As a shepherd seeketh out his flock in the day that he is among his sheep that are scattered; so will I seek out my sheep, and will deliver them out of all places where they have been scattered in the cloudy and dark day. And I will bring them out from the people, and gather them from the countries, and will bring them to their own land, and feed them upon the mountains of Israel by the rivers, and in all the inhabited places of the country. I will seek that which was lost, and bring again that which was driven away, and will bind up that which was broken, and will strengthen that which was sick; but I will destroy the fat and the strong; I will feed them with judgment."

first be filled, for it is not meet to take the children's bread, and to cast it unto the dogs." And she answered and said unto him, "Truth, Lord. Yet the dogs under the table eat of the children's crumbs which fall from their masters' table." Then Jesus answered and said unto her, "O woman, great is thy faith. For this saying go thy way, be it unto thee even as thou wilt, the devil is gone out of thy daughter."

And her daughter was made whole from that very hour. And when she was come to her house, she found the devil gone out, and her daughter laid upon the bed.

THE TREE OF LIFE

Chapter Forty

And again, departing from the coasts of Tyre and Zidon, he came unto the sea of Galilee, through the midst of the coasts of Decapolis, and went up into a mountain, and sat down there. And great multitudes came unto him, having with them those that were lame, blind, dumb, maimed, and many others, and cast them down at Jesus' feet, and he healed them.

And they bring unto him one that was deaf, and had an impediment in his speech, and they beseech him to put his hand upon him. And he took him aside from the multitude, and put his fingers into his ears, and he spit, and touched his tongue, and looking up to heaven, he sighed, and saith unto him, "Ephphatha," (that is, "Be opened.") And straightway his ears were opened, and the string of his tongue was loosed, and he spake plain. And he charged them that they should tell no man, but the more he charged them, so much the more a great deal they published it. And they were beyond measure astonished, saying, "He hath done all things well, he maketh both the deaf to hear, and the dumb to speak," insomuch that the multitude wondered, when they saw the dumb to speak, the maimed to be whole, the lame to walk, and the blind to see, and they glorified the God of Israel.

THE TREE OF LIFE

Chapter Forty One

In those days the multitude being very great, and having nothing to eat, Jesus called his disciples unto him, and saith unto them, "I have compassion on the multitude, because they continue with me now three days, and have nothing to eat, and if I send them away fasting to their own houses, they will faint by the way, for divers of them came from far."

And his disciples say unto him, "Whence should we have so much bread in the wilderness, as to fill so great a multitude?" And Jesus asked them, "How many loaves have ye?" And they said, "Seven, and a few little fishes."

And he commanded the multitude to sit down on the ground, and he took the seven loaves and the fishes, and gave thanks, and brake them, and gave to his disciples, and the disciples to the multitude. And they did all eat, and were filled,[353] and they took up

---

[353] Compare 2 Kings 4:42-44: "And there came a man from Baal-shalisha, and brought the man of God [Elisha] bread of the firstfruits, twenty loaves of barley, and full ears of corn in the husk thereof. And he said, 'Give unto the people, that they may eat.' And his servitor said, 'What, should I set this before an hundred men?' He said again, 'Give the people that they may eat, for thus saith the LORD, They shall eat, and shall leave thereof.' So he set it before them, and they did eat, and left thereof, according to the word of the LORD."
1 Kings 17:14-16: "For thus saith the LORD God of Israel, 'The barrel of meal shall not waste, neither shall the cruse of oil fail, until the day that the LORD sendeth rain upon the earth.' And she went and did according to the saying of Elijah; and she, and he, and her house, did eat many days. And the barrel of meal wasted not,

of the broken meat that was left seven baskets full. And they that had eaten were about four thousand men, beside women and children, and he sent them away.

neither did the cruse of oil fail, according to the word of the LORD, which he spake by Elijah."

2 Kings 4:1-7: "Now there cried a certain woman of the wives of the sons of the prophets unto Elisha, saying, 'Thy servant my husband is dead; and thou knowest that thy servant did fear the LORD; and the creditor is come to take unto him my two sons to be bondmen.' And Elisha said unto her, 'What shall I do for thee? Tell me, what hast thou in the house?' And she said, 'Thine handmaid hath not any thing in the house, save a pot of oil.' Then he said, 'Go, borrow thee vessels abroad of all thy neighbours, even empty vessels; borrow not a few. And when thou art come in, thou shalt shut the door upon thee and upon thy sons, and shalt pour out into all those vessels, and thou shalt set aside that which is full.' So she went from him, and shut the door upon her and upon her sons, who brought the vessels to her; and she poured out. And it came to pass, when the vessels were full, that she said unto her son, 'Bring me yet a vessel.' And he said unto her, 'There is not a vessel more.' And the oil stayed. Then she came and told the man of God. And he said, 'Go, sell the oil, and pay thy debt, and live thou and thy children of the rest.'"

THE TREE OF LIFE

Chapter Forty Two

And he sent away the multitude, and entered into a ship with his disciples, and came into the coasts of Magdala, into the parts of Dalmanutha. And the Pharisees also with the Sadducees came forth, and began to question with him, seeking of him a sign from heaven, tempting him. And he sighed deeply in his spirit, and saith, "Why doth this generation seek after a sign? Verily I say unto you, a *wicked*[354] *and adulterous*[355] *generation* seeketh after a sign, and there shall no sign be given unto this generation, but the sign of the prophet Jonah.[356] When it is evening, ye say, 'It will be fair weather, for the sky is red.' And in the morning, 'It will be foul weather to day, for the sky is red and lowring.' O ye hypocrites, ye can discern the face of the sky, but can ye not discern the signs of

---

[354] See Deuteronomy 1:35: "Surely there shall not one of these men of this evil generation see that good land, which I sware to give unto your fathers."
Deuteronomy 9:24: "Ye have been rebellious against the LORD from the day that I knew you."
Deuteronomy 32:5: "They have corrupted themselves, their spot is not the spot of his children; they are a perverse and crooked generation."
[355] See Jeremiah 3:20: "Surely as a wife treacherously departeth from her husband, so have ye dealt treacherously with me, O house of Israel, saith the LORD."
Hosea 1:2: "The beginning of the word of the LORD by Hosea. And the LORD said to Hosea, 'Go, take unto thee a wife of whoredoms and children of whoredoms; for the land hath committed great whoredom, departing from the LORD.'"
Hosea 9:1: "Rejoice not, O Israel, for joy, as other people; for thou hast gone a whoring from thy God, thou hast loved a reward upon every cornfloor."
[356] See Jonah 1:17: "Now the LORD had prepared a great fish to swallow up Jonah. And Jonah was in the belly of the fish three days and three nights."

the times?" And he left them, and entering into the ship again departed to the other side.

Now the disciples had forgotten to take bread, neither had they in the ship with them more than one loaf. And he charged them, saying, "Take heed, beware of the leaven of the Pharisees and of the Sadducees, and of the leaven of Herod." And they reasoned among themselves, saying, "It is because we have taken no bread." Which, when Jesus perceived, he said unto them, "O ye of little faith, why reason ye among yourselves, because ye have brought no bread? Perceive ye not yet, neither understand? Have ye your hearts yet hardened? *Having eyes, see ye not? And having ears, hear ye not?*[357] And do ye not remember? When I brake the five loaves among five thousand, how many baskets full of fragments took ye up?" They say unto him, "Twelve." "And when the seven among four thousand, how many baskets full of fragments took ye up?" And they said, "Seven." And he said unto them, "How is it that ye do not understand that I spake it not to you concerning bread, that ye should beware of the leaven of the Pharisees and of the Sadducees?" Then understood they how that he bade them not beware of the leaven of bread, but of the doctrine of the Pharisees and of the Sadducees.

And he cometh to Bethsaida, and they bring a blind man unto him, and besought him to touch him. And he took the blind man by the hand, and led him out of the town, and when he had spit on his eyes, and put his hands upon him, he asked him if he saw ought. And he looked up, and said, "I see men as trees, walking." After that he put his hands again upon his eyes, and made him look up, and he was restored, and saw every man clearly.

---

[357] Compare Jeremiah 5:21: "Hear now this, O foolish people, and without understanding; which have eyes, and see not; which have ears, and hear not."
Ezekiel 12:2: "Son of man, thou dwellest in the midst of a rebellious house, which have eyes to see, and see not; they have ears to hear, and hear not; for they are a rebellious house."

And he sent him away to his house, saying, "Neither go into the town, nor tell it to any in the town."

THE TREE OF LIFE

Chapter Forty Three

And Jesus went out, and his disciples, into the towns of Caesarea Philippi, and it came to pass, as he was alone praying by the way, he asked his disciples, saying unto them, "Whom do men say that I the Son of man am?"

And they answered, "Some say that thou art John the Baptist, some, Elijah, and others, Jeremiah, or one of the prophets is risen again." And he saith unto them, "But whom say ye that I am?" And Simon Peter answered and said, "Thou art the Christ,[358] the Son of the living God."[359] And Jesus answered and said unto him, "Blessed art thou, Simon bar Jonah, for flesh and blood hath not revealed it unto thee, but my Father which is in heaven.[360] And I say also unto thee, that thou art Peter, and upon this rock I will build my church, and the gates of hell shall not prevail against it. And I will give unto

---

[358] See Jeremiah 23:5: "Behold, the days come, saith the LORD, that I will raise unto David a righteous Branch, and a King shall reign and prosper, and shall execute judgment and justice in the earth."
[359] See 2 Esdras 13:29,32: "Behold, the days come, when the most High will begin to deliver them that are upon the earth. And the time shall be when these things shall come to pass, and the signs shall happen which I shewed thee before, and then shall my Son be declared, whom thou sawest as a man ascending."
[360] Compare Daniel 2:27-28: "Daniel answered in the presence of the king, and said, 'The secret which the king hath demanded cannot the wise men, the astrologers, the magicians, the soothsayers, shew unto the king; but there is a God in heaven that revealeth secrets, and maketh known to the king Nebuchadnezzar what shall be in the latter days. Thy dream, and the visions of thy head upon thy bed, are these;'"

thee the keys of the kingdom of heaven, and whatsoever thou shalt bind on earth shall be bound in heaven, and whatsoever thou shalt loose on earth shall be loosed in heaven."[361]

And he straitly charged them that they should tell no man that he was Jesus the Christ.

From that time forth began Jesus to shew unto his disciples, how that he must go unto Jerusalem, and be rejected of the elders and chief priests and scribes, and suffer many things of them,[362] and be killed,[363] and after three days rise again. And he spake that saying openly, and Peter took him, and began to rebuke him, saying, "Be it far from thee, Lord, this shall not be unto thee." But when he had turned about and looked on his disciples, he rebuked Peter, saying, "Get thee behind me, Satan, thou art an offence unto me, for thou savourest not the things that be of God, but those that be of men."[364]

---

[361] Compare Isaiah 22:22-23: "And the key of the house of David will I lay upon his shoulder; so he shall open, and none shall shut; and he shall shut, and none shall open."
[362] Compare Isaiah 53:3-5: "He is despised and rejected of men; a man of sorrows, and acquainted with grief. And we hid as it were our faces from him; he was despised, and we esteemed him not. Surely he hath borne our griefs, and carried our sorrows; yet we did esteem him stricken, smitten of God, and afflicted. But he was wounded for our transgressions, he was bruised for our iniquities; the chastisement of our peace was upon him; and with his stripes we are healed."
Proverbs 3:11-12: "My son, despise not the chastening of the LORD; neither be weary of his correction. For whom the LORD loveth he correcteth; even as a father the son in whom he delighteth."
[363] Compare 2 Esdras 7:29: "After these years shall my son Christ die, and all men that have life."
Zechariah 13:7: "Awake, O sword, against my shepherd, and against the man that is my fellow, saith the LORD of hosts; smite the shepherd, and the sheep shall be scattered; and I will turn mine hand upon the little ones."
[364] See Isaiah 53:10: "Yet it pleased the LORD to bruise him; he hath put him to grief; when thou shalt make his soul an offering for sin, he shall see his seed, he shall prolong his days, and the pleasure of the LORD shall prosper in his hand."
1 Samuel 2:6: "The LORD killeth, and maketh alive; he bringeth down to the grave, and bringeth up."
Genesis 22:1-2: "And it came to pass after these things, that God did tempt Abraham, and said unto him, 'Abraham;' and he said, 'Behold, here I am.' And he said, 'Take now thy son, thine only son Isaac, whom thou lovest, and get thee into

And when he had called the people unto him with his disciples also, he said unto them all, "If any man will come after me, let him deny himself, and take up his cross daily, and follow me. For whosoever will save his life shall lose it, but whosoever will lose his life for my sake and the gospel's, the same shall save it. For what is a man profited, if he shall gain the whole world, and lose his own soul, or be cast away? Or what shall a man give in exchange for his soul? For whosoever shall be ashamed of me and of my words in this adulterous[365] and sinful[366] generation, of him also shall the Son of man be ashamed, when he shall come in his own glory, and in the glory of his Father with his holy angels.[367] For then he shall *reward every man according to his works*.[368] But I tell you of a truth, that there be some standing here, which shall not taste of death,[369] till

---

the land of Moriah; and offer him there for a burnt offering upon one of the mountains which I will tell thee of.'"
[365] See Jeremiah 3:20: "Surely as a wife treacherously departeth from her husband, so have ye dealt treacherously with me, O house of Israel, saith the LORD."
Hosea 1:2: "The beginning of the word of the LORD by Hosea. And the LORD said to Hosea, 'Go, take unto thee a wife of whoredoms and children of whoredoms; for the land hath committed great whoredom, departing from the LORD.'"
Hosea 9:1: "Rejoice not, O Israel, for joy, as other people; for thou hast gone a whoring from thy God, thou hast loved a reward upon every cornfloor."
[366] See Deuteronomy 1:35: "Surely there shall not one of these men of this evil generation see that good land, which I sware to give unto your fathers."
Deuteronomy 9:24: "Ye have been rebellious against the LORD from the day that I knew you."
Deuteronomy 32:5: "They have corrupted themselves, their spot is not the spot of his children; they are a perverse and crooked generation."
[367] See Daniel 7:13-14: "I saw in the night visions, and, behold, one like the Son of man came with the clouds of heaven, and came to the Ancient of days, and they brought him near before him. And there was given him dominion, and glory, and a kingdom, that all people, nations, and languages, should serve him; his dominion is an everlasting dominion, which shall not pass away, and his kingdom that which shall not be destroyed."
[368] See Proverbs 24:12: "If thou sayest, 'Behold, we knew it not;' doth not he that pondereth the heart consider it? And he that keepeth thy soul, doth not he know it? And shall not he render to every man according to his works?'"
Jeremiah 17:10: "I the LORD search the heart, I try the reins, even to give every man according to his ways, and according to the fruit of his doings."
[369] Compare Genesis 5:22-24: "And Enoch walked with God after he begat Methuselah three hundred years, and begat sons and daughters. And all the days of

they have seen the Son of man coming in his kingdom with power."[370]

Enoch were three hundred sixty and five years. And Enoch walked with God; and he was not; for God took him."
2 Kings 2:1-6,11: "And it came to pass, when the LORD would take up Elijah into heaven by a whirlwind, that Elijah went with Elisha from Gilgal. And Elijah said unto Elisha, 'Tarry here, I pray thee; for the LORD hath sent me to Bethel.' And Elisha said unto him, 'As the LORD liveth, and as thy soul liveth, I will not leave thee.' So they went down to Bethel. And the sons of the prophets that were at Bethel came forth to Elisha, and said unto him, 'Knowest thou that the LORD will take away thy master from thy head to day?' And he said, 'Yea, I know it; hold ye your peace.' And Elijah said unto him, 'Elisha, tarry here, I pray thee; for the LORD hath sent me to Jericho.' And he said, 'As the LORD liveth, and as thy soul liveth, I will not leave thee.' So they came to Jericho. And the sons of the prophets that were at Jericho came to Elisha, and said unto him, 'Knowest thou that the LORD will take away thy master from thy head to day?' And he answered, 'Yea, I know it; hold ye your peace.' And Elijah said unto him, 'Tarry, I pray thee, here; for the LORD hath sent me to Jordan.' And he said, 'As the LORD liveth, and as thy soul liveth, I will not leave thee.' And they two went on. And it came to pass, as they still went on, and talked, that, behold, there appeared a chariot of fire, and horses of fire, and parted them both asunder; and Elijah went up by a whirlwind into heaven."
2 Esdras 14:7-9: "And now I say unto thee, that thou lay up in thy heart the signs that I have shewed, and the dreams that thou hast seen, and the interpretations which thou hast heard. For thou shalt be taken away from all, and from henceforth thou shalt remain with my Son, and with such as be like thee, until the times be ended."
[370] Compare 1 Samuel 2:10: "The adversaries of the LORD shall be broken to pieces; out of heaven shall he thunder upon them; the LORD shall judge the ends of the earth; and he shall give strength unto his king, and exalt the horn of his anointed."

THE TREE OF LIFE

Chapter Forty Four

And after six days Jesus taketh with him Peter, James, and John his brother, and leadeth them up into an high mountain apart by themselves to pray,[371] and as he prayed, he was transfigured before them. The fashion of his countenance was altered, his face did shine as the sun,[372] and his raiment became shining, exceeding white as snow, so as no fuller on earth can white them, and glistering.

And, behold, there appeared unto them in glory two men, which were Moses and Elijah, and they were talking with Jesus, and spake of his decease which he should accomplish at Jerusalem.

But Peter and they that were with him were heavy with sleep, and when they were awake, they saw his glory, and the two men that stood with him. And it came to pass, as they departed from him, Peter said unto Jesus, "Master, it is good for us to be here, if thou wilt, let us make three tabernacles, one for thee, and one for Moses,

---

[371] Compare Exodus 19:20: "And the LORD came down upon mount Sinai, on the top of the mount; and the LORD called Moses up to the top of the mount; and Moses went up."
[372] Compare Exodus 34:29-30,33: "And it came to pass, when Moses came down from mount Sinai with the two tables of testimony in Moses' hand, when he came down from the mount, that Moses wist not that the skin of his face shone while he talked with him. And when Aaron and all the children of Israel saw Moses, behold, the skin of his face shone; and they were afraid to come nigh him. And till Moses had done speaking with them, he put a vail on his face."

and one for Elijah." For he wist not what to say, for they were sore afraid.

While he yet spake, behold, there came a bright cloud, and overshadowed them,[373] and they feared as they entered into the cloud. And behold a voice came out of the cloud,[374] saying, "This is my beloved Son, in whom I am well pleased.[375] Hear ye him." And when the disciples heard it, they fell on their face, and were sore afraid.

And when the voice was past, Jesus came and touched them, and said, "Arise, and be not afraid." And, when they had lifted up their eyes and looked round about, they saw no man any more, save Jesus only with themselves. And as they came down from the mountain, he charged them that they should tell no man what things they had seen, saying, "Tell the vision to no man, until the Son of man be risen again from the dead." And they kept that saying close with themselves, and told no man in those days any of those things which they had seen, questioning one with another what the rising from the dead should mean.

And his disciples asked him, saying, "Why then say the scribes that Elijah must first come?" And Jesus answered and said unto them, "Elijah truly cometh first, and restoreth all things, as it is

---

[373] Compare Exodus 40:34-38: "Then a cloud covered the tent of the congregation, and the glory of the LORD filled the tabernacle. And Moses was not able to enter into the tent of the congregation, because the cloud abode thereon, and the glory of the LORD filled the tabernacle. And when the cloud was taken up from over the tabernacle, the children of Israel went onward in all their journeys. But if the cloud were not taken up, then they journeyed not till the day that it was taken up. For the cloud of the LORD was upon the tabernacle by day, and fire was on it by night, in the sight of all the house of Israel, throughout all their journeys."
[374] See 2 Samuel 22:14: "The LORD thundered from heaven, and the most High uttered his voice."
[375] See Isaiah 42:1: "Behold my servant, whom I uphold; mine elect, in whom my soul delighteth; I have put my spirit upon him; he shall bring forth judgment to the Gentiles."

THE TREE OF LIFE

written of him.[376] But I say unto you, that Elijah is come already, and they knew him not, but have done unto him whatsoever they listed. Likewise, so also shall the Son of man suffer many things of them, and be set at nought, as it is written of him."

Then the disciples understood that he spake unto them of John the Baptist.

---

[376] See Malachi 4:4-6: "Remember ye the law of Moses my servant, which I commanded unto him in Horeb for all Israel, with the statutes and judgments. Behold, I will send you Elijah the prophet before the coming of the great and dreadful day of the LORD; and he shall turn the heart of the fathers to the children, and the heart of the children to their fathers, lest I come and smite the earth with a curse."

THE TREE OF LIFE

Chapter Forty Five

And it came to pass, that on the next day, when they were come down from the hill to his disciples, he saw a great multitude about them, and the scribes questioning with them. And straightway all the people, when they beheld him, were greatly amazed, and running to him saluted him.

And Jesus asked the scribes, "What question ye with them?" And one of the multitude answered and said, "Master, I have brought unto thee my son, and I beseech thee, look upon him, for he is mine only child, and he is a lunatic, and sore vexed, which hath a dumb spirit that taketh him, and he suddenly crieth out, and it teareth him that he foameth again, and bruising him, hardly departeth from him. And wheresoever he taketh him, he teareth him, and he foameth, and gnasheth with his teeth, and pineth away. And I brought him to thy disciples that they should cast him out, and they could not cure him."[377] And Jesus answering said, "O *faithless and perverse generation*, how long shall I be with you? *How long shall I suffer you?*[378] Bring thy son hither unto me."

---

[377] Compare 2 Kings 4:8-37.
[378] Compare Deuteronomy 32:5: "They have corrupted themselves, their spot is not the spot of his children; they are a perverse and crooked generation."
Numbers 14:11: "And the LORD said unto Moses, 'How long will this people provoke me? And how long will it be ere they believe me, for all the signs which I have shewed among them?'"

And he asked his father, "How long is it ago since this came unto him?" And he said, "Of a child. And ofttimes it hath cast him into the fire, and into the waters, to destroy him, but if thou canst do any thing, have compassion on us, and help us." Jesus said unto him, "If thou canst believe, all things are possible to him that believeth." And straightway the father of the child cried out, and said with tears, "Lord, I believe, help thou mine unbelief." And they brought him unto him, and when he saw him, straightway the spirit threw him down, and tare him, and he fell on the ground, and wallowed, foaming. When Jesus saw that the people came running together, he rebuked the foul spirit, saying unto him, "Thou dumb and deaf spirit, I charge thee, come out of him, and enter no more into him." And the spirit cried, and rent him sore, and came out of him, and he was as one dead, insomuch that many said, "He is dead." But Jesus took him by the hand, and lifted him up, and he arose, and Jesus delivered him again to his father, and the child was cured from that very hour.

And when he was come into the house, then came the disciples to Jesus apart, and asked him privately, "Why could not we cast him out?" And Jesus said unto them, "Because of your unbelief. For verily I say unto you, if ye have faith as a grain of mustard seed, ye shall say unto this mountain, 'Remove hence to yonder place,' and it shall remove,[379] and ye might say unto this sycamine tree, 'Be thou plucked up by the root, and be thou planted in the sea,' and it should obey you, and nothing shall be impossible unto you." And the apostles said unto the Lord, "Increase our faith." And he said unto them, "This kind goeth not out but by prayer and fasting."

---

[379] Compare Job 9:2,5: "I know it is so of a truth; but how should man be just with God? Which removeth the mountains, and they know not; which overturneth them in his anger."
Zechariah 4:6-7: "Then he answered and spake unto me, saying, 'This is the word of the LORD unto Zerubbabel, saying, Not by might, nor by power, but by my spirit, saith the LORD of hosts. Who art thou, O great mountain? Before Zerubbabel thou shalt become a plain; and he shall bring forth the headstone thereof with shoutings, crying, "Grace, grace unto it."'"

Chapter Forty Six

Now the Jews' feast of tabernacles[380] was at hand. His brethren therefore said unto him, "Depart hence, and go into Judaea, that thy disciples also may see the works that thou doest. For there is no man that doeth any thing in secret, and he himself seeketh to be known openly. If thou do these things, shew thyself to the world." For neither did his brethren believe in him. Then Jesus said unto them, "Go ye up unto this feast, I go not up yet unto this feast, for my time is not yet full come, but your time is alway ready. The world cannot hate you, but me it hateth, because I testify of it, that the works thereof are evil."[381] When he had said these words unto them, he abode still in Galilee.

But when his brethren were gone up, then went he also up unto the feast, not openly, but as it were in secret. Then the Jews sought him at the feast, and said, "Where is he?" And there was much murmuring among the people concerning him, for some said,

---

[380] See Leviticus 23:33-43; Deuteronomy 16:13-15.
[381] Compare Psalms 69:7-9: "Because for thy sake I have borne reproach; shame hath covered my face. I am become a stranger unto my brethren, and an alien unto my mother's children. For the zeal of thine house hath eaten me up; and the reproaches of them that reproached thee are fallen upon me."
Isaiah 66:5: "Hear the word of the LORD, ye that tremble at his word; your brethren that hated you, that cast you out for my name's sake, said, 'Let the LORD be glorified;' but he shall appear to your joy, and they shall be ashamed."

"He is a good man," others said, "Nay, but he deceiveth the people." Howbeit no man spake openly of him for fear of the Jews.

Now about the midst of the feast Jesus went up into the temple, and taught. And the Jews marvelled, saying, "How knoweth this man letters, having never learned?" Jesus answered them, and said, "My doctrine is not mine, but his that sent me. If any man will do his will, he shall know of the doctrine, whether it be of God, or whether I speak of myself. He that speaketh of himself seeketh his own glory, but he that seeketh his glory that sent him, the same is true, and no unrighteousness is in him.[382] Did not Moses give you the law, and yet none of you keepeth the law? Why go ye about to kill me?" The people answered and said, "Thou hast a devil, who goeth about to kill thee?"

Jesus answered and said unto them, "I have done one work, and ye all marvel. Moses therefore gave unto you circumcision,[383] (not because it is of Moses, but of the fathers,)[384] and ye on the sabbath day circumcise a man. If a man on the sabbath day receive circumcision, that the law of Moses should not be broken, are ye angry at me, because I have made a man every whit whole on the

---

[382] Compare <u>Proverbs 27:2:</u> "Let another man praise thee, and not thine own mouth; a stranger, and not thine own lips."

[383] See <u>Leviticus 12:1-3:</u> "And the LORD spake unto Moses, saying, 'Speak unto the children of Israel, saying, "If a woman have conceived seed, and born a man child; then she shall be unclean seven days; according to the days of the separation for her infirmity shall she be unclean. And in the eighth day the flesh of his foreskin shall be circumcised.""'"

[384] See <u>Genesis 17:9-13:</u> "And God said unto Abraham, 'Thou shalt keep my covenant therefore, thou, and thy seed after thee in their generations. This is my covenant, which ye shall keep, between me and you and thy seed after thee. Every man child among you shall be circumcised. And ye shall circumcise the flesh of your foreskin; and it shall be a token of the covenant betwixt me and you. And he that is eight days old shall be circumcised among you, every man child in your generations, he that is born in the house, or bought with money of any stranger, which is not of thy seed. He that is born in thy house, and he that is bought with thy money, must needs be circumcised. And my covenant shall be in your flesh for an everlasting covenant.'"

sabbath day? Judge not according to the appearance, but judge righteous judgment."

Then said some of them of Jerusalem, "Is not this he, whom they seek to kill? But, lo, he speaketh boldly, and they say nothing unto him. Do the rulers know indeed that this is the very Christ?"[385] And some said, "Howbeit we know this man whence he is, but when Christ cometh, no man knoweth whence he is." Then cried Jesus in the temple as he taught, saying, "Ye both know me, and ye know whence I am, and I am not come of myself, but he that sent me is true, whom ye know not. But I know him, for I am from him, and he hath sent me."

Then they sought to take him, but no man laid hands on him, because his hour was not yet come. And many of the people believed on him, and said, "When Christ cometh, will he do more miracles than these which this man hath done?"[386]

The Pharisees heard that the people murmured such things concerning him, and the Pharisees and the chief priests sent officers to take him. Then said Jesus unto them, "Yet a little while am I with you, and then I go unto him that sent me. Ye shall seek me, and shall not find me, and where I am, thither ye cannot come."

Then said the Jews among themselves, "Whither will he go, that we shall not find him? Will he go unto the dispersed among the Gentiles, and teach the Gentiles? What manner of saying is this that he said, 'Ye shall seek me, and shall not find me, and where I am, thither ye cannot come?'"

---

[385] See Jeremiah 23:5: "Behold, the days come, saith the LORD, that I will raise unto David a righteous Branch, and a King shall reign and prosper, and shall execute judgment and justice in the earth."
[386] See Isaiah 35:5-6: "Then [in the days of Messiah] the eyes of the blind shall be opened, and the ears of the deaf shall be unstopped. Then shall the lame man leap as an hart, and the tongue of the dumb sing; for in the wilderness shall waters break out, and streams in the desert."

THE TREE OF LIFE

In the last day, that great day of the feast, Jesus stood and cried, saying, "If any man thirst, let him come unto me, and drink.[387] He that believeth on me, as the scripture hath said, out of his belly shall flow rivers of living water."[388] (But this spake he of the Spirit,[389] which they that believe on him should receive, for the Holy Ghost was not yet given, because that Jesus was not yet glorified.) Many of the people therefore, when they heard this saying, said, "Of a truth this is the Prophet,"[390] others said, "This is the Christ,"[391] but some said, "Shall Christ come out of Galilee? Hath not the scripture said that Christ cometh of the seed of David, and out of the town of Bethlehem, where David was?"[392] So there was a division among the

---

[387] Compare Isaiah 55:1-3: "Ho, every one that thirsteth, come ye to the waters, and he that hath no money; come ye, buy, and eat; yea, come, buy wine and milk without money and without price. Wherefore do ye spend money for that which is not bread? And your labour for that which satisfieth not? Hearken diligently unto me, and eat ye that which is good, and let your soul delight itself in fatness. Incline your ear, and come unto me; hear, and your soul shall live; and I will make an everlasting covenant with you, even the sure mercies of David."
Psalms 36:9: "For with thee is the fountain of life; in thy light shall we see light."
[388] Compare Proverbs 18:4: "The words of a man's mouth are as deep waters, and the wellspring of wisdom as a flowing brook."
Proverbs 14:27: "The fear of the LORD is a fountain of life, to depart from the snares of death."
Isaiah 58:11: "And the LORD shall guide thee continually, and satisfy thy soul in drought, and make fat thy bones; and thou shalt be like a watered garden, and like a spring of water, whose waters fail not."
2 Esdras 14:47: "For in [the wise] is the spring of understanding, the fountain of wisdom, and the stream of knowledge."
Sirach 21:13: "The knowledge of a wise man shall abound like a flood; and his counsel is like a pure fountain of life."
[389] Compare Isaiah 44:3: "For I will pour water upon him that is thirsty, and floods upon the dry ground. I will pour my spirit upon thy seed, and my blessing upon thine offspring."
[390] See Deuteronomy 18:15: "The LORD thy God will raise up unto thee a Prophet from the midst of thee, of thy brethren, like unto me; unto him ye shall hearken."
[391] See Jeremiah 23:5: "Behold, the days come, saith the LORD, that I will raise unto David a righteous Branch, and a King shall reign and prosper, and shall execute judgment and justice in the earth."
[392] See Micah 5:2: "But thou, Beth-lehem Ephratah, though thou be little among the thousands of Judah, yet out of thee shall he come forth unto me that is to be ruler in Israel; whose goings forth have been from of old, from everlasting."

people because of him. And some of them would have taken him, but no man laid hands on him.

Then came the officers to the chief priests and Pharisees, and they said unto them, "Why have ye not brought him?" The officers answered, "Never man spake like this man." Then answered them the Pharisees, "Are ye also deceived? Have any of the rulers or of the Pharisees believed on him? But this people who knoweth not the law are cursed." Nicodemus saith unto them, (he that came to Jesus by night, being one of them,) "Doth our law judge any man, before it hear him, and know what he doeth?"[393] They answered and said unto him, "Art thou also of Galilee? Search, and look, for out of Galilee ariseth no prophet." And every man went unto his own house.

Jesus went unto the mount of Olives. And early in the morning he came again into the temple, and all the people came unto him, and he sat down, and taught them. And the scribes and Pharisees brought unto him a woman taken in adultery, and when they had set her in the midst, they say unto him, "Master, this woman was taken in adultery, in the very act. Now Moses in the law commanded us, that such should be stoned,[394] but what sayest thou?" This they

---

1 Samuel 17:12: "Now David was the son of that Ephrathite of Bethlehemjudah, whose name was Jesse; and he had eight sons; and the man went among men for an old man in the days of Saul."
Isaiah 11:1: "And there shall come forth a rod out of the stem of Jesse, and a Branch shall grow out of his roots."
[393] Compare Deuteronomy 1:16-17: "And I charged your judges at that time, saying, 'Hear the causes between your brethren, and judge righteously between every man and his brother, and the stranger that is with him. Ye shall not respect persons in judgment; but ye shall hear the small as well as the great; ye shall not be afraid of the face of man; for the judgment is God's. And the cause that is too hard for you, bring it unto me, and I will hear it.'"
Proverbs 18:13: "He that answereth a matter before he heareth it, it is folly and shame unto him."
[394] See Leviticus 20:10: "And the man that committeth adultery with another man's wife, even he that committeth adultery with his neighbour's wife, the adulterer and the adulteress shall surely be put to death."

said, tempting him, that they might have to accuse him. But Jesus stooped down, and with his finger wrote on the ground, as though he heard them not. So when they continued asking him, he lifted up himself, and said unto them, "He that is without sin among you, let him first cast a stone at her."[395] And again he stooped down, and wrote on the ground. And they which heard it, being convicted by their own conscience, went out one by one, beginning at the eldest, even unto the last, and Jesus was left alone, and the woman standing in the midst. When Jesus had lifted up himself, and saw none but the woman, he said unto her, "Woman, where are those thine accusers? Hath no man condemned thee?" She said, "No man, Lord." And Jesus said unto her, "Neither do I condemn thee, go, and sin no more."

Then spake Jesus again, saying, "I am the light of the world, he that followeth me shall not walk in darkness, but shall have the light of life.[396]" The Pharisees therefore said unto him, "Thou bearest record of thyself, thy record is not true." Jesus answered and said unto them, "Though I bear record of myself, yet my record is true, for I know whence I came, and whither I go, but ye cannot tell whence I come, and whither I go. Ye judge after the flesh, I judge no man. And yet if I judge, my judgment is true, for I am not alone, but I and the Father that sent me. It is also written in your law, that 'the

---

Deuteronomy 22:22-24: "If a man be found lying with a woman married to an husband, then they shall both of them die, both the man that lay with the woman, and the woman; so shalt thou put away evil from Israel. If a damsel that is a virgin be betrothed unto an husband, and a man find her in the city, and lie with her; then ye shall bring them both out unto the gate of that city, and ye shall stone them with stones that they die; the damsel, because she cried not, being in the city; and the man, because he hath humbled his neighbour's wife. So thou shalt put away evil from among you."
[395] Compare <u>Sirach 18:20:</u> "Before judgment examine thyself, and in the day of visitation thou shalt find mercy."
[396] Compare <u>Malachi 4:2:</u> "But unto you that fear my name shall the Sun of righteousness arise with healing in his wings; and ye shall go forth, and grow up as calves of the stall."
<u>Psalms 36:9:</u> "For with thee is the fountain of life; in thy light shall we see light."

*testimony of two men is true.'*³⁹⁷ I am one that bear witness of myself, and the Father that sent me beareth witness of me." Then said they unto him, "Where is thy Father?" Jesus answered, "Ye neither know me, nor my Father,³⁹⁸ if ye had known me, ye should have known my Father also." These words spake Jesus in the treasury, as he taught in the temple, and no man laid hands on him, for his hour was not yet come. Then said Jesus again unto them, "I go my way, and ye shall seek me, and shall die in your sins, whither I go, ye cannot come." Then said the Jews, "Will he kill himself? Because he saith, 'Whither I go, ye cannot come.'" And he said unto them, "Ye are from beneath, I am from above. Ye are of this world, I am not of this world. I said therefore unto you, that ye shall die in your sins, for if ye believe not that I am he, ye shall die in your sins." Then said they unto him, "Who art thou?" And Jesus saith unto them, "Even the same that I said unto you from the beginning. I have many things to say and to judge of you, but he that sent me is true, and I speak to the world those things which I have heard of him." But they understood not that he spake to them of the Father.

Then said Jesus unto them, "When ye have lifted up the Son of man,³⁹⁹ then shall ye know that I am he, and that I do nothing of

---

³⁹⁷ "One witness shall not rise up against a man for any iniquity, or for any sin, in any sin that he sinneth; at the mouth of two witnesses, or at the mouth of three witnesses, shall the matter be established." – Deuteronomy 19:15
See also Deuteronomy 17:6.
³⁹⁸ See Deuteronomy 4:29: "But if from thence thou shalt seek the LORD thy God, thou shalt find him, if thou seek him with all thy heart and with all thy soul."
1 Chronicles 28:9: "And thou, Solomon my son, know thou the God of thy father, and serve him with a perfect heart and with a willing mind; for the LORD searcheth all hearts, and understandeth all the imaginations of the thoughts; if thou seek him, he will be found of thee; but if thou forsake him, he will cast thee off for ever."
³⁹⁹ See Isaiah 5:26: "And he will lift up an ensign to the nations from far, and will hiss unto them from the end of the earth; and, behold, they shall come with speed swiftly."
Isaiah 11:10: "And in that day there shall be a root of Jesse, which shall stand for an ensign of the people; to it shall the Gentiles seek; and his rest shall be glorious."

myself, but as my Father hath taught me, I speak these things. And he that sent me is with me, the Father hath not left me alone, for I do always those things that please him."

As he spake these words, many believed on him. Then said Jesus to those Jews which believed on him, "If ye continue in my word, then are ye my disciples indeed, and ye shall know the truth, and the truth shall make you free." They answered him, "We be Abraham's seed, and were never in bondage to any man, how sayest thou, 'Ye shall be made free?'" Jesus answered them, "Verily, verily, I say unto you, whosoever committeth sin is the servant of sin.[400] And the servant abideth not in the house for ever, but the Son abideth ever. If the Son therefore shall make you free, ye shall be free indeed.[401] I know that ye are Abraham's seed, but ye seek to kill me, because my word hath no place in you. I speak that which I have seen with my Father, and ye do that which ye have seen with your father." They answered and said unto him, "Abraham is our father."

Isaiah 18:3: "All ye inhabitants of the world, and dwellers on the earth, see ye, when he lifteth up an ensign on the mountains; and when he bloweth a trumpet, hear ye."
[400] Compare *2 Esdras* 16:77: "Woe be unto them that are bound with their sins, and covered with their iniquities like as a field is covered over with bushes, and the path thereof covered with thorns, that no man may travel through!"
Isaiah 50:1-2: "Thus saith the LORD, 'Where is the bill of your mother's divorcement, whom I have put away? Or which of my creditors is it to whom I have sold you? Behold, for your iniquities have ye sold yourselves, and for your transgressions is your mother put away. Wherefore, when I came, was there no man? When I called, was there none to answer? Is my hand shortened at all, that it cannot redeem? Or have I no power to deliver? Behold, at my rebuke I dry up the sea, I make the rivers a wilderness; their fish stinketh, because there is no water, and dieth for thirst.'"
[401] Compare Psalms 107:8-14: "Oh that men would praise the LORD for his goodness, and for his wonderful works to the children of men! For he satisfieth the longing soul, and filleth the hungry soul with goodness. Such as sit in darkness and in the shadow of death, being bound in affliction and iron; because they rebelled against the words of God, and contemned the counsel of the most High; therefore he brought down their heart with labour; they fell down, and there was none to help. Then they cried unto the LORD in their trouble, and he saved them out of their distresses. He brought them out of darkness and the shadow of death, and brake their bands in sunder."

Jesus saith unto them, "If ye were Abraham's children, ye would do the works of Abraham. But now ye seek to kill me, a man that hath told you the truth, which I have heard of God, this did not Abraham. Ye do the deeds of your father." Then said they to him, "We be not born of fornication, we have one Father, even God." Jesus said unto them, "If God were your Father, ye would love me, for I proceeded forth and came from God, neither came I of myself, but he sent me. Why do ye not understand my speech? Even because ye cannot hear my word. Ye are of your father the devil,[402] and the lusts of your father ye will do. He was a murderer from the beginning,[403] and abode not in the truth, because there is no truth in him. When he speaketh a lie, he speaketh of his own, for he is a liar, and the father of it.[404] And because I tell you the truth, ye believe me not. Which of you convinceth me of sin? And if I say the truth, why do ye not believe me? He that is of God heareth God's words, ye therefore hear them not, because ye are not of God."

Then answered the Jews, and said unto him, "Say we not well that thou art a Samaritan, and hast a devil?" Jesus answered, "I have not a devil, but I honour my Father, and ye do dishonour me. And I seek not mine own glory, there is one that seeketh and judgeth. Verily, verily, I say unto you, if a man keep my saying, he shall never

---

[402] Compare <u>1 Samuel 2:12:</u> "Now the sons of Eli were sons of Belial; they knew not the LORD."
[403] See <u>Wisdom 2:23-24:</u> "For God created man to be immortal, and made him to be an image of his own eternity. Nevertheless through envy of the devil came death into the world; and they that do hold of his side do find it."
<u>2 Esdras 1:26:</u> "Whensoever ye shall call upon me, I will not hear you; for ye have defiled your hands with blood, and your feet are swift to commit manslaughter."
See also <u>Genesis 4:1-24</u> (Cain and Abel).
[404] See <u>Genesis 3:1-4:</u> "Now the serpent was more subtil than any beast of the field which the LORD God had made. And he said unto the woman, 'Yea, hath God said, "Ye shall not eat of every tree of the garden?"' And the woman said unto the serpent, 'We may eat of the fruit of the trees of the garden. But of the fruit of the tree which is in the midst of the garden, God hath said, "Ye shall not eat of it, neither shall ye touch it, lest ye die."' And the serpent said unto the woman, 'Ye shall not surely die.'"

THE TREE OF LIFE

see death."[405] Then said the Jews unto him, "Now we know that thou hast a devil. Abraham is dead, and the prophets, and thou sayest, 'If a man keep my saying, he shall never taste of death.' Art thou greater than our father Abraham, which is dead? And the prophets who are dead? Whom makest thou thyself?"

Jesus answered, "If I honour myself, my honour is nothing, it is my Father that honoureth me, of whom ye say, that he is your God. Yet ye have not known him, but I know him, and if I should say, 'I know him not,' I shall be a liar like unto you, but I know him, and keep his saying. Your father Abraham rejoiced to see my day, and he saw it, and was glad." Then said the Jews unto him, "Thou art not yet fifty years old, and hast thou seen Abraham?"

Jesus said unto them, "Verily, verily, I say unto you, before Abraham was, *I am*."[406] Then took they up stones to cast at him,[407]

---

[405] Compare <u>Genesis 5:22-24:</u> "And Enoch walked with God after he begat Methuselah three hundred years, and begat sons and daughters. And all the days of Enoch were three hundred sixty and five years. And Enoch walked with God; and he was not; for God took him."
<u>2 Kings 2:1,11,15-17:</u> "And it came to pass, when the LORD would take up Elijah into heaven by a whirlwind, that Elijah went with Elisha from Gilgal. And it came to pass, as they still went on, and talked, that, behold, there appeared a chariot of fire, and horses of fire, and parted them both asunder; and Elijah went up by a whirlwind into heaven. And when the sons of the prophets which were to view at Jericho saw him, they said, 'The spirit of Elijah doth rest on Elisha.' And they came to meet him, and bowed themselves to the ground before him. And they said unto him, 'Behold now, there be with thy servants fifty strong men; let them go, we pray thee, and seek thy master; lest peradventure the Spirit of the LORD hath taken him up, and cast him upon some mountain, or into some valley.' And he said, 'Ye shall not send.' And when they urged him till he was ashamed, he said, 'Send.' They sent therefore fifty men; and they sought three days, but found him not."
<u>2 Esdras 14:7-9:</u> "And now I say unto thee, hat thou lay up in thy heart the signs that I have shewed, and the dreams that thou hast seen, and the interpretations which thou hast heard. For thou shalt be taken away from all, and from henceforth thou shalt remain with my Son, and with such as be like thee, until the times be ended."
[406] See <u>Exodus 3:13-14:</u> "And Moses said unto God, 'Behold, when I come unto the children of Israel, and shall say unto them, "The God of your fathers hath sent me unto you;" and they shall say to me, "What is his name?" What shall I say unto

but Jesus hid himself, and went out of the temple, going through the midst of them, and so passed by.

them?' And God said unto Moses, 'I AM THAT I AM;' and he said, 'Thus shalt thou say unto the children of Israel, "I AM hath sent me unto you."'"
407 See Leviticus 24:16: "And he that blasphemeth the name of the LORD, he shall surely be put to death, and all the congregation shall certainly stone him; as well the stranger, as he that is born in the land, when he blasphemeth the name of the LORD, shall be put to death."

THE TREE OF LIFE

Chapter Forty Seven

And they departed thence, and passed through Galilee, and he would not that any man should know it. And while they abode in Galilee, they were all amazed at the mighty power of God. But while they wondered every one at all things which Jesus did, he said unto his disciples, "Let these sayings sink down into your ears, for the Son of man shall be betrayed into the hands of men, and they shall kill him, and after that he is killed, he shall rise the third day." And they were exceeding sorry. But they understood not that saying, and it was hid from them,[408] that they perceived it not, and were afraid to ask him of that saying.

---

[408] Compare <u>Sirach 11:4:</u> "Boast not of thy clothing and raiment, and exalt not thyself in the day of honour; for the works of the Lord are wonderful, and his works among men are hidden."
<u>Deuteronomy 29:4:</u> "Yet the LORD hath not given you an heart to perceive, and eyes to see, and ears to hear, unto this day."

THE TREE OF LIFE

Chapter Forty Eight

And when they were come to Capernaum, they that received tribute money came to Peter, and said, "Doth not your master pay tribute?" He saith, "Yes." And when he was come into the house, Jesus prevented him, saying, "What thinkest thou, Simon? Of whom do the kings of the earth take custom or tribute? Of their own children, or of strangers?" Peter saith unto him, "Of strangers." Jesus saith unto him, "Then are the children free. Notwithstanding, lest we should offend them, go thou to the sea, and cast an hook, and take up the fish that first cometh up, and when thou hast opened his mouth, thou shalt find a piece of money, that take, and give unto them for me and thee."

And being in the house Jesus asked them, "What was it that ye disputed among yourselves by the way?" But they held their peace, for by the way they had disputed among themselves, who should be the greatest.

And Jesus, perceiving the thought of their heart, sat down, and called the twelve, and he saith unto them, "If any man desire to be first, the same shall be last of all, and servant of all." And he called a little child unto him, and set him in the midst of them, and when he had taken him in his arms, he said unto them, "Verily I say unto you, except ye be converted, and become as little children, ye shall not enter into the kingdom of heaven. Whosoever therefore shall humble himself as this little child,⁴⁰⁹ the same is greatest in the kingdom of heaven. For the Son of man is come to *save that which was lost.*⁴¹⁰ How think ye? If a man have an hundred sheep, and one of them be gone astray, doth he not leave the ninety and nine, and goeth into the mountains, and seeketh that which is gone astray? And if so be that he find it, verily I say unto you, he rejoiceth more of that sheep, than of the ninety and nine which went not astray. Even so it is not the will of your Father which is in heaven, that one of these little ones should perish. And take heed that ye despise not one of these little ones, for I say unto you, that in heaven their angels do always behold the face of my Father which is in heaven. And whoso shall receive one such little child in my name receiveth me, and whosoever shall receive me receiveth not me, but him that sent me, for he that is least among you all, the same shall be great."

And John answered him, saying, "Master, we saw one casting out devils in thy name, and he followeth not us, and we forbad him, because he followeth not us."

And Jesus said unto him, "Forbid him not, for there is no man which shall do a miracle in my name, that can lightly speak evil of me. For he that is not against us is on our part. Again I say unto you, that if two of you shall agree on earth as touching any thing that they shall ask, it shall be done for them of my Father which is in heaven. For where two or three are gathered together in my name, there am I in the midst of them. Verily I say unto you, whatsoever ye

---

[409] Compare Ecclesiastes 4:13: "Better is a poor and a wise child than an old and foolish king, who will no more be admonished."

[410] See Ezekiel 34:11,15-16: "For thus saith the Lord GOD; Behold, I, even I, will both search my sheep, and seek them out. I will feed my flock, and I will cause them to lie down, saith the Lord GOD. I will seek that which was lost, and bring again that which was driven away, and will bind up that which was broken, and will strengthen that which was sick; but I will destroy the fat and the strong; I will feed them with judgment."

See also Jeremiah 50:6: "My people hath been lost sheep; their shepherds have caused them to go astray, they have turned them away on the mountains; they have gone from mountain to hill, they have forgotten their restingplace."

shall bind on earth shall be bound in heaven, and whatsoever ye shall loose on earth shall be loosed in heaven. For whosoever shall give you a cup of water to drink in my name, because ye belong to Christ, verily I say unto you, he shall not lose his reward. But whoso shall offend one of these little ones which believe in me, it is better for him that a millstone were hanged about his neck, and he were drowned in the depth of the sea."

Then said he unto the disciples, "Woe unto the world because of offences! For it is impossible but that offences will come, but woe unto him, through whom they come!

"Wherefore if thy hand offend thee, cut it off, and cast it from thee, it is better for thee to enter into life maimed, than having two hands to go into hell, into *everlasting fire that never shall be quenched, where their worm dieth not.*[411] And if thy foot offend thee, cut it off, and cast it from thee, it is better for thee to enter halt into life, than having two feet to be cast into hell, into the *fire that never shall be quenched, where their worm dieth not.* And if thine eye offend thee, pluck it out, and cast it from thee, it is better for thee to enter into life with one eye, rather than having two eyes to be cast into hell fire, *where their worm dieth not.*

"Take heed to yourselves, if thy brother trespass against thee, rebuke him,[412] and if he repent, forgive him. And if he trespass against thee seven times in a day, and seven times in a day turn

---

[411] See Isaiah 66:24: "And they shall go forth, and look upon the carcases of the men that have transgressed against me; for their worm shall not die, neither shall their fire be quenched; and they shall be an abhorring unto all flesh."
See also Psalms 9:17: "The wicked shall be turned into hell, and all the nations that forget God."
Judith 16:17: "Woe to the nations that rise up against my kindred! The Lord Almighty will take vengeance of them in the day of judgment, in putting fire and worms in their flesh; and they shall feel them, and weep for ever."
Sirach 7:17: "Humble thyself greatly; for the vengeance of the ungodly is fire and worms."
[412] See Leviticus 19:17: "Thou shalt not hate thy brother in thine heart; thou shalt in any wise rebuke thy neighbour, and not suffer sin upon him."

again to thee, saying, 'I repent,' thou shalt forgive him. Moreover if thy brother shall trespass against thee, go and tell him his fault between thee and him alone, if he shall hear thee, thou hast gained thy brother. But if he will not hear thee, then take with thee one or two more, *that in the mouth of two or three witnesses every word may be established.*[413] And if he shall neglect to hear them, tell it unto the church,[414] but if he neglect to hear the church, let him be unto thee as an heathen man and a publican." Then came Peter to him, and said, "Lord, how oft shall my brother sin against me, and I forgive him? till seven times?" Jesus saith unto him, "I say not unto thee, 'Until seven times,' but, 'Until seventy times seven.'

"Therefore is the kingdom of heaven likened unto a certain king, which would take account of his servants. And when he had begun to reckon, one was brought unto him, which owed him ten thousand talents. But forasmuch as he had not to pay, his lord commanded him to be sold, and his wife, and children, and all that he had, and payment to be made. The servant therefore fell down, and worshipped him, saying, 'Lord, have patience with me, and I will pay thee all.' Then the lord of that servant was moved with compassion, and loosed him, and forgave him the debt. But the same servant went out, and found one of his fellowservants, which owed him an hundred pence, and he laid hands on him, and took him by the throat, saying, 'Pay me that thou owest.' And his fellowservant fell down at his feet, and besought him, saying, 'Have patience with me, and I will pay thee all.' And he would not, but went and cast him into prison, till he should pay the debt. So when his fellowservants

---

[413] See Deuteronomy 19:15: "One witness shall not rise up against a man for any iniquity, or for any sin, in any sin that he sinneth; at the mouth of two witnesses, or at the mouth of three witnesses, shall the matter be established."
[414] See Deuteronomy 17:8-9: "If there arise a matter too hard for thee in judgment, between blood and blood, between plea and plea, and between stroke and stroke, being matters of controversy within thy gates; then shalt thou arise, and get thee up into the place which the LORD thy God shall choose; And thou shalt come unto the priests the Levites, and unto the judge that shall be in those days, and inquire; and they shall shew thee the sentence of judgment."

saw what was done, they were very sorry, and came and told unto their lord all that was done. Then his lord, after that he had called him, said unto him, 'O thou wicked servant, I forgave thee all that debt, because thou desiredst me. Shouldest not thou also have had compassion on thy fellowservant, even as I had pity on thee?' And his lord was wroth, and delivered him to the tormentors, till he should pay all that was due unto him. So likewise shall my heavenly Father do also unto you, if ye from your hearts forgive not every one his brother their trespasses."

THE TREE OF LIFE

THE TREE OF LIFE

Chapter Forty Nine

And it came to pass, when the time was come that he should be received up, he stedfastly set his face to go to Jerusalem,[415] and sent messengers before his face. And they went, and entered into a village of the Samaritans, to make ready for him. And they did not receive him, because his face was as though he would go to Jerusalem. And when his disciples James and John saw this, they said, "Lord, wilt thou that we command fire to come down from heaven, and consume them, even as Elijah did?"[416] But he turned, and rebuked them, and said, "Ye know not what manner of spirit ye are of. For the Son of man is not come to destroy men's lives, but to save them."[417] And they went to another village.

---

[415] Compare Isaiah 50:6-7: "I gave my back to the smiters, and my cheeks to them that plucked off the hair; I hid not my face from shame and spitting. For the Lord GOD will help me; therefore shall I not be confounded; therefore have I set my face like a flint, and I know that I shall not be ashamed."
[416] See 2 Kings 1:9-12: "Then the king sent unto him a captain of fifty with his fifty. And he went up to him; and, behold, he sat on the top of an hill. And he spake unto him, 'Thou man of God, the king hath said, "Come down."' And Elijah answered and said to the captain of fifty, 'If I be a man of God, then let fire come down from heaven, and consume thee and thy fifty.' And there came down fire from heaven, and consumed him and his fifty. Again also he sent unto him another captain of fifty with his fifty. And he answered and said unto him, 'O man of God, thus hath the king said, "Come down quickly."' And Elijah answered and said unto them, 'If I be a man of God, let fire come down from heaven, and consume thee and thy fifty.' And the fire of God came down from heaven, and consumed him and his fifty."
[417] Compare Ezekiel 18:23,32: "Have I any pleasure at all that the wicked should die? saith the Lord GOD; and not that he should return from his ways, and live? For

And it came to pass, that Jesus departed from Galilee, and came into the coasts of Judaea by the farther side of Jordan, and the people resort unto him again, and, as he was wont, he taught them again. And great multitudes followed him, and he healed them there.

The Pharisees also came unto him, tempting him, and asking him, "Is it lawful for a man to put away his wife for every cause?" And he answered and said unto them, "What did Moses command you?" And they said, "Moses suffered to write a bill of divorcement, and to put her away."[418]

And he answered and said unto them, "Have ye not read, that from the beginning of the creation God made them *'male and female'*?[419] And said, *'For this cause shall a man leave father and mother, and shall cleave to his wife, and they twain shall be one flesh'*?[420] Wherefore they are no more twain, but one flesh. What therefore God hath joined together, let not man put asunder."[421]

They say unto him, "Why did Moses then command to give a writing of divorcement, and to put her away?" And Jesus answered and said unto them, "Because of the hardness of your hearts Moses

---

I have no pleasure in the death of him that dieth, saith the Lord GOD; wherefore turn yourselves, and live ye."
[418] See Deuteronomy 24:1-2: "When a man hath taken a wife, and married her, and it come to pass that she find no favour in his eyes, because he hath found some uncleanness in her; then let him write her a bill of divorcement, and give it in her hand, and send her out of his house. And when she is departed out of his house, she may go and be another man's wife."
[419] "So God created man in his own image, in the image of God created he him; male and female created he them." – Genesis 1:27
[420] "Therefore shall a man leave his father and his mother, and shall cleave unto his wife; and they shall be one flesh." – Genesis 2:24
[421] Compare Malachi 2:14-16: "Yet ye say, 'Wherefore?' Because the LORD hath been witness between thee and the wife of thy youth, against whom thou hast dealt treacherously; yet is she thy companion, and the wife of thy covenant. And did not he make one? Yet had he the residue of the spirit. And wherefore one? That he might seek a godly seed. Therefore take heed to your spirit, and let none deal treacherously against the wife of his youth. For the LORD, the God of Israel, saith that he hateth putting away; for one covereth violence with his garment, saith the LORD of hosts; therefore take heed to your spirit, that ye deal not treacherously."

suffered you to put away your wives, but from the beginning it was not so."

And in the house his disciples asked him again of the same matter. And he saith unto them, "Whosoever shall put away his wife, and marry another, committeth adultery against her. And I say unto you, whosoever shall put away his wife, except it be for fornication, and shall marry another, committeth adultery, and whosoever marrieth her that is put away from her husband committeth adultery. And if a woman shall put away her husband, and be married to another, she committeth adultery."[422]

His disciples say unto him, "If the case of the man be so with his wife, it is not good to marry." But he said unto them, "All men cannot receive this saying, save they to whom it is given. For there are some eunuchs, which were so born from their mother's womb, and there are some eunuchs, which were made eunuchs of men, and there be eunuchs, which have made themselves eunuchs for the kingdom of heaven's sake. He that is able to receive it, let him receive it."[423]

Then were there brought unto him little children, that he should put his hands on them,[424] and pray, but when his disciples

---

[422] Compare <u>Leviticus 21:13-14:</u> "And [a priest] shall take a wife in her virginity. A widow, or a divorced woman, or profane, or an harlot, these shall he not take; but he shall take a virgin of his own people to wife."
<u>Ezekiel 44:22:</u> "Neither shall [the priests] take for their wives a widow, nor her that is put away; but they shall take maidens of the seed of the house of Israel, or a widow that had a priest before."
<u>Exodus 19:5-6:</u> "Now therefore, if ye will obey my voice indeed, and keep my covenant, then ye shall be a peculiar treasure unto me above all people; for all the earth is mine. And ye shall be unto me a kingdom of priests, and an holy nation. These are the words which thou shalt speak unto the children of Israel."
[423] Compare <u>Ezekiel 3:27:</u> "But when I speak with thee, I will open thy mouth, and thou shalt say unto them, 'Thus saith the Lord GOD; He that heareth, let him hear; and he that forbeareth, let him forbear;' for they are a rebellious house."
[424] Compare <u>Deuteronomy 34:9:</u> "And Joshua the son of Nun was full of the spirit of wisdom; for Moses had laid his hands upon him; and the children of Israel hearkened unto him, and did as the LORD commanded Moses."

THE TREE OF LIFE

saw it, they rebuked those that brought them. But when Jesus saw it, he was much displeased, and called them unto him, said, "Suffer the little children to come unto me, and forbid them not, for of such is the kingdom of heaven. Verily I say unto you, whosoever shall not receive the kingdom of God as a little child[425] shall in no wise enter therein." And he took them up in his arms, put his hands upon them, and blessed them, and departed thence.

---

[425] Compare Ecclesiastes 4:13: "Better is a poor and a wise child than an old and foolish king, who will no more be admonished."

Chapter Fifty

And when he was gone forth into the way, there came a certain ruler running, and kneeled to him, and asked him, "Good Master, what good thing shall I do that I may inherit eternal life?" And Jesus said unto him, "Why callest thou me good? There is none good but one, that is, God.[426] But if thou wilt enter into life, keep the commandments." He saith unto him, "Which?" Jesus said, *"Thou shalt not kill, Thou shalt not commit adultery, Thou shalt not steal, Thou shalt not bear false witness, Honour thy father and thy mother,*[427] *and, Thou shalt love thy neighbour as thyself."*[428] The

---

[426] Compare *Sirach 18:2:* "The Lord only is righteous, and there is none other but he."
Psalms 14:2-3: "The LORD looked down from heaven upon the children of men, to see if there were any that did understand, and seek God. They are all gone aside, they are all together become filthy; there is none that doeth good, no, not one."
Psalms 118:1: "O give thanks unto the LORD; for he is good; because his mercy endureth for ever."
Psalms 145:9: "The LORD is good to all; and his tender mercies are over all his works."
[427] "Honour thy father and thy mother; that thy days may be long upon the land which the LORD thy God giveth thee. Thou shalt not kill. Thou shalt not commit adultery. Thou shalt not steal. Thou shalt not bear false witness against thy neighbour." – Exodus 20:12-16
"Honour thy father and thy mother, as the LORD thy God hath commanded thee; that thy days may be prolonged, and that it may go well with thee, in the land which the LORD thy God giveth thee. Thou shalt not kill. Neither shalt thou commit adultery. Neither shalt thou steal. Neither shalt thou bear false witness against thy neighbour." – Deuteronomy 5:16-20

young man answered and said unto him, "Master, all these things have I kept from my youth up, what lack I yet?"

Then Jesus beholding him loved him, and said unto him, "Yet lackest thou one thing. If thou wilt be perfect, go thy way, sell all that thou hast, and give to the poor, and thou shalt have treasure in heaven, and come, take up the cross, and follow me." But when the young man heard that saying, he was grieved, and went away very sorrowful, for he was very rich and had great possessions. And when Jesus saw that he was very sorrowful, he looked round about, and saith unto his disciples, "Verily I say unto you, that a rich man shall hardly enter into the kingdom of heaven." And the disciples were astonished at his words. But Jesus answereth again, and saith unto them, "Children, how hard is it for them that trust in riches to enter into the kingdom of God!⁴²⁹ It is easier for a camel to go

---

⁴²⁸ "Thou shalt not hate thy brother in thine heart; thou shalt in any wise rebuke thy neighbour, and not suffer sin upon him. Thou shalt not avenge, nor bear any grudge against the children of thy people, but thou shalt love thy neighbour as thyself; I am the LORD." – Leviticus 19:17-18
"Love thine own soul, and comfort thy heart, remove sorrow far from thee; for sorrow hath killed many, and there is no profit therein." – Sirach 30:23
⁴²⁹ Compare Proverbs 11:28: "He that trusteth in his riches shall fall; but the righteous shall flourish as a branch."
Psalms 49:6,11,14,16-19: "They that trust in their wealth, and boast themselves in the multitude of their riches; Their inward thought is, that their houses shall continue for ever, and their dwelling places to all generations; they call their lands after their own names. Like sheep they are laid in the grave; death shall feed on them; and the upright shall have dominion over them in the morning; and their beauty shall consume in the grave from their dwelling. Be not thou afraid when one is made rich, when the glory of his house is increased; for when he dieth he shall carry nothing away; his glory shall not descend after him. Though while he lived he blessed his soul; and men will praise thee, when thou doest well to thyself. He shall go to the generation of his fathers; they shall never see light."
Job 27:19: "The rich man shall lie down, but he shall not be gathered; he openeth his eyes, and he is not."
Job 21:7,13-15: "Wherefore do the wicked live, become old, yea, are mighty in power? They spend their days in wealth, and in a moment go down to the grave. Therefore they say unto God, 'Depart from us; for we desire not the knowledge of thy ways.' 'What is the Almighty, that we should serve him? And what profit should we have, if we pray unto him?'"

through the eye of a needle, than for a rich man to enter into the kingdom of God." When his disciples heard it, they were exceedingly astonished out of measure, saying among themselves, "Who then can be saved?"

But Jesus beheld them, and said unto them, "With men this is impossible, but not with God, for with God all things are possible."[430] Then answered Peter and said unto him, "Behold, we have forsaken all, and followed thee, what shall we have therefore?"

And Jesus said unto them, "Verily I say unto you, that ye which have followed me, in the regeneration when the Son of man shall sit in the throne of his glory,[431] ye also shall sit upon twelve thrones, judging the twelve tribes of Israel. And every one that hath forsaken houses, or parents, or brethren, or sisters, or father, or mother, or wife, or children, or lands, for my name's sake, shall receive an hundredfold now in this time, houses, and brethren, and sisters, and mothers, and children, and lands, with persecutions, and in the world to come eternal life. But many that are first shall be last, and the last shall be first."

Proverbs 30:8-9: "Remove far from me vanity and lies; give me neither poverty nor riches; feed me with food convenient for me. Lest I be full, and deny thee, and say, 'Who is the LORD?' or lest I be poor, and steal, and take the name of my God in vain."

[430] See Jeremiah 32:17: "Ah Lord GOD! behold, thou hast made the heaven and the earth by thy great power and stretched out arm, and there is nothing too hard for thee."

Tobit 4:8-10: "Give alms of thy substance; and when thou givest alms, let not thine eye be envious, neither turn thy face from any poor, and the face of God shall not be turned away from thee. If thou hast abundance give alms accordingly; if thou have but a little, be not afraid to give according to that little. For thou layest up a good treasure for thyself against the day of necessity. Because that alms do deliver from death, and suffereth not to come into darkness."

[431] See Daniel 7:13-14: "I saw in the night visions, and, behold, one like the Son of man came with the clouds of heaven, and came to the Ancient of days, and they brought him near before him. And there was given him dominion, and glory, and a kingdom, that all people, nations, and languages, should serve him; his dominion is an everlasting dominion, which shall not pass away, and his kingdom that which shall not be destroyed."

THE TREE OF LIFE

"For the kingdom of heaven is like unto a man that is an householder, which went out early in the morning to hire labourers into his vineyard. And when he had agreed with the labourers for a penny a day, he sent them into his vineyard. And he went out about the third hour, and saw others standing idle in the marketplace, and said unto them, 'Go ye also into the vineyard, and whatsoever is right I will give you.' And they went their way. Again he went out about the sixth and ninth hour, and did likewise. And about the eleventh hour he went out, and found others standing idle, and saith unto them, 'Why stand ye here all the day idle?' They say unto him, 'Because no man hath hired us.' He saith unto them, 'Go ye also into the vineyard, and whatsoever is right, that shall ye receive.' So when even was come, the lord of the vineyard saith unto his steward, 'Call the labourers, and give them their hire, beginning from the last unto the first.' And when they came that were hired about the eleventh hour, they received every man a penny. But when the first came, they supposed that they should have received more, and they likewise received every man a penny. And when they had received it, they murmured against the goodman of the house, saying, 'These last have wrought but one hour, and thou hast made them equal unto us, which have borne the burden and heat of the day.' But he answered one of them, and said, 'Friend, I do thee no wrong, didst not thou agree with me for a penny? Take that thine is, and go thy way, I will give unto this last, even as unto thee. Is it not lawful for me to do what I will with mine own? Is thine eye evil, because I am good?'"

And, "There was a certain rich man, which was clothed in purple and fine linen, and fared sumptuously every day. And there was a certain beggar named Lazarus, which was laid at his gate, full of sores, and desiring to be fed with the crumbs which fell from the rich man's table, moreover the dogs came and licked his sores. And it came to pass, that the beggar died, and was carried by the angels into Abraham's bosom, the rich man also died, and was buried, and in hell he lift up his eyes, being in torments, and seeth Abraham afar off, and Lazarus in his bosom. And he cried and said, 'Father Abraham, have mercy on me, and send Lazarus, that he may dip the tip of his finger in water, and cool my tongue, for I am tormented in this flame.' But Abraham said, 'Son, remember that thou in thy lifetime receivedst thy good things, and likewise Lazarus evil things, but now he is comforted, and thou art tormented. And beside all this, between us and you there is a great gulf fixed,[432] so that they which would pass from hence to you cannot, neither can they pass to us, that would come from thence.' Then he said, 'I pray thee therefore, father, that thou wouldest send him to my father's house, for I have five brethren, that he may testify unto them, lest they also come into this place of torment.' Abraham saith unto him, 'They have Moses and the prophets, let them hear them.' And he said, 'Nay, father Abraham, but if one went unto them from the dead, they will repent.' And he said unto him, 'If they hear not Moses and the prophets, neither will they be persuaded, though one rose from the dead.' So the last shall be first, and the first last, *for many be called, but few chosen.*"[433]

And the Pharisees also, who were covetous, heard all these things, and they derided him. And he said unto them, "Ye are they

---

[432] Compare Isaiah 59:2-3: "But your iniquities have separated between you and your God, and your sins have hid his face from you, that he will not hear. For your hands are defiled with blood, and your fingers with iniquity; your lips have spoken lies, your tongue hath muttered perverseness."
Job 11:7-9: "Canst thou by searching find out God? Canst thou find out the Almighty unto perfection? It is as high as heaven; what canst thou do? Deeper than hell; what canst thou know? The measure thereof is longer than the earth, and broader than the sea."
[433] See 2 Esdras 8:1-3: "And he answered me, saying, 'The most High hath made this world for many, but the world to come for few. I will tell thee a similitude, Esdras; as when thou askest the earth, it shall say unto thee, that it giveth much mould whereof earthen vessels are made, but little dust that gold cometh of; even so is the course of this present world. There be many created, but few shall be saved.'"

THE TREE OF LIFE

which justify yourselves before men,[434] but God knoweth your hearts,[435] for that which is highly esteemed among men is abomination in the sight of God.[436] The law and the prophets were until John, since that time the kingdom of God is preached, and every man presseth into it. And it is easier for heaven and earth to pass, than one tittle of the law to fail."[437]

---

[434] Compare Job 9:20: "If I justify myself, mine own mouth shall condemn me; if I say, 'I am perfect,' it shall also prove me perverse."
Sirach 7:5: "Justify not thyself before the Lord; and boast not of thy wisdom before the king."
[435] See 1 Samuel 16:7: "But the LORD said unto Samuel, 'Look not on his countenance, or on the height of his stature; because I have refused him; for the LORD seeth not as man seeth; for man looketh on the outward appearance, but the LORD looketh on the heart.'"
1 Chronicles 28:9: "And thou, Solomon my son, know thou the God of thy father, and serve him with a perfect heart and with a willing mind; for the LORD searcheth all hearts, and understandeth all the imaginations of the thoughts; if thou seek him, he will be found of thee; but if thou forsake him, he will cast thee off for ever."
2 Esdras 16:54,63: "Behold, the Lord knoweth all the works of men, their imaginations, their thoughts, and their hearts. Surely he knoweth your inventions, and what ye think in your hearts, even them that sin, and would hide their sin."
Wisdom 1:6: "For wisdom is a loving spirit; and will not acquit a blasphemer of his words; for God is witness of his reins, and a true beholder of his heart, and a hearer of his tongue."
[436] Compare Proverbs 14:12 (and 16:25): "There is a way which seemeth right unto a man, but the end thereof are the ways of death."
Isaiah 55:8-9: "For my thoughts are not your thoughts, neither are your ways my ways, saith the LORD. For as the heavens are higher than the earth, so are my ways higher than your ways, and my thoughts than your thoughts."
[437] Compare Isaiah 40:8: "The grass withereth, the flower fadeth; but the word of our God shall stand for ever."
Isaiah 51:6-8: "Lift up your eyes to the heavens, and look upon the earth beneath; for the heavens shall vanish away like smoke, and the earth shall wax old like a garment, and they that dwell therein shall die in like manner; but my salvation shall be for ever, and my righteousness shall not be abolished. Hearken unto me, ye that know righteousness, the people in whose heart is my law; fear ye not the reproach of men, neither be ye afraid of their revilings. For the moth shall eat them up like a garment, and the worm shall eat them like wool; but my righteousness shall be for ever, and my salvation from generation to generation."
2 Esdras 9:36-37: "For we that have received the law perish by sin, and our heart also which received it. Notwithstanding the law perisheth not, but remaineth in his force."

THE TREE OF LIFE

Chapter Fifty One

After these things the LORD appointed other seventy[438] also, and sent them two and two before his face into every city and place, whither he himself would come. Therefore said he

---

<u>Baruch 4:1:</u> "This is the book of the commandments of God, and the law that endureth for ever; all they that keep it shall come to life; but such as leave it shall die."

[438] Compare <u>Numbers 11:10-17,24-25:</u> "Then Moses heard the people weep throughout their families, every man in the door of his tent; and the anger of the LORD was kindled greatly; Moses also was displeased. And Moses said unto the LORD, 'Wherefore hast thou afflicted thy servant? And wherefore have I not found favour in thy sight, that thou layest the burden of all this people upon me? Have I conceived all this people? Have I begotten them, that thou shouldest say unto me, "Carry them in thy bosom, as a nursing father beareth the sucking child, unto the land which thou swarest unto their fathers?" Whence should I have flesh to give unto all this people? For they weep unto me, saying, "Give us flesh, that we may eat." I am not able to bear all this people alone, because it is too heavy for me. And if thou deal thus with me, kill me, I pray thee, out of hand, if I have found favour in thy sight; and let me not see my wretchedness.' And the LORD said unto Moses, 'Gather unto me seventy men of the elders of Israel, whom thou knowest to be the elders of the people, and officers over them; and bring them unto the tabernacle of the congregation, that they may stand there with thee. And I will come down and talk with thee there; and I will take of the spirit which is upon thee, and will put it upon them; and they shall bear the burden of the people with thee, that thou bear it not thyself alone.' And Moses went out, and told the people the words of the LORD, and gathered the seventy men of the elders of the people, and set them round about the tabernacle. And the LORD came down in a cloud, and spake unto him, and took of the spirit that was upon him, and gave it unto the seventy elders; and it came to pass, that, when the spirit rested upon them, they prophesied, and did not cease."

THE TREE OF LIFE

unto them, "The harvest truly is great, but the labourers are few, pray ye therefore the Lord of the harvest, that he would send forth labourers into his harvest.

"Go your ways, behold, I send you forth as lambs among wolves. Carry neither purse, nor scrip, nor shoes, and salute no man by the way. And into whatsoever house ye enter, first say, 'Peace be to this house.'[439] And if the son of peace be there, your peace shall rest upon it, if not, it shall turn to you again. And in the same house remain, eating and drinking such things as they give, for the labourer is worthy of his hire. Go not from house to house. And into whatsoever city ye enter, and they receive you, eat such things as are set before you, and heal the sick that are therein, and say unto them, 'The kingdom of God is come nigh unto you.' But into whatsoever city ye enter, and they receive you not, go your ways out into the streets of the same, and say, 'Even the very dust of your city, which cleaveth on us, we do wipe off against you, notwithstanding, be ye sure of this, that the kingdom of God is come nigh unto you.' But I say unto you, that it shall be more tolerable in that day for Sodom,[440] than for that city. He that heareth you heareth me, and he that despiseth you despiseth me, and he that despiseth me despiseth him that sent me."

---

[439] Compare <u>1 Samuel 25:5-6:</u> "And David sent out ten young men, and David said unto the young men, 'Get you up to Carmel, and go to Nabal, and greet him in my name. And thus shall ye say to him that liveth in prosperity, "Peace be both to thee, and peace be to thine house, and peace be unto all that thou hast."'"

[440] Compare <u>Ezekiel 16:49-50:</u> "Behold, this was the iniquity of thy sister Sodom, pride, fulness of bread, and abundance of idleness was in her and in her daughters, neither did she strengthen the hand of the poor and needy. And they were haughty, and committed abomination before me; therefore I took them away as I saw good." <u>Genesis 19:24-25:</u> "Then the LORD rained upon Sodom and upon Gomorrah brimstone and fire from the LORD out of heaven; and he overthrew those cities, and all the plain, and all the inhabitants of the cities, and that which grew upon the ground."

And he said unto them, "I beheld Satan as lightning fall from heaven.⁴⁴¹ Behold, I give unto you power to tread on serpents and scorpions, and over all the power of the enemy, and nothing shall by any means hurt you. Therefore I say unto you, take no thought for your life, what ye shall eat, neither for the body, what ye shall put on. The life is more than meat, and the body is more than raiment. Consider the ravens,⁴⁴² for they neither sow nor reap, which neither have storehouse nor barn, and God feedeth them, how much more are ye better than the fowls? And which of you with taking thought can add to his stature one cubit? If ye then be not able to do that thing which is least, why take ye thought for the rest? Consider the lilies how they grow, they toil not, they spin not, and yet I say unto you, that Solomon in all his glory⁴⁴³ was not arrayed like one of these. If then God so clothe the grass, which is to day in the field, and to morrow is cast into the oven, how much more will he clothe you, O ye of little faith? And seek ye not what ye shall eat, or what ye shall drink, neither be ye of doubtful mind. For all these things do the nations of the world seek after, and your Father knoweth that ye have need of these things. But rather seek ye the kingdom of God, and all these things shall be added unto you.⁴⁴⁴ Fear not, little flock,

---

⁴⁴¹ Compare Isaiah 14:12-15: "How art thou fallen from heaven, O Lucifer, son of the morning! How art thou cut down to the ground, which didst weaken the nations! For thou hast said in thine heart, 'I will ascend into heaven, I will exalt my throne above the stars of God. I will sit also upon the mount of the congregation, in the sides of the north. I will ascend above the heights of the clouds; I will be like the most High.' Yet thou shalt be brought down to hell, to the sides of the pit."
⁴⁴² See Psalms 147:7-9: "Sing unto the LORD with thanksgiving; sing praise upon the harp unto our God; who covereth the heaven with clouds, who prepareth rain for the earth, who maketh grass to grow upon the mountains. He giveth to the beast his food, and to the young ravens which cry."
⁴⁴³ See 1 Kings 10:1-29; 2 Chronicles 9:1-31.
⁴⁴⁴ See Deuteronomy 15:7-10: "If there be among you a poor man of one of thy brethren within any of thy gates in thy land which the LORD thy God giveth thee, thou shalt not harden thine heart, nor shut thine hand from thy poor brother. But thou shalt open thine hand wide unto him, and shalt surely lend him sufficient for his need, in that which he wanteth. Beware that there be not a thought in thy wicked heart, saying, 'The seventh year, the year of release, is at hand;' and thine eye be evil against thy poor brother, and thou givest him nought; and he cry unto

THE TREE OF LIFE

for it is your Father's good pleasure to give you the kingdom.[445] Sell that ye have, and give alms, provide yourselves bags which wax not old, a treasure in the heavens that faileth not, where no thief

---

the LORD against thee, and it be sin unto thee. Thou shalt surely give him, and thine heart shall not be grieved when thou givest unto him; because that for this thing the LORD thy God shall bless thee in all thy works, and in all that thou puttest thine hand unto."
Deuteronomy 28:1-6: "And it shall come to pass, if thou shalt hearken diligently unto the voice of the LORD thy God, to observe and to do all his commandments which I command thee this day, that the LORD thy God will set thee on high above all nations of the earth. And all these blessings shall come on thee, and overtake thee, if thou shalt hearken unto the voice of the LORD thy God. Blessed shalt thou be in the city, and blessed shalt thou be in the field. Blessed shall be the fruit of thy body, and the fruit of thy ground, and the fruit of thy cattle, the increase of thy kine, and the flocks of thy sheep. Blessed shall be thy basket and thy store. Blessed shalt thou be when thou comest in, and blessed shalt thou be when thou goest out."
Proverbs 3:9-10: "Honour the LORD with thy substance, and with the firstfruits of all thine increase. So shall thy barns be filled with plenty, and thy presses shall burst out with new wine."
Sirach 35:10-11: "Give unto the most High according as he hath enriched thee; and as thou hast gotten, give with a cheerful eye. For the Lord recompenseth, and will give thee seven times as much."
Tobit 12:8-13: "Prayer is good with fasting and alms and righteousness. A little with righteousness is better than much with unrighteousness. It is better to give alms than to lay up gold. Help the poor for the commandment's sake, and turn him not away because of his poverty. Lose thy money for thy brother and thy friend, and let it not rust under a stone to be lost. Lay up thy treasure according to the commandments of the most High, and it shall bring thee more profit than gold. Shut up alms in thy storehouses, and it shall deliver thee from all affliction. It shall fight for thee against thine enemies better than a mighty shield and strong spear."
[445] See Daniel 7:27: "And the kingdom and dominion, and the greatness of the kingdom under the whole heaven, shall be given to the people of the saints of the most High, whose kingdom is an everlasting kingdom, and all dominions shall serve and obey him."

approacheth, neither moth corrupteth.⁴⁴⁶ For where your treasure is, there will your heart be also.⁴⁴⁷

"Let your loins be girded about, and your lights burning. And ye yourselves like unto men that wait for their lord, when he will return from the wedding, that when he cometh and knocketh, they may open unto him immediately. Blessed are those servants, whom the lord when he cometh shall find watching, verily I say unto you, that he shall gird himself, and make them to sit down to meat, and will come forth and serve them.⁴⁴⁸ And if he shall come in the second watch, or come in the third watch, and find them so, blessed are those servants. And this know, that if the goodman of the house had known what hour the thief would come, he would have watched, and not have suffered his house to be broken through. Be ye therefore ready also, for the Son of man cometh at an hour when ye think not."

Then Peter said unto him, "Lord, speakest thou this parable unto us, or even to all?" And the Lord said, "Who then is that faithful and wise steward, whom his lord shall make ruler over his household, to give them their portion of meat in due season? Blessed is that servant, whom his lord when he cometh shall find so doing. Of a truth I say unto you, that he will make him ruler over all

---

⁴⁴⁶ Compare *Tobit* 4:7-10: "Give alms of thy substance; and when thou givest alms, let not thine eye be envious, neither turn thy face from any poor, and the face of God shall not be turned away from thee. If thou hast abundance give alms accordingly; if thou have but a little, be not afraid to give according to that little; for thou layest up a good treasure for thyself against the day of necessity. Because that alms do deliver from death, and suffereth not to come into darkness."
⁴⁴⁷ Compare Proverbs 23:7: "For as he thinketh in his heart, so is he. 'Eat and drink,' saith he to thee; but his heart is not with thee."
⁴⁴⁸ See Isaiah 25:6-8: "And in this mountain shall the LORD of hosts make unto all people a feast of fat things, a feast of wines on the lees, of fat things full of marrow, of wines on the lees well refined. And he will destroy in this mountain the face of the covering cast over all people, and the vail that is spread over all nations. He will swallow up death in victory; and the Lord GOD will wipe away tears from off all faces; and the rebuke of his people shall he take away from off all the earth; for the LORD hath spoken it."

that he hath. But if that servant say in his heart, 'My lord delayeth his coming,' and shall begin to beat the menservants and maidens, and to eat and drink, and to be drunken, the lord of that servant will come in a day when he looketh not for him, and at an hour when he is not aware, and will cut him in sunder, and will appoint him his portion with the unbelievers. And that servant, which knew his lord's will, and prepared not himself, neither did according to his will, shall be beaten with many stripes. But he that knew not, and did commit things worthy of stripes, shall be beaten with few stripes. For unto whomsoever much is given, of him shall be much required, and to whom men have committed much, of him they will ask the more."

And he said also to the people, "When ye see a cloud rise out of the west, straightway ye say, 'There cometh a shower,' and so it is. And when ye see the south wind blow, ye say, 'There will be heat,' and it cometh to pass. Ye hypocrites, ye can discern the face of the sky and of the earth, but how is it that ye do not discern this time? Yea, and why even of yourselves judge ye not what is right?

"When thou goest with thine adversary to the magistrate, as thou art in the way, give diligence that thou mayest be delivered from him, lest he hale thee to the judge, and the judge deliver thee to the officer, and the officer cast thee into prison. I tell thee, thou shalt not depart thence, till thou hast paid the very last mite."

Chapter Fifty Two

And there went great multitudes with him, and he turned, and said unto them, "If any man come to me, and hate not his father, and mother, and wife, and children, and brethren, and sisters, yea, and his own life also, he cannot be my disciple.[449] And whosoever doth not bear his cross, and come after me, cannot be my disciple. I am come to send fire on the earth,[450] and what will

---

[449] Compare Genesis 22:1-2,9-12,15-17: "And it came to pass after these things, that God did tempt Abraham, and said unto him, 'Abraham;' and he said, 'Behold, here I am.' And he said, 'Take now thy son, thine only son Isaac, whom thou lovest, and get thee into the land of Moriah; and offer him there for a burnt offering upon one of the mountains which I will tell thee of.' And they came to the place which God had told him of; and Abraham built an altar there, and laid the wood in order, and bound Isaac his son, and laid him on the altar upon the wood. And Abraham stretched forth his hand, and took the knife to slay his son. And the angel of the LORD called unto him out of heaven, and said, 'Abraham, Abraham;' and he said, 'Here am I.' And he said, 'Lay not thine hand upon the lad, neither do thou any thing unto him; for now I know that thou fearest God, seeing thou hast not withheld thy son, thine only son from me.' And the angel of the LORD called unto Abraham out of heaven the second time, and said, 'By myself have I sworn, saith the LORD, for because thou hast done this thing, and hast not withheld thy son, thine only son; that in blessing I will bless thee, and in multiplying I will multiply thy seed as the stars of the heaven, and as the sand which is upon the sea shore; and thy seed shall possess the gate of his enemies.'"
[450] Compare Isaiah 66:15-16: "For, behold, the LORD will come with fire, and with his chariots like a whirlwind, to render his anger with fury, and his rebuke with flames of fire. For by fire and by his sword will the LORD plead with all flesh; and the slain of the LORD shall be many."
2 Esdras 16:53-54,63-64: "Let not the sinner say that he hath not sinned; for God shall burn coals of fire upon his head, which saith before the Lord God and his

I, if it be already kindled? But I have a baptism to be baptized with, and how am I straitened till it be accomplished! Suppose ye that I am come to give peace on earth? I tell you, nay, but rather division. For from henceforth there shall be five in one house divided, three against two, and two against three. *The father shall be divided against the son, and the son against the father, the mother against the daughter, and the daughter against the mother, the mother in law against her daughter in law, and the daughter in law against her mother in law.*[451]

---

glory, 'I have not sinned.' Behold, the Lord knoweth all the works of men, their imaginations, their thoughts, and their hearts. Surely he knoweth your inventions, and what ye think in your hearts, even them that sin, and would hide their sin. Therefore hath the Lord exactly searched out all your works, and he will put you all to shame."

2 *Esdras* 13:3-4,10-11,20,26-29,37-38: "And I beheld, and, lo, that man waxed strong with the thousands of heaven; and when he turned his countenance to look, all the things trembled that were seen under him. And whensoever the voice went out of his mouth, all they burned that heard his voice, like as the earth faileth when it feeleth the fire. But only I saw that he sent out of his mouth as it had been a blast of fire, and out of his lips a flaming breath, and out of his tongue he cast out sparks and tempests. And they were all mixed together; the blast of fire, the flaming breath, and the great tempest; and fell with violence upon the multitude which was prepared to fight, and burned them up every one, so that upon a sudden of an innumerable multitude nothing was to be perceived, but only dust and smell of smoke. When I saw this I was afraid. And he said unto me, 'The same is he whom God the Highest hath kept a great season, which by his own self shall deliver his creature; and he shall order them that are left behind. And whereas thou sawest, that out of his mouth there came as a blast of wind, and fire, and storm; and that he held neither sword, nor any instrument of war, but that the rushing in of him destroyed the whole multitude that came to subdue him; this is the interpretation: Behold, the days come, when the most High will begin to deliver them that are upon the earth. And this my Son shall rebuke the wicked inventions of those nations, which for their wicked life are fallen into the tempest; And shall lay before them their evil thoughts, and the torments wherewith they shall begin to be tormented, which are like unto a flame, and he shall destroy them without labour by the law which is like unto me.'"

[451] See Micah 7:5-6: "Trust ye not in a friend, put ye not confidence in a guide; keep the doors of thy mouth from her that lieth in thy bosom. For the son dishonoureth the father, the daughter riseth up against her mother, the daughter in law against her mother in law; a man's enemies are the men of his own house."
See also Ezekiel 38:21: "And I will call for a sword against him throughout all my mountains, saith the Lord GOD; every man's sword shall be against his brother."

THE TREE OF LIFE

"For which of you, intending to build a tower, sitteth not down first, and counteth the cost, whether he have sufficient to finish it? Lest haply, after he hath laid the foundation, and is not able to finish it, all that behold it begin to mock him, saying, 'This man began to build, and was not able to finish.'

"Or what king, going to make war against another king, sitteth not down first, and consulteth whether he be able with ten thousand to meet him that cometh against him with twenty thousand? Or else, while the other is yet a great way off, he sendeth an ambassage, and desireth conditions of peace. So likewise, whosoever he be of you that forsaketh not all that he hath, he cannot be my disciple."[452]

---

[452] Compare <u>Sirach 7:36:</u> "Whatsoever thou takest in hand, remember the end, and thou shalt never do amiss."

THE TREE OF LIFE

THE TREE OF LIFE

Chapter Fifty Three

And it came to pass, that, as he was praying in a certain place, when he ceased, one of his disciples said unto him, "Lord, teach us to pray, as John also taught his disciples." And he said unto them, "When ye pray, say,

> 'Our Father which art in heaven,[453] hallowed be thy name.[454] Thy kingdom come.[455] Thy will be done, as

---

[453] Compare <u>Malachi 2:10:</u> "Have we not all one father? Hath not one God created us? Why do we deal treacherously every man against his brother, by profaning the covenant of our fathers?"
<u>2 Esdras 1:28-29:</u> "Thus saith the Almighty Lord, Have I not prayed you as a father his sons, as a mother her daughters, and a nurse her young babes, that ye would be my people, and I should be your God; that ye would be my children, and I should be your father?"
[454] Compare <u>Leviticus 22:31-33:</u> "Therefore shall ye keep my commandments, and do them. I am the LORD. Neither shall ye profane my holy name; but I will be hallowed among the children of Israel. I am the LORD which hallow you, that brought you out of the land of Egypt, to be your God. I am the LORD."
<u>Isaiah 57:15:</u> "For thus saith the high and lofty One that inhabiteth eternity, whose name is Holy; I dwell in the high and holy place, with him also that is of a contrite and humble spirit, to revive the spirit of the humble, and to revive the heart of the contrite ones."
<u>1 Kings 8:17:</u> "And it was in the heart of David my father to build an house for the name of the LORD God of Israel."
<u>Psalms 148:13:</u> "Let them praise the name of the LORD; for his name alone is excellent; his glory is above the earth and heaven."

in heaven, so in earth.[456] Give us day by day our daily bread.[457] And forgive us our sins, for we also forgive every one that is indebted to us.[458] And lead us not into temptation, but deliver us from evil.'"[459]

And he said unto them, "Which of you shall have a friend, and shall go unto him at midnight, and say unto him, 'Friend, lend me three loaves, for a friend of mine in his journey is come to me, and I have nothing to set before him.' And he from within shall answer and say, 'Trouble me not, the door is now shut, and my children are with me in bed, I cannot rise and give thee.' I say unto you, though he will not rise and give him because he is his friend, yet because of his importunity he will rise and give him as many as he needeth. And I say unto you, ask, and it shall be given you, seek, and ye shall find, knock, and it shall be opened unto you. For every one that asketh receiveth, and he that seeketh findeth, and to him that knocketh it shall be opened. If a son shall ask bread of any of you that is a father,

---

[455] Compare Daniel 2:44: "And in the days of these kings shall the God of heaven set up a kingdom, which shall never be destroyed. And the kingdom shall not be left to other people, but it shall break in pieces and consume all these kingdoms, and it shall stand for ever."
Numbers 14:21: "But as truly as I live, all the earth shall be filled with the glory of the LORD."
Joel 2:28-29: "And it shall come to pass afterward, that I will pour out my spirit upon all flesh; and your sons and your daughters shall prophesy, your old men shall dream dreams, your young men shall see visions; and also upon the servants and upon the handmaids in those days will I pour out my spirit."
[456] Compare Psalms 103:19-20: "The LORD hath prepared his throne in the heavens; and his kingdom ruleth over all. Bless the LORD, ye his angels, that excel in strength, that do his commandments, hearkening unto the voice of his word."
Prayer of Manasses 1:15: "Therefore I will praise thee for ever all the days of my life; for all the powers of the heavens do praise thee, and thine is the glory for ever and ever. Amen."
[457] Compare Exodus 16:4: "Then said the LORD unto Moses, 'Behold, I will rain bread from heaven for you; and the people shall go out and gather a certain rate every day, that I may prove them, whether they will walk in my law, or no.'"
[458] Compare Sirach 28:2: "Forgive thy neighbour the hurt that he hath done unto thee, so shall thy sins also be forgiven when thou prayest."
[459] Compare Psalms 140:1: "Deliver me, O LORD, from the evil man; preserve me from the violent man."

will he give him a stone? Or if he ask a fish, will he for a fish give him a serpent? Or if he shall ask an egg, will he offer him a scorpion? If ye then, being evil, know how to give good gifts unto your children, how much more shall your heavenly Father give the Holy Spirit to them that ask him?"[460]

---

[460] Compare Psalms 145:18: "The LORD is nigh unto all them that call upon him, to all that call upon him in truth."
Isaiah 55:6: "Seek ye the LORD while he may be found, call ye upon him while he is near."
Jeremiah 23:23-24: "Am I a God at hand, saith the LORD, and not a God afar off? Can any hide himself in secret places that I shall not see him? saith the LORD. Do not I fill heaven and earth? saith the LORD."

THE TREE OF LIFE

Chapter Fifty Four

There were present at that season some that told him of the Galilaeans, whose blood Pilate had mingled with their sacrifices. And Jesus answering said unto them, "Suppose ye that these Galilaeans were sinners above all the Galilaeans, because they suffered such things? I tell you, nay, but, except ye repent, ye shall all likewise perish. Or those eighteen, upon whom the tower in Siloam fell, and slew them, think ye that they were sinners above all men that dwelt in Jerusalem? I tell you, nay, but, except ye repent, ye shall all likewise perish."

He spake also this parable, "A certain man had a fig tree planted in his vineyard, and he came and sought fruit thereon, and found none. Then said he unto the dresser of his vineyard, 'Behold, these three years I come seeking fruit on this fig tree, and find none. Cut it down, why cumbereth it the ground?' And he answering said unto him, 'Lord, let it alone this year also, till I shall dig about it, and dung it, and if it bear fruit, well, and if not, then after that thou shalt cut it down.'"[461]

---

[461] Compare Isaiah 5:7: "For the vineyard of the LORD of hosts is the house of Israel, and the men of Judah his pleasant plant. And he looked for judgment, but behold oppression; for righteousness, but behold a cry."
2 Esdras 9:30-31: "And thou spakest saying, 'Hear me, O Israel; and mark my words, thou seed of Jacob. For, behold, I sow my law in you, and it shall bring fruit in you, and ye shall be honoured in it for ever.'"

THE TREE OF LIFE

Chapter Fifty Five

Now it came to pass, as they went, that he entered into a certain village, and a certain woman named Martha received him into her house. And she had a sister called Mary, which also sat at Jesus' feet, and heard his word. But Martha was cumbered about much serving, and came to him, and said, "Lord, dost thou not care that my sister hath left me to serve alone? Bid her therefore that she help me." And Jesus answered and said unto her, "Martha, Martha, thou art careful and troubled about many things, but one thing is needful, and Mary hath chosen that good part, which shall not be taken away from her."

THE TREE OF LIFE

Chapter Fifty Six

And the seventy returned again with joy, saying, "Lord, even the devils are subject unto us through thy name." And Jesus answered and said, "Notwithstanding in this rejoice not, that the spirits are subject unto you, but rather rejoice, because your names are written in heaven."[462]

In that hour Jesus rejoiced in spirit, and said, "I thank thee, O Father, Lord of heaven and earth, that thou hast hid these things from the wise and prudent, and hast revealed them unto babes, even so, Father, for so it seemed good in thy sight.

---

[462] See <u>Exodus 32:31-33:</u> "And Moses returned unto the LORD, and said, 'Oh, this people have sinned a great sin, and have made them gods of gold. Yet now, if thou wilt forgive their sin--; and if not, blot me, I pray thee, out of thy book which thou hast written.' And the LORD said unto Moses, 'Whosoever hath sinned against me, him will I blot out of my book.'"
<u>Psalms 69:28:</u> "Let them be blotted out of the book of the living, and not be written with the righteous."
<u>Daniel 12:1:</u> "And at that time shall Michael stand up, the great prince which standeth for the children of thy people; and there shall be a time of trouble, such as never was since there was a nation even to that same time; and at that time thy people shall be delivered, every one that shall be found written in the book."
<u>2 Esdras 14:34-35:</u> "Therefore if so be that ye will subdue your own understanding, and reform your hearts, ye shall be kept alive and after death ye shall obtain mercy. For after death shall the judgment come, when we shall live again; and then shall the names of the righteous be manifest, and the works of the ungodly shall be declared."

THE TREE OF LIFE

"All things are delivered to me of my Father, and no man knoweth who the Son is, but the Father, and who the Father is, but the Son, and he to whom the Son will reveal him. For no man hath seen the Father at any time, but the only begotten Son, which is in the bosom of the Father, he hath declared him."

And he turned him unto his disciples, and said privately, "Blessed are the eyes which see the things that ye see, for I tell you, that many prophets and kings have desired to see those things which ye see, and have not seen them, and to hear those things which ye hear, and have not heard them."[463]

And he said unto the disciples, "But the days will come, when ye shall desire to see one of the days of the Son of man, and ye shall not see it."

---

[463] Compare 2 Esdras 13:51-56: "Then said I, 'O Lord that bearest rule, shew me this: Wherefore have I seen the man coming up from the midst of the sea?' And he said unto me, 'Like as thou canst neither seek out nor know the things that are in the deep of the sea; even so can no man upon earth see my Son, or those that be with him, but in the day time. This is the interpretation of the dream which thou sawest, and whereby thou only art here lightened. For thou hast forsaken thine own way, and applied thy diligence unto my law, and sought it. Thy life hast thou ordered in wisdom, and hast called understanding thy mother. And therefore have I shewed thee the treasures of the Highest; after other three days I will speak other things unto thee, and declare unto thee mighty and wondrous things.'"

THE TREE OF LIFE

Chapter Fifty Seven

And, behold, a certain lawyer stood up, and tempted him, saying, "Master, what shall I do to inherit eternal life?" He said unto him, "What is written in the law? How readest thou?" And he answering said, "*Thou shalt love the Lord thy God with all thy heart, and with all thy soul, and with all thy strength, and with all thy mind,*⁴⁶⁴ and *thy neighbour as thyself.*"⁴⁶⁵ And he said unto him, "Thou hast answered right, this do, and thou shalt live."

But he, willing to justify himself, said unto Jesus, "And who is my neighbour?"

And Jesus answering said, "A certain man went down from Jerusalem to Jericho, and fell among thieves, which stripped him of

---

⁴⁶⁴ "And thou shalt love the LORD thy God with all thine heart, and with all thy soul, and with all thy might." – <u>Deuteronomy 6:5</u>
"And now, Israel, what doth the LORD thy God require of thee, but to fear the LORD thy God, to walk in all his ways, and to love him, and to serve the LORD thy God with all thy heart and with all thy soul," – <u>Deuteronomy 10:12</u>
"But take diligent heed to do the commandment and the law, which Moses the servant of the LORD charged you, to love the LORD your God, and to walk in all his ways, and to keep his commandments, and to cleave unto him, and to serve him with all your heart and with all your soul." – <u>Joshua 22:5</u>
⁴⁶⁵ "Thou shalt not hate thy brother in thine heart; thou shalt in any wise rebuke thy neighbour, and not suffer sin upon him. Thou shalt not avenge, nor bear any grudge against the children of thy people, but thou shalt love thy neighbour as thyself: I am the LORD." – <u>Leviticus 19:17-18</u>
"Love thine own soul, and comfort thy heart, remove sorrow far from thee; for sorrow hath killed many, and there is no profit therein." – *<u>Sirach 30:23</u>*

his raiment, and wounded him, and departed, leaving him half dead. And by chance, there came down a certain priest that way, and when he saw him, he passed by on the other side. And likewise a Levite, when he was at the place, came and looked on him, and passed by on the other side. But a certain Samaritan, as he journeyed, came where he was, and when he saw him, he had compassion on him, and went to him, and bound up his wounds, pouring in oil and wine, and set him on his own beast, and brought him to an inn, and took care of him. And on the morrow when he departed, he took out two pence, and gave them to the host, and said unto him, 'Take care of him, and whatsoever thou spendest more, when I come again, I will repay thee.' Which now of these three, thinkest thou, was neighbour unto him that fell among the thieves?" And he said, "He that shewed mercy on him." Then said Jesus unto him, "Go, and do thou likewise."

Chapter Fifty Eight

And as he spake, a certain Pharisee besought him to dine with him, and he went in, and sat down to meat. And when the Pharisee saw it, he marvelled that he had not first washed before dinner.

And the Lord said unto him, "Now do ye Pharisees make clean the outside of the cup and the platter, but your inward part is full of ravening and wickedness. Ye fools, did not he that made that which is without make that which is within also? But rather give alms of such things as ye have, and, behold, all things are clean unto you.[466]

"But woe unto you, Pharisees! For ye tithe mint and rue and all manner of herbs, and pass over judgment and the love of God. These ought ye to have done,[467] and not to leave the other undone. Woe unto you, Pharisees! For ye love the uppermost seats in the synagogues, and greetings in the markets. Woe unto you, scribes

---

[466] Compare <u>Tobit 12:9:</u> "For alms doth deliver from death, and shall purge away all sin. Those that exercise alms and righteousness shall be filled with life."
<u>Sirach 3:30:</u> "Water will quench a flaming fire; and alms maketh an atonement for sins."
[467] See <u>Leviticus 27:30:</u> "And all the tithe of the land, whether of the seed of the land, or of the fruit of the tree, is the LORD'S; it is holy unto the LORD."
<u>Deuteronomy 14:22-23:</u> "Thou shalt truly tithe all the increase of thy seed, that the field bringeth forth year by year. And thou shalt eat before the LORD thy God, in the place which he shall choose to place his name there, the tithe of thy corn, of thy wine, and of thine oil, and the firstlings of thy herds and of thy flocks; that thou mayest learn to fear the LORD thy God always."

and Pharisees, hypocrites!⁴⁶⁸ For ye are as graves which appear not, and the men that walk over them are not aware of them."⁴⁶⁹

Then answered one of the lawyers, and said unto him, "Master, thus saying thou reproachest us also." And he said, "Woe unto you also, ye lawyers! For ye lade men with burdens grievous to be borne, and ye yourselves touch not the burdens with one of your fingers. Woe unto you! For ye build the sepulchres of the prophets, and your fathers killed them. Truly ye bear witness that ye allow the deeds of your fathers, for they indeed killed them, and ye build their sepulchres. Therefore also said the wisdom of God, 'I will send them prophets and apostles, and some of them they shall slay and persecute,'⁴⁷⁰ Woe unto you, lawyers! For ye have taken away the key of knowledge, ye entered not in yourselves, and them that were entering in ye hindered."

And as he said these things unto them, the scribes and the Pharisees began to urge him vehemently, and to provoke him to speak of many things, laying wait for him, and seeking to catch something out of his mouth, that they might accuse him.

In the mean time, when there were gathered together an innumerable multitude of people, insomuch that they trode one upon another, he began to say unto his disciples first of all, "Beware ye of the leaven of the Pharisees, which is hypocrisy.⁴⁷¹ For there is nothing covered, that shall not be revealed, neither hid, that shall not be known. Therefore, whatsoever ye have spoken in darkness

---

⁴⁶⁸ Compare Job 13:16: "He also shall be my salvation; for an hypocrite shall not come before him."
Job 27:8: "For what is the hope of the hypocrite, though he hath gained, when God taketh away his soul?"
⁴⁶⁹ See Numbers 19:16: "And whosoever toucheth one that is slain with a sword in the open fields, or a dead body, or a bone of a man, or a grave, shall be unclean seven days."
⁴⁷⁰ See 1 Kings 18:13; 2 Chronicles 24:20-21, 16:10; Isaiah 66:5,13-14; Jeremiah 11:21, 20:2, 37:13-15; Daniel 6:13-16; Amos 7:10-13; et cetera.
⁴⁷¹ Compare Sirach 32:15: "He that seeketh the law shall be filled therewith; but the hypocrite will be offended thereat."

THE TREE OF LIFE

shall be heard in the light, and that which ye have spoken in the ear in closets shall be proclaimed upon the housetops.[472]

"And I say unto you my friends, be not afraid of them that kill the body, and after that have no more that they can do. But I will forewarn you whom ye shall fear, fear him, which after he hath killed, hath power to cast into hell, yea, I say unto you, fear him.[473]

"Are not five sparrows sold for two farthings, and not one of them is forgotten before God? But even the very hairs of your head are all numbered. Fear not therefore, ye are of more value than many sparrows."

---

[472] Compare Proverbs 20:27: "The spirit of man is the candle of the LORD, searching all the inward parts of the belly."
Ecclesiastes 12:14: "For God shall bring every work into judgment, with every secret thing, whether it be good, or whether it be evil."
2 Samuel 12:11-12: "Thus saith the LORD, 'Behold, I will raise up evil against thee out of thine own house, and I will take thy wives before thine eyes, and give them unto thy neighbour, and he shall lie with thy wives in the sight of this sun. For thou didst it secretly; but I will do this thing before all Israel, and before the sun.'"
Wisdom 1:8,11: "Therefore he that speaketh unrighteous things cannot be hid; neither shall vengeance, when it punisheth, pass by him. Therefore beware of murmuring, which is unprofitable; and refrain your tongue from backbiting; for there is no word so secret, that shall go for nought; and the mouth that belieth slayeth the soul."
Sirach 42:18-20: "He seeketh out the deep, and the heart, and considereth their crafty devices; for the Lord knoweth all that may be known, and he beholdeth the signs of the world. He declareth the things that are past, and for to come, and revealeth the steps of hidden things. No thought escapeth him, neither any word is hidden from him."
[473] Compare Isaiah 45:5,7: "I am the LORD, and there is none else, there is no God beside me; I girded thee, though thou hast not known me; I form the light, and create darkness; I make peace, and create evil; I the LORD do all these things."
Ecclesiastes 12:13: "Let us hear the conclusion of the whole matter: Fear God, and keep his commandments; for this is the whole duty of man."
Psalms 9:17: "The wicked shall be turned into hell, and all the nations that forget God."

THE TREE OF LIFE

And one of the company said unto him, "Master, speak to my brother, that he divide the inheritance with me." And he said unto him, "Man, who made me a judge or a divider over you?"[474]

And he said unto them, "Take heed, and beware of covetousness, for a man's life consisteth not in the abundance of the things which he possesseth." And he spake a parable unto them, saying, "The ground of a certain rich man brought forth plentifully. And he thought within himself, saying, 'What shall I do, because I have no room where to bestow my fruits?' And he said, 'This will I do, I will pull down my barns, and build greater, and there will I bestow all my fruits and my goods. And I will say to my soul, "Soul, thou hast much goods laid up for many years, take thine ease, *eat, drink, and be merry*.'"[475] But God said unto him, 'Thou fool, this night thy soul shall be required of thee, then whose shall those things be, which thou hast provided?'[476] So is he that layeth up treasure for himself, and is not rich toward God."[477]

---

[474] Compare Exodus 2:13-14: "And when he went out the second day, behold, two men of the Hebrews strove together; and he said to him that did the wrong, 'Wherefore smitest thou thy fellow?' And he said, 'Who made thee a prince and a judge over us? Intendest thou to kill me, as thou killedst the Egyptian?' And Moses feared, and said, 'Surely this thing is known.'"
[475] See Ecclesiastes 8:15: "Then I commended mirth, because a man hath no better thing under the sun, than to eat, and to drink, and to be merry; for that shall abide with him of his labour the days of his life, which God giveth him under the sun."
[476] Compare Job 21:13: "They spend their days in wealth, and in a moment go down to the grave."
Psalms 39:6: "Surely every man walketh in a vain shew; surely they are disquieted in vain; he heapeth up riches, and knoweth not who shall gather them."
[477] Compare Proverbs 13:7: "There is that maketh himself rich, yet hath nothing; there is that maketh himself poor, yet hath great riches."
Tobit 4:8-10: "If thou hast abundance give alms accordingly; if thou have but a little, be not afraid to give according to that little. For thou layest up a good treasure for thyself against the day of necessity. Because that alms do deliver from death, and suffereth not to come into darkness."

THE TREE OF LIFE

Chapter Fifty Nine

And he went through the cities and villages, teaching, and journeying toward Jerusalem. And he was teaching in one of the synagogues on the sabbath. And, behold, there was a woman which had a spirit of infirmity eighteen years, and was bowed together, and could in no wise lift up herself. And when Jesus saw her, he called her to him, and said unto her, "Woman, thou art loosed from thine infirmity." And he laid his hands on her, and immediately she was made straight,[478] and glorified God.

And the ruler of the synagogue answered with indignation, because that Jesus had healed on the sabbath day, and said unto the people, "There are six days in which men ought to work,[479] in them therefore come and be healed, and not on the sabbath day."

The Lord then answered him, and said, "Thou hypocrite, doth not each one of you on the sabbath loose his ox or his ass from the stall, and lead him away to watering? And ought not this woman, being a daughter of Abraham, whom Satan hath bound, lo, these eighteen years, be loosed from this bond on the sabbath day?"

---

[478] See Psalms 146:8: "The LORD openeth the eyes of the blind; the LORD raiseth them that are bowed down; the LORD loveth the righteous."
[479] See Exodus 20:9-10: "Six days shalt thou labour, and do all thy work. But the seventh day is the sabbath of the LORD thy God; in it thou shalt not do any work, thou, nor thy son, nor thy daughter, thy manservant, nor thy maidservant, nor thy cattle, nor thy stranger that is within thy gates."

THE TREE OF LIFE

And when he had said these things, all his adversaries were ashamed, and all the people rejoiced for all the glorious things that were done by him.

Then said one unto him, "Lord, are there few that be saved?"[480] And he said unto them, "Strive to enter in at the strait gate, for many, I say unto you, will seek to enter in, and shall not be able.[481] When once the master of the house is risen up, and hath shut the door, and ye begin to stand without, and to knock at the door, saying, 'Lord, Lord, open unto us,' he shall answer and say unto you, 'I know you not whence ye are.' Then shall ye begin to say, 'We have eaten and drunk in thy presence, and thou hast taught in our streets.' But he shall say, 'I tell you, I know you not whence ye

---

[480] See *2 Esdras 9:14-15:* "I have said before, and now do speak, and will speak it also hereafter, that there be many more of them which perish, than of them which shall be saved; like as a wave is greater than a drop."
2 Esdras 8:1-3: "And he answered me, saying, 'The most High hath made this world for many, but the world to come for few. I will tell thee a similitude, Esdras; as when thou askest the earth, it shall say unto thee, that it giveth much mould whereof earthen vessels are made, but little dust that gold cometh of; even so is the course of this present world. There be many created, but few shall be saved.'
2 Esdras 8:41: "For as the husbandman soweth much seed upon the ground, and planteth many trees, and yet the thing that is sown good in his season cometh not up, neither doth all that is planted take root; even so is it of them that are sown in the world; they shall not all be saved."
[481] Compare *2 Esdras 7:3-14:* "And I said, 'Speak on, my God.' Then said he unto me, 'The sea is set in a wide place, that it might be deep and great. But put the case the entrance were narrow, and like a river; who then could go into the sea to look upon it, and to rule it? If he went not through the narrow, how could he come into the broad? There is also another thing: A city is builded, and set upon a broad field, and is full of all good things; the entrance thereof is narrow, and is set in a dangerous place to fall, like as if there were a fire on the right hand, and on the left a deep water; and one only path between them both, even between the fire and the water, so small that there could but one man go there at once. If this city now were given unto a man for an inheritance, if he never shall pass the danger set before it, how shall he receive this inheritance?' And I said, 'It is so, Lord.' Then said he unto me, 'Even so also is Israel's portion. Because for their sakes I made the world; and when Adam transgressed my statutes, then was decreed that now is done. Then were the entrances of this world made narrow, full of sorrow and travail; they are but few and evil, full of perils, and very painful. For the entrances of the elder world were wide and sure, and brought immortal fruit. If then they that live labour not to enter these strait and vain things, they can never receive those that are laid up for them.'"

THE TREE OF LIFE

are, *depart from me, all ye workers of iniquity.*'[482] There shall be weeping and *gnashing of teeth*,[483] when ye shall see Abraham, and Isaac, and Jacob, and all the prophets, in the kingdom of God, and you yourselves thrust out.[484] And they shall come from the east, and from the west, and from the north, and from the south,[485] and shall sit down[486] in the kingdom of God. And, behold, there are last which shall be first, and there are first which shall be last."

---

[482] See Psalms 6:8: "Depart from me, all ye workers of iniquity; for the LORD hath heard the voice of my weeping."
[483] See Psalms 112:4,10: "Unto the upright there ariseth light in the darkness; he is gracious, and full of compassion, and righteous. The wicked shall see it, and be grieved; he shall gnash with his teeth, and melt away; the desire of the wicked shall perish."
[484] Compare Malachi 1:6-11: "A son honoureth his father, and a servant his master; if then I be a father, where is mine honour? And if I be a master, where is my fear? saith the LORD of hosts unto you, O priests, that despise my name. And ye say, 'Wherein have we despised thy name?' Ye offer polluted bread upon mine altar; and ye say, 'Wherein have we polluted thee?' In that ye say, 'The table of the LORD is contemptible.' Who is there even among you that would shut the doors for nought? neither do ye kindle fire on mine altar for nought. I have no pleasure in you, saith the LORD of hosts, neither will I accept an offering at your hand. For from the rising of the sun even unto the going down of the same my name shall be great among the Gentiles; and in every place incense shall be offered unto my name, and a pure offering; for my name shall be great among the heathen, saith the LORD of hosts."
2 Esdras 1:35-40: "Your houses will I give to a people that shall come; which not having heard of me yet shall believe me; to whom I have shewed no signs, yet they shall do that I have commanded them. They have seen no prophets, yet they shall call their sins to remembrance, and acknowledge them. I take to witness the grace of the people to come, whose little ones rejoice in gladness; and though they have not seen me with bodily eyes, yet in spirit they believe the thing that I say. And now, brother, behold what glory; and see the people that come from the east. Unto whom I will give for leaders, Abraham, Isaac, and Jacob, Hosea, Amos, and Micah, Joel, Obadiah, and Jonah, Nahum, and Habakkuk, Zephaniah, Haggai, Zechariah, and Malachi, which is called also an angel of the Lord."
[485] See Psalms 107:1-3: "O give thanks unto the LORD, for he is good; for his mercy endureth for ever. Let the redeemed of the LORD say so, whom he hath redeemed from the hand of the enemy; and gathered them out of the lands, from the east, and from the west, from the north, and from the south."
[486] See Isaiah 25:6-8: "And in this mountain shall the LORD of hosts make unto all people a feast of fat things, a feast of wines on the lees, of fat things full of marrow, of wines on the lees well refined. And he will destroy in this mountain the face of the covering cast over all people, and the vail that is spread over all nations. He will

THE TREE OF LIFE

The same day there came certain of the Pharisees, saying unto him, "Get thee out, and depart hence, for Herod will kill thee." And he said unto them, "Go ye, and tell that fox, 'Behold, I cast out devils, and I do cures to day and to morrow, and the third day I shall be perfected. Nevertheless I must walk to day, and to morrow, and the day following, for it cannot be that a prophet perish out of Jerusalem.'

"O Jerusalem, Jerusalem, which killest the prophets,[487] and stonest them that are sent unto thee, how often would I have gathered thy children together, *as a hen doth gather her brood under her wings*, and ye would not! Behold, your *house is left unto you desolate*,[488] and verily I say unto you, ye shall not see me, until the time come when ye shall say, '*Blessed is he that cometh in the name of the Lord.*'"[489]

---

swallow up death in victory; and the Lord GOD will wipe away tears from off all faces; and the rebuke of his people shall he take away from off all the earth; for the LORD hath spoken it."
[487] Compare <u>2 Esdras 15:52-56:</u> "Would I with jealousy have so proceeded against thee, saith the Lord, if thou hadst not always slain my chosen, exalting the stroke of thine hands, and saying over their dead, when thou wast drunken, 'Set forth the beauty of thy countenance?' The reward of thy whoredom shall be in thy bosom, therefore shalt thou receive recompence. Like as thou hast done unto my chosen, saith the Lord, even so shall God do unto thee, and shall deliver thee into mischief."
[488] Compare <u>2 Esdras 1:28-33:</u> "Thus saith the Almighty Lord, 'Have I not prayed you as a father his sons, as a mother her daughters, and a nurse her young babes, that ye would be my people, and I should be your God; that ye would be my children, and I should be your father? I gathered you together, as a hen gathereth her chickens under her wings; but now, what shall I do unto you? I will cast you out from my face. When ye offer unto me, I will turn my face from you; for your solemn feastdays, your new moons, and your circumcisions, have I forsaken. I sent unto you my servants the prophets, whom ye have taken and slain, and torn their bodies in pieces, whose blood I will require of your hands,' saith the Lord. Thus saith the Almighty Lord, 'Your house is desolate, I will cast you out as the wind doth stubble.'"
<u>Jeremiah 22:5:</u> "But if ye will not hear these words, I swear by myself, saith the LORD, that this house shall become a desolation."
[489] See <u>Psalms 118:25-26:</u> "Save now [Hosanna], I beseech thee, O LORD; O LORD, I beseech thee, send now prosperity. Blessed be he that cometh in the name of the LORD; we have blessed you out of the house of the LORD."

Chapter Sixty

And it came to pass, as he went into the house of one of the chief Pharisees to eat bread on the sabbath day, that they watched him. And, behold, there was a certain man before him which had the dropsy. And Jesus answering spake unto the lawyers and Pharisees, saying, "Is it lawful to heal on the sabbath day?" And they held their peace. And he took him, and healed him, and let him go, and answered them, saying, "Which of you shall have an ass or an ox fallen into a pit, and will not straightway pull him out on the sabbath day?" And they could not answer him again to these things.

And he put forth a parable to those which were bidden, when he marked how they chose out the chief rooms, saying unto them, "When thou art bidden of any man to a wedding, sit not down in the highest room,[490] lest a more honourable man than thou be bidden of him, and he that bade thee and him come and say to thee, 'Give this man place,' and thou begin with shame to take the lowest room. But when thou art bidden, go and sit down in the lowest room, that when he that bade thee cometh, he may say unto thee, 'Friend, *go up higher*,' then shalt thou have worship in the presence of them that sit at meat with thee.[491]

---

[490] Compare <u>Sirach 7:4:</u> "Seek not of the Lord preeminence, neither of the king the seat of honour."
[491] Compare <u>Proverbs 25:6-7:</u> "Put not forth thyself in the presence of the king, and stand not in the place of great men. For better it is that it be said unto thee, 'Come

"But which of you, having a servant plowing or feeding cattle, will say unto him by and by, when he is come from the field, 'Go and sit down to meat?' And will not rather say unto him, 'Make ready wherewith I may sup, and gird thyself, and serve me, till I have eaten and drunken, and afterward thou shalt eat and drink?' Doth he thank that servant because he did the things that were commanded him? I trow not. So likewise ye, when ye shall have done all those things which are commanded you, say, 'We are unprofitable servants, we have done that which was our duty to do.' For whosoever exalteth himself shall be abased, and he that humbleth himself shall be exalted."[492]

Then said he also to him that bade him, "When thou makest a dinner or a supper, call not thy friends, nor thy brethren, neither thy kinsmen, nor thy rich neighbours, lest they also bid thee again, and a

---

up hither;' than that thou shouldest be put lower in the presence of the prince whom thine eyes have seen."
[492] Compare Proverbs 16:18-19: "Pride goeth before destruction, and an haughty spirit before a fall. Better it is to be of an humble spirit with the lowly, than to divide the spoil with the proud."
Proverbs 29:23: "A man's pride shall bring him low; but honour shall uphold the humble in spirit."
Judges 6:14-16: "And the LORD looked upon [Gideon], and said, 'Go in this thy might, and thou shalt save Israel from the hand of the Midianites; have not I sent thee?' And he said unto him, 'Oh my Lord, wherewith shall I save Israel? Behold, my family is poor in Manasseh, and I am the least in my father's house.' And the LORD said unto him, 'Surely I will be with thee, and thou shalt smite the Midianites as one man.'"
Numbers 12:3: "(Now the man Moses was very meek, above all the men which were upon the face of the earth.)"
Exodus 4:10-12: "And Moses said unto the LORD, 'O my Lord, I am not eloquent, neither heretofore, nor since thou hast spoken unto thy servant; but I am slow of speech, and of a slow tongue.' And the LORD said unto him, 'Who hath made man's mouth? Or who maketh the dumb, or deaf, or the seeing, or the blind? Have not I the LORD? Now therefore go, and I will be with thy mouth, and teach thee what thou shalt say.'"
1 Samuel 16:6-7: "And it came to pass, when they were come, that [Samuel] looked on Eliab, and said, 'Surely the LORD'S anointed is before him.' But the LORD said unto Samuel, 'Look not on his countenance, or on the height of his stature; because I have refused him; for the LORD seeth not as man seeth; for man looketh on the outward appearance, but the LORD looketh on the heart.'"

recompence be made thee. But when thou makest a feast, call the poor, the maimed, the lame, the blind, and thou shalt be blessed, for they cannot recompense thee, for thou shalt be recompensed at the resurrection of the just."[493]

And when one of them that sat at meat with him heard these things, he said unto him, "Blessed is he that shall eat bread in the kingdom of God."[494]

Then said he unto him, "A certain man made a great supper, and bade many,[495] and sent his servant at supper time to say to them that were bidden, 'Come, for all things are now ready.' And they all with one consent began to make excuse.[496] The first said unto him, 'I have bought a piece of ground, and I must needs go and

---

[493] Compare Tobit 2:1-2: "Now when I was come home again, and my wife Anna was restored unto me, with my son Tobias, in the feast of Pentecost, which is the holy feast of the seven weeks, there was a good dinner prepared me, in the which I sat down to eat. And when I saw abundance of meat, I said to my son, 'Go and bring what poor man soever thou shalt find out of our brethren, who is mindful of the Lord; and, lo, I tarry for thee.'"

[494] See Isaiah 25:6-8: "And in this mountain shall the LORD of hosts make unto all people a feast of fat things, a feast of wines on the lees, of fat things full of marrow, of wines on the lees well refined. And he will destroy in this mountain the face of the covering cast over all people, and the vail that is spread over all nations. He will swallow up death in victory; and the Lord GOD will wipe away tears from off all faces; and the rebuke of his people shall he take away from off all the earth; for the LORD hath spoken it."

[495] Compare Proverbs 9:1-6: "Wisdom hath builded her house, she hath hewn out her seven pillars. She hath killed her beasts; she hath mingled her wine; she hath also furnished her table. She hath sent forth her maidens; she crieth upon the highest places of the city, 'Whoso is simple, let him turn in hither;' as for him that wanteth understanding, she saith to him, 'Come, eat of my bread, and drink of the wine which I have mingled. Forsake the foolish, and live; and go in the way of understanding.'"

[496] Compare Deuteronomy 20:5-7: "And the officers shall speak unto the people, saying, 'What man is there that hath built a new house, and hath not dedicated it? Let him go and return to his house, lest he die in the battle, and another man dedicate it. And what man is he that hath planted a vineyard, and hath not yet eaten of it? Let him also go and return unto his house, lest he die in the battle, and another man eat of it. And what man is there that hath betrothed a wife, and hath not taken her? Let him go and return unto his house, lest he die in the battle, and another man take her.'"

see it, I pray thee have me excused.' And another said, 'I have bought five yoke of oxen, and I go to prove them, I pray thee have me excused.' And another said, 'I have married a wife, and therefore I cannot come.' So that servant came, and shewed his lord these things. Then the master of the house being angry said to his servant, 'Go out quickly into the streets and lanes of the city, and bring in hither the poor, and the maimed, and the halt, and the blind.' And the servant said, 'Lord, it is done as thou hast commanded, and yet there is room.' And the lord said unto the servant, 'Go out into the highways and hedges, and compel them to come in, that my house may be filled. For I say unto you, that none of those men which were bidden shall taste of my supper.'"

Chapter Sixty One

Then drew near unto him all the publicans and sinners for to hear him. And the Pharisees and scribes murmured, saying, "This man receiveth sinners, and eateth with them." And he spake this parable unto them, saying, "What man of you, having an hundred sheep, if he lose one of them, doth not leave the ninety and nine in the wilderness, and go after that which is lost, until he find it? And when he hath found it, he layeth it on his shoulders, rejoicing. And when he cometh home, he calleth together his friends and neighbours, saying unto them, 'Rejoice with me, for I have found my sheep which was lost.' I say unto you, that likewise joy shall be in heaven over one sinner that repenteth, more than over ninety and nine just persons, which need no repentance.[497]

"Either what woman, having ten pieces of silver, if she lose one piece, doth not light a candle, and sweep the house, and seek diligently till she find it? And when she hath found it, she calleth her friends and her neighbours together, saying, 'Rejoice with me, for I have found the piece which I had lost.' Likewise, I say unto you,

---

[497] Compare _2 Esdras_ 7:59-61: "For this is the life whereof Moses spake unto the people while he lived, saying, 'Choose thee life, that thou mayest live.' Nevertheless they believed not him, nor yet the prophets after him, no nor me which have spoken unto them, that there should not be such heaviness in their destruction, as shall be joy over them that are persuaded to salvation."

there is joy in the presence of the angels of God over one sinner that repenteth."

And he said, "A certain man had two sons, and the younger of them said to his father, 'Father, give me the portion of goods that falleth to me.' And he divided unto them his living. And not many days after, the younger son gathered all together, and took his journey into a far country, and there wasted his substance with riotous living. And when he had spent all, there arose a mighty famine in that land, and he began to be in want. And he went and joined himself to a citizen of that country, and he sent him into his fields to feed swine. And he would fain have filled his belly with the husks that the swine did eat, and no man gave unto him. And when he came to himself, he said, 'How many hired servants of my father's have bread enough and to spare, and I perish with hunger! I will arise and go to my father, and will say unto him, "Father, I have sinned against heaven, and before thee, and am no more worthy to be called thy son, make me as one of thy hired servants."' And he arose, and came to his father. But when he was yet a great way off, his father saw him, and had compassion, and ran, and fell on his neck, and kissed him. And the son said unto him, 'Father, I have sinned against heaven, and in thy sight, and am no more worthy to be called thy son.' But the father said to his servants, 'Bring forth the best robe, and put it on him, and put a ring on his hand, and shoes on his feet. And bring hither the fatted calf, and kill it, and let us eat, and be merry. For this my son was dead, and is alive again, he was lost, and is found.' And they began to be merry. Now his elder son was in the field, and as he came and drew nigh to the house, he heard musick and dancing. And he called one of the servants, and asked what these things meant. And he said unto him, 'Thy brother is come, and thy father hath killed the fatted calf, because he hath received him safe and sound.' And he was angry, and would not go in, therefore came his father out, and intreated him. And he answering said to his father, 'Lo, these many years do I serve thee, neither transgressed I at any time thy commandment, and yet thou never gavest me a kid, that I might make merry with my friends, but as soon as this thy son was come, which hath devoured thy living with harlots, thou hast killed for him the fatted calf.' And he said unto him, 'Son, thou art ever with me, and all that I have is thine. It was meet that we should make merry, and be glad, for this thy brother was dead, and is alive again, and was lost, and is found.'"

THE TREE OF LIFE

Chapter Sixty Two

And it came to pass, as he went to Jerusalem, that he passed through the midst of Samaria and Galilee. And as he entered into a certain village, there met him ten men that were lepers, which stood afar off,[498] and they lifted up their voices, and said, "Jesus, Master, have mercy on us." And when he saw them, he said unto them, "Go shew yourselves unto the priests."[499] And it came to pass, that, as they went, they were cleansed. And one of them, when he saw that he was healed, turned back, and with a loud voice glorified God, and fell down on his face at his feet, giving him thanks, and he was a Samaritan. And Jesus answering said, "Were there not ten cleansed? But where are the nine? There are not found that returned to give glory to God, save this stranger." And he said unto him, "Arise, go thy way, thy faith hath made thee whole."

And as Jesus passed by, he saw a man which was blind from his birth. And his disciples asked him, saying, "Master, who did sin, this man, or his parents, that he was born blind?" Jesus answered, "Neither hath this man sinned, nor his parents, but that the works of God should be made manifest in him. I must work the works of him

---

[498] See Leviticus 13:46: "All the days wherein the plague shall be in him he shall be defiled; he is unclean. He shall dwell alone; without the camp shall his habitation be."
[499] See Leviticus 14:1-57.

that sent me,[500] while it is day,[501] the night cometh, when no man can work. As long as I am in the world, I am the light of the world."[502]

When he had thus spoken, he spat on the ground, and made clay of the spittle, and he anointed the eyes of the blind man with the clay, and said unto him, "Go, wash in the pool of Siloam, (which is by interpretation, Sent.)" He went his way therefore, and washed, and came seeing. The neighbours therefore, and they which before had seen him that he was blind, said, "Is not this he that sat and begged?" Some said, "This is he," others said, "He is like him," but he said, "I am he." Therefore said they unto him, "How were thine eyes opened?" He answered and said, "A man that is called Jesus made clay, and anointed mine eyes, and said unto me, 'Go to the pool of Siloam, and wash,' and I went and washed, and I received sight." Then said they unto him, "Where is he?" He said, "I know not."

They brought to the Pharisees him that aforetime was blind. And it was the sabbath day when Jesus made the clay, and opened his eyes. Then again the Pharisees also asked him how he had received his sight. He said unto them, "He put clay upon mine eyes, and I washed, and do see." Therefore said some of the Pharisees, "This man is not of God, because he keepeth not the sabbath day."

---

[500] See Psalms 146:5-10: "Happy is he that hath the God of Jacob for his help, whose hope is in the LORD his God; which made heaven, and earth, the sea, and all that therein is; which keepeth truth for ever; which executeth judgment for the oppressed; which giveth food to the hungry. The LORD looseth the prisoners; the LORD openeth the eyes of the blind; the LORD raiseth them that are bowed down; the LORD loveth the righteous; the LORD preserveth the strangers; he relieveth the fatherless and widow; but the way of the wicked he turneth upside down. The LORD shall reign for ever, even thy God, O Zion, unto all generations. Praise ye the LORD."
[501] Compare 2 Esdras 13:52: "And he said unto me, 'Like as thou canst neither seek out nor know the things that are in the deep of the sea; even so can no man upon earth see my Son, or those that be with him, but in the day time.'"
[502] See Malachi 4:2: "But unto you that fear my name shall the Sun of righteousness arise with healing in his wings; and ye shall go forth, and grow up as calves of the stall."

Others said, "How can a man that is a sinner do such miracles?" And there was a division among them. They say unto the blind man again, "What sayest thou of him, that he hath opened thine eyes?" He said, "He is a prophet."

But the Jews did not believe concerning him, that he had been blind, and received his sight, until they called the parents of him that had received his sight. And they asked them, saying, "Is this your son, who ye say was born blind? How then doth he now see?" His parents answered them and said, "We know that this is our son, and that he was born blind. But by what means he now seeth, we know not; or who hath opened his eyes, we know not; he is of age, ask him, he shall speak for himself." These words spake his parents, because they feared the Jews, for the Jews had agreed already, that if any man did confess that he was Christ, he should be put out of the synagogue.[503] Therefore said his parents, "He is of age, ask him." Then again called they the man that was blind, and said unto him, "Give God the praise, we know that this man is a sinner." He answered and said, "Whether he be a sinner or no, I know not, one thing I know, that, whereas I was blind, now I see." Then said they to him again, "What did he to thee? How opened he thine eyes?" He answered them, "I have told you already, and ye did not hear, wherefore would ye hear it again? Will ye also be his disciples?" Then they reviled him, and said, "Thou art his disciple, but we are Moses' disciples. We know that God spake unto Moses, as for this fellow, we know not from whence he is."

The man answered and said unto them, "Why herein is a marvellous thing, that ye know not from whence he is, and yet he hath opened mine eyes. Now we know that God heareth not sinners, but if any man be a worshipper of God, and doeth his will, him he heareth. Since the world began was it not heard that any man

---

[503] See Isaiah 66:5: "Hear the word of the LORD, ye that tremble at his word; your brethren that hated you, that cast you out for my name's sake, said, 'Let the LORD be glorified;' but he shall appear to your joy, and they shall be ashamed."

opened the eyes of one that was born blind. If this man were not of God, he could do nothing." They answered and said unto him, "Thou wast altogether born in sins, and dost thou teach us?" And they cast him out.

Jesus heard that they had cast him out, and when he had found him, he said unto him, "Dost thou believe on the Son of God?"[504] He answered and said, "Who is he, Lord, that I might believe on him?" And Jesus said unto him, "Thou hast both seen him, and it is he that talketh with thee." And he said, "Lord, I believe." And he worshipped him.

And Jesus said, "For judgment I am come into this world, that they which see not might see, and that they which see might be made blind."[505] And some of the Pharisees which were with him heard these words, and said unto him, "Are we blind also?" Jesus said unto them, "If ye were blind, ye should have no sin, but now ye say, 'We see,' therefore your sin remaineth.[506]

"Verily, verily, I say unto you, He that entereth not by the door into the sheepfold, but climbeth up some other way, the same is a thief and a robber. But he that entereth in by the door is the shepherd of the sheep. To him the porter openeth, and the sheep

---

[504] See *2 Esdras* 2:46-47: "Then said I unto the angel, 'What young person is it that crowneth them, and giveth them palms in their hands?' So he answered and said unto me, 'It is the Son of God, whom they have confessed in the world.' Then began I greatly to commend them that stood so stiffly for the name of the Lord."
[505] Compare Deuteronomy 29:2-4: "And Moses called unto all Israel, and said unto them, 'Ye have seen all that the LORD did before your eyes in the land of Egypt unto Pharaoh, and unto all his servants, and unto all his land; the great temptations which thine eyes have seen, the signs, and those great miracles; yet the LORD hath not given you an heart to perceive, and eyes to see, and ears to hear, unto this day.'"
Isaiah 44:18: "They have not known nor understood; for he hath shut their eyes, that they cannot see; and their hearts, that they cannot understand."
Isaiah 6:10: "Make the heart of this people fat, and make their ears heavy, and shut their eyes; lest they see with their eyes, and hear with their ears, and understand with their heart, and convert, and be healed."
[506] Compare *Wisdom* 2:21: "Such things they did imagine, and were deceived; for their own wickedness hath blinded them."

hear his voice, and he calleth his own sheep by name, and leadeth them out. And when he putteth forth his own sheep, he goeth before them, and the sheep follow him, for they know his voice. And a stranger will they not follow, but will flee from him, for they know not the voice of strangers."[507]

This parable spake Jesus unto them, but they understood not what things they were which he spake unto them.[508] Then said Jesus unto them again, "Verily, verily, I say unto you, I am the door of the sheep.[509] All that ever came before me are thieves and robbers, but the sheep did not hear them. I am the door, by me if any man enter in, he shall be saved, and shall go in and out, and find pasture. The thief cometh not, but for to steal, and to kill, and to destroy. I am come that they might have life, and that they might have it more abundantly. I am the good shepherd,[510] the good shepherd giveth

---

[507] Compare Psalms 23:1-2: "The LORD is my shepherd; I shall not want. He maketh me to lie down in green pastures; he leadeth me beside the still waters."
Psalms 80:1: "Give ear, O Shepherd of Israel, thou that leadest Joseph like a flock; thou that dwellest between the cherubims, shine forth."
[508] Compare Psalms 95:7-11: "For he is our God; and we are the people of his pasture, and the sheep of his hand. To day if ye will hear his voice, harden not your heart, as in the provocation, and as in the day of temptation in the wilderness; when your fathers tempted me, proved me, and saw my work. Forty years long was I grieved with this generation, and said, 'It is a people that do err in their heart, and they have not known my ways; unto whom I sware in my wrath that they should not enter into my rest.'"
[509] Compare Psalms 118:19-21: "Open to me the gates of righteousness; I will go into them, and I will praise the LORD; this gate of the LORD, into which the righteous shall enter. I will praise thee; for thou hast heard me, and art become my salvation."
[510] Compare Ezekiel 34:2-16: "Son of man, prophesy against the shepherds of Israel, prophesy, and say unto them, 'Thus saith the Lord GOD unto the shepherds; Woe be to the shepherds of Israel that do feed themselves! Should not the shepherds feed the flocks? Ye eat the fat, and ye clothe you with the wool, ye kill them that are fed; but ye feed not the flock. The diseased have ye not strengthened, neither have ye healed that which was sick, neither have ye bound up that which was broken, neither have ye brought again that which was driven away, neither have ye sought that which was lost; but with force and with cruelty have ye ruled them. And they were scattered, because there is no shepherd; and they became meat to all the beasts of the field, when they were scattered. My sheep wandered through all the mountains, and upon every high hill; yea, my flock was scattered

his life for the sheep. But he that is an hireling, and not the shepherd, whose own the sheep are not, seeth the wolf coming, and leaveth the sheep, and fleeth, and the wolf catcheth them, and scattereth the sheep. The hireling fleeth, because he is an hireling, and careth not for the sheep. I am the good shepherd, and know my sheep, and am known of mine. As the Father knoweth me, even so know I the Father, and I lay down my life for the sheep. And other sheep I have, which are not of this fold, them also I must bring, and they shall hear my voice, and there shall be one fold, and one shepherd.[511] Therefore doth my Father love me, because I lay down my life, that I might take it again. No man taketh it from me, but I lay

---

upon all the face of the earth, and none did search or seek after them. Therefore, ye shepherds, hear the word of the LORD: As I live, saith the Lord GOD, surely because my flock became a prey, and my flock became meat to every beast of the field, because there was no shepherd, neither did my shepherds search for my flock, but the shepherds fed themselves, and fed not my flock; therefore, O ye shepherds, hear the word of the LORD; Thus saith the Lord GOD; Behold, I am against the shepherds; and I will require my flock at their hand, and cause them to cease from feeding the flock; neither shall the shepherds feed themselves any more; for I will deliver my flock from their mouth, that they may not be meat for them. For thus saith the Lord GOD; Behold, I, even I, will both search my sheep, and seek them out. As a shepherd seeketh out his flock in the day that he is among his sheep that are scattered; so will I seek out my sheep, and will deliver them out of all places where they have been scattered in the cloudy and dark day. And I will bring them out from the people, and gather them from the countries, and will bring them to their own land, and feed them upon the mountains of Israel by the rivers, and in all the inhabited places of the country. I will feed them in a good pasture, and upon the high mountains of Israel shall their fold be; there shall they lie in a good fold, and in a fat pasture shall they feed upon the mountains of Israel. I will feed my flock, and I will cause them to lie down, saith the Lord GOD. I will seek that which was lost, and bring again that which was driven away, and will bind up that which was broken, and will strengthen that which was sick; but I will destroy the fat and the strong; I will feed them with judgment.'"
[511] Compare Ezekiel 34:23-24: "And I will set up one shepherd over them, and he shall feed them, even my servant David; he shall feed them, and he shall be their shepherd. And I the LORD will be their God, and my servant David a prince among them; I the LORD have spoken it."

it down of myself. I have power to lay it down, and I have power to take it again.[512] This commandment have I received of my Father."

There was a division therefore again among the Jews for these sayings. And many of them said, "He hath a devil, and is mad, why hear ye him?" Others said, "These are not the words of him that hath a devil. Can a devil open the eyes of the blind?"

And it was at Jerusalem the feast of the dedication,[513] and it was winter. And Jesus walked in the temple in Solomon's porch. Then came the Jews round about him, and said unto him, "How long dost thou make us to doubt? If thou be the Christ, tell us plainly." Jesus answered them, "I told you, and ye believed not, the works that I do in my Father's name, they bear witness of me. But ye believe not, because ye are not of my sheep, as I said unto you. My sheep hear my voice, and I know them, and they follow me. And I give unto them eternal life, and they shall never perish, neither shall any man pluck them out of my hand. My Father, which gave them me, is greater than all, and no man is able to pluck them out of my Father's hand. I and my Father are one." Then the Jews took up stones again to stone him.

Jesus answered them, "Many good works have I shewed you from my Father, for which of those works do ye stone me?" The Jews answered him, saying, "For a good work we stone thee not, but for blasphemy, and because that thou, being a man, makest thyself God."[514]

---

[512] Compare Deuteronomy 32:39-40: "See now that I, even I, am he, and there is no God with me; I kill, and I make alive; I wound, and I heal; neither is there any that can deliver out of my hand. For I lift up my hand to heaven, and say, 'I live for ever.'"
[513] See 1 Maccabees 4:52-59.
[514] See Leviticus 24:16: "And he that blasphemeth the name of the LORD, he shall surely be put to death, and all the congregation shall certainly stone him; as well the stranger, as he that is born in the land, when he blasphemeth the name of the LORD, shall be put to death."

Jesus answered them, "Is it not written in your law, *I said, Ye are gods?*'[515] If he called them gods, unto whom the word of God came, and the scripture cannot be broken, say ye of him, whom the Father hath sanctified, and sent into the world, 'Thou blasphemest,' because I said, 'I am the Son of God?' If I do not the works of my Father, believe me not. But if I do, though ye believe not me, believe the works,[516] that ye may know, and believe, that the Father is in me, and I in him." Therefore they sought again to take him, but he escaped out of their hand, and went away again beyond Jordan into the place where John at first baptized, and there he abode.

And many resorted unto him, and said, "John did no miracle, but all things that John spake of this man were true." And many believed on him there.

Compare Exodus 7:1: "And the LORD said unto Moses, 'See, I have made thee a god to Pharaoh; and Aaron thy brother shall be thy prophet.'"
Zechariah 12:8: "In that day shall the LORD defend the inhabitants of Jerusalem; and he that is feeble among them at that day shall be as David; and the house of David shall be as God, as the angel of the LORD before them."
[515] "I have said, 'Ye are gods; and all of you are children of the most High.'" – Psalms 82:6
[516] See Psalms 146:5-10: "Happy is he that hath the God of Jacob for his help, whose hope is in the LORD his God; which made heaven, and earth, the sea, and all that therein is; which keepeth truth for ever; which executeth judgment for the oppressed; which giveth food to the hungry. The LORD looseth the prisoners; the LORD openeth the eyes of the blind; the LORD raiseth them that are bowed down; the LORD loveth the righteous; the LORD preserveth the strangers; he relieveth the fatherless and widow; but the way of the wicked he turneth upside down. The LORD shall reign for ever, even thy God, O Zion, unto all generations. Praise ye the LORD."

THE TREE OF LIFE

Chapter Sixty Three

Now a certain man was sick, named Lazarus, of Bethany, the town of Mary (which anointed the Lord with ointment, and wiped his feet with her hair) and her sister Martha, whose brother Lazarus was sick. Therefore his sisters sent unto Jesus, saying, "Lord, behold, he whom thou lovest is sick." When Jesus heard that, he said, "This sickness is not unto death, but for the glory of God, that the Son of God might be glorified thereby."

Now Jesus loved Martha, and her sister Mary, and Lazarus. When he had heard therefore that he was sick, he abode two days still in the same place where he was. Then after that saith he to his disciples, "Let us go into Judaea again." His disciples say unto him, "Master, the Jews of late sought to stone thee, and goest thou thither again?" Jesus answered, "Are there not twelve hours in the day? If any man walk in the day, he stumbleth not, because he seeth the light of this world. But if a man walk in the night, he stumbleth, because there is no light in him."

These things said he, and after that he saith unto them, "Our friend Lazarus sleepeth,[517] but I go, that I may awake him out of sleep." Then said his disciples, "Lord, if he sleep, he shall do well."

---

[517] See Psalms 13:3: "Consider and hear me, O LORD my God; lighten mine eyes, lest I sleep the sleep of death."
Daniel 12:2: "And many of them that sleep in the dust of the earth shall awake, some to everlasting life, and some to shame and everlasting contempt."

THE TREE OF LIFE

Howbeit Jesus spake of his death, but they thought that he had spoken of taking of rest in sleep. Then said Jesus unto them plainly, "Lazarus is dead. And I am glad for your sakes that I was not there, to the intent ye may believe, nevertheless let us go unto him." Then said Thomas, which is called Didymus, unto his fellowdisciples, "Let us also go, that we may die with him."

Now Bethany was nigh unto Jerusalem, about fifteen furlongs off, and many of the Jews came to Martha and Mary, to comfort them concerning their brother. Then Martha, as soon as she heard that Jesus was coming, went and met him, but Mary sat still in the house. Then said Martha unto Jesus, "Lord, if thou hadst been here, my brother had not died. But I know, that even now, whatsoever thou wilt ask of God, God will give it thee." Jesus saith unto her, "Thy brother shall rise again." Martha saith unto him, "I know that he shall rise again in the resurrection at the last day."[518] Jesus said unto her, "I am the resurrection,[519] and the life, he that believeth in me, though he were dead, yet shall he live. And whosoever liveth and believeth in me shall never die. Believest thou this?" She saith unto

---

[518] Compare Daniel 12:2-3: "And many of them that sleep in the dust of the earth shall awake, some to everlasting life, and some to shame and everlasting contempt. And they that be wise shall shine as the brightness of the firmament; and they that turn many to righteousness as the stars for ever and ever."
[519] Compare Hosea 13:14: "I will ransom them from the power of the grave; I will redeem them from death. O death, I will be thy plagues; O grave, I will be thy destruction; repentance shall be hid from mine eyes."
Isaiah 26:19: "Thy dead men shall live, together with my dead body shall they arise. Awake and sing, ye that dwell in dust; for thy dew is as the dew of herbs, and the earth shall cast out the dead."
Ezekiel 37:12-14: "Therefore prophesy and say unto them, 'Thus saith the Lord GOD; Behold, O my people, I will open your graves, and cause you to come up out of your graves, and bring you into the land of Israel. And ye shall know that I am the LORD, when I have opened your graves, O my people, and brought you up out of your graves, and shall put my spirit in you, and ye shall live, and I shall place you in your own land; then shall ye know that I the LORD have spoken it, and performed it, saith the LORD.'"
2 Maccabees 7:9: "And when he was at the last gasp, he said, 'Thou like a fury takest us out of this present life, but the King of the world shall raise us up, who have died for his laws, unto everlasting life.'"

him, "Yea, Lord, I believe that thou art the Christ,[520] the Son of God,[521] which should come into the world." And when she had so said, she went her way, and called Mary her sister secretly, saying, "The Master is come, and calleth for thee." As soon as she heard that, she arose quickly, and came unto him.

Now Jesus was not yet come into the town, but was in that place where Martha met him. The Jews then which were with her in the house, and comforted her, when they saw Mary, that she rose up hastily and went out, followed her, saying, "She goeth unto the grave to weep there." Then when Mary was come where Jesus was, and saw him, she fell down at his feet, saying unto him, "Lord, if thou hadst been here, my brother had not died."

When Jesus therefore saw her weeping, and the Jews also weeping which came with her, he groaned in the spirit, and was troubled, and wept. Then said the Jews, "Behold how he loved him!" And some of them said, "Could not this man, which opened the eyes of the blind, have caused that even this man should not have died?" And Jesus said, "Where have ye laid him?" They said unto him, "Lord, come and see." Jesus therefore again groaning in himself cometh to the grave. It was a cave, and a stone lay upon it. Jesus said, "Take ye away the stone." Martha, the sister of him that was dead, saith unto him, "Lord, by this time he stinketh, for he hath been dead four days." Jesus saith unto her, "Said I not unto thee, that, if thou wouldest believe, thou shouldest see the glory of God?" Then they took away the stone from the place where the dead was laid.

---

[520] See Jeremiah 23:5: "Behold, the days come, saith the LORD, that I will raise unto David a righteous Branch, and a King shall reign and prosper, and shall execute judgment and justice in the earth."
[521] See 2 Esdras 13:29,32: "Behold, the days come, when the most High will begin to deliver them that are upon the earth. And the time shall be when these things shall come to pass, and the signs shall happen which I shewed thee before, and then shall my Son be declared, whom thou sawest as a man ascending."

And Jesus lifted up his eyes, and said, "Father, I thank thee that thou hast heard me. And I knew that thou hearest me always, but because of the people which stand by I said it, that they may believe that thou hast sent me." And when he thus had spoken, he cried with a loud voice, "Lazarus, come forth." And he that was dead came forth,[522] bound hand and foot with graveclothes, and his face was bound about with a napkin. Jesus saith unto them, "Loose him, and let him go." Then many of the Jews which came to Mary, and had seen the things which Jesus did, believed on him. But some of them went their ways to the Pharisees, and told them what things Jesus had done.

Then gathered the chief priests and the Pharisees a council, and said, "What do we? For this man doeth many miracles, and if we let him thus alone, all men will believe on him, and the Romans shall come and take away both our place and nation." And one of them, named Caiaphas, being the high priest that same year, said unto them, "Ye know nothing at all, nor consider that it is expedient for us, that one man should die for the people, and that the whole nation perish not." And this spake he not of himself, but being high priest that year, he prophesied that Jesus should die for that nation, and not for that nation only, but that also he should gather together in one the children of God that were scattered abroad.

Then from that day forth they took counsel together for to put him to death.

---

[522] Compare 1 Kings 17:1-24 (Elijah); 2 Kings 4:8-37 (Elisha).

Chapter Sixty Four

Jesus therefore walked no more openly among the Jews, but went thence unto a country near to the wilderness, into a city called Ephraim, and there continued with his disciples. And Jesus entered and passed through Jericho.

And, behold, there was a man named Zacchaeus, which was the chief among the publicans, and he was rich. And he sought to see Jesus who he was, and could not for the press, because he was little of stature. And he ran before, and climbed up into a sycamore tree to see him, for he was to pass that way.

And when Jesus came to the place, he looked up, and saw him, and said unto him, "Zacchaeus, make haste, and come down, for to day I must abide at thy house." And he made haste, and came down, and received him joyfully. And when they saw it, they all murmured, saying that he was gone to be guest with a man that is a sinner. And Jesus said, "This day is salvation come to this house, forasmuch as he also is a son of Abraham. For the Son of man is come to *seek and to save that which was lost.*"[523] And Zacchaeus stood, and said unto the Lord, "Behold, Lord, the half of my goods I give to the poor, and

---

[523] See Ezekiel 34:16: "I will seek that which was lost, and bring again that which was driven away, and will bind up that which was broken, and will strengthen that which was sick; but I will destroy the fat and the strong; I will feed them with judgment."

if I have taken any thing from any man by false accusation, I restore him fourfold."[524]

And as they heard these things, he added and spake a parable, because he was nigh to Jerusalem, and because they thought that the kingdom of God should immediately appear. He said therefore, "A certain nobleman went into a far country to receive for himself a kingdom, and to return. And he called his ten servants, and delivered them ten pounds, and said unto them, 'Occupy till I come.' But his citizens hated him, and sent a message after him, saying, 'We will not have this man to reign over us.' And it came to pass, that when he was returned, having received the kingdom, then he commanded these servants to be called unto him, to whom he had given the money, that he might know how much every man had gained by trading. Then came the first, saying, 'Lord, thy pound hath gained ten pounds.' And he said unto him, 'Well, thou good servant, because thou hast been faithful in a very little, have thou authority over ten cities.' And the second came, saying, 'Lord, thy pound hath gained five pounds.' And he said likewise to him, 'Be thou also over five cities.' And another came, saying, 'Lord, behold, here is thy pound, which I have kept laid up in a napkin. For I feared thee, because thou art an austere man, thou takest up that thou layedst not down, and reapest that thou didst not sow.' And he saith unto him, 'Out of thine own mouth will I judge thee, thou wicked servant. Thou knewest that I was an austere man, taking up that I laid not down, and reaping that I did not sow. Wherefore then gavest not thou my money into the bank, that at my coming I might have required mine own with usury?' And he said unto them that stood by, 'Take from him the pound, and give it to him that hath ten pounds.'"[525] And they said unto him, "But Lord, he hath ten pounds."

---

[524] Compare Exodus 22:1: "If a man shall steal an ox, or a sheep, and kill it, or sell it; he shall restore five oxen for an ox, and four sheep for a sheep."
[525] Compare Psalms 49:14: "Like sheep they are laid in the grave; death shall feed on them; and the upright shall have dominion over them in the morning; and their beauty shall consume in the grave from their dwelling."

THE TREE OF LIFE

And he said, "I say unto you, that unto every one which hath shall be given, and from him that hath not, even that he hath shall be taken away from him. But those mine enemies, which would not that I should reign over them, bring hither, and slay them before me.'"

THE TREE OF LIFE

THE TREE OF LIFE

Chapter Sixty Five

And it came to pass, that as he went out of Jericho with his disciples and a great number of people, blind Bartimaeus, the son of Timaeus, sat by the way side begging.

And hearing the multitude pass by, he asked what it meant. And they told him, that Jesus of Nazareth passeth by. And when he heard that it was Jesus of Nazareth, he began to cry out, and say, "Jesus, thou son of David,[526] have mercy on me." And they which went before rebuked him, that he should hold his peace, but he cried so much the more, "Thou son of David, have mercy on me!"

And Jesus stood still, and commanded him to be brought unto him. And they called the blind man, saying unto him, "Be of good comfort, rise, he calleth thee." And he, casting away his garment, rose, and came to Jesus, and when he was come near, Jesus asked him, and said, "What will ye that I shall do unto you?" And the blind man said unto him, "Lord, that I might receive my sight." And Jesus had compassion on him, and said unto him, "Receive thy sight, and go thy way, thy faith hath made thee whole." And immediately he received his sight, and followed Jesus in the way, glorifying God, and all the people, when they saw it, gave praise unto God.

---

[526] Compare Isaiah 35:5-6: "Then [in the days of Messiah] the eyes of the blind shall be opened, and the ears of the deaf shall be unstopped. Then shall the lame man leap as an hart, and the tongue of the dumb sing; for in the wilderness shall waters break out, and streams in the desert."

THE TREE OF LIFE

And when he had thus spoken, he went before, ascending up to Jerusalem, and as Jesus went before them, and they followed, they were afraid. And he took again the twelve disciples apart in the way, and began to tell them what things should happen unto him, saying, "Behold, we go up to Jerusalem, and all things that are written by the prophets concerning the Son of man shall be accomplished,[527] and he shall be betrayed unto the chief priests and

---

[527] See Isaiah 53:1-12: "Who hath believed our report? And to whom is the arm of the LORD revealed? For he shall grow up before him as a tender plant, and as a root out of a dry ground; he hath no form nor comeliness; and when we shall see him, there is no beauty that we should desire him. He is despised and rejected of men; a man of sorrows, and acquainted with grief; and we hid as it were our faces from him; he was despised, and we esteemed him not. Surely he hath borne our griefs, and carried our sorrows; yet we did esteem him stricken, smitten of God, and afflicted. But he was wounded for our transgressions, he was bruised for our iniquities; the chastisement of our peace was upon him; and with his stripes we are healed. All we like sheep have gone astray; we have turned every one to his own way; and the LORD hath laid on him the iniquity of us all. He was oppressed, and he was afflicted, yet he opened not his mouth; he is brought as a lamb to the slaughter, and as a sheep before her shearers is dumb, so he openeth not his mouth. He was taken from prison and from judgment; and who shall declare his generation? For he was cut off out of the land of the living; for the transgression of my people was he stricken. And he made his grave with the wicked, and with the rich in his death; because he had done no violence, neither was any deceit in his mouth. Yet it pleased the LORD to bruise him; he hath put him to grief; when thou shalt make his soul an offering for sin, he shall see his seed, he shall prolong his days, and the pleasure of the LORD shall prosper in his hand. He shall see of the travail of his soul, and shall be satisfied; by his knowledge shall my righteous servant justify many; for he shall bear their iniquities. Therefore will I divide him a portion with the great, and he shall divide the spoil with the strong; because he hath poured out his soul unto death; and he was numbered with the transgressors; and he bare the sin of many, and made intercession for the transgressors."
Psalms 22:1-19: "My God, my God, why hast thou forsaken me? Why art thou so far from helping me, and from the words of my roaring? O my God, I cry in the daytime, but thou hearest not; and in the night season, and am not silent. But thou art holy, O thou that inhabitest the praises of Israel. Our fathers trusted in thee; they trusted, and thou didst deliver them. They cried unto thee, and were delivered; they trusted in thee, and were not confounded. But I am a worm, and no man; a reproach of men, and despised of the people. All they that see me laugh me to scorn; they shoot out the lip, they shake the head saying, 'He trusted on the LORD that he would deliver him; let him deliver him, seeing he delighted in him.' But thou art he that took me out of the womb; thou didst make me hope when I was upon my mother's breasts. I was cast upon thee from the womb; thou art my God from my mother's

unto the scribes, and they shall condemn him to death, and shall deliver him to the Gentiles, and he shall be mocked, and spitefully entreated, and spitted on, and they shall scourge him, and crucify him, and put him to death, and the third day he shall rise again." And they understood none of these things, and this saying was hid from them,[528] neither knew they the things which were spoken.

---

belly. Be not far from me; for trouble is near; for there is none to help. Many bulls have compassed me; strong bulls of Bashan have beset me round. They gaped upon me with their mouths, as a ravening and a roaring lion. I am poured out like water, and all my bones are out of joint; my heart is like wax; it is melted in the midst of my bowels. My strength is dried up like a potsherd; and my tongue cleaveth to my jaws; and thou hast brought me into the dust of death. For dogs have compassed me; the assembly of the wicked have inclosed me; they pierced my hands and my feet. I may tell all my bones; they look and stare upon me. They part my garments among them, and cast lots upon my vesture. But be not thou far from me, O LORD; O my strength, haste thee to help me."
See also Isaiah 50:4-9.
[528] Compare Isaiah 44:18: "They have not known nor understood; for he hath shut their eyes, that they cannot see; and their hearts, that they cannot understand."

THE TREE OF LIFE

Chapter Sixty Six

Then came to him the mother of Zebedee's children with her sons, James and John, worshipping him, and desiring a certain thing of him, saying, "Master, we would that thou shouldest do for us whatsoever we shall desire." And he said unto them, "What would ye that I should do for you?" She saith unto him, "Grant that these my two sons may sit, the one on thy right hand, and the other on the left, in thy kingdom."

But Jesus answered and said, "Ye know not what ye ask. Are ye able to drink of the cup that I shall drink of, and to be baptized with the baptism that I am baptized with?" They say unto him, "We are able." And Jesus said unto them, "Ye shall drink indeed of my cup, and be baptized with the baptism that I am baptized with, but to sit on my right hand, and on my left, is not mine to give, but it shall be given to them for whom it is prepared of my Father."

And when the ten heard it, they were moved with indignation against James and John. But Jesus called them unto him, and said, "Ye know that the princes of the Gentiles exercise dominion over them, and their great ones exercise authority upon them. But it shall not be so among you, whosoever will be great among you, let him be your minister. And whosoever will be chief among you, let him be servant of all, even as the Son of man came not to be ministered unto, but to minister, and to give his life a ransom[529] for many."

---

[529] Compare <u>Isaiah 35:10:</u> "And the ransomed of the LORD shall return, and come to Zion with songs and everlasting joy upon their heads; they shall obtain joy and gladness, and sorrow and sighing shall flee away."
<u>Isaiah 44:22:</u> "I have blotted out, as a thick cloud, thy transgressions, and, as a cloud, thy sins; return unto me; for I have redeemed thee."
<u>Jeremiah 31:11:</u> "For the LORD hath redeemed Jacob, and ransomed him from the hand of him that was stronger than he."
<u>Hosea 13:14:</u> "I will ransom them from the power of the grave; I will redeem them from death. O death, I will be thy plagues; O grave, I will be thy destruction; repentance shall be hid from mine eyes."

THE TREE OF LIFE

Chapter Sixty Seven

Then Jesus six days before the passover[530] came to Bethany, where Lazarus was, whom he raised from the dead. There they made him a supper, and Martha served, but Lazarus was one of them that sat at the table with him.

Much people of the Jews therefore knew that he was there, and they came not for Jesus' sake only, but that they might see Lazarus also, whom he had raised from the dead. And the chief priests consulted that they might put Lazarus also to death, because that by reason of him many of the Jews went away, and believed on Jesus.

Now when Jesus was in Bethany, in the house of Simon the leper, as he sat at meat, there came unto him a woman, having an alabaster box of very precious ointment of spikenard, and she brake the box, and poured it on his head,[531] as he sat at meat.

---

[530] See Exodus 12:1-51; Leviticus 23:5-8; Numbers 28:16-25; Deuteronomy 16:1-8.
[531] Compare 1 Samuel 10:1: "Then Samuel took a vial of oil, and poured it upon his head, and kissed him, and said, 'Is it not because the LORD hath anointed thee to be captain over his inheritance?'"
1 Samuel 16:12-13: "And he sent, and brought him in. Now he was ruddy, and withal of a beautiful countenance, and goodly to look to. And the LORD said, 'Arise, anoint him; for this is he.' Then Samuel took the horn of oil, and anointed him in the midst of his brethren; and the Spirit of the LORD came upon David from that day forward. So Samuel rose up, and went to Ramah."

And there were some that had indignation within themselves, and they murmured against her, and one of his disciples, Judas Iscariot, Simon's son, which should betray him, said, "To what purpose is this waste? For this ointment might have been sold for more than three hundred pence, and been given to the poor." This he said, not that he cared for the poor, but because he was a thief, and had the bag, and bare what was put therein.

When Jesus understood it, he said, "Let her alone, why trouble ye the woman? For she hath wrought a good work upon me. She hath done what she could, for against the day of my burial hath she kept this, and she is come aforehand to anoint my body to the burying. And ye have the poor with you always, and whensoever ye will ye may do them good,[532] but me ye have not always. Verily I say unto you, wheresoever this gospel shall be preached throughout the whole world, this also, that this woman hath done, shall be spoken of for a memorial of her."

---

2 Kings 9:6: "And he arose, and went into the house; and he poured the oil on his head, and said unto him, 'Thus saith the LORD God of Israel, I have anointed thee king over the people of the LORD, even over Israel.'"
[532] See Deuteronomy 15:11: "For the poor shall never cease out of the land; therefore I command thee, saying, 'Thou shalt open thine hand wide unto thy brother, to thy poor, and to thy needy, in thy land.'"

Chapter Sixty Eight

On the next day they drew nigh unto Jerusalem, and were come to Bethphage and Bethany, unto the mount of Olives, then sent Jesus two disciples, saying unto them, "Go into the village over against you, and as soon as ye be entered into it, ye shall find an ass tied, and a colt tied with her, whereon never man sat, loose them, and bring them hither unto me. And if any man ask you, 'Why do ye this?' Thus shall ye say unto him, 'Because the Lord hath need of them.' And straightway he will send them hither."

And the disciples went, and did as Jesus commanded them, and found even as he had said unto them, the colt tied by the door without in a place where two ways met, and they loose him. And as they were loosing the colt, the owners thereof said unto them, "Why loose ye the colt?" And they said, "The Lord hath need of him." And they let them go.

And brought the ass, and the colt to Jesus, and put on them their clothes, and Jesus sat thereon. All this was done, that it might be fulfilled which was spoken by the prophet, saying, *"Tell ye the daughter of Zion, 'Behold, thy King cometh unto thee, meek, and sitting upon an ass, and a colt the foal of an ass.'"*[533] These things

---

[533] "Rejoice greatly, O daughter of Zion; shout, O daughter of Jerusalem; behold, thy King cometh unto thee; he is just, and having salvation; lowly, and riding upon an ass, and upon a colt the foal of an ass." – Zechariah 9:9

understood not his disciples at the first, but when Jesus was glorified, then remembered they that these things were written of him, and that they had done these things unto him.

And many went out of the country up to Jerusalem before the Jews' feast of unleavened bread, (which is called the passover), to purify themselves. And as much people were come to the feast, and they heard that Jesus was coming to Jerusalem, they went forth to meet him. And when he was come nigh, even now at the descent of the mount of Olives,[534] a very great multitude of the disciples spread their clothes in the way,[535] and others cut down branches off the palm trees, and strawed them in the way.[536] And the multitudes that went before, and they that followed, began to rejoice and praise God

---

See also Genesis 49:10-11: "The sceptre shall not depart from Judah, nor a lawgiver from between his feet, until Shiloh come; and unto him shall the gathering of the people be. Binding his foal unto the vine, and his ass's colt unto the choice vine; he washed his garments in wine, and his clothes in the blood of grapes."
1 Kings 1:38-40: "So Zadok the priest, and Nathan the prophet, and Benaiah the son of Jehoiada, and the Cherethites, and the Pelethites, went down, and caused Solomon to ride upon king David's mule, and brought him to Gihon. And Zadok the priest took an horn of oil out of the tabernacle, and anointed Solomon. And they blew the trumpet; and all the people said, 'God save king Solomon.' And all the people came up after him, and the people piped with pipes, and rejoiced with great joy, so that the earth rent with the sound of them."
[534] See Isaiah 52:7: "How beautiful upon the mountains are the feet of him that bringeth good tidings, that publisheth peace; that bringeth good tidings of good, that publisheth salvation; that saith unto Zion, 'Thy God reigneth!'"
Psalms 121:1: "I will lift up mine eyes unto the hills, from whence cometh my help."
[535] Compare 2 Kings 9:12-13: "And they said, 'It is false; tell us now.' And he said, 'Thus and thus spake he to me, saying, "Thus saith the LORD, I have anointed thee king over Israel."' Then they hasted, and took every man his garment, and put it under him on the top of the stairs, and blew with trumpets, saying, 'Jehu is king.'"
[536] Compare 1 Maccabees 13:51: "And [Simon] entered into it the three and twentieth day of the second month in the hundred seventy first year, with thanksgiving, and branches of palm trees, and with harps, and cymbals, and with viols, and hymns, and songs; because there was destroyed a great enemy out of Israel."
2 Maccabees 10:3,7: "And having cleansed the temple they made another altar, and striking stones they took fire out of them, and offered a sacrifice after two years, and set forth incense, and lights, and shewbread. Therefore they bare branches, and fair boughs, and palms also, and sang psalms unto him that had given them good success in cleansing his place."

THE TREE OF LIFE

with a loud voice for all the mighty works that they had seen, and cried, saying, "Hosanna to the son of David! Blessed is the King of Israel that cometh in the name of the Lord! Blessed be the kingdom of our father David, that cometh in the name of the Lord! Hosanna in the highest! Peace in heaven, and glory in the highest!"[537] And some of the Pharisees from among the multitude said unto him, "Master, rebuke thy disciples." And he answered and said unto them, "I tell you that, if these should hold their peace, *the stones would immediately cry out.*"[538]

And when he was come near, he beheld the city, and wept over it, saying, "If thou hadst known, even thou, at least in this thy day, the things which belong unto thy peace! But now they are hid from thine eyes. For the days shall come upon thee, that thine enemies shall cast a trench about thee, and *compass thee round, and keep thee in on every side, and shall lay thee even with the ground*, and thy children within thee, and they shall not leave in thee one stone upon another, because thou knewest not the time of thy visitation."[539] The people therefore that was with him when he

---

[537] See Psalms 118:17-27: "I shall not die, but live, and declare the works of the LORD. The LORD hath chastened me sore; but he hath not given me over unto death. Open to me the gates of righteousness; I will go into them, and I will praise the LORD. This gate of the LORD, into which the righteous shall enter. I will praise thee; for thou hast heard me, and art become my salvation. The stone which the builders refused is become the head stone of the corner. This is the LORD's doing; it is marvellous in our eyes. This is the day which the LORD hath made; we will rejoice and be glad in it. Save now [Hosanna], I beseech thee, O LORD; O LORD, I beseech thee, send now prosperity. Blessed be he that cometh in the name of the LORD; we have blessed you out of the house of the LORD. God is the LORD, which hath shewed us light; bind the sacrifice with cords, even unto the horns of the altar."
[538] Compare Habakkuk 2:11: "For the stone shall cry out of the wall, and the beam out of the timber shall answer it."
[539] Compare Isaiah 29:1-4: "Woe to Ariel, to Ariel, the city where David dwelt! Add ye year to year; let them kill sacrifices. Yet I will distress Ariel, and there shall be heaviness and sorrow; and it shall be unto me as Ariel. And I will camp against thee round about, and will lay siege against thee with a mount, and I will raise forts against thee. And thou shalt be brought down, and shalt speak out of the ground, and thy speech shall be low out of the dust, and thy voice shall be, as of one that

called Lazarus out of his grave, and raised him from the dead, bare record. (For this cause the people also met him, for that they heard that he had done this miracle.)

And when he was come into Jerusalem, all the city was moved, saying, "Who is this?" And the multitude said, "This is Jesus the prophet of Nazareth of Galilee." The Pharisees therefore said among themselves, "Perceive ye how ye prevail nothing? Behold, the world is gone after him." And there were certain Greeks among them that came up to worship at the feast, the same came therefore to Philip, which was of Bethsaida of Galilee, and desired him, saying, "Sir, we would see Jesus." Philip cometh and telleth Andrew, and again Andrew and Philip tell Jesus. And Jesus answered them, saying, "The hour is come, that the Son of man should be glorified. Verily, verily, I say unto you, except a corn of wheat fall into the ground and die, it abideth alone, but if it die, it bringeth forth much fruit. He that loveth his life shall lose it, and he that hateth his life in this world shall keep it unto life eternal. If any man serve me, let him follow me, and where I am, there shall also my servant be. If any man serve me, him will my Father honour. Now is my soul troubled, and what shall I say?

"Father, save me from this hour, but for this cause came I unto this hour: Father, glorify thy name." Then came there a voice from heaven,[540] saying, "I have both glorified it, and will glorify it again." The people therefore, that stood by, and heard it, said that it thundered, others said, "An angel spake to him." Jesus answered and said, "This voice came not because of me, but for your sakes. Now is the judgment of this world, now shall the prince of this world be cast out. And I, if *I be lifted up from the earth, will draw all men unto*

---

hath a familiar spirit, out of the ground, and thy speech shall whisper out of the dust."
[540] See 2 Samuel 22:14: "The LORD thundered from heaven, and the most High uttered his voice."

THE TREE OF LIFE

me."⁵⁴¹ This he said, signifying what death he should die. The people answered him, "We have heard out of the law that *Christ abideth for ever*,⁵⁴² and how sayest thou, the Son of man must be lifted up? Who is this Son of man?"

Then Jesus said unto them, "Yet a little while is the light with you. Walk while ye have the light, lest darkness come upon you, for he that walketh in darkness knoweth not whither he goeth. While ye

---

⁵⁴¹ See Isaiah 5:26: "And he will lift up an ensign to the nations from far, and will hiss unto them from the end of the earth; and, behold, they shall come with speed swiftly."
Isaiah 11:10: "And in that day there shall be a root of Jesse, which shall stand for an ensign of the people; to it shall the Gentiles seek; and his rest shall be glorious."
Isaiah 18:3: "All ye inhabitants of the world, and dwellers on the earth, see ye, when he lifteth up an ensign on the mountains; and when he bloweth a trumpet, hear ye."
Compare Numbers 21:8-9: "And the LORD said unto Moses, 'Make thee a fiery serpent, and set it upon a pole; and it shall come to pass, that every one that is bitten, when he looketh upon it, shall live.' And Moses made a serpent of brass, and put it upon a pole, and it came to pass, that if a serpent had bitten any man, when he beheld the serpent of brass, he lived."
⁵⁴² See Psalms 89:34-37: "My covenant will I not break, nor alter the thing that is gone out of my lips. Once have I sworn by my holiness that I will not lie unto David. His seed shall endure for ever, and his throne as the sun before me. It shall be established for ever as the moon, and as a faithful witness in heaven. Selah."
2 Samuel 7:16: "And thine house and thy kingdom shall be established for ever before thee; thy throne shall be established for ever."
Isaiah 9:6-7: "For unto us a child is born, unto us a son is given; and the government shall be upon his shoulder; and his name shall be called Wonderful, Counsellor, The mighty God, The everlasting Father, The Prince of Peace. Of the increase of his government and peace there shall be no end, upon the throne of David, and upon his kingdom, to order it, and to establish it with judgment and with justice from henceforth even for ever. The zeal of the LORD of hosts will perform this."
Daniel 2:44: "And in the days of these kings shall the God of heaven set up a kingdom, which shall never be destroyed; and the kingdom shall not be left to other people, but it shall break in pieces and consume all these kingdoms, and it shall stand for ever."
Daniel 7:13-14: "I saw in the night visions, and, behold, one like the Son of man came with the clouds of heaven, and came to the Ancient of days, and they brought him near before him. And there was given him dominion, and glory, and a kingdom, that all people, nations, and languages, should serve him; his dominion is an everlasting dominion, which shall not pass away, and his kingdom that which shall not be destroyed."

have light, believe in the light, that ye may be the children of light." These things spake Jesus, and departed, and did hide himself from them. But though he had done so many miracles before them, yet they believed not on him,⁵⁴³ that the saying of Isaiah the prophet might be fulfilled, which he spake, "Lord, who hath believed our report? And to whom hath the arm of the Lord been revealed?"⁵⁴⁴ Therefore they could not believe, because that Isaiah said again, "He hath blinded their eyes, and hardened their heart, that they should not see with their eyes, nor understand with their heart, and be converted, and I should heal them."⁵⁴⁵ These things said Isaiah, when he saw his glory, and spake of him.

Nevertheless among the chief rulers also many believed on him, but because of the Pharisees they did not confess him, lest they should be put out of the synagogue. For they loved the praise of men more than the praise of God.⁵⁴⁶ Jesus cried and said, "He that believeth on me, believeth not on me, but on him that sent me. And he that seeth me, seeth him that sent me. I am come a light into the world,⁵⁴⁷ that whosoever believeth on me should not abide in

---

⁵⁴³ Compare Deuteronomy 29:2-4: "And Moses called unto all Israel, and said unto them, 'Ye have seen all that the LORD did before your eyes in the land of Egypt unto Pharaoh, and unto all his servants, and unto all his land; the great temptations which thine eyes have seen, the signs, and those great miracles; yet the LORD hath not given you an heart to perceive, and eyes to see, and ears to hear, unto this day.'"
⁵⁴⁴ "Who hath believed our report? And to whom is the arm of the LORD revealed?" – Isaiah 53:1
⁵⁴⁵ "Make the heart of this people fat, and make their ears heavy, and shut their eyes; lest they see with their eyes, and hear with their ears, and understand with their heart, and convert, and be healed." – Isaiah 6:10
⁵⁴⁶ Compare Proverbs 29:25: "The fear of man bringeth a snare; but whoso putteth his trust in the LORD shall be safe."
Isaiah 66:5: "Hear the word of the LORD, ye that tremble at his word; your brethren that hated you, that cast you out for my name's sake, said, 'Let the LORD be glorified;' but he shall appear to your joy, and they shall be ashamed."
⁵⁴⁷ See Malachi 4:2: "But unto you that fear my name shall the Sun of righteousness arise with healing in his wings; and ye shall go forth, and grow up as calves of the stall."
Isaiah 60:1-3: "Arise, shine; for thy light is come, and the glory of the LORD is risen upon thee. For, behold, the darkness shall cover the earth, and gross darkness the

THE TREE OF LIFE

darkness. And if any man hear my words, and believe not, I judge him not, for I came not to judge the world, but to save the world. He that rejecteth me, and receiveth not my words, hath one that judgeth him, the word that I have spoken, the same shall judge him in the last day. For I have not spoken of myself, but the Father which sent me, he gave me a commandment, what I should say, and what I should speak. And I know that his commandment is life everlasting,[548] whatsoever I speak therefore, even as the Father said unto me, so I speak."

---

people; but the LORD shall arise upon thee, and his glory shall be seen upon thee. And the Gentiles shall come to thy light, and kings to the brightness of thy rising."
[548] Compare <u>Sirach 19:19:</u> "The knowledge of the commandments of the Lord is the doctrine of life; and they that do things that please him shall receive the fruit of the tree of immortality."
<u>Baruch 4:1:</u> "This is the book of the commandments of God, and the law that endureth for ever; all they that keep it shall come to life; but such as leave it shall die."

THE TREE OF LIFE

Chapter Sixty Nine

And they come to Jerusalem, and Jesus went into the temple of God, and began to cast out them that sold and bought in the temple, and overthrew the tables of the moneychangers, and the seats of them that sold doves, and would not suffer that any man should carry any vessel through the temple. And said unto them, "Is it not written, *'My house shall be called of all nations the house of prayer?'*[549] But ye have made it a *den of thieves.*"[550]

And the blind and the lame came to him in the temple, and he healed them. And when the chief priests and scribes saw the wonderful things that he did, and the children crying in the temple, and saying, "*Hosanna* to the son of David,"[551] they were sore displeased, and said unto him, "Hearest thou what these say?" And Jesus saith unto them, "Yea, have ye never read, *'Out of the mouth of babes and sucklings thou hast perfected praise?'*"[552] And the scribes and chief priests heard it, and sought how they might destroy him,

---

[549] "Even them will I bring to my holy mountain, and make them joyful in my house of prayer; their burnt offerings and their sacrifices shall be accepted upon mine altar; for mine house shall be called an house of prayer for all people." – Isaiah 56:7
[550] See Jeremiah 7:11: "Is this house, which is called by my name, become a den of robbers in your eyes? Behold, even I have seen it, saith the LORD."
[551] See Psalms 118:25: "Save now [Hosanna], I beseech thee, O LORD; O LORD, I beseech thee, send now prosperity."
[552] "Out of the mouth of babes and sucklings hast thou ordained strength because of thine enemies, that thou mightest still the enemy and the avenger." – Psalms 8:2

for they feared him, because all the people was astonished at his doctrine.

And when Jesus had looked round about upon all things, and now the eventide was come, he left them, and he went out of the city unto Bethany with the twelve, and he lodged there.

THE TREE OF LIFE

Chapter Seventy

Now in the morning as he returned into the city, when they were come from Bethany, he hungered. And when he saw a fig tree afar off in the way, he came to it, if haply he might find any thing thereon, and came, and found nothing but leaves only, for the time of figs was not yet, and said unto it, "Let no fruit grow on thee henceforward for ever." And his disciples heard it.

And all the people came early in the morning to him in the temple, for to hear him. And he taught daily in the temple. But the chief priests and the scribes and the chief of the people sought to destroy him, and could not find what they might do, for all the people were very attentive to hear him.

THE TREE OF LIFE

Chapter Seventy One

And the next day, in the morning, as they passed by, they saw the fig tree dried up from the roots. And Peter calling to remembrance saith unto him, "Master, behold, the fig tree which thou cursedst is withered away." And when the disciples saw it, they marvelled, saying, "How soon is the fig tree withered away!" And Jesus answering saith unto them, "Have faith in God, for verily I say unto you, if ye have faith, and doubt not, ye shall not only do this which is done to the fig tree, but also if ye shall say unto this mountain, 'Be thou removed, and be thou cast into the sea,' it shall be done.[553] For verily I say unto you, that whosoever shall not doubt in his heart, but shall believe that those things which he saith shall come to pass, he shall have whatsoever he saith. Therefore I say unto you, all things, whatsoever ye desire, when ye pray, believe that ye receive them, and ye shall have them. And when ye stand praying, forgive, if ye have ought against any, that your Father also

---

[553] Compare Job 9:2,5: "I know it is so of a truth; but how should man be just with God? Which removeth the mountains, and they know not; which overturneth them in his anger."
Zechariah 4:6-7: "Then he answered and spake unto me, saying, 'This is the word of the LORD unto Zerubbabel, saying, Not by might, nor by power, but by my spirit, saith the LORD of hosts. Who art thou, O great mountain? Before Zerubbabel thou shalt become a plain; and he shall bring forth the headstone thereof with shoutings, crying, "Grace, grace unto it."'"

which is in heaven may forgive you your trespasses.[554] But if ye do not forgive, neither will your Father which is in heaven forgive your trespasses."

---

[554] Compare *Sirach* 28:2: "Forgive thy neighbour the hurt that he hath done unto thee, so shall thy sins also be forgiven when thou prayest."

Chapter Seventy Two

And it came to pass, that on one of those days, as he taught the people in the temple, and preached the gospel, the chief priests and the scribes came upon him with the elders, and say unto him, "By what authority doest thou these things? And who gave thee this authority to do these things?"

And Jesus answered and said unto them, "I will also ask of you one question, which if ye answer me, in like wise I will tell you by what authority I do these things." And he answered and said unto them, "The baptism of John, was it from heaven, or of men? Answer me." And they reasoned with themselves, saying, "If we shall say, 'From heaven,' he will say unto us, 'Why then did ye not believe him?' But if we say, 'Of men,' all the people will stone us." For they feared the people, for all men counted John, that he was a prophet indeed. And they answered Jesus, and said, "We cannot tell whence it was." And Jesus answering said unto them, "Neither do I tell you by what authority I do these things. But what think ye? A certain man had two sons, and he came to the first, and said, 'Son, go work to day in my vineyard.' He answered and said, 'I will not,' but afterward he repented, and went. And he came to the second, and said likewise. And he answered and said, 'I go, sir,' and went not. Whether of them twain did the will of his father?" They say unto him, "The first." Jesus saith unto them, "Verily I say unto you, that the publicans and the harlots go into the kingdom of God before you.

For John came unto you in the way of righteousness, and ye believed him not, but the publicans and the harlots believed him, and ye, when ye had seen it, repented not afterward, that ye might believe him."

And he spake this parable unto certain which trusted in themselves that they were righteous,[555] and despised others: "Two men went up into the temple to pray, the one a Pharisee, and the other a publican. The Pharisee stood and prayed thus with himself, 'God, I thank thee, that I am not as other men are, extortioners, unjust, adulterers, or even as this publican. I fast twice in the week, I give tithes of all that I possess.' And the publican, standing afar off, would not lift up so much as his eyes unto heaven, but smote upon his breast, saying, 'God be merciful to me a sinner.' I tell you, this man went down to his house justified rather than the other,[556] for every one that exalteth himself shall be abased, and he that humbleth himself shall be exalted.[557] Whosoever shall seek to save his life shall lose it, and whosoever shall lose his life shall preserve it.

"Hear another parable: There was a certain householder, which planted a vineyard, and set an hedge round about it, and

---

[555] Compare Isaiah 65:2,5: "I have spread out my hands all the day unto a rebellious people, which walketh in a way that was not good, after their own thoughts; which say, 'Stand by thyself, come not near to me; for I am holier than thou.' These are a smoke in my nose, a fire that burneth all the day."
Ecclesiastes 7:16-17: "Be not righteous over much; neither make thyself over wise; why shouldest thou destroy thyself? Be not over much wicked, neither be thou foolish; why shouldest thou die before thy time?"
[556] Compare 2 Esdras 8:48-49: "In this also thou art marvellous before the most High; in that thou hast humbled thyself, as it becometh thee, and hast not judged thyself worthy to be much glorified among the righteous."
[557] Compare Proverbs 16:18-19: "Pride goeth before destruction, and an haughty spirit before a fall. Better it is to be of an humble spirit with the lowly, than to divide the spoil with the proud."
Proverbs 29:23: "A man's pride shall bring him low; but honour shall uphold the humble in spirit."

digged a winepress in it, and built a tower,[558] and let it out to husbandmen, and went into a far country for a long time. And when the time of the fruit drew near, he sent a servant to the husbandmen, that he might receive from the husbandmen of the fruit of the vineyard, but the husbandmen caught him, and beat him, and sent him away empty. And again he sent unto them another servant, and at him they cast stones, and wounded him in the head, and sent him away shamefully handled and empty. And again he sent a third, and they wounded him also, and cast him out. And again he sent another, and him they killed, and many others, beating some, and killing some. Then said the lord of the vineyard, 'What shall I do? I will send my beloved son, it may be they will reverence him when they see him.' Having yet therefore one son, his wellbeloved, he sent him also last unto them. But when the husbandmen saw the son, they reasoned among themselves, 'This is the heir, come, let us kill him, and let us seize on his inheritance, that it may be ours.' And they caught him, and cast him out of the vineyard, and killed him. When the lord therefore of the vineyard cometh, what therefore will he do unto those husbandmen?" They say unto him, "He will miserably destroy those wicked men, and will let out his vineyard unto other husbandmen, which shall render him

---

[558] Compare Isaiah 5:1-7: "Now will I sing to my wellbeloved a song of my beloved touching his vineyard. My wellbeloved hath a vineyard in a very fruitful hill; and he fenced it, and gathered out the stones thereof, and planted it with the choicest vine, and built a tower in the midst of it, and also made a winepress therein; and he looked that it should bring forth grapes, and it brought forth wild grapes. And now, O inhabitants of Jerusalem, and men of Judah, judge, I pray you, betwixt me and my vineyard. What could have been done more to my vineyard, that I have not done in it? Wherefore, when I looked that it should bring forth grapes, brought it forth wild grapes? And now go to; I will tell you what I will do to my vineyard: I will take away the hedge thereof, and it shall be eaten up; and break down the wall thereof, and it shall be trodden down. And I will lay it waste; it shall not be pruned, nor digged; but there shall come up briers and thorns. I will also command the clouds that they rain no rain upon it. For the vineyard of the LORD of hosts is the house of Israel, and the men of Judah his pleasant plant; and he looked for judgment, but behold oppression; for righteousness, but behold a cry."

the fruits in their seasons."⁵⁵⁹ And he beheld them, and said, "Therefore say I unto you, the kingdom of God shall be taken from you, and given to a nation bringing forth the fruits thereof."⁵⁶⁰ And when they heard it, they said, "God forbid." Jesus saith unto them, "Did ye never read in the scriptures, *'The stone which the builders rejected, the same is become the head of the corner, this is the Lord's doing, and it is marvellous in our eyes?'*⁵⁶¹ Whosoever shall fall upon

---

⁵⁵⁹ Compare 2 Esdras 9:30-31: "And thou spakest saying, 'Hear me, O Israel; and mark my words, thou seed of Jacob. For, behold, I sow my law in you, and it shall bring fruit in you, and ye shall be honoured in it for ever.'"

⁵⁶⁰ See Hosea 2:21-23: "And it shall come to pass in that day, I will hear, saith the LORD, I will hear the heavens, and they shall hear the earth; and the earth shall hear the corn, and the wine, and the oil; and they shall hear Jezreel. And I will sow her unto me in the earth; and I will have mercy upon her that had not obtained mercy; and I will say to them which were not my people, 'Thou art my people;' and they shall say, 'Thou art my God.'"

Malachi 1:6-11: "A son honoureth his father, and a servant his master; if then I be a father, where is mine honour? And if I be a master, where is my fear? saith the LORD of hosts unto you, O priests, that despise my name. And ye say, 'Wherein have we despised thy name?' Ye offer polluted bread upon mine altar; and ye say, 'Wherein have we polluted thee?' In that ye say, 'The table of the LORD is contemptible.' Who is there even among you that would shut the doors for nought? Neither do ye kindle fire on mine altar for nought. I have no pleasure in you, saith the LORD of hosts, neither will I accept an offering at your hand. For from the rising of the sun even unto the going down of the same my name shall be great among the Gentiles; and in every place incense shall be offered unto my name, and a pure offering; for my name shall be great among the heathen, saith the LORD of hosts."

2 Esdras 1:24-25,35-40: "What shall I do unto thee, O Jacob? Thou, Judah, wouldest not obey me. I will turn me to other nations, and unto those will I give my name, that they may keep my statutes. Seeing ye have forsaken me, I will forsake you also; when ye desire me to be gracious unto you, I shall have no mercy upon you. Your houses will I give to a people that shall come; which not having heard of me yet shall believe me; to whom I have shewed no signs, yet they shall do that I have commanded them. They have seen no prophets, yet they shall call their sins to remembrance, and acknowledge them. I take to witness the grace of the people to come, whose little ones rejoice in gladness; and though they have not seen me with bodily eyes, yet in spirit they believe the thing that I say. And now, brother, behold what glory; and see the people that come from the east; unto whom I will give for leaders, Abraham, Isaac, and Jacob, Hosea, Amos, and Micah, Joel, Obadiah, and Jonah, Nahum, and Habakkuk, Zephaniah, Haggai, Zechariah, and Malachi, which is called also an angel of the Lord."

⁵⁶¹ "The stone which the builders refused is become the head stone of the corner. This is the LORD's doing; it is marvellous in our eyes." – Psalms 118:22-23

that stone shall be broken, but on whomsoever it shall fall, it will grind him to powder."⁵⁶²

And when he was demanded of the Pharisees, when the kingdom of God should come, he answered them and said, "The kingdom of God cometh not with observation, neither shall they say, 'Lo here!' or, 'Lo there!' for, behold, the kingdom of God is within you."

And the chief priests and the scribes the same hour sought to lay hands on him, but they feared the multitude, because they took him for a prophet, for they knew that he had spoken the parable against them, and they left him, and went their way.

And Jesus answered and spake unto them again by parables, and said, "The kingdom of heaven is like unto a certain king, which made a marriage for his son,⁵⁶³ and sent forth his servants to call them that were bidden to the wedding, and they would not come. Again, he sent forth other servants, saying, 'Tell them which are

---

⁵⁶² Compare Isaiah 8:13-15: "Sanctify the LORD of hosts himself; and let him be your fear, and let him be your dread. And he shall be for a sanctuary; but for a stone of stumbling and for a rock of offence to both the houses of Israel, for a gin and for a snare to the inhabitants of Jerusalem. And many among them shall stumble, and fall, and be broken, and be snared, and be taken."
Isaiah 28:16: "Therefore thus saith the Lord GOD, 'Behold, I lay in Zion for a foundation a stone, a tried stone, a precious corner stone, a sure foundation; he that believeth shall not make haste.'"
Daniel 2:44-45: "And in the days of these kings shall the God of heaven set up a kingdom, which shall never be destroyed; and the kingdom shall not be left to other people, but it shall break in pieces and consume all these kingdoms, and it shall stand for ever. Forasmuch as thou sawest that the stone was cut out of the mountain without hands, and that it brake in pieces the iron, the brass, the clay, the silver, and the gold; the great God hath made known to the king what shall come to pass hereafter; and the dream is certain, and the interpretation thereof sure."
⁵⁶³ Compare Proverbs 9:1-6: "Wisdom hath builded her house, she hath hewn out her seven pillars. She hath killed her beasts; she hath mingled her wine; she hath also furnished her table. She hath sent forth her maidens; she crieth upon the highest places of the city, 'Whoso is simple, let him turn in hither;' as for him that wanteth understanding, she saith to him, 'Come, eat of my bread, and drink of the wine which I have mingled. Forsake the foolish, and live; and go in the way of understanding.'"

bidden, "Behold, I have prepared my dinner, my oxen and my fatlings are killed, and all things are ready, come unto the marriage."' But they made light of it, and went their ways, one to his farm, another to his merchandise, and the remnant took his servants, and entreated them spitefully, and slew them. But when the king heard thereof, he was wroth, and he sent forth his armies, and destroyed those murderers, and burned up their city. Then saith he to his servants, 'The wedding is ready, but they which were bidden were not worthy. Go ye therefore into the highways, and as many as ye shall find, bid to the marriage.' So those servants went out into the highways, and gathered together all, as many as they found, both bad and good, and the wedding was furnished with guests. And when the king came in to see the guests, he saw there a man which had not on a wedding garment. And he saith unto him, 'Friend, how camest thou in hither not having a wedding garment?' And he was speechless. Then said the king to the servants, 'Bind him hand and foot, and take him away, and cast him into outer darkness, there shall be weeping and *gnashing of teeth*.[564] For *many are called, but few are chosen*.'"[565]

And when the chief priests and Pharisees had heard his parables, they perceived that he spake of them, and they went and took counsel how they might entangle him in his talk. And they send forth unto him certain spies of the Pharisees and of the Herodians, which should feign themselves just men, that they might catch him in his words, that so they might deliver him unto the power and authority of the governor. And they sent them with the Herodians,

---

[564] See Psalms 112:4,10: "Unto the upright there ariseth light in the darkness; he is gracious, and full of compassion, and righteous. The wicked shall see it, and be grieved; he shall gnash with his teeth, and melt away; the desire of the wicked shall perish."

[565] See 2 Esdras 8:1-3: "And he answered me, saying, 'The most High hath made this world for many, but the world to come for few. I will tell thee a similitude, Esdras; as when thou askest the earth, it shall say unto thee, that it giveth much mould whereof earthen vessels are made, but little dust that gold cometh of; even so is the course of this present world. There be many created, but few shall be saved.'"

saying, "Master, we know that thou art true, neither carest thou for any man, for thou regardest not the person of any, but teachest the way of God truly.[566] Tell us therefore, what thinkest thou? Is it lawful to give tribute unto Caesar, or not? Shall we give, or shall we not give?" But he, knowing their hypocrisy, and perceiving their craftiness, said unto them, "Why tempt ye me, ye hypocrites? Bring me the tribute money, that I may see it." And they brought unto him a penny. And he saith unto them, "Whose is this image and superscription?" They answered and said, "Caesar's." Then saith he unto them, "Render therefore unto Caesar the things which are Caesar's, and unto God the things that are God's." And they marvelled at his answer. And when they could not take hold of his words before the people, they held their peace, and left him, and went their way.

The same day came to him the Sadducees, which say that there is no resurrection, and asked him, saying, "Master, Moses wrote unto us, '*If a man's brother die, and leave his wife behind him,*

---

[566] See *Wisdom 6:7*: "For he which is Lord over all shall fear no man's person, neither shall he stand in awe of any man's greatness; for he hath made the small and great, and careth for all alike."
Leviticus 19:15: "Ye shall do no unrighteousness in judgment; thou shalt not respect the person of the poor, nor honour the person of the mighty; but in righteousness shalt thou judge thy neighbour."
Deuteronomy 1:17: "Ye shall not respect persons in judgment; but ye shall hear the small as well as the great; ye shall not be afraid of the face of man; for the judgment is God's; and the cause that is too hard for you, bring it unto me, and I will hear it."
Isaiah 51:7: "Hearken unto me, ye that know righteousness, the people in whose heart is my law; fear ye not the reproach of men, neither be ye afraid of their revilings."
Deuteronomy 10:15-20: "Only the LORD had a delight in thy fathers to love them, and he chose their seed after them, even you above all people, as it is this day. Circumcise therefore the foreskin of your heart, and be no more stiffnecked. For the LORD your God is God of gods, and Lord of lords, a great God, a mighty, and a terrible, which regardeth not persons, nor taketh reward. He doth execute the judgment of the fatherless and widow, and loveth the stranger, in giving him food and raiment. Love ye therefore the stranger; for ye were strangers in the land of Egypt. Thou shalt fear the LORD thy God; him shalt thou serve, and to him shalt thou cleave, and swear by his name."

THE TREE OF LIFE

and leave no children, that his brother should take his wife, and raise up seed unto his brother.'[567] Now there were with us seven brethren, and the first, when he had married a wife, deceased, and, having no issue, left his wife unto his brother. And the second took her to wife, and he died childless. And the third likewise, and in like manner unto the seventh also,[568] and they left no children, and all died, and last of all, the woman died also. Therefore in the resurrection, when they shall rise, whose wife shall she be of the seven? For they all had her to wife." Jesus answered and said unto them, "Ye do err, because ye know not the scriptures, neither the power of God.[569] The

---

[567] "If brethren dwell together, and one of them die, and have no child, the wife of the dead shall not marry without unto a stranger; her husband's brother shall go in unto her, and take her to him to wife, and perform the duty of an husband's brother unto her. And it shall be, that the firstborn which she beareth shall succeed in the name of his brother which is dead, that his name be not put out of Israel." - Deuteronomy 25:5-6

[568] Compare Tobit 7:10-11: "'For it is meet that thou shouldest marry my daughter; nevertheless I will declare unto thee the truth. I have given my daughter in marriage to seven men, who died that night they came in unto her; nevertheless for the present be merry.' But Tobias said, 'I will eat nothing here, till we agree and swear one to another.'"

[569] See Isaiah 26:19,21: "Thy dead men shall live, together with my dead body shall they arise. Awake and sing, ye that dwell in dust; for thy dew is as the dew of herbs, and the earth shall cast out the dead. For, behold, the LORD cometh out of his place to punish the inhabitants of the earth for their iniquity; the earth also shall disclose her blood, and shall no more cover her slain."

Daniel 12:2: "And many of them that sleep in the dust of the earth shall awake, some to everlasting life, and some to shame and everlasting contempt."

Job 19:25-26: "For I know that my redeemer liveth, and that he shall stand at the latter day upon the earth. And though after my skin worms destroy this body, yet in my flesh shall I see God."

Hosea 13:14: "I will ransom them from the power of the grave; I will redeem them from death. O death, I will be thy plagues; O grave, I will be thy destruction; repentance shall be hid from mine eyes."

Wisdom 2:23: "For God created man to be immortal, and made him to be an image of his own eternity."

Ezekiel 37:12-14: "Therefore prophesy and say unto them, 'Thus saith the Lord GOD; Behold, O my people, I will open your graves, and cause you to come up out of your graves, and bring you into the land of Israel. And ye shall know that I am the LORD, when I have opened your graves, O my people, and brought you up out of your graves, and shall put my spirit in you, and ye shall live, and I shall place you in

THE TREE OF LIFE

children of this world marry, and are given in marriage, but they which shall be accounted worthy to obtain that world, and shall rise from the dead, they neither marry, nor are given in marriage, but are as the angels which are in heaven. Neither can they die any more, for they are equal unto the angels, and are the children of God, being the children of the resurrection. But as touching the resurrection of the dead, that they rise, have ye not read in the book of Moses that which was spoken unto you by God at the bush, saying, '*I am the God of Abraham, and the God of Isaac, and the God of Jacob?*'[570] God is not the God of the dead, but of the living, for all live unto him,[571] ye therefore do greatly err." And when the multitude heard this, they were astonished at his doctrine.

But when the Pharisees had heard that he had put the Sadducees to silence, they were gathered together. Then one of them, which was a lawyer, came, and having heard them reasoning together, and perceiving that he had answered them well, asked him a question, tempting him, and saying, "Master, which is the great commandment in the law?" And Jesus answered him, "The first of all the commandments is, '*Hear, O Israel, the Lord our God is one Lord. And thou shalt love the Lord thy God with all thy heart, and with all*

---

your own land; then shall ye know that I the LORD have spoken it, and performed it, saith the LORD.'"
2 Esdras 7:32: "And the earth shall restore those that are asleep in her, and so shall the dust those that dwell in silence, and the secret places shall deliver those souls that were committed unto them."
[570] "Moreover he said, 'I am the God of thy father, the God of Abraham, the God of Isaac, and the God of Jacob.' And Moses hid his face; for he was afraid to look upon God. And God said moreover unto Moses, 'Thus shalt thou say unto the children of Israel, "The LORD God of your fathers, the God of Abraham, the God of Isaac, and the God of Jacob, hath sent me unto you;" this is my name for ever, and this is my memorial unto all generations.'" – Exodus 3:6,15
[571] Compare Isaiah 24:23: "Then the moon shall be confounded, and the sun ashamed, when the LORD of hosts shall reign in mount Zion, and in Jerusalem, and before his ancients gloriously."

*thy soul, and with all thy mind, and with all thy strength.'*⁵⁷² This is the first and great commandment. And the second is like unto it, namely this, *'Thou shalt love thy neighbour as thyself.'*⁵⁷³ There is none other commandment greater than these. On these two commandments hang all the law and the prophets." Then certain of the scribes answering said, "Well, Master, thou hast said the truth, for there is one God, and there is none other but he, and to love him with all the heart, and with all the understanding, and with all the soul, and with all the strength, and to love his neighbour as himself, is more than all whole burnt offerings and sacrifices."⁵⁷⁴ And when Jesus saw that he answered discreetly, he said unto him, "Thou art not far from the kingdom of God."

And after that they durst not ask him any question at all.

While the Pharisees were gathered together, Jesus asked them while he taught in the temple, "What think ye of Christ? Whose son

---

⁵⁷² "Hear, O Israel: The LORD our God is one LORD. And thou shalt love the LORD thy God with all thine heart, and with all thy soul, and with all thy might." - <u>Deuteronomy 6.4-5</u>
⁵⁷³ "Thou shalt not hate thy brother in thine heart; thou shalt in any wise rebuke thy neighbour, and not suffer sin upon him. Thou shalt not avenge, nor bear any grudge against the children of thy people, but thou shalt love thy neighbour as thyself: I am the LORD." - <u>Leviticus 19:17-18</u>
"Love thine own soul, and comfort thy heart, remove sorrow far from thee; for sorrow hath killed many, and there is no profit therein." - <u>Sirach 30:23</u>
⁵⁷⁴ Compare <u>Hosea 6:6</u>: "For I desired mercy, and not sacrifice; and the knowledge of God more than burnt offerings."
<u>Micah 6:6-8</u>: "Wherewith shall I come before the LORD, and bow myself before the high God? Shall I come before him with burnt offerings, with calves of a year old? Will the LORD be pleased with thousands of rams, or with ten thousands of rivers of oil? Shall I give my firstborn for my transgression, the fruit of my body for the sin of my soul? He hath shewed thee, O man, what is good; and what doth the LORD require of thee, but to do justly, and to love mercy, and to walk humbly with thy God?"
<u>Ecclesiastes 12:13</u>: "Let us hear the conclusion of the whole matter: Fear God, and keep his commandments; for this is the whole duty of man."

is he?" They say unto him, "The son of David."[575] He saith unto them, "How then doth David by the Holy Ghost in the book of Psalms call him Lord, saying, *'The LORD said unto my Lord, "Sit thou on my right hand, till I make thine enemies thy footstool?"'*[576] If David therefore calleth him Lord, how is he then his son?" And the common people heard him gladly.

And no man was able to answer him a word, neither durst any man from that day forth ask him any more questions.

And Jesus sat over against the treasury, and beheld how the people cast their gifts into the treasury, and many that were rich cast in much. And there came a certain poor widow, casting in thither two mites, which make a farthing. And he called unto him his disciples, and saith unto them, "Verily I say unto you, that this poor widow hath cast more in, than all they which have cast into the treasury, for all they did cast in unto the offerings of God of their abundance, but she of her want did cast in all that she had, even all her living."

Then in the audience of all the people he said unto his disciples, saying, "The scribes and the Pharisees sit in Moses' seat. All therefore whatsoever they bid you observe, that observe and do, but do not ye after their works, for they say, and do not. For they bind heavy burdens and grievous to be borne, and lay them on men's shoulders, but they themselves will not move them with one of their fingers. And all their works they do for to be seen of men, for they make broad their phylacteries,[577] and enlarge the borders

---

[575] See Jeremiah 23:5: "Behold, the days come, saith the LORD, that I will raise unto David a righteous Branch, and a King shall reign and prosper, and shall execute judgment and justice in the earth."
[576] "The LORD said unto my Lord, 'Sit thou at my right hand, until I make thine enemies thy footstool.'" – Psalms 110:1
[577] See Exodus 13:9: "And it shall be for a sign unto thee upon thine hand, and for a memorial between thine eyes, that the LORD'S law may be in thy mouth; for with a strong hand hath the LORD brought thee out of Egypt."

of their garments.⁵⁷⁸ Beware of the scribes, which love to go in long robes, and love salutations in the marketplaces, and the highest seats in the synagogues, and the chief rooms at feasts, and to be called of men, 'Rabbi,' 'Rabbi.' But be not ye called Rabbi, for one is your Master, even Christ, and all ye are brethren. And call no man your father upon the earth, for one is your Father, which is in heaven.⁵⁷⁹ But he that is greatest among you shall be your servant. And whosoever shall exalt himself shall be abased, and he that shall humble himself shall be exalted.⁵⁸⁰

"But woe unto you, scribes and Pharisees, hypocrites! For ye shut up the kingdom of heaven against men, for ye neither go in yourselves, neither suffer ye them that are entering to go in.

"Woe unto you, scribes and Pharisees, hypocrites! For ye devour widows' houses, and for a pretence make long prayer, therefore ye shall receive the greater damnation.

Deuteronomy 6:6-8: "And these words, which I command thee this day, shall be in thine heart. And thou shalt teach them diligently unto thy children, and shalt talk of them when thou sittest in thine house, and when thou walkest by the way, and when thou liest down, and when thou risest up. And thou shalt bind them for a sign upon thine hand, and they shall be as frontlets between thine eyes."
Deuteronomy 11:18: "Therefore shall ye lay up these my words in your heart and in your soul, and bind them for a sign upon your hand, that they may be as frontlets between your eyes."
⁵⁷⁸ See Numbers 15:38: "Speak unto the children of Israel, and bid them that they make them fringes in the borders of their garments throughout their generations, and that they put upon the fringe of the borders a ribband of blue. And it shall be unto you for a fringe, that ye may look upon it, and remember all the commandments of the LORD, and do them; and that ye seek not after your own heart and your own eyes, after which ye use to go a whoring."
⁵⁷⁹ Compare *2 Esdras* 1:28-29: "Thus saith the Almighty Lord, 'Have I not prayed you as a father his sons, as a mother her daughters, and a nurse her young babes, that ye would be my people, and I should be your God; that ye would be my children, and I should be your father?'"
⁵⁸⁰ Compare Proverbs 16:18-19: "Pride goeth before destruction, and an haughty spirit before a fall. Better it is to be of an humble spirit with the lowly, than to divide the spoil with the proud."
Proverbs 29:23: "A man's pride shall bring him low; but honour shall uphold the humble in spirit."

"Woe unto you, scribes and Pharisees, hypocrites! For ye compass sea and land to make one proselyte, and when he is made, ye make him twofold more the child of hell than yourselves.

"Woe unto you, ye blind guides, which say, 'Whosoever shall swear by the temple, it is nothing, but whosoever shall swear by the gold of the temple, he is a debtor!' Ye fools and blind, for whether is greater, the gold, or the temple that sanctifieth the gold? And, 'Whosoever shall swear by the altar, it is nothing, but whosoever sweareth by the gift that is upon it, he is guilty.' Ye fools and blind, for whether is greater, the gift, or the altar that sanctifieth the gift?[581] Whoso therefore shall swear by the altar, sweareth by it, and by all things thereon. And whoso shall swear by the temple, sweareth by it, and by him that dwelleth therein. And he that shall swear by heaven, sweareth by the throne of God,[582] and by him that sitteth thereon.

"Woe unto you, scribes and Pharisees, hypocrites! For ye pay tithe of mint and anise and cummin, and have omitted the weightier matters of the law, judgment, mercy, and faith.[583] These ought ye to

---

[581] See Exodus 29:37: "Seven days thou shalt make an atonement for the altar, and sanctify it; and it shall be an altar most holy; whatsoever toucheth the altar shall be holy."
[582] See Isaiah 66:1: "Thus saith the LORD, The heaven is my throne, and the earth is my footstool; where is the house that ye build unto me? And where is the place of my rest?"
[583] Compare Isaiah 1:11-20: "To what purpose is the multitude of your sacrifices unto me? saith the LORD. I am full of the burnt offerings of rams, and the fat of fed beasts; and I delight not in the blood of bullocks, or of lambs, or of he goats. When ye come to appear before me, who hath required this at your hand, to tread my courts? Bring no more vain oblations; incense is an abomination unto me; the new moons and sabbaths, the calling of assemblies, I cannot away with; it is iniquity, even the solemn meeting. Your new moons and your appointed feasts my soul hateth. They are a trouble unto me; I am weary to bear them. And when ye spread forth your hands, I will hide mine eyes from you; yea, when ye make many prayers, I will not hear; your hands are full of blood. Wash you, make you clean; put away the evil of your doings from before mine eyes; cease to do evil; learn to do well; seek judgment, relieve the oppressed, judge the fatherless, plead for the widow. Come now, and let us reason together, saith the LORD. Though your sins be as

have done,[584] and not to leave the other undone. Ye blind guides, which strain at a gnat, and swallow a camel.

"Woe unto you, scribes and Pharisees, hypocrites! For ye make clean the outside of the cup and of the platter, but within they are full of extortion and excess. Thou blind Pharisee, cleanse first that which is within the cup and platter, that the outside of them may be clean also.

"Woe unto you, scribes and Pharisees, hypocrites! For ye are like unto whited sepulchres, which indeed appear beautiful outward, but are within full of dead men's bones, and of all

---

scarlet, they shall be as white as snow; though they be red like crimson, they shall be as wool. If ye be willing and obedient, ye shall eat the good of the land; but if ye refuse and rebel, ye shall be devoured with the sword; for the mouth of the LORD hath spoken it."
Isaiah 58:2-7: "Yet they seek me daily, and delight to know my ways, as a nation that did righteousness, and forsook not the ordinance of their God; they ask of me the ordinances of justice; they take delight in approaching to God. 'Wherefore have we fasted,' say they, 'and thou seest not? Wherefore have we afflicted our soul, and thou takest no knowledge?' Behold, in the day of your fast ye find pleasure, and exact all your labours. Behold, ye fast for strife and debate, and to smite with the fist of wickedness. Ye shall not fast as ye do this day, to make your voice to be heard on high. Is it such a fast that I have chosen? A day for a man to afflict his soul? Is it to bow down his head as a bulrush, and to spread sackcloth and ashes under him? Wilt thou call this a fast, and an acceptable day to the LORD? Is not this the fast that I have chosen? To loose the bands of wickedness, to undo the heavy burdens, and to let the oppressed go free, and that ye break every yoke? Is it not to deal thy bread to the hungry, and that thou bring the poor that are cast out to thy house? When thou seest the naked, that thou cover him; and that thou hide not thyself from thine own flesh?"
[584] See Leviticus 27:30: "And all the tithe of the land, whether of the seed of the land, or of the fruit of the tree, is the LORD'S; it is holy unto the LORD."
Deuteronomy 14:22-23: "Thou shalt truly tithe all the increase of thy seed, that the field bringeth forth year by year. And thou shalt eat before the LORD thy God, in the place which he shall choose to place his name there, the tithe of thy corn, of thy wine, and of thine oil, and the firstlings of thy herds and of thy flocks; that thou mayest learn to fear the LORD thy God always."

uncleanness.[585] Even so, ye also outwardly appear righteous unto men, but within ye are full of hypocrisy and iniquity.

"Woe unto you, scribes and Pharisees, hypocrites! Because ye build the tombs of the prophets, and garnish the sepulchres of the righteous, and say, 'If we had been in the days of our fathers, we would not have been partakers with them in the blood of the prophets.' Wherefore ye be witnesses unto yourselves, that ye are the children of them which killed the prophets. Fill ye up then the measure of your fathers.[586]

"Ye serpents, ye generation of vipers, how can ye escape the damnation of hell? Wherefore, behold, I send unto you prophets, and wise men, and scribes, and some of them ye shall kill and crucify, and some of them shall ye scourge in your synagogues, and persecute them from city to city,[587] that upon you may come all the righteous blood shed upon the earth,[588] from the blood of righteous

---

[585] Compare Psalms 5:9: "For there is no faithfulness in their mouth; their inward part is very wickedness; their throat is an open sepulchre; they flatter with their tongue."
[586] Compare Isaiah 30:9-11: "That this is a rebellious people, lying children, children that will not hear the law of the LORD; which say to the seers, 'See not;' and to the prophets, 'Prophesy not unto us right things, speak unto us smooth things, prophesy deceits; get you out of the way, turn aside out of the path, cause the Holy One of Israel to cease from before us.'"
[587] See 2 Chronicles 36:15-16: "And the LORD God of their fathers sent to them by his messengers, rising up betimes, and sending; because he had compassion on his people, and on his dwelling place. But they mocked the messengers of God, and despised his words, and misused his prophets, until the wrath of the LORD arose against his people, till there was no remedy."
[588] See 2 Esdras 1:32: "I sent unto you my servants the prophets, whom ye have taken and slain, and torn their bodies in pieces, whose blood I will require of your hands, saith the Lord."
2 Esdras 15:7-9: "Therefore saith the Lord, I will hold my tongue no more as touching their wickedness, which they profanely commit, neither will I suffer them in those things, in which they wickedly exercise themselves; behold, the innocent and righteous blood crieth unto me, and the souls of the just complain continually. And therefore, saith the Lord, I will surely avenge them, and receive unto me all the innocent blood from among them."

Abel[589] unto the blood of Zacharias son of Jehoiada, whom ye slew between the temple and the altar.[590] Verily I say unto you, all these things shall be required of this generation.[591]

"O Jerusalem, Jerusalem, thou that killest the prophets,[592] and stonest them which are sent unto thee, how often would I have gathered thy children together, *even as a hen gathereth her chickens under her wings*, and ye would not! Behold, *your house is left unto*

Deuteronomy 32:43: "Rejoice, O ye nations, with his people; for he will avenge the blood of his servants, and will render vengeance to his adversaries, and will be merciful unto his land, and to his people."
[589] See Genesis 4:8: "And Cain talked with Abel his brother; and it came to pass, when they were in the field, that Cain rose up against Abel his brother, and slew him."
[590] See 2 Chronicles 24:19-21: "Yet he sent prophets to them, to bring them again unto the LORD; and they testified against them; but they would not give ear. And the Spirit of God came upon Zechariah the son of Jehoiada the priest, which stood above the people, and said unto them, 'Thus saith God, Why transgress ye the commandments of the LORD, that ye cannot prosper? Because ye have forsaken the LORD, he hath also forsaken you.' And they conspired against him, and stoned him with stones at the commandment of the king in the court of the house of the LORD."
[591] Compare Deuteronomy 1:35: "Surely there shall not one of these men of this evil generation see that good land, which I sware to give unto your fathers."
Genesis 4:10: "And he said, 'What hast thou done? The voice of thy brother's blood crieth unto me from the ground.'"
2 Esdras 15:8-9: "I will hold my tongue no more as touching their wickedness, which they profanely commit, neither will I suffer them in those things, in which they wickedly exercise themselves. Behold, the innocent and righteous blood crieth unto me, and the souls of the just complain continually. And therefore, saith the Lord, I will surely avenge them, and receive unto me all the innocent blood from among them."
2 Maccabees 8:2-4: "And they called upon the Lord, that he would look upon the people that was trodden down of all; and also pity the temple profaned of ungodly men; and that he would have compassion upon the city, sore defaced, and ready to be made even with the ground; and hear the blood that cried unto him, and remember the wicked slaughter of harmless infants, and the blasphemies committed against his name; and that he would shew his hatred against the wicked."
[592] Compare 2 Esdras 15:52-56: "Would I with jealousy have so proceeded against thee, saith the Lord, if thou hadst not always slain my chosen, exalting the stroke of thine hands, and saying over their dead, when thou wast drunken, 'Set forth the beauty of thy countenance?' The reward of thy whoredom shall be in thy bosom, therefore shalt thou receive recompence. Like as thou hast done unto my chosen, saith the Lord, even so shall God do unto thee, and shall deliver thee into mischief."

*you desolate.*⁵⁹³ For I say unto you, ye shall not see me henceforth, till ye shall say, *'Blessed is he that cometh in the name of the Lord.'*"⁵⁹⁴

And Jesus went out, and departed from the temple, and his disciples came to him for to shew him the buildings of the temple. And as he went out of the temple, one of his disciples saith unto him, "Master, see what manner of stones and what buildings are here!" And as some spake of the temple, how it was adorned with goodly stones and gifts, he said, "Seest thou these great buildings? Verily I say unto you, as for these things which ye behold, the days will

---

⁵⁹³ Compare <u>2 Esdras 1:28-33:</u> "Thus saith the Almighty Lord, 'Have I not prayed you as a father his sons, as a mother her daughters, and a nurse her young babes, that ye would be my people, and I should be your God; that ye would be my children, and I should be your father? I gathered you together, as a hen gathereth her chickens under her wings; but now, what shall I do unto you? I will cast you out from my face. When ye offer unto me, I will turn my face from you; for your solemn feastdays, your new moons, and your circumcisions, have I forsaken. I sent unto you my servants the prophets, whom ye have taken and slain, and torn their bodies in pieces, whose blood I will require of your hands,' saith the Lord. Thus saith the Almighty Lord, 'Your house is desolate, I will cast you out as the wind doth stubble.'"
<u>Psalms 17:8-9:</u> "Keep me as the apple of the eye, hide me under the shadow of thy wings, from the wicked that oppress me, from my deadly enemies, who compass me about."
<u>Psalms 91:1-4:</u> "He that dwelleth in the secret place of the most High shall abide under the shadow of the Almighty. I will say of the LORD, 'He is my refuge and my fortress; my God; in him will I trust.' Surely he shall deliver thee from the snare of the fowler, and from the noisome pestilence. He shall cover thee with his feathers, and under his wings shalt thou trust; his truth shall be thy shield and buckler."
<u>Jeremiah 12:7-8,10-11:</u> "I have forsaken mine house, I have left mine heritage; I have given the dearly beloved of my soul into the hand of her enemies. Mine heritage is unto me as a lion in the forest; it crieth out against me; therefore have I hated it. Many pastors have destroyed my vineyard, they have trodden my portion under foot, they have made my pleasant portion a desolate wilderness. They have made it desolate, and being desolate it mourneth unto me; the whole land is made desolate, because no man layeth it to heart."
⁵⁹⁴ See <u>Psalms 118:25-26:</u> "Save now [Hosanna], I beseech thee, O LORD; O LORD, I beseech thee, send now prosperity. Blessed be he that cometh in the name of the LORD; we have blessed you out of the house of the LORD."

come, in the which there shall not be left one stone upon another, that shall not be thrown down."[595]

---

[595] See <u>Micah 3:12:</u> "Therefore shall Zion for your sake be plowed as a field, and Jerusalem shall become heaps, and the mountain of the house as the high places of the forest."

THE TREE OF LIFE

Chapter Seventy Three

And in the day time he was teaching in the temple, and at night he went out, and abode in the mount that is called the mount of Olives. And as he sat upon the mount of Olives over against the temple, Peter and James and John and Andrew asked him privately, saying, "Master, tell us, when shall these things be? And what shall be the sign when all these things shall be fulfilled?"

And Jesus answered and said unto them, "Take heed lest any man deceive you, for many shall come in my name, saying, 'I am Christ, and the time draweth near,' and shall deceive many, but go ye not therefore after them.

"But when ye shall hear of wars and commotions and *rumours of wars*, be ye not troubled,[596] for all such things must come to pass, but the end is not yet. For nation shall rise against nation, and kingdom against kingdom,[597] and there shall be famines, and pestilences, and earthquakes, in divers places, and fearful sights,

---

[596] See Jeremiah 51:45-46: "My people, go ye out of the midst of her, and deliver ye every man his soul from the fierce anger of the LORD. And lest your heart faint, and ye fear for the rumour that shall be heard in the land; a rumour shall both come one year, and after that in another year shall come a rumour, and violence in the land, ruler against ruler."
[597] Compare 2 Chronicles 15:5-6: "And in those times there was no peace to him that went out, nor to him that came in, but great vexations were upon all the inhabitants of the countries. And nation was destroyed of nation, and city of city; for God did vex them with all adversity."

and great signs shall there be from heaven. All these are the beginning of sorrows.

"But before all these, they shall lay their hands on you, and persecute you, delivering you up to the councils, and in the synagogues ye shall be beaten, and into prisons, being brought before kings and rulers for my name's sake, for a testimony against them.[598] Then shall they deliver you up to be afflicted, and shall kill you, and ye shall be hated of all nations for my name's sake.[599] And this gospel of the kingdom must first be preached in all the world for a witness unto all nations, and then shall the end come.

"And when they bring you, and deliver you up unto the synagogues, and unto magistrates, and powers, take ye no thought beforehand how or what thing ye shall answer, or what ye shall say, neither do ye premeditate, but whatsoever shall be given you in that hour, that speak ye, for it is not ye that speak, but the Holy Ghost.[600] For the Holy Ghost shall teach you in the same hour what ye ought to say. Settle it therefore in your hearts, not to meditate before what ye shall answer, for I will give you a mouth and wisdom, which all your adversaries shall not be able to gainsay nor resist.

---

[598] See Jeremiah 15:15: "O LORD, thou knowest; remember me, and visit me, and revenge me of my persecutors; take me not away in thy longsuffering; know that for thy sake I have suffered rebuke."
[599] Compare Isaiah 66:5: "Hear the word of the LORD, ye that tremble at his word; your brethren that hated you, that cast you out for my name's sake, said, 'Let the LORD be glorified;' but he shall appear to your joy, and they shall be ashamed."
Isaiah 51:7: "Hearken unto me, ye that know righteousness, the people in whose heart is my law; fear ye not the reproach of men, neither be ye afraid of their revilings."
Jeremiah 15:15: "O LORD, thou knowest; remember me, and visit me, and revenge me of my persecutors; take me not away in thy longsuffering; know that for thy sake I have suffered rebuke."
[600] Compare Jeremiah 1:9: "Then the LORD put forth his hand, and touched my mouth. And the LORD said unto me, 'Behold, I have put my words in thy mouth.'"
Exodus 4:11-12: "And the LORD said unto him, 'Who hath made man's mouth? Or who maketh the dumb, or deaf, or the seeing, or the blind? Have not I the LORD? Now therefore go, and I will be with thy mouth, and teach thee what thou shalt say.'"

"And ye shall be betrayed both by parents, and brethren, and kinsfolks, and friends, and some of you shall they cause to be put to death. And ye shall be hated of all men for my name's sake, but he that shall endure unto the end, the same shall be saved. And *there shall not an hair of your head perish.*[601] In your patience possess ye your souls.[602] And then shall many be offended, and shall betray one another, and shall hate one another. And many false prophets shall rise, and shall deceive many. And because iniquity shall abound, the love of many shall wax cold. Now the brother shall betray the brother to death, and the father the son, and children shall rise up against their parents, and shall cause them to be put to death.[603]

"And when ye shall see Jerusalem compassed with armies, then know that the desolation thereof is nigh. When ye therefore shall see the *abomination of desolation,* spoken of by Daniel the prophet, standing where it ought not, in the holy place,[604] (let him

---

[601] See 1 Kings 1:52: "And Solomon said, 'If he will shew himself a worthy man, there shall not an hair of him fall to the earth; but if wickedness shall be found in him, he shall die.'"
[602] Compare Sirach 2:1-5: "My son, if thou come to serve the Lord, prepare thy soul for temptation. Set thy heart aright, and constantly endure, and make not haste in time of trouble. Cleave unto him, and depart not away, that thou mayest be increased at thy last end. Whatsoever is brought upon thee take cheerfully, and be patient when thou art changed to a low estate. For gold is tried in the fire, and acceptable men in the furnace of adversity."
[603] Compare Micah 7:5-6: "Trust ye not in a friend, put ye not confidence in a guide, keep the doors of thy mouth from her that lieth in thy bosom. For the son dishonoureth the father, the daughter riseth up against her mother, the daughter in law against her mother in law; a man's enemies are the men of his own house."
Ezekiel 38:21: "And I will call for a sword against him throughout all my mountains, saith the Lord GOD; every man's sword shall be against his brother."
[604] See Daniel 9:26-27: "And after threescore and two weeks shall Messiah be cut off, but not for himself; and the people of the prince that shall come shall destroy the city and the sanctuary; and the end thereof shall be with a flood, and unto the end of the war desolations are determined. And he shall confirm the covenant with many for one week; and in the midst of the week he shall cause the sacrifice and the oblation to cease, and for the overspreading of abominations he shall make it desolate, even until the consummation, and that determined shall be poured upon the desolate."

that readeth understand,) then let them that are in Judaea flee to the mountains, and let them which are in the midst of it depart out, and let not them that are in the countries enter thereinto.[605] Let him which is on the housetop, and his stuff in the house, let him not come down into the house, neither enter therein, to take any thing out of his house. And he that is in the field, let him likewise not turn back again for to take up his clothes. For these be *the days of vengeance*,[606] that all things which are written may be fulfilled.[607]

<u>Daniel 11:31:</u> "And arms shall stand on his part, and they shall pollute the sanctuary of strength, and shall take away the daily sacrifice, and they shall place the abomination that maketh desolate."
See also <u>*1 Maccabees* 1:54-59:</u> "Now the fifteenth day of the month Casleu, in the hundred forty and fifth year, they set up the abomination of desolation upon the altar, and builded idol altars throughout the cities of Juda on every side; and burnt incense at the doors of their houses, and in the streets. And when they had rent in pieces the books of the law which they found, they burnt them with fire. And whosoever was found with any the book of the testament, or if any committed to the law, the king's commandment was, that they should put him to death. Thus did they by their authority unto the Israelites every month, to as many as were found in the cities. Now the five and twentieth day of the month they did sacrifice upon the idol altar, which was upon the altar of God."
<u>*1 Maccabees* 6:7:</u> "Also that they had pulled down the abomination, which he had set up upon the altar in Jerusalem, and that they had compassed about the sanctuary with high walls, as before, and his city Bethsura."
[605] See <u>Ezekiel 7:5-22.</u>
[606] See <u>Isaiah 63:3-4:</u> "I have trodden the winepress alone; and of the people there was none with me; for I will tread them in mine anger, and trample them in my fury; and their blood shall be sprinkled upon my garments, and I will stain all my raiment. For the day of vengeance is in mine heart, and the year of my redeemed is come."
<u>Hosea 9:7:</u> "The days of visitation are come, the days of recompence are come; Israel shall know it; the prophet is a fool, the spiritual man is mad, for the multitude of thine iniquity, and the great hatred."
<u>Zephaniah 1:14-18:</u> "The great day of the LORD is near, it is near, and hasteth greatly, even the voice of the day of the LORD; the mighty man shall cry there bitterly. That day is a day of wrath, a day of trouble and distress, a day of wasteness and desolation, a day of darkness and gloominess, a day of clouds and thick darkness, a day of the trumpet and alarm against the fenced cities, and against the high towers. And I will bring distress upon men, that they shall walk like blind men, because they have sinned against the LORD; and their blood shall be poured out as dust, and their flesh as the dung. Neither their silver nor their gold shall be able to deliver them in the day of the LORD'S wrath; but the whole land shall be devoured

THE TREE OF LIFE

And woe unto them that are with child, and to them that give suck in those days! For there shall be great distress in the land, and wrath upon this people, and they shall fall by the edge of the sword, and shall be led away captive into all nations, and Jerusalem shall be trodden down of the Gentiles, until the times of the Gentiles be fulfilled.

"And pray ye that your flight be not in the winter, neither on the sabbath day, for then shall be great tribulation, such as was not since the beginning of the world which God created unto this time, no, nor ever shall be. And except that the Lord had shortened those days, no flesh should be saved, but for the elect's sake, whom he hath chosen, he hath *shortened the days*.[608]

"Verily I say unto you, that this generation shall not pass, till all these things be fulfilled. Heaven and earth shall pass away, but my words shall not pass away.[609]

---

by the fire of his jealousy; for he shall make even a speedy riddance of all them that dwell in the land."
[607] See Isaiah 11:1-12:6, 25:6-8, 28:16-21, 34:1-35:10, 40:1-11, 59:20-63:5, 66:15-16; Jeremiah 23:1-8; Ezekiel 34:1-31; Daniel 2:44-45, 7:13-14, 9:24-27; Hosea 13:14; Micah 1:1-7:20; Zechariah 12:9-14:21; Malachi 4:1-6; Judith 16:15; et cetera.
[608] See 2 *Esdras* 2:13: "Go, and ye shall receive; pray for few days unto you, that they may be shortened; the kingdom is already prepared for you: watch."
Sirach 36:8: "Make the time short, remember the covenant, and let them declare thy wonderful works."
[609] Compare Isaiah 40:8: "The grass withereth, the flower fadeth; but the word of our God shall stand for ever."
Isaiah 51:6-8: "Lift up your eyes to the heavens, and look upon the earth beneath; for the heavens shall vanish away like smoke, and the earth shall wax old like a garment, and they that dwell therein shall die in like manner; but my salvation shall be for ever, and my righteousness shall not be abolished. Hearken unto me, ye that know righteousness, the people in whose heart is my law; fear ye not the reproach of men, neither be ye afraid of their revilings. For the moth shall eat them up like a garment, and the worm shall eat them like wool; but my righteousness shall be for ever, and my salvation from generation to generation."
Psalms 102:24-27: "I said, O my God, take me not away in the midst of my days; thy years are throughout all generations. Of old hast thou laid the foundation of the earth; and the heavens are the work of thy hands. They shall perish, but thou shalt endure; yea, all of them shall wax old like a garment; as a vesture shalt thou change

THE TREE OF LIFE

"Then if any man shall say unto you, 'Lo, here is Christ,' or, 'Lo, he is there,' believe him not. And if they shall say to you, 'See here,' or, 'See there,' go not after them, nor follow them. For there shall arise false Christs, and false prophets,[610] and shall shew great signs and wonders, to seduce and deceive, if it were possible, even the very elect.[611] Wherefore if they shall say unto you, 'Behold, he is in the desert,' go not forth, or 'Behold, he is in the secret chambers,' believe it not. For as the lightning cometh out of one part under heaven, and shineth even unto the other, so shall also the coming of the Son of man be.[612]

---

them, and they shall be changed. But thou art the same, and thy years shall have no end."
[610] Compare 1 Kings 22:19-23: "And he said, 'Hear thou therefore the word of the LORD: I saw the LORD sitting on his throne, and all the host of heaven standing by him on his right hand and on his left. And the LORD said, "Who shall persuade Ahab, that he may go up and fall at Ramoth-gilead?" And one said on this manner, and another said on that manner. And there came forth a spirit, and stood before the LORD, and said, "I will persuade him." And the LORD said unto him, "Wherewith?" And he said, "I will go forth, and I will be a lying spirit in the mouth of all his prophets." And he said, "Thou shalt persuade him, and prevail also; go forth, and do so." Now therefore, behold, the LORD hath put a lying spirit in the mouth of all these thy prophets, and the LORD hath spoken evil concerning thee.'"
Deuteronomy 13:1-3: "If there arise among you a prophet, or a dreamer of dreams, and giveth thee a sign or a wonder, and the sign or the wonder come to pass, whereof he spake unto thee, saying, 'Let us go after other gods, which thou hast not known, and let us serve them;' thou shalt not hearken unto the words of that prophet, or that dreamer of dreams; for the LORD your God proveth you, to know whether ye love the LORD your God with all your heart and with all your soul."
[611] Compare Daniel 11:35: "And some of them of understanding shall fall, to try them, and to purge, and to make them white, even to the time of the end; because it is yet for a time appointed."
[612] See Zechariah 9:14: "And the LORD shall be seen over them, and his arrow shall go forth as the lightning; and the LORD GOD shall blow the trumpet, and shall go with whirlwinds of the south."
Daniel 7:13-14: "I saw in the night visions, and, behold, one like the Son of man came with the clouds of heaven, and came to the Ancient of days, and they brought him near before him. And there was given him dominion, and glory, and a kingdom, that all people, nations, and languages, should serve him; his dominion is an everlasting dominion, which shall not pass away, and his kingdom that which shall not be destroyed."

"But first must he suffer many things, and be rejected of this generation. But take ye heed, behold, I have told you all things before.

"But in the days after that tribulation, there shall be signs in the sun, and in the moon, and in the stars. The sun shall be darkened, and the moon shall not give her light, and the stars of heaven shall fall, and the powers that are in heaven shall be shaken, and upon the earth distress of nations, with perplexity, the sea and the waves roaring, men's hearts failing them for fear of those things which are coming on the earth, and then shall all the tribes of the earth mourn.[613]

---

[613] Compare Isaiah 13:6-11: "Howl ye; for the day of the LORD is at hand; it shall come as a destruction from the Almighty. Therefore shall all hands be faint, and every man's heart shall melt. And they shall be afraid; pangs and sorrows shall take hold of them; they shall be in pain as a woman that travaileth. They shall be amazed one at another; their faces shall be as flames. Behold, the day of the LORD cometh, cruel both with wrath and fierce anger, to lay the land desolate; and he shall destroy the sinners thereof out of it. For the stars of heaven and the constellations thereof shall not give their light; the sun shall be darkened in his going forth, and the moon shall not cause her light to shine. And I will punish the world for their evil, and the wicked for their iniquity; and I will cause the arrogancy of the proud to cease, and will lay low the haughtiness of the terrible."
Isaiah 24:23: "Then the moon shall be confounded, and the sun ashamed, when the LORD of hosts shall reign in mount Zion, and in Jerusalem, and before his ancients gloriously."
Isaiah 29:6-7: "Thou shalt be visited of the LORD of hosts with thunder, and with earthquake, and great noise, with storm and tempest, and the flame of devouring fire. And the multitude of all the nations that fight against Ariel, even all that fight against her and her munition, and that distress her, shall be as a dream of a night vision."
Ezekiel 32:7-10: "And when I shall put thee out, I will cover the heaven, and make the stars thereof dark; I will cover the sun with a cloud, and the moon shall not give her light. All the bright lights of heaven will I make dark over thee, and set darkness upon thy land, saith the Lord GOD. I will also vex the hearts of many people, when I shall bring thy destruction among the nations, into the countries which thou hast not known. Yea, I will make many people amazed at thee, and their kings shall be horribly afraid for thee, when I shall brandish my sword before them; and they shall tremble at every moment, every man for his own life, in the day of thy fall."
Joel 2:2-11,30-31: "A day of darkness and of gloominess, a day of clouds and of thick darkness, as the morning spread upon the mountains; a great people and a

THE TREE OF LIFE

"And then shall appear the sign of the Son of man in heaven, and they shall see the Son of man coming in *the clouds of heaven with great power and glory*.[614] And he shall send his angels with a

---

strong; there hath not been ever the like, neither shall be any more after it, even to the years of many generations. A fire devoureth before them; and behind them a flame burneth; the land is as the garden of Eden before them, and behind them a desolate wilderness; yea, and nothing shall escape them. Like the noise of chariots on the tops of mountains shall they leap, like the noise of a flame of fire that devoureth the stubble, as a strong people set in battle array. Before their face the people shall be much pained; all faces shall gather blackness. They shall run to and fro in the city; they shall run upon the wall, they shall climb up upon the houses; they shall enter in at the windows like a thief. The earth shall quake before them; the heavens shall tremble; the sun and the moon shall be dark, and the stars shall withdraw their shining. And the LORD shall utter his voice before his army; for his camp is very great; for he is strong that executeth his word; for the day of the LORD is great and very terrible; and who can abide it? And I will shew wonders in the heavens and in the earth, blood, and fire, and pillars of smoke. The sun shall be turned into darkness, and the moon into blood, before the great and the terrible day of the LORD come."

Joel 3:15: "The sun and the moon shall be darkened, and the stars shall withdraw their shining."

Amos 5:17-20: "And in all vineyards shall be wailing; for I will pass through thee, saith the LORD. Woe unto you that desire the day of the LORD! To what end is it for you? The day of the LORD is darkness, and not light. As if a man did flee from a lion, and a bear met him; or went into the house, and leaned his hand on the wall, and a serpent bit him. Shall not the day of the LORD be darkness, and not light? Even very dark, and no brightness in it?"

See also Joshua 10:12-14; Isaiah 38:4-8.

[614] See Daniel 7:13-14: "I saw in the night visions, and, behold, one like the Son of man came with the clouds of heaven, and came to the Ancient of days, and they brought him near before him. And there was given him dominion, and glory, and a kingdom, that all people, nations, and languages, should serve him; his dominion is an everlasting dominion, which shall not pass away, and his kingdom that which shall not be destroyed."

Psalms 97:1-6: "The LORD reigneth; let the earth rejoice; let the multitude of isles be glad thereof. Clouds and darkness are round about him; righteousness and judgment are the habitation of his throne. A fire goeth before him, and burneth up his enemies round about. His lightnings enlightened the world; the earth saw, and trembled. The hills melted like wax at the presence of the LORD, at the presence of the Lord of the whole earth. The heavens declare his righteousness, and all the people see his glory."

Psalms 104:1-3: "Bless the LORD, O my soul. O LORD my God, thou art very great; thou art clothed with honour and majesty. Who coverest thyself with light as with a garment; who stretchest out the heavens like a curtain; who layeth the beams of his

THE TREE OF LIFE

great sound of a trumpet,[615] and they shall gather together his elect from the four winds, from the *uttermost part of the earth to the uttermost part of heaven*.[616] And when these things begin to come to

---

chambers in the waters; who maketh the clouds his chariot; who walketh upon the wings of the wind."
1 Samuel 2:10: "The adversaries of the LORD shall be broken to pieces; out of heaven shall he thunder upon them; the LORD shall judge the ends of the earth; and he shall give strength unto his king, and exalt the horn of his anointed."
[615] Compare Exodus 19:16-20: "And it came to pass on the third day in the morning, that there were thunders and lightnings, and a thick cloud upon the mount, and the voice of the trumpet exceeding loud; so that all the people that was in the camp trembled. And Moses brought forth the people out of the camp to meet with God; and they stood at the nether part of the mount. And mount Sinai was altogether on a smoke, because the LORD descended upon it in fire; and the smoke thereof ascended as the smoke of a furnace, and the whole mount quaked greatly. And when the voice of the trumpet sounded long, and waxed louder and louder, Moses spake, and God answered him by a voice. And the LORD came down upon mount Sinai, on the top of the mount; and the LORD called Moses up to the top of the mount; and Moses went up."
Isaiah 27:13: "And it shall come to pass in that day, that the great trumpet shall be blown, and they shall come which were ready to perish in the land of Assyria, and the outcasts in the land of Egypt, and shall worship the LORD in the holy mount at Jerusalem."
Isaiah 18:3: "All ye inhabitants of the world, and dwellers on the earth, see ye, when he lifteth up an ensign on the mountains; and when he bloweth a trumpet, hear ye."
Zechariah 9:14: "And the LORD shall be seen over them, and his arrow shall go forth as the lightning; and the LORD GOD shall blow the trumpet, and shall go with whirlwinds of the south."
[616] See Deuteronomy 30:3-4: "That then the LORD thy God will turn thy captivity, and have compassion upon thee, and will return and gather thee from all the nations, whither the LORD thy God hath scattered thee. If any of thine be driven out unto the outmost parts of heaven, from thence will the LORD thy God gather thee, and from thence will he fetch thee."
Isaiah 11:10-12, 18:3: "And in that day there shall be a root of Jesse, which shall stand for an ensign of the people; to it shall the Gentiles seek; and his rest shall be glorious. And it shall come to pass in that day, that the Lord shall set his hand again the second time to recover the remnant of his people, which shall be left, from Assyria, and from Egypt, and from Pathros, and from Cush, and from Elam, and from Shinar, and from Hamath, and from the islands of the sea. And he shall set up an ensign for the nations, and shall assemble the outcasts of Israel, and gather together the dispersed of Judah from the four corners of the earth. All ye inhabitants of the world, and dwellers on the earth, see ye, when he lifteth up an ensign on the mountains; and when he bloweth a trumpet, hear ye."

pass, then look up,[617] and lift up your heads, for your redemption drraweth nigh. And as it was in the days of Noah, so shall it be also in the days of the Son of man. For in the days that were before the flood they did eat, they drank, they married wives, and they were given in marriage, until the day that Noah entered into the ark, and they knew not until the flood came, and took them all away,[618] so shall also the coming of the Son of man be. Likewise also as it was in the days of Lot, they did eat, they drank, they bought, they sold, they planted, they builded, but the same day that Lot went out of Sodom it rained fire and brimstone from heaven, and destroyed them all.[619] Even thus shall it be in the day when the Son of man is revealed. Remember Lot's wife.[620]

"I tell you, in that night there shall be two men in one bed, the one shall be taken, and the other shall be left. Two women shall be grinding together at the mill, the one shall be taken, and the other left. Then shall two be in the field, the one shall be taken, and the other left."[621] And they answered and said unto him, "Where, Lord?" And he said unto them, "Wheresoever the carcase is, *there will the eagles be gathered together.*"[622]

---

[617] Compare Psalms 123:1-2: "Unto thee lift I up mine eyes, O thou that dwellest in the heavens. Behold, as the eyes of servants look unto the hand of their masters, and as the eyes of a maiden unto the hand of her mistress; so our eyes wait upon the LORD our God, until that he have mercy upon us."
[618] See Genesis 6:5-7:23.
[619] See Genesis 18:16-19:26.
[620] See Genesis 19:26: "But his wife looked back from behind him, and she became a pillar of salt."
[621] Compare Jeremiah 3:14-15: "Turn, O backsliding children, saith the LORD; for I am married unto you; and I will take you one of a city, and two of a family, and I will bring you to Zion. And I will give you pastors according to mine heart, which shall feed you with knowledge and understanding."
[622] See Isaiah 34:8,15: "For it is the day of the LORD'S vengeance, and the year of recompences for the controversy of Zion. There shall the great owl make her nest, and lay, and hatch, and gather under her shadow; there shall the vultures also be gathered, every one with her mate."

THE TREE OF LIFE

And he spake to them a parable, "Behold the fig tree, and all the trees, when her branch is yet tender, and now shoots forth leaves, ye see and know of your own selves that summer is now nigh at hand. So likewise ye, when ye shall see all these things come to pass, know that it is nigh at hand, even at the doors.

"But of that day and hour knoweth no man, no, not the angels which are in heaven, neither the Son, but my Father only. Take ye heed, watch and pray, for ye know not when the time is."

And he spake a parable unto them to this end, that men ought always to pray, and not to faint, saying, "There was in a city a judge, which feared not God, neither regarded man. And there was a widow in that city, and she came unto him, saying, 'Avenge me of mine adversary.' And he would not for a while, but afterward he said within himself, 'Though I fear not God, nor regard man, yet because this widow troubleth me, I will avenge her, lest by her continual coming she weary me.' Hear what the unjust judge saith. Shall not God avenge his own elect, which cry day and night unto him, though he bear long with them? I tell you that he will avenge them speedily.

"Nevertheless when the Son of man cometh, shall he find faith on the earth? Watch ye therefore, and pray always, that ye may be accounted worthy to escape all these things that shall come to pass, and to stand before the Son of man. And take heed to yourselves, lest at any time your hearts be overcharged with surfeiting, and drunkenness, and cares of this life, and that day come upon you unawares. For as a snare shall it come on all them that dwell on the face of the whole earth. For the Son of man is as a man taking a far journey, who left his house, and gave authority to his servants, and to every man his work, and commanded the porter to watch. Watch therefore, for ye know not what hour your Lord doth come, at even, or at midnight, or at the cockcrowing, or in the morning, lest coming suddenly he find you sleeping. But know this, that if the goodman of the house had known in what watch the thief would come, he would have watched, and would not have suffered his house to be broken up. Therefore be ye also ready, for in such an hour as ye think not the Son of man cometh. Who then is a faithful and wise servant, whom his lord hath made ruler over his household, to give them meat in due season? Blessed is that servant, whom his lord when he cometh shall find so doing. Verily I say unto you, that he shall make him ruler over all his goods. But if that evil servant shall say in his heart, 'My lord delayeth his coming,' and shall begin to smite his fellowservants, and to eat and drink with the drunken, the lord of that servant shall come in a day when he looketh not for him, and in an hour that he is not aware of, and shall cut him asunder, and appoint him his portion with the hypocrites, there shall be weeping and *gnashing of teeth*.[623]

"Then shall the kingdom of heaven be likened unto ten virgins, which took their lamps, and went forth to meet the bridegroom. And five of them were wise, and five were foolish. They that were foolish took their lamps, and took no oil with them. But the wise took oil in their vessels with their lamps. While the bridegroom tarried, they all slumbered and slept. And at midnight there was a cry made, 'Behold, the bridegroom cometh, go ye out to meet him.' Then all those virgins arose, and trimmed their lamps. And the foolish said unto the wise, 'Give us of your oil, for our lamps are gone out.'[624] But the wise answered, saying, 'Not so, lest there be not enough for us and you, but go ye rather to them that sell, and buy for yourselves.'

---

[623] See Psalms 112:4,10: "Unto the upright there ariseth light in the darkness; he is gracious, and full of compassion, and righteous. The wicked shall see it, and be grieved; he shall gnash with his teeth, and melt away; the desire of the wicked shall perish."
[624] Compare Psalms 119:105: "Thy word is a lamp unto my feet, and a light unto my path."
Proverbs 6:23: "For the commandment is a lamp; and the law is light; and reproofs of instruction are the way of life."
Proverbs 13:9: "The light of the righteous rejoiceth; but the lamp of the wicked shall be put out."

And while they went to buy, the bridegroom came, and they that were ready went in with him to the marriage, and the door was shut. Afterward came also the other virgins, saying, 'Lord, Lord, open to us.' But he answered and said, 'Verily I say unto you, I know you not.' Watch therefore, for ye know neither the day nor the hour wherein the Son of man cometh. And what I say unto you I say unto all: watch.[625]

"For the kingdom of heaven is as a man travelling into a far country, who called his own servants, and delivered unto them his goods. And unto one he gave five talents, to another two, and to another one, to every man according to his several ability, and straightway took his journey. Then he that had received the five talents went and traded with the same, and made them other five talents. And likewise he that had received two, he also gained other two. But he that had received one went and digged in the earth, and hid his lord's money. After a long time the lord of those servants cometh, and reckoneth with them. And so he that had received five talents came and brought other five talents, saying, 'Lord, thou deliveredst unto me five talents, behold, I have gained beside them five talents more.' His lord said unto him, 'Well done, thou good and faithful servant, thou hast been faithful over a few things, I will make thee ruler over many things, enter thou into the joy of thy lord.' He also that had received two talents came and said, 'Lord, thou deliveredst unto me two talents, behold, I have gained two other talents beside them.' His lord said unto him, 'Well done, good and faithful servant, thou hast been faithful over a few things, I will make thee ruler over many things, enter thou into the joy of thy lord.' Then he which had received the one talent came and said, 'Lord, I knew thee that thou art an hard man, reaping where thou hast not sown, and gathering where thou hast not strawed, and I was afraid, and went and hid thy talent in the earth, lo, there thou

---

[625] Compare *2 Esdras* 2:13: "Go, and ye shall receive; pray for few days unto you, that they may be shortened; the kingdom is already prepared for you: watch."

hast that is thine.' His lord answered and said unto him, 'Thou wicked and slothful servant, thou knewest that I reap where I sowed not, and gather where I have not strawed. Thou oughtest therefore to have put my money to the exchangers, and then at my coming I should have received mine own with usury. Take therefore the talent from him, and give it unto him which hath ten talents.[626] For unto every one that hath shall be given, and he shall have abundance, but from him that hath not shall be taken away even that which he hath. And cast ye the unprofitable servant into outer darkness, there shall be weeping and *gnashing of teeth*.'[627]

"When the Son of man shall come in his glory,[628] and all the holy angels with him, then shall he sit upon the throne of his glory, and before him shall be gathered all nations,[629] and he shall separate them one from another, as a shepherd divideth his sheep from the goats. And he shall set the sheep on his right hand, but the

---

[626] Compare Psalms 49:14: "Like sheep they are laid in the grave; death shall feed on them; and the upright shall have dominion over them in the morning; and their beauty shall consume in the grave from their dwelling."

[627] See Psalms 112:4,10: "Unto the upright there ariseth light in the darkness; he is gracious, and full of compassion, and righteous. The wicked shall see it, and be grieved; he shall gnash with his teeth, and melt away; the desire of the wicked shall perish."

[628] See Daniel 7:13-14: "I saw in the night visions, and, behold, one like the Son of man came with the clouds of heaven, and came to the Ancient of days, and they brought him near before him. And there was given him dominion, and glory, and a kingdom, that all people, nations, and languages, should serve him; his dominion is an everlasting dominion, which shall not pass away, and his kingdom that which shall not be destroyed."

[629] See Isaiah 66:18: "For I know their works and their thoughts; it shall come, that I will gather all nations and tongues; and they shall come, and see my glory."
Isaiah 2:2-4: "And it shall come to pass in the last days, that the mountain of the LORD'S house shall be established in the top of the mountains, and shall be exalted above the hills; and all nations shall flow unto it. And many people shall go and say, Come ye, and let us go up to the mountain of the LORD, to the house of the God of Jacob; and he will teach us of his ways, and we will walk in his paths; for out of Zion shall go forth the law, and the word of the LORD from Jerusalem. And he shall judge among the nations, and shall rebuke many people; and they shall beat their swords into plowshares, and their spears into pruninghooks; nation shall not lift up sword against nation, neither shall they learn war any more."

goats on the left. Then shall the King say unto them on his right hand, 'Come, ye blessed of my Father, inherit the kingdom prepared for you from the foundation of the world. For I was an hungred, and ye gave me meat, I was thirsty, and ye gave me drink, I was a stranger, and ye took me in, naked, and ye clothed me, I was sick, and ye visited me, I was in prison, and ye came unto me.'[630] Then shall the righteous answer him, saying, 'Lord, when saw we thee an hungred, and fed thee? Or thirsty, and gave thee drink? When saw we thee a stranger, and took thee in? Or naked, and clothed thee? Or when saw we thee sick, or in prison, and came unto thee?' And the King shall answer and say unto them, 'Verily I say unto you, inasmuch as ye have done it unto one of the least of these my brethren, ye have done it unto me.'[631] Then shall he say also unto them on the left hand, 'Depart from me, ye cursed, into everlasting fire, prepared for the devil and his angels. For I was an hungred, and ye gave me no meat, I was thirsty, and ye gave me no drink, I was a stranger, and ye took me not in, naked, and ye clothed me not, sick, and in prison, and ye visited me not.' Then shall they also answer him, saying, 'Lord, when saw we thee an hungred, or athirst, or a stranger, or naked, or sick, or in prison, and did not minister unto thee?' Then shall he answer them, saying, 'Verily I say unto you, inasmuch as ye did it not to one of the least of these, ye did it not to me.' And these shall go away into everlasting punishment, but the righteous into life eternal."[632]

---

[630] Compare Isaiah 58:6: "Is not this the fast that I have chosen? To loose the bands of wickedness, to undo the heavy burdens, and to let the oppressed go free, and that ye break every yoke? Is it not to deal thy bread to the hungry, and that thou bring the poor that are cast out to thy house? When thou seest the naked, that thou cover him; and that thou hide not thyself from thine own flesh?"
[631] See Isaiah 58:10-11: "And if thou draw out thy soul to the hungry, and satisfy the afflicted soul; then shall thy light rise in obscurity, and thy darkness be as the noonday; and the LORD shall guide thee continually, and satisfy thy soul in drought, and make fat thy bones; and thou shalt be like a watered garden, and like a spring of water, whose waters fail not."
[632] Compare Daniel 12:2-3: "And many of them that sleep in the dust of the earth shall awake, some to everlasting life, and some to shame and everlasting contempt.

THE TREE OF LIFE

And they that be wise shall shine as the brightness of the firmament; and they that turn many to righteousness as the stars for ever and ever."

Chapter Seventy Four

And it came to pass, when Jesus had finished all these sayings, he said unto his disciples, "Ye know that after two days is the feast of the passover,[633] and the Son of man is betrayed to be crucified."

Now after two days was the feast, and the chief priests, and the scribes, and the elders of the people, assembled unto the palace of the high priest, who was called Caiaphas, and consulted how they might take Jesus by subtilty, and kill him. But they said, "Not on the feast day, lest there be an uproar among the people," for they feared the people.

Then sought they for Jesus, and spake among themselves, as they stood in the temple, "What think ye, that he will not come to the feast?" Now both the chief priests and the Pharisees had given a commandment, that, if any man knew where he were, he should shew it, that they might take him.

Then entered Satan into Judas surnamed Iscariot, being of the number of the twelve, and he went his way, and communed with the chief priests and captains, how he might betray him unto them. And said unto them, "What will ye give me, and I will deliver him unto you?" And when they heard it, they were glad, and covenanted with him for thirty pieces of silver. And he promised, and from that time

---

[633] See Exodus 12:1-51; Leviticus 23:5-8; Numbers 28:16-25; Deuteronomy 16:1-8.

forth he sought how he might conveniently betray him unto them in the absence of the multitude.

Chapter Seventy Five

Then came the first day of unleavened bread, when the passover must be killed.[634] And he sent Peter and John, saying, "Go and prepare us the passover, that we may eat." And they said unto him, "Where wilt thou that we go and prepare that thou mayest eat the passover?" And he sendeth them forth, the two of his disciples, and saith unto them, "Go ye into the city, and when ye are entered into the city, there shall meet you a man bearing a pitcher of water, follow him into the house where he entereth in. And say unto him, 'The Master saith, "My time is at hand. I will keep the passover at thy house with my disciples. Where is the guestchamber, where I shall eat the passover?"' And he will shew you a large upper room furnished and prepared, there make ready for us."

---

[634] See Exodus 12:21,8: "Then Moses called for all the elders of Israel, and said unto them, 'Draw out and take you a lamb according to your families, and kill the passover. And they shall eat the flesh in that night, roast with fire, and unleavened bread; and with bitter herbs they shall eat it.'"

THE TREE OF LIFE

Chapter Seventy Six

And his disciples went forth, and came into the city, and found as he had said unto them, and they made ready the passover. Now before the feast of the passover, when Jesus knew that his hour was come that he should depart out of this world unto the Father, having loved his own which were in the world, he loved them unto the end.

Now when the hour was come, he sat down, and the twelve apostles with him. And he said unto them, "With desire I have desired to eat this passover with you before I suffer." And as they were eating, Jesus took bread, and gave thanks, and brake it, and gave unto the disciples, saying, "Take, eat. This is my body which is given for you.[635] This do in remembrance of me. For I say unto you, I will not any more eat thereof, until it be fulfilled in the kingdom of God." And he took the cup, and when he had given thanks, he gave it to them, saying, "Take this, and divide it among yourselves, drink ye all of it. This cup is the new testament in my blood,[636] which is shed

---

[635] Compare Exodus 29:31-33: "And thou shalt take the ram of the consecration, and seethe his flesh in the holy place. And Aaron and his sons shall eat the flesh of the ram, and the bread that is in the basket, by the door of the tabernacle of the congregation. And they shall eat those things wherewith the atonement was made, to consecrate and to sanctify them; but a stranger shall not eat thereof, because they are holy."

[636] See Jeremiah 31:31-34: "Behold, the days come, saith the LORD, that I will make a new covenant with the house of Israel, and with the house of Judah; not according to the covenant that I made with their fathers in the day that I took them by the

THE TREE OF LIFE

for you,[637] and for many,[638] for the remission of sins.[639] For I say unto you, I will not drink of the fruit of the vine, until that day when I drink it new with you in my Father's kingdom." And they all drank of it.[640]

And he said unto them, "The kings of the Gentiles exercise lordship over them, and they that exercise authority upon them are called benefactors. But ye shall not be so, but he that is greatest

---

hand to bring them out of the land of Egypt; which my covenant they brake, although I was an husband unto them, saith the LORD; but this shall be the covenant that I will make with the house of Israel; after those days, saith the LORD, I will put my law in their inward parts, and write it in their hearts; and will be their God, and they shall be my people. And they shall teach no more every man his neighbour, and every man his brother, saying, 'Know the LORD;' for they shall all know me, from the least of them unto the greatest of them, saith the LORD; for I will forgive their iniquity, and I will remember their sin no more."
Leviticus 17:11,14: "For the life of the flesh is in the blood; and I have given it to you upon the altar to make an atonement for your souls; for it is the blood that maketh an atonement for the soul. For it is the life of all flesh; the blood of it is for the life thereof; therefore I said unto the children of Israel, 'Ye shall eat the blood of no manner of flesh;' for the life of all flesh is the blood thereof; whosoever eateth it shall be cut off."
[637] Compare Exodus 24:7-8: "And he took the book of the covenant, and read in the audience of the people; and they said, 'All that the LORD hath said will we do, and be obedient.' And Moses took the blood, and sprinkled it on the people, and said, 'Behold the blood of the covenant, which the LORD hath made with you concerning all these words.'"
[638] Compare Isaiah 52:15: "So shall he sprinkle many nations; the kings shall shut their mouths at him; for that which had not been told them shall they see; and that which they had not heard shall they consider."
[639] Compare Exodus 30:1,3,6,10: "And thou shalt make an altar to burn incense upon; of shittim wood shalt thou make it. And thou shalt overlay it with pure gold, the top thereof, and the sides thereof round about, and the horns thereof; and thou shalt make unto it a crown of gold round about. And thou shalt put it before the vail that is by the ark of the testimony, before the mercy seat that is over the testimony, where I will meet with thee. And Aaron shall make an atonement upon the horns of it once in a year with the blood of the sin offering of atonements; once in the year shall he make atonement upon it throughout your generations; it is most holy unto the LORD."
[640] Compare Genesis 14:18-19: "And Melchizedek king of Salem brought forth bread and wine; and he was the priest of the most high God. And he blessed him, and said, 'Blessed be Abram of the most high God, possessor of heaven and earth. And blessed be the most high God, which hath delivered thine enemies into thy hand.' And he gave him tithes of all."

among you, let him be as the younger, and he that is chief, as he that doth serve. For whether is greater, he that sitteth at meat, or he that serveth? Is not he that sitteth at meat? But I am among you as he that serveth."[641]

And supper being ended, the devil having now put into the heart of Judas Iscariot, Simon's son, to betray him, Jesus knowing that the Father had given all things into his hands, and that he was come from God, and went to God, he riseth from supper, and laid aside his garments, and took a towel, and girded himself. After that he poureth water into a bason, and began to wash the disciples' feet, and to wipe them with the towel wherewith he was girded. Then cometh he to Simon Peter, and Peter saith unto him, "Lord, dost thou wash my feet?" Jesus answered and said unto him, "What I do, thou knowest not now, but thou shalt know hereafter." Peter saith unto him, "Thou shalt never wash my feet." Jesus answered him, "If I wash thee not, thou hast no part with me." Simon Peter saith unto him, "Lord, not my feet only, but also my hands and my head." Jesus saith to him, "He that is washed needeth not save to wash his feet, but is clean every whit, and ye are clean, but not all." For he knew who should betray him, therefore said he, "Ye are not all clean."

So after he had washed their feet, and had taken his garments, and was set down again, he said unto them, "Know ye what I have done to you? Ye are they which have continued with me in my temptations. And I appoint unto you a kingdom, as my Father hath appointed unto me. That ye may eat and drink at my table[642] in my

---

[641] Compare <u>Sirach 32:1-2:</u> "If thou be made the master of a feast, lift not thyself up, but be among them as one of the rest; take diligent care for them, and so sit down. And when thou hast done all thy office, take thy place, that thou mayest be merry with them, and receive a crown for thy well ordering of the feast."

[642] See <u>Isaiah 25:6-8:</u> "And in this mountain shall the LORD of hosts make unto all people a feast of fat things, a feast of wines on the lees, of fat things full of marrow, of wines on the lees well refined. And he will destroy in this mountain the face of the covering cast over all people, and the vail that is spread over all nations. He will swallow up death in victory; and the Lord GOD will wipe away tears from off all

kingdom, and sit on thrones judging the twelve tribes of Israel. Ye call me Master and Lord, and ye say well, for so I am. If I then, your Lord and Master, have washed your feet, ye also ought to wash one another's feet. For I have given you an example, that ye should do as I have done to you. Verily, verily, I say unto you, the servant is not greater than his lord, neither he that is sent greater than he that sent him. If ye know these things, happy are ye if ye do them. I speak not of you all, I know whom I have chosen, but that the scripture may be fulfilled, '*He that eateth bread with me hath lifted up his heel against me.*'[643] Now I tell you before it come, that, when it is come to pass, ye may believe that I am he." When Jesus had thus said, he was troubled in spirit, and testified, and said, "Verily, verily, I say unto you, that one of you which eateth with me shall betray me. Behold, the hand of him that betrayeth me is with me on the table. And truly the Son of man goeth, as it is written of him,[644] but woe unto that man by whom the Son of man is betrayed! It had been good for that man if he had never been born."

Then the disciples looked one on another, doubting of whom he spake. And they began to enquire among themselves, which of them it was that should do this thing. Now there was leaning on Jesus' bosom one of his disciples, whom Jesus loved, named John. Simon Peter therefore beckoned to him, that he should ask who it should be of whom he spake. He then lying on Jesus' breast saith unto him, "Lord, who is it?" And they began to be exceeding sorrowful, and to say unto him one by one, "Lord, is it I?" And he answered and said unto them, "It is one of the twelve. He it is, to whom I shall give a sop, when I have dipped it." And when he had dipped the sop, he gave it to Judas Iscariot, the son of Simon. Then

---

faces; and the rebuke of his people shall he take away from off all the earth; for the LORD hath spoken it."
[643] "Yea, mine own familiar friend, in whom I trusted, which did eat of my bread, hath lifted up his heel against me." – Psalms 41:9
[644] See Psalms 22:1-19, 34:19-20, 69:1-36, 110:1-7; Isaiah 50:4-9, 52:13-53:12; *et cetera.*

Judas, which betrayed him, answered and said, "Master, is it I?" He said unto him, "Thou hast said." And after the sop Satan entered into him. Then said Jesus unto him, "That thou doest, do quickly." Now no man at the table knew for what intent he spake this unto him. For some of them thought, because Judas had the bag, that Jesus had said unto him, "Buy those things that we have need of against the feast," or, that he should give something to the poor. He then, having received the sop, went immediately out, and it was night.

Therefore, when he was gone out, Jesus said, "Now is the Son of man glorified, and God is glorified in him. If God be glorified in him, God shall also straightway glorify him in himself. Little children, yet a little while I am with you. Ye shall seek me, and as I said unto the Jews, 'Whither I go, ye cannot come,' so now I say to you." Simon Peter said unto him, "Lord, whither goest thou?" Jesus answered him, "Whither I go, thou canst not follow me now, but thou shalt follow me afterwards." Peter said unto him, "Lord, why cannot I follow thee now? I will lay down my life for thy sake." And the Lord said, "Simon, Simon, behold, Satan hath desired to have you, that he may sift you as wheat. But I have prayed for thee, that thy faith fail not, and when thou art converted, strengthen thy brethren." Then saith Jesus unto them, "All ye shall be offended because of me this night, for it is written, *'I will smite the shepherd, and the sheep of the flock shall be scattered abroad.'*[645] But after I am risen again, I will go before you into Galilee." And Peter said unto him, "Lord, I am ready to go with thee, both into prison, and to death." Jesus answered him, "Wilt thou lay down thy life for my sake? Verily, verily, I say unto thee, Peter, the cock shall not crow this day, before that thou shalt thrice deny that thou knowest me." Peter answered and said unto him, "Though all men shall be offended because of thee, yet will I never be offended." And Jesus

---

[645] "Awake, O sword, against my shepherd, and against the man that is my fellow, saith the LORD of hosts; smite the shepherd, and the sheep shall be scattered; and I will turn mine hand upon the little ones." – Zechariah 13:7

THE TREE OF LIFE

saith unto him, "Verily I say unto thee, that this day, even in this night, before the cock crow twice, thou shalt deny me thrice." But he spake the more vehemently, "Though I should die with thee, yet will I not deny thee in any wise." Likewise also said all the disciples.

And Jesus said, "Let not your heart be troubled, ye believe in God, believe also in me. In my Father's house are many mansions, if it were not so, I would have told you. I go to prepare a place for you.[646] And if I go and prepare a place for you, I will come again, and receive you unto myself, that where I am, there ye may be also. And whither I go ye know, and the way ye know." Thomas saith unto him, "Lord, we know not whither thou goest, and how can we know the way?" Jesus saith unto him, "I am the way, the truth, and the life, no man cometh unto the Father, but by me. If ye had known me, ye should have known my Father also, and from henceforth ye know him, and have seen him." Philip saith unto him, "Lord, shew us the Father, and it sufficeth us." Jesus saith unto him, "Have I been so long time with you, and yet hast thou not known me, Philip? He that hath seen me hath seen the Father, and how sayest thou then, 'Shew us the Father?' Believest thou not that I am in the Father, and the Father in me? The words that I speak unto you I speak not of myself, but the Father that dwelleth in me, he doeth the works. Believe me that I am in the Father, and the Father in me, or else believe me for the very works' sake.[647] Verily, verily, I say unto you, he that

---

[646] Compare <u>2 Esdras 8:52-54:</u> "For unto you is paradise opened, the tree of life is planted, the time to come is prepared, plenteousness is made ready, a city is builded, and rest is allowed, yea, perfect goodness and wisdom. The root of evil is sealed up from you, weakness and the moth is hid from you, and corruption is fled into hell to be forgotten. Sorrows are passed, and in the end is shewed the treasure of immortality."

[647] See <u>Psalms 146:5-10:</u> "Happy is he that hath the God of Jacob for his help, whose hope is in the LORD his God; which made heaven, and earth, the sea, and all that therein is; which keepeth truth for ever; which executeth judgment for the oppressed; which giveth food to the hungry. The LORD looseth the prisoners; the LORD openeth the eyes of the blind; the LORD raiseth them that are bowed down; the LORD loveth the righteous; the LORD preserveth the strangers; he relieveth the fatherless and widow; but the way of the wicked he turneth upside down. The

believeth on me, the works that I do shall he do also, and greater works than these shall he do, because I go unto my Father.

"If ye love me, keep my commandments,[648] and I will pray the Father, and he shall give you another Comforter, that he may abide with you for ever, even the Spirit of truth, whom the world cannot receive, because it seeth him not, neither knoweth him, but ye know him, for he dwelleth with you, and shall be in you. I will not leave you comfortless, I will come to you.[649] Yet a little while, and the world seeth me no more, but ye see me. Because I live, ye shall live also. At that day ye shall know that I am in my Father, and ye in me, and I in you. He that hath my commandments, and keepeth them, he it is that loveth me, and he that loveth me shall be loved of my Father, and I will love him, and will manifest myself to him." Judas saith unto him, (not Iscariot), "Lord, how is it that thou wilt manifest thyself unto us, and not unto the world?" Jesus answered and said unto him, "If a man love me, he will keep my words, and my Father will love him, and we will come unto him, and make our abode with him.[650] He that loveth me not keepeth not my sayings. And the word

---

LORD shall reign for ever, even thy God, O Zion, unto all generations. Praise ye the LORD."
[648] Compare <u>Sirach 2:15:</u> "They that fear the Lord will not disobey his Word; and they that love him will keep his ways."
[649] Compare <u>Isaiah 42:6:</u> "I the LORD have called thee in righteousness, and will hold thine hand, and will keep thee, and give thee for a covenant of the people, for a light of the Gentiles."
[650] Compare <u>Leviticus 26:11-12:</u> "And I will set my tabernacle among you; and my soul shall not abhor you. And I will walk among you, and will be your God, and ye shall be my people."
<u>Exodus 29:45:</u> "And I will dwell among the children of Israel, and will be their God."
<u>Isaiah 4:4-6:</u> "When the Lord shall have washed away the filth of the daughters of Zion, and shall have purged the blood of Jerusalem from the midst thereof by the spirit of judgment, and by the spirit of burning. And the LORD will create upon every dwelling place of mount Zion, and upon her assemblies, a cloud and smoke by day, and the shining of a flaming fire by night; for upon all the glory shall be a defence. And there shall be a tabernacle for a shadow in the daytime from the heat, and for a place of refuge, and for a covert from storm and from rain."
<u>1 Chronicles 28:9:</u> "And thou, Solomon my son, know thou the God of thy father, and serve him with a perfect heart and with a willing mind; for the LORD searcheth

which ye hear is not mine, but the Father's which sent me. These things have I spoken unto you, being yet present with you. But the Comforter, which is the Holy Ghost, whom the Father will send in my name, he shall teach you all things, and bring all things to your remembrance, whatsoever I have said unto you. Peace I leave with you, my peace I give unto you, not as the world giveth, give I unto you. Let not your heart be troubled, neither let it be afraid.[651]

"Ye have heard how I said unto you, 'I go away, and come again unto you.' If ye loved me, ye would rejoice, because I said, 'I go unto the Father,' for my Father is greater than I. And now I have told you before it come to pass, that, when it is come to pass, ye might believe. Hereafter I will not talk much with you, for the prince of this world cometh, and hath nothing in me. But that the world may know that I love the Father, and as the Father gave me commandment, even so I do."

And he said unto them, "When I sent you without purse, and scrip, and shoes, *lacked ye any thing?*"[652] And they said, "Nothing." Then said he unto them, "But now, he that hath a purse, let him take it, and likewise his scrip, and he that hath no sword, let him sell his garment, and buy one. For I say unto you, that this that is written must yet be accomplished in me, 'And he was reckoned among the

---

all hearts, and understandeth all the imaginations of the thoughts; if thou seek him, he will be found of thee; but if thou forsake him, he will cast thee off for ever."
Jeremiah 29:11-13: "For I know the thoughts that I think toward you, saith the LORD, thoughts of peace, and not of evil, to give you an expected end. Then shall ye call upon me, and ye shall go and pray unto me, and I will hearken unto you. And ye shall seek me, and find me, when ye shall search for me with all your heart."
Wisdom 1:2: "For he will be found of them that tempt him not; and sheweth himself unto such as do not distrust him."
[651] Compare Psalms 46:10: "Be still, and know that I am God. I will be exalted among the heathen, I will be exalted in the earth."
[652] See Deuteronomy 2:7: "For the LORD thy God hath blessed thee in all the works of thy hand; he knoweth thy walking through this great wilderness; these forty years the LORD thy God hath been with thee; thou hast lacked nothing."
Sirach 40:26: "Riches and strength lift up the heart; but the fear of the Lord is above them both; there is no want in the fear of the Lord, and it needeth not to seek help."

transgressors,'[653] for the things concerning me have an end." And they said, "Lord, behold, here are two swords." And he said unto them, "It is enough. Arise, let us go hence."

---

[653] "Therefore will I divide him a portion with the great, and he shall divide the spoil with the strong; because he hath poured out his soul unto death; and he was numbered with the transgressors; and he bare the sin of many, and made intercession for the transgressors." – Isaiah 53:12

THE TREE OF LIFE

THE TREE OF LIFE

Chapter Seventy Seven

And when they had sung an hymn, they went out into the mount of Olives. And Jesus said, "I am the true vine, and my Father is the husbandman. Every branch in me that beareth not fruit he taketh away, and every branch that beareth fruit, he purgeth it, that it may bring forth more fruit. Now ye are clean through the word which I have spoken unto you. Abide in me, and I in you. As the branch cannot bear fruit of itself, except it abide in the vine, no more can ye, except ye abide in me. I am the vine, ye are the branches. He that abideth in me, and I in him, the same bringeth forth much fruit, for without me ye can do nothing. If a man abide not in me, he is cast forth as a branch, and is withered, and men gather them, and cast them into the fire, and they are burned. If ye abide in me, and my words abide in you,[654] ye shall ask what ye will, and it shall be done unto you. Herein is my Father glorified, that ye bear much fruit, so shall ye be my disciples. As the Father hath loved me, so have I loved you, continue ye in my love. If ye keep my commandments, ye shall abide in my love, even as I have kept my

---

[654] Compare Deuteronomy 6:6: "And these words, which I command thee this day, shall be in thine heart."
Isaiah 51:7: "Hearken unto me, ye that know righteousness, the people in whose heart is my law; fear ye not the reproach of men, neither be ye afraid of their revilings."
Wisdom 6:11: "Wherefore set your affection upon my words; desire them, and ye shall be instructed."

Father's commandments, and abide in his love. These things have I spoken unto you, that my joy might remain in you, and that your joy might be full. A new commandment I give unto you: that ye love one another. As I have loved you, that ye also love one another. By this shall all men know that ye are my disciples, if ye have love one to another. Greater love hath no man than this, that a man lay down his life for his friends. Ye are my friends, if ye do whatsoever I command you. Henceforth I call you not servants, for the servant knoweth not what his lord doeth, but I have called you friends, for all things that I have heard of my Father I have made known unto you. Ye have not chosen me, but I have chosen you, and ordained you, that ye should go and bring forth fruit, and that your fruit should remain, that whatsoever ye shall ask of the Father in my name, he may give it you. These things I command you, that ye love one another, as I have loved you. If the world hate you, ye know that it hated me before it hated you. If ye were of the world, the world would love his own, but because ye are not of the world, I have chosen you out of the world, therefore the world hateth you. Remember the word that I said unto you, 'The servant is not greater than his lord.' If they have persecuted me, they will also persecute you, if they have kept my saying, they will keep yours also.[655] But all these things will they do unto you for my name's sake, because they know not him that sent me. If I had not come and spoken unto them, they had not had sin, but now they have no cloak for their sin. He that hateth me hateth my Father also. If I had not done among them the works which none other man did, they had not had sin, but now have they both seen and hated both me and my Father. But this cometh to pass, that the word might be fulfilled that is written in

---

[655] Compare *Sirach* 2:1-5: "My son, if thou come to serve the Lord, prepare thy soul for temptation. Set thy heart aright, and constantly endure, and make not haste in time of trouble. Cleave unto him, and depart not away, that thou mayest be increased at thy last end. Whatsoever is brought upon thee take cheerfully, and be patient when thou art changed to a low estate. For gold is tried in the fire, and acceptable men in the furnace of adversity."

their law, *'They hated me without a cause.'*[656] But when the Comforter is come, whom I will send unto you from the Father, even the Spirit of truth, which proceedeth from the Father, he shall testify of me. And ye also shall bear witness, because ye have been with me from the beginning. These things have I spoken unto you, that ye should not be offended. They shall put you out of the synagogues, yea, the time cometh, that whosoever killeth you will think that he doeth God service.[657] And these things will they do unto you, because they have not known the Father, nor me. But these things have I told you, that when the time shall come, ye may remember that I told you of them. And these things I said not unto you at the beginning, because I was with you. But now I go my way to him that sent me, and none of you asketh me, 'Whither goest thou?'

"But because I have said these things unto you, sorrow hath filled your heart.[658] Nevertheless I tell you the truth. It is expedient for you that I go away, for if I go not away, the Comforter will not come unto you, but if I depart, I will send him unto you. And when he is come, he will reprove the world of sin, and of righteousness, and of judgment: of sin, because they believe not on me; of righteousness, because I go to my Father, and ye see me no more; of judgment, because the prince of this world is judged. I have yet many things to say unto you, but ye cannot bear them now. Howbeit when he, the Spirit of truth, is come, he will guide you into all truth, for he shall not speak of himself, but whatsoever he shall hear, that shall he speak, and he will shew you things to come. He shall glorify me, for he shall receive of mine, and shall shew it unto you. All things that the Father hath are mine, therefore said I, that he shall

---

[656] "They that hate me without a cause are more than the hairs of mine head; they that would destroy me, being mine enemies wrongfully, are mighty; then I restored that which I took not away." – Psalms 69:4

[657] Compare Isaiah 66:5: "Hear the word of the LORD, ye that tremble at his word; your brethren that hated you, that cast you out for my name's sake, said, 'Let the LORD be glorified;' but he shall appear to your joy, and they shall be ashamed."

[658] Compare Psalms 51:11: "Cast me not away from thy presence; and take not thy holy spirit from me."

take of mine, and shall shew it unto you. A little while, and ye shall not see me, and again, a little while, and ye shall see me, because I go to the Father."

Then said some of his disciples among themselves, "What is this that he saith unto us, 'A little while, and ye shall not see me, and again, a little while, and ye shall see me,' and, 'Because I go to the Father?'" They said therefore, "We cannot tell what he saith." Now Jesus knew that they were desirous to ask him, and said unto them, "Do ye enquire among yourselves of that I said, 'A little while, and ye shall not see me, and again, a little while, and ye shall see me?' Verily, verily, I say unto you, that ye shall weep and lament, but the world shall rejoice, and ye shall be sorrowful, but your sorrow shall be turned into joy. A woman when she is in travail hath sorrow, because her hour is come, but as soon as she is delivered of the child, she remembereth no more the anguish, for joy that a man is born into the world. And ye now therefore have sorrow, but I will see you again, and your heart shall rejoice, and your joy no man taketh from you. And in that day ye shall ask me nothing. Verily, verily, I say unto you, whatsoever ye shall ask the Father in my name, he will give it you. Hitherto have ye asked nothing in my name; ask, and ye shall receive, that your joy may be full. And whatsoever ye shall ask in my name, that will I do, that the Father may be glorified in the Son. If ye shall ask any thing in my name, I will do it.

"These things have I spoken unto you in proverbs, but the time cometh, when I shall no more speak unto you in proverbs, but I shall shew you plainly of the Father. At that day ye shall ask in my name, I say not unto you that I will pray the Father for you, for the Father himself loveth you, because ye have loved me, and have believed that I came out from God. I came forth from the Father, and am come into the world, again, I leave the world, and go to the Father." His disciples said unto him, "Lo, now speakest thou plainly, and speakest no proverb. Now are we sure that thou knowest all things, and needest not that any man should ask thee, by this we believe that thou camest forth from God." Jesus answered them, "Do ye now believe? Behold, the hour cometh, yea, is now come, that *ye shall be scattered, every man to his own*,[659] and shall leave me alone, and yet I am not alone, because the Father is with me. These things I have spoken unto you, that in me ye might have peace. In the world ye shall have tribulation, but be of good cheer, I have overcome the world."

---

[659] See 1 Kings 22:17: "And he said, 'I saw all Israel scattered upon the hills, as sheep that have not a shepherd;' and the LORD said, 'These have no master; let them return every man to his house in peace.'"

THE TREE OF LIFE

Chapter Seventy Eight

These words spake Jesus, and lifted up his eyes to heaven, and said, "Father, the hour is come, glorify thy Son, that thy Son also may glorify thee. As thou hast given him power over all flesh, that he should give eternal life to as many as thou hast given him. And this is life eternal, that they might know thee the only true God, and Jesus Christ, whom thou hast sent.[660] I have glorified thee on the earth, I have finished the work which thou gavest me to do. And now, O Father, glorify thou me with thine own self with the glory which I had with thee before the world was. I have manifested thy name unto the men which thou gavest me out of the world, thine they were, and thou gavest them me, and they have kept thy word. Now they have known that all things whatsoever thou hast given me are of thee. For I have given unto them the words which thou gavest me, and they have received them, and have known surely that I came out from thee, and they have believed that thou didst send me.

"I pray for them. I pray not for the world, but for them which thou hast given me, for they are thine. And all mine are thine, and thine are mine, and I am glorified in them. And now I am no more in the world, but these are in the world, and I come to thee. Holy Father, keep through thine own name those whom thou hast given me, that they may be one, as we are. While I was with them in the

---

[660] Compare *Wisdom* 15:3: "For to know thee is perfect righteousness; yea, to know thy power is the root of immortality."

world, I kept them in thy name, *those that thou gavest me I have kept, and none of them is lost,*[661] (but the son of perdition,) that the scripture might be fulfilled. And now come I to thee, and these things I speak in the world, that they might have my joy fulfilled in themselves. I have given them thy word, and the world hath hated them, because they are not of the world, even as I am not of the world. I pray not that thou shouldest take them out of the world, but that thou shouldest keep them from the evil. They are not of the world, even as I am not of the world. Sanctify them through thy truth, thy word is truth. As thou hast sent me into the world, even so have I also sent them into the world. And for their sakes I sanctify myself, that they also might be sanctified through the truth. Neither pray I for these alone, but for them also which shall believe on me through their word, that they all may be one, as thou, Father, art in me, and I in thee, that they also may be one in us, that the world may believe that thou hast sent me. And the glory which thou gavest me I have given them, that they may be one, even as we are one. I in them, and thou in me, that they may be made perfect in one, and that the world may know that thou hast sent me, and hast loved them, as thou hast loved me. Father, I will that they also, whom thou hast given me, be with me where I am, that they may behold my glory, which thou hast given me, for thou lovedst me before the foundation of the world. O righteous Father, the world hath not known thee, but I have known thee, and these have known that thou hast sent me. And I have declared unto them thy name, and will declare it, that the love wherewith thou hast loved me may be in them, and I in them."

---

[661] "As for the servants whom I have given thee, there shall not one of them perish; for I will require them from among thy number." – *2 Esdras* 2:26

Chapter Seventy Nine

When Jesus had spoken these words, he went forth with his disciples over the brook Kidron, as he was wont, to the mount of Olives, where was a garden, into the which he entered, and his disciples. And Judas also, which betrayed him, knew the place, for Jesus ofttimes resorted thither with his disciples.

And they came to a place which was named Gethsemane, and he saith to his disciples, "Sit ye here, while I go and pray yonder." And when he was at the place, he said unto them, "Pray that ye enter not into temptation." And he taketh with him Peter and James and John the two sons of Zebedee, and began to be sorrowful and very heavy. And saith unto them, "My soul is exceeding sorrowful unto death,[662] tarry ye here, and watch with me." And he went a little farther, and he was withdrawn from them about a stone's cast, fell on his face, and prayed, saying, "Abba, Father, all things are possible unto thee, if thou be willing, remove this cup[663] from me, nevertheless not what I will, but what thou wilt."[664]

---

[662] Compare Psalms 69:1-2: "Save me, O God; for the waters are come in unto my soul. I sink in deep mire, where there is no standing. I am come into deep waters, where the floods overflow me."
Psalms 119:28: "My soul melteth for heaviness; strengthen thou me according unto thy word."
[663] See Isaiah 51:17: "Awake, awake, stand up, O Jerusalem, which hast drunk at the hand of the LORD the cup of his fury; thou hast drunken the dregs of the cup of trembling, and wrung them out."

THE TREE OF LIFE

And there appeared an angel unto him from heaven, strengthening him. And being in an agony he prayed more earnestly,⁶⁶⁵ and his sweat was as it were great drops of blood falling down to the ground.⁶⁶⁶

<u>Isaiah 53:6,10-11:</u> "All we like sheep have gone astray; we have turned every one to his own way; and the LORD hath laid on him the iniquity of us all. Yet it pleased the LORD to bruise him; he hath put him to grief; when thou shalt make his soul an offering for sin, he shall see his seed, he shall prolong his days, and the pleasure of the LORD shall prosper in his hand. He shall see of the travail of his soul, and shall be satisfied; by his knowledge shall my righteous servant justify many; for he shall bear their iniquities."
<u>Psalms 18:4:</u> "The sorrows of death compassed me, and the floods of ungodly men made me afraid. The sorrows of hell compassed me about; the snares of death prevented me. In my distress I called upon the LORD, and cried unto my God; he heard my voice out of his temple, and my cry came before him, even into his ears."
⁶⁶⁴ Compare <u>Proverbs 3:5-8:</u> "Trust in the LORD with all thine heart; and lean not unto thine own understanding. In all thy ways acknowledge him, and he shall direct thy paths. Be not wise in thine own eyes; fear the LORD, and depart from evil."
<u>Numbers 16:28:</u> "And Moses said, 'Hereby ye shall know that the LORD hath sent me to do all these works; for I have not done them of mine own mind.'"
<u>Isaiah 50:5:</u> "The Lord GOD hath opened mine ear, and I was not rebellious, neither turned away back."
⁶⁶⁵ Compare <u>Psalms 88:1-9,13-18:</u> "O LORD God of my salvation, I have cried day and night before thee. Let my prayer come before thee; incline thine ear unto my cry; for my soul is full of troubles; and my life draweth nigh unto the grave. I am counted with them that go down into the pit. I am as a man that hath no strength. Free among the dead, like the slain that lie in the grave, whom thou rememberest no more; and they are cut off from thy hand. Thou hast laid me in the lowest pit, in darkness, in the deeps. Thy wrath lieth hard upon me, and thou hast afflicted me with all thy waves. Selah. Thou hast put away mine acquaintance far from me; thou hast made me an abomination unto them; I am shut up, and I cannot come forth. Mine eye mourneth by reason of affliction. LORD, I have called daily upon thee, I have stretched out my hands unto thee. But unto thee have I cried, O LORD; and in the morning shall my prayer prevent thee. LORD, why castest thou off my soul? Why hidest thou thy face from me? I am afflicted and ready to die from my youth up; while I suffer thy terrors I am distracted. Thy fierce wrath goeth over me; thy terrors have cut me off. They came round about me daily like water; they compassed me about together. Lover and friend hast thou put far from me, and mine acquaintance into darkness."
⁶⁶⁶ Compare <u>Genesis 49:10-11:</u> "The sceptre shall not depart from Judah, nor a lawgiver from between his feet, until Shiloh come; and unto him shall the gathering of the people be. Binding his foal unto the vine, and his ass's colt unto the choice vine; he washed his garments in wine, and his clothes in the blood of grapes."

And when he rose up from prayer, and was come to his disciples, he found them sleeping for sorrow, and said unto them, "Why sleep ye? Rise and pray, lest ye enter into temptation." And he saith unto Peter, "Simon, sleepest thou? Couldest not thou watch with me one hour? Watch ye and pray, that ye enter not into temptation. The spirit truly is ready, and willing, but the flesh is weak."

He went away again the second time, and prayed, saying, "O my Father, if this cup may not pass away from me, except I drink it, thy will be done." And when he returned, he found them asleep again, for their eyes were heavy, neither wist they what to answer him.

And he left them, and went away again, and prayed the third time, saying the same words. Then cometh he to his disciples the third time, and said unto them, "Sleep on now, and take your rest, it is enough."

And immediately, while he yet spake, cometh Judas, one of the twelve, having received a band of men and officers from the chief priests and the scribes and the Pharisees, and with him a great multitude with lanterns and torches and swords and staves. And he said unto his disciples, "Behold, the hour is at hand, and the Son of man is betrayed into the hands of sinners. Rise up, let us be going, behold, he that betrayeth me is at hand."

Jesus therefore, knowing all things that should come upon him, went forth, and said unto them, "Whom seek ye?" They answered him, "Jesus of Nazareth." Jesus saith unto them, "I am he." As soon then as he had said unto them, "I am he,"[667] they went

---

[667] See Exodus 3:13-14: "And Moses said unto God, 'Behold, when I come unto the children of Israel, and shall say unto them, "The God of your fathers hath sent me unto you;" and they shall say to me, "What is his name?" What shall I say unto them?' And God said unto Moses, 'I AM THAT I AM;' and he said, 'Thus shalt thou say unto the children of Israel, "I AM hath sent me unto you."'"

backward, and fell to the ground. Then asked he them again, "Whom seek ye?" And they said, "Jesus of Nazareth." Jesus answered, "I have told you that I am he, if therefore ye seek me, let these go their way," that the saying might be fulfilled, which he spake, "*Of them which thou gavest me have I lost none.*"⁶⁶⁸

Now he that betrayed him gave them a sign, saying, "Whomsoever I shall kiss, that same is he, take him, and hold him fast, and lead him away safely." And forthwith he came to Jesus, and said, "Hail, master," and Jesus said unto him, "Friend, wherefore art thou come?" And Judas kissed him, and he said, "Judas, betrayest thou the Son of man with a kiss?"⁶⁶⁹

Then came they, and laid hands on Jesus, and took him. When they which were about him saw what would follow, they said unto him, "Lord, shall we smite with the sword?" And Simon Peter having a sword stretched out his hand, and drew his sword, and smote the high priest's servant, and cut off his right ear. The servant's name was Malchus. Then said Jesus unto Peter, "Put up thy sword into his sheath, for all they that take the sword shall perish with the sword.⁶⁷⁰ The cup which my Father hath given me, shall I not drink it? Thinkest thou that I cannot now pray to my Father, and he shall presently give me more than twelve legions of angels?⁶⁷¹ But how

---

⁶⁶⁸ "As for the servants whom I have given thee, there shall not one of them perish; for I will require them from among thy number." – *2 Esdras* 2:26
⁶⁶⁹ Compare 2 Samuel 20:9-10: "And Joab said to Amasa, 'Art thou in health, my brother?' And Joab took Amasa by the beard with the right hand to kiss him. But Amasa took no heed to the sword that was in Joab's hand; so he smote him therewith in the fifth rib, and shed out his bowels to the ground, and struck him not again; and he died. So Joab and Abishai his brother pursued after Sheba the son of Bichri."
Proverbs 27:6: "Faithful are the wounds of a friend; but the kisses of an enemy are deceitful."
⁶⁷⁰ Compare Genesis 9:6: "Whoso sheddeth man's blood, by man shall his blood be shed; for in the image of God made he man."
⁶⁷¹ Compare Psalms 7:10: "My defence is of God, which saveth the upright in heart."
Psalms 34:7: "The angel of the LORD encampeth round about them that fear him, and delivereth them."

then shall the scriptures be fulfilled, that thus it must be?" And Jesus said unto the chief priests, and captains of the temple, and the elders, which were come to him, "Suffer ye thus far." And he touched his ear, and healed him. And said unto them, "Are ye come out, as against a thief, with swords and with staves for to take me? I sat daily with you teaching in the temple, and ye stretched forth no hands against me, to lay hold on me. But the scriptures must be fulfilled, and this is your hour, and the power of darkness." But all this was done, that the scriptures of the prophets might be fulfilled.[672]

---

2 Kings 19:35: "And it came to pass that night, that the angel of the LORD went out, and smote in the camp of the Assyrians an hundred fourscore and five thousand; and when they arose early in the morning, behold, they were all dead corpses."
2 Kings 6:15-17: "And when the servant of the man of God was risen early, and gone forth, behold, an host compassed the city both with horses and chariots. And his servant said unto him, 'Alas, my master! How shall we do?' And he answered, 'Fear not; for they that be with us are more than they that be with them.' And Elisha prayed, and said, 'LORD, I pray thee, open his eyes, that he may see.' And the LORD opened the eyes of the young man; and he saw; and, behold, the mountain was full of horses and chariots of fire round about Elisha."
[672] See Isaiah 53:1-12: "Who hath believed our report? And to whom is the arm of the LORD revealed? For he shall grow up before him as a tender plant, and as a root out of a dry ground; he hath no form nor comeliness; and when we shall see him, there is no beauty that we should desire him. He is despised and rejected of men; a man of sorrows, and acquainted with grief; and we hid as it were our faces from him; he was despised, and we esteemed him not. Surely he hath borne our griefs, and carried our sorrows; yet we did esteem him stricken, smitten of God, and afflicted. But he was wounded for our transgressions, he was bruised for our iniquities; the chastisement of our peace was upon him; and with his stripes we are healed. All we like sheep have gone astray; we have turned every one to his own way; and the LORD hath laid on him the iniquity of us all. He was oppressed, and he was afflicted, yet he opened not his mouth; he is brought as a lamb to the slaughter, and as a sheep before her shearers is dumb, so he openeth not his mouth. He was taken from prison and from judgment; and who shall declare his generation? For he was cut off out of the land of the living; for the transgression of my people was he stricken. And he made his grave with the wicked, and with the rich in his death; because he had done no violence, neither was any deceit in his mouth. Yet it pleased the LORD to bruise him; he hath put him to grief; when thou shalt make his soul an offering for sin, he shall see his seed, he shall prolong his days, and the pleasure of the LORD shall prosper in his hand. He shall see of the travail of his soul, and shall be satisfied; by his knowledge shall my righteous servant justify

Then all the disciples forsook him, and fled. And there followed him a certain young man, having a linen cloth cast about his naked body, and the young men laid hold on him, and he left the linen cloth, and fled from them naked.

---

many; for he shall bear their iniquities. Therefore will I divide him a portion with the great, and he shall divide the spoil with the strong; because he hath poured out his soul unto death; and he was numbered with the transgressors; and he bare the sin of many, and made intercession for the transgressors."
Psalms 22:1-19: "My God, my God, why hast thou forsaken me? Why art thou so far from helping me, and from the words of my roaring? O my God, I cry in the daytime, but thou hearest not; and in the night season, and am not silent. But thou art holy, O thou that inhabitest the praises of Israel. Our fathers trusted in thee; they trusted, and thou didst deliver them. They cried unto thee, and were delivered; they trusted in thee, and were not confounded. But I am a worm, and no man; a reproach of men, and despised of the people. All they that see me laugh me to scorn; they shoot out the lip, they shake the head saying, 'He trusted on the LORD that he would deliver him; let him deliver him, seeing he delighted in him.' But thou art he that took me out of the womb; thou didst make me hope when I was upon my mother's breasts. I was cast upon thee from the womb; thou art my God from my mother's belly. Be not far from me; for trouble is near; for there is none to help. Many bulls have compassed me; strong bulls of Bashan have beset me round. They gaped upon me with their mouths, as a ravening and a roaring lion. I am poured out like water, and all my bones are out of joint; my heart is like wax; it is melted in the midst of my bowels. My strength is dried up like a potsherd; and my tongue cleaveth to my jaws; and thou hast brought me into the dust of death. For dogs have compassed me; the assembly of the wicked have inclosed me; they pierced my hands and my feet. I may tell all my bones; they look and stare upon me. They part my garments among them, and cast lots upon my vesture. But be not thou far from me, O LORD; O my strength, haste thee to help me."

Chapter Eighty

Then the band and the captain and officers of the Jews took Jesus, and bound him, and led him away to Annas first, for he was father in law to Caiaphas, which was the high priest that same year. And Annas sent him bound unto Caiaphas the high priest. (And Caiaphas was he, which gave counsel to the Jews, that it was expedient that one man should die for the people.) And they led Jesus away to Caiaphas the high priest's house, and with him were assembled all the chief priests and the elders and the scribes.

And Simon Peter followed Jesus, and so did John, who was known unto the high priest, and he went in with Jesus into the palace of the high priest, to see the end.

The high priest then asked Jesus of his disciples, and of his doctrine. Jesus answered him, "I spake openly to the world, I ever taught in the synagogue, and in the temple, whither the Jews always resort, and in secret have I said nothing. Why askest thou me? Ask them which heard me, what I have said unto them, behold, they know what I said." And when he had thus spoken, one of the officers which stood by struck Jesus with the palm of his hand, saying, "Answerest thou the high priest so?" Jesus answered him, "If I have spoken evil, bear witness of the evil, but if well,[673] why smitest thou

---

[673] Compare Exodus 23:1-2: "Thou shalt not raise a false report; put not thine hand with the wicked to be an unrighteous witness. Thou shalt not follow a multitude to

me?" And the chief priests, and elders, and all the council sought for witness against Jesus to put him to death, and found none, yea, though many false witnesses came, yet found they none that agreed together. And there arose certain, and bare false witness against him, saying, "This fellow said, 'I am able to destroy the temple of God, and to build it in three days.'" And, "We heard him say, 'I will destroy this temple that is made with hands, and within three days I will build another made without hands.'" But neither so did their witness agree together.

And the high priest stood up in the midst, and asked Jesus, saying, "Answerest thou nothing? What is it which these witness against thee?" But he held his peace, and answered nothing. Again the high priest asked him, and said unto him, "Art thou the Christ,[674] the Son of the Blessed?"[675] But Jesus held his peace.[676]

And the high priest answered and said unto him, "I adjure thee by the living God, that thou tell us whether thou be the Christ, the Son of God. Art thou the Christ? Tell us." And he said unto them, "If I tell you, ye will not believe, and if I also ask you, ye will not answer me, nor let me go." Then said they all, "Art thou then the Son of God?" And Jesus saith unto him, "I am, and hereafter shall ye see the

---

do evil; neither shalt thou speak in a cause to decline after many to wrest judgment."
[674] See Jeremiah 23:5: "Behold, the days come, saith the LORD, that I will raise unto David a righteous Branch, and a King shall reign and prosper, and shall execute judgment and justice in the earth."
[675] See *2 Esdras* 13:29,32: "Behold, the days come, when the most High will begin to deliver them that are upon the earth. And the time shall be when these things shall come to pass, and the signs shall happen which I shewed thee before, and then shall my Son be declared, whom thou sawest as a man ascending."
[676] See Isaiah 53:7: "He was oppressed, and he was afflicted, yet he opened not his mouth; he is brought as a lamb to the slaughter, and as a sheep before her shearers is dumb, so he openeth not his mouth."

THE TREE OF LIFE

Son of man sitting on the right hand of the power of God,[677] and coming in the clouds of heaven."[678]

Then the high priest rent his clothes,[679] saying, "He hath spoken blasphemy, what further need have we of witnesses?

---

[677] See Psalms 80:17: "Let thy hand be upon the man of thy right hand, upon the son of man whom thou madest strong for thyself."
Psalms 110:1-2,4-6: "The LORD said unto my Lord, 'Sit thou at my right hand, until I make thine enemies thy footstool. The LORD shall send the rod of thy strength out of Zion; rule thou in the midst of thine enemies. The LORD hath sworn, and will not repent, "Thou art a priest for ever after the order of Melchizedek." The Lord at thy right hand shall strike through kings in the day of his wrath. He shall judge among the heathen, he shall fill the places with the dead bodies; he shall wound the heads over many countries.'"
1 Samuel 2:10: "The adversaries of the LORD shall be broken to pieces; out of heaven shall he thunder upon them; the LORD shall judge the ends of the earth; and he shall give strength unto his king, and exalt the horn of his anointed."
Exodus 15:6-7: "Thy right hand, O LORD, is become glorious in power; thy right hand, O LORD, hath dashed in pieces the enemy. And in the greatness of thine excellency thou hast overthrown them that rose up against thee; thou sentest forth thy wrath, which consumed them as stubble."
[678] See Daniel 7:13-14: "I saw in the night visions, and, behold, one like the Son of man came with the clouds of heaven, and came to the Ancient of days, and they brought him near before him. And there was given him dominion, and glory, and a kingdom, that all people, nations, and languages, should serve him; his dominion is an everlasting dominion, which shall not pass away, and his kingdom that which shall not be destroyed."
Psalms 97:1-6: "The LORD reigneth; let the earth rejoice; let the multitude of isles be glad thereof. Clouds and darkness are round about him; righteousness and judgment are the habitation of his throne. A fire goeth before him, and burneth up his enemies round about. His lightnings enlightened the world; the earth saw, and trembled. The hills melted like wax at the presence of the LORD, at the presence of the Lord of the whole earth. The heavens declare his righteousness, and all the people see his glory."
Psalms 104:1-3: "Bless the LORD, O my soul. O LORD my God, thou art very great; thou art clothed with honour and majesty. Who coverest thyself with light as with a garment; who stretchest out the heavens like a curtain; who layeth the beams of his chambers in the waters; who maketh the clouds his chariot; who walketh upon the wings of the wind."
See also Zechariah 14:4-9.
[679] See Leviticus 21:10: "And he that is the high priest among his brethren, upon whose head the anointing oil was poured, and that is consecrated to put on the garments, shall not uncover his head, nor rend his clothes."

Behold, now ye have heard his blasphemy of his own mouth. What think ye?" And they all answered and said, "He is guilty of death."[680]

And when the men that held Jesus had blindfolded him, they struck him on the face with the palms of their hands, and asked him, saying, "Prophesy unto us, thou Christ, who is it that smote thee?" Then did they spit in his face,[681] and buffeted him, and many other things blasphemously spake they against him.

---

[680] See Leviticus 24:16: "And he that blasphemeth the name of the LORD, he shall surely be put to death, and all the congregation shall certainly stone him; as well the stranger, as he that is born in the land, when he blasphemeth the name of the LORD, shall be put to death."

[681] See Isaiah 50:6: "I gave my back to the smiters, and my cheeks to them that plucked off the hair; I hid not my face from shame and spitting."

Chapter Eighty One

But Peter stood at the door without the palace of the high priest. Then went out that other disciple, John, which was known unto the high priest, and spake unto her that kept the door, and brought in Peter. And when they had kindled a fire in the midst of the hall, and were set down together, Peter sat down among them. And as Peter was beneath in the palace, there cometh a certain damsel unto him, one of the maids of the high priest, she it was that kept the door, and when she saw Peter as he sat warming himself by the fire, she earnestly looked upon him, and said, "Thou also wast with Jesus of Galilee, art not thou also one of this man's disciples?" But he denied before them all, saying, "Woman, I know him not, neither understand I what thou sayest."

And he went out into the porch, and the cock crew. And the servants and officers stood there, who had made a fire of coals, for it was cold, and they warmed themselves, and Simon Peter stood with them, and warmed himself. And when he was gone out into the porch, another maid saw him, and said unto them that were there, "This fellow was also with Jesus of Nazareth. Art not thou also one of his disciples?" And again he denied with an oath, "I do not know the man."

And about the space of one hour after, another that stood by confidently affirmed again to Peter, saying, "Surely thou art one of them, for thou art a Galilaean, and thy speech agreeth thereto." One of the servants of the high priest, being his kinsman whose ear Peter cut off, saith, "Did not I see thee in the garden with him?" But he began to curse and to swear, saying, "I know not this man of whom ye speak." And immediately, while he yet spake, the cock crew. And the Lord turned, and looked upon Peter, and Peter remembered the word of the Lord, how he had said unto him, "Before the cock crow twice, thou shalt deny me thrice." And when he thought thereon, he went out, and wept bitterly.

THE TREE OF LIFE

Chapter Eighty Two

And as soon as it was day, the elders of the people and the chief priests and the scribes came together, and bound Jesus, and the whole multitude of them arose, and carried him away, and delivered him to Pontius Pilate, the governor, to put him to death.

Then led they Jesus from Caiaphas unto the hall of judgment, and it was early, and they themselves went not into the judgment hall, lest they should be defiled, but that they might eat the passover.

Pilate then went out unto them, and said, "What accusation bring ye against this man?" They answered and said unto him, "If he were not a malefactor, we would not have delivered him up unto thee."

Then said Pilate unto them, "Take ye him, and judge him according to your law." The Jews therefore said unto him, "It is not lawful for us to put any man to death," that the saying of Jesus might be fulfilled, which he spake, signifying what death he should die. And when he was accused of the chief priests and elders, he answered nothing. And the chief priests accused him of many things, but he answered nothing.

Then said Pilate unto him, "Hearest thou not how many things they witness against thee?" And Pilate asked him again, saying,

"Answerest thou nothing? Behold how many things they witness against thee." But Jesus yet answered him never a word,[682] insomuch that Pilate marvelled greatly.

And they began to accuse him, saying, "We found this fellow perverting the nation, and forbidding to give tribute to Caesar, saying that he himself is Christ a King."[683]

Then Pilate entered into the judgment hall again, and called Jesus, and said unto him, "Art thou the King of the Jews?" Jesus answered him, "Sayest thou this thing of thyself, or did others tell it thee of me?" Pilate answered, "Am I a Jew? Thine own nation and the chief priests have delivered thee unto me. What hast thou done?" Jesus answered, "My kingdom is not of this world, if my kingdom were of this world, then would my servants fight, that I should not be delivered to the Jews, but now is my kingdom not from hence." And Jesus stood before the governor, and the governor asked him, saying, "Art thou a king then?" Jesus answered, "Thou sayest that I am a king. To this end was I born, and for this cause came I into the world, that I should bear witness unto the truth. Every one that is of the truth heareth my voice." Pilate saith unto him, "What is truth?"

And when he had said this, he went out again unto the chief priests and to the Jews, and saith unto them, "I find no fault at all in

---

[682] See Isaiah 53:7: "He was oppressed, and he was afflicted, yet he opened not his mouth; he is brought as a lamb to the slaughter, and as a sheep before her shearers is dumb, so he openeth not his mouth."
[683] See Genesis 49:10: "The sceptre shall not depart from Judah, nor a lawgiver from between his feet, until Shiloh come; and unto him shall the gathering of the people be."
Isaiah 9:6-7: "For unto us a child is born, unto us a son is given; and the government shall be upon his shoulder; and his name shall be called Wonderful, Counsellor, The mighty God, The everlasting Father, The Prince of Peace. Of the increase of his government and peace there shall be no end, upon the throne of David, and upon his kingdom, to order it, and to establish it with judgment and with justice from henceforth even for ever. The zeal of the LORD of hosts will perform this."

this man." And they were the more fierce, saying, "He stirreth up the people, teaching throughout all Jewry, beginning from Galilee to this place."

When Pilate heard of Galilee, he asked whether the man were a Galilaean. And as soon as he knew that he belonged unto Herod's jurisdiction, he sent him to Herod, who himself also was at Jerusalem at that time.

And when Herod saw Jesus, he was exceeding glad, for he was desirous to see him of a long season, because he had heard many things of him, and he hoped to have seen some miracle done by him. Then he questioned with him in many words, but he answered him nothing. And the chief priests and scribes stood and vehemently accused him.

And Herod with his men of war set him at nought, and mocked him, and arrayed him in a gorgeous robe, and sent him again to Pilate. And the same day Pilate and Herod were made friends together, for before they were at enmity between themselves.

And Pilate, when he had called together the chief priests and the rulers and the people, said unto them, "Ye have brought this man unto me, as one that perverteth the people, and, behold, I, having examined him before you, have found no fault in this man touching those things whereof ye accuse him, no, nor yet Herod, for I sent you to him, and, lo, nothing worthy of death is done unto him. I will therefore chastise him, and release him. But ye have a custom, that I should release unto you one prisoner, whomsoever you desire, at the passover. (For at that feast the governor of necessity must release unto the people a prisoner, whomsoever they desired.) Will ye therefore that I release unto you the King of the Jews?" (For he knew that the chief priests had delivered him for envy.)

And they had then a notable prisoner, called Barabbas, who for insurrection made in the city, and for murder, was cast into prison, which lay bound with them that had made insurrection with him. Therefore when they were gathered together, Pilate said unto them, "Whom will ye that I release unto you? Barabbas, or Jesus which is called Christ?"

But the chief priests and elders persuaded the multitude that they should ask Barabbas, and destroy Jesus. The governor answered and said unto them, "Whether of the twain will ye that I release unto you?" And the multitude cried out all at once, saying, "Away with this man, and release unto us Barabbas."

And when Pilate was set down on the judgment seat, his wife sent unto him, saying, "Have thou nothing to do with that just man, for I have suffered many things this day in a dream because of him." Pilate therefore, willing to release Jesus, spake again to them, saying, "What shall I do then with Jesus whom ye call the King of the Jews?" And they cried out, saying, "Crucify him, crucify him." And the governor said, "Why, what evil hath he done?" But they cried out the more, saying, "Let him be crucified." Then Pilate said unto them, "Why, what evil hath he done?" And they cried out the more exceedingly, "Crucify him." And he said unto them the third time, "Why, what evil hath he done? I have found no cause of death in him, I will therefore chastise him, and let him go." Then Pilate therefore took Jesus, and scourged him.[684]

Then the soldiers of the governor took Jesus into the common hall, called Praetorium, and gathered unto him the whole band of soldiers. And the soldiers stripped him, and they clothed him with a purple robe, and platted a crown of thorns, and put it about his head, and put a reed in his right hand, and they bowed the knee before him, and worshipped him, and mocked him, saying, "Hail,

---

[684] See Isaiah 53:5: "But he was wounded for our transgressions, he was bruised for our iniquities; the chastisement of our peace was upon him; and with his stripes we are healed."

King of the Jews!" and they smote him with their hands. And they spit upon him, and took the reed, and smote him on the head.[685]

Pilate therefore went forth again, and saith unto them, "Behold, I bring him forth to you, that ye may know that I find no fault in him."

Then came Jesus forth, wearing the crown of thorns, and the purple robe. And Pilate saith unto them, "Behold the man!" When the chief priests therefore and officers saw him, they cried out, saying, "Crucify him, crucify him." Pilate saith unto them, "Take ye him, and crucify him, for I find no fault in him."

The Jews answered him, "We have a law, and by our law he ought to die, because he made himself the Son of God."[686] When Pilate therefore heard that saying, he was the more afraid, and went again into the judgment hall, and saith unto Jesus, "Whence art thou?" But Jesus gave him no answer. Then saith Pilate unto him, "Speakest thou not unto me? Knowest thou not that I have power to crucify thee, and have power to release thee?" Jesus answered, "Thou couldest have no power at all against me, except it were given thee from above,[687] therefore he that delivered me unto thee hath the greater sin."

And from thenceforth Pilate sought to release him, but the Jews cried out, saying, "If thou let this man go, thou art not Caesar's friend, whosoever maketh himself a king speaketh against Caesar."

---

[685] See Isaiah 50:6: "I gave my back to the smiters, and my cheeks to them that plucked off the hair; I hid not my face from shame and spitting."
Isaiah 52:14: "As many were astonied at thee; his visage was so marred more than any man, and his form more than the sons of men."
[686] See Leviticus 24:16: "And he that blasphemeth the name of the LORD, he shall surely be put to death, and all the congregation shall certainly stone him; as well the stranger, as he that is born in the land, when he blasphemeth the name of the LORD, shall be put to death."
[687] See Wisdom 6:1-3: "Hear therefore, O ye kings, and understand; learn, ye that be judges of the ends of the earth. Give ear, ye that rule the people, and glory in the multitude of nations. For power is given you of the Lord, and sovereignty from the Highest, who shall try your works, and search out your counsels."

When Pilate therefore heard that saying, he brought Jesus forth, and sat down in the judgment seat in a place that is called the Pavement, (but in the Hebrew, Gabbatha). And it was the preparation of the passover, and he saith unto the Jews, "Behold your King!" But they cried out, "Away with him, away with him, crucify him." Pilate saith unto them, "Shall I crucify your King?" The chief priests answered, "We have no king but Caesar."[688] And they were instant with loud voices, requiring that he might be crucified. And the voices of them and of the chief priests prevailed.

When Pilate saw that he could prevail nothing, but that rather a tumult was made, he took water, and washed his hands before the multitude, saying, "I am innocent of the blood of this just person, see ye to it." Then answered all the people, and said, "His blood be on us, and on our children."[689]

And so Pilate, willing to content the people, gave sentence that it should be as they required, and he released Barabbas unto them, and delivered Jesus, when he had scourged him, to be crucified.

And after that they had mocked him, they took the purple robe off from him, and put his own clothes on him, and led him away to crucify him.

---

[688] See Isaiah 53:3-4: "He is despised and rejected of men; a man of sorrows, and acquainted with grief; and we hid as it were our faces from him; he was despised, and we esteemed him not. Surely he hath borne our griefs, and carried our sorrows; yet we did esteem him stricken, smitten of God, and afflicted."

[689] See Exodus 12:5-6: "Your lamb shall be without blemish, a male of the first year; ye shall take it out from the sheep, or from the goats; and ye shall keep it up until the fourteenth day of the same month; and the whole assembly of the congregation of Israel shall kill it in the evening."

Chapter Eighty Three

Then Judas, which had betrayed him, when he saw that he was condemned, repented himself, and brought again the thirty pieces of silver to the chief priests and elders, saying, "I have sinned in that I have betrayed the innocent blood."[690] And they said, "What is that to us? See thou to that." And he cast down the pieces of silver in the temple, and departed, and went and hanged himself.[691]

And the chief priests took the silver pieces, and said, "It is not lawful for to put them into the treasury, because it is the price of blood." And they took counsel, and bought with them the potter's field, to bury strangers in. Wherefore that field was called, the field of blood, unto this day. Then was fulfilled that which was spoken by Zechariah the prophet, saying, "*And they took the thirty pieces of silver, the price of him that was valued, whom they of the children of*

---

[690] Compare Deuteronomy 27:25: "'Cursed be he that taketh reward to slay an innocent person.' And all the people shall say, 'Amen.'"
Deuteronomy 19:10,12-13: "That innocent blood be not shed in thy land, which the LORD thy God giveth thee for an inheritance, and so blood be upon thee. Then the elders of his city shall send and fetch him thence, and deliver him into the hand of the avenger of blood, that he may die. Thine eye shall not pity him, but thou shalt put away the guilt of innocent blood from Israel, that it may go well with thee."
See also Proverbs 6:16-19; Psalms 94:20-21.
[691] Compare Deuteronomy 21:23: "And if a man have committed a sin worthy of death, and he be to be put to death, and thou hang him on a tree; his body shall not remain all night upon the tree, but thou shalt in any wise bury him that day; (for he that is hanged is accursed of God;) that thy land be not defiled, which the LORD thy God giveth thee for an inheritance."

Israel did value, and gave them for the potter's field, as the Lord appointed me."[692]

---

[692] "And I said unto them, 'If ye think good, give me my price; and if not, forbear.' So they weighed for my price thirty pieces of silver. And the LORD said unto me, 'Cast it unto the potter; a goodly price that I was prised at of them.' And I took the thirty pieces of silver, and cast them to the potter in the house of the LORD." – Zechariah 11:12-13

Chapter Eighty Four

And as they led him away, they came out, and found a man of Cyrene who passed by, coming out of the country, Simon by name, the father of Alexander and Rufus, and they compelled him, that he might bear his cross after Jesus.

And there followed him a great company of people, and of women, which also bewailed and lamented him. But Jesus turning unto them said, "Daughters of Jerusalem, weep not for me, but weep for yourselves, and for your children. For, behold, the days are coming, in the which they shall say, 'Blessed are the barren, and the wombs that never bare, and the paps which never gave suck.'[693]

---

[693] Compare Deuteronomy 28:49-57: "The LORD shall bring a nation against thee from far, from the end of the earth, as swift as the eagle flieth; a nation whose tongue thou shalt not understand; a nation of fierce countenance, which shall not regard the person of the old, nor shew favour to the young. And he shall eat the fruit of thy cattle, and the fruit of thy land, until thou be destroyed; which also shall not leave thee either corn, wine, or oil, or the increase of thy kine, or flocks of thy sheep, until he have destroyed thee. And he shall besiege thee in all thy gates, until thy high and fenced walls come down, wherein thou trustedst, throughout all thy land; and he shall besiege thee in all thy gates throughout all thy land, which the LORD thy God hath given thee. And thou shalt eat the fruit of thine own body, the flesh of thy sons and of thy daughters, which the LORD thy God hath given thee, in the siege, and in the straitness, wherewith thine enemies shall distress thee. So that the man that is tender among you, and very delicate, his eye shall be evil toward his brother, and toward the wife of his bosom, and toward the remnant of his children which he shall leave; so that he will not give to any of them of the flesh of his children whom he shall eat: because he hath nothing left him in the siege, and in the straitness, wherewith thine enemies shall distress thee in all thy gates. The tender

Then shall they begin to *say to the mountains, 'Fall on us,' and to the hills, 'Cover us.'*[694] For if they do these things in a green tree, what shall be done in the dry?"[695]

---

and delicate woman among you, which would not adventure to set the sole of her foot upon the ground for delicateness and tenderness, her eye shall be evil toward the husband of her bosom, and toward her son, and toward her daughter, and toward her young one that cometh out from between her feet, and toward her children which she shall bear; for she shall eat them for want of all things secretly in the siege and straitness, wherewith thine enemy shall distress thee in thy gates.

[694] See Hosea 10:8: "The high places also of Aven, the sin of Israel, shall be destroyed; the thorn and the thistle shall come up on their altars; and they shall say to the mountains, 'Cover us;' and to the hills, 'Fall on us.'"

[695] Compare Deuteronomy 31:27: "For I [Moses] know thy rebellion, and thy stiff neck; behold, while I am yet alive with you this day, ye have been rebellious against the LORD; and how much more after my death?"

Chapter Eighty Five

And he, bearing his cross, went forth into a place called in the Hebrew Golgotha, (which is, being interpreted, the place of a skull,) where they crucified him.[696] And there were also two other malefactors, led with him to be put to death. And when they were come to the place, which is called Calvary, and there they crucified him, and the malefactors, one on his right hand, and the other on his left. And the scripture was fulfilled, which saith, "*And he was numbered with the transgressors.*"[697] Then said Jesus, "Father, forgive them, for they know not what they do."

Then the soldiers, when they had crucified Jesus, took his garments, and made four parts, to every soldier a part, and also his coat. Now the coat was without seam, woven from the top throughout. They said therefore among themselves, "Let us not rend it, but cast lots for it, whose it shall be," that the scripture might be fulfilled, which saith, "*They parted my garments among them, and for my vesture they did cast lots.*"[698] These things therefore the soldiers

---

[696] See Psalms 22:16: "For dogs have compassed me; the assembly of the wicked have inclosed me; they pierced my hands and my feet."
[697] "Therefore will I divide him a portion with the great, and he shall divide the spoil with the strong; because he hath poured out his soul unto death; and he was numbered with the transgressors; and he bare the sin of many, and made intercession for the transgressors." – Isaiah 53:12
[698] "They part my garments among them, and cast lots upon my vesture." – Psalms 22:18

did. And it was the third hour, when they crucified him. And sitting down they watched him there.

And Pilate had written a title, the superscription of his accusation, and put it on the cross. And the writing was, THIS IS JESUS OF NAZARETH, THE KING OF THE JEWS. This title then read many of the Jews, for the place where Jesus was crucified was nigh to the city, and it was written in Hebrew, and Greek, and Latin.[699] Then said the chief priests of the Jews to Pilate, "Write not, 'The King of the Jews,' but that 'he said, "I am King of the Jews."'" Pilate answered, "What I have written I have written."

And they that passed by reviled him, wagging their heads, and saying, "Ah, thou that destroyest the temple, and buildest it in three days, save thyself. If thou be the Son of God, come down from the cross." And the people stood beholding.

And the rulers also with them derided him, saying, "He saved others, let him save himself, if he be Christ, the chosen of God."

And the soldiers also mocked him, coming to him, and offering him vinegar to drink mingled with gall,[700] and saying, "If thou be the king of the Jews, save thyself," and when he had tasted thereof, he would not drink, and received it not.

Likewise also the chief priests mocking him, with the scribes and elders, said, "He saved others, himself he cannot save. Let Christ the King of Israel descend now from the cross, that we may see, and

---

[699] See Isaiah 52:10: "The LORD hath made bare his holy arm in the eyes of all the nations; and all the ends of the earth shall see the salvation of our God."
Isaiah 5:26: "And he will lift up an ensign to the nations from far, and will hiss unto them from the end of the earth; and, behold, they shall come with speed swiftly."
Isaiah 11:10: "And in that day there shall be a root of Jesse, which shall stand for an ensign of the people; to it shall the Gentiles seek; and his rest shall be glorious."
[700] Compare Psalms 69:20-21: "Reproach hath broken my heart; and I am full of heaviness; and I looked for some to take pity, but there was none; and for comforters, but I found none. They gave me also gall for my meat; and in my thirst they gave me vinegar to drink."

we will believe him. He trusted in God, let him deliver him now,[701] if he will have him, for he said, 'I am the Son of God.'"[702]

And the thieves that were crucified with him reviled him. And one of the malefactors which were hanged, railed on him, saying, "If thou be Christ, save thyself and us." But the other answering rebuked him, saying, "Dost not thou fear God, seeing thou art in the same condemnation? And we indeed justly, for we receive the due reward of our deeds, but this man hath done nothing amiss." And he said unto Jesus, "Lord, remember me when thou comest into thy kingdom." And Jesus said unto him, "Verily I say unto thee, to day shalt thou be with me in paradise."

Now there stood by the cross of Jesus his mother, and his mother's sister, Mary the wife of Cleophas, and Mary Magdalene. When Jesus therefore saw his mother, and John standing by, whom he loved, he saith unto his mother, "Woman, behold thy son." Then saith he to John, "Behold thy mother." And from that hour John took her unto his own home.

---

[701] See Psalms 22:7-8: "All they that see me laugh me to scorn; they shoot out the lip, they shake the head saying, 'He trusted on the LORD that he would deliver him; let him deliver him, seeing he delighted in him.'"
Isaiah 53:4: "Surely he hath borne our griefs, and carried our sorrows; yet we did esteem him stricken, smitten of God, and afflicted."
[702] Compare Wisdom 2:1,12-20: "For the ungodly said, reasoning with themselves, but not aright, 'Our life is short and tedious, and in the death of a man there is no remedy; neither was there any man known to have returned from the grave. Therefore let us lie in wait for the righteous; because he is not for our turn, and he is clean contrary to our doings; he upbraideth us with our offending the law, and objecteth to our infamy the transgressions of our education. He professeth to have the knowledge of God; and he calleth himself the child of the Lord. He was made to reprove our thoughts. He is grievous unto us even to behold; for his life is not like other men's, his ways are of another fashion. We are esteemed of him as counterfeits; he abstaineth from our ways as from filthiness; he pronounceth the end of the just to be blessed, and maketh his boast that God is his father. Let us see if his words be true; and let us prove what shall happen in the end of him. For if the just man be the son of God, he will help him, and deliver him from the hand of his enemies. Let us examine him with despitefulness and torture, that we may know his meekness, and prove his patience. Let us condemn him with a shameful death; for by his own saying he shall be respected.'"

THE TREE OF LIFE

Now when the sixth hour was come, there was a darkness over all the earth until the ninth hour.[703] And at the ninth hour Jesus cried with a loud voice, saying, "Eli, Eli, lama sabachthani?" (which is, being interpreted, *"My God, my God, why hast thou forsaken me?"*)[704] And some of them that stood by, when they heard it, said, "Behold, he calleth for Elijah."

After this, Jesus knowing that all things were now accomplished, that the scripture might be fulfilled, saith, "I thirst." Now there was set a vessel full of vinegar, and straightway one of them ran, and filled a spunge with vinegar, and put it upon a hyssop,[705] and put it to his mouth, and gave him to drink, saying, "Let alone, let us see whether Elijah will come to take him down."

And when Jesus therefore had received the vinegar, he said, "It is finished." And Jesus cried with a loud voice, saying, "Father, *into thy hands I commend my spirit,*"[706] and having said thus, he bowed his head, and he yielded up the ghost.[707]

---

[703] Compare Exodus 20:21: "And the people stood afar off, and Moses drew near unto the thick darkness where God was."
1 Kings 8:12: "Then spake Solomon, 'The LORD said that he would dwell in thick darkness.'"
[704] See Psalms 22:1: "My God, my God, why hast thou forsaken me? Why art thou so far from helping me, and from the words of my roaring?"
See also Psalms 22:1-19.
[705] Compare Exodus 12:21-22: "Then Moses called for all the elders of Israel, and said unto them, 'Draw out and take you a lamb according to your families, and kill the passover. And ye shall take a bunch of hyssop, and dip it in the blood that is in the bason, and strike the lintel and the two side posts with the blood that is in the bason; and none of you shall go out at the door of his house until the morning.'"
[706] See Psalms 31:5: "Into thine hand I commit my spirit; thou hast redeemed me, O LORD God of truth."
Ecclesiastes 12:7: "Then shall the dust return to the earth as it was; and the spirit shall return unto God who gave it."
[707] See *2 Esdras* 7:29: "After these years shall my son Christ die, and all men that have life."
Isaiah 53:8,12: "He was taken from prison and from judgment; and who shall declare his generation? For he was cut off out of the land of the living; for the transgression of my people was he stricken. Therefore will I divide him a portion with the great, and he shall divide the spoil with the strong; because he hath

And the veil of the temple was rent in twain from the top to the bottom,[708] and the earth did quake, and the rocks rent.[709]

Now when the centurion, which stood over against him, and they that were with him, watching Jesus, saw the earthquake, and those things that were done, and saw that he so cried out, and gave up the ghost, they feared greatly, and glorified God, saying, "Truly this was the Son of God." And all the people that came together to that sight, beholding the things which were done, smote their breasts, and returned.

And all his acquaintance, and the women that followed him from Galilee, stood afar off, beholding these things, among whom was Mary Magdalene, and Mary the mother of James the less and of Joses, and Salome the mother of Zebedee's children, and many other women which came up with him unto Jerusalem, who followed him, and ministered unto him.

---

poured out his soul unto death; and he was numbered with the transgressors; and he bare the sin of many, and made intercession for the transgressors."
[708] Compare <u>Isaiah 25:7-8</u>: "And he will destroy in this mountain the face of the covering cast over all people, and the vail that is spread over all nations. He will swallow up death in victory; and the Lord GOD will wipe away tears from off all faces; and the rebuke of his people shall he take away from off all the earth; for the LORD hath spoken it."
<u>Genesis 37:34</u>: "And Jacob rent his clothes, and put sackcloth upon his loins, and mourned for his son many days."
<u>Isaiah 64:1-2</u>: "Oh that thou wouldest rend the heavens, that thou wouldest come down, that the mountains might flow down at thy presence, as when the melting fire burneth, the fire causeth the waters to boil, to make thy name known to thine adversaries, that the nations may tremble at thy presence!"
[709] Compare <u>2 Samuel 22:5-10 (and Psalms 18:4-9)</u>: "When the waves of death compassed me, the floods of ungodly men made me afraid; the sorrows of hell compassed me about; the snares of death prevented me; in my distress I called upon the LORD, and cried to my God; and he did hear my voice out of his temple, and my cry did enter into his ears. Then the earth shook and trembled; the foundations of heaven moved and shook, because he was wroth. There went up a smoke out of his nostrils, and fire out of his mouth devoured; coals were kindled by it. He bowed the heavens also, and came down; and darkness was under his feet."

THE TREE OF LIFE

THE TREE OF LIFE

Chapter Eighty Six

The Jews therefore, because it was the preparation, that the bodies should not remain upon the cross on the sabbath day, for that sabbath day was an high day, besought Pilate that their legs might be broken, and that they might be taken away.[710] Then came the soldiers, and brake the legs of the first, and of the other which was crucified with him. But when they came to Jesus, and saw that he was dead already, they brake not his legs. But one of the soldiers with a spear pierced his side, and forthwith came there out blood and water. And he that saw it bare record, and his record is true, and he knoweth that he saith true, that ye might believe. For these things were done, that the scripture should be fulfilled, "*A bone of him shall not be broken.*"[711] And again another scripture saith, "*They shall look on him whom they pierced.*"[712]

---

[710] Compare Deuteronomy 21:22-23: "And if a man have committed a sin worthy of death, and he be to be put to death, and thou hang him on a tree, his body shall not remain all night upon the tree, but thou shalt in any wise bury him that day; (for he that is hanged is accursed of God;) that thy land be not defiled, which the LORD thy God giveth thee for an inheritance."
[711] "He keepeth all his bones; not one of them is broken." – Psalms 34:20
Compare Exodus 12:21,43,46: "Then Moses called for all the elders of Israel, and said unto them, 'Draw out and take you a lamb according to your families, and kill the passover.' And the LORD said unto Moses and Aaron, 'This is the ordinance of the Passover; there shall no stranger eat thereof; in one house shall it be eaten; thou shalt not carry forth ought of the flesh abroad out of the house; neither shall ye break a bone thereof.'"

And, behold, there was a rich man named Joseph, an honourable counsellor, and he was a good man, and a just, (the same had not consented to the counsel and deed of them,) he was of Arimathaea, a city of the Jews, who also himself was Jesus' disciple (but secretly for fear of the Jews,) who also waited for the kingdom of God. And now when the even was come, because it was the preparation, that is, the day before the sabbath, this man went in boldly unto Pilate, and besought him that he might take away the body of Jesus. And Pilate marvelled if he were already dead, and calling unto him the centurion, he asked him whether he had been any while dead. And when he knew it of the centurion, Pilate commanded the body to be delivered to Joseph.

He bought fine linen, and came therefore, and took the body of Jesus down. And there came also Nicodemus, which at the first came to Jesus by night, and brought a mixture of myrrh and aloes, about an hundred pound weight. Then took they the body of Jesus, and wound it in clean linen clothes with the spices, as the manner of the Jews is to bury.

Now in the place where he was crucified there was a garden, and in the garden a new sepulchre, wherein never man before was laid. And when Joseph had taken the body, he laid it in his own new tomb,[713] which he had hewn out of the rock, and he rolled a great stone to the door of the sepulchre, and departed.

Numbers 9:12: "They shall leave none of it unto the morning, nor break any bone of it; according to all the ordinances of the passover they shall keep it."
[712] "And I will pour upon the house of David, and upon the inhabitants of Jerusalem, the spirit of grace and of supplications; and they shall look upon me whom they have pierced, and they shall mourn for him, as one mourneth for his only son, and shall be in bitterness for him, as one that is in bitterness for his firstborn." - Zechariah 12:10
See also Psalms 22:16: "For dogs have compassed me; the assembly of the wicked have inclosed me; they pierced my hands and my feet."
[713] See Isaiah 53:9: "And he made his grave with the wicked, and with the rich in his death; because he had done no violence, neither was any deceit in his mouth."

And that day was the preparation, and the sabbath drew on. And the women also, which came with him from Galilee, Mary Magdalene and Mary the mother of Joses, followed after, and beheld the sepulchre, and how his body was laid. And there was Mary Magdalene, and the other Mary, sitting over against the sepulchre. There laid they Jesus therefore because of the Jews' preparation day, for the sepulchre was nigh at hand.

THE TREE OF LIFE

Chapter Eighty Seven

And the women returned, and prepared spices and ointments, and rested the sabbath day according to the commandment.[714] Now the next day, that followed the day of the preparation, the chief priests and Pharisees came together unto Pilate, saying, "Sir, we remember that that deceiver said, while he was yet alive, 'After three days I will rise again.' Command therefore that the sepulchre be made sure until the third day, lest his disciples come by night, and steal him away, and say unto the people, 'He is risen from the dead,' so the last error shall be worse than the first." Pilate said unto them, "Ye have a watch, go your way, make it as sure as ye can." So they went, and made the sepulchre sure, sealing the stone, and setting a watch.[715]

---

[714] See Exodus 20:9-10: "Six days shalt thou labour, and do all thy work; but the seventh day is the sabbath of the LORD thy God; in it thou shalt not do any work, thou, nor thy son, nor thy daughter, thy manservant, nor thy maidservant, nor thy cattle, nor thy stranger that is within thy gates."
[715] Compare Daniel 6:16-17: "Then the king commanded, and they brought Daniel, and cast him into the den of lions. Now the king spake and said unto Daniel, 'Thy God whom thou servest continually, he will deliver thee.' And a stone was brought and laid upon the mouth of the den; and the king sealed it with his own signet, and with the signet of his lords; that the purpose might not be changed concerning Daniel."

THE TREE OF LIFE

Chapter Eighty Eight

And, behold, there was a great earthquake, for the angel of the Lord descended from heaven, and came and rolled back the stone from the door, and sat upon it. His countenance was like lightning, and his raiment white as snow, and for fear of him the keepers did shake, and became as dead men.

And Mary Magdalene, and Mary the mother of James, and Salome, and Joanna, and certain others with them, had bought sweet spices, that they might come and anoint him. And now upon the first day of the week, very early in the morning as the rising of the sun began to dawn, they came unto the sepulchre, bringing the spices which they had prepared.

And they said among themselves, "Who shall roll us away the stone from the door of the sepulchre?" And when they looked, they found the stone rolled away from the sepulchre, and they were much perplexed thereabout, for it was very great. And it came to pass, as they were much perplexed, behold, they saw a young man sitting on the right side, clothed in a long white and shining garment, and they were afraid, and bowed down their faces to the earth. And he saith unto them, "Be not affrighted. For I know that ye seek Jesus of Nazareth, which was crucified. Why seek ye the living among the dead? He is not here, for he is risen, as he said. Come, behold the place where the Lord lay."

And they entered into the sepulchre, and found not the body of the Lord Jesus. And the angel said unto them, "Remember how he spake unto you when he was yet in Galilee, saying, 'The Son of man must be delivered into the hands of sinful men, and be crucified, and the third day rise again?'" And they remembered his words. And the angel said, "But go your way quickly, and tell his disciples and Peter that he is risen from the dead, and that he goeth before you into Galilee. There shall ye see him, as he said unto you. Lo, I have told you."

And they departed quickly from the sepulchre with fear and great joy, and did run to bring his disciples word. Now when they were going, behold, some of the watch came into the city, and shewed unto the chief priests all the things that were done. And when they were assembled with the elders, and had taken counsel, they gave large money unto the soldiers, saying, "Say ye, 'His disciples came by night, and stole him away while we slept.' And if this come to the governor's ears, we will persuade him, and secure you." So they took the money, and did as they were taught, and this saying is commonly reported among the Jews until this day.

And they went out quickly, and fled from the sepulchre, for they trembled and were amazed, neither said they any thing to any man, for they were afraid. And they cometh to Simon Peter, and to John, and Mary saith unto them, "They have taken away the LORD out of the sepulchre, and we know not where they have laid him." Peter therefore arose, and John, and came to the sepulchre. So they ran both together, and John did outrun Peter, and came first to the sepulchre. And he stooping down, and looking in, saw the linen clothes laid by themselves, yet went he not in. Then cometh Simon Peter following him, and went into the sepulchre, and seeth the linen clothes lie, and the napkin, that was about his head, not lying with the linen clothes, but wrapped together in a place by itself. Then went in also John, which came first to the sepulchre, and he saw, and believed. For as yet they knew not the scripture, that he must rise again from the dead.⁷¹⁶

Then the disciples went away again unto their own home, wondering in themselves at that which was come to pass.

But Mary stood without at the sepulchre weeping, and as she wept, she stooped down, and looked into the sepulchre, and seeth two angels in white sitting, the one at the head, and the other at the feet, where the body of Jesus had lain. And they say unto her, "Woman, why weepest thou?" She saith unto them, "Because they have taken away my LORD, and I know not where they have laid him." And when she had thus said, she turned herself back, and saw Jesus standing, and knew not that it was Jesus. (Now when Jesus was risen early the first day of the week, he appeared first to Mary Magdalene, out of whom he had cast seven devils.) And Jesus saith unto her, "Woman, why weepest thou? Whom seekest thou?" She, supposing him to be the gardener, saith unto him, "Sir, if thou have borne him hence, tell me where thou hast laid him, and I will take him away." Jesus saith unto her, "Mary." And she turned herself, and saith unto him, "Rabboni," (which is to say, Master). Jesus saith unto her, "Touch me not, for I am not yet ascended to my Father, but go to my brethren, and say unto them, 'I ascend unto my Father, and your Father, and to my God, and your God.'"

And she went and told the women that had been with him from Galilee, as they mourned and wept. And they all went to tell his disciples, and behold, as they went, Jesus met them, saying, "All hail." And they came and held him by the feet, and worshipped him. Then said Jesus unto them, "Be not afraid, go tell my brethren that they go into Galilee, and there shall they see me."

---

⁷¹⁶ Compare Isaiah 25:8: "He will swallow up death in victory; and the Lord GOD will wipe away tears from off all faces; and the rebuke of his people shall he take away from off all the earth; for the LORD hath spoken it."
Psalms 49:15: "But God will redeem my soul from the power of the grave; for he shall receive me. Selah."

And they all returned, and told all these things unto the eleven, and to all the rest, that they had seen the LORD, and that he had spoken these things unto them. It was Mary Magdalene, and Joanna, and Mary the mother of James, and other women that were with them, which told these things unto the apostles. And they, when they had heard that he was alive, and had been seen of them, their words seemed to them as idle tales, and they believed them not.

THE TREE OF LIFE

Chapter Eighty Nine

After that he appeared in another form unto two of them, as they walked, and went into the country. And, behold, two of them went that same day to a village called Emmaus, which was from Jerusalem about threescore furlongs. And they talked together of all these things which had happened. And it came to pass, that, while they communed together and reasoned, Jesus himself drew near, and went with them. But their eyes were holden that they should not know him.[717] And he said unto them, "What manner of communications are these that ye have one to another, as ye walk, and are sad?" And the one of them, whose name was Cleopas, answering said unto him, "Art thou only a stranger in Jerusalem, and hast not known the things which are come to pass

---

[717] Compare 2 Kings 6:11-14,18-20: "Therefore the heart of the king of Syria was sore troubled for this thing; and he called his servants, and said unto them, 'Will ye not shew me which of us is for the king of Israel?' And one of his servants said, 'None, my lord, O king; but Elisha, the prophet that is in Israel, telleth the king of Israel the words that thou speakest in thy bedchamber.' And he said, 'Go and spy where he is, that I may send and fetch him.' And it was told him, saying, 'Behold, he is in Dothan.' Therefore sent he thither horses, and chariots, and a great host; and they came by night, and compassed the city about. And when they came down to him, Elisha prayed unto the LORD, and said, 'Smite this people, I pray thee, with blindness.' And he smote them with blindness according to the word of Elisha. And Elisha said unto them, 'This is not the way, neither is this the city; follow me, and I will bring you to the man whom ye seek.' But he led them to Samaria. And it came to pass, when they were come into Samaria, that Elisha said, 'LORD, open the eyes of these men, that they may see.' And the LORD opened their eyes, and they saw; and, behold, they were in the midst of Samaria."

there in these days?" And he said unto them, "What things?" And they said unto him, "Concerning Jesus of Nazareth, which was a prophet mighty in deed and word before God and all the people. And how the chief priests and our rulers delivered him to be condemned to death, and have crucified him. But we trusted that it had been he which should have redeemed Israel, and beside all this, to day is the third day since these things were done. Yea, and certain women also of our company made us astonished, which were early at the sepulchre, and when they found not his body, they came, saying that they had also seen a vision of angels, which said that he was alive. And certain of them which were with us went to the sepulchre, and found it even so as the women had said, but him they saw not." Then he said unto them, "O fools, and slow of heart to believe all that the prophets have spoken. Ought not Christ to have suffered these things, and to enter into his glory?" And beginning at Moses and all the prophets, he expounded unto them in all the scriptures the things concerning himself.[718]

And they drew nigh unto the village, whither they went, and he made as though he would have gone further. But they constrained him, saying, "Abide with us, for it is toward evening, and the day is far spent." And he went in to tarry with them. And it came to pass, as he sat at meat with them, he took bread, and blessed it, and brake, and gave to them. And their eyes were opened, and they knew him, and he vanished out of their sight. And they said one to another, "Did not our heart burn within us, while he talked with us by the way, and while he opened to us the scriptures?" And they rose up the same hour, and returned to Jerusalem, and found the eleven gathered together, and them that were with them, saying,

---

[718] See Genesis 3:13-15, 49:10-12; Deuteronomy 18:15-19; Job 19:23-27; Psalms 22:1-19, 34:19-20, 69:1-36, 110:1-7, 112:1-10, 118:20-26; Isaiah 8:13-15, 9:1-8, 11:1-12:6, 25:6-8, 28:16-21, 34:1-35:10, 40:1-11, 42:1-7, 49:13-16, 50:4-9, 52:13-53:12, 59:20-63:5, 66:15-16; Jeremiah 23:1-8; Ezekiel 34:1-31; Daniel 2:44-45, 7:13-14, 9:24-27; Hosea 13:14; Micah 5:2-4; Zechariah 12:9-14:21; Malachi 4:1-6; 2 Maccabees 7:1-42; et cetera.

"The Lord is risen indeed, and hath appeared to Simon." And they told what things were done in the way, and how he was known of them in breaking of bread, neither believed they them.

THE TREE OF LIFE

Chapter Ninety

Then the same day at evening, being the first day of the week, when the doors were shut where the disciples were assembled for fear of the Jews, and as they thus spake, came Jesus himself and stood in the midst of them, and saith unto them, "Peace be unto you." But they were terrified and affrighted, and supposed that they had seen a spirit. And he said unto them, "Why are ye troubled? And why do thoughts arise in your hearts?[719] Behold my hands and my feet, that it is I myself, handle me, and see, for a spirit hath not flesh and bones, as ye see me have." And when he had thus spoken, he shewed them his hands and his feet, and his side. Then were the disciples glad, when they saw the LORD. And while they yet believed not for joy, and wondered, he said unto them, "Have ye here any meat?" And they gave him a piece of a broiled fish, and of an honeycomb. And he took it, and did eat before them. And as they sat at meat, he upbraided them for their unbelief and hardness of heart, because they believed not them which had seen him after he was risen. And he said unto them, "These are the

---

[719] Compare Psalms 139:1-2: "O LORD, thou hast searched me, and known me. Thou knowest my downsitting and mine uprising, thou understandest my thought afar off."
Jeremiah 17:10: "I the LORD search the heart, I try the reins, even to give every man according to his ways, and according to the fruit of his doings."
2 Esdras 16:54,63: "Behold, the Lord knoweth all the works of men, their imaginations, their thoughts, and their hearts. Surely he knoweth your inventions, and what ye think in your hearts, even them that sin, and would hide their sin."

words which I spake unto you, while I was yet with you, that all things must be fulfilled, which were written in the law of Moses, and in the prophets, and in the psalms, concerning me."[720] Then opened he their understanding, that they might understand the scriptures, and said unto them, "Thus it is written, and thus it behoved Christ to suffer, and to rise from the dead the third day, and that repentance and remission of sins should be preached in his name among all nations, beginning at Jerusalem. And ye are witnesses of these things."

But Thomas, one of the eleven, called Didymus, was not with them when Jesus came. The other disciples therefore said unto him, "We have seen the LORD." But he said unto them, "Except I shall see in his hands the print of the nails, and put my finger into the print of the nails, and thrust my hand into his side, I will not believe."

And after eight days again his disciples were within, and Thomas with them, then came Jesus, the doors being shut, and stood in the midst, and said, "Peace be unto you." And when they saw him, they worshipped him, but some doubted. Then saith he to Thomas, "Reach hither thy finger, and behold my hands,[721] and reach hither thy hand, and thrust it into my side, and be not faithless, but believing." And Thomas answered and said unto him, "My LORD and my God." Jesus saith unto him, "Thomas, because thou hast seen me,

---

[720] See Genesis 3:13-15, 49:10-12; Deuteronomy 18:15-19; Job 19:23-27; Psalms 22:1-19, 34:19-20, 69:1-36, 110:1-7, 112:1-10, 118:20-26; Isaiah 8:13-15, 9:1-8, 11:1-12:6, 25:6-8, 28:16-21, 34:1-35:10, 40:1-11, 42:1-7, 49:13-16, 50:4-9, 52:13-53:12, 59:20-63:5, 66:15-16; Jeremiah 23:1-8; Ezekiel 34:1-31; Daniel 2:44-45; 7:13-14, 9:24-27; Hosea 13:14; Micah 5:2-4; Zechariah 12:9-14:21; Malachi 4:1-6; 2 Maccabees 7:1-42; et cetera.
[721] See Isaiah 49:15-16: "Can a woman forget her sucking child, that she should not have compassion on the son of her womb? Yea, they may forget, yet will I not forget thee. Behold, I have graven thee upon the palms of my hands; thy walls are continually before me."
Zechariah 13:6: "And one shall say unto him, 'What are these wounds in thine hands?' Then he shall answer, 'Those with which I was wounded in the house of my friends.'"

thou hast believed, blessed are they that have not seen, and yet have believed."

Then said Jesus to them again, "Peace be unto you. As my Father hath sent me, even so send I you. And, behold, I send the promise of my Father upon you, but tarry ye in the city of Jerusalem, until ye be endued with power from on high."

And when he had said this, he breathed on them,[722] and saith unto them, "Receive ye the Holy Ghost. Whose soever sins ye remit, they are remitted unto them, and whose soever sins ye retain, they are retained."

And he led them out as far as to Bethany, and he lifted up his hands, and blessed them.[723] And it came to pass, while he blessed them, he was parted from them, and carried up into heaven, and sat on the right hand of God.[724] And they worshipped him, and returned to Jerusalem with great joy.

---

[722] Compare Genesis 2:7: "And the LORD God formed man of the dust of the ground, and breathed into his nostrils the breath of life; and man became a living soul."
1 Samuel 10:6: "And the Spirit of the LORD will come upon thee, and thou shalt prophesy with them, and shalt be turned into another man."
Job 33:4: "The Spirit of God hath made me, and the breath of the Almighty hath given me life."
[723] Compare Leviticus 9:22: "And Aaron lifted up his hand toward the people, and blessed them, and came down from offering of the sin offering, and the burnt offering, and peace offerings."
Numbers 6:23-26: "Speak unto Aaron and unto his sons, saying, 'On this wise ye shall bless the children of Israel, saying unto them, "The LORD bless thee, and keep thee. The LORD make his face shine upon thee, and be gracious unto thee. The LORD lift up his countenance upon thee, and give thee peace."'"
Sirach 50:20: "Then he went down, and lifted up his hands over the whole congregation of the children of Israel, to give the blessing of the Lord with his lips, and to rejoice in his name."
[724] See Psalms 110:1-2,4-6: "The LORD said unto my Lord, 'Sit thou at my right hand, until I make thine enemies thy footstool. The LORD shall send the rod of thy strength out of Zion; rule thou in the midst of thine enemies. The LORD hath sworn, and will not repent, "Thou art a priest for ever after the order of Melchizedek." The Lord at thy right hand shall strike through kings in the day of his wrath. He shall judge among the heathen, he shall fill the places with the dead bodies; he shall wound the heads over many countries.'"

THE TREE OF LIFE

And the graves were opened,[725] and many bodies of the saints which slept arose, and came out of the graves after his resurrection, and went into the holy city, and appeared unto many.

Psalms 80:17: "Let thy hand be upon the man of thy right hand, upon the son of man whom thou madest strong for thyself."
1 Samuel 2:10: "The adversaries of the LORD shall be broken to pieces; out of heaven shall he thunder upon them; the LORD shall judge the ends of the earth; and he shall give strength unto his king, and exalt the horn of his anointed."
Psalms 89:26-27: "He shall cry unto me, 'Thou art my father, my God, and the rock of my salvation.' Also I will make him my firstborn, higher than the kings of the earth."
Isaiah 52:13: "Behold, my servant shall deal prudently, he shall be exalted and extolled, and be very high."
[725] See Ezekiel 37:12-14: "Therefore prophesy and say unto them, 'Thus saith the Lord GOD; Behold, O my people, I will open your graves, and cause you to come up out of your graves, and bring you into the land of Israel. And ye shall know that I am the LORD, when I have opened your graves, O my people, and brought you up out of your graves, and shall put my spirit in you, and ye shall live, and I shall place you in your own land; then shall ye know that I the LORD have spoken it, and performed it, saith the LORD.'"
Isaiah 24:23: "Then the moon shall be confounded, and the sun ashamed, when the LORD of hosts shall reign in mount Zion, and in Jerusalem, and before his ancients gloriously."
Hosea 13:14: "I will ransom them from the power of the grave; I will redeem them from death. O death, I will be thy plagues. O grave, I will be thy destruction; repentance shall be hid from mine eyes."
Job 19:25-26: "For I know that my redeemer liveth, and that he shall stand at the latter day upon the earth. And though after my skin worms destroy this body, yet in my flesh shall I see God."
Isaiah 26:19,21: "Thy dead men shall live, together with my dead body shall they arise. Awake and sing, ye that dwell in dust; for thy dew is as the dew of herbs, and the earth shall cast out the dead. For, behold, the LORD cometh out of his place to punish the inhabitants of the earth for their iniquity; the earth also shall disclose her blood, and shall no more cover her slain."
Daniel 12:2: "And many of them that sleep in the dust of the earth shall awake, some to everlasting life, and some to shame and everlasting contempt."
Isaiah 25:8: "He will swallow up death in victory; and the Lord GOD will wipe away tears from off all faces; and the rebuke of his people shall he take away from off all the earth; for the LORD hath spoken it."
2 Esdras 2:11-12,16: "Their glory also will I take unto me, and give these the everlasting tabernacles, which I had prepared for them. They shall have the Tree of Life for an ointment of sweet savour; they shall neither labour, nor be weary. And those that be dead will I raise up again from their places, and bring them out of the graves; for I have known my name in Israel."

THE TREE OF LIFE

After these things Jesus shewed himself again to the disciples at the sea of Tiberias, and on this wise shewed he himself. There were together Simon Peter, and Thomas called Didymus, and Nathanael of Cana in Galilee, and the sons of Zebedee, and two other of his disciples. Simon Peter saith unto them, "I go a fishing." They say unto him, "We also go with thee." They went forth, and entered into a ship immediately, and that night they caught nothing. But when the morning was now come, Jesus stood on the shore, but the disciples knew not that it was Jesus. Then Jesus saith unto them, "Children, have ye any meat?" They answered him, "No." And he said unto them, "Cast the net on the right side of the ship, and ye shall find." They cast therefore, and now they were not able to draw it for the multitude of fishes. Therefore John saith unto Peter, "It is the Lord." Now when Simon Peter heard that it was the Lord, he girt his fisher's coat unto him, (for he was naked,) and did cast himself into the sea. And the other disciples came in a little ship, for they were not far from land, but as it were two hundred cubits, dragging the net with fishes. As soon then as they were come to land, they saw a fire of coals there, and fish laid thereon, and bread. Jesus saith unto them, "Bring of the fish which ye have now caught." Simon Peter went up, and drew the net to land full of great fishes, an hundred and fifty and three, and for all there were so many, yet was not the net broken. Jesus saith unto them, "Come and dine." And none of the

---

2 Esdras 4:40-42: "So he answered me, and said, 'Go thy way to a woman with child, and ask of her when she hath fulfilled her nine months, if her womb may keep the birth any longer within her.' Then said I, 'No, Lord, that can she not.' And he said unto me, 'In the grave the chambers of souls are like the womb of a woman; for like as a woman that travaileth maketh haste to escape the necessity of the travail; even so do these places haste to deliver those things that are committed unto them.'"

2 Esdras 7:32: "And the earth shall restore those that are asleep in her, and so shall the dust those that dwell in silence, and the secret places shall deliver those souls that were committed unto them."

2 Maccabees 7:9: "And when he was at the last gasp, he said, 'Thou like a fury takest us out of this present life, but the King of the world shall raise us up, who have died for his laws, unto everlasting life.'"

disciples durst ask him, "Who art thou?" knowing that it was the Lord.

Jesus then cometh, and taketh bread, and giveth them, and fish likewise. This is now the third time that Jesus shewed himself to his disciples, after that he was risen from the dead. So when they had dined, Jesus saith to Simon Peter, "Simon, son of Jonah, lovest thou me more than these?" He saith unto him, "Yea, Lord, thou knowest that I love thee." He saith unto him, "Feed my lambs." He saith to him again the second time, "Simon, son of Jonah, lovest thou me?" He saith unto him, "Yea, Lord, thou knowest that I love thee." He saith unto him, "Feed my sheep." He saith unto him the third time, "Simon, son of Jonah, lovest thou me?" Peter was grieved because he said unto him the third time, "Lovest thou me?" And he said unto him, "Lord, thou knowest all things, thou knowest that I love thee." Jesus saith unto him, "Feed my sheep. Verily, verily, I say unto thee, when thou wast young, thou girdedst thyself, and walkedst whither thou wouldest, but when thou shalt be old, thou shalt stretch forth thy hands, and another shall gird thee, and carry thee whither thou wouldest not." This spake he, signifying by what death he should glorify God. And when he had spoken this, he saith unto him, "Follow me." Then Peter, turning about, seeth John following, (which also leaned on his breast at supper, and said, "Lord, which is he that betrayeth thee?") Peter seeing him saith to Jesus, "Lord, and what shall this man do?" Jesus saith unto him, "If I will that he tarry till I come, what is that to thee? Follow thou me." Then went this saying abroad among the brethren, that that disciple should not die, yet Jesus said not unto him, "He shall not die," but, "If I will that he tarry till I come, what is that to thee?" This is the disciple which testifieth of these things, and wrote these things, and we know that his testimony is true.

Then the eleven disciples went away into Galilee, into a mountain where Jesus had appointed them. And Jesus came and spake unto them, saying, "All power is given unto me in heaven and

THE TREE OF LIFE

in earth."[726] And he said unto them, "Go ye into all the world,[727] and preach the gospel to every creature. He that believeth and is baptized shall be saved, but he that believeth not shall be damned. And these signs shall follow them that believe: in my name shall they cast out devils, they shall speak with new tongues, they shall take up serpents, and if they drink any deadly thing, it shall not hurt them, they shall lay hands on the sick, and they shall recover. Go ye therefore, and teach all nations,[728] baptizing them in the name of the Father, and of the Son, and of the Holy Ghost, teaching them to observe all things whatsoever I have commanded you, and, lo, I am with you alway, even unto the end of the world.[729] Amen."

---

[726] See Daniel 7:13-14: "I saw in the night visions, and, behold, one like the Son of man came with the clouds of heaven, and came to the Ancient of days, and they brought him near before him. And there was given him dominion, and glory, and a kingdom, that all people, nations, and languages, should serve him; his dominion is an everlasting dominion, which shall not pass away, and his kingdom that which shall not be destroyed."
1 Samuel 2:10: "The adversaries of the LORD shall be broken to pieces; out of heaven shall he thunder upon them; the LORD shall judge the ends of the earth; and he shall give strength unto his king, and exalt the horn of his anointed."
[727] Compare Jeremiah 10:6-7: "Forasmuch as there is none like unto thee, O LORD; thou art great, and thy name is great in might. Who would not fear thee, O King of nations? For to thee doth it appertain; forasmuch as among all the wise men of the nations, and in all their kingdoms, there is none like unto thee."
Zechariah 14:9: "And the LORD shall be king over all the earth; in that day shall there be one LORD, and his name one."
[728] Compare Isaiah 60:2-3: "For, behold, the darkness shall cover the earth, and gross darkness the people; but the LORD shall arise upon thee, and his glory shall be seen upon thee. And the Gentiles shall come to thy light, and kings to the brightness of thy rising."
[729] Compare Isaiah 42:6: "I the LORD have called thee in righteousness, and will hold thine hand, and will keep thee, and give thee for a covenant of the people, for a light of the Gentiles."
1 Kings 8:57: "The LORD our God be with us, as he was with our fathers; let him not leave us, nor forsake us."
Exodus 3:10-12: "'Come now therefore, and I will send thee unto Pharaoh, that thou mayest bring forth my people the children of Israel out of Egypt.' And Moses said unto God, 'Who am I, that I should go unto Pharaoh, and that I should bring forth the children of Israel out of Egypt?' And he said, 'Certainly I will be with thee; and this shall be a token unto thee, that I have sent thee; when thou hast brought forth the people out of Egypt, ye shall serve God upon this mountain.'"

THE TREE OF LIFE

And they went forth, and preached every where, the Lord working with them, and confirming the word with signs following, and were continually in the temple, praising and blessing God.

Amen.

Jeremiah 1:8-9: "'Be not afraid of their faces; for I am with thee to deliver thee, saith the LORD.' Then the LORD put forth his hand, and touched my mouth. And the LORD said unto me, 'Behold, I have put my words in thy mouth.'"

Epilogue

And many other signs truly did Jesus in the presence of his disciples, which are not written in this book. But these are written, that ye might believe that Jesus is the Christ, the Son of God, and that believing ye might have life through his name. And there are also many other things which Jesus did, the which, if they should be written every one, I suppose that even the world itself could not contain the books that should be written.

Amen.

THE TREE OF LIFE

Appendix

Generations

The book of the generation of Jesus Christ, the son of David, the son of Abraham:

Abraham begat Isaac, and Isaac begat Jacob, and Jacob begat Judas and his brethren, and Judas begat Phares and Zara of Thamar, and Phares begat Esrom, and Esrom begat Aram, and Aram begat Aminadab, and Aminadab begat Naasson, and Naasson begat Salmon, and Salmon begat Booz of Rachab, and Booz begat Obed of Ruth, and Obed begat Jesse, and Jesse begat David the king, and David the king begat Solomon of her that had been the wife of Urias, and Solomon begat Roboam, and Roboam begat Abia, and Abia begat Asa, and Asa begat Josaphat, and Josaphat begat Joram, and Joram begat Ozias, and Ozias begat Joatham, and Joatham begat Achaz, and Achaz begat Ezekias, and Ezekias begat Manasses, and Manasses begat Amon, and Amon begat Josias, and Josias begat Jechonias and his brethren, about the time they were carried away to Babylon, and after they were brought to Babylon, Jechonias begat Salathiel, and Salathiel begat Zorobabel, and Zorobabel begat Abiud, and Abiud begat Eliakim, and Eliakim begat Azor, and Azor begat Sadoc, and Sadoc begat Achim, and Achim begat Eliud, and Eliud begat Eleazar, and Eleazar begat Matthan, and Matthan begat Jacob, and Jacob begat Joseph the husband of Mary, of whom was born

THE TREE OF LIFE

Jesus, who is called Christ. So all the generations from Abraham to David are fourteen generations, and from David until the carrying away into Babylon are fourteen generations, and from the carrying away into Babylon unto Christ are fourteen generations.

And Jesus was (as was supposed) the son of Joseph, which was the son of Heli, which was the son of Matthat, which was the son of Levi, which was the son of Melchi, which was the son of Janna, which was the son of Joseph, which was the son of Mattathias, which was the son of Amos, which was the son of Naum, which was the son of Esli, which was the son of Nagge, which was the son of Maath, which was the son of Mattathias, which was the son of Semei, which was the son of Joseph, which was the son of Juda, which was the son of Joanna, which was the son of Rhesa, which was the son of Zorobabel, which was the son of Salathiel, which was the son of Neri, which was the son of Melchi, which was the son of Addi, which was the son of Cosam, which was the son of Elmodam, which was the son of Er, which was the son of Jose, which was the son of Eliezer, which was the son of Jorim, which was the son of Matthat, which was the son of Levi, which was the son of Simeon, which was the son of Juda, which was the son of Joseph, which was the son of Jonan, which was the son of Eliakim, which was the son of Melea, which was the son of Menan, which was the son of Mattatha, which was the son of Nathan, which was the son of David, which was the son of Jesse, which was the son of Obed, which was the son of Booz, which was the son of Salmon, which was the son of Naasson, which was the son of Aminadab, which was the son of Aram, which was the son of Esrom, which was the son of Phares, which was the son of Juda, which was the son of Jacob, which was the son of Isaac, which was the son of Abraham, which was the son of Thara, which was the son of Nachor, which was the son of Saruch, which was the son of Ragau, which was the son of Phalec, which was the son of Heber, which was the son of Sala, which was the son of Cainan, which was the son of Arphaxad, which was the son of Sem, which was the son

THE TREE OF LIFE

of Noe, which was the son of Lamech, which was the son of Mathusala, which was the son of Enoch, which was the son of Jared, which was the son of Maleleel, which was the son of Cainan, which was the son of Enos, which was the son of Seth, which was the son of Adam, which was the son of God.

THE TREE OF LIFE

THE TREE OF LIFE

Afterword

Source Material

Following is the author's arrangement of every verse used in creating the foregoing. All 3,779 verses from the four gospels of the King James Version of the Bible are represented, as is indicated in the left most column of the table.

#	Verse	Verse Content
1	John1:1	In the beginning was the Word, and the Word was with God, and the Word was God.
2	John1:2	The same was in the beginning with God.
3	John1:3	All things were made by him; and without him was not any thing made that was made.
4	John1:4	In him was life; and the life was the light of men.
5	John1:5	And the light shineth in darkness; and the darkness comprehended it not.
6	Mark1:1	The beginning of the gospel of Jesus Christ, the Son of God;
7	Luke1:1	Forasmuch as many have taken in hand to set forth in order a declaration of those things which are most surely believed among us,
8	Luke1:2	Even as they delivered them unto us, which from the beginning were eyewitnesses, and ministers of the word;
9	Luke1:3	It seemed good to me also, having had perfect understanding of all things from the very first, to write unto thee in order, most excellent Theophilus,
10	Luke1:4	That thou mightest know the certainty of those things, wherein thou hast been instructed.
11	Luke1:5	There was in the days of Herod, the king of Judaea, a certain priest named Zacharias, of the course of Abia: and his wife was of the daughters of Aaron, and her name was Elisabeth.
12	Luke1:6	And they were both righteous before God, walking in all the commandments and ordinances of the Lord blameless.
13	Luke1:7	And they had no child, because that Elisabeth was barren, and they both were now well stricken in years.
14	Luke1:8	And it came to pass, that while he executed the priest's office before God in the order of his course,

THE TREE OF LIFE

15	Luke1:9	According to the custom of the priest's office, his lot was to burn incense when he went into the temple of the Lord.
16	Luke1:10	And the whole multitude of the people were praying without at the time of incense.
17	Luke1:11	And there appeared unto him an angel of the Lord standing on the right side of the altar of incense.
18	Luke1:12	And when Zacharias saw him, he was troubled, and fear fell upon him.
19	Luke1:13	But the angel said unto him, Fear not, Zacharias: for thy prayer is heard; and thy wife Elisabeth shall bear thee a son, and thou shalt call his name John.
20	Luke1:14	And thou shalt have joy and gladness; and many shall rejoice at his birth.
21	Luke1:15	For he shall be great in the sight of the Lord, and shall drink neither wine nor strong drink; and he shall be filled with the Holy Ghost, even from his mother's womb.
22	Luke1:16	And many of the children of Israel shall he turn to the Lord their God.
23	Luke1:17	And he shall go before him in the spirit and power of Elias, to turn the hearts of the fathers to the children, and the disobedient to the wisdom of the just; to make ready a people prepared for the Lord.
24	Luke1:18	And Zacharias said unto the angel, Whereby shall I know this? for I am an old man, and my wife well stricken in years.
25	Luke1:19	And the angel answering said unto him, I am Gabriel, that stand in the presence of God; and am sent to speak unto thee, and to shew thee these glad tidings.
26	Luke1:20	And, behold, thou shalt be dumb, and not able to speak, until the day that these things shall be performed, because thou believest not my words, which shall be fulfilled in their season.
27	Luke1:21	And the people waited for Zacharias, and marvelled that he tarried so long in the temple.
28	Luke1:22	And when he came out, he could not speak unto them: and they perceived that he had seen a vision in the temple: for he beckoned unto them, and remained speechless.
29	Luke1:23	And it came to pass, that, as soon as the days of his ministration were accomplished, he departed to his own house.
30	Luke1:24	And after those days his wife Elisabeth conceived, and hid herself five months, saying,
31	Luke1:25	Thus hath the Lord dealt with me in the days wherein he looked on me, to take away my reproach among men.
32	Luke1:26	And in the sixth month the angel Gabriel was sent from God unto a city of Galilee, named Nazareth,
33	Luke1:27	To a virgin espoused to a man whose name was Joseph, of the house of David; and the virgin's name was Mary.
34	Luke1:28	And the angel came in unto her, and said, Hail, thou that art highly favoured, the Lord is with thee: blessed art thou among women.
35	Luke1:29	And when she saw him, she was troubled at his saying, and cast in her mind what manner of salutation this should be.
36	Luke1:30	And the angel said unto her, Fear not, Mary: for thou hast found favour with God.
37	Luke1:31	And, behold, thou shalt conceive in thy womb, and bring forth a son, and shalt call his name JESUS.
38	Luke1:32	He shall be great, and shall be called the Son of the Highest: and the Lord God shall give unto him the throne of his father David:
39	Luke1:33	And he shall reign over the house of Jacob for ever; and of his kingdom there shall be no end.
40	Luke1:34	Then said Mary unto the angel, How shall this be, seeing I know not a man?
41	Luke1:35	And the angel answered and said unto her, The Holy Ghost shall come upon thee, and the power of the Highest shall overshadow thee: therefore also that

THE TREE OF LIFE

		holy thing which shall be born of thee shall be called the Son of God.
42	Luke1:36	And, behold, thy cousin Elisabeth, she hath also conceived a son in her old age: and this is the sixth month with her, who was called barren.
43	Luke1:37	For with God nothing shall be impossible.
44	Luke1:38	And Mary said, Behold the handmaid of the Lord; be it unto me according to thy word. And the angel departed from her.
45	Luke1:39	And Mary arose in those days, and went into the hill country with haste, into a city of Juda;
46	Luke1:40	And entered into the house of Zacharias, and saluted Elisabeth.
47	Luke1:41	And it came to pass, that, when Elisabeth heard the salutation of Mary, the babe leaped in her womb; and Elisabeth was filled with the Holy Ghost:
48	Luke1:42	And she spake out with a loud voice, and said, Blessed art thou among women, and blessed is the fruit of thy womb.
49	Luke1:43	And whence is this to me, that the mother of my Lord should come to me?
50	Luke1:44	For, lo, as soon as the voice of thy salutation sounded in mine ears, the babe leaped in my womb for joy.
51	Luke1:45	And blessed is she that believed: for there shall be a performance of those things which were told her from the Lord.
52	Luke1:46	And Mary said, My soul doth magnify the Lord,
53	Luke1:47	And my spirit hath rejoiced in God my Saviour.
54	Luke1:48	For he hath regarded the low estate of his handmaiden: for, behold, from henceforth all generations shall call me blessed.
55	Luke1:49	For he that is mighty hath done to me great things; and holy is his name.
56	Luke1:50	And his mercy is on them that fear him from generation to generation.
57	Luke1:51	He hath shewed strength with his arm; he hath scattered the proud in the imagination of their hearts.
58	Luke1:52	He hath put down the mighty from their seats, and exalted them of low degree.
59	Luke1:53	He hath filled the hungry with good things; and the rich he hath sent empty away.
60	Luke1:54	He hath holpen his servant Israel, in remembrance of his mercy;
61	Luke1:55	As he spake to our fathers, to Abraham, and to his seed for ever.
62	Luke1:56	And Mary abode with her about three months, and returned to her own house.
63	Matt1:18	Now the birth of Jesus Christ was on this wise: When as his mother Mary was espoused to Joseph, before they came together, she was found with child of the Holy Ghost.
64	Matt1:19	Then Joseph her husband, being a just man, and not willing to make her a publick example, was minded to put her away privily.
65	Matt1:20	But while he thought on these things, behold, the angel of the LORD appeared unto him in a dream, saying, Joseph, thou son of David, fear not to take unto thee Mary thy wife: for that which is conceived in her is of the Holy Ghost.
66	Matt1:21	And she shall bring forth a son, and thou shalt call his name JESUS: for he shall save his people from their sins.
67	Matt1:22	Now all this was done, that it might be fulfilled which was spoken of the Lord by the prophet, saying,
68	Matt1:23	Behold, a virgin shall be with child, and shall bring forth a son, and they shall call his name Emmanuel, which being interpreted is, God with us.
69	Matt1:24	Then Joseph being raised from sleep did as the angel of the Lord had bidden him, and took unto him his wife:
70	Matt1:25	And knew her not till she had brought forth her firstborn son: and he called his name JESUS.
71	Luke1:57	Now Elisabeth's full time came that she should be delivered; and she brought forth a son.
72	Luke1:58	And her neighbours and her cousins heard how the Lord had shewed great mercy upon her; and they rejoiced with her.

THE TREE OF LIFE

73	Luke1:59	And it came to pass, that on the eighth day they came to circumcise the child; and they called him Zacharias, after the name of his father.
74	Luke1:60	And his mother answered and said, Not so; but he shall be called John.
75	Luke1:61	And they said unto her, There is none of thy kindred that is called by this name.
76	Luke1:62	And they made signs to his father, how he would have him called.
77	Luke1:63	And he asked for a writing table, and wrote, saying, His name is John. And they marvelled all.
78	Luke1:64	And his mouth was opened immediately, and his tongue loosed, and he spake, and praised God.
79	Luke1:65	And fear came on all that dwelt round about them: and all these sayings were noised abroad throughout all the hill country of Judaea.
80	Luke1:66	And all they that heard them laid them up in their hearts, saying, What manner of child shall this be! And the hand of the Lord was with him.
81	Luke1:67	And his father Zacharias was filled with the Holy Ghost, and prophesied, saying,
82	Luke1:68	Blessed be the Lord God of Israel; for he hath visited and redeemed his people,
83	Luke1:69	And hath raised up an horn of salvation for us in the house of his servant David;
84	Luke1:70	As he spake by the mouth of his holy prophets, which have been since the world began:
85	Luke1:71	That we should be saved from our enemies, and from the hand of all that hate us;
86	Luke1:72	To perform the mercy promised to our fathers, and to remember his holy covenant;
87	Luke1:73	The oath which he sware to our father Abraham,
88	Luke1:74	That he would grant unto us, that we being delivered out of the hand of our enemies might serve him without fear,
89	Luke1:75	In holiness and righteousness before him, all the days of our life.
90	Luke1:76	And thou, child, shalt be called the prophet of the Highest: for thou shalt go before the face of the Lord to prepare his ways;
91	Luke1:77	To give knowledge of salvation unto his people by the remission of their sins,
92	Luke1:78	Through the tender mercy of our God; whereby the dayspring from on high hath visited us,
93	Luke1:79	To give light to them that sit in darkness and in the shadow of death, to guide our feet into the way of peace.
94	Luke1:80	And the child grew, and waxed strong in spirit, and was in the deserts till the day of his shewing unto Israel.
95	Luke2:1	And it came to pass in those days, that there went out a decree from Caesar Augustus, that all the world should be taxed.
96	Luke2:2	(And this taxing was first made when Cyrenius was governor of Syria.)
97	Luke2:3	And all went to be taxed, every one into his own city.
98	Luke2:4	And Joseph also went up from Galilee, out of the city of Nazareth, into Judaea, unto the city of David, which is called Bethlehem; (because he was of the house and lineage of David:)
99	Luke2:5	To be taxed with Mary his espoused wife, being great with child.
100	Luke2:6	And so it was, that, while they were there, the days were accomplished that she should be delivered.
101	Luke2:7	And she brought forth her firstborn son, and wrapped him in swaddling clothes, and laid him in a manger; because there was no room for them in the inn.
102	Luke2:8	And there were in the same country shepherds abiding in the field, keeping watch over their flock by night.
103	Luke2:9	And, lo, the angel of the Lord came upon them, and the glory of the Lord shone round about them: and they were sore afraid.
104	Luke2:10	And the angel said unto them, Fear not: for, behold, I bring you good tidings of great joy, which shall be to all people.

THE TREE OF LIFE

105	Luke2:11	For unto you is born this day in the city of David a Saviour, which is Christ the Lord.
106	Luke2:12	And this shall be a sign unto you; Ye shall find the babe wrapped in swaddling clothes, lying in a manger.
107	Luke2:13	And suddenly there was with the angel a multitude of the heavenly host praising God, and saying,
108	Luke2:14	Glory to God in the highest, and on earth peace, good will toward men.
109	Luke2:15	And it came to pass, as the angels were gone away from them into heaven, the shepherds said one to another, Let us now go even unto Bethlehem, and see this thing which is come to pass, which the Lord hath made known unto us.
110	Luke2:16	And they came with haste, and found Mary, and Joseph, and the babe lying in a manger.
111	Luke2:17	And when they had seen it, they made known abroad the saying which was told them concerning this child.
112	Luke2:18	And all they that heard it wondered at those things which were told them by the shepherds.
113	Luke2:19	But Mary kept all these things, and pondered them in her heart.
114	Luke2:20	And the shepherds returned, glorifying and praising God for all the things that they had heard and seen, as it was told unto them.
115	Luke2:21	And when eight days were accomplished for the circumcising of the child, his name was called JESUS, which was so named of the angel before he was conceived in the womb.
116	Luke2:22	And when the days of her purification according to the law of Moses were accomplished, they brought him to Jerusalem, to present him to the Lord;
117	Luke2:23	(As it is written in the law of the LORD, Every male that openeth the womb shall be called holy to the Lord;)
118	Luke2:24	And to offer a sacrifice according to that which is said in the law of the Lord, A pair of turtledoves, or two young pigeons.
119	Luke2:25	And, behold, there was a man in Jerusalem, whose name was Simeon; and the same man was just and devout, waiting for the consolation of Israel: and the Holy Ghost was upon him.
120	Luke2:26	And it was revealed unto him by the Holy Ghost, that he should not see death, before he had seen the Lord's Christ.
121	Luke2:27	And he came by the Spirit into the temple: and when the parents brought in the child Jesus, to do for him after the custom of the law,
122	Luke2:28	Then took he him up in his arms, and blessed God, and said,
123	Luke2:29	Lord, now lettest thou thy servant depart in peace, according to thy word:
124	Luke2:30	For mine eyes have seen thy salvation,
125	Luke2:31	Which thou hast prepared before the face of all people;
126	Luke2:32	A light to lighten the Gentiles, and the glory of thy people Israel.
127	Luke2:33	And Joseph and his mother marvelled at those things which were spoken of him.
128	Luke2:34	And Simeon blessed them, and said unto Mary his mother, Behold, this child is set for the fall and rising again of many in Israel; and for a sign which shall be spoken against;
129	Luke2:35	(Yea, a sword shall pierce through thy own soul also,) that the thoughts of many hearts may be revealed.
130	Luke2:36	And there was one Anna, a prophetess, the daughter of Phanuel, of the tribe of Aser: she was of a great age, and had lived with an husband seven years from her virginity;
131	Luke2:37	And she was a widow of about fourscore and four years, which departed not from the temple, but served God with fastings and prayers night and day.
132	Luke2:38	And she coming in that instant gave thanks likewise unto the Lord, and spake of him to all them that looked for redemption in Jerusalem.

THE TREE OF LIFE

133	Luke2:39	And when they had performed all things according to the law of the Lord, they returned into Galilee, to their own city Nazareth.
134	Matt2:1	Now when Jesus was born in Bethlehem of Judaea in the days of Herod the king, behold, there came wise men from the east to Jerusalem,
135	Matt2:2	Saying, Where is he that is born King of the Jews? for we have seen his star in the east, and are come to worship him.
136	Matt2:3	When Herod the king had heard these things, he was troubled, and all Jerusalem with him.
137	Matt2:4	And when he had gathered all the chief priests and scribes of the people together, he demanded of them where Christ should be born.
138	Matt2:5	And they said unto him, In Bethlehem of Judaea: for thus it is written by the prophet,
139	Matt2:6	And thou Bethlehem, in the land of Juda, art not the least among the princes of Juda: for out of thee shall come a Governor, that shall rule my people Israel.
140	Matt2:7	Then Herod, when he had privily called the wise men, enquired of them diligently what time the star appeared.
141	Matt2:8	And he sent them to Bethlehem, and said, Go and search diligently for the young child; and when ye have found him, bring me word again, that I may come and worship him also.
142	Matt2:9	When they had heard the king, they departed; and, lo, the star, which they saw in the east, went before them, till it came and stood over where the young child was.
143	Matt2:10	When they saw the star, they rejoiced with exceeding great joy.
144	Matt2:11	And when they were come into the house, they saw the young child with Mary his mother, and fell down, and worshipped him: and when they had opened their treasures, they presented unto him gifts; gold, and frankincense, and myrrh.
145	Matt2:12	And being warned of God in a dream that they should not return to Herod, they departed into their own country another way.
146	Matt2:13	And when they were departed, behold, the angel of the Lord appeareth to Joseph in a dream, saying, Arise, and take the young child and his mother, and flee into Egypt, and be thou there until I bring thee word: for Herod will seek the young child to destroy him.
147	Matt2:14	When he arose, he took the young child and his mother by night, and departed into Egypt:
148	Matt2:15	And was there until the death of Herod: that it might be fulfilled which was spoken of the Lord by the prophet, saying, Out of Egypt have I called my son.
149	Matt2:16	Then Herod, when he saw that he was mocked of the wise men, was exceeding wroth, and sent forth, and slew all the children that were in Bethlehem, and in all the coasts thereof, from two years old and under, according to the time which he had diligently enquired of the wise men.
150	Matt2:17	Then was fulfilled that which was spoken by Jeremy the prophet, saying,
151	Matt2:18	In Rama was there a voice heard, lamentation, and weeping, and great mourning, Rachel weeping for her children, and would not be comforted, because they are not.
152	Matt2:19	But when Herod was dead, behold, an angel of the Lord appeareth in a dream to Joseph in Egypt,
153	Matt2:20	Saying, Arise, and take the young child and his mother, and go into the land of Israel: for they are dead which sought the young child's life.
154	Matt2:21	And he arose, and took the young child and his mother, and came into the land of Israel.
155	Matt2:22	But when he heard that Archelaus did reign in Judaea in the room of his father Herod, he was afraid to go thither: notwithstanding, being warned of God in a dream, he turned aside into the parts of Galilee:
156	Matt2:23	And he came and dwelt in a city called Nazareth: that it might be fulfilled which

THE TREE OF LIFE

		was spoken by the prophets, He shall be called a Nazarene.
157	Luke2:40	And the child grew, and waxed strong in spirit, filled with wisdom: and the grace of God was upon him.
158	Luke2:41	Now his parents went to Jerusalem every year at the feast of the passover.
159	Luke2:42	And when he was twelve years old, they went up to Jerusalem after the custom of the feast.
160	Luke2:43	And when they had fulfilled the days, as they returned, the child Jesus tarried behind in Jerusalem; and Joseph and his mother knew not of it.
161	Luke2:44	But they, supposing him to have been in the company, went a day's journey; and they sought him among their kinsfolk and acquaintance.
162	Luke2:45	And when they found him not, they turned back again to Jerusalem, seeking him.
163	Luke2:46	And it came to pass, that after three days they found him in the temple, sitting in the midst of the doctors, both hearing them, and asking them questions.
164	Luke2:47	And all that heard him were astonished at his understanding and answers.
165	Luke2:48	And when they saw him, they were amazed: and his mother said unto him, Son, why hast thou thus dealt with us? behold, thy father and I have sought thee sorrowing.
166	Luke2:49	And he said unto them, How is it that ye sought me? wist ye not that I must be about my Father's business?
167	Luke2:50	And they understood not the saying which he spake unto them.
168	Luke2:51	And he went down with them, and came to Nazareth, and was subject unto them: but his mother kept all these sayings in her heart.
169	Luke2:52	And Jesus increased in wisdom and stature, and in favour with God and man.
170	Luke3:1	Now in the fifteenth year of the reign of Tiberius Caesar, Pontius Pilate being governor of Judaea, and Herod being tetrarch of Galilee, and his brother Philip tetrarch of Ituraea and of the region of Trachonitis, and Lysanias the tetrarch of Abilene,
171	Luke3:2	Annas and Caiaphas being the high priests, the word of God came unto John the son of Zacharias in the wilderness.
172	John1:6	There was a man sent from God, whose name was John.
173	Matt3:1	In those days came John the Baptist, preaching in the wilderness of Judaea,
174	Luke3:3	And he came into all the country about Jordan, preaching the baptism of repentance for the remission of sins;
175	Mark1:4	John did baptize in the wilderness, and preach the baptism of repentance for the remission of sins.
176	John1:7	The same came for a witness, to bear witness of the Light, that all men through him might believe.
177	John1:8	He was not that Light, but was sent to bear witness of that Light.
178	John1:9	That was the true Light, which lighteth every man that cometh into the world.
179	John1:10	He was in the world, and the world was made by him, and the world knew him not.
180	John1:11	He came unto his own, and his own received him not.
181	John1:12	But as many as received him, to them gave he power to become the sons of God, even to them that believe on his name:
182	John1:13	Which were born, not of blood, nor of the will of the flesh, nor of the will of man, but of God.
183	John1:14	And the Word was made flesh, and dwelt among us, (and we beheld his glory, the glory as of the only begotten of the Father,) full of grace and truth.
184	John1:16	And of his fulness have all we received, and grace for grace.
185	John1:17	For the law was given by Moses, but grace and truth came by Jesus Christ.
186	Matt3:4	And the same John had his raiment of camel's hair, and a leathern girdle about his loins; and his meat was locusts and wild honey.
187	Mark1:6	And John was clothed with camel's hair, and with a girdle of a skin about his

THE TREE OF LIFE

		loins; and he did eat locusts and wild honey;
188	Matt3:5	Then went out to him Jerusalem, and all Judaea, and all the region round about Jordan,
189	Matt3:6	And were baptized of him in Jordan, confessing their sins.
190	Mark1:5	And there went out unto him all the land of Judaea, and they of Jerusalem, and were all baptized of him in the river of Jordan, confessing their sins.
191	Luke3:7	Then said he to the multitude that came forth to be baptized of him, O generation of vipers, who hath warned you to flee from the wrath to come?
192	Matt3:7	But when he saw many of the Pharisees and Sadducees come to his baptism, he said unto them, O generation of vipers, who hath warned you to flee from the wrath to come?
193	Matt3:8	Bring forth therefore fruits meet for repentance:
194	Luke3:8	Bring forth therefore fruits worthy of repentance, and begin not to say within yourselves, We have Abraham to our father: for I say unto you, That God is able of these stones to raise up children unto Abraham.
195	Matt3:9	And think not to say within yourselves, We have Abraham to our father: for I say unto you, that God is able of these stones to raise up children unto Abraham.
196	Luke3:9	And now also the axe is laid unto the root of the trees: every tree therefore which bringeth not forth good fruit is hewn down, and cast into the fire.
197	Matt3:10	And now also the axe is laid unto the root of the trees: therefore every tree which bringeth not forth good fruit is hewn down, and cast into the fire.
198	Matt3:2	And saying, Repent ye: for the kingdom of heaven is at hand.
199	Luke3:10	And the people asked him, saying, What shall we do then?
200	Luke3:11	He answereth and saith unto them, He that hath two coats, let him impart to him that hath none; and he that hath meat, let him do likewise.
201	Luke3:12	Then came also publicans to be baptized, and said unto him, Master, what shall we do?
202	Luke3:13	And he said unto them, Exact no more than that which is appointed you.
203	Luke3:14	And the soldiers likewise demanded of him, saying, And what shall we do? And he said unto them, Do violence to no man, neither accuse any falsely; and be content with your wages.
204	John1:19	And this is the record of John, when the Jews sent priests and Levites from Jerusalem to ask him, Who art thou?
205	Luke3:15	And as the people were in expectation, and all men mused in their hearts of John, whether he were the Christ, or not;
206	John1:20	And he confessed, and denied not; but confessed, I am not the Christ.
207	John1:21	And they asked him, What then? Art thou Elias? And he saith, I am not. Art thou that prophet? And he answered, No.
208	John1:22	Then said they unto him, Who art thou? that we may give an answer to them that sent us. What sayest thou of thyself?
209	Mark1:2	As it is written in the prophets, Behold, I send my messenger before thy face, which shall prepare thy way before thee.
210	John1:23	He said, I am the voice of one crying in the wilderness, Make straight the way of the Lord, as said the prophet Esaias.
211	Mark1:3	The voice of one crying in the wilderness, Prepare ye the way of the Lord, make his paths straight.
212	Matt3:3	For this is he that was spoken of by the prophet Esaias, saying, The voice of one crying in the wilderness, Prepare ye the way of the Lord, make his paths straight.
213	Luke3:4	As it is written in the book of the words of Esaias the prophet, saying, The voice of one crying in the wilderness, Prepare ye the way of the Lord, make his paths straight.
214	Luke3:5	Every valley shall be filled, and every mountain and hill shall be brought low; and the crooked shall be made straight, and the rough ways shall be made smooth;

THE TREE OF LIFE

215	Luke3:6	And all flesh shall see the salvation of God.
216	John1:24	And they which were sent were of the Pharisees.
217	John1:25	And they asked him, and said unto him, Why baptizest thou then, if thou be not that Christ, nor Elias, neither that prophet?
218	John1:26	John answered them, saying, I baptize with water: but there standeth one among you, whom ye know not;
219	John1:27	He it is, who coming after me is preferred before me, whose shoe's latchet I am not worthy to unloose.
220	Mark1:7	And preached, saying, There cometh one mightier than I after me, the latchet of whose shoes I am not worthy to stoop down and unloose.
221	Luke3:16	John answered, saying unto them all, I indeed baptize you with water; but one mightier than I cometh, the latchet of whose shoes I am not worthy to unloose: he shall baptize you with the Holy Ghost and with fire:
222	Matt3:11	I indeed baptize you with water unto repentance: but he that cometh after me is mightier than I, whose shoes I am not worthy to bear: he shall baptize you with the Holy Ghost, and with fire:
223	Mark1:8	I indeed have baptized you with water: but he shall baptize you with the Holy Ghost.
224	Matt3:12	Whose fan is in his hand, and he will throughly purge his floor, and gather his wheat into the garner; but he will burn up the chaff with unquenchable fire.
225	Luke3:17	Whose fan is in his hand, and he will throughly purge his floor, and will gather the wheat into his garner; but the chaff he will burn with fire unquenchable.
226	Luke3:18	And many other things in his exhortation preached he unto the people.
227	John1:28	These things were done in Bethabara beyond Jordan, where John was baptizing.
228	John1:29	The next day John seeth Jesus coming unto him, and saith, Behold the Lamb of God, which taketh away the sin of the world.
229	Matt3:13	Then cometh Jesus from Galilee to Jordan unto John, to be baptized of him.
230	Mark1:9	And it came to pass in those days, that Jesus came from Nazareth of Galilee, and was baptized of John in Jordan.
231	John1:15	John bare witness of him, and cried, saying, This was he of whom I spake, He that cometh after me is preferred before me: for he was before me.
232	John1:30	This is he of whom I said, After me cometh a man which is preferred before me: for he was before me.
233	John1:31	And I knew him not: but that he should be made manifest to Israel, therefore am I come baptizing with water.
234	Matt3:14	But John forbad him, saying, I have need to be baptized of thee, and comest thou to me?
235	Matt3:15	And Jesus answering said unto him, Suffer it to be so now: for thus it becometh us to fulfil all righteousness. Then he suffered him.
236	Luke3:21	Now when all the people were baptized, it came to pass, that Jesus also being baptized, and praying, the heaven was opened,
237	Matt3:16	And Jesus, when he was baptized, went up straightway out of the water: and, lo, the heavens were opened unto him, and he saw the Spirit of God descending like a dove, and lighting upon him:
238	Mark1:10	And straightway coming up out of the water, he saw the heavens opened, and the Spirit like a dove descending upon him:
239	Mark1:11	And there came a voice from heaven, saying, Thou art my beloved Son, in whom I am well pleased.
240	John1:32	And John bare record, saying, I saw the Spirit descending from heaven like a dove, and it abode upon him.
241	John1:33	And I knew him not: but he that sent me to baptize with water, the same said unto me, Upon whom thou shalt see the Spirit descending, and remaining on him, the same is he which baptizeth with the Holy Ghost.

THE TREE OF LIFE

242	John1:34	And I saw, and bare record that this is the Son of God.
243	Luke3:22	And the Holy Ghost descended in a bodily shape like a dove upon him, and a voice came from heaven, which said, Thou art my beloved Son; in thee I am well pleased.
244	Matt3:17	And lo a voice from heaven, saying, This is my beloved Son, in whom I am well pleased.
245	Luke4:1	And Jesus being full of the Holy Ghost returned from Jordan, and was led by the Spirit into the wilderness,
246	Mark1:12	And immediately the Spirit driveth him into the wilderness.
247	Matt4:1	Then was Jesus led up of the Spirit into the wilderness to be tempted of the devil.
248	Mark1:13	And he was there in the wilderness forty days, tempted of Satan; and was with the wild beasts; and the angels ministered unto him.
249	Matt4:2	And when he had fasted forty days and forty nights, he was afterward an hungred.
250	Luke4:2	Being forty days tempted of the devil. And in those days he did eat nothing: and when they were ended, he afterward hungered.
251	Matt4:3	And when the tempter came to him, he said, If thou be the Son of God, command that these stones be made bread.
252	Luke4:3	And the devil said unto him, If thou be the Son of God, command this stone that it be made bread.
253	Matt4:4	But he answered and said, It is written, Man shall not live by bread alone, but by every word that proceedeth out of the mouth of God.
254	Luke4:4	And Jesus answered him, saying, It is written, That man shall not live by bread alone, but by every word of God.
255	Matt4:5	Then the devil taketh him up into the holy city, and setteth him on a pinnacle of the temple,
256	Luke4:9	And he brought him to Jerusalem, and set him on a pinnacle of the temple, and said unto him, If thou be the Son of God, cast thyself down from hence:
257	Matt4:6	And saith unto him, If thou be the Son of God, cast thyself down: for it is written, He shall give his angels charge concerning thee: and in their hands they shall bear thee up, lest at any time thou dash thy foot against a stone.
258	Luke4:10	For it is written, He shall give his angels charge over thee, to keep thee:
259	Luke4:11	And in their hands they shall bear thee up, lest at any time thou dash thy foot against a stone.
260	Matt4:7	Jesus said unto him, It is written again, Thou shalt not tempt the Lord thy God.
261	Luke4:12	And Jesus answering said unto him, It is said, Thou shalt not tempt the Lord thy God.
262	Luke4:5	And the devil, taking him up into an high mountain, shewed unto him all the kingdoms of the world in a moment of time.
263	Matt4:8	Again, the devil taketh him up into an exceeding high mountain, and sheweth him all the kingdoms of the world, and the glory of them;
264	Matt4:9	And saith unto him, All these things will I give thee, if thou wilt fall down and worship me.
265	Luke4:6	And the devil said unto him, All this power will I give thee, and the glory of them: for that is delivered unto me; and to whomsoever I will I give it.
266	Luke4:7	If thou therefore wilt worship me, all shall be thine.
267	Matt4:10	Then saith Jesus unto him, Get thee hence, Satan: for it is written, Thou shalt worship the Lord thy God, and him only shalt thou serve.
268	Luke4:8	And Jesus answered and said unto him, Get thee behind me, Satan: for it is written, Thou shalt worship the Lord thy God, and him only shalt thou serve.
269	Luke4:13	And when the devil had ended all the temptation, he departed from him for a season.
270	Matt4:11	Then the devil leaveth him, and, behold, angels came and ministered unto him.

THE TREE OF LIFE

271	John1:35	Again the next day after John stood, and two of his disciples;
272	John1:36	And looking upon Jesus as he walked, he saith, Behold the Lamb of God!
273	John1:37	And the two disciples heard him speak, and they followed Jesus.
274	John1:38	Then Jesus turned, and saw them following, and saith unto them, What seek ye? They said unto him, Rabbi, (which is to say, being interpreted, Master,) where dwellest thou?
275	John1:39	He saith unto them, Come and see. They came and saw where he dwelt, and abode with him that day: for it was about the tenth hour.
276	John1:40	One of the two which heard John speak, and followed him, was Andrew, Simon Peter's brother.
277	John1:41	He first findeth his own brother Simon, and saith unto him, We have found the Messias, which is, being interpreted, the Christ.
278	John1:42	And he brought him to Jesus. And when Jesus beheld him, he said, Thou art Simon the son of Jona: thou shalt be called Cephas, which is by interpretation, A stone.
279	John1:43	The day following Jesus would go forth into Galilee, and findeth Philip, and saith unto him, Follow me.
280	John1:44	Now Philip was of Bethsaida, the city of Andrew and Peter.
281	John1:45	Philip findeth Nathanael, and saith unto him, We have found him, of whom Moses in the law, and the prophets, did write, Jesus of Nazareth, the son of Joseph.
282	John1:46	And Nathanael said unto him, Can there any good thing come out of Nazareth? Philip saith unto him, Come and see.
283	John1:47	Jesus saw Nathanael coming to him, and saith of him, Behold an Israelite indeed, in whom is no guile!
284	John1:48	Nathanael saith unto him, Whence knowest thou me? Jesus answered and said unto him, Before that Philip called thee, when thou wast under the fig tree, I saw thee.
285	John1:49	Nathanael answered and saith unto him, Rabbi, thou art the Son of God; thou art the King of Israel.
286	John1:50	Jesus answered and said unto him, Because I said unto thee, I saw thee under the fig tree, believest thou? thou shalt see greater things than these.
287	John1:51	And he saith unto him, Verily, verily, I say unto you, Hereafter ye shall see heaven open, and the angels of God ascending and descending upon the Son of man.
288	John2:1	And the third day there was a marriage in Cana of Galilee; and the mother of Jesus was there:
289	John2:2	And both Jesus was called, and his disciples, to the marriage.
290	John2:3	And when they wanted wine, the mother of Jesus saith unto him, They have no wine.
291	John2:4	Jesus saith unto her, Woman, what have I to do with thee? mine hour is not yet come.
292	John2:5	His mother saith unto the servants, Whatsoever he saith unto you, do it.
293	John2:6	And there were set there six waterpots of stone, after the manner of the purifying of the Jews, containing two or three firkins apiece.
294	John2:7	Jesus saith unto them, Fill the waterpots with water. And they filled them up to the brim.
295	John2:8	And he saith unto them, Draw out now, and bear unto the governor of the feast. And they bare it.
296	John2:9	When the ruler of the feast had tasted the water that was made wine, and knew not whence it was: (but the servants which drew the water knew;) the governor of the feast called the bridegroom,
297	John2:10	And saith unto him, Every man at the beginning doth set forth good wine; and when men have well drunk, then that which is worse: but thou hast kept the good

THE TREE OF LIFE

		wine until now.
298	Luke5:39	No man also having drunk old wine straightway desireth new: for he saith, The old is better.
299	John2:11	This beginning of miracles did Jesus in Cana of Galilee, and manifested forth his glory; and his disciples believed on him.
300	John2:12	After this he went down to Capernaum, he, and his mother, and his brethren, and his disciples: and they continued there not many days.
301	John2:13	And the Jews' passover was at hand, and Jesus went up to Jerusalem,
302	John2:14	And found in the temple those that sold oxen and sheep and doves, and the changers of money sitting:
303	John2:15	And when he had made a scourge of small cords, he drove them all out of the temple, and the sheep, and the oxen; and poured out the changers' money, and overthrew the tables;
304	John2:16	And said unto them that sold doves, Take these things hence; make not my Father's house an house of merchandise.
305	John2:17	And his disciples remembered that it was written, The zeal of thine house hath eaten me up.
306	John2:18	Then answered the Jews and said unto him, What sign shewest thou unto us, seeing that thou doest these things?
307	John2:19	Jesus answered and said unto them, Destroy this temple, and in three days I will raise it up.
308	John2:20	Then said the Jews, Forty and six years was this temple in building, and wilt thou rear it up in three days?
309	John2:21	But he spake of the temple of his body.
310	John2:22	When therefore he was risen from the dead, his disciples remembered that he had said this unto them; and they believed the scripture, and the word which Jesus had said.
311	John2:23	Now when he was in Jerusalem at the passover, in the feast day, many believed in his name, when they saw the miracles which he did.
312	John2:24	But Jesus did not commit himself unto them, because he knew all men,
313	John2:25	And needed not that any should testify of man: for he knew what was in man.
314	John3:1	There was a man of the Pharisees, named Nicodemus, a ruler of the Jews:
315	John3:2	The same came to Jesus by night, and said unto him, Rabbi, we know that thou art a teacher come from God: for no man can do these miracles that thou doest, except God be with him.
316	John3:3	Jesus answered and said unto him, Verily, verily, I say unto thee, Except a man be born again, he cannot see the kingdom of God.
317	John3:4	Nicodemus saith unto him, How can a man be born when he is old? can he enter the second time into his mother's womb, and be born?
318	John3:5	Jesus answered, Verily, verily, I say unto thee, Except a man be born of water and of the Spirit, he cannot enter into the kingdom of God.
319	John3:6	That which is born of the flesh is flesh; and that which is born of the Spirit is spirit.
320	John3:7	Marvel not that I said unto thee, Ye must be born again.
321	John3:8	The wind bloweth where it listeth, and thou hearest the sound thereof, but canst not tell whence it cometh, and whither it goeth: so is every one that is born of the Spirit.
322	John3:9	Nicodemus answered and said unto him, How can these things be?
323	John3:10	Jesus answered and said unto him, Art thou a master of Israel, and knowest not these things?
324	John3:11	Verily, verily, I say unto thee, We speak that we do know, and testify that we have seen; and ye receive not our witness.
325	John3:12	If I have told you earthly things, and ye believe not, how shall ye believe, if I tell you of heavenly things?

THE TREE OF LIFE

326	John3:13	And no man hath ascended up to heaven, but he that came down from heaven, even the Son of man which is in heaven.
327	John3:14	And as Moses lifted up the serpent in the wilderness, even so must the Son of man be lifted up:
328	John3:15	That whosoever believeth in him should not perish, but have eternal life.
329	John3:16	For God so loved the world, that he gave his only begotten Son, that whosoever believeth in him should not perish, but have everlasting life.
330	John3:17	For God sent not his Son into the world to condemn the world; but that the world through him might be saved.
331	John3:18	He that believeth on him is not condemned: but he that believeth not is condemned already, because he hath not believed in the name of the only begotten Son of God.
332	John3:19	And this is the condemnation, that light is come into the world, and men loved darkness rather than light, because their deeds were evil.
333	John3:20	For every one that doeth evil hateth the light, neither cometh to the light, lest his deeds should be reproved.
334	John3:21	But he that doeth truth cometh to the light, that his deeds may be made manifest, that they are wrought in God.
335	John3:22	After these things came Jesus and his disciples into the land of Judaea; and there he tarried with them, and baptized.
336	John4:2	(Though Jesus himself baptized not, but his disciples,)
337	John3:23	And John also was baptizing in Aenon near to Salim, because there was much water there: and they came, and were baptized.
338	John3:24	For John was not yet cast into prison.
339	John3:25	Then there arose a question between some of John's disciples and the Jews about purifying.
340	John3:26	And they came unto John, and said unto him, Rabbi, he that was with thee beyond Jordan, to whom thou barest witness, behold, the same baptizeth, and all men come to him.
341	John3:27	John answered and said, A man can receive nothing, except it be given him from heaven.
342	John3:28	Ye yourselves bear me witness, that I said, I am not the Christ, but that I am sent before him.
343	John3:29	He that hath the bride is the bridegroom: but the friend of the bridegroom, which standeth and heareth him, rejoiceth greatly because of the bridegroom's voice: this my joy therefore is fulfilled.
344	John3:30	He must increase, but I must decrease.
345	John3:31	He that cometh from above is above all: he that is of the earth is earthly, and speaketh of the earth: he that cometh from heaven is above all.
346	John3:32	And what he hath seen and heard, that he testifieth; and no man receiveth his testimony.
347	John3:33	He that hath received his testimony hath set to his seal that God is true.
348	John3:34	For he whom God hath sent speaketh the words of God: for God giveth not the Spirit by measure unto him.
349	John3:35	The Father loveth the Son, and hath given all things into his hand.
350	John3:36	He that believeth on the Son hath everlasting life: and he that believeth not the Son shall not see life; but the wrath of God abideth on him.
351	John4:1	When therefore the LORD knew how the Pharisees had heard that Jesus made and baptized more disciples than John,
352	John4:3	He left Judaea, and departed again into Galilee.
353	John4:4	And he must needs go through Samaria.
354	John4:5	Then cometh he to a city of Samaria, which is called Sychar, near to the parcel of ground that Jacob gave to his son Joseph.

THE TREE OF LIFE

355	John4:6	Now Jacob's well was there. Jesus therefore, being wearied with his journey, sat thus on the well: and it was about the sixth hour.
356	John4:7	There cometh a woman of Samaria to draw water: Jesus saith unto her, Give me to drink.
357	John4:8	(For his disciples were gone away unto the city to buy meat.)
358	John4:9	Then saith the woman of Samaria unto him, How is it that thou, being a Jew, askest drink of me, which am a woman of Samaria? for the Jews have no dealings with the Samaritans.
359	John4:10	Jesus answered and said unto her, If thou knewest the gift of God, and who it is that saith to thee, Give me to drink; thou wouldest have asked of him, and he would have given thee living water.
360	John4:11	The woman saith unto him, Sir, thou hast nothing to draw with, and the well is deep: from whence then hast thou that living water?
361	John4:12	Art thou greater than our father Jacob, which gave us the well, and drank thereof himself, and his children, and his cattle?
362	John4:13	Jesus answered and said unto her, Whosoever drinketh of this water shall thirst again:
363	John4:14	But whosoever drinketh of the water that I shall give him shall never thirst; but the water that I shall give him shall be in him a well of water springing up into everlasting life.
364	John4:15	The woman saith unto him, Sir, give me this water, that I thirst not, neither come hither to draw.
365	John4:16	Jesus saith unto her, Go, call thy husband, and come hither.
366	John4:17	The woman answered and said, I have no husband. Jesus said unto her, Thou hast well said, I have no husband:
367	John4:18	For thou hast had five husbands; and he whom thou now hast is not thy husband: in that saidst thou truly.
368	John4:19	The woman saith unto him, Sir, I perceive that thou art a prophet.
369	John4:20	Our fathers worshipped in this mountain; and ye say, that in Jerusalem is the place where men ought to worship.
370	John4:21	Jesus saith unto her, Woman, believe me, the hour cometh, when ye shall neither in this mountain, nor yet at Jerusalem, worship the Father.
371	John4:22	Ye worship ye know not what: we know what we worship: for salvation is of the Jews.
372	John4:23	But the hour cometh, and now is, when the true worshippers shall worship the Father in spirit and in truth: for the Father seeketh such to worship him.
373	John4:24	God is a Spirit: and they that worship him must worship him in spirit and in truth.
374	John4:25	The woman saith unto him, I know that Messias cometh, which is called Christ: when he is come, he will tell us all things.
375	John4:26	Jesus saith unto her, I that speak unto thee am he.
376	John4:27	And upon this came his disciples, and marvelled that he talked with the woman: yet no man said, What seekest thou? or, Why talkest thou with her?
377	John4:28	The woman then left her waterpot, and went her way into the city, and saith to the men,
378	John4:29	Come, see a man, which told me all things that ever I did: is not this the Christ?
379	John4:30	Then they went out of the city, and came unto him.
380	John4:31	In the mean while his disciples prayed him, saying, Master, eat.
381	John4:32	But he said unto them, I have meat to eat that ye know not of.
382	John4:33	Therefore said the disciples one to another, Hath any man brought him ought to eat?
383	John4:34	Jesus saith unto them, My meat is to do the will of him that sent me, and to finish his work.
384	John4:35	Say not ye, There are yet four months, and then cometh harvest? behold, I say

THE TREE OF LIFE

		unto you, Lift up your eyes, and look on the fields; for they are white already to harvest.
385	John4:36	And he that reapeth receiveth wages, and gathereth fruit unto life eternal: that both he that soweth and he that reapeth may rejoice together.
386	John4:37	And herein is that saying true, One soweth, and another reapeth.
387	John4:38	I sent you to reap that whereon ye bestowed no labour: other men laboured, and ye are entered into their labours.
388	John4:39	And many of the Samaritans of that city believed on him for the saying of the woman, which testified, He told me all that ever I did.
389	John4:40	So when the Samaritans were come unto him, they besought him that he would tarry with them: and he abode there two days.
390	John4:41	And many more believed because of his own word;
391	John4:42	And said unto the woman, Now we believe, not because of thy saying: for we have heard him ourselves, and know that this is indeed the Christ, the Saviour of the world.
392	John4:43	Now after two days he departed thence, and went into Galilee.
393	Matt4:12	Now when Jesus had heard that John was cast into prison, he departed into Galilee;
394	Mark1:14	Now after that John was put in prison, Jesus came into Galilee, preaching the gospel of the kingdom of God,
395	Luke4:14	And Jesus returned in the power of the Spirit into Galilee: and there went out a fame of him through all the region round about.
396	Mark1:15	And saying, The time is fulfilled, and the kingdom of God is at hand: repent ye, and believe the gospel.
397	John4:45	Then when he was come into Galilee, the Galilaeans received him, having seen all the things that he did at Jerusalem at the feast: for they also went unto the feast.
398	Luke4:15	And he taught in their synagogues, being glorified of all.
399	Matt4:13	And leaving Nazareth, he came and dwelt in Capernaum, which is upon the sea coast, in the borders of Zabulon and Nephthalim:
400	Matt4:14	That it might be fulfilled which was spoken by Esaias the prophet, saying,
401	Matt4:15	The land of Zabulon, and the land of Nephthalim, by the way of the sea, beyond Jordan, Galilee of the Gentiles;
402	Matt4:16	The people which sat in darkness saw great light; and to them which sat in the region and shadow of death light is sprung up.
403	Matt4:17	From that time Jesus began to preach, and to say, Repent: for the kingdom of heaven is at hand.
404	Luke5:1	And it came to pass, that, as the people pressed upon him to hear the word of God, he stood by the lake of Gennesaret,
405	Matt4:18	And Jesus, walking by the sea of Galilee, saw two brethren, Simon called Peter, and Andrew his brother, casting a net into the sea: for they were fishers.
406	Mark1:16	Now as he walked by the sea of Galilee, he saw Simon and Andrew his brother casting a net into the sea: for they were fishers.
407	Luke5:2	And saw two ships standing by the lake: but the fishermen were gone out of them, and were washing their nets.
408	Luke5:3	And he entered into one of the ships, which was Simon's, and prayed him that he would thrust out a little from the land. And he sat down, and taught the people out of the ship.
409	Luke5:4	Now when he had left speaking, he said unto Simon, Launch out into the deep, and let down your nets for a draught.
410	Luke5:5	And Simon answering said unto him, Master, we have toiled all the night, and have taken nothing: nevertheless at thy word I will let down the net.
411	Luke5:6	And when they had this done, they inclosed a great multitude of fishes: and their

THE TREE OF LIFE

		net brake.
412	Luke5:7	And they beckoned unto their partners, which were in the other ship, that they should come and help them. And they came, and filled both the ships, so that they began to sink.
413	Luke5:8	When Simon Peter saw it, he fell down at Jesus' knees, saying, Depart from me; for I am a sinful man, O Lord.
414	Luke5:9	For he was astonished, and all that were with him, at the draught of the fishes which they had taken:
415	Luke5:10	And so was also James, and John, the sons of Zebedee, which were partners with Simon. And Jesus said unto Simon, Fear not; from henceforth thou shalt catch men.
416	Mark1:17	And Jesus said unto them, Come ye after me, and I will make you to become fishers of men.
417	Matt4:19	And he saith unto them, Follow me, and I will make you fishers of men.
418	Luke5:11	And when they had brought their ships to land, they forsook all, and followed him.
419	Matt4:20	And they straightway left their nets, and followed him.
420	Mark1:18	And straightway they forsook their nets, and followed him.
421	Matt4:21	And going on from thence, he saw other two brethren, James the son of Zebedee, and John his brother, in a ship with Zebedee their father, mending their nets; and he called them.
422	Mark1:19	And when he had gone a little farther thence, he saw James the son of Zebedee, and John his brother, who also were in the ship mending their nets.
423	Matt4:22	And they immediately left the ship and their father, and followed him.
424	Mark1:20	And straightway he called them: and they left their father Zebedee in the ship with the hired servants, and went after him.
425	John4:46	So Jesus came again into Cana of Galilee, where he made the water wine. And there was a certain nobleman, whose son was sick at Capernaum.
426	John4:47	When he heard that Jesus was come out of Judaea into Galilee, he went unto him, and besought him that he would come down, and heal his son: for he was at the point of death.
427	John4:48	Then said Jesus unto him, Except ye see signs and wonders, ye will not believe.
428	John4:49	The nobleman saith unto him, Sir, come down ere my child die.
429	John4:50	Jesus saith unto him, Go thy way; thy son liveth. And the man believed the word that Jesus had spoken unto him, and he went his way.
430	John4:51	And as he was now going down, his servants met him, and told him, saying, Thy son liveth.
431	John4:52	Then enquired he of them the hour when he began to amend. And they said unto him, Yesterday at the seventh hour the fever left him.
432	John4:53	So the father knew that it was at the same hour, in the which Jesus said unto him, Thy son liveth: and himself believed, and his whole house.
433	John4:54	This is again the second miracle that Jesus did, when he was come out of Judaea into Galilee.
434	Luke4:16	And he came to Nazareth, where he had been brought up: and, as his custom was, he went into the synagogue on the sabbath day, and stood up for to read.
435	Luke4:17	And there was delivered unto him the book of the prophet Esaias. And when he had opened the book, he found the place where it was written,
436	Luke4:18	The Spirit of the Lord is upon me, because he hath anointed me to preach the gospel to the poor; he hath sent me to heal the brokenhearted, to preach deliverance to the captives, and recovering of sight to the blind, to set at liberty them that are bruised,
437	Luke4:19	To preach the acceptable year of the Lord.
438	Luke4:20	And he closed the book, and he gave it again to the minister, and sat down. And the eyes of all them that were in the synagogue were fastened on him.

THE TREE OF LIFE

439	Luke4:21	And he began to say unto them, This day is this scripture fulfilled in your ears.
440	Luke4:22	And all bare him witness, and wondered at the gracious words which proceeded out of his mouth. And they said, Is not this Joseph's son?
441	Luke4:23	And he said unto them, Ye will surely say unto me this proverb, Physician, heal thyself: whatsoever we have heard done in Capernaum, do also here in thy country.
442	Luke4:24	And he said, Verily I say unto you, No prophet is accepted in his own country.
443	Luke4:25	But I tell you of a truth, many widows were in Israel in the days of Elias, when the heaven was shut up three years and six months, when great famine was throughout all the land;
444	Luke4:26	But unto none of them was Elias sent, save unto Sarepta, a city of Sidon, unto a woman that was a widow.
445	Luke4:27	And many lepers were in Israel in the time of Eliseus the prophet; and none of them was cleansed, saving Naaman the Syrian.
446	Luke4:28	And all they in the synagogue, when they heard these things, were filled with wrath,
447	Luke4:29	And rose up, and thrust him out of the city, and led him unto the brow of the hill whereon their city was built, that they might cast him down headlong.
448	Luke4:30	But he passing through the midst of them went his way,
449	Luke4:31	And came down to Capernaum, a city of Galilee, and taught them on the sabbath days.
450	Mark1:21	And they went into Capernaum; and straightway on the sabbath day he entered into the synagogue, and taught.
451	Mark1:22	And they were astonished at his doctrine: for he taught them as one that had authority, and not as the scribes.
452	Luke4:32	And they were astonished at his doctrine: for his word was with power.
453	Luke4:33	And in the synagogue there was a man, which had a spirit of an unclean devil, and cried out with a loud voice,
454	Mark1:23	And there was in their synagogue a man with an unclean spirit; and he cried out,
455	Luke4:34	Saying, Let us alone; what have we to do with thee, thou Jesus of Nazareth? art thou come to destroy us? I know thee who thou art; the Holy One of God.
456	Mark1:24	Saying, Let us alone; what have we to do with thee, thou Jesus of Nazareth? art thou come to destroy us? I know thee who thou art, the Holy One of God.
457	Mark1:25	And Jesus rebuked him, saying, Hold thy peace, and come out of him.
458	Luke4:35	And Jesus rebuked him, saying, Hold thy peace, and come out of him. And when the devil had thrown him in the midst, he came out of him, and hurt him not.
459	Mark1:26	And when the unclean spirit had torn him, and cried with a loud voice, he came out of him.
460	Luke4:36	And they were all amazed, and spake among themselves, saying, What a word is this! for with authority and power he commandeth the unclean spirits, and they come out.
461	Mark1:27	And they were all amazed, insomuch that they questioned among themselves, saying, What thing is this? what new doctrine is this? for with authority commandeth he even the unclean spirits, and they do obey him.
462	Luke4:37	And the fame of him went out into every place of the country round about.
463	Mark1:28	And immediately his fame spread abroad throughout all the region round about Galilee.
464	Mark1:29	And forthwith, when they were come out of the synagogue, they entered into the house of Simon and Andrew, with James and John.
465	Luke4:38	And he arose out of the synagogue, and entered into Simon's house. And Simon's wife's mother was taken with a great fever; and they besought him for her.
466	Matt8:14	And when Jesus was come into Peter's house, he saw his wife's mother laid, and

THE TREE OF LIFE

		sick of a fever.
467	Mark1:30	But Simon's wife's mother lay sick of a fever, and anon they tell him of her.
468	Luke4:39	And he stood over her, and rebuked the fever; and it left her: and immediately she arose and ministered unto them.
469	Matt8:15	And he touched her hand, and the fever left her: and she arose, and ministered unto them.
470	Mark1:31	And he came and took her by the hand, and lifted her up; and immediately the fever left her, and she ministered unto them.
471	Matt8:16	When the even was come, they brought unto him many that were possessed with devils: and he cast out the spirits with his word, and healed all that were sick:
472	Mark1:32	And at even, when the sun did set, they brought unto him all that were diseased, and them that were possessed with devils.
473	Luke4:40	Now when the sun was setting, all they that had any sick with divers diseases brought them unto him; and he laid his hands on every one of them, and healed them.
474	Matt8:17	That it might be fulfilled which was spoken by Esaias the prophet, saying, Himself took our infirmities, and bare our sicknesses.
475	Mark1:33	And all the city was gathered together at the door.
476	Mark1:34	And he healed many that were sick of divers diseases, and cast out many devils; and suffered not the devils to speak, because they knew him.
477	Luke4:41	And devils also came out of many, crying out, and saying, Thou art Christ the Son of God. And he rebuking them suffered them not to speak: for they knew that he was Christ.
478	Mark1:35	And in the morning, rising up a great while before day, he went out, and departed into a solitary place, and there prayed.
479	Mark1:36	And Simon and they that were with him followed after him.
480	Mark1:37	And when they had found him, they said unto him, All men seek for thee.
481	Mark1:38	And he said unto them, Let us go into the next towns, that I may preach there also: for therefore came I forth.
482	Luke4:42	And when it was day, he departed and went into a desert place: and the people sought him, and came unto him, and stayed him, that he should not depart from them.
483	Luke4:43	And he said unto them, I must preach the kingdom of God to other cities also: for therefore am I sent.
484	Luke4:44	And he preached in the synagogues of Galilee.
485	Mark1:39	And he preached in their synagogues throughout all Galilee, and cast out devils.
486	Matt4:23	And Jesus went about all Galilee, teaching in their synagogues, and preaching the gospel of the kingdom, and healing all manner of sickness and all manner of disease among the people.
487	Matt4:24	And his fame went throughout all Syria: and they brought unto him all sick people that were taken with divers diseases and torments, and those which were possessed with devils, and those which were lunatick, and those that had the palsy; and he healed them.
488	Matt4:25	And there followed him great multitudes of people from Galilee, and from Decapolis, and from Jerusalem, and from Judaea, and from beyond Jordan.
489	Luke6:17	And he came down with them, and stood in the plain, and the company of his disciples, and a great multitude of people out of all Judaea and Jerusalem, and from the sea coast of Tyre and Sidon, which came to hear him, and to be healed of their diseases;
490	Luke6:18	And they that were vexed with unclean spirits: and they were healed.
491	Luke6:19	And the whole multitude sought to touch him: for there went virtue out of him, and healed them all.
492	Matt5:1	And seeing the multitudes, he went up into a mountain: and when he was set, his

THE TREE OF LIFE

		disciples came unto him:
493	Matt5:2	And he opened his mouth, and taught them, saying,
494	Luke6:20	And he lifted up his eyes on his disciples, and said, Blessed be ye poor: for yours is the kingdom of God.
495	Matt5:3	Blessed are the poor in spirit: for theirs is the kingdom of heaven.
496	Matt5:4	Blessed are they that mourn: for they shall be comforted.
497	Matt5:5	Blessed are the meek: for they shall inherit the earth.
498	Matt5:6	Blessed are they which do hunger and thirst after righteousness: for they shall be filled.
499	Luke6:21	Blessed are ye that hunger now: for ye shall be filled. Blessed are ye that weep now: for ye shall laugh.
500	Matt5:7	Blessed are the merciful: for they shall obtain mercy.
501	Matt5:8	Blessed are the pure in heart: for they shall see God.
502	Matt5:9	Blessed are the peacemakers: for they shall be called the children of God.
503	Matt5:10	Blessed are they which are persecuted for righteousness' sake: for theirs is the kingdom of heaven.
504	Matt5:11	Blessed are ye, when men shall revile you, and persecute you, and shall say all manner of evil against you falsely, for my sake.
505	Luke6:22	Blessed are ye, when men shall hate you, and when they shall separate you from their company, and shall reproach you, and cast out your name as evil, for the Son of man's sake.
506	Matt5:12	Rejoice, and be exceeding glad: for great is your reward in heaven: for so persecuted they the prophets which were before you.
507	Luke6:23	Rejoice ye in that day, and leap for joy: for, behold, your reward is great in heaven: for in the like manner did their fathers unto the prophets.
508	Luke6:24	But woe unto you that are rich! for ye have received your consolation.
509	Luke6:25	Woe unto you that are full! for ye shall hunger. Woe unto you that laugh now! for ye shall mourn and weep.
510	Luke6:26	Woe unto you, when all men shall speak well of you! for so did their fathers to the false prophets.
511	Mark9:49	For every one shall be salted with fire, and every sacrifice shall be salted with salt.
512	Matt5:13	Ye are the salt of the earth: but if the salt have lost his savour, wherewith shall it be salted? it is thenceforth good for nothing, but to be cast out, and to be trodden under foot of men.
513	Mark9:50	Salt is good: but if the salt have lost his saltness, wherewith will ye season it? Have salt in yourselves, and have peace one with another.
514	Luke14:34	Salt is good: but if the salt have lost his savour, wherewith shall it be seasoned?
515	Luke14:35	It is neither fit for the land, nor yet for the dunghill; but men cast it out. He that hath ears to hear, let him hear.
516	Luke5:36	And he spake also a parable unto them; No man putteth a piece of a new garment upon an old; if otherwise, then both the new maketh a rent, and the piece that was taken out of the new agreeth not with the old.
517	Mark2:21	No man also seweth a piece of new cloth on an old garment: else the new piece that filled it up taketh away from the old, and the rent is made worse.
518	Matt9:16	No man putteth a piece of new cloth unto an old garment, for that which is put in to fill it up taketh from the garment, and the rent is made worse.
519	Luke5:37	And no man putteth new wine into old bottles; else the new wine will burst the bottles, and be spilled, and the bottles shall perish.
520	Mark2:22	And no man putteth new wine into old bottles: else the new wine doth burst the bottles, and the wine is spilled, and the bottles will be marred: but new wine must be put into new bottles.
521	Matt9:17	Neither do men put new wine into old bottles: else the bottles break, and the wine

THE TREE OF LIFE

		runneth out, and the bottles perish: but they put new wine into new bottles, and both are preserved.
522	Luke5:38	But new wine must be put into new bottles; and both are preserved.
523	Matt5:14	Ye are the light of the world. A city that is set on an hill cannot be hid.
524	Luke11:33	No man, when he hath lighted a candle, putteth it in a secret place, neither under a bushel, but on a candlestick, that they which come in may see the light.
525	Matt5:15	Neither do men light a candle, and put it under a bushel, but on a candlestick; and it giveth light unto all that are in the house.
526	Matt5:16	Let your light so shine before men, that they may see your good works, and glorify your Father which is in heaven.
527	Matt5:17	Think not that I am come to destroy the law, or the prophets: I am not come to destroy, but to fulfil.
528	Matt5:18	For verily I say unto you, Till heaven and earth pass, one jot or one tittle shall in no wise pass from the law, till all be fulfilled.
529	Matt5:19	Whosoever therefore shall break one of these least commandments, and shall teach men so, he shall be called the least in the kingdom of heaven: but whosoever shall do and teach them, the same shall be called great in the kingdom of heaven.
530	Matt5:20	For I say unto you, That except your righteousness shall exceed the righteousness of the scribes and Pharisees, ye shall in no case enter into the kingdom of heaven.
531	Matt5:21	Ye have heard that it was said by them of old time, Thou shalt not kill; and whosoever shall kill shall be in danger of the judgment:
532	Matt5:22	But I say unto you, That whosoever is angry with his brother without a cause shall be in danger of the judgment: and whosoever shall say to his brother, Raca, shall be in danger of the council: but whosoever shall say, Thou fool, shall be in danger of hell fire.
533	Matt5:23	Therefore if thou bring thy gift to the altar, and there rememberest that thy brother hath ought against thee;
534	Matt5:24	Leave there thy gift before the altar, and go thy way; first be reconciled to thy brother, and then come and offer thy gift.
535	Matt5:25	Agree with thine adversary quickly, whiles thou art in the way with him; lest at any time the adversary deliver thee to the judge, and the judge deliver thee to the officer, and thou be cast into prison.
536	Matt5:26	Verily I say unto thee, Thou shalt by no means come out thence, till thou hast paid the uttermost farthing.
537	Matt5:27	Ye have heard that it was said by them of old time, Thou shalt not commit adultery:
538	Matt5:28	But I say unto you, That whosoever looketh on a woman to lust after her hath committed adultery with her already in his heart.
539	Matt5:29	And if thy right eye offend thee, pluck it out, and cast it from thee: for it is profitable for thee that one of thy members should perish, and not that thy whole body should be cast into hell.
540	Matt5:30	And if thy right hand offend thee, cut it off, and cast it from thee: for it is profitable for thee that one of thy members should perish, and not that thy whole body should be cast into hell.
541	Matt5:31	It hath been said, Whosoever shall put away his wife, let him give her a writing of divorcement:
542	Matt5:32	But I say unto you, That whosoever shall put away his wife, saving for the cause of fornication, causeth her to commit adultery: and whosoever shall marry her that is divorced committeth adultery.
543	Matt5:33	Again, ye have heard that it hath been said by them of old time, Thou shalt not forswear thyself, but shalt perform unto the Lord thine oaths:

THE TREE OF LIFE

544	Matt5:34	But I say unto you, Swear not at all; neither by heaven; for it is God's throne:
545	Matt5:35	Nor by the earth; for it is his footstool: neither by Jerusalem; for it is the city of the great King.
546	Matt5:36	Neither shalt thou swear by thy head, because thou canst not make one hair white or black.
547	Matt5:37	But let your communication be, Yea, yea; Nay, nay: for whatsoever is more than these cometh of evil.
548	Matt5:38	Ye have heard that it hath been said, An eye for an eye, and a tooth for a tooth:
549	Matt5:39	But I say unto you, That ye resist not evil: but whosoever shall smite thee on thy right cheek, turn to him the other also.
550	Luke6:29	And unto him that smiteth thee on the one cheek offer also the other; and him that taketh away thy cloak forbid not to take thy coat also.
551	Matt5:40	And if any man will sue thee at the law, and take away thy coat, let him have thy cloak also.
552	Matt5:41	And whosoever shall compel thee to go a mile, go with him twain.
553	Matt5:42	Give to him that asketh thee, and from him that would borrow of thee turn not thou away.
554	Luke6:30	Give to every man that asketh of thee; and of him that taketh away thy goods ask them not again.
555	Matt5:43	Ye have heard that it hath been said, Thou shalt love thy neighbour, and hate thine enemy.
556	Matt5:44	But I say unto you, Love your enemies, bless them that curse you, do good to them that hate you, and pray for them which despitefully use you, and persecute you;
557	Luke6:27	But I say unto you which hear, Love your enemies, do good to them which hate you,
558	Luke6:28	Bless them that curse you, and pray for them which despitefully use you.
559	Luke6:31	And as ye would that men should do to you, do ye also to them likewise.
560	Matt7:12	Therefore all things whatsoever ye would that men should do to you, do ye even so to them: for this is the law and the prophets.
561	Matt7:13	Enter ye in at the strait gate: for wide is the gate, and broad is the way, that leadeth to destruction, and many there be which go in thereat:
562	Matt7:14	Because strait is the gate, and narrow is the way, which leadeth unto life, and few there be that find it.
563	Matt5:45	That ye may be the children of your Father which is in heaven: for he maketh his sun to rise on the evil and on the good, and sendeth rain on the just and on the unjust.
564	Matt5:46	For if ye love them which love you, what reward have ye? do not even the publicans the same?
565	Luke6:32	For if ye love them which love you, what thank have ye? for sinners also love those that love them.
566	Luke6:33	And if ye do good to them which do good to you, what thank have ye? for sinners also do even the same.
567	Luke6:34	And if ye lend to them of whom ye hope to receive, what thank have ye? for sinners also lend to sinners, to receive as much again.
568	Matt5:47	And if ye salute your brethren only, what do ye more than others? do not even the publicans so?
569	Luke6:35	But love ye your enemies, and do good, and lend, hoping for nothing again; and your reward shall be great, and ye shall be the children of the Highest: for he is kind unto the unthankful and to the evil.
570	Luke6:36	Be ye therefore merciful, as your Father also is merciful.
571	Matt5:48	Be ye therefore perfect, even as your Father which is in heaven is perfect.
572	Luke6:40	The disciple is not above his master: but every one that is perfect shall be as his

THE TREE OF LIFE

		master.
573	Luke6:46	And why call ye me, Lord, Lord, and do not the things which I say?
574	Matt7:21	Not every one that saith unto me, Lord, Lord, shall enter into the kingdom of heaven; but he that doeth the will of my Father which is in heaven.
575	Matt7:22	Many will say to me in that day, Lord, Lord, have we not prophesied in thy name? and in thy name have cast out devils? and in thy name done many wonderful works?
576	Matt7:23	And then will I profess unto them, I never knew you: depart from me, ye that work iniquity.
577	Matt7:7	Ask, and it shall be given you; seek, and ye shall find; knock, and it shall be opened unto you:
578	Matt7:8	For every one that asketh receiveth; and he that seeketh findeth; and to him that knocketh it shall be opened.
579	Matt7:9	Or what man is there of you, whom if his son ask bread, will he give him a stone?
580	Matt7:10	Or if he ask a fish, will he give him a serpent?
581	Matt7:11	If ye then, being evil, know how to give good gifts unto your children, how much more shall your Father which is in heaven give good things to them that ask him?
582	Matt7:1	Judge not, that ye be not judged.
583	Matt7:2	For with what judgment ye judge, ye shall be judged: and with what measure ye mete, it shall be measured to you again.
584	Luke6:37	Judge not, and ye shall not be judged: condemn not, and ye shall not be condemned: forgive, and ye shall be forgiven:
585	Matt6:14	For if ye forgive men their trespasses, your heavenly Father will also forgive you:
586	Matt6:15	But if ye forgive not men their trespasses, neither will your Father forgive your trespasses.
587	Matt7:6	Give not that which is holy unto the dogs, neither cast ye your pearls before swine, lest they trample them under their feet, and turn again and rend you.
588	Matt6:1	Take heed that ye do not your alms before men, to be seen of them: otherwise ye have no reward of your Father which is in heaven.
589	Matt6:2	Therefore when thou doest thine alms, do not sound a trumpet before thee, as the hypocrites do in the synagogues and in the streets, that they may have glory of men. Verily I say unto you, They have their reward.
590	Matt6:3	But when thou doest alms, let not thy left hand know what thy right hand doeth:
591	Matt6:4	That thine alms may be in secret: and thy Father which seeth in secret himself shall reward thee openly.
592	Matt6:5	And when thou prayest, thou shalt not be as the hypocrites are: for they love to pray standing in the synagogues and in the corners of the streets, that they may be seen of men. Verily I say unto you, They have their reward.
593	Matt6:6	But thou, when thou prayest, enter into thy closet, and when thou hast shut thy door, pray to thy Father which is in secret; and thy Father which seeth in secret shall reward thee openly.
594	Matt6:7	But when ye pray, use not vain repetitions, as the heathen do: for they think that they shall be heard for their much speaking.
595	Matt6:8	Be not ye therefore like unto them: for your Father knoweth what things ye have need of, before ye ask him.
596	Matt6:9	After this manner therefore pray ye: Our Father which art in heaven, Hallowed be thy name.
597	Matt6:10	Thy kingdom come. Thy will be done in earth, as it is in heaven.
598	Matt6:11	Give us this day our daily bread.
599	Matt6:12	And forgive us our debts, as we forgive our debtors.
600	Matt6:13	And lead us not into temptation, but deliver us from evil: For thine is the kingdom, and the power, and the glory, for ever. Amen.
601	Matt6:16	Moreover when ye fast, be not, as the hypocrites, of a sad countenance: for they

THE TREE OF LIFE

		disfigure their faces, that they may appear unto men to fast. Verily I say unto you, They have their reward.
602	Matt6:17	But thou, when thou fastest, anoint thine head, and wash thy face;
603	Matt6:18	That thou appear not unto men to fast, but unto thy Father which is in secret: and thy Father, which seeth in secret, shall reward thee openly.
604	Matt7:15	Beware of false prophets, which come to you in sheep's clothing, but inwardly they are ravening wolves.
605	Matt7:16	Ye shall know them by their fruits. Do men gather grapes of thorns, or figs of thistles?
606	Matt7:17	Even so every good tree bringeth forth good fruit; but a corrupt tree bringeth forth evil fruit.
607	Luke6:43	For a good tree bringeth not forth corrupt fruit; neither doth a corrupt tree bring forth good fruit.
608	Matt7:18	A good tree cannot bring forth evil fruit, neither can a corrupt tree bring forth good fruit.
609	Luke6:44	For every tree is known by his own fruit. For of thorns men do not gather figs, nor of a bramble bush gather they grapes.
610	Matt7:19	Every tree that bringeth not forth good fruit is hewn down, and cast into the fire.
611	Luke6:45	A good man out of the good treasure of his heart bringeth forth that which is good; and an evil man out of the evil treasure of his heart bringeth forth that which is evil: for of the abundance of the heart his mouth speaketh.
612	Matt7:20	Wherefore by their fruits ye shall know them.
613	Matt6:19	Lay not up for yourselves treasures upon earth, where moth and rust doth corrupt, and where thieves break through and steal:
614	Matt6:20	But lay up for yourselves treasures in heaven, where neither moth nor rust doth corrupt, and where thieves do not break through nor steal:
615	Luke6:38	Give, and it shall be given unto you; good measure, pressed down, and shaken together, and running over, shall men give into your bosom. For with the same measure that ye mete withal it shall be measured to you again.
616	Matt6:21	For where your treasure is, there will your heart be also.
617	Luke6:41	And why beholdest thou the mote that is in thy brother's eye, but perceivest not the beam that is in thine own eye?
618	Matt7:3	And why beholdest thou the mote that is in thy brother's eye, but considerest not the beam that is in thine own eye?
619	Matt7:4	Or how wilt thou say to thy brother, Let me pull out the mote out of thine eye; and, behold, a beam is in thine own eye?
620	Luke6:42	Either how canst thou say to thy brother, Brother, let me pull out the mote that is in thine eye, when thou thyself beholdest not the beam that is in thine own eye? Thou hypocrite, cast out first the beam out of thine own eye, and then shalt thou see clearly to pull out the mote that is in thy brother's eye.
621	Matt7:5	Thou hypocrite, first cast out the beam out of thine own eye; and then shalt thou see clearly to cast out the mote out of thy brother's eye.
622	Matt6:22	The light of the body is the eye: if therefore thine eye be single, thy whole body shall be full of light.
623	Luke11:36	If thy whole body therefore be full of light, having no part dark, the whole shall be full of light, as when the bright shining of a candle doth give thee light.
624	Luke6:39	And he spake a parable unto them, Can the blind lead the blind? shall they not both fall into the ditch?
625	Luke11:34	The light of the body is the eye: therefore when thine eye is single, thy whole body also is full of light; but when thine eye is evil, thy body also is full of darkness.
626	Matt6:23	But if thine eye be evil, thy whole body shall be full of darkness. If therefore the light that is in thee be darkness, how great is that darkness!

THE TREE OF LIFE

627	Luke11:35	Take heed therefore that the light which is in thee be not darkness.
628	Luke16:1	And he said also unto his disciples, There was a certain rich man, which had a steward; and the same was accused unto him that he had wasted his goods.
629	Luke16:2	And he called him, and said unto him, How is it that I hear this of thee? give an account of thy stewardship; for thou mayest be no longer steward.
630	Luke16:3	Then the steward said within himself, What shall I do? for my lord taketh away from me the stewardship: I cannot dig; to beg I am ashamed.
631	Luke16:4	I am resolved what to do, that, when I am put out of the stewardship, they may receive me into their houses.
632	Luke16:5	So he called every one of his lord's debtors unto him, and said unto the first, How much owest thou unto my lord?
633	Luke16:6	And he said, An hundred measures of oil. And he said unto him, Take thy bill, and sit down quickly, and write fifty.
634	Luke16:7	Then said he to another, And how much owest thou? And he said, An hundred measures of wheat. And he said unto him, Take thy bill, and write fourscore.
635	Luke16:8	And the lord commended the unjust steward, because he had done wisely: for the children of this world are in their generation wiser than the children of light.
636	Luke16:9	And I say unto you, Make to yourselves friends of the mammon of unrighteousness; that, when ye fail, they may receive you into everlasting habitations.
637	Luke16:10	He that is faithful in that which is least is faithful also in much: and he that is unjust in the least is unjust also in much.
638	Luke16:11	If therefore ye have not been faithful in the unrighteous mammon, who will commit to your trust the true riches?
639	Luke16:12	And if ye have not been faithful in that which is another man's, who shall give you that which is your own?
640	Matt6:24	No man can serve two masters: for either he will hate the one, and love the other; or else he will hold to the one, and despise the other. Ye cannot serve God and mammon.
641	Luke16:13	No servant can serve two masters: for either he will hate the one, and love the other; or else he will hold to the one, and despise the other. Ye cannot serve God and mammon.
642	Matt6:25	Therefore I say unto you, Take no thought for your life, what ye shall eat, or what ye shall drink; nor yet for your body, what ye shall put on. Is not the life more than meat, and the body than raiment?
643	Matt6:26	Behold the fowls of the air: for they sow not, neither do they reap, nor gather into barns; yet your heavenly Father feedeth them. Are ye not much better than they?
644	Matt6:27	Which of you by taking thought can add one cubit unto his stature?
645	Matt6:28	And why take ye thought for raiment? Consider the lilies of the field, how they grow; they toil not, neither do they spin:
646	Matt6:29	And yet I say unto you, That even Solomon in all his glory was not arrayed like one of these.
647	Matt6:30	Wherefore, if God so clothe the grass of the field, which to day is, and to morrow is cast into the oven, shall he not much more clothe you, O ye of little faith?
648	Matt6:31	Therefore take no thought, saying, What shall we eat? or, What shall we drink? or, Wherewithal shall we be clothed?
649	Matt6:32	(For after all these things do the Gentiles seek:) for your heavenly Father knoweth that ye have need of all these things.
650	Matt6:33	But seek ye first the kingdom of God, and his righteousness; and all these things shall be added unto you.
651	Matt6:34	Take therefore no thought for the morrow: for the morrow shall take thought for the things of itself. Sufficient unto the day is the evil thereof.
652	Luke6:47	Whosoever cometh to me, and heareth my sayings, and doeth them, I will shew

THE TREE OF LIFE

		you to whom he is like:
653	Matt7:24	Therefore whosoever heareth these sayings of mine, and doeth them, I will liken him unto a wise man, which built his house upon a rock:
654	Luke6:48	He is like a man which built an house, and digged deep, and laid the foundation on a rock: and when the flood arose, the stream beat vehemently upon that house, and could not shake it: for it was founded upon a rock.
655	Matt7:25	And the rain descended, and the floods came, and the winds blew, and beat upon that house; and it fell not: for it was founded upon a rock.
656	Matt7:26	And every one that heareth these sayings of mine, and doeth them not, shall be likened unto a foolish man, which built his house upon the sand:
657	Luke6:49	But he that heareth, and doeth not, is like a man that without a foundation built an house upon the earth; against which the stream did beat vehemently, and immediately it fell; and the ruin of that house was great.
658	Matt7:27	And the rain descended, and the floods came, and the winds blew, and beat upon that house; and it fell: and great was the fall of it.
659	Matt7:28	And it came to pass, when Jesus had ended these sayings, the people were astonished at his doctrine:
660	Matt7:29	For he taught them as one having authority, and not as the scribes.
661	Matt8:1	When he was come down from the mountain, great multitudes followed him.
662	Luke5:12	And it came to pass, when he was in a certain city, behold a man full of leprosy: who seeing Jesus fell on his face, and besought him, saying, Lord, if thou wilt, thou canst make me clean.
663	Mark1:40	And there came a leper to him, beseeching him, and kneeling down to him, and saying unto him, If thou wilt, thou canst make me clean.
664	Matt8:2	And, behold, there came a leper and worshipped him, saying, Lord, if thou wilt, thou canst make me clean.
665	Mark1:41	And Jesus, moved with compassion, put forth his hand, and touched him, and saith unto him, I will; be thou clean.
666	Matt8:3	And Jesus put forth his hand, and touched him, saying, I will; be thou clean. And immediately his leprosy was cleansed.
667	Luke5:13	And he put forth his hand, and touched him, saying, I will: be thou clean. And immediately the leprosy departed from him.
668	Mark1:42	And as soon as he had spoken, immediately the leprosy departed from him, and he was cleansed.
669	Mark1:43	And he straitly charged him, and forthwith sent him away;
670	Mark1:44	And saith unto him, See thou say nothing to any man: but go thy way, shew thyself to the priest, and offer for thy cleansing those things which Moses commanded, for a testimony unto them.
671	Luke5:14	And he charged him to tell no man: but go, and shew thyself to the priest, and offer for thy cleansing, according as Moses commanded, for a testimony unto them.
672	Matt8:4	And Jesus saith unto him, See thou tell no man; but go thy way, shew thyself to the priest, and offer the gift that Moses commanded, for a testimony unto them.
673	Luke5:15	But so much the more went there a fame abroad of him: and great multitudes came together to hear, and to be healed by him of their infirmities.
674	Mark1:45	But he went out, and began to publish it much, and to blaze abroad the matter, insomuch that Jesus could no more openly enter into the city, but was without in desert places: and they came to him from every quarter.
675	Luke5:16	And he withdrew himself into the wilderness, and prayed.
676	Matt8:18	Now when Jesus saw great multitudes about him, he gave commandment to depart unto the other side.
677	Luke9:57	And it came to pass, that, as they went in the way, a certain man said unto him, Lord, I will follow thee whithersoever thou goest.

THE TREE OF LIFE

678	Matt8:19	And a certain scribe came, and said unto him, Master, I will follow thee whithersoever thou goest.
679	Matt8:20	And Jesus saith unto him, The foxes have holes, and the birds of the air have nests; but the Son of man hath not where to lay his head.
680	Luke9:58	And Jesus said unto him, Foxes have holes, and birds of the air have nests; but the Son of man hath not where to lay his head.
681	Luke9:59	And he said unto another, Follow me. But he said, Lord, suffer me first to go and bury my father.
682	Matt8:21	And another of his disciples said unto him, Lord, suffer me first to go and bury my father.
683	Matt8:22	But Jesus said unto him, Follow me; and let the dead bury their dead.
684	Luke9:60	Jesus said unto him, Let the dead bury their dead: but go thou and preach the kingdom of God.
685	Luke9:61	And another also said, Lord, I will follow thee; but let me first go bid them farewell, which are at home at my house.
686	Luke9:62	And Jesus said unto him, No man, having put his hand to the plough, and looking back, is fit for the kingdom of God.
687	Matt9:1	And he entered into a ship, and passed over, and came into his own city.
688	Luke5:17	And it came to pass on a certain day, as he was teaching, that there were Pharisees and doctors of the law sitting by, which were come out of every town of Galilee, and Judaea, and Jerusalem: and the power of the Lord was present to heal them.
689	Mark2:1	And again he entered into Capernaum after some days; and it was noised that he was in the house.
690	Mark2:2	And straightway many were gathered together, insomuch that there was no room to receive them, no, not so much as about the door: and he preached the word unto them.
691	Mark2:3	And they come unto him, bringing one sick of the palsy, which was borne of four.
692	Luke5:18	And, behold, men brought in a bed a man which was taken with a palsy: and they sought means to bring him in, and to lay him before him.
693	Mark2:4	And when they could not come nigh unto him for the press, they uncovered the roof where he was: and when they had broken it up, they let down the bed wherein the sick of the palsy lay.
694	Luke5:19	And when they could not find by what way they might bring him in because of the multitude, they went upon the housetop, and let him down through the tiling with his couch into the midst before Jesus.
695	Luke5:20	And when he saw their faith, he said unto him, Man, thy sins are forgiven thee.
696	Mark2:5	When Jesus saw their faith, he said unto the sick of the palsy, Son, thy sins be forgiven thee.
697	Matt9:2	And, behold, they brought to him a man sick of the palsy, lying on a bed: and Jesus seeing their faith said unto the sick of the palsy; Son, be of good cheer; thy sins be forgiven thee.
698	Mark2:6	But there were certain of the scribes sitting there, and reasoning in their hearts,
699	Luke5:21	And the scribes and the Pharisees began to reason, saying, Who is this which speaketh blasphemies? Who can forgive sins, but God alone?
700	Matt9:3	And, behold, certain of the scribes said within themselves, This man blasphemeth.
701	Mark2:7	Why doth this man thus speak blasphemies? who can forgive sins but God only?
702	Mark2:8	And immediately when Jesus perceived in his spirit that they so reasoned within themselves, he said unto them, Why reason ye these things in your hearts?
703	Luke5:22	But when Jesus perceived their thoughts, he answering said unto them, What reason ye in your hearts?
704	Matt9:4	And Jesus knowing their thoughts said, Wherefore think ye evil in your hearts?

THE TREE OF LIFE

705	Matt9:5	For whether is easier, to say, Thy sins be forgiven thee; or to say, Arise, and walk?
706	Mark2:9	Whether is it easier to say to the sick of the palsy, Thy sins be forgiven thee; or to say, Arise, and take up thy bed, and walk?
707	Luke5:23	Whether is easier, to say, Thy sins be forgiven thee; or to say, Rise up and walk?
708	Mark2:10	But that ye may know that the Son of man hath power on earth to forgive sins, (he saith to the sick of the palsy,)
709	Mark2:11	I say unto thee, Arise, and take up thy bed, and go thy way into thine house.
710	Matt9:6	But that ye may know that the Son of man hath power on earth to forgive sins, (then saith he to the sick of the palsy,) Arise, take up thy bed, and go unto thine house.
711	Luke5:24	But that ye may know that the Son of man hath power upon earth to forgive sins, (he said unto the sick of the palsy,) I say unto thee, Arise, and take up thy couch, and go into thine house.
712	Matt9:7	And he arose, and departed to his house.
713	Luke5:25	And immediately he rose up before them, and took up that whereon he lay, and departed to his own house, glorifying God.
714	Mark2:12	And immediately he arose, took up the bed, and went forth before them all; insomuch that they were all amazed, and glorified God, saying, We never saw it on this fashion.
715	Matt9:8	But when the multitudes saw it, they marvelled, and glorified God, which had given such power unto men.
716	Luke5:26	And they were all amazed, and they glorified God, and were filled with fear, saying, We have seen strange things to day.
717	Mark2:13	And he went forth again by the sea side; and all the multitude resorted unto him, and he taught them.
718	Matt9:9	And as Jesus passed forth from thence, he saw a man, named Matthew, sitting at the receipt of custom: and he saith unto him, Follow me. And he arose, and followed him.
719	Mark2:14	And as he passed by, he saw Levi the son of Alphaeus sitting at the receipt of custom, and said unto him, Follow me. And he arose and followed him.
720	Luke5:27	And after these things he went forth, and saw a publican, named Levi, sitting at the receipt of custom: and he said unto him, Follow me.
721	Luke5:28	And he left all, rose up, and followed him.
722	Luke5:29	And Levi made him a great feast in his own house: and there was a great company of publicans and of others that sat down with them.
723	Mark2:15	And it came to pass, that, as Jesus sat at meat in his house, many publicans and sinners sat also together with Jesus and his disciples: for there were many, and they followed him.
724	Matt9:10	And it came to pass, as Jesus sat at meat in the house, behold, many publicans and sinners came and sat down with him and his disciples.
725	Luke5:30	But their scribes and Pharisees murmured against his disciples, saying, Why do ye eat and drink with publicans and sinners?
726	Mark2:16	And when the scribes and Pharisees saw him eat with publicans and sinners, they said unto his disciples, How is it that he eateth and drinketh with publicans and sinners?
727	Matt9:11	And when the Pharisees saw it, they said unto his disciples, Why eateth your Master with publicans and sinners?
728	Matt9:12	But when Jesus heard that, he said unto them, They that be whole need not a physician, but they that are sick.
729	Luke5:31	And Jesus answering said unto them, They that are whole need not a physician; but they that are sick.
730	Mark2:17	When Jesus heard it, he saith unto them, They that are whole have no need of

THE TREE OF LIFE

		the physician, but they that are sick: I came not to call the righteous, but sinners to repentance.
731	Luke5:32	I came not to call the righteous, but sinners to repentance.
732	Matt9:13	But go ye and learn what that meaneth, I will have mercy, and not sacrifice: for I am not come to call the righteous, but sinners to repentance.
733	Matt9:14	Then came to him the disciples of John, saying, Why do we and the Pharisees fast oft, but thy disciples fast not?
734	Mark2:18	And the disciples of John and of the Pharisees used to fast: and they come and say unto him, Why do the disciples of John and of the Pharisees fast, but thy disciples fast not?
735	Luke5:33	And they said unto him, Why do the disciples of John fast often, and make prayers, and likewise the disciples of the Pharisees; but thine eat and drink?
736	Luke5:34	And he said unto them, Can ye make the children of the bridechamber fast, while the bridegroom is with them?
737	Mark2:19	And Jesus said unto them, Can the children of the bridechamber fast, while the bridegroom is with them? as long as they have the bridegroom with them, they cannot fast.
738	Luke5:35	But the days will come, when the bridegroom shall be taken away from them, and then shall they fast in those days.
739	Mark2:20	But the days will come, when the bridegroom shall be taken away from them, and then shall they fast in those days.
740	Matt9:15	And Jesus said unto them, Can the children of the bridechamber mourn, as long as the bridegroom is with them? but the days will come, when the bridegroom shall be taken from them, and then shall they fast.
741	John5:1	After this there was a feast of the Jews; and Jesus went up to Jerusalem.
742	John5:2	Now there is at Jerusalem by the sheep market a pool, which is called in the Hebrew tongue Bethesda, having five porches.
743	John5:3	In these lay a great multitude of impotent folk, of blind, halt, withered, waiting for the moving of the water.
744	John5:4	For an angel went down at a certain season into the pool, and troubled the water: whosoever then first after the troubling of the water stepped in was made whole of whatsoever disease he had.
745	John5:5	And a certain man was there, which had an infirmity thirty and eight years.
746	John5:6	When Jesus saw him lie, and knew that he had been now a long time in that case, he saith unto him, Wilt thou be made whole?
747	John5:7	The impotent man answered him, Sir, I have no man, when the water is troubled, to put me into the pool: but while I am coming, another steppeth down before me.
748	John5:8	Jesus saith unto him, Rise, take up thy bed, and walk.
749	John5:9	And immediately the man was made whole, and took up his bed, and walked: and on the same day was the sabbath.
750	John5:10	The Jews therefore said unto him that was cured, It is the sabbath day: it is not lawful for thee to carry thy bed.
751	John5:11	He answered them, He that made me whole, the same said unto me, Take up thy bed, and walk.
752	John5:12	Then asked they him, What man is that which said unto thee, Take up thy bed, and walk?
753	John5:13	And he that was healed wist not who it was: for Jesus had conveyed himself away, a multitude being in that place.
754	John5:14	Afterward Jesus findeth him in the temple, and said unto him, Behold, thou art made whole: sin no more, lest a worse thing come unto thee.
755	John5:15	The man departed, and told the Jews that it was Jesus, which had made him whole.
756	John5:16	And therefore did the Jews persecute Jesus, and sought to slay him, because he

THE TREE OF LIFE

		had done these things on the sabbath day.
757	John5:17	But Jesus answered them, My Father worketh hitherto, and I work.
758	John5:19	Then answered Jesus and said unto them, Verily, verily, I say unto you, The Son can do nothing of himself, but what he seeth the Father do: for what things soever he doeth, these also doeth the Son likewise.
759	John5:20	For the Father loveth the Son, and sheweth him all things that himself doeth: and he will shew him greater works than these, that ye may marvel.
760	John5:21	For as the Father raiseth up the dead, and quickeneth them; even so the Son quickeneth whom he will.
761	John5:22	For the Father judgeth no man, but hath committed all judgment unto the Son:
762	John5:23	That all men should honour the Son, even as they honour the Father. He that honoureth not the Son honoureth not the Father which hath sent him.
763	John5:24	Verily, verily, I say unto you, He that heareth my word, and believeth on him that sent me, hath everlasting life, and shall not come into condemnation; but is passed from death unto life.
764	John5:25	Verily, verily, I say unto you, The hour is coming, and now is, when the dead shall hear the voice of the Son of God: and they that hear shall live.
765	John5:26	For as the Father hath life in himself; so hath he given to the Son to have life in himself;
766	John5:27	And hath given him authority to execute judgment also, because he is the Son of man.
767	John5:28	Marvel not at this: for the hour is coming, in the which all that are in the graves shall hear his voice,
768	John5:29	And shall come forth; they that have done good, unto the resurrection of life; and they that have done evil, unto the resurrection of damnation.
769	John5:30	I can of mine own self do nothing: as I hear, I judge: and my judgment is just; because I seek not mine own will, but the will of the Father which hath sent me.
770	John5:31	If I bear witness of myself, my witness is not true.
771	John5:32	There is another that beareth witness of me; and I know that the witness which he witnesseth of me is true.
772	John5:33	Ye sent unto John, and he bare witness unto the truth.
773	John5:34	But I receive not testimony from man: but these things I say, that ye might be saved.
774	John5:35	He was a burning and a shining light: and ye were willing for a season to rejoice in his light.
775	John5:36	But I have greater witness than that of John: for the works which the Father hath given me to finish, the same works that I do, bear witness of me, that the Father hath sent me.
776	John5:37	And the Father himself, which hath sent me, hath borne witness of me. Ye have neither heard his voice at any time, nor seen his shape.
777	John5:38	And ye have not his word abiding in you: for whom he hath sent, him ye believe not.
778	John5:39	Search the scriptures; for in them ye think ye have eternal life: and they are they which testify of me.
779	John5:40	And ye will not come to me, that ye might have life.
780	John5:41	I receive not honour from men.
781	John5:42	But I know you, that ye have not the love of God in you.
782	John5:43	I am come in my Father's name, and ye receive me not: if another shall come in his own name, him ye will receive.
783	John5:44	How can ye believe, which receive honour one of another, and seek not the honour that cometh from God only?
784	John5:45	Do not think that I will accuse you to the Father: there is one that accuseth you, even Moses, in whom ye trust.

THE TREE OF LIFE

785	John5:46	For had ye believed Moses, ye would have believed me: for he wrote of me.
786	John5:47	But if ye believe not his writings, how shall ye believe my words?
787	John5:18	Therefore the Jews sought the more to kill him, because he not only had broken the sabbath, but said also that God was his Father, making himself equal with God.
788	John6:1	After these things Jesus went over the sea of Galilee, which is the sea of Tiberias.
789	John6:2	And a great multitude followed him, because they saw his miracles which he did on them that were diseased.
790	Matt12:1	At that time Jesus went on the sabbath day through the corn; and his disciples were an hungred, and began to pluck the ears of corn, and to eat.
791	Mark2:23	And it came to pass, that he went through the corn fields on the sabbath day; and his disciples began, as they went, to pluck the ears of corn.
792	Luke6:1	And it came to pass on the second sabbath after the first, that he went through the corn fields; and his disciples plucked the ears of corn, and did eat, rubbing them in their hands.
793	Matt12:2	But when the Pharisees saw it, they said unto him, Behold, thy disciples do that which is not lawful to do upon the sabbath day.
794	Mark2:24	And the Pharisees said unto him, Behold, why do they on the sabbath day that which is not lawful?
795	Luke6:2	And certain of the Pharisees said unto them, Why do ye that which is not lawful to do on the sabbath days?
796	Mark2:25	And he said unto them, Have ye never read what David did, when he had need, and was an hungred, he, and they that were with him?
797	Luke6:3	And Jesus answering them said, Have ye not read so much as this, what David did, when himself was an hungred, and they which were with him;
798	Matt12:3	But he said unto them, Have ye not read what David did, when he was an hungred, and they that were with him;
799	Mark2:26	How he went into the house of God in the days of Abiathar the high priest, and did eat the shewbread, which is not lawful to eat but for the priests, and gave also to them which were with him?
800	Luke6:4	How he went into the house of God, and did take and eat the shewbread, and gave also to them that were with him; which it is not lawful to eat but for the priests alone?
801	Matt12:4	How he entered into the house of God, and did eat the shewbread, which was not lawful for him to eat, neither for them which were with him, but only for the priests?
802	Matt12:5	Or have ye not read in the law, how that on the sabbath days the priests in the temple profane the sabbath, and are blameless?
803	Matt12:6	But I say unto you, That in this place is one greater than the temple.
804	Matt12:7	But if ye had known what this meaneth, I will have mercy, and not sacrifice, ye would not have condemned the guiltless.
805	Mark2:27	And he said unto them, The sabbath was made for man, and not man for the sabbath:
806	Mark2:28	Therefore the Son of man is Lord also of the sabbath.
807	Luke6:5	And he said unto them, That the Son of man is Lord also of the sabbath.
808	Matt12:8	For the Son of man is Lord even of the sabbath day.
809	Matt12:9	And when he was departed thence, he went into their synagogue:
810	Luke6:6	And it came to pass also on another sabbath, that he entered into the synagogue and taught: and there was a man whose right hand was withered.
811	Mark3:1	And he entered again into the synagogue; and there was a man there which had a withered hand.
812	Luke6:7	And the scribes and Pharisees watched him, whether he would heal on the

THE TREE OF LIFE

		sabbath day; that they might find an accusation against him.
813	Mark3:2	And they watched him, whether he would heal him on the sabbath day; that they might accuse him.
814	Luke6:8	But he knew their thoughts, and said to the man which had the withered hand, Rise up, and stand forth in the midst. And he arose and stood forth.
815	Mark3:3	And he saith unto the man which had the withered hand, Stand forth.
816	Matt12:10	And, behold, there was a man which had his hand withered. And they asked him, saying, Is it lawful to heal on the sabbath days? that they might accuse him.
817	Luke6:9	Then said Jesus unto them, I will ask you one thing; Is it lawful on the sabbath days to do good, or to do evil? to save life, or to destroy it?
818	Mark3:4	And he saith unto them, Is it lawful to do good on the sabbath days, or to do evil? to save life, or to kill? But they held their peace.
819	Matt12:11	And he said unto them, What man shall there be among you, that shall have one sheep, and if it fall into a pit on the sabbath day, will he not lay hold on it, and lift it out?
820	Matt12:12	How much then is a man better than a sheep? Wherefore it is lawful to do well on the sabbath days.
821	Mark3:5	And when he had looked round about on them with anger, being grieved for the hardness of their hearts, he saith unto the man, Stretch forth thine hand. And he stretched it out: and his hand was restored whole as the other.
822	Luke6:10	And looking round about upon them all, he said unto the man, Stretch forth thy hand. And he did so: and his hand was restored whole as the other.
823	Matt12:13	Then saith he to the man, Stretch forth thine hand. And he stretched it forth; and it was restored whole, like as the other.
824	Luke6:11	And they were filled with madness; and communed one with another what they might do to Jesus.
825	Matt12:14	Then the Pharisees went out, and held a council against him, how they might destroy him.
826	Mark3:6	And the Pharisees went forth, and straightway took counsel with the Herodians against him, how they might destroy him.
827	Matt12:15	But when Jesus knew it, he withdrew himself from thence: and great multitudes followed him, and he healed them all;
828	Mark3:7	But Jesus withdrew himself with his disciples to the sea: and a great multitude from Galilee followed him, and from Judaea,
829	Mark3:8	And from Jerusalem, and from Idumaea, and from beyond Jordan; and they about Tyre and Sidon, a great multitude, when they had heard what great things he did, came unto him.
830	Mark3:9	And he spake to his disciples, that a small ship should wait on him because of the multitude, lest they should throng him.
831	Mark3:10	For he had healed many; insomuch that they pressed upon him for to touch him, as many as had plagues.
832	Mark3:11	And unclean spirits, when they saw him, fell down before him, and cried, saying, Thou art the Son of God.
833	Mark3:12	And he straitly charged them that they should not make him known.
834	Matt12:16	And charged them that they should not make him known:
835	Matt12:17	That it might be fulfilled which was spoken by Esaias the prophet, saying,
836	Matt12:18	Behold my servant, whom I have chosen; my beloved, in whom my soul is well pleased: I will put my spirit upon him, and he shall shew judgment to the Gentiles.
837	Matt12:19	He shall not strive, nor cry; neither shall any man hear his voice in the streets.
838	Matt12:20	A bruised reed shall he not break, and smoking flax shall he not quench, till he send forth judgment unto victory.
839	Matt12:21	And in his name shall the Gentiles trust.
840	Luke7:36	And one of the Pharisees desired him that he would eat with him. And he went

THE TREE OF LIFE

		into the Pharisee's house, and sat down to meat.
841	Luke7:37	And, behold, a woman in the city, which was a sinner, when she knew that Jesus sat at meat in the Pharisee's house, brought an alabaster box of ointment,
842	John12:3	Then took Mary a pound of ointment of spikenard, very costly, and anointed the feet of Jesus, and wiped his feet with her hair: and the house was filled with the odour of the ointment.
843	Luke7:38	And stood at his feet behind him weeping, and began to wash his feet with tears, and did wipe them with the hairs of her head, and kissed his feet, and anointed them with the ointment.
844	Luke7:39	Now when the Pharisee which had bidden him saw it, he spake within himself, saying, This man, if he were a prophet, would have known who and what manner of woman this is that toucheth him: for she is a sinner.
845	Luke7:40	And Jesus answering said unto him, Simon, I have somewhat to say unto thee. And he saith, Master, say on.
846	Luke7:41	There was a certain creditor which had two debtors: the one owed five hundred pence, and the other fifty.
847	Luke7:42	And when they had nothing to pay, he frankly forgave them both. Tell me therefore, which of them will love him most?
848	Luke7:43	Simon answered and said, I suppose that he, to whom he forgave most. And he said unto him, Thou hast rightly judged.
849	Luke7:44	And he turned to the woman, and said unto Simon, Seest thou this woman? I entered into thine house, thou gavest me no water for my feet: but she hath washed my feet with tears, and wiped them with the hairs of her head.
850	Luke7:45	Thou gavest me no kiss: but this woman since the time I came in hath not ceased to kiss my feet.
851	Luke7:46	My head with oil thou didst not anoint: but this woman hath anointed my feet with ointment.
852	Luke7:47	Wherefore I say unto thee, Her sins, which are many, are forgiven; for she loved much: but to whom little is forgiven, the same loveth little.
853	Luke7:48	And he said unto her, Thy sins are forgiven.
854	Luke7:49	And they that sat at meat with him began to say within themselves, Who is this that forgiveth sins also?
855	Luke7:50	And he said to the woman, Thy faith hath saved thee; go in peace.
856	Luke8:1	And it came to pass afterward, that he went throughout every city and village, preaching and shewing the glad tidings of the kingdom of God: and the twelve were with him,
857	Luke8:2	And certain women, which had been healed of evil spirits and infirmities, Mary called Magdalene, out of whom went seven devils,
858	Luke8:3	And Joanna the wife of Chuza Herod's steward, and Susanna, and many others, which ministered unto him of their substance.
859	Matt9:35	And Jesus went about all the cities and villages, teaching in their synagogues, and preaching the gospel of the kingdom, and healing every sickness and every disease among the people.
860	Matt9:36	But when he saw the multitudes, he was moved with compassion on them, because they fainted, and were scattered abroad, as sheep having no shepherd.
861	Matt9:37	Then saith he unto his disciples, The harvest truly is plenteous, but the labourers are few;
862	Matt9:38	Pray ye therefore the Lord of the harvest, that he will send forth labourers into his harvest.
863	Luke6:12	And it came to pass in those days, that he went out into a mountain to pray, and continued all night in prayer to God.
864	Mark3:13	And he goeth up into a mountain, and calleth unto him whom he would: and they came unto him.

THE TREE OF LIFE

865	John6:3	And Jesus went up into a mountain, and there he sat with his disciples.
866	Luke6:13	And when it was day, he called unto him his disciples: and of them he chose twelve, whom also he named apostles;
867	Mark3:14	And he ordained twelve, that they should be with him, and that he might send them forth to preach,
868	Luke9:1	Then he called his twelve disciples together, and gave them power and authority over all devils, and to cure diseases.
869	Matt10:1	And when he had called unto him his twelve disciples, he gave them power against unclean spirits, to cast them out, and to heal all manner of sickness and all manner of disease.
870	Mark3:15	And to have power to heal sicknesses, and to cast out devils:
871	Matt10:2	Now the names of the twelve apostles are these; The first, Simon, who is called Peter, and Andrew his brother; James the son of Zebedee, and John his brother;
872	Mark3:16	And Simon he surnamed Peter;
873	Luke6:14	Simon, (whom he also named Peter,) and Andrew his brother, James and John, Philip and Bartholomew,
874	Mark3:17	And James the son of Zebedee, and John the brother of James; and he surnamed them Boanerges, which is, The sons of thunder:
875	Luke6:15	Matthew and Thomas, James the son of Alphaeus, and Simon called Zelotes,
876	Matt10:3	Philip, and Bartholomew; Thomas, and Matthew the publican; James the son of Alphaeus, and Lebbaeus, whose surname was Thaddaeus;
877	Mark3:18	And Andrew, and Philip, and Bartholomew, and Matthew, and Thomas, and James the son of Alphaeus, and Thaddaeus, and Simon the Canaanite,
878	Matt10:4	Simon the Canaanite, and Judas Iscariot, who also betrayed him.
879	Luke6:16	And Judas the brother of James, and Judas Iscariot, which also was the traitor.
880	Mark3:19	And Judas Iscariot, which also betrayed him: and they went into an house.
881	Mark6:7	And he called unto him the twelve, and began to send them forth by two and two; and gave them power over unclean spirits;
882	Luke9:2	And he sent them to preach the kingdom of God, and to heal the sick.
883	Matt10:5	These twelve Jesus sent forth, and commanded them, saying, Go not into the way of the Gentiles, and into any city of the Samaritans enter ye not:
884	Matt10:6	But go rather to the lost sheep of the house of Israel.
885	Matt10:7	And as ye go, preach, saying, The kingdom of heaven is at hand.
886	Matt10:8	Heal the sick, cleanse the lepers, raise the dead, cast out devils: freely ye have received, freely give.
887	Luke9:3	And he said unto them, Take nothing for your journey, neither staves, nor scrip, neither bread, neither money; neither have two coats apiece.
888	Matt10:9	Provide neither gold, nor silver, nor brass in your purses,
889	Mark6:8	And commanded them that they should take nothing for their journey, save a staff only; no scrip, no bread, no money in their purse:
890	Matt10:10	Nor scrip for your journey, neither two coats, neither shoes, nor yet staves: for the workman is worthy of his meat.
891	Mark6:9	But be shod with sandals; and not put on two coats.
892	Matt10:11	And into whatsoever city or town ye shall enter, enquire who in it is worthy; and there abide till ye go thence.
893	Matt10:12	And when ye come into an house, salute it.
894	Matt10:13	And if the house be worthy, let your peace come upon it: but if it be not worthy, let your peace return to you.
895	Mark6:10	And he said unto them, In what place soever ye enter into an house, there abide till ye depart from that place.
896	Luke9:4	And whatsoever house ye enter into, there abide, and thence depart.
897	Matt10:14	And whosoever shall not receive you, nor hear your words, when ye depart out of

THE TREE OF LIFE

		that house or city, shake off the dust of your feet.
898	Luke9:5	And whosoever will not receive you, when ye go out of that city, shake off the very dust from your feet for a testimony against them.
899	Mark6:11	And whosoever shall not receive you, nor hear you, when ye depart thence, shake off the dust under your feet for a testimony against them. Verily I say unto you, It shall be more tolerable for Sodom and Gomorrha in the day of judgment, than for that city.
900	Matt10:15	Verily I say unto you, It shall be more tolerable for the land of Sodom and Gomorrha in the day of judgment, than for that city.
901	Matt10:16	Behold, I send you forth as sheep in the midst of wolves: be ye therefore wise as serpents, and harmless as doves.
902	Matt10:17	But beware of men: for they will deliver you up to the councils, and they will scourge you in their synagogues;
903	Matt10:18	And ye shall be brought before governors and kings for my sake, for a testimony against them and the Gentiles.
904	Matt10:19	But when they deliver you up, take no thought how or what ye shall speak: for it shall be given you in that same hour what ye shall speak.
905	Matt10:20	For it is not ye that speak, but the Spirit of your Father which speaketh in you.
906	Matt10:21	And the brother shall deliver up the brother to death, and the father the child: and the children shall rise up against their parents, and cause them to be put to death.
907	Matt10:22	And ye shall be hated of all men for my name's sake: but he that endureth to the end shall be saved.
908	Matt10:23	But when they persecute you in this city, flee ye into another: for verily I say unto you, Ye shall not have gone over the cities of Israel, till the Son of man be come.
909	Matt10:24	The disciple is not above his master, nor the servant above his lord.
910	Matt10:25	It is enough for the disciple that he be as his master, and the servant as his lord. If they have called the master of the house Beelzebub, how much more shall they call them of his household?
911	Matt10:26	Fear them not therefore: for there is nothing covered, that shall not be revealed; and hid, that shall not be known.
912	Matt10:27	What I tell you in darkness, that speak ye in light: and what ye hear in the ear, that preach ye upon the housetops.
913	Matt10:28	And fear not them which kill the body, but are not able to kill the soul: but rather fear him which is able to destroy both soul and body in hell.
914	Matt10:29	Are not two sparrows sold for a farthing? and one of them shall not fall on the ground without your Father.
915	Matt10:31	Fear ye not therefore, ye are of more value than many sparrows.
916	Matt10:30	But the very hairs of your head are all numbered.
917	Matt10:32	Whosoever therefore shall confess me before men, him will I confess also before my Father which is in heaven.
918	Matt10:33	But whosoever shall deny me before men, him will I also deny before my Father which is in heaven.
919	Matt10:34	Think not that I am come to send peace on earth: I came not to send peace, but a sword.
920	Matt10:35	For I am come to set a man at variance against his father, and the daughter against her mother, and the daughter in law against her mother in law.
921	Matt10:36	And a man's foes shall be they of his own household.
922	Matt10:37	He that loveth father or mother more than me is not worthy of me: and he that loveth son or daughter more than me is not worthy of me.
923	Matt10:38	And he that taketh not his cross, and followeth after me, is not worthy of me.
924	Matt10:39	He that findeth his life shall lose it: and he that loseth his life for my sake shall find it.

THE TREE OF LIFE

925	Matt10:40	He that receiveth you receiveth me, and he that receiveth me receiveth him that sent me.
926	John13:20	Verily, verily, I say unto you, He that receiveth whomsoever I send receiveth me; and he that receiveth me receiveth him that sent me.
927	Matt10:41	He that receiveth a prophet in the name of a prophet shall receive a prophet's reward; and he that receiveth a righteous man in the name of a righteous man shall receive a righteous man's reward.
928	Matt10:42	And whosoever shall give to drink unto one of these little ones a cup of cold water only in the name of a disciple, verily I say unto you, he shall in no wise lose his reward.
929	Luke9:6	And they departed, and went through the towns, preaching the gospel, and healing every where.
930	Mark6:12	And they went out, and preached that men should repent.
931	Mark6:13	And they cast out many devils, and anointed with oil many that were sick, and healed them.
932	Matt11:1	And it came to pass, when Jesus had made an end of commanding his twelve disciples, he departed thence to teach and to preach in their cities.
933	Luke7:1	Now when he had ended all his sayings in the audience of the people, he entered into Capernaum.
934	Matt8:5	And when Jesus was entered into Capernaum, there came unto him a centurion, beseeching him,
935	Luke7:2	And a certain centurion's servant, who was dear unto him, was sick, and ready to die.
936	Luke7:3	And when he heard of Jesus, he sent unto him the elders of the Jews, beseeching him that he would come and heal his servant.
937	Matt8:6	And saying, Lord, my servant lieth at home sick of the palsy, grievously tormented.
938	Luke7:4	And when they came to Jesus, they besought him instantly, saying, That he was worthy for whom he should do this:
939	Luke7:5	For he loveth our nation, and he hath built us a synagogue.
940	Matt8:7	And Jesus saith unto him, I will come and heal him.
941	Luke7:6	Then Jesus went with them. And when he was now not far from the house, the centurion sent friends to him, saying unto him, Lord, trouble not thyself: for I am not worthy that thou shouldest enter under my roof:
942	Matt8:8	The centurion answered and said, Lord, I am not worthy that thou shouldest come under my roof: but speak the word only, and my servant shall be healed.
943	Luke7:7	Wherefore neither thought I myself worthy to come unto thee: but say in a word, and my servant shall be healed.
944	Matt8:9	For I am a man under authority, having soldiers under me: and I say to this man, Go, and he goeth; and to another, Come, and he cometh; and to my servant, Do this, and he doeth it.
945	Luke7:8	For I also am a man set under authority, having under me soldiers, and I say unto one, Go, and he goeth; and to another, Come, and he cometh; and to my servant, Do this, and he doeth it.
946	Matt8:10	When Jesus heard it, he marvelled, and said to them that followed, Verily I say unto you, I have not found so great faith, no, not in Israel.
947	Luke7:9	When Jesus heard these things, he marvelled at him, and turned him about, and said unto the people that followed him, I say unto you, I have not found so great faith, no, not in Israel.
948	Matt8:11	And I say unto you, That many shall come from the east and west, and shall sit down with Abraham, and with Isaac, and Jacob, in the kingdom of heaven.
949	Matt8:12	But the children of the kingdom shall be cast out into outer darkness: there shall be weeping and gnashing of teeth.

THE TREE OF LIFE

950	Matt8:13	And Jesus said unto the centurion, Go thy way; and as thou hast believed, so be it done unto thee. And his servant was healed in the selfsame hour.
951	Luke7:10	And they that were sent, returning to the house, found the servant whole that had been sick.
952	Luke7:11	And it came to pass the day after, that he went into a city called Nain; and many of his disciples went with him, and much people.
953	Luke7:12	Now when he came nigh to the gate of the city, behold, there was a dead man carried out, the only son of his mother, and she was a widow: and much people of the city was with her.
954	Luke7:13	And when the Lord saw her, he had compassion on her, and said unto her, Weep not.
955	Luke7:14	And he came and touched the bier: and they that bare him stood still. And he said, Young man, I say unto thee, Arise.
956	Luke7:15	And he that was dead sat up, and began to speak. And he delivered him to his mother.
957	Luke7:16	And there came a fear on all: and they glorified God, saying, That a great prophet is risen up among us; and, That God hath visited his people.
958	Luke7:17	And this rumour of him went forth throughout all Judaea, and throughout all the region round about.
959	Luke7:18	And the disciples of John shewed him of all these things.
960	Matt11:2	Now when John had heard in the prison the works of Christ, he sent two of his disciples,
961	Luke7:19	And John calling unto him two of his disciples sent them to Jesus, saying, Art thou he that should come? or look we for another?
962	Luke7:20	When the men were come unto him, they said, John Baptist hath sent us unto thee, saying, Art thou he that should come? or look we for another?
963	Matt11:3	And said unto him, Art thou he that should come, or do we look for another?
964	Luke7:21	And in that same hour he cured many of their infirmities and plagues, and of evil spirits; and unto many that were blind he gave sight.
965	Matt11:4	Jesus answered and said unto them, Go and shew John again those things which ye do hear and see:
966	Luke7:22	Then Jesus answering said unto them, Go your way, and tell John what things ye have seen and heard; how that the blind see, the lame walk, the lepers are cleansed, the deaf hear, the dead are raised, to the poor the gospel is preached.
967	Matt11:5	The blind receive their sight, and the lame walk, the lepers are cleansed, and the deaf hear, the dead are raised up, and the poor have the gospel preached to them.
968	Matt11:6	And blessed is he, whosoever shall not be offended in me.
969	Luke7:23	And blessed is he, whosoever shall not be offended in me.
970	Matt11:7	And as they departed, Jesus began to say unto the multitudes concerning John, What went ye out into the wilderness to see? A reed shaken with the wind?
971	Luke7:24	And when the messengers of John were departed, he began to speak unto the people concerning John, What went ye out into the wilderness for to see? A reed shaken with the wind?
972	Matt11:8	But what went ye out for to see? A man clothed in soft raiment? behold, they that wear soft clothing are in kings' houses.
973	Luke7:25	But what went ye out for to see? A man clothed in soft raiment? Behold, they which are gorgeously apparelled, and live delicately, are in kings' courts.
974	Matt11:9	But what went ye out for to see? A prophet? yea, I say unto you, and more than a prophet.
975	Luke7:26	But what went ye out for to see? A prophet? Yea, I say unto you, and much more than a prophet.
976	Matt11:10	For this is he, of whom it is written, Behold, I send my messenger before thy face,

THE TREE OF LIFE

		which shall prepare thy way before thee.
977	Luke7:27	This is he, of whom it is written, Behold, I send my messenger before thy face, which shall prepare thy way before thee.
978	Matt11:11	Verily I say unto you, Among them that are born of women there hath not risen a greater than John the Baptist: notwithstanding he that is least in the kingdom of heaven is greater than he.
979	Luke7:28	For I say unto you, Among those that are born of women there is not a greater prophet than John the Baptist: but he that is least in the kingdom of God is greater than he.
980	Matt11:12	And from the days of John the Baptist until now the kingdom of heaven suffereth violence, and the violent take it by force.
981	Matt11:13	For all the prophets and the law prophesied until John.
982	Matt11:14	And if ye will receive it, this is Elias, which was for to come.
983	Matt11:15	He that hath ears to hear, let him hear.
984	Luke7:29	And all the people that heard him, and the publicans, justified God, being baptized with the baptism of John.
985	Luke7:30	But the Pharisees and lawyers rejected the counsel of God against themselves, being not baptized of him.
986	Luke7:31	And the Lord said, Whereunto then shall I liken the men of this generation? and to what are they like?
987	Matt11:16	But whereunto shall I liken this generation? It is like unto children sitting in the markets, and calling unto their fellows,
988	Luke7:32	They are like unto children sitting in the marketplace, and calling one to another, and saying, We have piped unto you, and ye have not danced; we have mourned to you, and ye have not wept.
989	Matt11:17	And saying, We have piped unto you, and ye have not danced; we have mourned unto you, and ye have not lamented.
990	Luke7:33	For John the Baptist came neither eating bread nor drinking wine; and ye say, He hath a devil.
991	Matt11:18	For John came neither eating nor drinking, and they say, He hath a devil.
992	Luke7:34	The Son of man is come eating and drinking; and ye say, Behold a gluttonous man, and a winebibber, a friend of publicans and sinners!
993	Matt11:19	The Son of man came eating and drinking, and they say, Behold a man gluttonous, and a winebibber, a friend of publicans and sinners. But wisdom is justified of her children.
994	Luke7:35	But wisdom is justified of all her children.
995	Matt11:20	Then began he to upbraid the cities wherein most of his mighty works were done, because they repented not:
996	Matt11:21	Woe unto thee, Chorazin! woe unto thee, Bethsaida! for if the mighty works, which were done in you, had been done in Tyre and Sidon, they would have repented long ago in sackcloth and ashes.
997	Luke10:13	Woe unto thee, Chorazin! woe unto thee, Bethsaida! for if the mighty works had been done in Tyre and Sidon, which have been done in you, they had a great while ago repented, sitting in sackcloth and ashes.
998	Matt11:22	But I say unto you, It shall be more tolerable for Tyre and Sidon at the day of judgment, than for you.
999	Luke10:14	But it shall be more tolerable for Tyre and Sidon at the judgment, than for you.
1000	Luke10:15	And thou, Capernaum, which art exalted to heaven, shalt be thrust down to hell.
1001	Matt11:23	And thou, Capernaum, which art exalted unto heaven, shalt be brought down to hell: for if the mighty works, which have been done in thee, had been done in Sodom, it would have remained until this day.
1002	Matt11:24	But I say unto you, That it shall be more tolerable for the land of Sodom in the day of judgment, than for thee.

THE TREE OF LIFE

1003	Matt11:25	At that time Jesus answered and said, I thank thee, O Father, Lord of heaven and earth, because thou hast hid these things from the wise and prudent, and hast revealed them unto babes.
1004	Matt11:26	Even so, Father: for so it seemed good in thy sight.
1005	Matt11:27	All things are delivered unto me of my Father: and no man knoweth the Son, but the Father; neither knoweth any man the Father, save the Son, and he to whomsoever the Son will reveal him.
1006	Matt11:28	Come unto me, all ye that labour and are heavy laden, and I will give you rest.
1007	Matt11:29	Take my yoke upon you, and learn of me; for I am meek and lowly in heart: and ye shall find rest unto your souls.
1008	Matt11:30	For my yoke is easy, and my burden is light.
1009	Mark3:20	And the multitude cometh together again, so that they could not so much as eat bread.
1010	Mark3:21	And when his friends heard of it, they went out to lay hold on him: for they said, He is beside himself.
1011	Matt12:22	Then was brought unto him one possessed with a devil, blind, and dumb: and he healed him, insomuch that the blind and dumb both spake and saw.
1012	Luke11:14	And he was casting out a devil, and it was dumb. And it came to pass, when the devil was gone out, the dumb spake; and the people wondered.
1013	Matt12:23	And all the people were amazed, and said, Is not this the son of David?
1014	Matt12:24	But when the Pharisees heard it, they said, This fellow doth not cast out devils, but by Beelzebub the prince of the devils.
1015	Mark3:22	And the scribes which came down from Jerusalem said, He hath Beelzebub, and by the prince of the devils casteth he out devils.
1016	Luke11:15	But some of them said, He casteth out devils through Beelzebub the chief of the devils.
1017	Matt12:25	And Jesus knew their thoughts, and said unto them, Every kingdom divided against itself is brought to desolation; and every city or house divided against itself shall not stand:
1018	Luke11:17	But he, knowing their thoughts, said unto them, Every kingdom divided against itself is brought to desolation; and a house divided against a house falleth.
1019	Mark3:23	And he called them unto him, and said unto them in parables, How can Satan cast out Satan?
1020	Matt12:26	And if Satan cast out Satan, he is divided against himself; how shall then his kingdom stand?
1021	Luke11:18	If Satan also be divided against himself, how shall his kingdom stand? because ye say that I cast out devils through Beelzebub.
1022	Mark3:24	And if a kingdom be divided against itself, that kingdom cannot stand.
1023	Mark3:25	And if a house be divided against itself, that house cannot stand.
1024	Mark3:26	And if Satan rise up against himself, and be divided, he cannot stand, but hath an end.
1025	Matt12:27	And if I by Beelzebub cast out devils, by whom do your children cast them out? therefore they shall be your judges.
1026	Luke11:19	And if I by Beelzebub cast out devils, by whom do your sons cast them out? therefore shall they be your judges.
1027	Matt12:28	But if I cast out devils by the Spirit of God, then the kingdom of God is come unto you.
1028	Luke11:20	But if I with the finger of God cast out devils, no doubt the kingdom of God is come upon you.
1029	Luke11:21	When a strong man armed keepeth his palace, his goods are in peace:
1030	Luke11:22	But when a stronger than he shall come upon him, and overcome him, he taketh from him all his armour wherein he trusted, and divideth his spoils.
1031	Mark3:27	No man can enter into a strong man's house, and spoil his goods, except he will

THE TREE OF LIFE

		first bind the strong man; and then he will spoil his house.
1032	Matt12:29	Or else how can one enter into a strong man's house, and spoil his goods, except he first bind the strong man? and then he will spoil his house.
1033	Matt12:43	When the unclean spirit is gone out of a man, he walketh through dry places, seeking rest, and findeth none.
1034	Luke11:24	When the unclean spirit is gone out of a man, he walketh through dry places, seeking rest; and finding none, he saith, I will return unto my house whence I came out.
1035	Matt12:44	Then he saith, I will return into my house from whence I came out; and when he is come, he findeth it empty, swept, and garnished.
1036	Luke11:25	And when he cometh, he findeth it swept and garnished.
1037	Luke11:26	Then goeth he, and taketh to him seven other spirits more wicked than himself; and they enter in, and dwell there: and the last state of that man is worse than the first.
1038	Matt12:45	Then goeth he, and taketh with himself seven other spirits more wicked than himself, and they enter in and dwell there: and the last state of that man is worse than the first. Even so shall it be also unto this wicked generation.
1039	Luke11:23	He that is not with me is against me: and he that gathereth not with me scattereth.
1040	Matt12:30	He that is not with me is against me; and he that gathereth not with me scattereth abroad.
1041	Luke12:8	Also I say unto you, Whosoever shall confess me before men, him shall the Son of man also confess before the angels of God:
1042	Luke12:9	But he that denieth me before men shall be denied before the angels of God.
1043	Mark3:28	Verily I say unto you, All sins shall be forgiven unto the sons of men, and blasphemies wherewith soever they shall blaspheme:
1044	Matt12:31	Wherefore I say unto you, All manner of sin and blasphemy shall be forgiven unto men: but the blasphemy against the Holy Ghost shall not be forgiven unto men.
1045	Luke12:10	And whosoever shall speak a word against the Son of man, it shall be forgiven him: but unto him that blasphemeth against the Holy Ghost it shall not be forgiven.
1046	Mark3:29	But he that shall blaspheme against the Holy Ghost hath never forgiveness, but is in danger of eternal damnation:
1047	Matt12:32	And whosoever speaketh a word against the Son of man, it shall be forgiven him: but whosoever speaketh against the Holy Ghost, it shall not be forgiven him, neither in this world, neither in the world to come.
1048	Mark3:30	Because they said, He hath an unclean spirit.
1049	Matt12:33	Either make the tree good, and his fruit good; or else make the tree corrupt, and his fruit corrupt: for the tree is known by his fruit.
1050	Matt12:34	O generation of vipers, how can ye, being evil, speak good things? for out of the abundance of the heart the mouth speaketh.
1051	Matt12:35	A good man out of the good treasure of the heart bringeth forth good things: and an evil man out of the evil treasure bringeth forth evil things.
1052	Matt12:36	But I say unto you, That every idle word that men shall speak, they shall give account thereof in the day of judgment.
1053	Matt12:37	For by thy words thou shalt be justified, and by thy words thou shalt be condemned.
1054	Luke11:27	And it came to pass, as he spake these things, a certain woman of the company lifted up her voice, and said unto him, Blessed is the womb that bare thee, and the paps which thou hast sucked.
1055	Luke11:28	But he said, Yea rather, blessed are they that hear the word of God, and keep it.
1056	Matt12:38	Then certain of the scribes and of the Pharisees answered, saying, Master, we would see a sign from thee.

THE TREE OF LIFE

1057	Luke11:16	And others, tempting him, sought of him a sign from heaven.
1058	Luke11:29	And when the people were gathered thick together, he began to say, This is an evil generation: they seek a sign; and there shall no sign be given it, but the sign of Jonas the prophet.
1059	Matt12:39	But he answered and said unto them, An evil and adulterous generation seeketh after a sign; and there shall no sign be given to it, but the sign of the prophet Jonas:
1060	Luke11:30	For as Jonas was a sign unto the Ninevites, so shall also the Son of man be to this generation.
1061	Matt12:40	For as Jonas was three days and three nights in the whale's belly; so shall the Son of man be three days and three nights in the heart of the earth.
1062	Luke11:32	The men of Nineve shall rise up in the judgment with this generation, and shall condemn it: for they repented at the preaching of Jonas; and, behold, a greater than Jonas is here.
1063	Matt12:41	The men of Nineveh shall rise in judgment with this generation, and shall condemn it: because they repented at the preaching of Jonas; and, behold, a greater than Jonas is here.
1064	Luke11:31	The queen of the south shall rise up in the judgment with the men of this generation, and condemn them: for she came from the utmost parts of the earth to hear the wisdom of Solomon; and, behold, a greater than Solomon is here.
1065	Matt12:42	The queen of the south shall rise up in the judgment with this generation, and shall condemn it: for she came from the uttermost parts of the earth to hear the wisdom of Solomon; and, behold, a greater than Solomon is here.
1066	Matt12:46	While he yet talked to the people, behold, his mother and his brethren stood without, desiring to speak with him.
1067	Luke8:19	Then came to him his mother and his brethren, and could not come at him for the press.
1068	Mark3:31	There came then his brethren and his mother, and, standing without, sent unto him, calling him.
1069	Mark3:32	And the multitude sat about him, and they said unto him, Behold, thy mother and thy brethren without seek for thee.
1070	Luke8:20	And it was told him by certain which said, Thy mother and thy brethren stand without, desiring to see thee.
1071	Matt12:47	Then one said unto him, Behold, thy mother and thy brethren stand without, desiring to speak with thee.
1072	Mark3:33	And he answered them, saying, Who is my mother, or my brethren?
1073	Matt12:48	But he answered and said unto him that told him, Who is my mother? and who are my brethren?
1074	Mark3:34	And he looked round about on them which sat about him, and said, Behold my mother and my brethren!
1075	Matt12:49	And he stretched forth his hand toward his disciples, and said, Behold my mother and my brethren!
1076	Luke8:21	And he answered and said unto them, My mother and my brethren are these which hear the word of God, and do it.
1077	Matt12:50	For whosoever shall do the will of my Father which is in heaven, the same is my brother, and sister, and mother.
1078	Mark3:35	For whosoever shall do the will of God, the same is my brother, and my sister, and mother.
1079	Matt13:1	The same day went Jesus out of the house, and sat by the sea side.
1080	Mark4:1	And he began again to teach by the sea side: and there was gathered unto him a great multitude, so that he entered into a ship, and sat in the sea; and the whole multitude was by the sea on the land.
1081	Matt13:2	And great multitudes were gathered together unto him, so that he went into a

THE TREE OF LIFE

		ship, and sat; and the whole multitude stood on the shore.
1082	Mark4:2	And he taught them many things by parables, and said unto them in his doctrine,
1083	Luke8:4	And when much people were gathered together, and were come to him out of every city, he spake by a parable:
1084	Matt13:3	And he spake many things unto them in parables, saying, Behold, a sower went forth to sow;
1085	Mark4:3	Hearken; Behold, there went out a sower to sow:
1086	Luke8:5	A sower went out to sow his seed: and as he sowed, some fell by the way side; and it was trodden down, and the fowls of the air devoured it.
1087	Mark4:4	And it came to pass, as he sowed, some fell by the way side, and the fowls of the air came and devoured it up.
1088	Matt13:4	And when he sowed, some seeds fell by the way side, and the fowls came and devoured them up:
1089	Luke8:6	And some fell upon a rock; and as soon as it was sprung up, it withered away, because it lacked moisture.
1090	Mark4:5	And some fell on stony ground, where it had not much earth; and immediately it sprang up, because it had no depth of earth:
1091	Matt13:5	Some fell upon stony places, where they had not much earth: and forthwith they sprung up, because they had no deepness of earth:
1092	Matt13:6	And when the sun was up, they were scorched; and because they had no root, they withered away.
1093	Mark4:6	But when the sun was up, it was scorched; and because it had no root, it withered away.
1094	Matt13:7	And some fell among thorns; and the thorns sprung up, and choked them:
1095	Luke8:7	And some fell among thorns; and the thorns sprang up with it, and choked it.
1096	Mark4:7	And some fell among thorns, and the thorns grew up, and choked it, and it yielded no fruit.
1097	Matt13:8	But other fell into good ground, and brought forth fruit, some an hundredfold, some sixtyfold, some thirtyfold.
1098	Mark4:8	And other fell on good ground, and did yield fruit that sprang up and increased; and brought forth, some thirty, and some sixty, and some an hundred.
1099	Luke8:8	And other fell on good ground, and sprang up, and bare fruit an hundredfold. And when he had said these things, he cried, He that hath ears to hear, let him hear.
1100	Mark4:9	And he said unto them, He that hath ears to hear, let him hear.
1101	Matt13:9	Who hath ears to hear, let him hear.
1102	Mark4:10	And when he was alone, they that were about him with the twelve asked of him the parable.
1103	Luke8:9	And his disciples asked him, saying, What might this parable be?
1104	Mark4:13	And he said unto them, Know ye not this parable? and how then will ye know all parables?
1105	Matt13:18	Hear ye therefore the parable of the sower.
1106	Luke8:11	Now the parable is this: The seed is the word of God.
1107	Mark4:14	The sower soweth the word.
1108	Matt13:19	When any one heareth the word of the kingdom, and understandeth it not, then cometh the wicked one, and catcheth away that which was sown in his heart. This is he which received seed by the way side.
1109	Mark4:15	And these are they by the way side, where the word is sown; but when they have heard, Satan cometh immediately, and taketh away the word that was sown in their hearts.
1110	Luke8:12	Those by the way side are they that hear; then cometh the devil, and taketh away the word out of their hearts, lest they should believe and be saved.
1111	Mark4:16	And these are they likewise which are sown on stony ground; who, when they have heard the word, immediately receive it with gladness;

THE TREE OF LIFE

1112	Matt13:20	But he that received the seed into stony places, the same is he that heareth the word, and anon with joy receiveth it;
1113	Luke8:13	They on the rock are they, which, when they hear, receive the word with joy; and these have no root, which for a while believe, and in time of temptation fall away.
1114	Matt13:21	Yet hath he not root in himself, but dureth for a while: for when tribulation or persecution ariseth because of the word, by and by he is offended.
1115	Mark4:17	And have no root in themselves, and so endure but for a time: afterward, when affliction or persecution ariseth for the word's sake, immediately they are offended.
1116	Mark4:18	And these are they which are sown among thorns; such as hear the word,
1117	Luke8:14	And that which fell among thorns are they, which, when they have heard, go forth, and are choked with cares and riches and pleasures of this life, and bring no fruit to perfection.
1118	Matt13:22	He also that received seed among the thorns is he that heareth the word; and the care of this world, and the deceitfulness of riches, choke the word, and he becometh unfruitful.
1119	Mark4:19	And the cares of this world, and the deceitfulness of riches, and the lusts of other things entering in, choke the word, and it becometh unfruitful.
1120	Luke8:15	But that on the good ground are they, which in an honest and good heart, having heard the word, keep it, and bring forth fruit with patience.
1121	Matt13:23	But he that received seed into the good ground is he that heareth the word, and understandeth it; which also beareth fruit, and bringeth forth, some an hundredfold, some sixty, some thirty.
1122	Mark4:20	And these are they which are sown on good ground; such as hear the word, and receive it, and bring forth fruit, some thirtyfold, some sixty, and some an hundred.
1123	Matt13:10	And the disciples came, and said unto him, Why speakest thou unto them in parables?
1124	Matt13:11	He answered and said unto them, Because it is given unto you to know the mysteries of the kingdom of heaven, but to them it is not given.
1125	Mark4:11	And he said unto them, Unto you it is given to know the mystery of the kingdom of God: but unto them that are without, all these things are done in parables:
1126	Matt13:12	For whosoever hath, to him shall be given, and he shall have more abundance: but whosoever hath not, from him shall be taken away even that he hath.
1127	Matt13:14	And in them is fulfilled the prophecy of Esaias, which saith, By hearing ye shall hear, and shall not understand; and seeing ye shall see, and shall not perceive:
1128	Matt13:15	For this people's heart is waxed gross, and their ears are dull of hearing, and their eyes they have closed; lest at any time they should see with their eyes and hear with their ears, and should understand with their heart, and should be converted, and I should heal them.
1129	Luke8:10	And he said, Unto you it is given to know the mysteries of the kingdom of God: but to others in parables; that seeing they might not see, and hearing they might not understand.
1130	Matt13:13	Therefore speak I to them in parables: because they seeing see not; and hearing they hear not, neither do they understand.
1131	Mark4:12	That seeing they may see, and not perceive; and hearing they may hear, and not understand; lest at any time they should be converted, and their sins should be forgiven them.
1132	Matt13:16	But blessed are your eyes, for they see: and your ears, for they hear.
1133	Matt13:17	For verily I say unto you, That many prophets and righteous men have desired to see those things which ye see, and have not seen them; and to hear those things which ye hear, and have not heard them.
1134	Mark4:21	And he said unto them, Is a candle brought to be put under a bushel, or under a bed? and not to be set on a candlestick?

THE TREE OF LIFE

1135	Luke8:16	No man, when he hath lighted a candle, covereth it with a vessel, or putteth it under a bed; but setteth it on a candlestick, that they which enter in may see the light.
1136	Mark4:22	For there is nothing hid, which shall not be manifested; neither was any thing kept secret, but that it should come abroad.
1137	Luke8:17	For nothing is secret, that shall not be made manifest; neither any thing hid, that shall not be known and come abroad.
1138	Mark4:23	If any man have ears to hear, let him hear.
1139	Mark4:24	And he said unto them, Take heed what ye hear: with what measure ye mete, it shall be measured to you: and unto you that hear shall more be given.
1140	Luke8:18	Take heed therefore how ye hear: for whosoever hath, to him shall be given; and whosoever hath not, from him shall be taken even that which he seemeth to have.
1141	Mark4:25	For he that hath, to him shall be given: and he that hath not, from him shall be taken even that which he hath.
1142	Mark4:26	And he said, So is the kingdom of God, as if a man should cast seed into the ground;
1143	Mark4:27	And should sleep, and rise night and day, and the seed should spring and grow up, he knoweth not how.
1144	Mark4:28	For the earth bringeth forth fruit of herself; first the blade, then the ear, after that the full corn in the ear.
1145	Mark4:29	But when the fruit is brought forth, immediately he putteth in the sickle, because the harvest is come.
1146	Luke13:18	Then said he, Unto what is the kingdom of God like? and whereunto shall I resemble it?
1147	Matt13:24	Another parable put he forth unto them, saying, The kingdom of heaven is likened unto a man which sowed good seed in his field:
1148	Matt13:25	But while men slept, his enemy came and sowed tares among the wheat, and went his way.
1149	Matt13:26	But when the blade was sprung up, and brought forth fruit, then appeared the tares also.
1150	Matt13:27	So the servants of the householder came and said unto him, Sir, didst not thou sow good seed in thy field? from whence then hath it tares?
1151	Matt13:28	He said unto them, An enemy hath done this. The servants said unto him, Wilt thou then that we go and gather them up?
1152	Matt13:29	But he said, Nay; lest while ye gather up the tares, ye root up also the wheat with them.
1153	Matt13:30	Let both grow together until the harvest: and in the time of harvest I will say to the reapers, Gather ye together first the tares, and bind them in bundles to burn them: but gather the wheat into my barn.
1154	Mark4:30	And he said, Whereunto shall we liken the kingdom of God? or with what comparison shall we compare it?
1155	Matt13:31	Another parable put he forth unto them, saying, The kingdom of heaven is like to a grain of mustard seed, which a man took, and sowed in his field:
1156	Luke13:19	It is like a grain of mustard seed, which a man took, and cast into his garden; and it grew, and waxed a great tree; and the fowls of the air lodged in the branches of it.
1157	Mark4:31	It is like a grain of mustard seed, which, when it is sown in the earth, is less than all the seeds that be in the earth:
1158	Matt13:32	Which indeed is the least of all seeds: but when it is grown, it is the greatest among herbs, and becometh a tree, so that the birds of the air come and lodge in the branches thereof.
1159	Mark4:32	But when it is sown, it groweth up, and becometh greater than all herbs, and

THE TREE OF LIFE

		shooteth out great branches; so that the fowls of the air may lodge under the shadow of it.
1160	Luke13:20	And again he said, Whereunto shall I liken the kingdom of God?
1161	Matt13:33	Another parable spake he unto them; The kingdom of heaven is like unto leaven, which a woman took, and hid in three measures of meal, till the whole was leavened.
1162	Luke13:21	It is like leaven, which a woman took and hid in three measures of meal, till the whole was leavened.
1163	Mark4:33	And with many such parables spake he the word unto them, as they were able to hear it.
1164	Matt13:34	All these things spake Jesus unto the multitude in parables; and without a parable spake he not unto them:
1165	Matt13:35	That it might be fulfilled which was spoken by the prophet, saying, I will open my mouth in parables; I will utter things which have been kept secret from the foundation of the world.
1166	Mark4:34	But without a parable spake he not unto them: and when they were alone, he expounded all things to his disciples.
1167	Matt13:36	Then Jesus sent the multitude away, and went into the house: and his disciples came unto him, saying, Declare unto us the parable of the tares of the field.
1168	Matt13:37	He answered and said unto them, He that soweth the good seed is the Son of man;
1169	Matt13:38	The field is the world; the good seed are the children of the kingdom; but the tares are the children of the wicked one;
1170	Matt13:39	The enemy that sowed them is the devil; the harvest is the end of the world; and the reapers are the angels.
1171	Matt13:40	As therefore the tares are gathered and burned in the fire; so shall it be in the end of this world.
1172	Matt13:41	The Son of man shall send forth his angels, and they shall gather out of his kingdom all things that offend, and them which do iniquity;
1173	Matt13:42	And shall cast them into a furnace of fire: there shall be wailing and gnashing of teeth.
1174	Matt13:43	Then shall the righteous shine forth as the sun in the kingdom of their Father. Who hath ears to hear, let him hear.
1175	Matt13:44	Again, the kingdom of heaven is like unto treasure hid in a field; the which when a man hath found, he hideth, and for joy thereof goeth and selleth all that he hath, and buyeth that field.
1176	Matt13:45	Again, the kingdom of heaven is like unto a merchant man, seeking goodly pearls:
1177	Matt13:46	Who, when he had found one pearl of great price, went and sold all that he had, and bought it.
1178	Matt13:47	Again, the kingdom of heaven is like unto a net, that was cast into the sea, and gathered of every kind:
1179	Matt13:48	Which, when it was full, they drew to shore, and sat down, and gathered the good into vessels, but cast the bad away.
1180	Matt13:49	So shall it be at the end of the world: the angels shall come forth, and sever the wicked from among the just,
1181	Matt13:50	And shall cast them into the furnace of fire: there shall be wailing and gnashing of teeth.
1182	Matt13:51	Jesus saith unto them, Have ye understood all these things? They say unto him, Yea, Lord.
1183	Matt13:52	Then said he unto them, Therefore every scribe which is instructed unto the kingdom of heaven is like unto a man that is an householder, which bringeth forth out of his treasure things new and old.

THE TREE OF LIFE

1184	Matt13:53	And it came to pass, that when Jesus had finished these parables, he departed thence.
1185	Mark4:35	And the same day, when the even was come, he saith unto them, Let us pass over unto the other side.
1186	Luke8:22	Now it came to pass on a certain day, that he went into a ship with his disciples: and he said unto them, Let us go over unto the other side of the lake. And they launched forth.
1187	Mark4:36	And when they had sent away the multitude, they took him even as he was in the ship. And there were also with him other little ships.
1188	Matt8:23	And when he was entered into a ship, his disciples followed him.
1189	Luke8:23	But as they sailed he fell asleep: and there came down a storm of wind on the lake; and they were filled with water, and were in jeopardy.
1190	Mark4:37	And there arose a great storm of wind, and the waves beat into the ship, so that it was now full.
1191	Matt8:24	And, behold, there arose a great tempest in the sea, insomuch that the ship was covered with the waves: but he was asleep.
1192	Mark4:38	And he was in the hinder part of the ship, asleep on a pillow: and they awake him, and say unto him, Master, carest thou not that we perish?
1193	Matt8:25	And his disciples came to him, and awoke him, saying, Lord, save us: we perish.
1194	Luke8:24	And they came to him, and awoke him, saying, Master, master, we perish. Then he arose, and rebuked the wind and the raging of the water: and they ceased, and there was a calm.
1195	Matt8:26	And he saith unto them, Why are ye fearful, O ye of little faith? Then he arose, and rebuked the winds and the sea; and there was a great calm.
1196	Mark4:39	And he arose, and rebuked the wind, and said unto the sea, Peace, be still. And the wind ceased, and there was a great calm.
1197	Mark4:40	And he said unto them, Why are ye so fearful? how is it that ye have no faith?
1198	Luke8:25	And he said unto them, Where is your faith? And they being afraid wondered, saying one to another, What manner of man is this! for he commandeth even the winds and water, and they obey him.
1199	Mark4:41	And they feared exceedingly, and said one to another, What manner of man is this, that even the wind and the sea obey him?
1200	Matt8:27	But the men marvelled, saying, What manner of man is this, that even the winds and the sea obey him!
1201	Mark5:1	And they came over unto the other side of the sea, into the country of the Gadarenes.
1202	Luke8:26	And they arrived at the country of the Gadarenes, which is over against Galilee.
1203	Matt8:28	And when he was come to the other side into the country of the Gergesenes, there met him two possessed with devils, coming out of the tombs, exceeding fierce, so that no man might pass by that way.
1204	Mark5:2	And when he was come out of the ship, immediately there met him out of the tombs a man with an unclean spirit,
1205	Luke8:27	And when he went forth to land, there met him out of the city a certain man, which had devils long time, and ware no clothes, neither abode in any house, but in the tombs.
1206	Mark5:3	Who had his dwelling among the tombs; and no man could bind him, no, not with chains:
1207	Mark5:4	Because that he had been often bound with fetters and chains, and the chains had been plucked asunder by him, and the fetters broken in pieces: neither could any man tame him.
1208	Mark5:5	And always, night and day, he was in the mountains, and in the tombs, crying, and cutting himself with stones.
1209	Mark5:6	But when he saw Jesus afar off, he ran and worshipped him,

THE TREE OF LIFE

1210	Luke8:28	When he saw Jesus, he cried out, and fell down before him, and with a loud voice said, What have I to do with thee, Jesus, thou Son of God most high? I beseech thee, torment me not.
1211	Matt8:29	And, behold, they cried out, saying, What have we to do with thee, Jesus, thou Son of God? art thou come hither to torment us before the time?
1212	Mark5:7	And cried with a loud voice, and said, What have I to do with thee, Jesus, thou Son of the most high God? I adjure thee by God, that thou torment me not.
1213	Mark5:8	For he said unto him, Come out of the man, thou unclean spirit.
1214	Luke8:29	(For he had commanded the unclean spirit to come out of the man. For oftentimes it had caught him: and he was kept bound with chains and in fetters; and he brake the bands, and was driven of the devil into the wilderness.)
1215	Mark5:9	And he asked him, What is thy name? And he answered, saying, My name is Legion: for we are many.
1216	Luke8:30	And Jesus asked him, saying, What is thy name? And he said, Legion: because many devils were entered into him.
1217	Mark5:10	And he besought him much that he would not send them away out of the country.
1218	Luke8:31	And they besought him that he would not command them to go out into the deep.
1219	Matt8:30	And there was a good way off from them an herd of many swine feeding.
1220	Mark5:11	Now there was there nigh unto the mountains a great herd of swine feeding.
1221	Matt8:31	So the devils besought him, saying, If thou cast us out, suffer us to go away into the herd of swine.
1222	Mark5:12	And all the devils besought him, saying, Send us into the swine, that we may enter into them.
1223	Luke8:32	And there was there an herd of many swine feeding on the mountain: and they besought him that he would suffer them to enter into them. And he suffered them.
1224	Luke8:33	Then went the devils out of the man, and entered into the swine: and the herd ran violently down a steep place into the lake, and were choked.
1225	Mark5:13	And forthwith Jesus gave them leave. And the unclean spirits went out, and entered into the swine: and the herd ran violently down a steep place into the sea, (they were about two thousand;) and were choked in the sea.
1226	Matt8:32	And he said unto them, Go. And when they were come out, they went into the herd of swine: and, behold, the whole herd of swine ran violently down a steep place into the sea, and perished in the waters.
1227	Mark5:14	And they that fed the swine fled, and told it in the city, and in the country. And they went out to see what it was that was done.
1228	Luke8:34	When they that fed them saw what was done, they fled, and went and told it in the city and in the country.
1229	Luke8:35	Then they went out to see what was done; and came to Jesus, and found the man, out of whom the devils were departed, sitting at the feet of Jesus, clothed, and in his right mind: and they were afraid.
1230	Mark5:15	And they come to Jesus, and see him that was possessed with the devil, and had the legion, sitting, and clothed, and in his right mind: and they were afraid.
1231	Mark5:16	And they that saw it told them how it befell to him that was possessed with the devil, and also concerning the swine.
1232	Luke8:36	They also which saw it told them by what means he that was possessed of the devils was healed.
1233	Matt8:33	And they that kept them fled, and went their ways into the city, and told every thing, and what was befallen to the possessed of the devils.
1234	Luke8:37	Then the whole multitude of the country of the Gadarenes round about besought him to depart from them; for they were taken with great fear: and he went up into the ship, and returned back again.
1235	Matt8:34	And, behold, the whole city came out to meet Jesus: and when they saw him, they besought him that he would depart out of their coasts.

THE TREE OF LIFE

1236	Mark5:17	And they began to pray him to depart out of their coasts.
1237	Mark5:18	And when he was come into the ship, he that had been possessed with the devil prayed him that he might be with him.
1238	Luke8:38	Now the man out of whom the devils were departed besought him that he might be with him: but Jesus sent him away, saying,
1239	Luke8:39	Return to thine own house, and shew how great things God hath done unto thee. And he went his way, and published throughout the whole city how great things Jesus had done unto him.
1240	Mark5:19	Howbeit Jesus suffered him not, but saith unto him, Go home to thy friends, and tell them how great things the Lord hath done for thee, and hath had compassion on thee.
1241	Mark5:20	And he departed, and began to publish in Decapolis how great things Jesus had done for him: and all men did marvel.
1242	Mark5:21	And when Jesus was passed over again by ship unto the other side, much people gathered unto him: and he was nigh unto the sea.
1243	Luke8:40	And it came to pass, that, when Jesus was returned, the people gladly received him: for they were all waiting for him.
1244	Mark5:22	And, behold, there cometh one of the rulers of the synagogue, Jairus by name; and when he saw him, he fell at his feet,
1245	Luke8:41	And, behold, there came a man named Jairus, and he was a ruler of the synagogue: and he fell down at Jesus' feet, and besought him that he would come into his house:
1246	Matt9:18	While he spake these things unto them, behold, there came a certain ruler, and worshipped him, saying, My daughter is even now dead: but come and lay thy hand upon her, and she shall live.
1247	Mark5:23	And besought him greatly, saying, My little daughter lieth at the point of death: I pray thee, come and lay thy hands on her, that she may be healed; and she shall live.
1248	Luke8:42	For he had one only daughter, about twelve years of age, and she lay a dying. But as he went the people thronged him.
1249	Matt9:19	And Jesus arose, and followed him, and so did his disciples.
1250	Mark5:24	And Jesus went with him; and much people followed him, and thronged him.
1251	Mark5:25	And a certain woman, which had an issue of blood twelve years,
1252	Luke8:43	And a woman having an issue of blood twelve years, which had spent all her living upon physicians, neither could be healed of any,
1253	Mark5:26	And had suffered many things of many physicians, and had spent all that she had, and was nothing bettered, but rather grew worse,
1254	Matt9:20	And, behold, a woman, which was diseased with an issue of blood twelve years, came behind him, and touched the hem of his garment:
1255	Mark5:27	When she had heard of Jesus, came in the press behind, and touched his garment.
1256	Luke8:44	Came behind him, and touched the border of his garment: and immediately her issue of blood stanched.
1257	Matt9:21	For she said within herself, If I may but touch his garment, I shall be whole.
1258	Mark5:28	For she said, If I may touch but his clothes, I shall be whole.
1259	Mark5:29	And straightway the fountain of her blood was dried up; and she felt in her body that she was healed of that plague.
1260	Mark5:30	And Jesus, immediately knowing in himself that virtue had gone out of him, turned him about in the press, and said, Who touched my clothes?
1261	Luke8:45	And Jesus said, Who touched me? When all denied, Peter and they that were with him said, Master, the multitude throng thee and press thee, and sayest thou, Who touched me?
1262	Mark5:31	And his disciples said unto him, Thou seest the multitude thronging thee, and

THE TREE OF LIFE

		sayest thou, Who touched me?
1263	Luke8:46	And Jesus said, Somebody hath touched me: for I perceive that virtue is gone out of me.
1264	Mark5:32	And he looked round about to see her that had done this thing.
1265	Luke8:47	And when the woman saw that she was not hid, she came trembling, and falling down before him, she declared unto him before all the people for what cause she had touched him, and how she was healed immediately.
1266	Mark5:33	But the woman fearing and trembling, knowing what was done in her, came and fell down before him, and told him all the truth.
1267	Matt9:22	But Jesus turned him about, and when he saw her, he said, Daughter, be of good comfort; thy faith hath made thee whole. And the woman was made whole from that hour.
1268	Luke8:48	And he said unto her, Daughter, be of good comfort: thy faith hath made thee whole; go in peace.
1269	Mark5:34	And he said unto her, Daughter, thy faith hath made thee whole; go in peace, and be whole of thy plague.
1270	Luke8:49	While he yet spake, there cometh one from the ruler of the synagogue's house, saying to him, Thy daughter is dead; trouble not the Master.
1271	Mark5:35	While he yet spake, there came from the ruler of the synagogue's house certain which said, Thy daughter is dead: why troublest thou the Master any further?
1272	Mark5:36	As soon as Jesus heard the word that was spoken, he saith unto the ruler of the synagogue, Be not afraid, only believe.
1273	Luke8:50	But when Jesus heard it, he answered him, saying, Fear not: believe only, and she shall be made whole.
1274	Mark5:38	And he cometh to the house of the ruler of the synagogue, and seeth the tumult, and them that wept and wailed greatly.
1275	Matt9:23	And when Jesus came into the ruler's house, and saw the minstrels and the people making a noise,
1276	Luke8:51	And when he came into the house, he suffered no man to go in, save Peter, and James, and John, and the father and the mother of the maiden.
1277	Mark5:37	And he suffered no man to follow him, save Peter, and James, and John the brother of James.
1278	Mark5:39	And when he was come in, he saith unto them, Why make ye this ado, and weep? the damsel is not dead, but sleepeth.
1279	Luke8:52	And all wept, and bewailed her: but he said, Weep not; she is not dead, but sleepeth.
1280	Matt9:24	He said unto them, Give place: for the maid is not dead, but sleepeth. And they laughed him to scorn.
1281	Luke8:53	And they laughed him to scorn, knowing that she was dead.
1282	Mark5:40	And they laughed him to scorn. But when he had put them all out, he taketh the father and the mother of the damsel, and them that were with him, and entereth in where the damsel was lying.
1283	Luke8:54	And he put them all out, and took her by the hand, and called, saying, Maid, arise.
1284	Mark5:41	And he took the damsel by the hand, and said unto her, Talitha cumi; which is, being interpreted, Damsel, I say unto thee, arise.
1285	Luke8:55	And her spirit came again, and she arose straightway: and he commanded to give her meat.
1286	Matt9:25	But when the people were put forth, he went in, and took her by the hand, and the maid arose.
1287	Mark5:42	And straightway the damsel arose, and walked; for she was of the age of twelve years. And they were astonished with a great astonishment.
1288	Luke8:56	And her parents were astonished: but he charged them that they should tell no

THE TREE OF LIFE

		man what was done.
1289	Mark5:43	And he charged them straitly that no man should know it; and commanded that something should be given her to eat.
1290	Matt9:26	And the fame hereof went abroad into all that land.
1291	Matt9:27	And when Jesus departed thence, two blind men followed him, crying, and saying, Thou son of David, have mercy on us.
1292	Matt9:28	And when he was come into the house, the blind men came to him: and Jesus saith unto them, Believe ye that I am able to do this? They said unto him, Yea, Lord.
1293	Matt9:29	Then touched he their eyes, saying, According to your faith be it unto you.
1294	Matt9:30	And their eyes were opened; and Jesus straitly charged them, saying, See that no man know it.
1295	Matt9:31	But they, when they were departed, spread abroad his fame in all that country.
1296	Matt9:32	As they went out, behold, they brought to him a dumb man possessed with a devil.
1297	Matt9:33	And when the devil was cast out, the dumb spake: and the multitudes marvelled, saying, It was never so seen in Israel.
1298	Matt9:34	But the Pharisees said, He casteth out devils through the prince of the devils.
1299	Mark6:1	And he went out from thence, and came into his own country; and his disciples follow him.
1300	Matt13:54	And when he was come into his own country, he taught them in their synagogue, insomuch that they were astonished, and said, Whence hath this man this wisdom, and these mighty works?
1301	Mark6:2	And when the sabbath day was come, he began to teach in the synagogue: and many hearing him were astonished, saying, From whence hath this man these things? and what wisdom is this which is given unto him, that even such mighty works are wrought by his hands?
1302	Matt13:55	Is not this the carpenter's son? is not his mother called Mary? and his brethren, James, and Joses, and Simon, and Judas?
1303	Matt13:56	And his sisters, are they not all with us? Whence then hath this man all these things?
1304	Mark6:3	Is not this the carpenter, the son of Mary, the brother of James, and Joses, and of Juda, and Simon? and are not his sisters here with us? And they were offended at him.
1305	Matt13:57	And they were offended in him. But Jesus said unto them, A prophet is not without honour, save in his own country, and in his own house.
1306	Mark6:4	But Jesus said unto them, A prophet is not without honour, but in his own country, and among his own kin, and in his own house.
1307	John4:44	For Jesus himself testified, that a prophet hath no honour in his own country.
1308	Matt13:58	And he did not many mighty works there because of their unbelief.
1309	Mark6:5	And he could there do no mighty work, save that he laid his hands upon a few sick folk, and healed them.
1310	Mark6:6	And he marvelled because of their unbelief. And he went round about the villages, teaching.
1311	Matt14:1	At that time Herod the tetrarch heard of the fame of Jesus,
1312	Luke9:9	And Herod said, John have I beheaded: but who is this, of whom I hear such things? And he desired to see him.
1313	Luke9:7	Now Herod the tetrarch heard of all that was done by him: and he was perplexed, because that it was said of some, that John was risen from the dead;
1314	Mark6:15	Others said, That it is Elias. And others said, That it is a prophet, or as one of the prophets.
1315	Luke9:8	And of some, that Elias had appeared; and of others, that one of the old prophets was risen again.

THE TREE OF LIFE

1316	Mark6:16	But when Herod heard thereof, he said, It is John, whom I beheaded: he is risen from the dead.
1317	Mark6:14	And king Herod heard of him; (for his name was spread abroad:) and he said, That John the Baptist was risen from the dead, and therefore mighty works do shew forth themselves in him.
1318	Matt14:2	And said unto his servants, This is John the Baptist; he is risen from the dead; and therefore mighty works do shew forth themselves in him.
1319	Mark6:20	For Herod feared John, knowing that he was a just man and an holy, and observed him; and when he heard him, he did many things, and heard him gladly.
1320	Matt14:3	For Herod had laid hold on John, and bound him, and put him in prison for Herodias' sake, his brother Philip's wife.
1321	Mark6:17	For Herod himself had sent forth and laid hold upon John, and bound him in prison for Herodias' sake, his brother Philip's wife: for he had married her.
1322	Matt14:4	For John said unto him, It is not lawful for thee to have her.
1323	Mark6:18	For John had said unto Herod, It is not lawful for thee to have thy brother's wife.
1324	Luke3:19	But Herod the tetrarch, being reproved by him for Herodias his brother Philip's wife, and for all the evils which Herod had done,
1325	Mark6:19	Therefore Herodias had a quarrel against him, and would have killed him; but she could not:
1326	Luke3:20	Added yet this above all, that he shut up John in prison.
1327	Matt14:5	And when he would have put him to death, he feared the multitude, because they counted him as a prophet.
1328	Mark6:21	And when a convenient day was come, that Herod on his birthday made a supper to his lords, high captains, and chief estates of Galilee;
1329	Matt14:6	But when Herod's birthday was kept, the daughter of Herodias danced before them, and pleased Herod.
1330	Mark6:22	And when the daughter of the said Herodias came in, and danced, and pleased Herod and them that sat with him, the king said unto the damsel, Ask of me whatsoever thou wilt, and I will give it thee.
1331	Mark6:23	And he sware unto her, Whatsoever thou shalt ask of me, I will give it thee, unto the half of my kingdom.
1332	Matt14:7	Whereupon he promised with an oath to give her whatsoever she would ask.
1333	Mark6:24	And she went forth, and said unto her mother, What shall I ask? And she said, The head of John the Baptist.
1334	Matt14:8	And she, being before instructed of her mother, said, Give me here John Baptist's head in a charger.
1335	Mark6:25	And she came in straightway with haste unto the king, and asked, saying, I will that thou give me by and by in a charger the head of John the Baptist.
1336	Matt14:9	And the king was sorry: nevertheless for the oath's sake, and them which sat with him at meat, he commanded it to be given her.
1337	Mark6:26	And the king was exceeding sorry; yet for his oath's sake, and for their sakes which sat with him, he would not reject her.
1338	Mark6:27	And immediately the king sent an executioner, and commanded his head to be brought: and he went and beheaded him in the prison,
1339	Matt14:10	And he sent, and beheaded John in the prison.
1340	Matt14:11	And his head was brought in a charger, and given to the damsel: and she brought it to her mother.
1341	Mark6:28	And brought his head in a charger, and gave it to the damsel: and the damsel gave it to her mother.
1342	Mark6:29	And when his disciples heard of it, they came and took up his corpse, and laid it in a tomb.
1343	Matt14:12	And his disciples came, and took up the body, and buried it, and went and told Jesus.

THE TREE OF LIFE

1344	Luke9:10	And the apostles, when they were returned, told him all that they had done. And he took them, and went aside privately into a desert place belonging to the city called Bethsaida.
1345	Mark6:30	And the apostles gathered themselves together unto Jesus, and told him all things, both what they had done, and what they had taught.
1346	Mark6:31	And he said unto them, Come ye yourselves apart into a desert place, and rest a while: for there were many coming and going, and they had no leisure so much as to eat.
1347	Mark6:32	And they departed into a desert place by ship privately.
1348	Matt14:13	When Jesus heard of it, he departed thence by ship into a desert place apart: and when the people had heard thereof, they followed him on foot out of the cities.
1349	Mark6:33	And the people saw them departing, and many knew him, and ran afoot thither out of all cities, and outwent them, and came together unto him.
1350	Luke9:11	And the people, when they knew it, followed him: and he received them, and spake unto them of the kingdom of God, and healed them that had need of healing.
1351	Matt14:14	And Jesus went forth, and saw a great multitude, and was moved with compassion toward them, and he healed their sick.
1352	Mark6:34	And Jesus, when he came out, saw much people, and was moved with compassion toward them, because they were as sheep not having a shepherd: and he began to teach them many things.
1353	Luke9:12	And when the day began to wear away, then came the twelve, and said unto him, Send the multitude away, that they may go into the towns and country round about, and lodge, and get victuals: for we are here in a desert place.
1354	Matt14:15	And when it was evening, his disciples came to him, saying, This is a desert place, and the time is now past; send the multitude away, that they may go into the villages, and buy themselves victuals.
1355	Mark6:35	And when the day was now far spent, his disciples came unto him, and said, This is a desert place, and now the time is far passed:
1356	Mark6:36	Send them away, that they may go into the country round about, and into the villages, and buy themselves bread: for they have nothing to eat.
1357	John6:4	And the passover, a feast of the Jews, was nigh.
1358	Matt14:16	But Jesus said unto them, They need not depart; give ye them to eat.
1359	John6:5	When Jesus then lifted up his eyes, and saw a great company come unto him, he saith unto Philip, Whence shall we buy bread, that these may eat?
1360	John6:6	And this he said to prove him: for he himself knew what he would do.
1361	John6:7	Philip answered him, Two hundred pennyworth of bread is not sufficient for them, that every one of them may take a little.
1362	John6:8	One of his disciples, Andrew, Simon Peter's brother, saith unto him,
1363	John6:9	There is a lad here, which hath five barley loaves, and two small fishes: but what are they among so many?
1364	Mark6:37	He answered and said unto them, Give ye them to eat. And they say unto him, Shall we go and buy two hundred pennyworth of bread, and give them to eat?
1365	Luke9:13	But he said unto them, Give ye them to eat. And they said, We have no more but five loaves and two fishes; except we should go and buy meat for all this people.
1366	Matt14:17	And they say unto him, We have here but five loaves, and two fishes.
1367	Mark6:38	He saith unto them, How many loaves have ye? go and see. And when they knew, they say, Five, and two fishes.
1368	Matt14:18	He said, Bring them hither to me.
1369	Mark6:39	And he commanded them to make all sit down by companies upon the green grass.
1370	Luke9:14	For they were about five thousand men. And he said to his disciples, Make them sit down by fifties in a company.

THE TREE OF LIFE

1371	John6:10	And Jesus said, Make the men sit down. Now there was much grass in the place. So the men sat down, in number about five thousand.
1372	Mark6:40	And they sat down in ranks, by hundreds, and by fifties.
1373	Luke9:15	And they did so, and made them all sit down.
1374	Matt14:19	And he commanded the multitude to sit down on the grass, and took the five loaves, and the two fishes, and looking up to heaven, he blessed, and brake, and gave the loaves to his disciples, and the disciples to the multitude.
1375	Mark6:41	And when he had taken the five loaves and the two fishes, he looked up to heaven, and blessed, and brake the loaves, and gave them to his disciples to set before them; and the two fishes divided he among them all.
1376	Luke9:16	Then he took the five loaves and the two fishes, and looking up to heaven, he blessed them, and brake, and gave to the disciples to set before the multitude.
1377	John6:11	And Jesus took the loaves; and when he had given thanks, he distributed to the disciples, and the disciples to them that were set down; and likewise of the fishes as much as they would.
1378	John6:12	When they were filled, he said unto his disciples, Gather up the fragments that remain, that nothing be lost.
1379	Luke9:17	And they did eat, and were all filled: and there was taken up of fragments that remained to them twelve baskets.
1380	John6:13	Therefore they gathered them together, and filled twelve baskets with the fragments of the five barley loaves, which remained over and above unto them that had eaten.
1381	Mark6:42	And they did all eat, and were filled.
1382	Mark6:43	And they took up twelve baskets full of the fragments, and of the fishes.
1383	Matt14:20	And they did all eat, and were filled: and they took up of the fragments that remained twelve baskets full.
1384	Mark6:44	And they that did eat of the loaves were about five thousand men.
1385	Matt14:21	And they that had eaten were about five thousand men, beside women and children.
1386	Matt14:22	And straightway Jesus constrained his disciples to get into a ship, and to go before him unto the other side, while he sent the multitudes away.
1387	Mark6:45	And straightway he constrained his disciples to get into the ship, and to go to the other side before unto Bethsaida, while he sent away the people.
1388	John6:14	Then those men, when they had seen the miracle that Jesus did, said, This is of a truth that prophet that should come into the world.
1389	John6:15	When Jesus therefore perceived that they would come and take him by force, to make him a king, he departed again into a mountain himself alone.
1390	Mark6:46	And when he had sent them away, he departed into a mountain to pray.
1391	Matt14:23	And when he had sent the multitudes away, he went up into a mountain apart to pray: and when the evening was come, he was there alone.
1392	John6:16	And when even was now come, his disciples went down unto the sea,
1393	John6:17	And entered into a ship, and went over the sea toward Capernaum. And it was now dark, and Jesus was not come to them.
1394	Mark6:47	And when even was come, the ship was in the midst of the sea, and he alone on the land.
1395	Matt14:24	But the ship was now in the midst of the sea, tossed with waves: for the wind was contrary.
1396	John6:18	And the sea arose by reason of a great wind that blew.
1397	Mark6:48	And he saw them toiling in rowing; for the wind was contrary unto them: and about the fourth watch of the night he cometh unto them, walking upon the sea, and would have passed by them.
1398	Matt14:25	And in the fourth watch of the night Jesus went unto them, walking on the sea.
1399	John6:19	So when they had rowed about five and twenty or thirty furlongs, they see Jesus

THE TREE OF LIFE

		walking on the sea, and drawing nigh unto the ship: and they were afraid.
1400	Matt14:26	And when the disciples saw him walking on the sea, they were troubled, saying, It is a spirit; and they cried out for fear.
1401	Mark6:49	But when they saw him walking upon the sea, they supposed it had been a spirit, and cried out:
1402	Mark6:50	For they all saw him, and were troubled. And immediately he talked with them, and saith unto them, Be of good cheer: it is I; be not afraid.
1403	Matt14:27	But straightway Jesus spake unto them, saying, Be of good cheer; it is I; be not afraid.
1404	John6:20	But he saith unto them, It is I; be not afraid.
1405	Matt14:28	And Peter answered him and said, Lord, if it be thou, bid me come unto thee on the water.
1406	Matt14:29	And he said, Come. And when Peter was come down out of the ship, he walked on the water, to go to Jesus.
1407	Matt14:30	But when he saw the wind boisterous, he was afraid; and beginning to sink, he cried, saying, Lord, save me.
1408	Matt14:31	And immediately Jesus stretched forth his hand, and caught him, and said unto him, O thou of little faith, wherefore didst thou doubt?
1409	Matt14:33	Then they that were in the ship came and worshipped him, saying, Of a truth thou art the Son of God.
1410	Matt14:32	And when they were come into the ship, the wind ceased.
1411	Mark6:51	And he went up unto them into the ship; and the wind ceased: and they were sore amazed in themselves beyond measure, and wondered.
1412	Mark6:52	For they considered not the miracle of the loaves: for their heart was hardened.
1413	John6:21	Then they willingly received him into the ship: and immediately the ship was at the land whither they went.
1414	Matt14:34	And when they were gone over, they came into the land of Gennesaret.
1415	Mark6:53	And when they had passed over, they came into the land of Gennesaret, and drew to the shore.
1416	Mark6:54	And when they were come out of the ship, straightway they knew him,
1417	Matt14:35	And when the men of that place had knowledge of him, they sent out into all that country round about, and brought unto him all that were diseased;
1418	Mark6:55	And ran through that whole region round about, and began to carry about in beds those that were sick, where they heard he was.
1419	Mark6:56	And whithersoever he entered, into villages, or cities, or country, they laid the sick in the streets, and besought him that they might touch if it were but the border of his garment: and as many as touched him were made whole.
1420	Matt14:36	And besought him that they might only touch the hem of his garment: and as many as touched were made perfectly whole.
1421	John6:22	The day following, when the people which stood on the other side of the sea saw that there was none other boat there, save that one whereinto his disciples were entered, and that Jesus went not with his disciples into the boat, but that his disciples were gone away alone;
1422	John6:23	(Howbeit there came other boats from Tiberias nigh unto the place where they did eat bread, after that the Lord had given thanks:)
1423	John6:24	When the people therefore saw that Jesus was not there, neither his disciples, they also took shipping, and came to Capernaum, seeking for Jesus.
1424	John6:25	And when they had found him on the other side of the sea, they said unto him, Rabbi, when camest thou hither?
1425	John6:26	Jesus answered them and said, Verily, verily, I say unto you, Ye seek me, not because ye saw the miracles, but because ye did eat of the loaves, and were filled.
1426	John6:27	Labour not for the meat which perisheth, but for that meat which endureth unto

THE TREE OF LIFE

		everlasting life, which the Son of man shall give unto you: for him hath God the Father sealed.
1427	John6:28	Then said they unto him, What shall we do, that we might work the works of God?
1428	John6:29	Jesus answered and said unto them, This is the work of God, that ye believe on him whom he hath sent.
1429	John6:30	They said therefore unto him, What sign shewest thou then, that we may see, and believe thee? what dost thou work?
1430	John6:31	Our fathers did eat manna in the desert; as it is written, He gave them bread from heaven to eat.
1431	John6:32	Then Jesus said unto them, Verily, verily, I say unto you, Moses gave you not that bread from heaven; but my Father giveth you the true bread from heaven.
1432	John6:33	For the bread of God is he which cometh down from heaven, and giveth life unto the world.
1433	John6:34	Then said they unto him, Lord, evermore give us this bread.
1434	John6:35	And Jesus said unto them, I am the bread of life: he that cometh to me shall never hunger; and he that believeth on me shall never thirst.
1435	John6:36	But I said unto you, That ye also have seen me, and believe not.
1436	John6:37	All that the Father giveth me shall come to me; and him that cometh to me I will in no wise cast out.
1437	John6:38	For I came down from heaven, not to do mine own will, but the will of him that sent me.
1438	John6:39	And this is the Father's will which hath sent me, that of all which he hath given me I should lose nothing, but should raise it up again at the last day.
1439	John6:40	And this is the will of him that sent me, that every one which seeth the Son, and believeth on him, may have everlasting life: and I will raise him up at the last day.
1440	John6:41	The Jews then murmured at him, because he said, I am the bread which came down from heaven.
1441	John6:42	And they said, Is not this Jesus, the son of Joseph, whose father and mother we know? how is it then that he saith, I came down from heaven?
1442	John6:43	Jesus therefore answered and said unto them, Murmur not among yourselves.
1443	John6:44	No man can come to me, except the Father which hath sent me draw him: and I will raise him up at the last day.
1444	John6:45	It is written in the prophets, And they shall be all taught of God. Every man therefore that hath heard, and hath learned of the Father, cometh unto me.
1445	John6:46	Not that any man hath seen the Father, save he which is of God, he hath seen the Father.
1446	John6:47	Verily, verily, I say unto you, He that believeth on me hath everlasting life.
1447	John6:48	I am that bread of life.
1448	John6:49	Your fathers did eat manna in the wilderness, and are dead.
1449	John6:50	This is the bread which cometh down from heaven, that a man may eat thereof, and not die.
1450	John6:51	I am the living bread which came down from heaven: if any man eat of this bread, he shall live for ever: and the bread that I will give is my flesh, which I will give for the life of the world.
1451	John6:52	The Jews therefore strove among themselves, saying, How can this man give us his flesh to eat?
1452	John6:53	Then Jesus said unto them, Verily, verily, I say unto you, Except ye eat the flesh of the Son of man, and drink his blood, ye have no life in you.
1453	John6:54	Whoso eateth my flesh, and drinketh my blood, hath eternal life; and I will raise him up at the last day.
1454	John6:55	For my flesh is meat indeed, and my blood is drink indeed.
1455	John6:56	He that eateth my flesh, and drinketh my blood, dwelleth in me, and I in him.

THE TREE OF LIFE

1456	John6:57	As the living Father hath sent me, and I live by the Father: so he that eateth me, even he shall live by me.
1457	John6:58	This is that bread which came down from heaven: not as your fathers did eat manna, and are dead: he that eateth of this bread shall live for ever.
1458	John6:59	These things said he in the synagogue, as he taught in Capernaum.
1459	John6:60	Many therefore of his disciples, when they had heard this, said, This is an hard saying; who can hear it?
1460	John6:61	When Jesus knew in himself that his disciples murmured at it, he said unto them, Doth this offend you?
1461	John6:62	What and if ye shall see the Son of man ascend up where he was before?
1462	John6:63	It is the spirit that quickeneth; the flesh profiteth nothing: the words that I speak unto you, they are spirit, and they are life.
1463	John6:64	But there are some of you that believe not. For Jesus knew from the beginning who they were that believed not, and who should betray him.
1464	John6:65	And he said, Therefore said I unto you, that no man can come unto me, except it were given unto him of my Father.
1465	John6:66	From that time many of his disciples went back, and walked no more with him.
1466	John6:67	Then said Jesus unto the twelve, Will ye also go away?
1467	John6:68	Then Simon Peter answered him, Lord, to whom shall we go? thou hast the words of eternal life.
1468	John6:69	And we believe and are sure that thou art that Christ, the Son of the living God.
1469	John6:70	Jesus answered them, Have not I chosen you twelve, and one of you is a devil?
1470	John6:71	He spake of Judas Iscariot the son of Simon: for he it was that should betray him, being one of the twelve.
1471	John7:1	After these things Jesus walked in Galilee: for he would not walk in Jewry, because the Jews sought to kill him.
1472	Mark7:1	Then came together unto him the Pharisees, and certain of the scribes, which came from Jerusalem.
1473	Mark7:2	And when they saw some of his disciples eat bread with defiled, that is to say, with unwashen, hands, they found fault.
1474	Mark7:3	For the Pharisees, and all the Jews, except they wash their hands oft, eat not, holding the tradition of the elders.
1475	Mark7:4	And when they come from the market, except they wash, they eat not. And many other things there be, which they have received to hold, as the washing of cups, and pots, brasen vessels, and of tables.
1476	Matt15:1	Then came to Jesus scribes and Pharisees, which were of Jerusalem, saying,
1477	Mark7:5	Then the Pharisees and scribes asked him, Why walk not thy disciples according to the tradition of the elders, but eat bread with unwashen hands?
1478	Matt15:2	Why do thy disciples transgress the tradition of the elders? for they wash not their hands when they eat bread.
1479	Matt15:3	But he answered and said unto them, Why do ye also transgress the commandment of God by your tradition?
1480	Mark7:9	And he said unto them, Full well ye reject the commandment of God, that ye may keep your own tradition.
1481	Matt15:4	For God commanded, saying, Honour thy father and mother: and, He that curseth father or mother, let him die the death.
1482	Mark7:10	For Moses said, Honour thy father and thy mother; and, Whoso curseth father or mother, let him die the death:
1483	Matt15:5	But ye say, Whosoever shall say to his father or his mother, It is a gift, by whatsoever thou mightest be profited by me;
1484	Mark7:11	But ye say, If a man shall say to his father or mother, It is Corban, that is to say, a gift, by whatsoever thou mightest be profited by me; he shall be free.
1485	Matt15:6	And honour not his father or his mother, he shall be free. Thus have ye made the

THE TREE OF LIFE

		commandment of God of none effect by your tradition.
1486	Mark7:12	And ye suffer him no more to do ought for his father or his mother;
1487	Mark7:13	Making the word of God of none effect through your tradition, which ye have delivered: and many such like things do ye.
1488	Mark7:6	He answered and said unto them, Well hath Esaias prophesied of you hypocrites, as it is written, This people honoureth me with their lips, but their heart is far from me.
1489	Matt15:7	Ye hypocrites, well did Esaias prophesy of you, saying,
1490	Matt15:8	This people draweth nigh unto me with their mouth, and honoureth me with their lips; but their heart is far from me.
1491	Mark7:7	Howbeit in vain do they worship me, teaching for doctrines the commandments of men.
1492	Matt15:9	But in vain they do worship me, teaching for doctrines the commandments of men.
1493	Mark7:8	For laying aside the commandment of God, ye hold the tradition of men, as the washing of pots and cups: and many other such like things ye do.
1494	Mark7:14	And when he had called all the people unto him, he said unto them, Hearken unto me every one of you, and understand:
1495	Matt15:10	And he called the multitude, and said unto them, Hear, and understand:
1496	Mark7:15	There is nothing from without a man, that entering into him can defile him: but the things which come out of him, those are they that defile the man.
1497	Matt15:11	Not that which goeth into the mouth defileth a man; but that which cometh out of the mouth, this defileth a man.
1498	Mark7:16	If any man have ears to hear, let him hear.
1499	Matt15:12	Then came his disciples, and said unto him, Knowest thou that the Pharisees were offended, after they heard this saying?
1500	Matt15:13	But he answered and said, Every plant, which my heavenly Father hath not planted, shall be rooted up.
1501	Matt15:14	Let them alone: they be blind leaders of the blind. And if the blind lead the blind, both shall fall into the ditch.
1502	Mark7:17	And when he was entered into the house from the people, his disciples asked him concerning the parable.
1503	Matt15:15	Then answered Peter and said unto him, Declare unto us this parable.
1504	Matt15:16	And Jesus said, Are ye also yet without understanding?
1505	Mark7:18	And he saith unto them, Are ye so without understanding also? Do ye not perceive, that whatsoever thing from without entereth into the man, it cannot defile him;
1506	Matt15:17	Do not ye yet understand, that whatsoever entereth in at the mouth goeth into the belly, and is cast out into the draught?
1507	Mark7:19	Because it entereth not into his heart, but into the belly, and goeth out into the draught, purging all meats?
1508	Matt15:18	But those things which proceed out of the mouth come forth from the heart; and they defile the man.
1509	Mark7:20	And he said, That which cometh out of the man, that defileth the man.
1510	Matt15:19	For out of the heart proceed evil thoughts, murders, adulteries, fornications, thefts, false witness, blasphemies:
1511	Mark7:21	For from within, out of the heart of men, proceed evil thoughts, adulteries, fornications, murders,
1512	Mark7:22	Thefts, covetousness, wickedness, deceit, lasciviousness, an evil eye, blasphemy, pride, foolishness:
1513	Mark7:23	All these evil things come from within, and defile the man.
1514	Matt15:20	These are the things which defile a man: but to eat with unwashen hands defileth not a man.

THE TREE OF LIFE

1515	Matt15:21	Then Jesus went thence, and departed into the coasts of Tyre and Sidon.
1516	Mark7:24	And from thence he arose, and went into the borders of Tyre and Sidon, and entered into an house, and would have no man know it: but he could not be hid.
1517	Mark7:25	For a certain woman, whose young daughter had an unclean spirit, heard of him, and came and fell at his feet:
1518	Mark7:26	The woman was a Greek, a Syrophenician by nation; and she besought him that he would cast forth the devil out of her daughter.
1519	Matt15:22	And, behold, a woman of Canaan came out of the same coasts, and cried unto him, saying, Have mercy on me, O Lord, thou son of David; my daughter is grievously vexed with a devil.
1520	Matt15:23	But he answered her not a word. And his disciples came and besought him, saying, Send her away; for she crieth after us.
1521	Matt15:24	But he answered and said, I am not sent but unto the lost sheep of the house of Israel.
1522	Matt15:25	Then came she and worshipped him, saying, Lord, help me.
1523	Matt15:26	But he answered and said, It is not meet to take the children's bread, and to cast it to dogs.
1524	Mark7:27	But Jesus said unto her, Let the children first be filled: for it is not meet to take the children's bread, and to cast it unto the dogs.
1525	Matt15:27	And she said, Truth, Lord: yet the dogs eat of the crumbs which fall from their masters' table.
1526	Mark7:28	And she answered and said unto him, Yes, Lord: yet the dogs under the table eat of the children's crumbs.
1527	Mark7:29	And he said unto her, For this saying go thy way; the devil is gone out of thy daughter.
1528	Matt15:28	Then Jesus answered and said unto her, O woman, great is thy faith: be it unto thee even as thou wilt. And her daughter was made whole from that very hour.
1529	Mark7:30	And when she was come to her house, she found the devil gone out, and her daughter laid upon the bed.
1530	Mark7:31	And again, departing from the coasts of Tyre and Sidon, he came unto the sea of Galilee, through the midst of the coasts of Decapolis.
1531	Matt15:29	And Jesus departed from thence, and came nigh unto the sea of Galilee; and went up into a mountain, and sat down there.
1532	Matt15:30	And great multitudes came unto him, having with them those that were lame, blind, dumb, maimed, and many others, and cast them down at Jesus' feet; and he healed them:
1533	Mark7:32	And they bring unto him one that was deaf, and had an impediment in his speech; and they beseech him to put his hand upon him.
1534	Mark7:33	And he took him aside from the multitude, and put his fingers into his ears, and he spit, and touched his tongue;
1535	Mark7:34	And looking up to heaven, he sighed, and saith unto him, Ephphatha, that is, Be opened.
1536	Mark7:35	And straightway his ears were opened, and the string of his tongue was loosed, and he spake plain.
1537	Mark7:36	And he charged them that they should tell no man: but the more he charged them, so much the more a great deal they published it;
1538	Mark7:37	And were beyond measure astonished, saying, He hath done all things well: he maketh both the deaf to hear, and the dumb to speak.
1539	Matt15:31	Insomuch that the multitude wondered, when they saw the dumb to speak, the maimed to be whole, the lame to walk, and the blind to see: and they glorified the God of Israel.
1540	Mark8:1	In those days the multitude being very great, and having nothing to eat, Jesus called his disciples unto him, and saith unto them,

THE TREE OF LIFE

1541	Matt15:32	Then Jesus called his disciples unto him, and said, I have compassion on the multitude, because they continue with me now three days, and have nothing to eat: and I will not send them away fasting, lest they faint in the way.
1542	Mark8:2	I have compassion on the multitude, because they have now been with me three days, and have nothing to eat:
1543	Mark8:3	And if I send them away fasting to their own houses, they will faint by the way: for divers of them came from far.
1544	Matt15:33	And his disciples say unto him, Whence should we have so much bread in the wilderness, as to fill so great a multitude?
1545	Mark8:4	And his disciples answered him, From whence can a man satisfy these men with bread here in the wilderness?
1546	Matt15:34	And Jesus saith unto them, How many loaves have ye? And they said, Seven, and a few little fishes.
1547	Mark8:5	And he asked them, How many loaves have ye? And they said, Seven.
1548	Matt15:35	And he commanded the multitude to sit down on the ground.
1549	Mark8:6	And he commanded the people to sit down on the ground: and he took the seven loaves, and gave thanks, and brake, and gave to his disciples to set before them; and they did set them before the people.
1550	Mark8:7	And they had a few small fishes: and he blessed, and commanded to set them also before them.
1551	Matt15:36	And he took the seven loaves and the fishes, and gave thanks, and brake them, and gave to his disciples, and the disciples to the multitude.
1552	Mark8:8	So they did eat, and were filled: and they took up of the broken meat that was left seven baskets.
1553	Matt15:37	And they did all eat, and were filled: and they took up of the broken meat that was left seven baskets full.
1554	Mark8:9	And they that had eaten were about four thousand: and he sent them away.
1555	Matt15:38	And they that did eat were four thousand men, beside women and children.
1556	Matt15:39	And he sent away the multitude, and took ship, and came into the coasts of Magdala.
1557	Mark8:10	And straightway he entered into a ship with his disciples, and came into the parts of Dalmanutha.
1558	Matt16:1	The Pharisees also with the Sadducees came, and tempting desired him that he would shew them a sign from heaven.
1559	Mark8:11	And the Pharisees came forth, and began to question with him, seeking of him a sign from heaven, tempting him.
1560	Mark8:12	And he sighed deeply in his spirit, and saith, Why doth this generation seek after a sign? verily I say unto you, There shall no sign be given unto this generation.
1561	Matt16:2	He answered and said unto them, When it is evening, ye say, It will be fair weather: for the sky is red.
1562	Matt16:3	And in the morning, It will be foul weather to day: for the sky is red and lowring. O ye hypocrites, ye can discern the face of the sky; but can ye not discern the signs of the times?
1563	Matt16:4	A wicked and adulterous generation seeketh after a sign; and there shall no sign be given unto it, but the sign of the prophet Jonas. And he left them, and departed.
1564	Mark8:13	And he left them, and entering into the ship again departed to the other side.
1565	Mark8:14	Now the disciples had forgotten to take bread, neither had they in the ship with them more than one loaf.
1566	Matt16:5	And when his disciples were come to the other side, they had forgotten to take bread.
1567	Mark8:15	And he charged them, saying, Take heed, beware of the leaven of the Pharisees, and of the leaven of Herod.

THE TREE OF LIFE

1568	Matt16:6	Then Jesus said unto them, Take heed and beware of the leaven of the Pharisees and of the Sadducees.
1569	Mark8:16	And they reasoned among themselves, saying, It is because we have no bread.
1570	Matt16:7	And they reasoned among themselves, saying, It is because we have taken no bread.
1571	Matt16:8	Which when Jesus perceived, he said unto them, O ye of little faith, why reason ye among yourselves, because ye have brought no bread?
1572	Mark8:17	And when Jesus knew it, he saith unto them, Why reason ye, because ye have no bread? perceive ye not yet, neither understand? have ye your heart yet hardened?
1573	Mark8:18	Having eyes, see ye not? and having ears, hear ye not? and do ye not remember?
1574	Mark8:19	When I brake the five loaves among five thousand, how many baskets full of fragments took ye up? They say unto him, Twelve.
1575	Matt16:9	Do ye not yet understand, neither remember the five loaves of the five thousand, and how many baskets ye took up?
1576	Mark8:20	And when the seven among four thousand, how many baskets full of fragments took ye up? And they said, Seven.
1577	Matt16:10	Neither the seven loaves of the four thousand, and how many baskets ye took up?
1578	Mark8:21	And he said unto them, How is it that ye do not understand?
1579	Matt16:11	How is it that ye do not understand that I spake it not to you concerning bread, that ye should beware of the leaven of the Pharisees and of the Sadducees?
1580	Matt16:12	Then understood they how that he bade them not beware of the leaven of bread, but of the doctrine of the Pharisees and of the Sadducees.
1581	Mark8:22	And he cometh to Bethsaida; and they bring a blind man unto him, and besought him to touch him.
1582	Mark8:23	And he took the blind man by the hand, and led him out of the town; and when he had spit on his eyes, and put his hands upon him, he asked him if he saw ought.
1583	Mark8:24	And he looked up, and said, I see men as trees, walking.
1584	Mark8:25	After that he put his hands again upon his eyes, and made him look up: and he was restored, and saw every man clearly.
1585	Mark8:26	And he sent him away to his house, saying, Neither go into the town, nor tell it to any in the town.
1586	Mark8:27	And Jesus went out, and his disciples, into the towns of Caesarea Philippi: and by the way he asked his disciples, saying unto them, Whom do men say that I am?
1587	Matt16:13	When Jesus came into the coasts of Caesarea Philippi, he asked his disciples, saying, Whom do men say that I the Son of man am?
1588	Luke9:18	And it came to pass, as he was alone praying, his disciples were with him: and he asked them, saying, Whom say the people that I am?
1589	Mark8:28	And they answered, John the Baptist: but some say, Elias; and others, One of the prophets.
1590	Matt16:14	And they said, Some say that thou art John the Baptist: some, Elias; and others, Jeremias, or one of the prophets.
1591	Luke9:19	They answering said, John the Baptist; but some say, Elias; and others say, that one of the old prophets is risen again.
1592	Matt16:15	He saith unto them, But whom say ye that I am?
1593	Mark8:29	And he saith unto them, But whom say ye that I am? And Peter answereth and saith unto him, Thou art the Christ.
1594	Luke9:20	He said unto them, But whom say ye that I am? Peter answering said, The Christ of God.
1595	Matt16:16	And Simon Peter answered and said, Thou art the Christ, the Son of the living

THE TREE OF LIFE

		God.
1596	Matt16:17	And Jesus answered and said unto him, Blessed art thou, Simon Barjona: for flesh and blood hath not revealed it unto thee, but my Father which is in heaven.
1597	Matt16:18	And I say also unto thee, That thou art Peter, and upon this rock I will build my church; and the gates of hell shall not prevail against it.
1598	Matt16:19	And I will give unto thee the keys of the kingdom of heaven: and whatsoever thou shalt bind on earth shall be bound in heaven: and whatsoever thou shalt loose on earth shall be loosed in heaven.
1599	Matt16:20	Then charged he his disciples that they should tell no man that he was Jesus the Christ.
1600	Mark8:30	And he charged them that they should tell no man of him.
1601	Luke9:21	And he straitly charged them, and commanded them to tell no man that thing;
1602	Matt16:21	From that time forth began Jesus to shew unto his disciples, how that he must go unto Jerusalem, and suffer many things of the elders and chief priests and scribes, and be killed, and be raised again the third day.
1603	Mark8:31	And he began to teach them, that the Son of man must suffer many things, and be rejected of the elders, and of the chief priests, and scribes, and be killed, and after three days rise again.
1604	Luke9:22	Saying, The Son of man must suffer many things, and be rejected of the elders and chief priests and scribes, and be slain, and be raised the third day.
1605	Mark8:32	And he spake that saying openly. And Peter took him, and began to rebuke him.
1606	Matt16:22	Then Peter took him, and began to rebuke him, saying, Be it far from thee, Lord: this shall not be unto thee.
1607	Mark8:33	But when he had turned about and looked on his disciples, he rebuked Peter, saying, Get thee behind me, Satan: for thou savourest not the things that be of God, but the things that be of men.
1608	Matt16:23	But he turned, and said unto Peter, Get thee behind me, Satan: thou art an offence unto me: for thou savourest not the things that be of God, but those that be of men.
1609	Mark8:34	And when he had called the people unto him with his disciples also, he said unto them, Whosoever will come after me, let him deny himself, and take up his cross, and follow me.
1610	Luke9:23	And he said to them all, If any man will come after me, let him deny himself, and take up his cross daily, and follow me.
1611	Matt16:24	Then said Jesus unto his disciples, If any man will come after me, let him deny himself, and take up his cross, and follow me.
1612	Luke9:24	For whosoever will save his life shall lose it: but whosoever will lose his life for my sake, the same shall save it.
1613	Matt16:25	For whosoever will save his life shall lose it: and whosoever will lose his life for my sake shall find it.
1614	Mark8:35	For whosoever will save his life shall lose it; but whosoever shall lose his life for my sake and the gospel's, the same shall save it.
1615	Luke9:25	For what is a man advantaged, if he gain the whole world, and lose himself, or be cast away?
1616	Mark8:36	For what shall it profit a man, if he shall gain the whole world, and lose his own soul?
1617	Matt16:26	For what is a man profited, if he shall gain the whole world, and lose his own soul? or what shall a man give in exchange for his soul?
1618	Mark8:37	Or what shall a man give in exchange for his soul?
1619	Luke9:26	For whosoever shall be ashamed of me and of my words, of him shall the Son of man be ashamed, when he shall come in his own glory, and in his Father's, and of the holy angels.
1620	Mark8:38	Whosoever therefore shall be ashamed of me and of my words in this adulterous

THE TREE OF LIFE

		and sinful generation; of him also shall the Son of man be ashamed, when he cometh in the glory of his Father with the holy angels.
1621	Matt16:27	For the Son of man shall come in the glory of his Father with his angels; and then he shall reward every man according to his works.
1622	Luke9:27	But I tell you of a truth, there be some standing here, which shall not taste of death, till they see the kingdom of God.
1623	Mark9:1	And he said unto them, Verily I say unto you, That there be some of them that stand here, which shall not taste of death, till they have seen the kingdom of God come with power.
1624	Matt16:28	Verily I say unto you, There be some standing here, which shall not taste of death, till they see the Son of man coming in his kingdom.
1625	Matt17:1	And after six days Jesus taketh Peter, James, and John his brother, and bringeth them up into an high mountain apart,
1626	Luke9:28	And it came to pass about an eight days after these sayings, he took Peter and John and James, and went up into a mountain to pray.
1627	Mark9:2	And after six days Jesus taketh with him Peter, and James, and John, and leadeth them up into an high mountain apart by themselves: and he was transfigured before them.
1628	Luke9:29	And as he prayed, the fashion of his countenance was altered, and his raiment was white and glistering.
1629	Matt17:2	And was transfigured before them: and his face did shine as the sun, and his raiment was white as the light.
1630	Mark9:3	And his raiment became shining, exceeding white as snow; so as no fuller on earth can white them.
1631	Mark9:4	And there appeared unto them Elias with Moses: and they were talking with Jesus.
1632	Matt17:3	And, behold, there appeared unto them Moses and Elias talking with him.
1633	Luke9:30	And, behold, there talked with him two men, which were Moses and Elias:
1634	Luke9:31	Who appeared in glory, and spake of his decease which he should accomplish at Jerusalem.
1635	Luke9:32	But Peter and they that were with him were heavy with sleep: and when they were awake, they saw his glory, and the two men that stood with him.
1636	Luke9:33	And it came to pass, as they departed from him, Peter said unto Jesus, Master, it is good for us to be here: and let us make three tabernacles; one for thee, and one for Moses, and one for Elias: not knowing what he said.
1637	Mark9:5	And Peter answered and said to Jesus, Master, it is good for us to be here: and let us make three tabernacles; one for thee, and one for Moses, and one for Elias.
1638	Matt17:4	Then answered Peter, and said unto Jesus, Lord, it is good for us to be here: if thou wilt, let us make here three tabernacles; one for thee, and one for Moses, and one for Elias.
1639	Mark9:6	For he wist not what to say; for they were sore afraid.
1640	Luke9:34	While he thus spake, there came a cloud, and overshadowed them: and they feared as they entered into the cloud.
1641	Matt17:5	While he yet spake, behold, a bright cloud overshadowed them: and behold a voice out of the cloud, which said, This is my beloved Son, in whom I am well pleased; hear ye him.
1642	Mark9:7	And there was a cloud that overshadowed them: and a voice came out of the cloud, saying, This is my beloved Son: hear him.
1643	Luke9:35	And there came a voice out of the cloud, saying, This is my beloved Son: hear him.
1644	Matt17:6	And when the disciples heard it, they fell on their face, and were sore afraid.
1645	Matt17:7	And Jesus came and touched them, and said, Arise, and be not afraid.

THE TREE OF LIFE

1646	Mark9:8	And suddenly, when they had looked round about, they saw no man any more, save Jesus only with themselves.
1647	Matt17:8	And when they had lifted up their eyes, they saw no man, save Jesus only.
1648	Luke9:36	And when the voice was past, Jesus was found alone. And they kept it close, and told no man in those days any of those things which they had seen.
1649	Matt17:9	And as they came down from the mountain, Jesus charged them, saying, Tell the vision to no man, until the Son of man be risen again from the dead.
1650	Mark9:9	And as they came down from the mountain, he charged them that they should tell no man what things they had seen, till the Son of man were risen from the dead.
1651	Mark9:10	And they kept that saying with themselves, questioning one with another what the rising from the dead should mean.
1652	Matt17:10	And his disciples asked him, saying, Why then say the scribes that Elias must first come?
1653	Mark9:11	And they asked him, saying, Why say the scribes that Elias must first come?
1654	Matt17:11	And Jesus answered and said unto them, Elias truly shall first come, and restore all things.
1655	Mark9:12	And he answered and told them, Elias verily cometh first, and restoreth all things; and how it is written of the Son of man, that he must suffer many things, and be set at nought.
1656	Mark9:13	But I say unto you, That Elias is indeed come, and they have done unto him whatsoever they listed, as it is written of him.
1657	Matt17:12	But I say unto you, That Elias is come already, and they knew him not, but have done unto him whatsoever they listed. Likewise shall also the Son of man suffer of them.
1658	Matt17:13	Then the disciples understood that he spake unto them of John the Baptist.
1659	Luke9:37	And it came to pass, that on the next day, when they were come down from the hill, much people met him.
1660	Mark9:14	And when he came to his disciples, he saw a great multitude about them, and the scribes questioning with them.
1661	Mark9:15	And straightway all the people, when they beheld him, were greatly amazed, and running to him saluted him.
1662	Mark9:16	And he asked the scribes, What question ye with them?
1663	Matt17:14	And when they were come to the multitude, there came to him a certain man, kneeling down to him, and saying,
1664	Matt17:15	Lord, have mercy on my son: for he is lunatick, and sore vexed: for ofttimes he falleth into the fire, and oft into the water.
1665	Mark9:17	And one of the multitude answered and said, Master, I have brought unto thee my son, which hath a dumb spirit;
1666	Luke9:38	And, behold, a man of the company cried out, saying, Master, I beseech thee, look upon my son: for he is mine only child.
1667	Luke9:39	And, lo, a spirit taketh him, and he suddenly crieth out; and it teareth him that he foameth again, and bruising him hardly departeth from him.
1668	Mark9:18	And wheresoever he taketh him, he teareth him: and he foameth, and gnasheth with his teeth, and pineth away: and I spake to thy disciples that they should cast him out; and they could not.
1669	Matt17:16	And I brought him to thy disciples, and they could not cure him.
1670	Luke9:40	And I besought thy disciples to cast him out; and they could not.
1671	Luke9:41	And Jesus answering said, O faithless and perverse generation, how long shall I be with you, and suffer you? Bring thy son hither.
1672	Mark9:19	He answereth him, and saith, O faithless generation, how long shall I be with you? how long shall I suffer you? bring him unto me.
1673	Matt17:17	Then Jesus answered and said, O faithless and perverse generation, how long shall I be with you? how long shall I suffer you? bring him hither to me.

THE TREE OF LIFE

1674	Mark9:20	And they brought him unto him: and when he saw him, straightway the spirit tare him; and he fell on the ground, and wallowed foaming.
1675	Mark9:21	And he asked his father, How long is it ago since this came unto him? And he said, Of a child.
1676	Mark9:22	And ofttimes it hath cast him into the fire, and into the waters, to destroy him: but if thou canst do any thing, have compassion on us, and help us.
1677	Mark9:23	Jesus said unto him, If thou canst believe, all things are possible to him that believeth.
1678	Mark9:24	And straightway the father of the child cried out, and said with tears, Lord, I believe; help thou mine unbelief.
1679	Luke9:42	And as he was yet a coming, the devil threw him down, and tare him. And Jesus rebuked the unclean spirit, and healed the child, and delivered him again to his father.
1680	Mark9:25	When Jesus saw that the people came running together, he rebuked the foul spirit, saying unto him, Thou dumb and deaf spirit, I charge thee, come out of him, and enter no more into him.
1681	Matt17:18	And Jesus rebuked the devil; and he departed out of him: and the child was cured from that very hour.
1682	Mark9:26	And the spirit cried, and rent him sore, and came out of him: and he was as one dead; insomuch that many said, He is dead.
1683	Mark9:27	But Jesus took him by the hand, and lifted him up; and he arose.
1684	Matt17:19	Then came the disciples to Jesus apart, and said, Why could not we cast him out?
1685	Mark9:28	And when he was come into the house, his disciples asked him privately, Why could not we cast him out?
1686	Matt17:20	And Jesus said unto them, Because of your unbelief: for verily I say unto you, If ye have faith as a grain of mustard seed, ye shall say unto this mountain, Remove hence to yonder place; and it shall remove; and nothing shall be impossible unto you.
1687	Luke17:6	And the Lord said, If ye had faith as a grain of mustard seed, ye might say unto this sycamine tree, Be thou plucked up by the root, and be thou planted in the sea; and it should obey you.
1688	Luke17:5	And the apostles said unto the Lord, Increase our faith.
1689	Mark9:29	And he said unto them, This kind can come forth by nothing, but by prayer and fasting.
1690	Matt17:21	Howbeit this kind goeth not out but by prayer and fasting.
1691	John7:2	Now the Jews' feast of tabernacles was at hand.
1692	John7:3	His brethren therefore said unto him, Depart hence, and go into Judaea, that thy disciples also may see the works that thou doest.
1693	John7:4	For there is no man that doeth any thing in secret, and he himself seeketh to be known openly. If thou do these things, shew thyself to the world.
1694	John7:5	For neither did his brethren believe in him.
1695	John7:8	Go ye up unto this feast: I go not up yet unto this feast: for my time is not yet full come.
1696	John7:6	Then Jesus said unto them, My time is not yet come: but your time is alway ready.
1697	John7:7	The world cannot hate you; but me it hateth, because I testify of it, that the works thereof are evil.
1698	John7:9	When he had said these words unto them, he abode still in Galilee.
1699	John7:10	But when his brethren were gone up, then went he also up unto the feast, not openly, but as it were in secret.
1700	John7:11	Then the Jews sought him at the feast, and said, Where is he?
1701	John7:12	And there was much murmuring among the people concerning him: for some

THE TREE OF LIFE

		said, He is a good man: others said, Nay; but he deceiveth the people.
1702	John7:13	Howbeit no man spake openly of him for fear of the Jews.
1703	John7:14	Now about the midst of the feast Jesus went up into the temple, and taught.
1704	John7:15	And the Jews marvelled, saying, How knoweth this man letters, having never learned?
1705	John7:16	Jesus answered them, and said, My doctrine is not mine, but his that sent me.
1706	John7:17	If any man will do his will, he shall know of the doctrine, whether it be of God, or whether I speak of myself.
1707	John7:18	He that speaketh of himself seeketh his own glory: but he that seeketh his glory that sent him, the same is true, and no unrighteousness is in him.
1708	John7:19	Did not Moses give you the law, and yet none of you keepeth the law? Why go ye about to kill me?
1709	John7:20	The people answered and said, Thou hast a devil: who goeth about to kill thee?
1710	John7:21	Jesus answered and said unto them, I have done one work, and ye all marvel.
1711	John7:22	Moses therefore gave unto you circumcision; (not because it is of Moses, but of the fathers;) and ye on the sabbath day circumcise a man.
1712	John7:23	If a man on the sabbath day receive circumcision, that the law of Moses should not be broken; are ye angry at me, because I have made a man every whit whole on the sabbath day?
1713	John7:24	Judge not according to the appearance, but judge righteous judgment.
1714	John7:25	Then said some of them of Jerusalem, Is not this he, whom they seek to kill?
1715	John7:26	But, lo, he speaketh boldly, and they say nothing unto him. Do the rulers know indeed that this is the very Christ?
1716	John7:27	Howbeit we know this man whence he is: but when Christ cometh, no man knoweth whence he is.
1717	John7:28	Then cried Jesus in the temple as he taught, saying, Ye both know me, and ye know whence I am: and I am not come of myself, but he that sent me is true, whom ye know not.
1718	John7:29	But I know him: for I am from him, and he hath sent me.
1719	John7:30	Then they sought to take him: but no man laid hands on him, because his hour was not yet come.
1720	John7:31	And many of the people believed on him, and said, When Christ cometh, will he do more miracles than these which this man hath done?
1721	John7:32	The Pharisees heard that the people murmured such things concerning him; and the Pharisees and the chief priests sent officers to take him.
1722	John7:33	Then said Jesus unto them, Yet a little while am I with you, and then I go unto him that sent me.
1723	John7:34	Ye shall seek me, and shall not find me: and where I am, thither ye cannot come.
1724	John7:35	Then said the Jews among themselves, Whither will he go, that we shall not find him? will he go unto the dispersed among the Gentiles, and teach the Gentiles?
1725	John7:36	What manner of saying is this that he said, Ye shall seek me, and shall not find me: and where I am, thither ye cannot come?
1726	John7:37	In the last day, that great day of the feast, Jesus stood and cried, saying, If any man thirst, let him come unto me, and drink.
1727	John7:38	He that believeth on me, as the scripture hath said, out of his belly shall flow rivers of living water.
1728	John7:39	(But this spake he of the Spirit, which they that believe on him should receive: for the Holy Ghost was not yet given; because that Jesus was not yet glorified.)
1729	John7:40	Many of the people therefore, when they heard this saying, said, Of a truth this is the Prophet.
1730	John7:41	Others said, This is the Christ. But some said, Shall Christ come out of Galilee?
1731	John7:42	Hath not the scripture said, That Christ cometh of the seed of David, and out of the town of Bethlehem, where David was?

THE TREE OF LIFE

1732	John7:43	So there was a division among the people because of him.
1733	John7:44	And some of them would have taken him; but no man laid hands on him.
1734	John7:45	Then came the officers to the chief priests and Pharisees; and they said unto them, Why have ye not brought him?
1735	John7:46	The officers answered, Never man spake like this man.
1736	John7:47	Then answered them the Pharisees, Are ye also deceived?
1737	John7:48	Have any of the rulers or of the Pharisees believed on him?
1738	John7:49	But this people who knoweth not the law are cursed.
1739	John7:50	Nicodemus saith unto them, (he that came to Jesus by night, being one of them,)
1740	John7:51	Doth our law judge any man, before it hear him, and know what he doeth?
1741	John7:52	They answered and said unto him, Art thou also of Galilee? Search, and look: for out of Galilee ariseth no prophet.
1742	John7:53	And every man went unto his own house.
1743	John8:1	Jesus went unto the mount of Olives.
1744	John8:2	And early in the morning he came again into the temple, and all the people came unto him; and he sat down, and taught them.
1745	John8:3	And the scribes and Pharisees brought unto him a woman taken in adultery; and when they had set her in the midst,
1746	John8:4	They say unto him, Master, this woman was taken in adultery, in the very act.
1747	John8:5	Now Moses in the law commanded us, that such should be stoned: but what sayest thou?
1748	John8:6	This they said, tempting him, that they might have to accuse him. But Jesus stooped down, and with his finger wrote on the ground, as though he heard them not.
1749	John8:7	So when they continued asking him, he lifted up himself, and said unto them, He that is without sin among you, let him first cast a stone at her.
1750	John8:8	And again he stooped down, and wrote on the ground.
1751	John8:9	And they which heard it, being convicted by their own conscience, went out one by one, beginning at the eldest, even unto the last: and Jesus was left alone, and the woman standing in the midst.
1752	John8:10	When Jesus had lifted up himself, and saw none but the woman, he said unto her, Woman, where are those thine accusers? hath no man condemned thee?
1753	John8:11	She said, No man, Lord. And Jesus said unto her, Neither do I condemn thee: go, and sin no more.
1754	John8:12	Then spake Jesus again unto them, saying, I am the light of the world: he that followeth me shall not walk in darkness, but shall have the light of life.
1755	John8:13	The Pharisees therefore said unto him, Thou bearest record of thyself; thy record is not true.
1756	John8:14	Jesus answered and said unto them, Though I bear record of myself, yet my record is true: for I know whence I came, and whither I go; but ye cannot tell whence I come, and whither I go.
1757	John8:15	Ye judge after the flesh; I judge no man.
1758	John8:16	And yet if I judge, my judgment is true: for I am not alone, but I and the Father that sent me.
1759	John8:17	It is also written in your law, that the testimony of two men is true.
1760	John8:18	I am one that bear witness of myself, and the Father that sent me beareth witness of me.
1761	John8:19	Then said they unto him, Where is thy Father? Jesus answered, Ye neither know me, nor my Father: if ye had known me, ye should have known my Father also.
1762	John8:20	These words spake Jesus in the treasury, as he taught in the temple: and no man laid hands on him; for his hour was not yet come.
1763	John8:21	Then said Jesus again unto them, I go my way, and ye shall seek me, and shall die in your sins: whither I go, ye cannot come.

THE TREE OF LIFE

1764	John8:22	Then said the Jews, Will he kill himself? because he saith, Whither I go, ye cannot come.
1765	John8:23	And he said unto them, Ye are from beneath; I am from above: ye are of this world; I am not of this world.
1766	John8:24	I said therefore unto you, that ye shall die in your sins: for if ye believe not that I am he, ye shall die in your sins.
1767	John8:25	Then said they unto him, Who art thou? And Jesus saith unto them, Even the same that I said unto you from the beginning.
1768	John8:26	I have many things to say and to judge of you: but he that sent me is true; and I speak to the world those things which I have heard of him.
1769	John8:27	They understood not that he spake to them of the Father.
1770	John8:28	Then said Jesus unto them, When ye have lifted up the Son of man, then shall ye know that I am he, and that I do nothing of myself; but as my Father hath taught me, I speak these things.
1771	John8:29	And he that sent me is with me: the Father hath not left me alone; for I do always those things that please him.
1772	John8:30	As he spake these words, many believed on him.
1773	John8:31	Then said Jesus to those Jews which believed on him, If ye continue in my word, then are ye my disciples indeed;
1774	John8:32	And ye shall know the truth, and the truth shall make you free.
1775	John8:33	They answered him, We be Abraham's seed, and were never in bondage to any man: how sayest thou, Ye shall be made free?
1776	John8:34	Jesus answered them, Verily, verily, I say unto you, Whosoever committeth sin is the servant of sin.
1777	John8:35	And the servant abideth not in the house for ever: but the Son abideth ever.
1778	John8:36	If the Son therefore shall make you free, ye shall be free indeed.
1779	John8:37	I know that ye are Abraham's seed; but ye seek to kill me, because my word hath no place in you.
1780	John8:38	I speak that which I have seen with my Father: and ye do that which ye have seen with your father.
1781	John8:39	They answered and said unto him, Abraham is our father. Jesus saith unto them, If ye were Abraham's children, ye would do the works of Abraham.
1782	John8:40	But now ye seek to kill me, a man that hath told you the truth, which I have heard of God: this did not Abraham.
1783	John8:41	Ye do the deeds of your father. Then said they to him, We be not born of fornication; we have one Father, even God.
1784	John8:42	Jesus said unto them, If God were your Father, ye would love me: for I proceeded forth and came from God; neither came I of myself, but he sent me.
1785	John8:43	Why do ye not understand my speech? even because ye cannot hear my word.
1786	John8:44	Ye are of your father the devil, and the lusts of your father ye will do. He was a murderer from the beginning, and abode not in the truth, because there is no truth in him. When he speaketh a lie, he speaketh of his own: for he is a liar, and the father of it.
1787	John8:45	And because I tell you the truth, ye believe me not.
1788	John8:46	Which of you convinceth me of sin? And if I say the truth, why do ye not believe me?
1789	John8:47	He that is of God heareth God's words: ye therefore hear them not, because ye are not of God.
1790	John8:48	Then answered the Jews, and said unto him, Say we not well that thou art a Samaritan, and hast a devil?
1791	John8:49	Jesus answered, I have not a devil; but I honour my Father, and ye do dishonour me.
1792	John8:50	And I seek not mine own glory: there is one that seeketh and judgeth.

THE TREE OF LIFE

1793	John8:51	Verily, verily, I say unto you, If a man keep my saying, he shall never see death.
1794	John8:52	Then said the Jews unto him, Now we know that thou hast a devil. Abraham is dead, and the prophets; and thou sayest, If a man keep my saying, he shall never taste of death.
1795	John8:53	Art thou greater than our father Abraham, which is dead? and the prophets are dead: whom makest thou thyself?
1796	John8:54	Jesus answered, If I honour myself, my honour is nothing: it is my Father that honoureth me; of whom ye say, that he is your God:
1797	John8:55	Yet ye have not known him; but I know him: and if I should say, I know him not, I shall be a liar like unto you: but I know him, and keep his saying.
1798	John8:56	Your father Abraham rejoiced to see my day: and he saw it, and was glad.
1799	John8:57	Then said the Jews unto him, Thou art not yet fifty years old, and hast thou seen Abraham?
1800	John8:58	Jesus said unto them, Verily, verily, I say unto you, Before Abraham was, I am.
1801	John8:59	Then took they up stones to cast at him: but Jesus hid himself, and went out of the temple, going through the midst of them, and so passed by.
1802	Mark9:30	And they departed thence, and passed through Galilee; and he would not that any man should know it.
1803	Luke9:43	And they were all amazed at the mighty power of God. But while they wondered every one at all things which Jesus did, he said unto his disciples,
1804	Luke9:44	Let these sayings sink down into your ears: for the Son of man shall be delivered into the hands of men.
1805	Mark9:31	For he taught his disciples, and said unto them, The Son of man is delivered into the hands of men, and they shall kill him; and after that he is killed, he shall rise the third day.
1806	Matt17:22	And while they abode in Galilee, Jesus said unto them, The Son of man shall be betrayed into the hands of men:
1807	Matt17:23	And they shall kill him, and the third day he shall be raised again. And they were exceeding sorry.
1808	Mark9:32	But they understood not that saying, and were afraid to ask him.
1809	Luke9:45	But they understood not this saying, and it was hid from them, that they perceived it not: and they feared to ask him of that saying.
1810	Matt17:24	And when they were come to Capernaum, they that received tribute money came to Peter, and said, Doth not your master pay tribute?
1811	Matt17:25	He saith, Yes. And when he was come into the house, Jesus prevented him, saying, What thinkest thou, Simon? of whom do the kings of the earth take custom or tribute? of their own children, or of strangers?
1812	Matt17:26	Peter saith unto him, Of strangers. Jesus saith unto him, Then are the children free.
1813	Matt17:27	Notwithstanding, lest we should offend them, go thou to the sea, and cast an hook, and take up the fish that first cometh up; and when thou hast opened his mouth, thou shalt find a piece of money: that take, and give unto them for me and thee.
1814	Mark9:33	And he came to Capernaum: and being in the house he asked them, What was it that ye disputed among yourselves by the way?
1815	Luke22:24	And there was also a strife among them, which of them should be accounted the greatest.
1816	Mark9:34	But they held their peace: for by the way they had disputed among themselves, who should be the greatest.
1817	Luke9:46	Then there arose a reasoning among them, which of them should be greatest.
1818	Matt18:1	At the same time came the disciples unto Jesus, saying, Who is the greatest in the kingdom of heaven?
1819	Mark9:35	And he sat down, and called the twelve, and saith unto them, If any man desire to

THE TREE OF LIFE

		be first, the same shall be last of all, and servant of all.
1820	Luke9:47	And Jesus, perceiving the thought of their heart, took a child, and set him by him,
1821	Matt18:2	And Jesus called a little child unto him, and set him in the midst of them,
1822	Mark9:36	And he took a child, and set him in the midst of them: and when he had taken him in his arms, he said unto them,
1823	Matt18:3	And said, Verily I say unto you, Except ye be converted, and become as little children, ye shall not enter into the kingdom of heaven.
1824	Matt18:4	Whosoever therefore shall humble himself as this little child, the same is greatest in the kingdom of heaven.
1825	Matt18:11	For the Son of man is come to save that which was lost.
1826	Matt18:12	How think ye? if a man have an hundred sheep, and one of them be gone astray, doth he not leave the ninety and nine, and goeth into the mountains, and seeketh that which is gone astray?
1827	Matt18:13	And if so be that he find it, verily I say unto you, he rejoiceth more of that sheep, than of the ninety and nine which went not astray.
1828	Matt18:14	Even so it is not the will of your Father which is in heaven, that one of these little ones should perish.
1829	Matt18:10	Take heed that ye despise not one of these little ones; for I say unto you, That in heaven their angels do always behold the face of my Father which is in heaven.
1830	Matt18:5	And whoso shall receive one such little child in my name receiveth me.
1831	Luke9:48	And said unto them, Whosoever shall receive this child in my name receiveth me: and whosoever shall receive me receiveth him that sent me: for he that is least among you all, the same shall be great.
1832	Mark9:37	Whosoever shall receive one of such children in my name, receiveth me: and whosoever shall receive me, receiveth not me, but him that sent me.
1833	Mark9:38	And John answered him, saying, Master, we saw one casting out devils in thy name, and he followeth not us: and we forbad him, because he followeth not us.
1834	Luke9:49	And John answered and said, Master, we saw one casting out devils in thy name; and we forbad him, because he followeth not with us.
1835	Luke9:50	And Jesus said unto him, Forbid him not: for he that is not against us is for us.
1836	Mark9:39	But Jesus said, Forbid him not: for there is no man which shall do a miracle in my name, that can lightly speak evil of me.
1837	Mark9:40	For he that is not against us is on our part.
1838	Matt18:19	Again I say unto you, That if two of you shall agree on earth as touching any thing that they shall ask, it shall be done for them of my Father which is in heaven.
1839	Matt18:20	For where two or three are gathered together in my name, there am I in the midst of them.
1840	Matt18:18	Verily I say unto you, Whatsoever ye shall bind on earth shall be bound in heaven: and whatsoever ye shall loose on earth shall be loosed in heaven.
1841	Mark9:41	For whosoever shall give you a cup of water to drink in my name, because ye belong to Christ, verily I say unto you, he shall not lose his reward.
1842	Matt18:6	But whoso shall offend one of these little ones which believe in me, it were better for him that a millstone were hanged about his neck, and that he were drowned in the depth of the sea.
1843	Mark9:42	And whosoever shall offend one of these little ones that believe in me, it is better for him that a millstone were hanged about his neck, and he were cast into the sea.
1844	Luke17:2	It were better for him that a millstone were hanged about his neck, and he cast into the sea, than that he should offend one of these little ones.
1845	Matt18:7	Woe unto the world because of offences! for it must needs be that offences come; but woe to that man by whom the offence cometh!
1846	Luke17:1	Then said he unto the disciples, It is impossible but that offences will come: but woe unto him, through whom they come!

THE TREE OF LIFE

1847	Matt18:8	Wherefore if thy hand or thy foot offend thee, cut them off, and cast them from thee: it is better for thee to enter into life halt or maimed, rather than having two hands or two feet to be cast into everlasting fire.
1848	Mark9:43	And if thy hand offend thee, cut it off: it is better for thee to enter into life maimed, than having two hands to go into hell, into the fire that never shall be quenched:
1849	Mark9:44	Where their worm dieth not, and the fire is not quenched.
1850	Mark9:45	And if thy foot offend thee, cut it off: it is better for thee to enter halt into life, than having two feet to be cast into hell, into the fire that never shall be quenched:
1851	Mark9:46	Where their worm dieth not, and the fire is not quenched.
1852	Matt18:9	And if thine eye offend thee, pluck it out, and cast it from thee: it is better for thee to enter into life with one eye, rather than having two eyes to be cast into hell fire.
1853	Mark9:47	And if thine eye offend thee, pluck it out: it is better for thee to enter into the kingdom of God with one eye, than having two eyes to be cast into hell fire:
1854	Mark9:48	Where their worm dieth not, and the fire is not quenched.
1855	Luke17:3	Take heed to yourselves: If thy brother trespass against thee, rebuke him; and if he repent, forgive him.
1856	Luke17:4	And if he trespass against thee seven times in a day, and seven times in a day turn again to thee, saying, I repent; thou shalt forgive him.
1857	Matt18:15	Moreover if thy brother shall trespass against thee, go and tell him his fault between thee and him alone: if he shall hear thee, thou hast gained thy brother.
1858	Matt18:16	But if he will not hear thee, then take with thee one or two more, that in the mouth of two or three witnesses every word may be established.
1859	Matt18:17	And if he shall neglect to hear them, tell it unto the church: but if he neglect to hear the church, let him be unto thee as an heathen man and a publican.
1860	Matt18:21	Then came Peter to him, and said, Lord, how oft shall my brother sin against me, and I forgive him? till seven times?
1861	Matt18:22	Jesus saith unto him, I say not unto thee, Until seven times: but, Until seventy times seven.
1862	Matt18:23	Therefore is the kingdom of heaven likened unto a certain king, which would take account of his servants.
1863	Matt18:24	And when he had begun to reckon, one was brought unto him, which owed him ten thousand talents.
1864	Matt18:25	But forasmuch as he had not to pay, his lord commanded him to be sold, and his wife, and children, and all that he had, and payment to be made.
1865	Matt18:26	The servant therefore fell down, and worshipped him, saying, Lord, have patience with me, and I will pay thee all.
1866	Matt18:27	Then the lord of that servant was moved with compassion, and loosed him, and forgave him the debt.
1867	Matt18:28	But the same servant went out, and found one of his fellowservants, which owed him an hundred pence: and he laid hands on him, and took him by the throat, saying, Pay me that thou owest.
1868	Matt18:29	And his fellowservant fell down at his feet, and besought him, saying, Have patience with me, and I will pay thee all.
1869	Matt18:30	And he would not: but went and cast him into prison, till he should pay the debt.
1870	Matt18:31	So when his fellowservants saw what was done, they were very sorry, and came and told unto their lord all that was done.
1871	Matt18:32	Then his lord, after that he had called him, said unto him, O thou wicked servant, I forgave thee all that debt, because thou desiredst me:
1872	Matt18:33	Shouldest not thou also have had compassion on thy fellowservant, even as I had pity on thee?
1873	Matt18:34	And his lord was wroth, and delivered him to the tormentors, till he should pay all that was due unto him.
1874	Matt18:35	So likewise shall my heavenly Father do also unto you, if ye from your hearts

THE TREE OF LIFE

		forgive not every one his brother their trespasses.
1875	Luke9:51	And it came to pass, when the time was come that he should be received up, he stedfastly set his face to go to Jerusalem,
1876	Luke9:52	And sent messengers before his face: and they went, and entered into a village of the Samaritans, to make ready for him.
1877	Luke9:53	And they did not receive him, because his face was as though he would go to Jerusalem.
1878	Luke9:54	And when his disciples James and John saw this, they said, Lord, wilt thou that we command fire to come down from heaven, and consume them, even as Elias did?
1879	Luke9:55	But he turned, and rebuked them, and said, Ye know not what manner of spirit ye are of.
1880	Luke9:56	For the Son of man is not come to destroy men's lives, but to save them. And they went to another village.
1881	Matt19:1	And it came to pass, that when Jesus had finished these sayings, he departed from Galilee, and came into the coasts of Judaea beyond Jordan;
1882	Mark10:1	And he arose from thence, and cometh into the coasts of Judaea by the farther side of Jordan: and the people resort unto him again; and, as he was wont, he taught them again.
1883	Matt19:2	And great multitudes followed him; and he healed them there.
1884	Matt19:3	The Pharisees also came unto him, tempting him, and saying unto him, Is it lawful for a man to put away his wife for every cause?
1885	Mark10:2	And the Pharisees came to him, and asked him, Is it lawful for a man to put away his wife? tempting him.
1886	Mark10:3	And he answered and said unto them, What did Moses command you?
1887	Mark10:4	And they said, Moses suffered to write a bill of divorcement, and to put her away.
1888	Matt19:4	And he answered and said unto them, Have ye not read, that he which made them at the beginning made them male and female,
1889	Mark10:6	But from the beginning of the creation God made them male and female.
1890	Mark10:7	For this cause shall a man leave his father and mother, and cleave to his wife;
1891	Matt19:5	And said, For this cause shall a man leave father and mother, and shall cleave to his wife: and they twain shall be one flesh?
1892	Mark10:8	And they twain shall be one flesh: so then they are no more twain, but one flesh.
1893	Matt19:6	Wherefore they are no more twain, but one flesh. What therefore God hath joined together, let not man put asunder.
1894	Mark10:9	What therefore God hath joined together, let not man put asunder.
1895	Matt19:7	They say unto him, Why did Moses then command to give a writing of divorcement, and to put her away?
1896	Mark10:5	And Jesus answered and said unto them, For the hardness of your heart he wrote you this precept.
1897	Matt19:8	He saith unto them, Moses because of the hardness of your hearts suffered you to put away your wives: but from the beginning it was not so.
1898	Mark10:10	And in the house his disciples asked him again of the same matter.
1899	Mark10:11	And he saith unto them, Whosoever shall put away his wife, and marry another, committeth adultery against her.
1900	Matt19:9	And I say unto you, Whosoever shall put away his wife, except it be for fornication, and shall marry another, committeth adultery: and whoso marrieth her which is put away doth commit adultery.
1901	Luke16:18	Whosoever putteth away his wife, and marrieth another, committeth adultery: and whosoever marrieth her that is put away from her husband committeth adultery.
1902	Mark10:12	And if a woman shall put away her husband, and be married to another, she committeth adultery.
1903	Matt19:10	His disciples say unto him, If the case of the man be so with his wife, it is not

THE TREE OF LIFE

		good to marry.
1904	Matt19:11	But he said unto them, All men cannot receive this saying, save they to whom it is given.
1905	Matt19:12	For there are some eunuchs, which were so born from their mother's womb: and there are some eunuchs, which were made eunuchs of men: and there be eunuchs, which have made themselves eunuchs for the kingdom of heaven's sake. He that is able to receive it, let him receive it.
1906	Matt19:13	Then were there brought unto him little children, that he should put his hands on them, and pray: and the disciples rebuked them.
1907	Mark10:13	And they brought young children to him, that he should touch them: and his disciples rebuked those that brought them.
1908	Luke18:15	And they brought unto him also infants, that he would touch them: but when his disciples saw it, they rebuked them.
1909	Mark10:14	But when Jesus saw it, he was much displeased, and said unto them, Suffer the little children to come unto me, and forbid them not: for of such is the kingdom of God.
1910	Matt19:14	But Jesus said, Suffer little children, and forbid them not, to come unto me: for of such is the kingdom of heaven.
1911	Luke18:16	But Jesus called them unto him, and said, Suffer little children to come unto me, and forbid them not: for of such is the kingdom of God.
1912	Luke18:17	Verily I say unto you, Whosoever shall not receive the kingdom of God as a little child shall in no wise enter therein.
1913	Mark10:15	Verily I say unto you, Whosoever shall not receive the kingdom of God as a little child, he shall not enter therein.
1914	Mark10:16	And he took them up in his arms, put his hands upon them, and blessed them.
1915	Matt19:15	And he laid his hands on them, and departed thence.
1916	Mark10:17	And when he was gone forth into the way, there came one running, and kneeled to him, and asked him, Good Master, what shall I do that I may inherit eternal life?
1917	Matt19:16	And, behold, one came and said unto him, Good Master, what good thing shall I do, that I may have eternal life?
1918	Luke18:18	And a certain ruler asked him, saying, Good Master, what shall I do to inherit eternal life?
1919	Luke18:19	And Jesus said unto him, Why callest thou me good? none is good, save one, that is, God.
1920	Mark10:18	And Jesus said unto him, Why callest thou me good? there is none good but one, that is, God.
1921	Matt19:17	And he said unto him, Why callest thou me good? there is none good but one, that is, God: but if thou wilt enter into life, keep the commandments.
1922	Matt19:18	He saith unto him, Which? Jesus said, Thou shalt do no murder, Thou shalt not commit adultery, Thou shalt not steal, Thou shalt not bear false witness,
1923	Luke18:20	Thou knowest the commandments, Do not commit adultery, Do not kill, Do not steal, Do not bear false witness, Honour thy father and thy mother.
1924	Mark10:19	Thou knowest the commandments, Do not commit adultery, Do not kill, Do not steal, Do not bear false witness, Defraud not, Honour thy father and mother.
1925	Matt19:19	Honour thy father and thy mother: and, Thou shalt love thy neighbour as thyself.
1926	Mark10:20	And he answered and said unto him, Master, all these have I observed from my youth.
1927	Luke18:21	And he said, All these have I kept from my youth up.
1928	Matt19:20	The young man saith unto him, All these things have I kept from my youth up: what lack I yet?
1929	Mark10:21	Then Jesus beholding him loved him, and said unto him, One thing thou lackest: go thy way, sell whatsoever thou hast, and give to the poor, and thou shalt have

THE TREE OF LIFE

		treasure in heaven: and come, take up the cross, and follow me.
1930	Luke18:22	Now when Jesus heard these things, he said unto him, Yet lackest thou one thing: sell all that thou hast, and distribute unto the poor, and thou shalt have treasure in heaven: and come, follow me.
1931	Matt19:21	Jesus said unto him, If thou wilt be perfect, go and sell that thou hast, and give to the poor, and thou shalt have treasure in heaven: and come and follow me.
1932	Mark10:22	And he was sad at that saying, and went away grieved: for he had great possessions.
1933	Matt19:22	But when the young man heard that saying, he went away sorrowful: for he had great possessions.
1934	Luke18:23	And when he heard this, he was very sorrowful: for he was very rich.
1935	Luke18:24	And when Jesus saw that he was very sorrowful, he said, How hardly shall they that have riches enter into the kingdom of God!
1936	Mark10:23	And Jesus looked round about, and saith unto his disciples, How hardly shall they that have riches enter into the kingdom of God!
1937	Matt19:23	Then said Jesus unto his disciples, Verily I say unto you, That a rich man shall hardly enter into the kingdom of heaven.
1938	Mark10:24	And the disciples were astonished at his words. But Jesus answereth again, and saith unto them, Children, how hard is it for them that trust in riches to enter into the kingdom of God!
1939	Mark10:25	It is easier for a camel to go through the eye of a needle, than for a rich man to enter into the kingdom of God.
1940	Matt19:24	And again I say unto you, It is easier for a camel to go through the eye of a needle, than for a rich man to enter into the kingdom of God.
1941	Luke18:25	For it is easier for a camel to go through a needle's eye, than for a rich man to enter into the kingdom of God.
1942	Matt19:25	When his disciples heard it, they were exceedingly amazed, saying, Who then can be saved?
1943	Mark10:26	And they were astonished out of measure, saying among themselves, Who then can be saved?
1944	Luke18:26	And they that heard it said, Who then can be saved?
1945	Matt19:26	But Jesus beheld them, and said unto them, With men this is impossible; but with God all things are possible.
1946	Mark10:27	And Jesus looking upon them saith, With men it is impossible, but not with God: for with God all things are possible.
1947	Luke18:27	And he said, The things which are impossible with men are possible with God.
1948	Mark10:28	Then Peter began to say unto him, Lo, we have left all, and have followed thee.
1949	Luke18:28	Then Peter said, Lo, we have left all, and followed thee.
1950	Matt19:27	Then answered Peter and said unto him, Behold, we have forsaken all, and followed thee; what shall we have therefore?
1951	Matt19:28	And Jesus said unto them, Verily I say unto you, That ye which have followed me, in the regeneration when the Son of man shall sit in the throne of his glory, ye also shall sit upon twelve thrones, judging the twelve tribes of Israel.
1952	Luke18:29	And he said unto them, Verily I say unto you, There is no man that hath left house, or parents, or brethren, or wife, or children, for the kingdom of God's sake,
1953	Mark10:29	And Jesus answered and said, Verily I say unto you, There is no man that hath left house, or brethren, or sisters, or father, or mother, or wife, or children, or lands, for my sake, and the gospel's,
1954	Matt19:29	And every one that hath forsaken houses, or brethren, or sisters, or father, or mother, or wife, or children, or lands, for my name's sake, shall receive an hundredfold, and shall inherit everlasting life.
1955	Luke18:30	Who shall not receive manifold more in this present time, and in the world to come life everlasting.

THE TREE OF LIFE

1956	Mark10:30	But he shall receive an hundredfold now in this time, houses, and brethren, and sisters, and mothers, and children, and lands, with persecutions; and in the world to come eternal life.
1957	Matt19:30	But many that are first shall be last; and the last shall be first.
1958	Mark10:31	But many that are first shall be last; and the last first.
1959	Matt20:1	For the kingdom of heaven is like unto a man that is an householder, which went out early in the morning to hire labourers into his vineyard.
1960	Matt20:2	And when he had agreed with the labourers for a penny a day, he sent them into his vineyard.
1961	Matt20:3	And he went out about the third hour, and saw others standing idle in the marketplace,
1962	Matt20:4	And said unto them; Go ye also into the vineyard, and whatsoever is right I will give you. And they went their way.
1963	Matt20:5	Again he went out about the sixth and ninth hour, and did likewise.
1964	Matt20:6	And about the eleventh hour he went out, and found others standing idle, and saith unto them, Why stand ye here all the day idle?
1965	Matt20:7	They say unto him, Because no man hath hired us. He saith unto them, Go ye also into the vineyard; and whatsoever is right, that shall ye receive.
1966	Matt20:8	So when even was come, the lord of the vineyard saith unto his steward, Call the labourers, and give them their hire, beginning from the last unto the first.
1967	Matt20:9	And when they came that were hired about the eleventh hour, they received every man a penny.
1968	Matt20:10	But when the first came, they supposed that they should have received more; and they likewise received every man a penny.
1969	Matt20:11	And when they had received it, they murmured against the goodman of the house,
1970	Matt20:12	Saying, These last have wrought but one hour, and thou hast made them equal unto us, which have borne the burden and heat of the day.
1971	Matt20:13	But he answered one of them, and said, Friend, I do thee no wrong: didst not thou agree with me for a penny?
1972	Matt20:14	Take that thine is, and go thy way: I will give unto this last, even as unto thee.
1973	Matt20:15	Is it not lawful for me to do what I will with mine own? Is thine eye evil, because I am good?
1974	Luke16:19	There was a certain rich man, which was clothed in purple and fine linen, and fared sumptuously every day:
1975	Luke16:20	And there was a certain beggar named Lazarus, which was laid at his gate, full of sores,
1976	Luke16:21	And desiring to be fed with the crumbs which fell from the rich man's table: moreover the dogs came and licked his sores.
1977	Luke16:22	And it came to pass, that the beggar died, and was carried by the angels into Abraham's bosom: the rich man also died, and was buried;
1978	Luke16:23	And in hell he lift up his eyes, being in torments, and seeth Abraham afar off, and Lazarus in his bosom.
1979	Luke16:24	And he cried and said, Father Abraham, have mercy on me, and send Lazarus, that he may dip the tip of his finger in water, and cool my tongue; for I am tormented in this flame.
1980	Luke16:25	But Abraham said, Son, remember that thou in thy lifetime receivedst thy good things, and likewise Lazarus evil things: but now he is comforted, and thou art tormented.
1981	Luke16:26	And beside all this, between us and you there is a great gulf fixed: so that they which would pass from hence to you cannot; neither can they pass to us, that would come from thence.
1982	Luke16:27	Then he said, I pray thee therefore, father, that thou wouldest send him to my

THE TREE OF LIFE

		father's house:
1983	Luke16:28	For I have five brethren; that he may testify unto them, lest they also come into this place of torment.
1984	Luke16:29	Abraham saith unto him, They have Moses and the prophets; let them hear them.
1985	Luke16:30	And he said, Nay, father Abraham: but if one went unto them from the dead, they will repent.
1986	Luke16:31	And he said unto him, If they hear not Moses and the prophets, neither will they be persuaded, though one rose from the dead.
1987	Matt20:16	So the last shall be first, and the first last: for many be called, but few chosen.
1988	Luke16:14	And the Pharisees also, who were covetous, heard all these things: and they derided him.
1989	Luke16:15	And he said unto them, Ye are they which justify yourselves before men; but God knoweth your hearts: for that which is highly esteemed among men is abomination in the sight of God.
1990	Luke16:16	The law and the prophets were until John: since that time the kingdom of God is preached, and every man presseth into it.
1991	Luke16:17	And it is easier for heaven and earth to pass, than one tittle of the law to fail.
1992	Luke10:1	After these things the LORD appointed other seventy also, and sent them two and two before his face into every city and place, whither he himself would come.
1993	Luke10:2	Therefore said he unto them, The harvest truly is great, but the labourers are few: pray ye therefore the Lord of the harvest, that he would send forth labourers into his harvest.
1994	Luke10:3	Go your ways: behold, I send you forth as lambs among wolves.
1995	Luke10:4	Carry neither purse, nor scrip, nor shoes: and salute no man by the way.
1996	Luke10:5	And into whatsoever house ye enter, first say, Peace be to this house.
1997	Luke10:6	And if the son of peace be there, your peace shall rest upon it: if not, it shall turn to you again.
1998	Luke10:7	And in the same house remain, eating and drinking such things as they give: for the labourer is worthy of his hire. Go not from house to house.
1999	Luke10:8	And into whatsoever city ye enter, and they receive you, eat such things as are set before you:
2000	Luke10:9	And heal the sick that are therein, and say unto them, The kingdom of God is come nigh unto you.
2001	Luke10:10	But into whatsoever city ye enter, and they receive you not, go your ways out into the streets of the same, and say,
2002	Luke10:11	Even the very dust of your city, which cleaveth on us, we do wipe off against you: notwithstanding be ye sure of this, that the kingdom of God is come nigh unto you.
2003	Luke10:12	But I say unto you, that it shall be more tolerable in that day for Sodom, than for that city.
2004	Luke10:16	He that heareth you heareth me; and he that despiseth you despiseth me; and he that despiseth me despiseth him that sent me.
2005	Luke10:18	And he said unto them, I beheld Satan as lightning fall from heaven.
2006	Luke10:19	Behold, I give unto you power to tread on serpents and scorpions, and over all the power of the enemy: and nothing shall by any means hurt you.
2007	Luke12:22	And he said unto his disciples, Therefore I say unto you, Take no thought for your life, what ye shall eat; neither for the body, what ye shall put on.
2008	Luke12:23	The life is more than meat, and the body is more than raiment.
2009	Luke12:24	Consider the ravens: for they neither sow nor reap; which neither have storehouse nor barn; and God feedeth them: how much more are ye better than the fowls?
2010	Luke12:25	And which of you with taking thought can add to his stature one cubit?
2011	Luke12:26	If ye then be not able to do that thing which is least, why take ye thought for the

THE TREE OF LIFE

		rest?
2012	Luke12:27	Consider the lilies how they grow: they toil not, they spin not; and yet I say unto you, that Solomon in all his glory was not arrayed like one of these.
2013	Luke12:28	If then God so clothe the grass, which is to day in the field, and to morrow is cast into the oven; how much more will he clothe you, O ye of little faith?
2014	Luke12:29	And seek not ye what ye shall eat, or what ye shall drink, neither be ye of doubtful mind.
2015	Luke12:30	For all these things do the nations of the world seek after: and your Father knoweth that ye have need of these things.
2016	Luke12:31	But rather seek ye the kingdom of God; and all these things shall be added unto you.
2017	Luke12:32	Fear not, little flock; for it is your Father's good pleasure to give you the kingdom.
2018	Luke12:33	Sell that ye have, and give alms; provide yourselves bags which wax not old, a treasure in the heavens that faileth not, where no thief approacheth, neither moth corrupteth.
2019	Luke12:34	For where your treasure is, there will your heart be also.
2020	Luke12:35	Let your loins be girded about, and your lights burning;
2021	Luke12:36	And ye yourselves like unto men that wait for their lord, when he will return from the wedding; that when he cometh and knocketh, they may open unto him immediately.
2022	Luke12:37	Blessed are those servants, whom the lord when he cometh shall find watching: verily I say unto you, that he shall gird himself, and make them to sit down to meat, and will come forth and serve them.
2023	Luke12:38	And if he shall come in the second watch, or come in the third watch, and find them so, blessed are those servants.
2024	Luke12:39	And this know, that if the goodman of the house had known what hour the thief would come, he would have watched, and not have suffered his house to be broken through.
2025	Luke12:40	Be ye therefore ready also: for the Son of man cometh at an hour when ye think not.
2026	Luke12:41	Then Peter said unto him, Lord, speakest thou this parable unto us, or even to all?
2027	Luke12:42	And the Lord said, Who then is that faithful and wise steward, whom his lord shall make ruler over his household, to give them their portion of meat in due season?
2028	Luke12:43	Blessed is that servant, whom his lord when he cometh shall find so doing.
2029	Luke12:44	Of a truth I say unto you, that he will make him ruler over all that he hath.
2030	Luke12:45	But and if that servant say in his heart, My lord delayeth his coming; and shall begin to beat the menservants and maidens, and to eat and drink, and to be drunken;
2031	Luke12:46	The lord of that servant will come in a day when he looketh not for him, and at an hour when he is not aware, and will cut him in sunder, and will appoint him his portion with the unbelievers.
2032	Luke12:47	And that servant, which knew his lord's will, and prepared not himself, neither did according to his will, shall be beaten with many stripes.
2033	Luke12:48	But he that knew not, and did commit things worthy of stripes, shall be beaten with few stripes. For unto whomsoever much is given, of him shall be much required: and to whom men have committed much, of him they will ask the more.
2034	Luke12:54	And he said also to the people, When ye see a cloud rise out of the west, straightway ye say, There cometh a shower; and so it is.
2035	Luke12:55	And when ye see the south wind blow, ye say, There will be heat; and it cometh to pass.
2036	Luke12:56	Ye hypocrites, ye can discern the face of the sky and of the earth; but how is it that ye do not discern this time?

THE TREE OF LIFE

2037	Luke12:57	Yea, and why even of yourselves judge ye not what is right?
2038	Luke12:58	When thou goest with thine adversary to the magistrate, as thou art in the way, give diligence that thou mayest be delivered from him; lest he hale thee to the judge, and the judge deliver thee to the officer, and the officer cast thee into prison.
2039	Luke12:59	I tell thee, thou shalt not depart thence, till thou hast paid the very last mite.
2040	Luke14:25	And there went great multitudes with him: and he turned, and said unto them,
2041	Luke14:26	If any man come to me, and hate not his father, and mother, and wife, and children, and brethren, and sisters, yea, and his own life also, he cannot be my disciple.
2042	Luke14:27	And whosoever doth not bear his cross, and come after me, cannot be my disciple.
2043	Luke12:49	I am come to send fire on the earth; and what will I, if it be already kindled?
2044	Luke12:50	But I have a baptism to be baptized with; and how am I straitened till it be accomplished!
2045	Luke12:51	Suppose ye that I am come to give peace on earth? I tell you, Nay; but rather division:
2046	Luke12:52	For from henceforth there shall be five in one house divided, three against two, and two against three.
2047	Luke12:53	The father shall be divided against the son, and the son against the father; the mother against the daughter, and the daughter against the mother; the mother in law against her daughter in law, and the daughter in law against her mother in law.
2048	Luke14:28	For which of you, intending to build a tower, sitteth not down first, and counteth the cost, whether he have sufficient to finish it?
2049	Luke14:29	Lest haply, after he hath laid the foundation, and is not able to finish it, all that behold it begin to mock him,
2050	Luke14:30	Saying, This man began to build, and was not able to finish.
2051	Luke14:31	Or what king, going to make war against another king, sitteth not down first, and consulteth whether he be able with ten thousand to meet him that cometh against him with twenty thousand?
2052	Luke14:32	Or else, while the other is yet a great way off, he sendeth an ambassage, and desireth conditions of peace.
2053	Luke14:33	So likewise, whosoever he be of you that forsaketh not all that he hath, he cannot be my disciple.
2054	Luke11:1	And it came to pass, that, as he was praying in a certain place, when he ceased, one of his disciples said unto him, Lord, teach us to pray, as John also taught his disciples.
2055	Luke11:2	And he said unto them, When ye pray, say, Our Father which art in heaven, Hallowed be thy name. Thy kingdom come. Thy will be done, as in heaven, so in earth.
2056	Luke11:3	Give us day by day our daily bread.
2057	Luke11:4	And forgive us our sins; for we also forgive every one that is indebted to us. And lead us not into temptation; but deliver us from evil.
2058	Luke11:5	And he said unto them, Which of you shall have a friend, and shall go unto him at midnight, and say unto him, Friend, lend me three loaves;
2059	Luke11:6	For a friend of mine in his journey is come to me, and I have nothing to set before him?
2060	Luke11:7	And he from within shall answer and say, Trouble me not: the door is now shut, and my children are with me in bed; I cannot rise and give thee.
2061	Luke11:8	I say unto you, Though he will not rise and give him, because he is his friend, yet because of his importunity he will rise and give him as many as he needeth.
2062	Luke11:9	And I say unto you, Ask, and it shall be given you; seek, and ye shall find; knock,

THE TREE OF LIFE

		and it shall be opened unto you.
2063	Luke11:10	For every one that asketh receiveth; and he that seeketh findeth; and to him that knocketh it shall be opened.
2064	Luke11:11	If a son shall ask bread of any of you that is a father, will he give him a stone? or if he ask a fish, will he for a fish give him a serpent?
2065	Luke11:12	Or if he shall ask an egg, will he offer him a scorpion?
2066	Luke11:13	If ye then, being evil, know how to give good gifts unto your children: how much more shall your heavenly Father give the Holy Spirit to them that ask him?
2067	Luke13:1	There were present at that season some that told him of the Galilaeans, whose blood Pilate had mingled with their sacrifices.
2068	Luke13:2	And Jesus answering said unto them, Suppose ye that these Galilaeans were sinners above all the Galilaeans, because they suffered such things?
2069	Luke13:3	I tell you, Nay: but, except ye repent, ye shall all likewise perish.
2070	Luke13:4	Or those eighteen, upon whom the tower in Siloam fell, and slew them, think ye that they were sinners above all men that dwelt in Jerusalem?
2071	Luke13:5	I tell you, Nay: but, except ye repent, ye shall all likewise perish.
2072	Luke13:6	He spake also this parable; A certain man had a fig tree planted in his vineyard; and he came and sought fruit thereon, and found none.
2073	Luke13:7	Then said he unto the dresser of his vineyard, Behold, these three years I come seeking fruit on this fig tree, and find none: cut it down; why cumbereth it the ground?
2074	Luke13:8	And he answering said unto him, Lord, let it alone this year also, till I shall dig about it, and dung it:
2075	Luke13:9	And if it bear fruit, well: and if not, then after that thou shalt cut it down.
2076	Luke10:38	Now it came to pass, as they went, that he entered into a certain village: and a certain woman named Martha received him into her house.
2077	Luke10:39	And she had a sister called Mary, which also sat at Jesus' feet, and heard his word.
2078	Luke10:40	But Martha was cumbered about much serving, and came to him, and said, Lord, dost thou not care that my sister hath left me to serve alone? bid her therefore that she help me.
2079	Luke10:41	And Jesus answered and said unto her, Martha, Martha, thou art careful and troubled about many things:
2080	Luke10:42	But one thing is needful: and Mary hath chosen that good part, which shall not be taken away from her.
2081	Luke10:17	And the seventy returned again with joy, saying, Lord, even the devils are subject unto us through thy name.
2082	Luke10:20	Notwithstanding in this rejoice not, that the spirits are subject unto you; but rather rejoice, because your names are written in heaven.
2083	Luke10:21	In that hour Jesus rejoiced in spirit, and said, I thank thee, O Father, Lord of heaven and earth, that thou hast hid these things from the wise and prudent, and hast revealed them unto babes: even so, Father; for so it seemed good in thy sight.
2084	Luke10:22	All things are delivered to me of my Father: and no man knoweth who the Son is, but the Father; and who the Father is, but the Son, and he to whom the Son will reveal him.
2085	John1:18	No man hath seen God at any time; the only begotten Son, which is in the bosom of the Father, he hath declared him.
2086	Luke10:23	And he turned him unto his disciples, and said privately, Blessed are the eyes which see the things that ye see:
2087	Luke10:24	For I tell you, that many prophets and kings have desired to see those things which ye see, and have not seen them; and to hear those things which ye hear, and have not heard them.

THE TREE OF LIFE

2088	Luke17:22	And he said unto the disciples, The days will come, when ye shall desire to see one of the days of the Son of man, and ye shall not see it.
2089	Luke10:25	And, behold, a certain lawyer stood up, and tempted him, saying, Master, what shall I do to inherit eternal life?
2090	Luke10:26	He said unto him, What is written in the law? how readest thou?
2091	Luke10:27	And he answering said, Thou shalt love the Lord thy God with all thy heart, and with all thy soul, and with all thy strength, and with all thy mind; and thy neighbour as thyself.
2092	Luke10:28	And he said unto him, Thou hast answered right: this do, and thou shalt live.
2093	Luke10:29	But he, willing to justify himself, said unto Jesus, And who is my neighbour?
2094	Luke10:30	And Jesus answering said, A certain man went down from Jerusalem to Jericho, and fell among thieves, which stripped him of his raiment, and wounded him, and departed, leaving him half dead.
2095	Luke10:31	And by chance there came down a certain priest that way: and when he saw him, he passed by on the other side.
2096	Luke10:32	And likewise a Levite, when he was at the place, came and looked on him, and passed by on the other side.
2097	Luke10:33	But a certain Samaritan, as he journeyed, came where he was: and when he saw him, he had compassion on him,
2098	Luke10:34	And went to him, and bound up his wounds, pouring in oil and wine, and set him on his own beast, and brought him to an inn, and took care of him.
2099	Luke10:35	And on the morrow when he departed, he took out two pence, and gave them to the host, and said unto him, Take care of him; and whatsoever thou spendest more, when I come again, I will repay thee.
2100	Luke10:36	Which now of these three, thinkest thou, was neighbour unto him that fell among the thieves?
2101	Luke10:37	And he said, He that shewed mercy on him. Then said Jesus unto him, Go, and do thou likewise.
2102	Luke11:37	And as he spake, a certain Pharisee besought him to dine with him: and he went in, and sat down to meat.
2103	Luke11:38	And when the Pharisee saw it, he marvelled that he had not first washed before dinner.
2104	Luke11:39	And the Lord said unto him, Now do ye Pharisees make clean the outside of the cup and the platter; but your inward part is full of ravening and wickedness.
2105	Luke11:40	Ye fools, did not he that made that which is without make that which is within also?
2106	Luke11:41	But rather give alms of such things as ye have; and, behold, all things are clean unto you.
2107	Luke11:42	But woe unto you, Pharisees! for ye tithe mint and rue and all manner of herbs, and pass over judgment and the love of God: these ought ye to have done, and not to leave the other undone.
2108	Luke11:43	Woe unto you, Pharisees! for ye love the uppermost seats in the synagogues, and greetings in the markets.
2109	Luke11:44	Woe unto you, scribes and Pharisees, hypocrites! for ye are as graves which appear not, and the men that walk over them are not aware of them.
2110	Luke11:45	Then answered one of the lawyers, and said unto him, Master, thus saying thou reproachest us also.
2111	Luke11:46	And he said, Woe unto you also, ye lawyers! for ye lade men with burdens grievous to be borne, and ye yourselves touch not the burdens with one of your fingers.
2112	Luke11:47	Woe unto you! for ye build the sepulchres of the prophets, and your fathers killed them.
2113	Luke11:48	Truly ye bear witness that ye allow the deeds of your fathers: for they indeed

THE TREE OF LIFE

		killed them, and ye build their sepulchres.
2114	Luke11:49	Therefore also said the wisdom of God, I will send them prophets and apostles, and some of them they shall slay and persecute:
2115	Luke11:52	Woe unto you, lawyers! for ye have taken away the key of knowledge: ye entered not in yourselves, and them that were entering in ye hindered.
2116	Luke11:53	And as he said these things unto them, the scribes and the Pharisees began to urge him vehemently, and to provoke him to speak of many things:
2117	Luke11:54	Laying wait for him, and seeking to catch something out of his mouth, that they might accuse him.
2118	Luke12:1	In the mean time, when there were gathered together an innumerable multitude of people, insomuch that they trode one upon another, he began to say unto his disciples first of all, Beware ye of the leaven of the Pharisees, which is hypocrisy.
2119	Luke12:2	For there is nothing covered, that shall not be revealed; neither hid, that shall not be known.
2120	Luke12:3	Therefore whatsoever ye have spoken in darkness shall be heard in the light; and that which ye have spoken in the ear in closets shall be proclaimed upon the housetops.
2121	Luke12:4	And I say unto you my friends, Be not afraid of them that kill the body, and after that have no more that they can do.
2122	Luke12:5	But I will forewarn you whom ye shall fear: Fear him, which after he hath killed hath power to cast into hell; yea, I say unto you, Fear him.
2123	Luke12:6	Are not five sparrows sold for two farthings, and not one of them is forgotten before God?
2124	Luke12:7	But even the very hairs of your head are all numbered. Fear not therefore: ye are of more value than many sparrows.
2125	Luke12:13	And one of the company said unto him, Master, speak to my brother, that he divide the inheritance with me.
2126	Luke12:14	And he said unto him, Man, who made me a judge or a divider over you?
2127	Luke12:15	And he said unto them, Take heed, and beware of covetousness: for a man's life consisteth not in the abundance of the things which he possesseth.
2128	Luke12:16	And he spake a parable unto them, saying, The ground of a certain rich man brought forth plentifully:
2129	Luke12:17	And he thought within himself, saying, What shall I do, because I have no room where to bestow my fruits?
2130	Luke12:18	And he said, This will I do: I will pull down my barns, and build greater; and there will I bestow all my fruits and my goods.
2131	Luke12:19	And I will say to my soul, Soul, thou hast much goods laid up for many years; take thine ease, eat, drink, and be merry.
2132	Luke12:20	But God said unto him, Thou fool, this night thy soul shall be required of thee: then whose shall those things be, which thou hast provided?
2133	Luke12:21	So is he that layeth up treasure for himself, and is not rich toward God.
2134	Luke13:22	And he went through the cities and villages, teaching, and journeying toward Jerusalem.
2135	Luke13:10	And he was teaching in one of the synagogues on the sabbath.
2136	Luke13:11	And, behold, there was a woman which had a spirit of infirmity eighteen years, and was bowed together, and could in no wise lift up herself.
2137	Luke13:12	And when Jesus saw her, he called her to him, and said unto her, Woman, thou art loosed from thine infirmity.
2138	Luke13:13	And he laid his hands on her: and immediately she was made straight, and glorified God.
2139	Luke13:14	And the ruler of the synagogue answered with indignation, because that Jesus had healed on the sabbath day, and said unto the people, There are six days in which men ought to work: in them therefore come and be healed, and not on the

		sabbath day.
2140	Luke13:15	The Lord then answered him, and said, Thou hypocrite, doth not each one of you on the sabbath loose his ox or his ass from the stall, and lead him away to watering?
2141	Luke13:16	And ought not this woman, being a daughter of Abraham, whom Satan hath bound, lo, these eighteen years, be loosed from this bond on the sabbath day?
2142	Luke13:17	And when he had said these things, all his adversaries were ashamed: and all the people rejoiced for all the glorious things that were done by him.
2143	Luke13:23	Then said one unto him, Lord, are there few that be saved? And he said unto them,
2144	Luke13:24	Strive to enter in at the strait gate: for many, I say unto you, will seek to enter in, and shall not be able.
2145	Luke13:25	When once the master of the house is risen up, and hath shut to the door, and ye begin to stand without, and to knock at the door, saying, Lord, Lord, open unto us; and he shall answer and say unto you, I know you not whence ye are:
2146	Luke13:26	Then shall ye begin to say, We have eaten and drunk in thy presence, and thou hast taught in our streets.
2147	Luke13:27	But he shall say, I tell you, I know you not whence ye are; depart from me, all ye workers of iniquity.
2148	Luke13:28	There shall be weeping and gnashing of teeth, when ye shall see Abraham, and Isaac, and Jacob, and all the prophets, in the kingdom of God, and you yourselves thrust out.
2149	Luke13:29	And they shall come from the east, and from the west, and from the north, and from the south, and shall sit down in the kingdom of God.
2150	Luke13:30	And, behold, there are last which shall be first, and there are first which shall be last.
2151	Luke13:31	The same day there came certain of the Pharisees, saying unto him, Get thee out, and depart hence: for Herod will kill thee.
2152	Luke13:32	And he said unto them, Go ye, and tell that fox, Behold, I cast out devils, and I do cures to day and to morrow, and the third day I shall be perfected.
2153	Luke13:33	Nevertheless I must walk to day, and to morrow, and the day following: for it cannot be that a prophet perish out of Jerusalem.
2154	Luke13:34	O Jerusalem, Jerusalem, which killest the prophets, and stonest them that are sent unto thee; how often would I have gathered thy children together, as a hen doth gather her brood under her wings, and ye would not!
2155	Luke13:35	Behold, your house is left unto you desolate: and verily I say unto you, Ye shall not see me, until the time come when ye shall say, Blessed is he that cometh in the name of the Lord.
2156	Luke14:1	And it came to pass, as he went into the house of one of the chief Pharisees to eat bread on the sabbath day, that they watched him.
2157	Luke14:2	And, behold, there was a certain man before him which had the dropsy.
2158	Luke14:3	And Jesus answering spake unto the lawyers and Pharisees, saying, Is it lawful to heal on the sabbath day?
2159	Luke14:4	And they held their peace. And he took him, and healed him, and let him go;
2160	Luke14:5	And answered them, saying, Which of you shall have an ass or an ox fallen into a pit, and will not straightway pull him out on the sabbath day?
2161	Luke14:6	And they could not answer him again to these things.
2162	Luke14:7	And he put forth a parable to those which were bidden, when he marked how they chose out the chief rooms; saying unto them,
2163	Luke14:8	When thou art bidden of any man to a wedding, sit not down in the highest room; lest a more honourable man than thou be bidden of him;
2164	Luke14:9	And he that bade thee and him come and say to thee, Give this man place; and thou begin with shame to take the lowest room.

THE TREE OF LIFE

2165	Luke14:10	But when thou art bidden, go and sit down in the lowest room; that when he that bade thee cometh, he may say unto thee, Friend, go up higher: then shalt thou have worship in the presence of them that sit at meat with thee.
2166	Luke17:7	But which of you, having a servant plowing or feeding cattle, will say unto him by and by, when he is come from the field, Go and sit down to meat?
2167	Luke17:8	And will not rather say unto him, Make ready wherewith I may sup, and gird thyself, and serve me, till I have eaten and drunken; and afterward thou shalt eat and drink?
2168	Luke17:9	Doth he thank that servant because he did the things that were commanded him? I trow not.
2169	Luke17:10	So likewise ye, when ye shall have done all those things which are commanded you, say, We are unprofitable servants: we have done that which was our duty to do.
2170	Luke14:11	For whosoever exalteth himself shall be abased; and he that humbleth himself shall be exalted.
2171	Luke14:12	Then said he also to him that bade him, When thou makest a dinner or a supper, call not thy friends, nor thy brethren, neither thy kinsmen, nor thy rich neighbours; lest they also bid thee again, and a recompence be made thee.
2172	Luke14:13	But when thou makest a feast, call the poor, the maimed, the lame, the blind:
2173	Luke14:14	And thou shalt be blessed; for they cannot recompense thee: for thou shalt be recompensed at the resurrection of the just.
2174	Luke14:15	And when one of them that sat at meat with him heard these things, he said unto him, Blessed is he that shall eat bread in the kingdom of God.
2175	Luke14:16	Then said he unto him, A certain man made a great supper, and bade many:
2176	Luke14:17	And sent his servant at supper time to say to them that were bidden, Come; for all things are now ready.
2177	Luke14:18	And they all with one consent began to make excuse. The first said unto him, I have bought a piece of ground, and I must needs go and see it: I pray thee have me excused.
2178	Luke14:19	And another said, I have bought five yoke of oxen, and I go to prove them: I pray thee have me excused.
2179	Luke14:20	And another said, I have married a wife, and therefore I cannot come.
2180	Luke14:21	So that servant came, and shewed his lord these things. Then the master of the house being angry said to his servant, Go out quickly into the streets and lanes of the city, and bring in hither the poor, and the maimed, and the halt, and the blind.
2181	Luke14:22	And the servant said, Lord, it is done as thou hast commanded, and yet there is room.
2182	Luke14:23	And the lord said unto the servant, Go out into the highways and hedges, and compel them to come in, that my house may be filled.
2183	Luke14:24	For I say unto you, That none of those men which were bidden shall taste of my supper.
2184	Luke15:1	Then drew near unto him all the publicans and sinners for to hear him.
2185	Luke15:2	And the Pharisees and scribes murmured, saying, This man receiveth sinners, and eateth with them.
2186	Luke15:3	And he spake this parable unto them, saying,
2187	Luke15:4	What man of you, having an hundred sheep, if he lose one of them, doth not leave the ninety and nine in the wilderness, and go after that which is lost, until he find it?
2188	Luke15:5	And when he hath found it, he layeth it on his shoulders, rejoicing.
2189	Luke15:6	And when he cometh home, he calleth together his friends and neighbours, saying unto them, Rejoice with me; for I have found my sheep which was lost.
2190	Luke15:7	I say unto you, that likewise joy shall be in heaven over one sinner that repenteth, more than over ninety and nine just persons, which need no repentance.

THE TREE OF LIFE

2191	Luke15:8	Either what woman having ten pieces of silver, if she lose one piece, doth not light a candle, and sweep the house, and seek diligently till she find it?
2192	Luke15:9	And when she hath found it, she calleth her friends and her neighbours together, saying, Rejoice with me; for I have found the piece which I had lost.
2193	Luke15:10	Likewise, I say unto you, there is joy in the presence of the angels of God over one sinner that repenteth.
2194	Luke15:11	And he said, A certain man had two sons:
2195	Luke15:12	And the younger of them said to his father, Father, give me the portion of goods that falleth to me. And he divided unto them his living.
2196	Luke15:13	And not many days after the younger son gathered all together, and took his journey into a far country, and there wasted his substance with riotous living.
2197	Luke15:14	And when he had spent all, there arose a mighty famine in that land; and he began to be in want.
2198	Luke15:15	And he went and joined himself to a citizen of that country; and he sent him into his fields to feed swine.
2199	Luke15:16	And he would fain have filled his belly with the husks that the swine did eat: and no man gave unto him.
2200	Luke15:17	And when he came to himself, he said, How many hired servants of my father's have bread enough and to spare, and I perish with hunger!
2201	Luke15:18	I will arise and go to my father, and will say unto him, Father, I have sinned against heaven, and before thee,
2202	Luke15:19	And am no more worthy to be called thy son: make me as one of thy hired servants.
2203	Luke15:20	And he arose, and came to his father. But when he was yet a great way off, his father saw him, and had compassion, and ran, and fell on his neck, and kissed him.
2204	Luke15:21	And the son said unto him, Father, I have sinned against heaven, and in thy sight, and am no more worthy to be called thy son.
2205	Luke15:22	But the father said to his servants, Bring forth the best robe, and put it on him; and put a ring on his hand, and shoes on his feet:
2206	Luke15:23	And bring hither the fatted calf, and kill it; and let us eat, and be merry:
2207	Luke15:24	For this my son was dead, and is alive again; he was lost, and is found. And they began to be merry.
2208	Luke15:25	Now his elder son was in the field: and as he came and drew nigh to the house, he heard musick and dancing.
2209	Luke15:26	And he called one of the servants, and asked what these things meant.
2210	Luke15:27	And he said unto him, Thy brother is come; and thy father hath killed the fatted calf, because he hath received him safe and sound.
2211	Luke15:28	And he was angry, and would not go in: therefore came his father out, and intreated him.
2212	Luke15:29	And he answering said to his father, Lo, these many years do I serve thee, neither transgressed I at any time thy commandment: and yet thou never gavest me a kid, that I might make merry with my friends:
2213	Luke15:30	But as soon as this thy son was come, which hath devoured thy living with harlots, thou hast killed for him the fatted calf.
2214	Luke15:31	And he said unto him, Son, thou art ever with me, and all that I have is thine.
2215	Luke15:32	It was meet that we should make merry, and be glad: for this thy brother was dead, and is alive again; and was lost, and is found.
2216	Luke17:11	And it came to pass, as he went to Jerusalem, that he passed through the midst of Samaria and Galilee.
2217	Luke17:12	And as he entered into a certain village, there met him ten men that were lepers, which stood afar off:
2218	Luke17:13	And they lifted up their voices, and said, Jesus, Master, have mercy on us.

THE TREE OF LIFE

2219	Luke17:14	And when he saw them, he said unto them, Go shew yourselves unto the priests. And it came to pass, that, as they went, they were cleansed.
2220	Luke17:15	And one of them, when he saw that he was healed, turned back, and with a loud voice glorified God,
2221	Luke17:16	And fell down on his face at his feet, giving him thanks: and he was a Samaritan.
2222	Luke17:17	And Jesus answering said, Were there not ten cleansed? but where are the nine?
2223	Luke17:18	There are not found that returned to give glory to God, save this stranger.
2224	Luke17:19	And he said unto him, Arise, go thy way: thy faith hath made thee whole.
2225	John9:1	And as Jesus passed by, he saw a man which was blind from his birth.
2226	John9:2	And his disciples asked him, saying, Master, who did sin, this man, or his parents, that he was born blind?
2227	John9:3	Jesus answered, Neither hath this man sinned, nor his parents: but that the works of God should be made manifest in him.
2228	John9:4	I must work the works of him that sent me, while it is day: the night cometh, when no man can work.
2229	John9:5	As long as I am in the world, I am the light of the world.
2230	John9:6	When he had thus spoken, he spat on the ground, and made clay of the spittle, and he anointed the eyes of the blind man with the clay,
2231	John9:7	And said unto him, Go, wash in the pool of Siloam, (which is by interpretation, Sent.) He went his way therefore, and washed, and came seeing.
2232	John9:8	The neighbours therefore, and they which before had seen him that he was blind, said, Is not this he that sat and begged?
2233	John9:9	Some said, This is he: others said, He is like him: but he said, I am he.
2234	John9:10	Therefore said they unto him, How were thine eyes opened?
2235	John9:11	He answered and said, A man that is called Jesus made clay, and anointed mine eyes, and said unto me, Go to the pool of Siloam, and wash: and I went and washed, and I received sight.
2236	John9:12	Then said they unto him, Where is he? He said, I know not.
2237	John9:13	They brought to the Pharisees him that aforetime was blind.
2238	John9:14	And it was the sabbath day when Jesus made the clay, and opened his eyes.
2239	John9:15	Then again the Pharisees also asked him how he had received his sight. He said unto them, He put clay upon mine eyes, and I washed, and do see.
2240	John9:16	Therefore said some of the Pharisees, This man is not of God, because he keepeth not the sabbath day. Others said, How can a man that is a sinner do such miracles? And there was a division among them.
2241	John9:17	They say unto the blind man again, What sayest thou of him, that he hath opened thine eyes? He said, He is a prophet.
2242	John9:18	But the Jews did not believe concerning him, that he had been blind, and received his sight, until they called the parents of him that had received his sight.
2243	John9:19	And they asked them, saying, Is this your son, who ye say was born blind? how then doth he now see?
2244	John9:20	His parents answered them and said, We know that this is our son, and that he was born blind:
2245	John9:21	But by what means he now seeth, we know not; or who hath opened his eyes, we know not: he is of age; ask him: he shall speak for himself.
2246	John9:22	These words spake his parents, because they feared the Jews: for the Jews had agreed already, that if any man did confess that he was Christ, he should be put out of the synagogue.
2247	John9:23	Therefore said his parents, He is of age; ask him.
2248	John9:24	Then again called they the man that was blind, and said unto him, Give God the praise: we know that this man is a sinner.
2249	John9:25	He answered and said, Whether he be a sinner or no, I know not: one thing I know, that, whereas I was blind, now I see.

THE TREE OF LIFE

2250	John9:26	Then said they to him again, What did he to thee? how opened he thine eyes?
2251	John9:27	He answered them, I have told you already, and ye did not hear: wherefore would ye hear it again? will ye also be his disciples?
2252	John9:28	Then they reviled him, and said, Thou art his disciple; but we are Moses' disciples.
2253	John9:29	We know that God spake unto Moses: as for this fellow, we know not from whence he is.
2254	John9:30	The man answered and said unto them, Why herein is a marvellous thing, that ye know not from whence he is, and yet he hath opened mine eyes.
2255	John9:31	Now we know that God heareth not sinners: but if any man be a worshipper of God, and doeth his will, him he heareth.
2256	John9:32	Since the world began was it not heard that any man opened the eyes of one that was born blind.
2257	John9:33	If this man were not of God, he could do nothing.
2258	John9:34	They answered and said unto him, Thou wast altogether born in sins, and dost thou teach us? And they cast him out.
2259	John9:35	Jesus heard that they had cast him out; and when he had found him, he said unto him, Dost thou believe on the Son of God?
2260	John9:36	He answered and said, Who is he, Lord, that I might believe on him?
2261	John9:37	And Jesus said unto him, Thou hast both seen him, and it is he that talketh with thee.
2262	John9:38	And he said, Lord, I believe. And he worshipped him.
2263	John9:39	And Jesus said, For judgment I am come into this world, that they which see not might see; and that they which see might be made blind.
2264	John9:40	And some of the Pharisees which were with him heard these words, and said unto him, Are we blind also?
2265	John9:41	Jesus said unto them, If ye were blind, ye should have no sin: but now ye say, We see; therefore your sin remaineth.
2266	John10:1	Verily, verily, I say unto you, He that entereth not by the door into the sheepfold, but climbeth up some other way, the same is a thief and a robber.
2267	John10:2	But he that entereth in by the door is the shepherd of the sheep.
2268	John10:3	To him the porter openeth; and the sheep hear his voice: and he calleth his own sheep by name, and leadeth them out.
2269	John10:4	And when he putteth forth his own sheep, he goeth before them, and the sheep follow him: for they know his voice.
2270	John10:5	And a stranger will they not follow, but will flee from him: for they know not the voice of strangers.
2271	John10:6	This parable spake Jesus unto them: but they understood not what things they were which he spake unto them.
2272	John10:7	Then said Jesus unto them again, Verily, verily, I say unto you, I am the door of the sheep.
2273	John10:8	All that ever came before me are thieves and robbers: but the sheep did not hear them.
2274	John10:9	I am the door: by me if any man enter in, he shall be saved, and shall go in and out, and find pasture.
2275	John10:10	The thief cometh not, but for to steal, and to kill, and to destroy: I am come that they might have life, and that they might have it more abundantly.
2276	John10:11	I am the good shepherd: the good shepherd giveth his life for the sheep.
2277	John10:12	But he that is an hireling, and not the shepherd, whose own the sheep are not, seeth the wolf coming, and leaveth the sheep, and fleeth: and the wolf catcheth them, and scattereth the sheep.
2278	John10:13	The hireling fleeth, because he is an hireling, and careth not for the sheep.
2279	John10:14	I am the good shepherd, and know my sheep, and am known of mine.

THE TREE OF LIFE

2280	John10:15	As the Father knoweth me, even so know I the Father: and I lay down my life for the sheep.
2281	John10:16	And other sheep I have, which are not of this fold: them also I must bring, and they shall hear my voice; and there shall be one fold, and one shepherd.
2282	John10:17	Therefore doth my Father love me, because I lay down my life, that I might take it again.
2283	John10:18	No man taketh it from me, but I lay it down of myself. I have power to lay it down, and I have power to take it again. This commandment have I received of my Father.
2284	John10:19	There was a division therefore again among the Jews for these sayings.
2285	John10:20	And many of them said, He hath a devil, and is mad; why hear ye him?
2286	John10:21	Others said, These are not the words of him that hath a devil. Can a devil open the eyes of the blind?
2287	John10:22	And it was at Jerusalem the feast of the dedication, and it was winter.
2288	John10:23	And Jesus walked in the temple in Solomon's porch.
2289	John10:24	Then came the Jews round about him, and said unto him, How long dost thou make us to doubt? If thou be the Christ, tell us plainly.
2290	John10:25	Jesus answered them, I told you, and ye believed not: the works that I do in my Father's name, they bear witness of me.
2291	John10:26	But ye believe not, because ye are not of my sheep, as I said unto you.
2292	John10:27	My sheep hear my voice, and I know them, and they follow me:
2293	John10:28	And I give unto them eternal life; and they shall never perish, neither shall any man pluck them out of my hand.
2294	John10:29	My Father, which gave them me, is greater than all; and no man is able to pluck them out of my Father's hand.
2295	John10:30	I and my Father are one.
2296	John10:31	Then the Jews took up stones again to stone him.
2297	John10:32	Jesus answered them, Many good works have I shewed you from my Father; for which of those works do ye stone me?
2298	John10:33	The Jews answered him, saying, For a good work we stone thee not; but for blasphemy; and because that thou, being a man, makest thyself God.
2299	John10:34	Jesus answered them, Is it not written in your law, I said, Ye are gods?
2300	John10:35	If he called them gods, unto whom the word of God came, and the scripture cannot be broken;
2301	John10:36	Say ye of him, whom the Father hath sanctified, and sent into the world, Thou blasphemest; because I said, I am the Son of God?
2302	John10:37	If I do not the works of my Father, believe me not.
2303	John10:38	But if I do, though ye believe not me, believe the works: that ye may know, and believe, that the Father is in me, and I in him.
2304	John10:39	Therefore they sought again to take him: but he escaped out of their hand,
2305	John10:40	And went away again beyond Jordan into the place where John at first baptized; and there he abode.
2306	John10:41	And many resorted unto him, and said, John did no miracle: but all things that John spake of this man were true.
2307	John10:42	And many believed on him there.
2308	John11:1	Now a certain man was sick, named Lazarus, of Bethany, the town of Mary and her sister Martha.
2309	John11:2	(It was that Mary which anointed the Lord with ointment, and wiped his feet with her hair, whose brother Lazarus was sick.)
2310	John11:3	Therefore his sisters sent unto him, saying, Lord, behold, he whom thou lovest is sick.
2311	John11:4	When Jesus heard that, he said, This sickness is not unto death, but for the glory of God, that the Son of God might be glorified thereby.

THE TREE OF LIFE

2312	John11:5	Now Jesus loved Martha, and her sister, and Lazarus.
2313	John11:6	When he had heard therefore that he was sick, he abode two days still in the same place where he was.
2314	John11:7	Then after that saith he to his disciples, Let us go into Judaea again.
2315	John11:8	His disciples say unto him, Master, the Jews of late sought to stone thee; and goest thou thither again?
2316	John11:9	Jesus answered, Are there not twelve hours in the day? If any man walk in the day, he stumbleth not, because he seeth the light of this world.
2317	John11:10	But if a man walk in the night, he stumbleth, because there is no light in him.
2318	John11:11	These things said he: and after that he saith unto them, Our friend Lazarus sleepeth; but I go, that I may awake him out of sleep.
2319	John11:12	Then said his disciples, Lord, if he sleep, he shall do well.
2320	John11:13	Howbeit Jesus spake of his death: but they thought that he had spoken of taking of rest in sleep.
2321	John11:14	Then said Jesus unto them plainly, Lazarus is dead.
2322	John11:15	And I am glad for your sakes that I was not there, to the intent ye may believe; nevertheless let us go unto him.
2323	John11:16	Then said Thomas, which is called Didymus, unto his fellowdisciples, Let us also go, that we may die with him.
2324	John11:18	Now Bethany was nigh unto Jerusalem, about fifteen furlongs off:
2325	John11:19	And many of the Jews came to Martha and Mary, to comfort them concerning their brother.
2326	John11:20	Then Martha, as soon as she heard that Jesus was coming, went and met him: but Mary sat still in the house.
2327	John11:21	Then said Martha unto Jesus, Lord, if thou hadst been here, my brother had not died.
2328	John11:22	But I know, that even now, whatsoever thou wilt ask of God, God will give it thee.
2329	John11:23	Jesus saith unto her, Thy brother shall rise again.
2330	John11:24	Martha saith unto him, I know that he shall rise again in the resurrection at the last day.
2331	John11:25	Jesus said unto her, I am the resurrection, and the life: he that believeth in me, though he were dead, yet shall he live:
2332	John11:26	And whosoever liveth and believeth in me shall never die. Believest thou this?
2333	John11:27	She saith unto him, Yea, Lord: I believe that thou art the Christ, the Son of God, which should come into the world.
2334	John11:28	And when she had so said, she went her way, and called Mary her sister secretly, saying, The Master is come, and calleth for thee.
2335	John11:29	As soon as she heard that, she arose quickly, and came unto him.
2336	John11:30	Now Jesus was not yet come into the town, but was in that place where Martha met him.
2337	John11:31	The Jews then which were with her in the house, and comforted her, when they saw Mary, that she rose up hastily and went out, followed her, saying, She goeth unto the grave to weep there.
2338	John11:32	Then when Mary was come where Jesus was, and saw him, she fell down at his feet, saying unto him, Lord, if thou hadst been here, my brother had not died.
2339	John11:33	When Jesus therefore saw her weeping, and the Jews also weeping which came with her, he groaned in the spirit, and was troubled,
2340	John11:35	Jesus wept.
2341	John11:36	Then said the Jews, Behold how he loved him!
2342	John11:37	And some of them said, Could not this man, which opened the eyes of the blind, have caused that even this man should not have died?
2343	John11:34	And said, Where have ye laid him? They said unto him, Lord, come and see.

THE TREE OF LIFE

2344	John11:38	Jesus therefore again groaning in himself cometh to the grave. It was a cave, and a stone lay upon it.
2345	John11:39	Jesus said, Take ye away the stone. Martha, the sister of him that was dead, saith unto him, Lord, by this time he stinketh: for he hath been dead four days.
2346	John11:17	Then when Jesus came, he found that he had lain in the grave four days already.
2347	John11:40	Jesus saith unto her, Said I not unto thee, that, if thou wouldest believe, thou shouldest see the glory of God?
2348	John11:41	Then they took away the stone from the place where the dead was laid. And Jesus lifted up his eyes, and said, Father, I thank thee that thou hast heard me.
2349	John11:42	And I knew that thou hearest me always: but because of the people which stand by I said it, that they may believe that thou hast sent me.
2350	John11:43	And when he thus had spoken, he cried with a loud voice, Lazarus, come forth.
2351	John11:44	And he that was dead came forth, bound hand and foot with graveclothes: and his face was bound about with a napkin. Jesus saith unto them, Loose him, and let him go.
2352	John11:45	Then many of the Jews which came to Mary, and had seen the things which Jesus did, believed on him.
2353	John11:46	But some of them went their ways to the Pharisees, and told them what things Jesus had done.
2354	John11:47	Then gathered the chief priests and the Pharisees a council, and said, What do we? for this man doeth many miracles.
2355	John11:48	If we let him thus alone, all men will believe on him: and the Romans shall come and take away both our place and nation.
2356	John11:49	And one of them, named Caiaphas, being the high priest that same year, said unto them, Ye know nothing at all,
2357	John11:50	Nor consider that it is expedient for us, that one man should die for the people, and that the whole nation perish not.
2358	John11:51	And this spake he not of himself: but being high priest that year, he prophesied that Jesus should die for that nation;
2359	John11:52	And not for that nation only, but that also he should gather together in one the children of God that were scattered abroad.
2360	John11:53	Then from that day forth they took counsel together for to put him to death.
2361	John11:54	Jesus therefore walked no more openly among the Jews; but went thence unto a country near to the wilderness, into a city called Ephraim, and there continued with his disciples.
2362	Luke19:1	And Jesus entered and passed through Jericho.
2363	Luke19:2	And, behold, there was a man named Zacchaeus, which was the chief among the publicans, and he was rich.
2364	Luke19:3	And he sought to see Jesus who he was; and could not for the press, because he was little of stature.
2365	Luke19:4	And he ran before, and climbed up into a sycomore tree to see him: for he was to pass that way.
2366	Luke19:5	And when Jesus came to the place, he looked up, and saw him, and said unto him, Zacchaeus, make haste, and come down; for to day I must abide at thy house.
2367	Luke19:6	And he made haste, and came down, and received him joyfully.
2368	Luke19:7	And when they saw it, they all murmured, saying, That he was gone to be guest with a man that is a sinner.
2369	Luke19:9	And Jesus said unto him, This day is salvation come to this house, forsomuch as he also is a son of Abraham.
2370	Luke19:10	For the Son of man is come to seek and to save that which was lost.
2371	Luke19:8	And Zacchaeus stood, and said unto the Lord; Behold, Lord, the half of my goods I give to the poor; and if I have taken any thing from any man by false accusation,

THE TREE OF LIFE

		I restore him fourfold.
2372	Luke19:11	And as they heard these things, he added and spake a parable, because he was nigh to Jerusalem, and because they thought that the kingdom of God should immediately appear.
2373	Luke19:12	He said therefore, A certain nobleman went into a far country to receive for himself a kingdom, and to return.
2374	Luke19:13	And he called his ten servants, and delivered them ten pounds, and said unto them, Occupy till I come.
2375	Luke19:14	But his citizens hated him, and sent a message after him, saying, We will not have this man to reign over us.
2376	Luke19:15	And it came to pass, that when he was returned, having received the kingdom, then he commanded these servants to be called unto him, to whom he had given the money, that he might know how much every man had gained by trading.
2377	Luke19:16	Then came the first, saying, Lord, thy pound hath gained ten pounds.
2378	Luke19:17	And he said unto him, Well, thou good servant: because thou hast been faithful in a very little, have thou authority over ten cities.
2379	Luke19:18	And the second came, saying, Lord, thy pound hath gained five pounds.
2380	Luke19:19	And he said likewise to him, Be thou also over five cities.
2381	Luke19:20	And another came, saying, Lord, behold, here is thy pound, which I have kept laid up in a napkin:
2382	Luke19:21	For I feared thee, because thou art an austere man: thou takest up that thou layedst not down, and reapest that thou didst not sow.
2383	Luke19:22	And he saith unto him, Out of thine own mouth will I judge thee, thou wicked servant. Thou knewest that I was an austere man, taking up that I laid not down, and reaping that I did not sow:
2384	Luke19:23	Wherefore then gavest not thou my money into the bank, that at my coming I might have required mine own with usury?
2385	Luke19:24	And he said unto them that stood by, Take from him the pound, and give it to him that hath ten pounds.
2386	Luke19:25	(And they said unto him, Lord, he hath ten pounds.)
2387	Luke19:26	For I say unto you, That unto every one which hath shall be given; and from him that hath not, even that he hath shall be taken away from him.
2388	Luke19:27	But those mine enemies, which would not that I should reign over them, bring hither, and slay them before me.
2389	Matt20:29	And as they departed from Jericho, a great multitude followed him.
2390	Luke18:35	And it came to pass, that as he was come nigh unto Jericho, a certain blind man sat by the way side begging:
2391	Mark10:46	And they came to Jericho: and as he went out of Jericho with his disciples and a great number of people, blind Bartimaeus, the son of Timaeus, sat by the highway side begging.
2392	Luke18:36	And hearing the multitude pass by, he asked what it meant.
2393	Luke18:37	And they told him, that Jesus of Nazareth passeth by.
2394	Matt20:30	And, behold, two blind men sitting by the way side, when they heard that Jesus passed by, cried out, saying, Have mercy on us, O Lord, thou son of David.
2395	Mark10:47	And when he heard that it was Jesus of Nazareth, he began to cry out, and say, Jesus, thou son of David, have mercy on me.
2396	Luke18:38	And he cried, saying, Jesus, thou son of David, have mercy on me.
2397	Matt20:31	And the multitude rebuked them, because they should hold their peace: but they cried the more, saying, Have mercy on us, O Lord, thou son of David.
2398	Mark10:48	And many charged him that he should hold his peace: but he cried the more a great deal, Thou son of David, have mercy on me.
2399	Luke18:39	And they which went before rebuked him, that he should hold his peace: but he cried so much the more, Thou son of David, have mercy on me.

THE TREE OF LIFE

2400	Mark10:49	And Jesus stood still, and commanded him to be called. And they call the blind man, saying unto him, Be of good comfort, rise; he calleth thee.
2401	Mark10:50	And he, casting away his garment, rose, and came to Jesus.
2402	Luke18:40	And Jesus stood, and commanded him to be brought unto him: and when he was come near, he asked him,
2403	Matt20:32	And Jesus stood still, and called them, and said, What will ye that I shall do unto you?
2404	Luke18:41	Saying, What wilt thou that I shall do unto thee? And he said, Lord, that I may receive my sight.
2405	Mark10:51	And Jesus answered and said unto him, What wilt thou that I should do unto thee? The blind man said unto him, Lord, that I might receive my sight.
2406	Matt20:33	They say unto him, Lord, that our eyes may be opened.
2407	Luke18:42	And Jesus said unto him, Receive thy sight: thy faith hath saved thee.
2408	Matt20:34	So Jesus had compassion on them, and touched their eyes: and immediately their eyes received sight, and they followed him.
2409	Mark10:52	And Jesus said unto him, Go thy way; thy faith hath made thee whole. And immediately he received his sight, and followed Jesus in the way.
2410	Luke18:43	And immediately he received his sight, and followed him, glorifying God: and all the people, when they saw it, gave praise unto God.
2411	Luke19:28	And when he had thus spoken, he went before, ascending up to Jerusalem.
2412	Mark10:32	And they were in the way going up to Jerusalem; and Jesus went before them: and they were amazed; and as they followed, they were afraid. And he took again the twelve, and began to tell them what things should happen unto him,
2413	Matt20:17	And Jesus going up to Jerusalem took the twelve disciples apart in the way, and said unto them,
2414	Matt20:18	Behold, we go up to Jerusalem; and the Son of man shall be betrayed unto the chief priests and unto the scribes, and they shall condemn him to death,
2415	Luke18:31	Then he took unto him the twelve, and said unto them, Behold, we go up to Jerusalem, and all things that are written by the prophets concerning the Son of man shall be accomplished.
2416	Mark10:33	Saying, Behold, we go up to Jerusalem; and the Son of man shall be delivered unto the chief priests, and unto the scribes; and they shall condemn him to death, and shall deliver him to the Gentiles:
2417	Luke18:32	For he shall be delivered unto the Gentiles, and shall be mocked, and spitefully entreated, and spitted on:
2418	Luke18:33	And they shall scourge him, and put him to death: and the third day he shall rise again.
2419	Matt20:19	And shall deliver him to the Gentiles to mock, and to scourge, and to crucify him: and the third day he shall rise again.
2420	Mark10:34	And they shall mock him, and shall scourge him, and shall spit upon him, and shall kill him: and the third day he shall rise again.
2421	Luke18:34	And they understood none of these things: and this saying was hid from them, neither knew they the things which were spoken.
2422	Matt20:20	Then came to him the mother of Zebedee's children with her sons, worshipping him, and desiring a certain thing of him.
2423	Mark10:35	And James and John, the sons of Zebedee, come unto him, saying, Master, we would that thou shouldest do for us whatsoever we shall desire.
2424	Mark10:36	And he said unto them, What would ye that I should do for you?
2425	Matt20:21	And he said unto her, What wilt thou? She saith unto him, Grant that these my two sons may sit, the one on thy right hand, and the other on the left, in thy kingdom.
2426	Mark10:37	They said unto him, Grant unto us that we may sit, one on thy right hand, and the other on thy left hand, in thy glory.

THE TREE OF LIFE

2427	Mark10:38	But Jesus said unto them, Ye know not what ye ask: can ye drink of the cup that I drink of? and be baptized with the baptism that I am baptized with?
2428	Matt20:22	But Jesus answered and said, Ye know not what ye ask. Are ye able to drink of the cup that I shall drink of, and to be baptized with the baptism that I am baptized with? They say unto him, We are able.
2429	Mark10:39	And they said unto him, We can. And Jesus said unto them, Ye shall indeed drink of the cup that I drink of; and with the baptism that I am baptized withal shall ye be baptized:
2430	Matt20:23	And he saith unto them, Ye shall drink indeed of my cup, and be baptized with the baptism that I am baptized with: but to sit on my right hand, and on my left, is not mine to give, but it shall be given to them for whom it is prepared of my Father.
2431	Mark10:40	But to sit on my right hand and on my left hand is not mine to give; but it shall be given to them for whom it is prepared.
2432	Matt20:24	And when the ten heard it, they were moved with indignation against the two brethren.
2433	Mark10:41	And when the ten heard it, they began to be much displeased with James and John.
2434	Matt20:25	But Jesus called them unto him, and said, Ye know that the princes of the Gentiles exercise dominion over them, and they that are great exercise authority upon them.
2435	Mark10:42	But Jesus called them to him, and saith unto them, Ye know that they which are accounted to rule over the Gentiles exercise lordship over them; and their great ones exercise authority upon them.
2436	Matt20:26	But it shall not be so among you: but whosoever will be great among you, let him be your minister;
2437	Mark10:43	But so shall it not be among you: but whosoever will be great among you, shall be your minister:
2438	Matt20:27	And whosoever will be chief among you, let him be your servant:
2439	Mark10:44	And whosoever of you will be the chiefest, shall be servant of all.
2440	Matt20:28	Even as the Son of man came not to be ministered unto, but to minister, and to give his life a ransom for many.
2441	Mark10:45	For even the Son of man came not to be ministered unto, but to minister, and to give his life a ransom for many.
2442	John12:1	Then Jesus six days before the passover came to Bethany, where Lazarus was, which had been dead, whom he raised from the dead.
2443	John12:2	There they made him a supper; and Martha served: but Lazarus was one of them that sat at the table with him.
2444	John12:9	Much people of the Jews therefore knew that he was there: and they came not for Jesus' sake only, but that they might see Lazarus also, whom he had raised from the dead.
2445	John12:10	But the chief priests consulted that they might put Lazarus also to death;
2446	John12:11	Because that by reason of him many of the Jews went away, and believed on Jesus.
2447	Matt26:6	Now when Jesus was in Bethany, in the house of Simon the leper,
2448	Mark14:3	And being in Bethany in the house of Simon the leper, as he sat at meat, there came a woman having an alabaster box of ointment of spikenard very precious; and she brake the box, and poured it on his head.
2449	Matt26:7	There came unto him a woman having an alabaster box of very precious ointment, and poured it on his head, as he sat at meat.
2450	Mark14:4	And there were some that had indignation within themselves, and said, Why was this waste of the ointment made?
2451	Matt26:8	But when his disciples saw it, they had indignation, saying, To what purpose is

THE TREE OF LIFE

		this waste?
2452	John12:4	Then saith one of his disciples, Judas Iscariot, Simon's son, which should betray him,
2453	John12:5	Why was not this ointment sold for three hundred pence, and given to the poor?
2454	Matt26:9	For this ointment might have been sold for much, and given to the poor.
2455	Mark14:5	For it might have been sold for more than three hundred pence, and have been given to the poor. And they murmured against her.
2456	John12:6	This he said, not that he cared for the poor; but because he was a thief, and had the bag, and bare what was put therein.
2457	Matt26:10	When Jesus understood it, he said unto them, Why trouble ye the woman? for she hath wrought a good work upon me.
2458	Mark14:6	And Jesus said, Let her alone; why trouble ye her? she hath wrought a good work on me.
2459	John12:7	Then said Jesus, Let her alone: against the day of my burying hath she kept this.
2460	Matt26:12	For in that she hath poured this ointment on my body, she did it for my burial.
2461	Mark14:8	She hath done what she could: she is come aforehand to anoint my body to the burying.
2462	Matt26:11	For ye have the poor always with you; but me ye have not always.
2463	John12:8	For the poor always ye have with you; but me ye have not always.
2464	Mark14:7	For ye have the poor with you always, and whensoever ye will ye may do them good: but me ye have not always.
2465	Matt26:13	Verily I say unto you, Wheresoever this gospel shall be preached in the whole world, there shall also this, that this woman hath done, be told for a memorial of her.
2466	Mark14:9	Verily I say unto you, Wheresoever this gospel shall be preached throughout the whole world, this also that she hath done shall be spoken of for a memorial of her.
2467	John12:12	On the next day much people that were come to the feast, when they heard that Jesus was coming to Jerusalem,
2468	Matt21:1	And when they drew nigh unto Jerusalem, and were come to Bethphage, unto the mount of Olives, then sent Jesus two disciples,
2469	Mark11:1	And when they came nigh to Jerusalem, unto Bethphage and Bethany, at the mount of Olives, he sendeth forth two of his disciples,
2470	Luke19:29	And it came to pass, when he was come nigh to Bethphage and Bethany, at the mount called the mount of Olives, he sent two of his disciples,
2471	Matt21:2	Saying unto them, Go into the village over against you, and straightway ye shall find an ass tied, and a colt with her: loose them, and bring them unto me.
2472	Mark11:2	And saith unto them, Go your way into the village over against you: and as soon as ye be entered into it, ye shall find a colt tied, whereon never man sat; loose him, and bring him.
2473	Luke19:30	Saying, Go ye into the village over against you; in the which at your entering ye shall find a colt tied, whereon yet never man sat: loose him, and bring him hither.
2474	Luke19:31	And if any man ask you, Why do ye loose him? thus shall ye say unto him, Because the Lord hath need of him.
2475	Matt21:3	And if any man say ought unto you, ye shall say, The Lord hath need of them; and straightway he will send them.
2476	Mark11:3	And if any man say unto you, Why do ye this? say ye that the Lord hath need of him; and straightway he will send him hither.
2477	Matt21:6	And the disciples went, and did as Jesus commanded them,
2478	Luke19:32	And they that were sent went their way, and found even as he had said unto them.
2479	Mark11:4	And they went their way, and found the colt tied by the door without in a place where two ways met; and they loose him.

THE TREE OF LIFE

2480	Luke19:33	And as they were loosing the colt, the owners thereof said unto them, Why loose ye the colt?
2481	Mark11:5	And certain of them that stood there said unto them, What do ye, loosing the colt?
2482	Luke19:34	And they said, The Lord hath need of him.
2483	Mark11:6	And they said unto them even as Jesus had commanded: and they let them go.
2484	Matt21:7	And brought the ass, and the colt, and put on them their clothes, and they set him thereon.
2485	Luke19:35	And they brought him to Jesus: and they cast their garments upon the colt, and they set Jesus thereon.
2486	Mark11:7	And they brought the colt to Jesus, and cast their garments on him; and he sat upon him.
2487	John12:14	And Jesus, when he had found a young ass, sat thereon; as it is written,
2488	John12:15	Fear not, daughter of Sion: behold, thy King cometh, sitting on an ass's colt.
2489	Matt21:4	All this was done, that it might be fulfilled which was spoken by the prophet, saying,
2490	Matt21:5	Tell ye the daughter of Sion, Behold, thy King cometh unto thee, meek, and sitting upon an ass, and a colt the foal of an ass.
2491	John12:16	These things understood not his disciples at the first: but when Jesus was glorified, then remembered they that these things were written of him, and that they had done these things unto him.
2492	John11:55	And the Jews' passover was nigh at hand: and many went out of the country up to Jerusalem before the passover, to purify themselves.
2493	Luke19:37	And when he was come nigh, even now at the descent of the mount of Olives, the whole multitude of the disciples began to rejoice and praise God with a loud voice for all the mighty works that they had seen;
2494	Luke19:36	And as he went, they spread their clothes in the way.
2495	Mark11:8	And many spread their garments in the way: and others cut down branches off the trees, and strawed them in the way.
2496	Matt21:8	And a very great multitude spread their garments in the way; others cut down branches from the trees, and strawed them in the way.
2497	John12:13	Took branches of palm trees, and went forth to meet him, and cried, Hosanna: Blessed is the King of Israel that cometh in the name of the Lord.
2498	Mark11:9	And they that went before, and they that followed, cried, saying, Hosanna; Blessed is he that cometh in the name of the Lord:
2499	Mark11:10	Blessed be the kingdom of our father David, that cometh in the name of the Lord: Hosanna in the highest.
2500	Matt21:9	And the multitudes that went before, and that followed, cried, saying, Hosanna to the son of David: Blessed is he that cometh in the name of the Lord; Hosanna in the highest.
2501	Luke19:38	Saying, Blessed be the King that cometh in the name of the Lord: peace in heaven, and glory in the highest.
2502	Luke19:39	And some of the Pharisees from among the multitude said unto him, Master, rebuke thy disciples.
2503	Luke19:40	And he answered and said unto them, I tell you that, if these should hold their peace, the stones would immediately cry out.
2504	Luke19:41	And when he was come near, he beheld the city, and wept over it,
2505	Luke19:42	Saying, If thou hadst known, even thou, at least in this thy day, the things which belong unto thy peace! but now they are hid from thine eyes.
2506	Luke19:43	For the days shall come upon thee, that thine enemies shall cast a trench about thee, and compass thee round, and keep thee in on every side,
2507	Luke19:44	And shall lay thee even with the ground, and thy children within thee; and they shall not leave in thee one stone upon another; because thou knewest not the

THE TREE OF LIFE

		time of thy visitation.
2508	John12:17	The people therefore that was with him when he called Lazarus out of his grave, and raised him from the dead, bare record.
2509	John12:18	For this cause the people also met him, for that they heard that he had done this miracle.
2510	Matt21:10	And when he was come into Jerusalem, all the city was moved, saying, Who is this?
2511	Matt21:11	And the multitude said, This is Jesus the prophet of Nazareth of Galilee.
2512	John12:19	The Pharisees therefore said among themselves, Perceive ye how ye prevail nothing? behold, the world is gone after him.
2513	John12:20	And there were certain Greeks among them that came up to worship at the feast:
2514	John12:21	The same came therefore to Philip, which was of Bethsaida of Galilee, and desired him, saying, Sir, we would see Jesus.
2515	John12:22	Philip cometh and telleth Andrew: and again Andrew and Philip tell Jesus.
2516	John12:23	And Jesus answered them, saying, The hour is come, that the Son of man should be glorified.
2517	John12:24	Verily, verily, I say unto you, Except a corn of wheat fall into the ground and die, it abideth alone: but if it die, it bringeth forth much fruit.
2518	John12:25	He that loveth his life shall lose it; and he that hateth his life in this world shall keep it unto life eternal.
2519	John12:26	If any man serve me, let him follow me; and where I am, there shall also my servant be: if any man serve me, him will my Father honour.
2520	John12:27	Now is my soul troubled; and what shall I say? Father, save me from this hour: but for this cause came I unto this hour.
2521	John12:28	Father, glorify thy name. Then came there a voice from heaven, saying, I have both glorified it, and will glorify it again.
2522	John12:29	The people therefore, that stood by, and heard it, said that it thundered: others said, An angel spake to him.
2523	John12:30	Jesus answered and said, This voice came not because of me, but for your sakes.
2524	John12:31	Now is the judgment of this world: now shall the prince of this world be cast out.
2525	John12:32	And I, if I be lifted up from the earth, will draw all men unto me.
2526	John12:33	This he said, signifying what death he should die.
2527	John12:34	The people answered him, We have heard out of the law that Christ abideth for ever: and how sayest thou, The Son of man must be lifted up? who is this Son of man?
2528	John12:35	Then Jesus said unto them, Yet a little while is the light with you. Walk while ye have the light, lest darkness come upon you: for he that walketh in darkness knoweth not whither he goeth.
2529	John12:36	While ye have light, believe in the light, that ye may be the children of light. These things spake Jesus, and departed, and did hide himself from them.
2530	John12:37	But though he had done so many miracles before them, yet they believed not on him:
2531	John12:38	That the saying of Esaias the prophet might be fulfilled, which he spake, Lord, who hath believed our report? and to whom hath the arm of the Lord been revealed?
2532	John12:39	Therefore they could not believe, because that Esaias said again,
2533	John12:40	He hath blinded their eyes, and hardened their heart; that they should not see with their eyes, nor understand with their heart, and be converted, and I should heal them.
2534	John12:41	These things said Esaias, when he saw his glory, and spake of him.
2535	John12:42	Nevertheless among the chief rulers also many believed on him; but because of the Pharisees they did not confess him, lest they should be put out of the

THE TREE OF LIFE

		synagogue:
2536	John12:43	For they loved the praise of men more than the praise of God.
2537	John12:44	Jesus cried and said, He that believeth on me, believeth not on me, but on him that sent me.
2538	John12:45	And he that seeth me seeth him that sent me.
2539	John12:46	I am come a light into the world, that whosoever believeth on me should not abide in darkness.
2540	John12:47	And if any man hear my words, and believe not, I judge him not: for I came not to judge the world, but to save the world.
2541	John12:48	He that rejecteth me, and receiveth not my words, hath one that judgeth him: the word that I have spoken, the same shall judge him in the last day.
2542	John12:49	For I have not spoken of myself; but the Father which sent me, he gave me a commandment, what I should say, and what I should speak.
2543	John12:50	And I know that his commandment is life everlasting: whatsoever I speak therefore, even as the Father said unto me, so I speak.
2544	Luke19:45	And he went into the temple, and began to cast out them that sold therein, and them that bought;
2545	Mark11:15	And they come to Jerusalem: and Jesus went into the temple, and began to cast out them that sold and bought in the temple, and overthrew the tables of the moneychangers, and the seats of them that sold doves;
2546	Matt21:12	And Jesus went into the temple of God, and cast out all them that sold and bought in the temple, and overthrew the tables of the moneychangers, and the seats of them that sold doves,
2547	Mark11:16	And would not suffer that any man should carry any vessel through the temple.
2548	Matt21:13	And said unto them, It is written, My house shall be called the house of prayer; but ye have made it a den of thieves.
2549	Luke19:46	Saying unto them, It is written, My house is the house of prayer: but ye have made it a den of thieves.
2550	Mark11:17	And he taught, saying unto them, Is it not written, My house shall be called of all nations the house of prayer? but ye have made it a den of thieves.
2551	Matt21:14	And the blind and the lame came to him in the temple; and he healed them.
2552	Matt21:15	And when the chief priests and scribes saw the wonderful things that he did, and the children crying in the temple, and saying, Hosanna to the son of David; they were sore displeased,
2553	Matt21:16	And said unto him, Hearest thou what these say? And Jesus saith unto them, Yea; have ye never read, Out of the mouth of babes and sucklings thou hast perfected praise?
2554	Mark11:18	And the scribes and chief priests heard it, and sought how they might destroy him: for they feared him, because all the people was astonished at his doctrine.
2555	Mark11:11	And Jesus entered into Jerusalem, and into the temple: and when he had looked round about upon all things, and now the eventide was come, he went out unto Bethany with the twelve.
2556	Matt21:17	And he left them, and went out of the city into Bethany; and he lodged there.
2557	Mark11:19	And when even was come, he went out of the city.
2558	Matt21:18	Now in the morning as he returned into the city, he hungered.
2559	Mark11:12	And on the morrow, when they were come from Bethany, he was hungry:
2560	Mark11:13	And seeing a fig tree afar off having leaves, he came, if haply he might find any thing thereon: and when he came to it, he found nothing but leaves; for the time of figs was not yet.
2561	Matt21:19	And when he saw a fig tree in the way, he came to it, and found nothing thereon, but leaves only, and said unto it, Let no fruit grow on thee henceforward for ever. And presently the fig tree withered away.
2562	Mark11:14	And Jesus answered and said unto it, No man eat fruit of thee hereafter for ever.

THE TREE OF LIFE

		And his disciples heard it.
2563	Luke21:38	And all the people came early in the morning to him in the temple, for to hear him.
2564	Luke19:47	And he taught daily in the temple. But the chief priests and the scribes and the chief of the people sought to destroy him,
2565	Luke19:48	And could not find what they might do: for all the people were very attentive to hear him.
2566	Mark11:20	And in the morning, as they passed by, they saw the fig tree dried up from the roots.
2567	Mark11:21	And Peter calling to remembrance saith unto him, Master, behold, the fig tree which thou cursedst is withered away.
2568	Matt21:20	And when the disciples saw it, they marvelled, saying, How soon is the fig tree withered away!
2569	Mark11:22	And Jesus answering saith unto them, Have faith in God.
2570	Matt21:21	Jesus answered and said unto them, Verily I say unto you, If ye have faith, and doubt not, ye shall not only do this which is done to the fig tree, but also if ye shall say unto this mountain, Be thou removed, and be thou cast into the sea; it shall be done.
2571	Mark11:23	For verily I say unto you, That whosoever shall say unto this mountain, Be thou removed, and be thou cast into the sea; and shall not doubt in his heart, but shall believe that those things which he saith shall come to pass; he shall have whatsoever he saith.
2572	Mark11:24	Therefore I say unto you, What things soever ye desire, when ye pray, believe that ye receive them, and ye shall have them.
2573	Matt21:22	And all things, whatsoever ye shall ask in prayer, believing, ye shall receive.
2574	Mark11:25	And when ye stand praying, forgive, if ye have ought against any: that your Father also which is in heaven may forgive you your trespasses.
2575	Mark11:26	But if ye do not forgive, neither will your Father which is in heaven forgive your trespasses.
2576	Luke20:1	And it came to pass, that on one of those days, as he taught the people in the temple, and preached the gospel, the chief priests and the scribes came upon him with the elders,
2577	Mark11:27	And they come again to Jerusalem: and as he was walking in the temple, there come to him the chief priests, and the scribes, and the elders,
2578	Matt21:23	And when he was come into the temple, the chief priests and the elders of the people came unto him as he was teaching, and said, By what authority doest thou these things? and who gave thee this authority?
2579	Mark11:28	And say unto him, By what authority doest thou these things? and who gave thee this authority to do these things?
2580	Luke20:2	And spake unto him, saying, Tell us, by what authority doest thou these things? or who is he that gave thee this authority?
2581	Matt21:24	And Jesus answered and said unto them, I also will ask you one thing, which if ye tell me, I in like wise will tell you by what authority I do these things.
2582	Mark11:29	And Jesus answered and said unto them, I will also ask of you one question, and answer me, and I will tell you by what authority I do these things.
2583	Luke20:3	And he answered and said unto them, I will also ask you one thing; and answer me:
2584	Luke20:4	The baptism of John, was it from heaven, or of men?
2585	Mark11:30	The baptism of John, was it from heaven, or of men? answer me.
2586	Matt21:25	The baptism of John, whence was it? from heaven, or of men? And they reasoned with themselves, saying, If we shall say, From heaven; he will say unto us, Why did ye not then believe him?
2587	Mark11:31	And they reasoned with themselves, saying, If we shall say, From heaven; he will say, Why then did ye not believe him?

THE TREE OF LIFE

2588	Luke20:5	And they reasoned with themselves, saying, If we shall say, From heaven; he will say, Why then believed ye him not?
2589	Matt21:26	But if we shall say, Of men; we fear the people; for all hold John as a prophet.
2590	Luke20:6	But and if we say, Of men; all the people will stone us: for they be persuaded that John was a prophet.
2591	Mark11:32	But if we shall say, Of men; they feared the people: for all men counted John, that he was a prophet indeed.
2592	Luke20:7	And they answered, that they could not tell whence it was.
2593	Luke20:8	And Jesus said unto them, Neither tell I you by what authority I do these things.
2594	Matt21:27	And they answered Jesus, and said, We cannot tell. And he said unto them, Neither tell I you by what authority I do these things.
2595	Mark11:33	And they answered and said unto Jesus, We cannot tell. And Jesus answering saith unto them, Neither do I tell you by what authority I do these things.
2596	Matt21:28	But what think ye? A certain man had two sons; and he came to the first, and said, Son, go work to day in my vineyard.
2597	Matt21:29	He answered and said, I will not: but afterward he repented, and went.
2598	Matt21:30	And he came to the second, and said likewise. And he answered and said, I go, sir: and went not.
2599	Matt21:31	Whether of them twain did the will of his father? They say unto him, The first. Jesus saith unto them, Verily I say unto you, That the publicans and the harlots go into the kingdom of God before you.
2600	Matt21:32	For John came unto you in the way of righteousness, and ye believed him not: but the publicans and the harlots believed him: and ye, when ye had seen it, repented not afterward, that ye might believe him.
2601	Luke18:9	And he spake this parable unto certain which trusted in themselves that they were righteous, and despised others:
2602	Luke18:10	Two men went up into the temple to pray; the one a Pharisee, and the other a publican.
2603	Luke18:11	The Pharisee stood and prayed thus with himself, God, I thank thee, that I am not as other men are, extortioners, unjust, adulterers, or even as this publican.
2604	Luke18:12	I fast twice in the week, I give tithes of all that I possess.
2605	Luke18:13	And the publican, standing afar off, would not lift up so much as his eyes unto heaven, but smote upon his breast, saying, God be merciful to me a sinner.
2606	Luke18:14	I tell you, this man went down to his house justified rather than the other: for every one that exalteth himself shall be abased; and he that humbleth himself shall be exalted.
2607	Luke17:33	Whosoever shall seek to save his life shall lose it; and whosoever shall lose his life shall preserve it.
2608	Matt21:33	Hear another parable: There was a certain householder, which planted a vineyard, and hedged it round about, and digged a winepress in it, and built a tower, and let it out to husbandmen, and went into a far country:
2609	Mark12:1	And he began to speak unto them by parables. A certain man planted a vineyard, and set an hedge about it, and digged a place for the winefat, and built a tower, and let it out to husbandmen, and went into a far country.
2610	Luke20:9	Then began he to speak to the people this parable; A certain man planted a vineyard, and let it forth to husbandmen, and went into a far country for a long time.
2611	Matt21:34	And when the time of the fruit drew near, he sent his servants to the husbandmen, that they might receive the fruits of it.
2612	Mark12:2	And at the season he sent to the husbandmen a servant, that he might receive from the husbandmen of the fruit of the vineyard.
2613	Luke20:10	And at the season he sent a servant to the husbandmen, that they should give him of the fruit of the vineyard: but the husbandmen beat him, and sent him away

THE TREE OF LIFE

		empty.
2614	Mark12:3	And they caught him, and beat him, and sent him away empty.
2615	Luke20:11	And again he sent another servant: and they beat him also, and entreated him shamefully, and sent him away empty.
2616	Mark12:4	And again he sent unto them another servant; and at him they cast stones, and wounded him in the head, and sent him away shamefully handled.
2617	Luke20:12	And again he sent a third: and they wounded him also, and cast him out.
2618	Matt21:35	And the husbandmen took his servants, and beat one, and killed another, and stoned another.
2619	Matt21:36	Again, he sent other servants more than the first: and they did unto them likewise.
2620	Mark12:5	And again he sent another; and him they killed, and many others; beating some, and killing some.
2621	Luke20:13	Then said the lord of the vineyard, What shall I do? I will send my beloved son: it may be they will reverence him when they see him.
2622	Mark12:6	Having yet therefore one son, his wellbeloved, he sent him also last unto them, saying, They will reverence my son.
2623	Matt21:37	But last of all he sent unto them his son, saying, They will reverence my son.
2624	Matt21:38	But when the husbandmen saw the son, they said among themselves, This is the heir; come, let us kill him, and let us seize on his inheritance.
2625	Luke20:14	But when the husbandmen saw him, they reasoned among themselves, saying, This is the heir: come, let us kill him, that the inheritance may be ours.
2626	Mark12:7	But those husbandmen said among themselves, This is the heir; come, let us kill him, and the inheritance shall be our's.
2627	Matt21:39	And they caught him, and cast him out of the vineyard, and slew him.
2628	Mark12:8	And they took him, and killed him, and cast him out of the vineyard.
2629	Luke20:15	So they cast him out of the vineyard, and killed him. What therefore shall the lord of the vineyard do unto them?
2630	Matt21:40	When the lord therefore of the vineyard cometh, what will he do unto those husbandmen?
2631	Mark12:9	What shall therefore the lord of the vineyard do? he will come and destroy the husbandmen, and will give the vineyard unto others.
2632	Matt21:41	They say unto him, He will miserably destroy those wicked men, and will let out his vineyard unto other husbandmen, which shall render him the fruits in their seasons.
2633	Luke20:16	He shall come and destroy these husbandmen, and shall give the vineyard to others. And when they heard it, they said, God forbid.
2634	Matt21:43	Therefore say I unto you, The kingdom of God shall be taken from you, and given to a nation bringing forth the fruits thereof.
2635	Luke20:17	And he beheld them, and said, What is this then that is written, The stone which the builders rejected, the same is become the head of the corner?
2636	Matt21:42	Jesus saith unto them, Did ye never read in the scriptures, The stone which the builders rejected, the same is become the head of the corner: this is the Lord's doing, and it is marvellous in our eyes?
2637	Mark12:10	And have ye not read this scripture; The stone which the builders rejected is become the head of the corner:
2638	Mark12:11	This was the Lord's doing, and it is marvellous in our eyes?
2639	Luke20:18	Whosoever shall fall upon that stone shall be broken; but on whomsoever it shall fall, it will grind him to powder.
2640	Matt21:44	And whosoever shall fall on this stone shall be broken: but on whomsoever it shall fall, it will grind him to powder.
2641	Luke17:20	And when he was demanded of the Pharisees, when the kingdom of God should come, he answered them and said, The kingdom of God cometh not with

THE TREE OF LIFE

		observation:
2642	Luke17:21	Neither shall they say, Lo here! or, lo there! for, behold, the kingdom of God is within you.
2643	Luke20:19	And the chief priests and the scribes the same hour sought to lay hands on him; and they feared the people: for they perceived that he had spoken this parable against them.
2644	Matt21:46	But when they sought to lay hands on him, they feared the multitude, because they took him for a prophet.
2645	Mark12:12	And they sought to lay hold on him, but feared the people: for they knew that he had spoken the parable against them: and they left him, and went their way.
2646	Matt22:1	And Jesus answered and spake unto them again by parables, and said,
2647	Matt22:2	The kingdom of heaven is like unto a certain king, which made a marriage for his son,
2648	Matt22:3	And sent forth his servants to call them that were bidden to the wedding: and they would not come.
2649	Matt22:4	Again, he sent forth other servants, saying, Tell them which are bidden, Behold, I have prepared my dinner: my oxen and my fatlings are killed, and all things are ready: come unto the marriage.
2650	Matt22:5	But they made light of it, and went their ways, one to his farm, another to his merchandise:
2651	Matt22:6	And the remnant took his servants, and entreated them spitefully, and slew them.
2652	Matt22:7	But when the king heard thereof, he was wroth: and he sent forth his armies, and destroyed those murderers, and burned up their city.
2653	Matt22:8	Then saith he to his servants, The wedding is ready, but they which were bidden were not worthy.
2654	Matt22:9	Go ye therefore into the highways, and as many as ye shall find, bid to the marriage.
2655	Matt22:10	So those servants went out into the highways, and gathered together all as many as they found, both bad and good: and the wedding was furnished with guests.
2656	Matt22:11	And when the king came in to see the guests, he saw there a man which had not on a wedding garment:
2657	Matt22:12	And he saith unto him, Friend, how camest thou in hither not having a wedding garment? And he was speechless.
2658	Matt22:13	Then said the king to the servants, Bind him hand and foot, and take him away, and cast him into outer darkness; there shall be weeping and gnashing of teeth.
2659	Matt22:14	For many are called, but few are chosen.
2660	Matt21:45	And when the chief priests and Pharisees had heard his parables, they perceived that he spake of them.
2661	Matt22:15	Then went the Pharisees, and took counsel how they might entangle him in his talk.
2662	Mark12:13	And they send unto him certain of the Pharisees and of the Herodians, to catch him in his words.
2663	Luke20:20	And they watched him, and sent forth spies, which should feign themselves just men, that they might take hold of his words, that so they might deliver him unto the power and authority of the governor.
2664	Matt22:16	And they sent out unto him their disciples with the Herodians, saying, Master, we know that thou art true, and teachest the way of God in truth, neither carest thou for any man: for thou regardest not the person of men.
2665	Luke20:21	And they asked him, saying, Master, we know that thou sayest and teachest rightly, neither acceptest thou the person of any, but teachest the way of God truly:
2666	Mark12:14	And when they were come, they say unto him, Master, we know that thou art true, and carest for no man: for thou regardest not the person of men, but

THE TREE OF LIFE

		teachest the way of God in truth: Is it lawful to give tribute to Caesar, or not?
2667	Luke20:22	Is it lawful for us to give tribute unto Caesar, or no?
2668	Matt22:17	Tell us therefore, What thinkest thou? Is it lawful to give tribute unto Caesar, or not?
2669	Mark12:15	Shall we give, or shall we not give? But he, knowing their hypocrisy, said unto them, Why tempt ye me? bring me a penny, that I may see it.
2670	Luke20:23	But he perceived their craftiness, and said unto them, Why tempt ye me?
2671	Matt22:18	But Jesus perceived their wickedness, and said, Why tempt ye me, ye hypocrites?
2672	Matt22:19	Shew me the tribute money. And they brought unto him a penny.
2673	Matt22:20	And he saith unto them, Whose is this image and superscription?
2674	Luke20:24	Shew me a penny. Whose image and superscription hath it? They answered and said, Caesar's.
2675	Mark12:16	And they brought it. And he saith unto them, Whose is this image and superscription? And they said unto him, Caesar's.
2676	Matt22:21	They say unto him, Caesar's. Then saith he unto them, Render therefore unto Caesar the things which are Caesar's; and unto God the things that are God's.
2677	Luke20:25	And he said unto them, Render therefore unto Caesar the things which be Caesar's, and unto God the things which be God's.
2678	Mark12:17	And Jesus answering said unto them, Render to Caesar the things that are Caesar's, and to God the things that are God's. And they marvelled at him.
2679	Luke20:26	And they could not take hold of his words before the people: and they marvelled at his answer, and held their peace.
2680	Matt22:22	When they had heard these words, they marvelled, and left him, and went their way.
2681	Matt22:23	The same day came to him the Saducees, which say that there is no resurrection, and asked him,
2682	Luke20:27	Then came to him certain of the Saducees, which deny that there is any resurrection; and they asked him,
2683	Mark12:18	Then come unto him the Sadducees, which say there is no resurrection; and they asked him, saying,
2684	Mark12:19	Master, Moses wrote unto us, If a man's brother die, and leave his wife behind him, and leave no children, that his brother should take his wife, and raise up seed unto his brother.
2685	Matt22:24	Saying, Master, Moses said, If a man die, having no children, his brother shall marry his wife, and raise up seed unto his brother.
2686	Luke20:28	Saying, Master, Moses wrote unto us, If any man's brother die, having a wife, and he die without children, that his brother should take his wife, and raise up seed unto his brother.
2687	Mark12:20	Now there were seven brethren: and the first took a wife, and dying left no seed.
2688	Luke20:29	There were therefore seven brethren: and the first took a wife, and died without children.
2689	Matt22:25	Now there were with us seven brethren: and the first, when he had married a wife, deceased, and, having no issue, left his wife unto his brother:
2690	Luke20:30	And the second took her to wife, and he died childless.
2691	Mark12:21	And the second took her, and died, neither left he any seed: and the third likewise.
2692	Matt22:26	Likewise the second also, and the third, unto the seventh.
2693	Luke20:31	And the third took her; and in like manner the seven also: and they left no children, and died.
2694	Mark12:22	And the seven had her, and left no seed: last of all the woman died also.
2695	Luke20:32	Last of all the woman died also.
2696	Matt22:27	And last of all the woman died also.

2697	Matt22:28	Therefore in the resurrection whose wife shall she be of the seven? for they all had her.
2698	Luke20:33	Therefore in the resurrection whose wife of them is she? for seven had her to wife.
2699	Mark12:23	In the resurrection therefore, when they shall rise, whose wife shall she be of them? for the seven had her to wife.
2700	Matt22:29	Jesus answered and said unto them, Ye do err, not knowing the scriptures, nor the power of God.
2701	Mark12:24	And Jesus answering said unto them, Do ye not therefore err, because ye know not the scriptures, neither the power of God?
2702	Luke20:34	And Jesus answering said unto them, The children of this world marry, and are given in marriage:
2703	Luke20:35	But they which shall be accounted worthy to obtain that world, and the resurrection from the dead, neither marry, nor are given in marriage:
2704	Matt22:30	For in the resurrection they neither marry, nor are given in marriage, but are as the angels of God in heaven.
2705	Mark12:25	For when they shall rise from the dead, they neither marry, nor are given in marriage; but are as the angels which are in heaven.
2706	Luke20:36	Neither can they die any more: for they are equal unto the angels; and are the children of God, being the children of the resurrection.
2707	Luke20:37	Now that the dead are raised, even Moses shewed at the bush, when he calleth the Lord the God of Abraham, and the God of Isaac, and the God of Jacob.
2708	Matt22:31	But as touching the resurrection of the dead, have ye not read that which was spoken unto you by God, saying,
2709	Mark12:26	And as touching the dead, that they rise: have ye not read in the book of Moses, how in the bush God spake unto him, saying, I am the God of Abraham, and the God of Isaac, and the God of Jacob?
2710	Matt22:32	I am the God of Abraham, and the God of Isaac, and the God of Jacob? God is not the God of the dead, but of the living.
2711	Luke20:38	For he is not a God of the dead, but of the living: for all live unto him.
2712	Mark12:27	He is not the God of the dead, but the God of the living: ye therefore do greatly err.
2713	Matt22:33	And when the multitude heard this, they were astonished at his doctrine.
2714	Matt22:34	But when the Pharisees had heard that he had put the Sadducees to silence, they were gathered together.
2715	Matt22:35	Then one of them, which was a lawyer, asked him a question, tempting him, and saying,
2716	Mark12:28	And one of the scribes came, and having heard them reasoning together, and perceiving that he had answered them well, asked him, Which is the first commandment of all?
2717	Matt22:36	Master, which is the great commandment in the law?
2718	Mark12:29	And Jesus answered him, The first of all the commandments is, Hear, O Israel; The Lord our God is one Lord:
2719	Mark12:30	And thou shalt love the Lord thy God with all thy heart, and with all thy soul, and with all thy mind, and with all thy strength: this is the first commandment.
2720	Matt22:37	Jesus said unto him, Thou shalt love the Lord thy God with all thy heart, and with all thy soul, and with all thy mind.
2721	Matt22:38	This is the first and great commandment.
2722	Matt22:39	And the second is like unto it, Thou shalt love thy neighbour as thyself.
2723	Mark12:31	And the second is like, namely this, Thou shalt love thy neighbour as thyself. There is none other commandment greater than these.
2724	Matt22:40	On these two commandments hang all the law and the prophets.
2725	Luke20:39	Then certain of the scribes answering said, Master, thou hast well said.

THE TREE OF LIFE

2726	Mark12:32	And the scribe said unto him, Well, Master, thou hast said the truth: for there is one God; and there is none other but he:
2727	Mark12:33	And to love him with all the heart, and with all the understanding, and with all the soul, and with all the strength, and to love his neighbour as himself, is more than all whole burnt offerings and sacrifices.
2728	Mark12:34	And when Jesus saw that he answered discreetly, he said unto him, Thou art not far from the kingdom of God. And no man after that durst ask him any question.
2729	Luke20:40	And after that they durst not ask him any question at all.
2730	Matt22:41	While the Pharisees were gathered together, Jesus asked them,
2731	Luke20:41	And he said unto them, How say they that Christ is David's son?
2732	Mark12:35	And Jesus answered and said, while he taught in the temple, How say the scribes that Christ is the son of David?
2733	Matt22:42	Saying, What think ye of Christ? whose son is he? They say unto him, The son of David.
2734	Matt22:43	He saith unto them, How then doth David in spirit call him Lord, saying,
2735	Matt22:44	The LORD said unto my Lord, Sit thou on my right hand, till I make thine enemies thy footstool?
2736	Mark12:36	For David himself said by the Holy Ghost, The LORD said to my Lord, Sit thou on my right hand, till I make thine enemies thy footstool.
2737	Luke20:42	And David himself saith in the book of Psalms, The LORD said unto my Lord, Sit thou on my right hand,
2738	Luke20:43	Till I make thine enemies thy footstool.
2739	Matt22:45	If David then call him Lord, how is he his son?
2740	Luke20:44	David therefore calleth him Lord, how is he then his son?
2741	Mark12:37	David therefore himself calleth him Lord; and whence is he then his son? And the common people heard him gladly.
2742	Matt22:46	And no man was able to answer him a word, neither durst any man from that day forth ask him any more questions.
2743	Mark12:41	And Jesus sat over against the treasury, and beheld how the people cast money into the treasury: and many that were rich cast in much.
2744	Luke21:1	And he looked up, and saw the rich men casting their gifts into the treasury.
2745	Mark12:42	And there came a certain poor widow, and she threw in two mites, which make a farthing.
2746	Luke21:2	And he saw also a certain poor widow casting in thither two mites.
2747	Mark12:43	And he called unto him his disciples, and saith unto them, Verily I say unto you, That this poor widow hath cast more in, than all they which have cast into the treasury:
2748	Luke21:3	And he said, Of a truth I say unto you, that this poor widow hath cast in more than they all:
2749	Mark12:44	For all they did cast in of their abundance; but she of her want did cast in all that she had, even all her living.
2750	Luke21:4	For all these have of their abundance cast in unto the offerings of God: but she of her penury hath cast in all the living that she had.
2751	Luke20:45	Then in the audience of all the people he said unto his disciples,
2752	Matt23:1	Then spake Jesus to the multitude, and to his disciples,
2753	Matt23:2	Saying, The scribes and the Pharisees sit in Moses' seat:
2754	Matt23:3	All therefore whatsoever they bid you observe, that observe and do; but do not ye after their works: for they say, and do not.
2755	Matt23:4	For they bind heavy burdens and grievous to be borne, and lay them on men's shoulders; but they themselves will not move them with one of their fingers.
2756	Matt23:5	But all their works they do for to be seen of men: they make broad their phylacteries, and enlarge the borders of their garments,
2757	Mark12:38	And he said unto them in his doctrine, Beware of the scribes, which love to go in

THE TREE OF LIFE

2758	Luke20:46	long clothing, and love salutations in the marketplaces, Beware of the scribes, which desire to walk in long robes, and love greetings in the markets, and the highest seats in the synagogues, and the chief rooms at feasts;
2759	Mark12:39	And the chief seats in the synagogues, and the uppermost rooms at feasts:
2760	Matt23:6	And love the uppermost rooms at feasts, and the chief seats in the synagogues,
2761	Matt23:7	And greetings in the markets, and to be called of men, Rabbi, Rabbi.
2762	Matt23:8	But be not ye called Rabbi: for one is your Master, even Christ; and all ye are brethren.
2763	Matt23:9	And call no man your father upon the earth: for one is your Father, which is in heaven.
2764	Matt23:10	Neither be ye called masters: for one is your Master, even Christ.
2765	Matt23:11	But he that is greatest among you shall be your servant.
2766	Matt23:12	And whosoever shall exalt himself shall be abased; and he that shall humble himself shall be exalted.
2767	Matt23:13	But woe unto you, scribes and Pharisees, hypocrites! for ye shut up the kingdom of heaven against men: for ye neither go in yourselves, neither suffer ye them that are entering to go in.
2768	Matt23:14	Woe unto you, scribes and Pharisees, hypocrites! for ye devour widows' houses, and for a pretence make long prayer: therefore ye shall receive the greater damnation.
2769	Mark12:40	Which devour widows' houses, and for a pretence make long prayers: these shall receive greater damnation.
2770	Luke20:47	Which devour widows' houses, and for a shew make long prayers: the same shall receive greater damnation.
2771	Matt23:15	Woe unto you, scribes and Pharisees, hypocrites! for ye compass sea and land to make one proselyte, and when he is made, ye make him twofold more the child of hell than yourselves.
2772	Matt23:16	Woe unto you, ye blind guides, which say, Whosoever shall swear by the temple, it is nothing; but whosoever shall swear by the gold of the temple, he is a debtor!
2773	Matt23:17	Ye fools and blind: for whether is greater, the gold, or the temple that sanctifieth the gold?
2774	Matt23:18	And, Whosoever shall swear by the altar, it is nothing; but whosoever sweareth by the gift that is upon it, he is guilty.
2775	Matt23:19	Ye fools and blind: for whether is greater, the gift, or the altar that sanctifieth the gift?
2776	Matt23:20	Whoso therefore shall swear by the altar, sweareth by it, and by all things thereon.
2777	Matt23:21	And whoso shall swear by the temple, sweareth by it, and by him that dwelleth therein.
2778	Matt23:22	And he that shall swear by heaven, sweareth by the throne of God, and by him that sitteth thereon.
2779	Matt23:23	Woe unto you, scribes and Pharisees, hypocrites! for ye pay tithe of mint and anise and cummin, and have omitted the weightier matters of the law, judgment, mercy, and faith: these ought ye to have done, and not to leave the other undone.
2780	Matt23:24	Ye blind guides, which strain at a gnat, and swallow a camel.
2781	Matt23:25	Woe unto you, scribes and Pharisees, hypocrites! for ye make clean the outside of the cup and of the platter, but within they are full of extortion and excess.
2782	Matt23:26	Thou blind Pharisee, cleanse first that which is within the cup and platter, that the outside of them may be clean also.
2783	Matt23:27	Woe unto you, scribes and Pharisees, hypocrites! for ye are like unto whited sepulchres, which indeed appear beautiful outward, but are within full of dead men's bones, and of all uncleanness.

THE TREE OF LIFE

2784	Matt23:28	Even so ye also outwardly appear righteous unto men, but within ye are full of hypocrisy and iniquity.
2785	Matt23:29	Woe unto you, scribes and Pharisees, hypocrites! because ye build the tombs of the prophets, and garnish the sepulchres of the righteous,
2786	Matt23:30	And say, If we had been in the days of our fathers, we would not have been partakers with them in the blood of the prophets.
2787	Matt23:31	Wherefore ye be witnesses unto yourselves, that ye are the children of them which killed the prophets.
2788	Matt23:32	Fill ye up then the measure of your fathers.
2789	Matt23:33	Ye serpents, ye generation of vipers, how can ye escape the damnation of hell?
2790	Matt23:34	Wherefore, behold, I send unto you prophets, and wise men, and scribes: and some of them ye shall kill and crucify; and some of them shall ye scourge in your synagogues, and persecute them from city to city:
2791	Luke11:50	That the blood of all the prophets, which was shed from the foundation of the world, may be required of this generation;
2792	Matt23:35	That upon you may come all the righteous blood shed upon the earth, from the blood of righteous Abel unto the blood of Zacharias son of Barachias, whom ye slew between the temple and the altar.
2793	Luke11:51	From the blood of Abel unto the blood of Zacharias, which perished between the altar and the temple: verily I say unto you, It shall be required of this generation.
2794	Matt23:36	Verily I say unto you, All these things shall come upon this generation.
2795	Matt23:37	O Jerusalem, Jerusalem, thou that killest the prophets, and stonest them which are sent unto thee, how often would I have gathered thy children together, even as a hen gathereth her chickens under her wings, and ye would not!
2796	Matt23:38	Behold, your house is left unto you desolate.
2797	Matt23:39	For I say unto you, Ye shall not see me henceforth, till ye shall say, Blessed is he that cometh in the name of the Lord.
2798	Matt24:1	And Jesus went out, and departed from the temple: and his disciples came to him for to shew him the buildings of the temple.
2799	Mark13:1	And as he went out of the temple, one of his disciples saith unto him, Master, see what manner of stones and what buildings are here!
2800	Luke21:5	And as some spake of the temple, how it was adorned with goodly stones and gifts, he said,
2801	Luke21:6	As for these things which ye behold, the days will come, in the which there shall not be left one stone upon another, that shall not be thrown down.
2802	Mark13:2	And Jesus answering said unto him, Seest thou these great buildings? there shall not be left one stone upon another, that shall not be thrown down.
2803	Matt24:2	And Jesus said unto them, See ye not all these things? verily I say unto you, There shall not be left here one stone upon another, that shall not be thrown down.
2804	Luke21:37	And in the day time he was teaching in the temple; and at night he went out, and abode in the mount that is called the mount of Olives.
2805	Matt24:3	And as he sat upon the mount of Olives, the disciples came unto him privately, saying, Tell us, when shall these things be? and what shall be the sign of thy coming, and of the end of the world?
2806	Mark13:3	And as he sat upon the mount of Olives over against the temple, Peter and James and John and Andrew asked him privately,
2807	Luke21:7	And they asked him, saying, Master, but when shall these things be? and what sign will there be when these things shall come to pass?
2808	Mark13:4	Tell us, when shall these things be? and what shall be the sign when all these things shall be fulfilled?
2809	Matt24:4	And Jesus answered and said unto them, Take heed that no man deceive you.
2810	Mark13:5	And Jesus answering them began to say, Take heed lest any man deceive you:

THE TREE OF LIFE

2811	Luke21:8	And he said, Take heed that ye be not deceived: for many shall come in my name, saying, I am Christ; and the time draweth near: go ye not therefore after them.
2812	Mark13:6	For many shall come in my name, saying, I am Christ; and shall deceive many.
2813	Matt24:5	For many shall come in my name, saying, I am Christ; and shall deceive many.
2814	Luke21:9	But when ye shall hear of wars and commotions, be not terrified: for these things must first come to pass; but the end is not by and by.
2815	Mark13:7	And when ye shall hear of wars and rumours of wars, be ye not troubled: for such things must needs be; but the end shall not be yet.
2816	Matt24:6	And ye shall hear of wars and rumours of wars: see that ye be not troubled: for all these things must come to pass, but the end is not yet.
2817	Matt24:7	For nation shall rise against nation, and kingdom against kingdom: and there shall be famines, and pestilences, and earthquakes, in divers places.
2818	Luke21:10	Then said he unto them, Nation shall rise against nation, and kingdom against kingdom:
2819	Luke21:11	And great earthquakes shall be in divers places, and famines, and pestilences; and fearful sights and great signs shall there be from heaven.
2820	Mark13:8	For nation shall rise against nation, and kingdom against kingdom: and there shall be earthquakes in divers places, and there shall be famines and troubles: these are the beginnings of sorrows.
2821	Matt24:8	All these are the beginning of sorrows.
2822	Luke21:12	But before all these, they shall lay their hands on you, and persecute you, delivering you up to the synagogues, and into prisons, being brought before kings and rulers for my name's sake.
2823	Matt24:9	Then shall they deliver you up to be afflicted, and shall kill you: and ye shall be hated of all nations for my name's sake.
2824	Mark13:9	But take heed to yourselves: for they shall deliver you up to councils; and in the synagogues ye shall be beaten: and ye shall be brought before rulers and kings for my sake, for a testimony against them.
2825	Luke21:13	And it shall turn to you for a testimony.
2826	Matt24:14	And this gospel of the kingdom shall be preached in all the world for a witness unto all nations; and then shall the end come.
2827	Mark13:10	And the gospel must first be published among all nations.
2828	Luke12:11	And when they bring you unto the synagogues, and unto magistrates, and powers, take ye no thought how or what thing ye shall answer, or what ye shall say:
2829	Mark13:11	But when they shall lead you, and deliver you up, take no thought beforehand what ye shall speak, neither do ye premeditate: but whatsoever shall be given you in that hour, that speak ye: for it is not ye that speak, but the Holy Ghost.
2830	Luke12:12	For the Holy Ghost shall teach you in the same hour what ye ought to say.
2831	Luke21:14	Settle it therefore in your hearts, not to meditate before what ye shall answer:
2832	Luke21:15	For I will give you a mouth and wisdom, which all your adversaries shall not be able to gainsay nor resist.
2833	Luke21:16	And ye shall be betrayed both by parents, and brethren, and kinsfolks, and friends; and some of you shall they cause to be put to death.
2834	Luke21:17	And ye shall be hated of all men for my name's sake.
2835	Mark13:13	And ye shall be hated of all men for my name's sake: but he that shall endure unto the end, the same shall be saved.
2836	Matt24:13	But he that shall endure unto the end, the same shall be saved.
2837	Luke21:18	But there shall not an hair of your head perish.
2838	Luke21:19	In your patience possess ye your souls.
2839	Matt24:10	And then shall many be offended, and shall betray one another, and shall hate one another.

THE TREE OF LIFE

2840	Matt24:11	And many false prophets shall rise, and shall deceive many.
2841	Matt24:12	And because iniquity shall abound, the love of many shall wax cold.
2842	Mark13:12	Now the brother shall betray the brother to death, and the father the son; and children shall rise up against their parents, and shall cause them to be put to death.
2843	Luke21:20	And when ye shall see Jerusalem compassed with armies, then know that the desolation thereof is nigh.
2844	Matt24:15	When ye therefore shall see the abomination of desolation, spoken of by Daniel the prophet, stand in the holy place, (whoso readeth, let him understand:)
2845	Mark13:14	But when ye shall see the abomination of desolation, spoken of by Daniel the prophet, standing where it ought not, (let him that readeth understand,) then let them that be in Judaea flee to the mountains:
2846	Matt24:16	Then let them which be in Judaea flee into the mountains:
2847	Luke21:21	Then let them which are in Judaea flee to the mountains; and let them which are in the midst of it depart out; and let not them that are in the countries enter thereinto.
2848	Matt24:17	Let him which is on the housetop not come down to take any thing out of his house:
2849	Mark13:15	And let him that is on the housetop not go down into the house, neither enter therein, to take any thing out of his house:
2850	Luke17:31	In that day, he which shall be upon the housetop, and his stuff in the house, let him not come down to take it away: and he that is in the field, let him likewise not return back.
2851	Mark13:16	And let him that is in the field not turn back again for to take up his garment.
2852	Matt24:18	Neither let him which is in the field return back to take his clothes.
2853	Luke21:22	For these be the days of vengeance, that all things which are written may be fulfilled.
2854	Matt24:19	And woe unto them that are with child, and to them that give suck in those days!
2855	Mark13:17	But woe to them that are with child, and to them that give suck in those days!
2856	Luke21:23	But woe unto them that are with child, and to them that give suck, in those days! for there shall be great distress in the land, and wrath upon this people.
2857	Luke21:24	And they shall fall by the edge of the sword, and shall be led away captive into all nations: and Jerusalem shall be trodden down of the Gentiles, until the times of the Gentiles be fulfilled.
2858	Mark13:18	And pray ye that your flight be not in the winter.
2859	Matt24:20	But pray ye that your flight be not in the winter, neither on the sabbath day:
2860	Matt24:21	For then shall be great tribulation, such as was not since the beginning of the world to this time, no, nor ever shall be.
2861	Mark13:19	For in those days shall be affliction, such as was not from the beginning of the creation which God created unto this time, neither shall be.
2862	Matt24:22	And except those days should be shortened, there should no flesh be saved: but for the elect's sake those days shall be shortened.
2863	Mark13:20	And except that the Lord had shortened those days, no flesh should be saved: but for the elect's sake, whom he hath chosen, he hath shortened the days.
2864	Matt24:34	Verily I say unto you, This generation shall not pass, till all these things be fulfilled.
2865	Mark13:30	Verily I say unto you, that this generation shall not pass, till all these things be done.
2866	Luke21:32	Verily I say unto you, This generation shall not pass away, till all be fulfilled.
2867	Matt24:35	Heaven and earth shall pass away, but my words shall not pass away.
2868	Mark13:31	Heaven and earth shall pass away: but my words shall not pass away.
2869	Luke21:33	Heaven and earth shall pass away: but my words shall not pass away.
2870	Matt24:23	Then if any man shall say unto you, Lo, here is Christ, or there; believe it not.

THE TREE OF LIFE

2871	Mark13:21	And then if any man shall say to you, Lo, here is Christ; or, lo, he is there; believe him not:
2872	Luke17:23	And they shall say to you, See here; or, see there: go not after them, nor follow them.
2873	Matt24:24	For there shall arise false Christs, and false prophets, and shall shew great signs and wonders; insomuch that, if it were possible, they shall deceive the very elect.
2874	Mark13:22	For false Christs and false prophets shall rise, and shall shew signs and wonders, to seduce, if it were possible, even the elect.
2875	Matt24:26	Wherefore if they shall say unto you, Behold, he is in the desert; go not forth: behold, he is in the secret chambers; believe it not.
2876	Matt24:27	For as the lightning cometh out of the east, and shineth even unto the west; so shall also the coming of the Son of man be.
2877	Luke17:24	For as the lightning, that lighteneth out of the one part under heaven, shineth unto the other part under heaven; so shall also the Son of man be in his day.
2878	Luke17:25	But first must he suffer many things, and be rejected of this generation.
2879	Mark13:23	But take ye heed: behold, I have foretold you all things.
2880	Matt24:25	Behold, I have told you before.
2881	Matt24:29	Immediately after the tribulation of those days shall the sun be darkened, and the moon shall not give her light, and the stars shall fall from heaven, and the powers of the heavens shall be shaken:
2882	Mark13:24	But in those days, after that tribulation, the sun shall be darkened, and the moon shall not give her light,
2883	Mark13:25	And the stars of heaven shall fall, and the powers that are in heaven shall be shaken.
2884	Luke21:25	And there shall be signs in the sun, and in the moon, and in the stars; and upon the earth distress of nations, with perplexity; the sea and the waves roaring;
2885	Luke21:26	Men's hearts failing them for fear, and for looking after those things which are coming on the earth: for the powers of heaven shall be shaken.
2886	Matt24:30	And then shall appear the sign of the Son of man in heaven: and then shall all the tribes of the earth mourn, and they shall see the Son of man coming in the clouds of heaven with power and great glory.
2887	Mark13:26	And then shall they see the Son of man coming in the clouds with great power and glory.
2888	Luke21:27	And then shall they see the Son of man coming in a cloud with power and great glory.
2889	Matt24:31	And he shall send his angels with a great sound of a trumpet, and they shall gather together his elect from the four winds, from one end of heaven to the other.
2890	Mark13:27	And then shall he send his angels, and shall gather together his elect from the four winds, from the uttermost part of the earth to the uttermost part of heaven.
2891	Luke21:28	And when these things begin to come to pass, then look up, and lift up your heads; for your redemption draweth nigh.
2892	Luke17:26	And as it was in the days of Noe, so shall it be also in the days of the Son of man.
2893	Matt24:37	But as the days of Noe were, so shall also the coming of the Son of man be.
2894	Matt24:38	For as in the days that were before the flood they were eating and drinking, marrying and giving in marriage, until the day that Noe entered into the ark,
2895	Luke17:27	They did eat, they drank, they married wives, they were given in marriage, until the day that Noe entered into the ark, and the flood came, and destroyed them all.
2896	Matt24:39	And knew not until the flood came, and took them all away; so shall also the coming of the Son of man be.
2897	Luke17:28	Likewise also as it was in the days of Lot; they did eat, they drank, they bought, they sold, they planted, they builded;

THE TREE OF LIFE

2898	Luke17:29	But the same day that Lot went out of Sodom it rained fire and brimstone from heaven, and destroyed them all.
2899	Luke17:30	Even thus shall it be in the day when the Son of man is revealed.
2900	Luke17:32	Remember Lot's wife.
2901	Luke17:34	I tell you, in that night there shall be two men in one bed; the one shall be taken, and the other shall be left.
2902	Matt24:41	Two women shall be grinding at the mill; the one shall be taken, and the other left.
2903	Luke17:35	Two women shall be grinding together; the one shall be taken, and the other left.
2904	Luke17:36	Two men shall be in the field; the one shall be taken, and the other left.
2905	Matt24:40	Then shall two be in the field; the one shall be taken, and the other left.
2906	Luke17:37	And they answered and said unto him, Where, Lord? And he said unto them, Wheresoever the body is, thither will the eagles be gathered together.
2907	Matt24:28	For wheresoever the carcase is, there will the eagles be gathered together.
2908	Luke21:29	And he spake to them a parable; Behold the fig tree, and all the trees;
2909	Matt24:32	Now learn a parable of the fig tree; When his branch is yet tender, and putteth forth leaves, ye know that summer is nigh:
2910	Mark13:28	Now learn a parable of the fig tree; When her branch is yet tender, and putteth forth leaves, ye know that summer is near:
2911	Luke21:30	When they now shoot forth, ye see and know of your own selves that summer is now nigh at hand.
2912	Luke21:31	So likewise ye, when ye see these things come to pass, know ye that the kingdom of God is nigh at hand.
2913	Matt24:33	So likewise ye, when ye shall see all these things, know that it is near, even at the doors.
2914	Mark13:29	So ye in like manner, when ye shall see these things come to pass, know that it is nigh, even at the doors.
2915	Mark13:32	But of that day and that hour knoweth no man, no, not the angels which are in heaven, neither the Son, but the Father.
2916	Matt24:36	But of that day and hour knoweth no man, no, not the angels of heaven, but my Father only.
2917	Mark13:33	Take ye heed, watch and pray: for ye know not when the time is.
2918	Luke18:1	And he spake a parable unto them to this end, that men ought always to pray, and not to faint;
2919	Luke18:2	Saying, There was in a city a judge, which feared not God, neither regarded man:
2920	Luke18:3	And there was a widow in that city; and she came unto him, saying, Avenge me of mine adversary.
2921	Luke18:4	And he would not for a while: but afterward he said within himself, Though I fear not God, nor regard man;
2922	Luke18:5	Yet because this widow troubleth me, I will avenge her, lest by her continual coming she weary me.
2923	Luke18:6	And the Lord said, Hear what the unjust judge saith.
2924	Luke18:7	And shall not God avenge his own elect, which cry day and night unto him, though he bear long with them?
2925	Luke18:8	I tell you that he will avenge them speedily. Nevertheless when the Son of man cometh, shall he find faith on the earth?
2926	Luke21:36	Watch ye therefore, and pray always, that ye may be accounted worthy to escape all these things that shall come to pass, and to stand before the Son of man.
2927	Luke21:34	And take heed to yourselves, lest at any time your hearts be overcharged with surfeiting, and drunkenness, and cares of this life, and so that day come upon you unawares.
2928	Luke21:35	For as a snare shall it come on all them that dwell on the face of the whole earth.
2929	Mark13:34	For the Son of man is as a man taking a far journey, who left his house, and gave

THE TREE OF LIFE

		authority to his servants, and to every man his work, and commanded the porter to watch.
2930	Matt24:42	Watch therefore: for ye know not what hour your Lord doth come.
2931	Mark13:35	Watch ye therefore: for ye know not when the master of the house cometh, at even, or at midnight, or at the cockcrowing, or in the morning:
2932	Mark13:36	Lest coming suddenly he find you sleeping.
2933	Matt24:43	But know this, that if the goodman of the house had known in what watch the thief would come, he would have watched, and would not have suffered his house to be broken up.
2934	Matt24:44	Therefore be ye also ready: for in such an hour as ye think not the Son of man cometh.
2935	Matt24:45	Who then is a faithful and wise servant, whom his lord hath made ruler over his household, to give them meat in due season?
2936	Matt24:46	Blessed is that servant, whom his lord when he cometh shall find so doing.
2937	Matt24:47	Verily I say unto you, That he shall make him ruler over all his goods.
2938	Matt24:48	But and if that evil servant shall say in his heart, My lord delayeth his coming;
2939	Matt24:49	And shall begin to smite his fellowservants, and to eat and drink with the drunken;
2940	Matt24:50	The lord of that servant shall come in a day when he looketh not for him, and in an hour that he is not aware of,
2941	Matt24:51	And shall cut him asunder, and appoint him his portion with the hypocrites: there shall be weeping and gnashing of teeth.
2942	Matt25:1	Then shall the kingdom of heaven be likened unto ten virgins, which took their lamps, and went forth to meet the bridegroom.
2943	Matt25:2	And five of them were wise, and five were foolish.
2944	Matt25:3	They that were foolish took their lamps, and took no oil with them:
2945	Matt25:4	But the wise took oil in their vessels with their lamps.
2946	Matt25:5	While the bridegroom tarried, they all slumbered and slept.
2947	Matt25:6	And at midnight there was a cry made, Behold, the bridegroom cometh; go ye out to meet him.
2948	Matt25:7	Then all those virgins arose, and trimmed their lamps.
2949	Matt25:8	And the foolish said unto the wise, Give us of your oil; for our lamps are gone out.
2950	Matt25:9	But the wise answered, saying, Not so; lest there be not enough for us and you: but go ye rather to them that sell, and buy for yourselves.
2951	Matt25:10	And while they went to buy, the bridegroom came; and they that were ready went in with him to the marriage: and the door was shut.
2952	Matt25:11	Afterward came also the other virgins, saying, Lord, Lord, open to us.
2953	Matt25:12	But he answered and said, Verily I say unto you, I know you not.
2954	Matt25:13	Watch therefore, for ye know neither the day nor the hour wherein the Son of man cometh.
2955	Mark13:37	And what I say unto you I say unto all, Watch.
2956	Matt25:14	For the kingdom of heaven is as a man travelling into a far country, who called his own servants, and delivered unto them his goods.
2957	Matt25:15	And unto one he gave five talents, to another two, and to another one; to every man according to his several ability; and straightway took his journey.
2958	Matt25:16	Then he that had received the five talents went and traded with the same, and made them other five talents.
2959	Matt25:17	And likewise he that had received two, he also gained other two.
2960	Matt25:18	But he that had received one went and digged in the earth, and hid his lord's money.
2961	Matt25:19	After a long time the lord of those servants cometh, and reckoneth with them.
2962	Matt25:20	And so he that had received five talents came and brought other five talents, saying, Lord, thou deliveredst unto me five talents: behold, I have gained beside

THE TREE OF LIFE

		them five talents more.
2963	Matt25:21	His lord said unto him, Well done, thou good and faithful servant: thou hast been faithful over a few things, I will make thee ruler over many things: enter thou into the joy of thy lord.
2964	Matt25:22	He also that had received two talents came and said, Lord, thou deliveredst unto me two talents: behold, I have gained two other talents beside them.
2965	Matt25:23	His lord said unto him, Well done, good and faithful servant; thou hast been faithful over a few things, I will make thee ruler over many things: enter thou into the joy of thy lord.
2966	Matt25:24	Then he which had received the one talent came and said, Lord, I knew thee that thou art an hard man, reaping where thou hast not sown, and gathering where thou hast not strawed:
2967	Matt25:25	And I was afraid, and went and hid thy talent in the earth: lo, there thou hast that is thine.
2968	Matt25:26	His lord answered and said unto him, Thou wicked and slothful servant, thou knewest that I reap where I sowed not, and gather where I have not strawed:
2969	Matt25:27	Thou oughtest therefore to have put my money to the exchangers, and then at my coming I should have received mine own with usury.
2970	Matt25:28	Take therefore the talent from him, and give it unto him which hath ten talents.
2971	Matt25:29	For unto every one that hath shall be given, and he shall have abundance: but from him that hath not shall be taken away even that which he hath.
2972	Matt25:30	And cast ye the unprofitable servant into outer darkness: there shall be weeping and gnashing of teeth.
2973	Matt25:31	When the Son of man shall come in his glory, and all the holy angels with him, then shall he sit upon the throne of his glory:
2974	Matt25:32	And before him shall be gathered all nations: and he shall separate them one from another, as a shepherd divideth his sheep from the goats:
2975	Matt25:33	And he shall set the sheep on his right hand, but the goats on the left.
2976	Matt25:34	Then shall the King say unto them on his right hand, Come, ye blessed of my Father, inherit the kingdom prepared for you from the foundation of the world:
2977	Matt25:35	For I was an hungred, and ye gave me meat: I was thirsty, and ye gave me drink: I was a stranger, and ye took me in:
2978	Matt25:36	Naked, and ye clothed me: I was sick, and ye visited me: I was in prison, and ye came unto me.
2979	Matt25:37	Then shall the righteous answer him, saying, Lord, when saw we thee an hungred, and fed thee? or thirsty, and gave thee drink?
2980	Matt25:38	When saw we thee a stranger, and took thee in? or naked, and clothed thee?
2981	Matt25:39	Or when saw we thee sick, or in prison, and came unto thee?
2982	Matt25:40	And the King shall answer and say unto them, Verily I say unto you, Inasmuch as ye have done it unto one of the least of these my brethren, ye have done it unto me.
2983	Matt25:41	Then shall he say also unto them on the left hand, Depart from me, ye cursed, into everlasting fire, prepared for the devil and his angels:
2984	Matt25:42	For I was an hungred, and ye gave me no meat: I was thirsty, and ye gave me no drink:
2985	Matt25:43	I was a stranger, and ye took me not in: naked, and ye clothed me not: sick, and in prison, and ye visited me not.
2986	Matt25:44	Then shall they also answer him, saying, Lord, when saw we thee an hungred, or athirst, or a stranger, or naked, or sick, or in prison, and did not minister unto thee?
2987	Matt25:45	Then shall he answer them, saying, Verily I say unto you, Inasmuch as ye did it not to one of the least of these, ye did it not to me.
2988	Matt25:46	And these shall go away into everlasting punishment: but the righteous into life

THE TREE OF LIFE

		eternal.
2989	Matt26:1	And it came to pass, when Jesus had finished all these sayings, he said unto his disciples,
2990	Matt26:2	Ye know that after two days is the feast of the passover, and the Son of man is betrayed to be crucified.
2991	Luke22:1	Now the feast of unleavened bread drew nigh, which is called the Passover.
2992	Mark14:1	After two days was the feast of the passover, and of unleavened bread: and the chief priests and the scribes sought how they might take him by craft, and put him to death.
2993	Matt26:3	Then assembled together the chief priests, and the scribes, and the elders of the people, unto the palace of the high priest, who was called Caiaphas,
2994	Luke22:2	And the chief priests and scribes sought how they might kill him; for they feared the people.
2995	Matt26:4	And consulted that they might take Jesus by subtilty, and kill him.
2996	Mark14:2	But they said, Not on the feast day, lest there be an uproar of the people.
2997	Matt26:5	But they said, Not on the feast day, lest there be an uproar among the people.
2998	John11:56	Then sought they for Jesus, and spake among themselves, as they stood in the temple, What think ye, that he will not come to the feast?
2999	John11:57	Now both the chief priests and the Pharisees had given a commandment, that, if any man knew where he were, he should shew it, that they might take him.
3000	Luke22:3	Then entered Satan into Judas surnamed Iscariot, being of the number of the twelve.
3001	Matt26:14	Then one of the twelve, called Judas Iscariot, went unto the chief priests,
3002	Mark14:10	And Judas Iscariot, one of the twelve, went unto the chief priests, to betray him unto them.
3003	Luke22:4	And he went his way, and communed with the chief priests and captains, how he might betray him unto them.
3004	Matt26:15	And said unto them, What will ye give me, and I will deliver him unto you? And they covenanted with him for thirty pieces of silver.
3005	Luke22:5	And they were glad, and covenanted to give him money.
3006	Mark14:11	And when they heard it, they were glad, and promised to give him money. And he sought how he might conveniently betray him.
3007	Luke22:6	And he promised, and sought opportunity to betray him unto them in the absence of the multitude.
3008	Matt26:16	And from that time he sought opportunity to betray him.
3009	Luke22:7	Then came the day of unleavened bread, when the passover must be killed.
3010	Luke22:8	And he sent Peter and John, saying, Go and prepare us the passover, that we may eat.
3011	Mark14:12	And the first day of unleavened bread, when they killed the passover, his disciples said unto him, Where wilt thou that we go and prepare that thou mayest eat the passover?
3012	Matt26:17	Now the first day of the feast of unleavened bread the disciples came to Jesus, saying unto him, Where wilt thou that we prepare for thee to eat the passover?
3013	Luke22:9	And they said unto him, Where wilt thou that we prepare?
3014	Mark14:13	And he sendeth forth two of his disciples, and saith unto them, Go ye into the city, and there shall meet you a man bearing a pitcher of water: follow him.
3015	Luke22:10	And he said unto them, Behold, when ye are entered into the city, there shall a man meet you, bearing a pitcher of water; follow him into the house where he entereth in.
3016	Matt26:18	And he said, Go into the city to such a man, and say unto him, The Master saith, My time is at hand; I will keep the passover at thy house with my disciples.
3017	Mark14:14	And wheresoever he shall go in, say ye to the goodman of the house, The Master saith, Where is the guestchamber, where I shall eat the passover with my

THE TREE OF LIFE

		disciples?
3018	Luke22:11	And ye shall say unto the goodman of the house, The Master saith unto thee, Where is the guestchamber, where I shall eat the passover with my disciples?
3019	Luke22:12	And he shall shew you a large upper room furnished: there make ready.
3020	Mark14:15	And he will shew you a large upper room furnished and prepared: there make ready for us.
3021	Mark14:16	And his disciples went forth, and came into the city, and found as he had said unto them: and they made ready the passover.
3022	Luke22:13	And they went, and found as he had said unto them: and they made ready the passover.
3023	Matt26:19	And the disciples did as Jesus had appointed them; and they made ready the passover.
3024	John13:1	Now before the feast of the passover, when Jesus knew that his hour was come that he should depart out of this world unto the Father, having loved his own which were in the world, he loved them unto the end.
3025	Mark14:17	And in the evening he cometh with the twelve.
3026	Matt26:20	Now when the even was come, he sat down with the twelve.
3027	Luke22:14	And when the hour was come, he sat down, and the twelve apostles with him.
3028	Luke22:15	And he said unto them, With desire I have desired to eat this passover with you before I suffer:
3029	Luke22:19	And he took bread, and gave thanks, and brake it, and gave unto them, saying, This is my body which is given for you: this do in remembrance of me.
3030	Mark14:22	And as they did eat, Jesus took bread, and blessed, and brake it, and gave to them, and said, Take, eat: this is my body.
3031	Matt26:26	And as they were eating, Jesus took bread, and blessed it, and brake it, and gave it to the disciples, and said, Take, eat; this is my body.
3032	Luke22:16	For I say unto you, I will not any more eat thereof, until it be fulfilled in the kingdom of God.
3033	Luke22:17	And he took the cup, and gave thanks, and said, Take this, and divide it among yourselves:
3034	Mark14:23	And he took the cup, and when he had given thanks, he gave it to them: and they all drank of it.
3035	Matt26:27	And he took the cup, and gave thanks, and gave it to them, saying, Drink ye all of it;
3036	Luke22:20	Likewise also the cup after supper, saying, This cup is the new testament in my blood, which is shed for you.
3037	Mark14:24	And he said unto them, This is my blood of the new testament, which is shed for many.
3038	Matt26:28	For this is my blood of the new testament, which is shed for many for the remission of sins.
3039	Luke22:18	For I say unto you, I will not drink of the fruit of the vine, until the kingdom of God shall come.
3040	Mark14:25	Verily I say unto you, I will drink no more of the fruit of the vine, until that day that I drink it new in the kingdom of God.
3041	Matt26:29	But I say unto you, I will not drink henceforth of this fruit of the vine, until that day when I drink it new with you in my Father's kingdom.
3042	Luke22:25	And he said unto them, The kings of the Gentiles exercise lordship over them; and they that exercise authority upon them are called benefactors.
3043	Luke22:26	But ye shall not be so: but he that is greatest among you, let him be as the younger; and he that is chief, as he that doth serve.
3044	Luke22:27	For whether is greater, he that sitteth at meat, or he that serveth? is not he that sitteth at meat? but I am among you as he that serveth.
3045	John13:2	And supper being ended, the devil having now put into the heart of Judas

THE TREE OF LIFE

		Iscariot, Simon's son, to betray him;
3046	John13:3	Jesus knowing that the Father had given all things into his hands, and that he was come from God, and went to God;
3047	John13:4	He riseth from supper, and laid aside his garments; and took a towel, and girded himself.
3048	John13:5	After that he poureth water into a bason, and began to wash the disciples' feet, and to wipe them with the towel wherewith he was girded.
3049	John13:6	Then cometh he to Simon Peter: and Peter saith unto him, Lord, dost thou wash my feet?
3050	John13:7	Jesus answered and said unto him, What I do thou knowest not now; but thou shalt know hereafter.
3051	John13:8	Peter saith unto him, Thou shalt never wash my feet. Jesus answered him, If I wash thee not, thou hast no part with me.
3052	John13:9	Simon Peter saith unto him, Lord, not my feet only, but also my hands and my head.
3053	John13:10	Jesus saith to him, He that is washed needeth not save to wash his feet, but is clean every whit: and ye are clean, but not all.
3054	John13:11	For he knew who should betray him; therefore said he, Ye are not all clean.
3055	John13:12	So after he had washed their feet, and had taken his garments, and was set down again, he said unto them, Know ye what I have done to you?
3056	Luke22:28	Ye are they which have continued with me in my temptations.
3057	Luke22:29	And I appoint unto you a kingdom, as my Father hath appointed unto me;
3058	Luke22:30	That ye may eat and drink at my table in my kingdom, and sit on thrones judging the twelve tribes of Israel.
3059	John13:13	Ye call me Master and Lord: and ye say well; for so I am.
3060	John13:14	If I then, your Lord and Master, have washed your feet; ye also ought to wash one another's feet.
3061	John13:15	For I have given you an example, that ye should do as I have done to you.
3062	John13:16	Verily, verily, I say unto you, The servant is not greater than his lord; neither he that is sent greater than he that sent him.
3063	John13:17	If ye know these things, happy are ye if ye do them.
3064	John13:18	I speak not of you all: I know whom I have chosen: but that the scripture may be fulfilled, He that eateth bread with me hath lifted up his heel against me.
3065	John13:19	Now I tell you before it come, that, when it is come to pass, ye may believe that I am he.
3066	John13:21	When Jesus had thus said, he was troubled in spirit, and testified, and said, Verily, verily, I say unto you, that one of you shall betray me.
3067	Mark14:18	And as they sat and did eat, Jesus said, Verily I say unto you, One of you which eateth with me shall betray me.
3068	Matt26:21	And as they did eat, he said, Verily I say unto you, that one of you shall betray me.
3069	Luke22:21	But, behold, the hand of him that betrayeth me is with me on the table.
3070	Luke22:22	And truly the Son of man goeth, as it was determined: but woe unto that man by whom he is betrayed!
3071	Mark14:21	The Son of man indeed goeth, as it is written of him: but woe to that man by whom the Son of man is betrayed! good were it for that man if he had never been born.
3072	Matt26:24	The Son of man goeth as it is written of him: but woe unto that man by whom the Son of man is betrayed! it had been good for that man if he had not been born.
3073	John13:22	Then the disciples looked one on another, doubting of whom he spake.
3074	Luke22:23	And they began to enquire among themselves, which of them it was that should do this thing.
3075	John13:23	Now there was leaning on Jesus' bosom one of his disciples, whom Jesus loved.

THE TREE OF LIFE

3076	John13:24	Simon Peter therefore beckoned to him, that he should ask who it should be of whom he spake.
3077	John13:25	He then lying on Jesus' breast saith unto him, Lord, who is it?
3078	Mark14:19	And they began to be sorrowful, and to say unto him one by one, Is it I? and another said, Is it I?
3079	Matt26:22	And they were exceeding sorrowful, and began every one of them to say unto him, Lord, is it I?
3080	Mark14:20	And he answered and said unto them, It is one of the twelve, that dippeth with me in the dish.
3081	Matt26:23	And he answered and said, He that dippeth his hand with me in the dish, the same shall betray me.
3082	John13:26	Jesus answered, He it is, to whom I shall give a sop, when I have dipped it. And when he had dipped the sop, he gave it to Judas Iscariot, the son of Simon.
3083	Matt26:25	Then Judas, which betrayed him, answered and said, Master, is it I? He said unto him, Thou hast said.
3084	John13:27	And after the sop Satan entered into him. Then said Jesus unto him, That thou doest, do quickly.
3085	John13:28	Now no man at the table knew for what intent he spake this unto him.
3086	John13:29	For some of them thought, because Judas had the bag, that Jesus had said unto him, Buy those things that we have need of against the feast; or, that he should give something to the poor.
3087	John13:30	He then having received the sop went immediately out: and it was night.
3088	John13:31	Therefore, when he was gone out, Jesus said, Now is the Son of man glorified, and God is glorified in him.
3089	John13:32	If God be glorified in him, God shall also glorify him in himself, and shall straightway glorify him.
3090	John13:33	Little children, yet a little while I am with you. Ye shall seek me: and as I said unto the Jews, Whither I go, ye cannot come; so now I say to you.
3091	John13:36	Simon Peter said unto him, Lord, whither goest thou? Jesus answered him, Whither I go, thou canst not follow me now; but thou shalt follow me afterwards.
3092	John13:37	Peter said unto him, Lord, why cannot I follow thee now? I will lay down my life for thy sake.
3093	Luke22:31	And the Lord said, Simon, Simon, behold, Satan hath desired to have you, that he may sift you as wheat:
3094	Luke22:32	But I have prayed for thee, that thy faith fail not: and when thou art converted, strengthen thy brethren.
3095	Mark14:27	And Jesus saith unto them, All ye shall be offended because of me this night: for it is written, I will smite the shepherd, and the sheep shall be scattered.
3096	Matt26:31	Then saith Jesus unto them, All ye shall be offended because of me this night: for it is written, I will smite the shepherd, and the sheep of the flock shall be scattered abroad.
3097	Matt26:32	But after I am risen again, I will go before you into Galilee.
3098	Mark14:28	But after that I am risen, I will go before you into Galilee.
3099	Luke22:33	And he said unto him, Lord, I am ready to go with thee, both into prison, and to death.
3100	John13:38	Jesus answered him, Wilt thou lay down thy life for my sake? Verily, verily, I say unto thee, The cock shall not crow, till thou hast denied me thrice.
3101	Luke22:34	And he said, I tell thee, Peter, the cock shall not crow this day, before that thou shalt thrice deny that thou knowest me.
3102	Mark14:29	But Peter said unto him, Although all shall be offended, yet will not I.
3103	Matt26:33	Peter answered and said unto him, Though all men shall be offended because of thee, yet will I never be offended.
3104	Mark14:30	And Jesus saith unto him, Verily I say unto thee, That this day, even in this night,

THE TREE OF LIFE

		before the cock crow twice, thou shalt deny me thrice.
3105	Matt26:34	Jesus said unto him, Verily I say unto thee, That this night, before the cock crow, thou shalt deny me thrice.
3106	Matt26:35	Peter said unto him, Though I should die with thee, yet will I not deny thee. Likewise also said all the disciples.
3107	Mark14:31	But he spake the more vehemently, If I should die with thee, I will not deny thee in any wise. Likewise also said they all.
3108	John14:1	Let not your heart be troubled: ye believe in God, believe also in me.
3109	John14:2	In my Father's house are many mansions: if it were not so, I would have told you. I go to prepare a place for you.
3110	John14:3	And if I go and prepare a place for you, I will come again, and receive you unto myself; that where I am, there ye may be also.
3111	John14:4	And whither I go ye know, and the way ye know.
3112	John14:5	Thomas saith unto him, Lord, we know not whither thou goest; and how can we know the way?
3113	John14:6	Jesus saith unto him, I am the way, the truth, and the life: no man cometh unto the Father, but by me.
3114	John14:7	If ye had known me, ye should have known my Father also: and from henceforth ye know him, and have seen him.
3115	John14:8	Philip saith unto him, Lord, shew us the Father, and it sufficeth us.
3116	John14:9	Jesus said unto him, Have I been so long time with you, and yet hast thou not known me, Philip? he that hath seen me hath seen the Father; and how sayest thou then, Shew us the Father?
3117	John14:10	Believest thou not that I am in the Father, and the Father in me? the words that I speak unto you I speak not of myself: but the Father that dwelleth in me, he doeth the works.
3118	John14:11	Believe me that I am in the Father, and the Father in me: or else believe me for the very works' sake.
3119	John14:12	Verily, verily, I say unto you, He that believeth on me, the works that I do shall he do also; and greater works than these shall he do; because I go unto my Father.
3120	John14:15	If ye love me, keep my commandments.
3121	John14:16	And I will pray the Father, and he shall give you another Comforter, that he may abide with you for ever;
3122	John14:17	Even the Spirit of truth; whom the world cannot receive, because it seeth him not, neither knoweth him: but ye know him; for he dwelleth with you, and shall be in you.
3123	John14:18	I will not leave you comfortless: I will come to you.
3124	John14:19	Yet a little while, and the world seeth me no more; but ye see me: because I live, ye shall live also.
3125	John14:20	At that day ye shall know that I am in my Father, and ye in me, and I in you.
3126	John14:21	He that hath my commandments, and keepeth them, he it is that loveth me: and he that loveth me shall be loved of my Father, and I will love him, and will manifest myself to him.
3127	John14:22	Judas saith unto him, not Iscariot, Lord, how is it that thou wilt manifest thyself unto us, and not unto the world?
3128	John14:23	Jesus answered and said unto him, If a man love me, he will keep my words: and my Father will love him, and we will come unto him, and make our abode with him.
3129	John14:24	He that loveth me not keepeth not my sayings: and the word which ye hear is not mine, but the Father's which sent me.
3130	John14:25	These things have I spoken unto you, being yet present with you.
3131	John14:26	But the Comforter, which is the Holy Ghost, whom the Father will send in my name, he shall teach you all things, and bring all things to your remembrance,

THE TREE OF LIFE

		whatsoever I have said unto you.
3132	John14:27	Peace I leave with you, my peace I give unto you: not as the world giveth, give I unto you. Let not your heart be troubled, neither let it be afraid.
3133	John14:28	Ye have heard how I said unto you, I go away, and come again unto you. If ye loved me, ye would rejoice, because I said, I go unto the Father: for my Father is greater than I.
3134	John14:29	And now I have told you before it come to pass, that, when it is come to pass, ye might believe.
3135	John14:30	Hereafter I will not talk much with you: for the prince of this world cometh, and hath nothing in me.
3136	John14:31	But that the world may know that I love the Father; and as the Father gave me commandment, even so I do. Arise, let us go hence.
3137	Luke22:35	And he said unto them, When I sent you without purse, and scrip, and shoes, lacked ye any thing? And they said, Nothing.
3138	Luke22:36	Then said he unto them, But now, he that hath a purse, let him take it, and likewise his scrip: and he that hath no sword, let him sell his garment, and buy one.
3139	Luke22:37	For I say unto you, that this that is written must yet be accomplished in me, And he was reckoned among the transgressors: for the things concerning me have an end.
3140	Luke22:38	And they said, Lord, behold, here are two swords. And he said unto them, It is enough.
3141	Matt26:30	And when they had sung an hymn, they went out into the mount of Olives.
3142	Mark14:26	And when they had sung an hymn, they went out into the mount of Olives.
3143	John15:1	I am the true vine, and my Father is the husbandman.
3144	John15:2	Every branch in me that beareth not fruit he taketh away: and every branch that beareth fruit, he purgeth it, that it may bring forth more fruit.
3145	John15:3	Now ye are clean through the word which I have spoken unto you.
3146	John15:4	Abide in me, and I in you. As the branch cannot bear fruit of itself, except it abide in the vine; no more can ye, except ye abide in me.
3147	John15:5	I am the vine, ye are the branches: He that abideth in me, and I in him, the same bringeth forth much fruit: for without me ye can do nothing.
3148	John15:6	If a man abide not in me, he is cast forth as a branch, and is withered; and men gather them, and cast them into the fire, and they are burned.
3149	John15:7	If ye abide in me, and my words abide in you, ye shall ask what ye will, and it shall be done unto you.
3150	John15:8	Herein is my Father glorified, that ye bear much fruit; so shall ye be my disciples.
3151	John15:9	As the Father hath loved me, so have I loved you: continue ye in my love.
3152	John15:10	If ye keep my commandments, ye shall abide in my love; even as I have kept my Father's commandments, and abide in his love.
3153	John15:11	These things have I spoken unto you, that my joy might remain in you, and that your joy might be full.
3154	John13:34	A new commandment I give unto you, That ye love one another; as I have loved you, that ye also love one another.
3155	John15:12	This is my commandment, That ye love one another, as I have loved you.
3156	John13:35	By this shall all men know that ye are my disciples, if ye have love one to another.
3157	John15:13	Greater love hath no man than this, that a man lay down his life for his friends.
3158	John15:14	Ye are my friends, if ye do whatsoever I command you.
3159	John15:15	Henceforth I call you not servants; for the servant knoweth not what his lord doeth: but I have called you friends; for all things that I have heard of my Father I have made known unto you.
3160	John15:16	Ye have not chosen me, but I have chosen you, and ordained you, that ye should

THE TREE OF LIFE

		go and bring forth fruit, and that your fruit should remain: that whatsoever ye shall ask of the Father in my name, he may give it you.
3161	John15:17	These things I command you, that ye love one another.
3162	John15:18	If the world hate you, ye know that it hated me before it hated you.
3163	John15:19	If ye were of the world, the world would love his own: but because ye are not of the world, but I have chosen you out of the world, therefore the world hateth you.
3164	John15:20	Remember the word that I said unto you, The servant is not greater than his lord. If they have persecuted me, they will also persecute you; if they have kept my saying, they will keep yours also.
3165	John15:21	But all these things will they do unto you for my name's sake, because they know not him that sent me.
3166	John15:22	If I had not come and spoken unto them, they had not had sin: but now they have no cloak for their sin.
3167	John15:23	He that hateth me hateth my Father also.
3168	John15:24	If I had not done among them the works which none other man did, they had not had sin: but now have they both seen and hated both me and my Father.
3169	John15:25	But this cometh to pass, that the word might be fulfilled that is written in their law, They hated me without a cause.
3170	John15:26	But when the Comforter is come, whom I will send unto you from the Father, even the Spirit of truth, which proceedeth from the Father, he shall testify of me:
3171	John15:27	And ye also shall bear witness, because ye have been with me from the beginning.
3172	John16:1	These things have I spoken unto you, that ye should not be offended.
3173	John16:2	They shall put you out of the synagogues: yea, the time cometh, that whosoever killeth you will think that he doeth God service.
3174	John16:3	And these things will they do unto you, because they have not known the Father, nor me.
3175	John16:4	But these things have I told you, that when the time shall come, ye may remember that I told you of them. And these things I said not unto you at the beginning, because I was with you.
3176	John16:5	But now I go my way to him that sent me; and none of you asketh me, Whither goest thou?
3177	John16:6	But because I have said these things unto you, sorrow hath filled your heart.
3178	John16:7	Nevertheless I tell you the truth; It is expedient for you that I go away: for if I go not away, the Comforter will not come unto you; but if I depart, I will send him unto you.
3179	John16:8	And when he is come, he will reprove the world of sin, and of righteousness, and of judgment:
3180	John16:9	Of sin, because they believe not on me;
3181	John16:10	Of righteousness, because I go to my Father, and ye see me no more;
3182	John16:11	Of judgment, because the prince of this world is judged.
3183	John16:12	I have yet many things to say unto you, but ye cannot bear them now.
3184	John16:13	Howbeit when he, the Spirit of truth, is come, he will guide you into all truth: for he shall not speak of himself; but whatsoever he shall hear, that shall he speak: and he will shew you things to come.
3185	John16:14	He shall glorify me: for he shall receive of mine, and shall shew it unto you.
3186	John16:15	All things that the Father hath are mine: therefore said I, that he shall take of mine, and shall shew it unto you.
3187	John16:16	A little while, and ye shall not see me: and again, a little while, and ye shall see me, because I go to the Father.
3188	John16:17	Then said some of his disciples among themselves, What is this that he saith unto us, A little while, and ye shall not see me: and again, a little while, and ye shall see me: and, Because I go to the Father?

THE TREE OF LIFE

3189	John16:18	They said therefore, What is this that he saith, A little while? we cannot tell what he saith.
3190	John16:19	Now Jesus knew that they were desirous to ask him, and said unto them, Do ye enquire among yourselves of that I said, A little while, and ye shall not see me: and again, a little while, and ye shall see me?
3191	John16:20	Verily, verily, I say unto you, That ye shall weep and lament, but the world shall rejoice: and ye shall be sorrowful, but your sorrow shall be turned into joy.
3192	John16:21	A woman when she is in travail hath sorrow, because her hour is come: but as soon as she is delivered of the child, she remembereth no more the anguish, for joy that a man is born into the world.
3193	John16:22	And ye now therefore have sorrow: but I will see you again, and your heart shall rejoice, and your joy no man taketh from you.
3194	John16:23	And in that day ye shall ask me nothing. Verily, verily, I say unto you, Whatsoever ye shall ask the Father in my name, he will give it you.
3195	John16:24	Hitherto have ye asked nothing in my name: ask, and ye shall receive, that your joy may be full.
3196	John14:13	And whatsoever ye shall ask in my name, that will I do, that the Father may be glorified in the Son.
3197	John14:14	If ye shall ask any thing in my name, I will do it.
3198	John16:25	These things have I spoken unto you in proverbs: but the time cometh, when I shall no more speak unto you in proverbs, but I shall shew you plainly of the Father.
3199	John16:26	At that day ye shall ask in my name: and I say not unto you, that I will pray the Father for you:
3200	John16:27	For the Father himself loveth you, because ye have loved me, and have believed that I came out from God.
3201	John16:28	I came forth from the Father, and am come into the world: again, I leave the world, and go to the Father.
3202	John16:29	His disciples said unto him, Lo, now speakest thou plainly, and speakest no proverb.
3203	John16:30	Now are we sure that thou knowest all things, and needest not that any man should ask thee: by this we believe that thou camest forth from God.
3204	John16:31	Jesus answered them, Do ye now believe?
3205	John16:32	Behold, the hour cometh, yea, is now come, that ye shall be scattered, every man to his own, and shall leave me alone: and yet I am not alone, because the Father is with me.
3206	John16:33	These things I have spoken unto you, that in me ye might have peace. In the world ye shall have tribulation: but be of good cheer; I have overcome the world.
3207	John17:1	These words spake Jesus, and lifted up his eyes to heaven, and said, Father, the hour is come; glorify thy Son, that thy Son also may glorify thee:
3208	John17:2	As thou hast given him power over all flesh, that he should give eternal life to as many as thou hast given him.
3209	John17:3	And this is life eternal, that they might know thee the only true God, and Jesus Christ, whom thou hast sent.
3210	John17:4	I have glorified thee on the earth: I have finished the work which thou gavest me to do.
3211	John17:5	And now, O Father, glorify thou me with thine own self with the glory which I had with thee before the world was.
3212	John17:6	I have manifested thy name unto the men which thou gavest me out of the world: thine they were, and thou gavest them me; and they have kept thy word.
3213	John17:7	Now they have known that all things whatsoever thou hast given me are of thee.
3214	John17:8	For I have given unto them the words which thou gavest me; and they have received them, and have known surely that I came out from thee, and they have

THE TREE OF LIFE

		believed that thou didst send me.
3215	John17:9	I pray for them: I pray not for the world, but for them which thou hast given me; for they are thine.
3216	John17:10	And all mine are thine, and thine are mine; and I am glorified in them.
3217	John17:11	And now I am no more in the world, but these are in the world, and I come to thee. Holy Father, keep through thine own name those whom thou hast given me, that they may be one, as we are.
3218	John17:12	While I was with them in the world, I kept them in thy name: those that thou gavest me I have kept, and none of them is lost, but the son of perdition; that the scripture might be fulfilled.
3219	John17:13	And now come I to thee; and these things I speak in the world, that they might have my joy fulfilled in themselves.
3220	John17:14	I have given them thy word; and the world hath hated them, because they are not of the world, even as I am not of the world.
3221	John17:15	I pray not that thou shouldest take them out of the world, but that thou shouldest keep them from the evil.
3222	John17:16	They are not of the world, even as I am not of the world.
3223	John17:17	Sanctify them through thy truth: thy word is truth.
3224	John17:18	As thou hast sent me into the world, even so have I also sent them into the world.
3225	John17:19	And for their sakes I sanctify myself, that they also might be sanctified through the truth.
3226	John17:20	Neither pray I for these alone, but for them also which shall believe on me through their word;
3227	John17:21	That they all may be one; as thou, Father, art in me, and I in thee, that they also may be one in us: that the world may believe that thou hast sent me.
3228	John17:22	And the glory which thou gavest me I have given them; that they may be one, even as we are one:
3229	John17:23	I in them, and thou in me, that they may be made perfect in one; and that the world may know that thou hast sent me, and hast loved them, as thou hast loved me.
3230	John17:24	Father, I will that they also, whom thou hast given me, be with me where I am; that they may behold my glory, which thou hast given me: for thou lovedst me before the foundation of the world.
3231	John17:25	O righteous Father, the world hath not known thee: but I have known thee, and these have known that thou hast sent me.
3232	John17:26	And I have declared unto them thy name, and will declare it: that the love wherewith thou hast loved me may be in them, and I in them.
3233	John18:1	When Jesus had spoken these words, he went forth with his disciples over the brook Cedron, where was a garden, into the which he entered, and his disciples.
3234	Luke22:39	And he came out, and went, as he was wont, to the mount of Olives; and his disciples also followed him.
3235	John18:2	And Judas also, which betrayed him, knew the place: for Jesus ofttimes resorted thither with his disciples.
3236	Mark14:32	And they came to a place which was named Gethsemane: and he saith to his disciples, Sit ye here, while I shall pray.
3237	Matt26:36	Then cometh Jesus with them unto a place called Gethsemane, and saith unto the disciples, Sit ye here, while I go and pray yonder.
3238	Luke22:40	And when he was at the place, he said unto them, Pray that ye enter not into temptation.
3239	Mark14:33	And he taketh with him Peter and James and John, and began to be sore amazed, and to be very heavy;
3240	Matt26:37	And he took with him Peter and the two sons of Zebedee, and began to be sorrowful and very heavy.

THE TREE OF LIFE

3241	Mark14:34	And saith unto them, My soul is exceeding sorrowful unto death: tarry ye here, and watch.
3242	Matt26:38	Then saith he unto them, My soul is exceeding sorrowful, even unto death: tarry ye here, and watch with me.
3243	Matt26:39	And he went a little farther, and fell on his face, and prayed, saying, O my Father, if it be possible, let this cup pass from me: nevertheless not as I will, but as thou wilt.
3244	Luke22:41	And he was withdrawn from them about a stone's cast, and kneeled down, and prayed,
3245	Luke22:42	Saying, Father, if thou be willing, remove this cup from me: nevertheless not my will, but thine, be done.
3246	Mark14:35	And he went forward a little, and fell on the ground, and prayed that, if it were possible, the hour might pass from him.
3247	Mark14:36	And he said, Abba, Father, all things are possible unto thee; take away this cup from me: nevertheless not what I will, but what thou wilt.
3248	Luke22:43	And there appeared an angel unto him from heaven, strengthening him.
3249	Luke22:44	And being in an agony he prayed more earnestly: and his sweat was as it were great drops of blood falling down to the ground.
3250	Luke22:45	And when he rose up from prayer, and was come to his disciples, he found them sleeping for sorrow,
3251	Luke22:46	And said unto them, Why sleep ye? rise and pray, lest ye enter into temptation.
3252	Matt26:40	And he cometh unto the disciples, and findeth them asleep, and saith unto Peter, What, could ye not watch with me one hour?
3253	Mark14:37	And he cometh, and findeth them sleeping, and saith unto Peter, Simon, sleepest thou? couldest not thou watch one hour?
3254	Mark14:38	Watch ye and pray, lest ye enter into temptation. The spirit truly is ready, but the flesh is weak.
3255	Matt26:41	Watch and pray, that ye enter not into temptation: the spirit indeed is willing, but the flesh is weak.
3256	Matt26:42	He went away again the second time, and prayed, saying, O my Father, if this cup may not pass away from me, except I drink it, thy will be done.
3257	Mark14:39	And again he went away, and prayed, and spake the same words.
3258	Matt26:43	And he came and found them asleep again: for their eyes were heavy.
3259	Mark14:40	And when he returned, he found them asleep again, (for their eyes were heavy,) neither wist they what to answer him.
3260	Matt26:44	And he left them, and went away again, and prayed the third time, saying the same words.
3261	Matt26:45	Then cometh he to his disciples, and saith unto them, Sleep on now, and take your rest: behold, the hour is at hand, and the Son of man is betrayed into the hands of sinners.
3262	Mark14:41	And he cometh the third time, and saith unto them, Sleep on now, and take your rest: it is enough, the hour is come; behold, the Son of man is betrayed into the hands of sinners.
3263	Matt26:47	And while he yet spake, lo, Judas, one of the twelve, came, and with him a great multitude with swords and staves, from the chief priests and elders of the people.
3264	Mark14:43	And immediately, while he yet spake, cometh Judas, one of the twelve, and with him a great multitude with swords and staves, from the chief priests and the scribes and the elders.
3265	John18:3	Judas then, having received a band of men and officers from the chief priests and Pharisees, cometh thither with lanterns and torches and weapons.
3266	Luke22:47	And while he yet spake, behold a multitude, and he that was called Judas, one of the twelve, went before them, and drew near unto Jesus to kiss him.
3267	Matt26:46	Rise, let us be going: behold, he is at hand that doth betray me.

THE TREE OF LIFE

3268	Mark14:42	Rise up, let us go; lo, he that betrayeth me is at hand.
3269	John18:4	Jesus therefore, knowing all things that should come upon him, went forth, and said unto them, Whom seek ye?
3270	John18:5	They answered him, Jesus of Nazareth. Jesus saith unto them, I am he. And Judas also, which betrayed him, stood with them.
3271	John18:6	As soon then as he had said unto them, I am he, they went backward, and fell to the ground.
3272	John18:7	Then asked he them again, Whom seek ye? And they said, Jesus of Nazareth.
3273	John18:8	Jesus answered, I have told you that I am he: if therefore ye seek me, let these go their way:
3274	John18:9	That the saying might be fulfilled, which he spake, Of them which thou gavest me have I lost none.
3275	Matt26:48	Now he that betrayed him gave them a sign, saying, Whomsoever I shall kiss, that same is he: hold him fast.
3276	Mark14:44	And he that betrayed him had given them a token, saying, Whomsoever I shall kiss, that same is he; take him, and lead him away safely.
3277	Matt26:49	And forthwith he came to Jesus, and said, Hail, master; and kissed him.
3278	Mark14:45	And as soon as he was come, he goeth straightway to him, and saith, Master, master; and kissed him.
3279	Luke22:48	But Jesus said unto him, Judas, betrayest thou the Son of man with a kiss?
3280	Matt26:50	And Jesus said unto him, Friend, wherefore art thou come? Then came they, and laid hands on Jesus, and took him.
3281	Mark14:46	And they laid their hands on him, and took him.
3282	Luke22:49	When they which were about him saw what would follow, they said unto him, Lord, shall we smite with the sword?
3283	John18:10	Then Simon Peter having a sword drew it, and smote the high priest's servant, and cut off his right ear. The servant's name was Malchus.
3284	Matt26:51	And, behold, one of them which were with Jesus stretched out his hand, and drew his sword, and struck a servant of the high priest's, and smote off his ear.
3285	Mark14:47	And one of them that stood by drew a sword, and smote a servant of the high priest, and cut off his ear.
3286	Luke22:50	And one of them smote the servant of the high priest, and cut off his right ear.
3287	John18:11	Then said Jesus unto Peter, Put up thy sword into the sheath: the cup which my Father hath given me, shall I not drink it?
3288	Matt26:52	Then said Jesus unto him, Put up again thy sword into his place: for all they that take the sword shall perish with the sword.
3289	Matt26:53	Thinkest thou that I cannot now pray to my Father, and he shall presently give me more than twelve legions of angels?
3290	Matt26:54	But how then shall the scriptures be fulfilled, that thus it must be?
3291	Luke22:51	And Jesus answered and said, Suffer ye thus far. And he touched his ear, and healed him.
3292	Luke22:52	Then Jesus said unto the chief priests, and captains of the temple, and the elders, which were come to him, Be ye come out, as against a thief, with swords and staves?
3293	Mark14:48	And Jesus answered and said unto them, Are ye come out, as against a thief, with swords and with staves to take me?
3294	Matt26:55	In that same hour said Jesus to the multitudes, Are ye come out as against a thief with swords and staves for to take me? I sat daily with you teaching in the temple, and ye laid no hold on me.
3295	Mark14:49	I was daily with you in the temple teaching, and ye took me not: but the scriptures must be fulfilled.
3296	Luke22:53	When I was daily with you in the temple, ye stretched forth no hands against me: but this is your hour, and the power of darkness.

THE TREE OF LIFE

3297	Matt26:56	But all this was done, that the scriptures of the prophets might be fulfilled. Then all the disciples forsook him, and fled.
3298	Mark14:50	And they all forsook him, and fled.
3299	Mark14:51	And there followed him a certain young man, having a linen cloth cast about his naked body; and the young men laid hold on him:
3300	Mark14:52	And he left the linen cloth, and fled from them naked.
3301	John18:12	Then the band and the captain and officers of the Jews took Jesus, and bound him,
3302	John18:13	And led him away to Annas first; for he was father in law to Caiaphas, which was the high priest that same year.
3303	Matt26:57	And they that had laid hold on Jesus led him away to Caiaphas the high priest, where the scribes and the elders were assembled.
3304	John18:24	Now Annas had sent him bound unto Caiaphas the high priest.
3305	John18:14	Now Caiaphas was he, which gave counsel to the Jews, that it was expedient that one man should die for the people.
3306	Mark14:53	And they led Jesus away to the high priest: and with him were assembled all the chief priests and the elders and the scribes.
3307	Luke22:54	Then took they him, and led him, and brought him into the high priest's house. And Peter followed afar off.
3308	John18:15	And Simon Peter followed Jesus, and so did another disciple: that disciple was known unto the high priest, and went in with Jesus into the palace of the high priest.
3309	Matt26:58	But Peter followed him afar off unto the high priest's palace, and went in, and sat with the servants, to see the end.
3310	Mark14:54	And Peter followed him afar off, even into the palace of the high priest: and he sat with the servants, and warmed himself at the fire.
3311	John18:19	The high priest then asked Jesus of his disciples, and of his doctrine.
3312	John18:20	Jesus answered him, I spake openly to the world; I ever taught in the synagogue, and in the temple, whither the Jews always resort; and in secret have I said nothing.
3313	John18:21	Why askest thou me? ask them which heard me, what I have said unto them: behold, they know what I said.
3314	John18:22	And when he had thus spoken, one of the officers which stood by struck Jesus with the palm of his hand, saying, Answerest thou the high priest so?
3315	John18:23	Jesus answered him, If I have spoken evil, bear witness of the evil: but if well, why smitest thou me?
3316	Mark14:55	And the chief priests and all the council sought for witness against Jesus to put him to death; and found none.
3317	Matt26:59	Now the chief priests, and elders, and all the council, sought false witness against Jesus, to put him to death;
3318	Matt26:60	But found none: yea, though many false witnesses came, yet found they none. At the last came two false witnesses,
3319	Mark14:56	For many bare false witness against him, but their witness agreed not together.
3320	Mark14:57	And there arose certain, and bare false witness against him, saying,
3321	Matt26:61	And said, This fellow said, I am able to destroy the temple of God, and to build it in three days.
3322	Mark14:58	We heard him say, I will destroy this temple that is made with hands, and within three days I will build another made without hands.
3323	Mark14:59	But neither so did their witness agree together.
3324	Matt26:62	And the high priest arose, and said unto him, Answerest thou nothing? what is it which these witness against thee?
3325	Mark14:60	And the high priest stood up in the midst, and asked Jesus, saying, Answerest thou nothing? what is it which these witness against thee?

THE TREE OF LIFE

3326	Mark14:61	But he held his peace, and answered nothing. Again the high priest asked him, and said unto him, Art thou the Christ, the Son of the Blessed?
3327	Matt26:63	But Jesus held his peace. And the high priest answered and said unto him, I adjure thee by the living God, that thou tell us whether thou be the Christ, the Son of God.
3328	Luke22:67	Art thou the Christ? tell us. And he said unto them, If I tell you, ye will not believe:
3329	Luke22:68	And if I also ask you, ye will not answer me, nor let me go.
3330	Luke22:70	Then said they all, Art thou then the Son of God? And he said unto them, Ye say that I am.
3331	Matt26:64	Jesus saith unto him, Thou hast said: nevertheless I say unto you, Hereafter shall ye see the Son of man sitting on the right hand of power, and coming in the clouds of heaven.
3332	Mark14:62	And Jesus said, I am: and ye shall see the Son of man sitting on the right hand of power, and coming in the clouds of heaven.
3333	Luke22:69	Hereafter shall the Son of man sit on the right hand of the power of God.
3334	Mark14:63	Then the high priest rent his clothes, and saith, What need we any further witnesses?
3335	Luke22:71	And they said, What need we any further witness? for we ourselves have heard of his own mouth.
3336	Matt26:65	Then the high priest rent his clothes, saying, He hath spoken blasphemy; what further need have we of witnesses? behold, now ye have heard his blasphemy.
3337	Mark14:64	Ye have heard the blasphemy: what think ye? And they all condemned him to be guilty of death.
3338	Matt26:66	What think ye? They answered and said, He is guilty of death.
3339	Luke22:63	And the men that held Jesus mocked him, and smote him.
3340	Luke22:64	And when they had blindfolded him, they struck him on the face, and asked him, saying, Prophesy, who is it that smote thee?
3341	Matt26:67	Then did they spit in his face, and buffeted him; and others smote him with the palms of their hands,
3342	Mark14:65	And some began to spit on him, and to cover his face, and to buffet him, and to say unto him, Prophesy: and the servants did strike him with the palms of their hands.
3343	Matt26:68	Saying, Prophesy unto us, thou Christ, Who is he that smote thee?
3344	Luke22:65	And many other things blasphemously spake they against him.
3345	John18:16	But Peter stood at the door without. Then went out that other disciple, which was known unto the high priest, and spake unto her that kept the door, and brought in Peter.
3346	Luke22:55	And when they had kindled a fire in the midst of the hall, and were set down together, Peter sat down among them.
3347	Matt26:69	Now Peter sat without in the palace: and a damsel came unto him, saying, Thou also wast with Jesus of Galilee.
3348	Mark14:66	And as Peter was beneath in the palace, there cometh one of the maids of the high priest:
3349	Mark14:67	And when she saw Peter warming himself, she looked upon him, and said, And thou also wast with Jesus of Nazareth.
3350	Luke22:56	But a certain maid beheld him as he sat by the fire, and earnestly looked upon him, and said, This man was also with him.
3351	John18:17	Then saith the damsel that kept the door unto Peter, Art not thou also one of this man's disciples? He saith, I am not.
3352	Luke22:57	And he denied him, saying, Woman, I know him not.
3353	Matt26:70	But he denied before them all, saying, I know not what thou sayest.
3354	Mark14:68	But he denied, saying, I know not, neither understand I what thou sayest. And he went out into the porch; and the cock crew.

THE TREE OF LIFE

3355	Matt26:71	And when he was gone out into the porch, another maid saw him, and said unto them that were there, This fellow was also with Jesus of Nazareth.
3356	John18:18	And the servants and officers stood there, who had made a fire of coals; for it was cold: and they warmed themselves: and Peter stood with them, and warmed himself.
3357	John18:25	And Simon Peter stood and warmed himself. They said therefore unto him, Art not thou also one of his disciples? He denied it, and said, I am not.
3358	Mark14:69	And a maid saw him again, and began to say to them that stood by, This is one of them.
3359	Luke22:58	And after a little while another saw him, and said, Thou art also of them. And Peter said, Man, I am not.
3360	Matt26:72	And again he denied with an oath, I do not know the man.
3361	Mark14:70	And he denied it again. And a little after, they that stood by said again to Peter, Surely thou art one of them: for thou art a Galilaean, and thy speech agreeth thereto.
3362	Luke22:59	And about the space of one hour after another confidently affirmed, saying, Of a truth this fellow also was with him: for he is a Galilaean.
3363	Matt26:73	And after a while came unto him they that stood by, and said to Peter, Surely thou also art one of them; for thy speech bewrayeth thee.
3364	John18:26	One of the servants of the high priest, being his kinsman whose ear Peter cut off, saith, Did not I see thee in the garden with him?
3365	Mark14:71	But he began to curse and to swear, saying, I know not this man of whom ye speak.
3366	Matt26:74	Then began he to curse and to swear, saying, I know not the man. And immediately the cock crew.
3367	Luke22:60	And Peter said, Man, I know not what thou sayest. And immediately, while he yet spake, the cock crew.
3368	John18:27	Peter then denied again: and immediately the cock crew.
3369	Luke22:61	And the Lord turned, and looked upon Peter. And Peter remembered the word of the Lord, how he had said unto him, Before the cock crow, thou shalt deny me thrice.
3370	Mark14:72	And the second time the cock crew. And Peter called to mind the word that Jesus said unto him, Before the cock crow twice, thou shalt deny me thrice. And when he thought thereon, he wept.
3371	Matt26:75	And Peter remembered the word of Jesus, which said unto him, Before the cock crow, thou shalt deny me thrice. And he went out, and wept bitterly.
3372	Luke22:62	And Peter went out, and wept bitterly.
3373	Luke22:66	And as soon as it was day, the elders of the people and the chief priests and the scribes came together, and led him into their council, saying,
3374	Matt27:1	When the morning was come, all the chief priests and elders of the people took counsel against Jesus to put him to death:
3375	Mark15:1	And straightway in the morning the chief priests held a consultation with the elders and scribes and the whole council, and bound Jesus, and carried him away, and delivered him to Pilate.
3376	Matt27:2	And when they had bound him, they led him away, and delivered him to Pontius Pilate the governor.
3377	Luke23:1	And the whole multitude of them arose, and led him unto Pilate.
3378	John18:28	Then led they Jesus from Caiaphas unto the hall of judgment: and it was early; and they themselves went not into the judgment hall, lest they should be defiled; but that they might eat the passover.
3379	John18:29	Pilate then went out unto them, and said, What accusation bring ye against this man?
3380	John18:30	They answered and said unto him, If he were not a malefactor, we would not

THE TREE OF LIFE

		have delivered him up unto thee.
3381	John18:31	Then said Pilate unto them, Take ye him, and judge him according to your law. The Jews therefore said unto him, It is not lawful for us to put any man to death:
3382	John18:32	That the saying of Jesus might be fulfilled, which he spake, signifying what death he should die.
3383	Matt27:12	And when he was accused of the chief priests and elders, he answered nothing.
3384	Mark15:3	And the chief priests accused him of many things: but he answered nothing.
3385	Matt27:13	Then said Pilate unto him, Hearest thou not how many things they witness against thee?
3386	Mark15:4	And Pilate asked him again, saying, Answerest thou nothing? behold how many things they witness against thee.
3387	Mark15:5	But Jesus yet answered nothing; so that Pilate marvelled.
3388	Matt27:14	And he answered him to never a word; insomuch that the governor marvelled greatly.
3389	Luke23:2	And they began to accuse him, saying, We found this fellow perverting the nation, and forbidding to give tribute to Caesar, saying that he himself is Christ a King.
3390	John18:33	Then Pilate entered into the judgment hall again, and called Jesus, and said unto him, Art thou the King of the Jews?
3391	John18:34	Jesus answered him, Sayest thou this thing of thyself, or did others tell it thee of me?
3392	John18:35	Pilate answered, Am I a Jew? Thine own nation and the chief priests have delivered thee unto me: what hast thou done?
3393	John18:36	Jesus answered, My kingdom is not of this world: if my kingdom were of this world, then would my servants fight, that I should not be delivered to the Jews: but now is my kingdom not from hence.
3394	Matt27:11	And Jesus stood before the governor: and the governor asked him, saying, Art thou the King of the Jews? And Jesus said unto him, Thou sayest.
3395	Mark15:2	And Pilate asked him, Art thou the King of the Jews? And he answering said unto him, Thou sayest it.
3396	Luke23:3	And Pilate asked him, saying, Art thou the King of the Jews? And he answered him and said, Thou sayest it.
3397	John18:37	Pilate therefore said unto him, Art thou a king then? Jesus answered, Thou sayest that I am a king. To this end was I born, and for this cause came I into the world, that I should bear witness unto the truth. Every one that is of the truth heareth my voice.
3398	John18:38	Pilate saith unto him, What is truth? And when he had said this, he went out again unto the Jews, and saith unto them, I find in him no fault at all.
3399	Luke23:4	Then said Pilate to the chief priests and to the people, I find no fault in this man.
3400	Luke23:5	And they were the more fierce, saying, He stirreth up the people, teaching throughout all Jewry, beginning from Galilee to this place.
3401	Luke23:6	When Pilate heard of Galilee, he asked whether the man were a Galilaean.
3402	Luke23:7	And as soon as he knew that he belonged unto Herod's jurisdiction, he sent him to Herod, who himself also was at Jerusalem at that time.
3403	Luke23:8	And when Herod saw Jesus, he was exceeding glad: for he was desirous to see him of a long season, because he had heard many things of him; and he hoped to have seen some miracle done by him.
3404	Luke23:9	Then he questioned with him in many words; but he answered him nothing.
3405	Luke23:10	And the chief priests and scribes stood and vehemently accused him.
3406	Luke23:11	And Herod with his men of war set him at nought, and mocked him, and arrayed him in a gorgeous robe, and sent him again to Pilate.
3407	Luke23:12	And the same day Pilate and Herod were made friends together: for before they were at enmity between themselves.
3408	Luke23:13	And Pilate, when he had called together the chief priests and the rulers and the

THE TREE OF LIFE

		people,
3409	Luke23:14	Said unto them, Ye have brought this man unto me, as one that perverteth the people: and, behold, I, having examined him before you, have found no fault in this man touching those things whereof ye accuse him:
3410	Luke23:15	No, nor yet Herod: for I sent you to him; and, lo, nothing worthy of death is done unto him.
3411	Luke23:16	I will therefore chastise him, and release him.
3412	Luke23:17	(For of necessity he must release one unto them at the feast.)
3413	John18:39	But ye have a custom, that I should release unto you one at the passover: will ye therefore that I release unto you the King of the Jews?
3414	Mark15:9	But Pilate answered them, saying, Will ye that I release unto you the King of the Jews?
3415	Mark15:10	For he knew that the chief priests had delivered him for envy.
3416	Matt27:18	For he knew that for envy they had delivered him.
3417	Matt27:15	Now at that feast the governor was wont to release unto the people a prisoner, whom they would.
3418	Mark15:6	Now at that feast he released unto them one prisoner, whomsoever they desired.
3419	Matt27:16	And they had then a notable prisoner, called Barabbas.
3420	Luke23:19	(Who for a certain sedition made in the city, and for murder, was cast into prison.)
3421	Mark15:7	And there was one named Barabbas, which lay bound with them that had made insurrection with him, who had committed murder in the insurrection.
3422	Matt27:17	Therefore when they were gathered together, Pilate said unto them, Whom will ye that I release unto you? Barabbas, or Jesus which is called Christ?
3423	Matt27:20	But the chief priests and elders persuaded the multitude that they should ask Barabbas, and destroy Jesus.
3424	Matt27:21	The governor answered and said unto them, Whether of the twain will ye that I release unto you? They said, Barabbas.
3425	Mark15:11	But the chief priests moved the people, that he should rather release Barabbas unto them.
3426	Mark15:8	And the multitude crying aloud began to desire him to do as he had ever done unto them.
3427	Luke23:18	And they cried out all at once, saying, Away with this man, and release unto us Barabbas:
3428	John18:40	Then cried they all again, saying, Not this man, but Barabbas. Now Barabbas was a robber.
3429	Matt27:19	When he was set down on the judgment seat, his wife sent unto him, saying, Have thou nothing to do with that just man: for I have suffered many things this day in a dream because of him.
3430	Luke23:20	Pilate therefore, willing to release Jesus, spake again to them.
3431	Matt27:22	Pilate saith unto them, What shall I do then with Jesus which is called Christ? They all say unto him, Let him be crucified.
3432	Mark15:12	And Pilate answered and said again unto them, What will ye then that I shall do unto him whom ye call the King of the Jews?
3433	Mark15:13	And they cried out again, Crucify him.
3434	Luke23:21	But they cried, saying, Crucify him, crucify him.
3435	Matt27:23	And the governor said, Why, what evil hath he done? But they cried out the more, saying, Let him be crucified.
3436	Mark15:14	Then Pilate said unto them, Why, what evil hath he done? And they cried out the more exceedingly, Crucify him.
3437	Luke23:22	And he said unto them the third time, Why, what evil hath he done? I have found no cause of death in him: I will therefore chastise him, and let him go.
3438	John19:1	Then Pilate therefore took Jesus, and scourged him.
3439	Matt27:27	Then the soldiers of the governor took Jesus into the common hall, and gathered

THE TREE OF LIFE

		unto him the whole band of soldiers.
3440	Mark15:16	And the soldiers led him away into the hall, called Praetorium; and they call together the whole band.
3441	John19:2	And the soldiers platted a crown of thorns, and put it on his head, and they put on him a purple robe,
3442	Matt27:28	And they stripped him, and put on him a scarlet robe.
3443	Mark15:17	And they clothed him with purple, and platted a crown of thorns, and put it about his head,
3444	Matt27:29	And when they had platted a crown of thorns, they put it upon his head, and a reed in his right hand: and they bowed the knee before him, and mocked him, saying, Hail, King of the Jews!
3445	Mark15:18	And began to salute him, Hail, King of the Jews!
3446	John19:3	And said, Hail, King of the Jews! and they smote him with their hands.
3447	Matt27:30	And they spit upon him, and took the reed, and smote him on the head.
3448	Mark15:19	And they smote him on the head with a reed, and did spit upon him, and bowing their knees worshipped him.
3449	John19:4	Pilate therefore went forth again, and saith unto them, Behold, I bring him forth to you, that ye may know that I find no fault in him.
3450	John19:5	Then came Jesus forth, wearing the crown of thorns, and the purple robe. And Pilate saith unto them, Behold the man!
3451	John19:6	When the chief priests therefore and officers saw him, they cried out, saying, Crucify him, crucify him. Pilate saith unto them, Take ye him, and crucify him: for I find no fault in him.
3452	John19:7	The Jews answered him, We have a law, and by our law he ought to die, because he made himself the Son of God.
3453	John19:8	When Pilate therefore heard that saying, he was the more afraid;
3454	John19:9	And went again into the judgment hall, and saith unto Jesus, Whence art thou? But Jesus gave him no answer.
3455	John19:10	Then saith Pilate unto him, Speakest thou not unto me? knowest thou not that I have power to crucify thee, and have power to release thee?
3456	John19:11	Jesus answered, Thou couldest have no power at all against me, except it were given thee from above: therefore he that delivered me unto thee hath the greater sin.
3457	John19:12	And from thenceforth Pilate sought to release him: but the Jews cried out, saying, If thou let this man go, thou art not Caesar's friend: whosoever maketh himself a king speaketh against Caesar.
3458	John19:13	When Pilate therefore heard that saying, he brought Jesus forth, and sat down in the judgment seat in a place that is called the Pavement, but in the Hebrew, Gabbatha.
3459	John19:14	And it was the preparation of the passover, and about the sixth hour: and he saith unto the Jews, Behold your King!
3460	John19:15	But they cried out, Away with him, away with him, crucify him. Pilate saith unto them, Shall I crucify your King? The chief priests answered, We have no king but Caesar.
3461	Luke23:23	And they were instant with loud voices, requiring that he might be crucified. And the voices of them and of the chief priests prevailed.
3462	Matt27:24	When Pilate saw that he could prevail nothing, but that rather a tumult was made, he took water, and washed his hands before the multitude, saying, I am innocent of the blood of this just person: see ye to it.
3463	Matt27:25	Then answered all the people, and said, His blood be on us, and on our children.
3464	Mark15:15	And so Pilate, willing to content the people, released Barabbas unto them, and delivered Jesus, when he had scourged him, to be crucified.
3465	Luke23:24	And Pilate gave sentence that it should be as they required.

THE TREE OF LIFE

3466	Luke23:25	And he released unto them him that for sedition and murder was cast into prison, whom they had desired; but he delivered Jesus to their will.
3467	Matt27:26	Then released he Barabbas unto them: and when he had scourged Jesus, he delivered him to be crucified.
3468	Matt27:31	And after that they had mocked him, they took the robe off from him, and put his own raiment on him, and led him away to crucify him.
3469	Mark15:20	And when they had mocked him, they took off the purple from him, and put his own clothes on him, and led him out to crucify him.
3470	John19:16	Then delivered he him therefore unto them to be crucified. And they took Jesus, and led him away.
3471	Matt27:3	Then Judas, which had betrayed him, when he saw that he was condemned, repented himself, and brought again the thirty pieces of silver to the chief priests and elders,
3472	Matt27:4	Saying, I have sinned in that I have betrayed the innocent blood. And they said, What is that to us? see thou to that.
3473	Matt27:5	And he cast down the pieces of silver in the temple, and departed, and went and hanged himself.
3474	Matt27:6	And the chief priests took the silver pieces, and said, It is not lawful for to put them into the treasury, because it is the price of blood.
3475	Matt27:7	And they took counsel, and bought with them the potter's field, to bury strangers in.
3476	Matt27:8	Wherefore that field was called, The field of blood, unto this day.
3477	Matt27:9	Then was fulfilled that which was spoken by Jeremy the prophet, saying, And they took the thirty pieces of silver, the price of him that was valued, whom they of the children of Israel did value;
3478	Matt27:10	And gave them for the potter's field, as the Lord appointed me.
3479	Mark15:21	And they compel one Simon a Cyrenian, who passed by, coming out of the country, the father of Alexander and Rufus, to bear his cross.
3480	Matt27:32	And as they came out, they found a man of Cyrene, Simon by name: him they compelled to bear his cross.
3481	Luke23:26	And as they led him away, they laid hold upon one Simon, a Cyrenian, coming out of the country, and on him they laid the cross, that he might bear it after Jesus.
3482	Luke23:27	And there followed him a great company of people, and of women, which also bewailed and lamented him.
3483	Luke23:28	But Jesus turning unto them said, Daughters of Jerusalem, weep not for me, but weep for yourselves, and for your children.
3484	Luke23:29	For, behold, the days are coming, in the which they shall say, Blessed are the barren, and the wombs that never bare, and the paps which never gave suck.
3485	Luke23:30	Then shall they begin to say to the mountains, Fall on us; and to the hills, Cover us.
3486	Luke23:31	For if they do these things in a green tree, what shall be done in the dry?
3487	John19:17	And he bearing his cross went forth into a place called the place of a skull, which is called in the Hebrew Golgotha:
3488	Mark15:22	And they bring him unto the place Golgotha, which is, being interpreted, The place of a skull.
3489	Matt27:33	And when they were come unto a place called Golgotha, that is to say, a place of a skull,
3490	John19:18	Where they crucified him, and two other with him, on either side one, and Jesus in the midst.
3491	Matt27:38	Then were there two thieves crucified with him, one on the right hand, and another on the left.
3492	Luke23:32	And there were also two other, malefactors, led with him to be put to death.

THE TREE OF LIFE

3493	Luke23:33	And when they were come to the place, which is called Calvary, there they crucified him, and the malefactors, one on the right hand, and the other on the left.
3494	Mark15:27	And with him they crucify two thieves; the one on his right hand, and the other on his left.
3495	Mark15:28	And the scripture was fulfilled, which saith, And he was numbered with the transgressors.
3496	Luke23:34	Then said Jesus, Father, forgive them; for they know not what they do. And they parted his raiment, and cast lots.
3497	Matt27:35	And they crucified him, and parted his garments, casting lots: that it might be fulfilled which was spoken by the prophet, They parted my garments among them, and upon my vesture did they cast lots.
3498	Mark15:24	And when they had crucified him, they parted his garments, casting lots upon them, what every man should take.
3499	John19:23	Then the soldiers, when they had crucified Jesus, took his garments, and made four parts, to every soldier a part; and also his coat: now the coat was without seam, woven from the top throughout.
3500	John19:24	They said therefore among themselves, Let us not rend it, but cast lots for it, whose it shall be: that the scripture might be fulfilled, which saith, They parted my raiment among them, and for my vesture they did cast lots. These things therefore the soldiers did.
3501	Mark15:25	And it was the third hour, and they crucified him.
3502	Matt27:36	And sitting down they watched him there;
3503	Mark15:26	And the superscription of his accusation was written over, THE KING OF THE JEWS.
3504	John19:19	And Pilate wrote a title, and put it on the cross. And the writing was, JESUS OF NAZARETH THE KING OF THE JEWS.
3505	Matt27:37	And set up over his head his accusation written, THIS IS JESUS THE KING OF THE JEWS.
3506	John19:20	This title then read many of the Jews: for the place where Jesus was crucified was nigh to the city: and it was written in Hebrew, and Greek, and Latin.
3507	Luke23:38	And a superscription also was written over him in letters of Greek, and Latin, and Hebrew, THIS IS THE KING OF THE JEWS.
3508	John19:21	Then said the chief priests of the Jews to Pilate, Write not, The King of the Jews; but that he said, I am King of the Jews.
3509	John19:22	Pilate answered, What I have written I have written.
3510	Matt27:39	And they that passed by reviled him, wagging their heads,
3511	Mark15:29	And they that passed by railed on him, wagging their heads, and saying, Ah, thou that destroyest the temple, and buildest it in three days,
3512	Matt27:40	And saying, Thou that destroyest the temple, and buildest it in three days, save thyself. If thou be the Son of God, come down from the cross.
3513	Mark15:30	Save thyself, and come down from the cross.
3514	Luke23:35	And the people stood beholding. And the rulers also with them derided him, saying, He saved others; let him save himself, if he be Christ, the chosen of God.
3515	Luke23:36	And the soldiers also mocked him, coming to him, and offering him vinegar,
3516	Luke23:37	And saying, If thou be the king of the Jews, save thyself.
3517	Matt27:34	They gave him vinegar to drink mingled with gall: and when he had tasted thereof, he would not drink.
3518	Mark15:23	And they gave him to drink wine mingled with myrrh: but he received it not.
3519	Matt27:41	Likewise also the chief priests mocking him, with the scribes and elders, said,
3520	Matt27:42	He saved others; himself he cannot save. If he be the King of Israel, let him now come down from the cross, and we will believe him.
3521	Mark15:31	Likewise also the chief priests mocking said among themselves with the scribes,

THE TREE OF LIFE

		He saved others; himself he cannot save.
3522	Matt27:43	He trusted in God; let him deliver him now, if he will have him: for he said, I am the Son of God.
3523	Mark15:32	Let Christ the King of Israel descend now from the cross, that we may see and believe. And they that were crucified with him reviled him.
3524	Matt27:44	The thieves also, which were crucified with him, cast the same in his teeth.
3525	Luke23:39	And one of the malefactors which were hanged railed on him, saying, If thou be Christ, save thyself and us.
3526	Luke23:40	But the other answering rebuked him, saying, Dost not thou fear God, seeing thou art in the same condemnation?
3527	Luke23:41	And we indeed justly; for we receive the due reward of our deeds: but this man hath done nothing amiss.
3528	Luke23:42	And he said unto Jesus, Lord, remember me when thou comest into thy kingdom.
3529	Luke23:43	And Jesus said unto him, Verily I say unto thee, To day shalt thou be with me in paradise.
3530	John19:25	Now there stood by the cross of Jesus his mother, and his mother's sister, Mary the wife of Cleophas, and Mary Magdalene.
3531	John19:26	When Jesus therefore saw his mother, and the disciple standing by, whom he loved, he saith unto his mother, Woman, behold thy son!
3532	John19:27	Then saith he to the disciple, Behold thy mother! And from that hour that disciple took her unto his own home.
3533	Matt27:45	Now from the sixth hour there was darkness over all the land unto the ninth hour.
3534	Mark15:33	And when the sixth hour was come, there was darkness over the whole land until the ninth hour.
3535	Luke23:44	And it was about the sixth hour, and there was a darkness over all the earth until the ninth hour.
3536	Matt27:46	And about the ninth hour Jesus cried with a loud voice, saying, Eli, Eli, lama sabachthani? that is to say, My God, my God, why hast thou forsaken me?
3537	Matt27:47	Some of them that stood there, when they heard that, said, This man calleth for Elias.
3538	Mark15:34	And at the ninth hour Jesus cried with a loud voice, saying, Eloi, Eloi, lama sabachthani? which is, being interpreted, My God, my God, why hast thou forsaken me?
3539	Mark15:35	And some of them that stood by, when they heard it, said, Behold, he calleth Elias.
3540	John19:28	After this, Jesus knowing that all things were now accomplished, that the scripture might be fulfilled, saith, I thirst.
3541	John19:29	Now there was set a vessel full of vinegar: and they filled a spunge with vinegar, and put it upon hyssop, and put it to his mouth.
3542	Matt27:48	And straightway one of them ran, and took a spunge, and filled it with vinegar, and put it on a reed, and gave him to drink.
3543	Matt27:49	The rest said, Let be, let us see whether Elias will come to save him.
3544	Mark15:36	And one ran and filled a spunge full of vinegar, and put it on a reed, and gave him to drink, saying, Let alone; let us see whether Elias will come to take him down.
3545	John19:30	When Jesus therefore had received the vinegar, he said, It is finished: and he bowed his head, and gave up the ghost.
3546	Luke23:46	And when Jesus had cried with a loud voice, he said, Father, into thy hands I commend my spirit: and having said thus, he gave up the ghost.
3547	Mark15:37	And Jesus cried with a loud voice, and gave up the ghost.
3548	Matt27:50	Jesus, when he had cried again with a loud voice, yielded up the ghost.
3549	Luke23:45	And the sun was darkened, and the veil of the temple was rent in the midst.
3550	Mark15:38	And the veil of the temple was rent in twain from the top to the bottom.
3551	Matt27:51	And, behold, the veil of the temple was rent in twain from the top to the bottom;

THE TREE OF LIFE

		and the earth did quake, and the rocks rent;
3552	Matt27:54	Now when the centurion, and they that were with him, watching Jesus, saw the earthquake, and those things that were done, they feared greatly, saying, Truly this was the Son of God.
3553	Mark15:39	And when the centurion, which stood over against him, saw that he so cried out, and gave up the ghost, he said, Truly this man was the Son of God.
3554	Luke23:47	Now when the centurion saw what was done, he glorified God, saying, Certainly this was a righteous man.
3555	Luke23:48	And all the people that came together to that sight, beholding the things which were done, smote their breasts, and returned.
3556	Luke23:49	And all his acquaintance, and the women that followed him from Galilee, stood afar off, beholding these things.
3557	Mark15:40	There were also women looking on afar off: among whom was Mary Magdalene, and Mary the mother of James the less and of Joses, and Salome;
3558	Mark15:41	(Who also, when he was in Galilee, followed him, and ministered unto him;) and many other women which came up with him unto Jerusalem.
3559	Matt27:55	And many women were there beholding afar off, which followed Jesus from Galilee, ministering unto him:
3560	Matt27:56	Among which was Mary Magdalene, and Mary the mother of James and Joses, and the mother of Zebedee's children.
3561	John19:31	The Jews therefore, because it was the preparation, that the bodies should not remain upon the cross on the sabbath day, (for that sabbath day was an high day,) besought Pilate that their legs might be broken, and that they might be taken away.
3562	John19:32	Then came the soldiers, and brake the legs of the first, and of the other which was crucified with him.
3563	John19:33	But when they came to Jesus, and saw that he was dead already, they brake not his legs:
3564	John19:34	But one of the soldiers with a spear pierced his side, and forthwith came there out blood and water.
3565	John19:35	And he that saw it bare record, and his record is true: and he knoweth that he saith true, that ye might believe.
3566	John19:36	For these things were done, that the scripture should be fulfilled, A bone of him shall not be broken.
3567	John19:37	And again another scripture saith, They shall look on him whom they pierced.
3568	Luke23:50	And, behold, there was a man named Joseph, a counsellor; and he was a good man, and a just:
3569	Luke23:51	(The same had not consented to the counsel and deed of them;) he was of Arimathaea, a city of the Jews: who also himself waited for the kingdom of God.
3570	Mark15:42	And now when the even was come, because it was the preparation, that is, the day before the sabbath,
3571	Mark15:43	Joseph of Arimathaea, an honourable counsellor, which also waited for the kingdom of God, came, and went in boldly unto Pilate, and craved the body of Jesus.
3572	Luke23:52	This man went unto Pilate, and begged the body of Jesus.
3573	Mark15:44	And Pilate marvelled if he were already dead: and calling unto him the centurion, he asked him whether he had been any while dead.
3574	Mark15:45	And when he knew it of the centurion, he gave the body to Joseph.
3575	Matt27:57	When the even was come, there came a rich man of Arimathaea, named Joseph, who also himself was Jesus' disciple:
3576	Matt27:58	He went to Pilate, and begged the body of Jesus. Then Pilate commanded the body to be delivered.
3577	John19:38	And after this Joseph of Arimathaea, being a disciple of Jesus, but secretly for

THE TREE OF LIFE

		fear of the Jews, besought Pilate that he might take away the body of Jesus: and Pilate gave him leave. He came therefore, and took the body of Jesus.
3578	John19:39	And there came also Nicodemus, which at the first came to Jesus by night, and brought a mixture of myrrh and aloes, about an hundred pound weight.
3579	Matt27:59	And when Joseph had taken the body, he wrapped it in a clean linen cloth,
3580	John19:40	Then took they the body of Jesus, and wound it in linen clothes with the spices, as the manner of the Jews is to bury.
3581	Mark15:46	And he bought fine linen, and took him down, and wrapped him in the linen, and laid him in a sepulchre which was hewn out of a rock, and rolled a stone unto the door of the sepulchre.
3582	John19:41	Now in the place where he was crucified there was a garden; and in the garden a new sepulchre, wherein was never man yet laid.
3583	Luke23:53	And he took it down, and wrapped it in linen, and laid it in a sepulchre that was hewn in stone, wherein never man before was laid.
3584	Matt27:60	And laid it in his own new tomb, which he had hewn out in the rock: and he rolled a great stone to the door of the sepulchre, and departed.
3585	Luke23:54	And that day was the preparation, and the sabbath drew on.
3586	Luke23:55	And the women also, which came with him from Galilee, followed after, and beheld the sepulchre, and how his body was laid.
3587	Mark15:47	And Mary Magdalene and Mary the mother of Joses beheld where he was laid.
3588	Matt27:61	And there was Mary Magdalene, and the other Mary, sitting over against the sepulchre.
3589	John19:42	There laid they Jesus therefore because of the Jews' preparation day; for the sepulchre was nigh at hand.
3590	Luke23:56	And they returned, and prepared spices and ointments; and rested the sabbath day according to the commandment.
3591	Matt27:62	Now the next day, that followed the day of the preparation, the chief priests and Pharisees came together unto Pilate,
3592	Matt27:63	Saying, Sir, we remember that that deceiver said, while he was yet alive, After three days I will rise again.
3593	Matt27:64	Command therefore that the sepulchre be made sure until the third day, lest his disciples come by night, and steal him away, and say unto the people, He is risen from the dead: so the last error shall be worse than the first.
3594	Matt27:65	Pilate said unto them, Ye have a watch: go your way, make it as sure as ye can.
3595	Matt27:66	So they went, and made the sepulchre sure, sealing the stone, and setting a watch.
3596	Matt28:2	And, behold, there was a great earthquake: for the angel of the Lord descended from heaven, and came and rolled back the stone from the door, and sat upon it.
3597	Matt28:3	His countenance was like lightning, and his raiment white as snow:
3598	Matt28:4	And for fear of him the keepers did shake, and became as dead men.
3599	Mark16:1	And when the sabbath was past, Mary Magdalene, and Mary the mother of James, and Salome, had bought sweet spices, that they might come and anoint him.
3600	Matt28:1	In the end of the sabbath, as it began to dawn toward the first day of the week, came Mary Magdalene and the other Mary to see the sepulchre.
3601	Luke24:1	Now upon the first day of the week, very early in the morning, they came unto the sepulchre, bringing the spices which they had prepared, and certain others with them.
3602	Mark16:2	And very early in the morning the first day of the week, they came unto the sepulchre at the rising of the sun.
3603	Mark16:3	And they said among themselves, Who shall roll us away the stone from the door of the sepulchre?
3604	John20:1	The first day of the week cometh Mary Magdalene early, when it was yet dark,

THE TREE OF LIFE

		unto the sepulchre, and seeth the stone taken away from the sepulchre.
3605	Luke24:2	And they found the stone rolled away from the sepulchre.
3606	Mark16:4	And when they looked, they saw that the stone was rolled away: for it was very great.
3607	Luke24:4	And it came to pass, as they were much perplexed thereabout, behold, two men stood by them in shining garments:
3608	Mark16:5	And entering into the sepulchre, they saw a young man sitting on the right side, clothed in a long white garment; and they were affrighted.
3609	Luke24:5	And as they were afraid, and bowed down their faces to the earth, they said unto them, Why seek ye the living among the dead?
3610	Matt28:5	And the angel answered and said unto the women, Fear not ye: for I know that ye seek Jesus, which was crucified.
3611	Mark16:6	And he saith unto them, Be not affrighted: Ye seek Jesus of Nazareth, which was crucified: he is risen; he is not here: behold the place where they laid him.
3612	Matt28:6	He is not here: for he is risen, as he said. Come, see the place where the Lord lay.
3613	Luke24:3	And they entered in, and found not the body of the Lord Jesus.
3614	Luke24:6	He is not here, but is risen: remember how he spake unto you when he was yet in Galilee,
3615	Luke24:7	Saying, The Son of man must be delivered into the hands of sinful men, and be crucified, and the third day rise again.
3616	Luke24:8	And they remembered his words,
3617	Mark16:7	But go your way, tell his disciples and Peter that he goeth before you into Galilee: there shall ye see him, as he said unto you.
3618	Matt28:7	And go quickly, and tell his disciples that he is risen from the dead; and, behold, he goeth before you into Galilee; there shall ye see him: lo, I have told you.
3619	Matt28:8	And they departed quickly from the sepulchre with fear and great joy; and did run to bring his disciples word.
3620	Matt28:11	Now when they were going, behold, some of the watch came into the city, and shewed unto the chief priests all the things that were done.
3621	Matt28:12	And when they were assembled with the elders, and had taken counsel, they gave large money unto the soldiers,
3622	Matt28:13	Saying, Say ye, His disciples came by night, and stole him away while we slept.
3623	Matt28:14	And if this come to the governor's ears, we will persuade him, and secure you.
3624	Matt28:15	So they took the money, and did as they were taught: and this saying is commonly reported among the Jews until this day.
3625	Mark16:8	And they went out quickly, and fled from the sepulchre; for they trembled and were amazed: neither said they any thing to any man; for they were afraid.
3626	John20:2	Then she runneth, and cometh to Simon Peter, and to the other disciple, whom Jesus loved, and saith unto them, They have taken away the LORD out of the sepulchre, and we know not where they have laid him.
3627	John20:3	Peter therefore went forth, and that other disciple, and came to the sepulchre.
3628	John20:4	So they ran both together: and the other disciple did outrun Peter, and came first to the sepulchre.
3629	John20:5	And he stooping down, and looking in, saw the linen clothes lying; yet went he not in.
3630	John20:6	Then cometh Simon Peter following him, and went into the sepulchre, and seeth the linen clothes lie,
3631	John20:7	And the napkin, that was about his head, not lying with the linen clothes, but wrapped together in a place by itself.
3632	John20:8	Then went in also that other disciple, which came first to the sepulchre, and he saw, and believed.
3633	John20:9	For as yet they knew not the scripture, that he must rise again from the dead.

THE TREE OF LIFE

3634	John20:10	Then the disciples went away again unto their own home.
3635	Luke24:12	Then arose Peter, and ran unto the sepulchre; and stooping down, he beheld the linen clothes laid by themselves, and departed, wondering in himself at that which was come to pass.
3636	John20:11	But Mary stood without at the sepulchre weeping: and as she wept, she stooped down, and looked into the sepulchre,
3637	John20:12	And seeth two angels in white sitting, the one at the head, and the other at the feet, where the body of Jesus had lain.
3638	John20:13	And they say unto her, Woman, why weepest thou? She saith unto them, Because they have taken away my LORD, and I know not where they have laid him.
3639	John20:14	And when she had thus said, she turned herself back, and saw Jesus standing, and knew not that it was Jesus.
3640	Mark16:9	Now when Jesus was risen early the first day of the week, he appeared first to Mary Magdalene, out of whom he had cast seven devils.
3641	John20:15	Jesus saith unto her, Woman, why weepest thou? whom seekest thou? She, supposing him to be the gardener, saith unto him, Sir, if thou have borne him hence, tell me where thou hast laid him, and I will take him away.
3642	John20:16	Jesus saith unto her, Mary. She turned herself, and saith unto him, Rabboni; which is to say, Master.
3643	John20:17	Jesus saith unto her, Touch me not; for I am not yet ascended to my Father: but go to my brethren, and say unto them, I ascend unto my Father, and your Father; and to my God, and your God.
3644	Mark16:10	And she went and told them that had been with him, as they mourned and wept.
3645	Matt28:9	And as they went to tell his disciples, behold, Jesus met them, saying, All hail. And they came and held him by the feet, and worshipped him.
3646	Matt28:10	Then said Jesus unto them, Be not afraid: go tell my brethren that they go into Galilee, and there shall they see me.
3647	Luke24:9	And returned from the sepulchre, and told all these things unto the eleven, and to all the rest.
3648	John20:18	Mary Magdalene came and told the disciples that she had seen the LORD, and that he had spoken these things unto her.
3649	Luke24:10	It was Mary Magdalene, and Joanna, and Mary the mother of James, and other women that were with them, which told these things unto the apostles.
3650	Mark16:11	And they, when they had heard that he was alive, and had been seen of her, believed not.
3651	Luke24:11	And their words seemed to them as idle tales, and they believed them not.
3652	Mark16:12	After that he appeared in another form unto two of them, as they walked, and went into the country.
3653	Luke24:13	And, behold, two of them went that same day to a village called Emmaus, which was from Jerusalem about threescore furlongs.
3654	Luke24:14	And they talked together of all these things which had happened.
3655	Luke24:15	And it came to pass, that, while they communed together and reasoned, Jesus himself drew near, and went with them.
3656	Luke24:16	But their eyes were holden that they should not know him.
3657	Luke24:17	And he said unto them, What manner of communications are these that ye have one to another, as ye walk, and are sad?
3658	Luke24:18	And the one of them, whose name was Cleopas, answering said unto him, Art thou only a stranger in Jerusalem, and hast not known the things which are come to pass there in these days?
3659	Luke24:19	And he said unto them, What things? And they said unto him, Concerning Jesus of Nazareth, which was a prophet mighty in deed and word before God and all the people:

THE TREE OF LIFE

3660	Luke24:20	And how the chief priests and our rulers delivered him to be condemned to death, and have crucified him.
3661	Luke24:21	But we trusted that it had been he which should have redeemed Israel: and beside all this, to day is the third day since these things were done.
3662	Luke24:22	Yea, and certain women also of our company made us astonished, which were early at the sepulchre;
3663	Luke24:23	And when they found not his body, they came, saying, that they had also seen a vision of angels, which said that he was alive.
3664	Luke24:24	And certain of them which were with us went to the sepulchre, and found it even so as the women had said: but him they saw not.
3665	Luke24:25	Then he said unto them, O fools, and slow of heart to believe all that the prophets have spoken:
3666	Luke24:26	Ought not Christ to have suffered these things, and to enter into his glory?
3667	Luke24:27	And beginning at Moses and all the prophets, he expounded unto them in all the scriptures the things concerning himself.
3668	Luke24:28	And they drew nigh unto the village, whither they went: and he made as though he would have gone further.
3669	Luke24:29	But they constrained him, saying, Abide with us: for it is toward evening, and the day is far spent. And he went in to tarry with them.
3670	Luke24:30	And it came to pass, as he sat at meat with them, he took bread, and blessed it, and brake, and gave to them.
3671	Luke24:31	And their eyes were opened, and they knew him; and he vanished out of their sight.
3672	Luke24:32	And they said one to another, Did not our heart burn within us, while he talked with us by the way, and while he opened to us the scriptures?
3673	Luke24:33	And they rose up the same hour, and returned to Jerusalem, and found the eleven gathered together, and them that were with them,
3674	Luke24:34	Saying, The Lord is risen indeed, and hath appeared to Simon.
3675	Luke24:35	And they told what things were done in the way, and how he was known of them in breaking of bread.
3676	Mark16:13	And they went and told it unto the residue: neither believed they them.
3677	John20:19	Then the same day at evening, being the first day of the week, when the doors were shut where the disciples were assembled for fear of the Jews, came Jesus and stood in the midst, and saith unto them, Peace be unto you.
3678	Luke24:36	And as they thus spake, Jesus himself stood in the midst of them, and saith unto them, Peace be unto you.
3679	Luke24:37	But they were terrified and affrighted, and supposed that they had seen a spirit.
3680	Luke24:38	And he said unto them, Why are ye troubled? and why do thoughts arise in your hearts?
3681	Luke24:39	Behold my hands and my feet, that it is I myself: handle me, and see; for a spirit hath not flesh and bones, as ye see me have.
3682	Luke24:40	And when he had thus spoken, he shewed them his hands and his feet.
3683	John20:20	And when he had so said, he shewed unto them his hands and his side. Then were the disciples glad, when they saw the LORD.
3684	Luke24:41	And while they yet believed not for joy, and wondered, he said unto them, Have ye here any meat?
3685	Luke24:42	And they gave him a piece of a broiled fish, and of an honeycomb.
3686	Luke24:43	And he took it, and did eat before them.
3687	Mark16:14	Afterward he appeared unto the eleven as they sat at meat, and upbraided them with their unbelief and hardness of heart, because they believed not them which had seen him after he was risen.
3688	Luke24:44	And he said unto them, These are the words which I spake unto you, while I was yet with you, that all things must be fulfilled, which were written in the law of

THE TREE OF LIFE

		Moses, and in the prophets, and in the psalms, concerning me.
3689	Luke24:45	Then opened he their understanding, that they might understand the scriptures,
3690	Luke24:46	And said unto them, Thus it is written, and thus it behoved Christ to suffer, and to rise from the dead the third day:
3691	Luke24:47	And that repentance and remission of sins should be preached in his name among all nations, beginning at Jerusalem.
3692	Luke24:48	And ye are witnesses of these things.
3693	John20:24	But Thomas, one of the twelve, called Didymus, was not with them when Jesus came.
3694	John20:25	The other disciples therefore said unto him, We have seen the LORD. But he said unto them, Except I shall see in his hands the print of the nails, and put my finger into the print of the nails, and thrust my hand into his side, I will not believe.
3695	John20:26	And after eight days again his disciples were within, and Thomas with them: then came Jesus, the doors being shut, and stood in the midst, and said, Peace be unto you.
3696	Matt28:17	And when they saw him, they worshipped him: but some doubted.
3697	John20:27	Then saith he to Thomas, Reach hither thy finger, and behold my hands; and reach hither thy hand, and thrust it into my side: and be not faithless, but believing.
3698	John20:28	And Thomas answered and said unto him, My LORD and my God.
3699	John20:29	Jesus saith unto him, Thomas, because thou hast seen me, thou hast believed: blessed are they that have not seen, and yet have believed.
3700	John20:21	Then said Jesus to them again, Peace be unto you: as my Father hath sent me, even so send I you.
3701	Luke24:49	And, behold, I send the promise of my Father upon you: but tarry ye in the city of Jerusalem, until ye be endued with power from on high.
3702	John20:22	And when he had said this, he breathed on them, and saith unto them, Receive ye the Holy Ghost:
3703	John20:23	Whose soever sins ye remit, they are remitted unto them; and whose soever sins ye retain, they are retained.
3704	Luke24:50	And he led them out as far as to Bethany, and he lifted up his hands, and blessed them.
3705	Luke24:51	And it came to pass, while he blessed them, he was parted from them, and carried up into heaven.
3706	Mark16:19	So then after the Lord had spoken unto them, he was received up into heaven, and sat on the right hand of God.
3707	Luke24:52	And they worshipped him, and returned to Jerusalem with great joy:
3708	Matt27:52	And the graves were opened; and many bodies of the saints which slept arose,
3709	Matt27:53	And came out of the graves after his resurrection, and went into the holy city, and appeared unto many.
3710	John21:1	After these things Jesus shewed himself again to the disciples at the sea of Tiberias; and on this wise shewed he himself.
3711	John21:2	There were together Simon Peter, and Thomas called Didymus, and Nathanael of Cana in Galilee, and the sons of Zebedee, and two other of his disciples.
3712	John21:3	Simon Peter saith unto them, I go a fishing. They say unto him, We also go with thee. They went forth, and entered into a ship immediately; and that night they caught nothing.
3713	John21:4	But when the morning was now come, Jesus stood on the shore: but the disciples knew not that it was Jesus.
3714	John21:5	Then Jesus saith unto them, Children, have ye any meat? They answered him, No.
3715	John21:6	And he said unto them, Cast the net on the right side of the ship, and ye shall find. They cast therefore, and now they were not able to draw it for the multitude

THE TREE OF LIFE

		of fishes.
3716	John21:7	Therefore that disciple whom Jesus loved saith unto Peter, It is the Lord. Now when Simon Peter heard that it was the Lord, he girt his fisher's coat unto him, (for he was naked,) and did cast himself into the sea.
3717	John21:8	And the other disciples came in a little ship; (for they were not far from land, but as it were two hundred cubits,) dragging the net with fishes.
3718	John21:9	As soon then as they were come to land, they saw a fire of coals there, and fish laid thereon, and bread.
3719	John21:10	Jesus saith unto them, Bring of the fish which ye have now caught.
3720	John21:11	Simon Peter went up, and drew the net to land full of great fishes, an hundred and fifty and three: and for all there were so many, yet was not the net broken.
3721	John21:12	Jesus saith unto them, Come and dine. And none of the disciples durst ask him, Who art thou? knowing that it was the Lord.
3722	John21:13	Jesus then cometh, and taketh bread, and giveth them, and fish likewise.
3723	John21:14	This is now the third time that Jesus shewed himself to his disciples, after that he was risen from the dead.
3724	John21:15	So when they had dined, Jesus saith to Simon Peter, Simon, son of Jonas, lovest thou me more than these? He saith unto him, Yea, Lord; thou knowest that I love thee. He saith unto him, Feed my lambs.
3725	John21:16	He saith to him again the second time, Simon, son of Jonas, lovest thou me? He saith unto him, Yea, Lord; thou knowest that I love thee. He saith unto him, Feed my sheep.
3726	John21:17	He saith unto him the third time, Simon, son of Jonas, lovest thou me? Peter was grieved because he said unto him the third time, Lovest thou me? And he said unto him, Lord, thou knowest all things; thou knowest that I love thee. Jesus saith unto him, Feed my sheep.
3727	John21:18	Verily, verily, I say unto thee, When thou wast young, thou girdedst thyself, and walkedst whither thou wouldest: but when thou shalt be old, thou shalt stretch forth thy hands, and another shall gird thee, and carry thee whither thou wouldest not.
3728	John21:19	This spake he, signifying by what death he should glorify God. And when he had spoken this, he saith unto him, Follow me.
3729	John21:20	Then Peter, turning about, seeth the disciple whom Jesus loved following; which also leaned on his breast at supper, and said, Lord, which is he that betrayeth thee?
3730	John21:21	Peter seeing him saith to Jesus, Lord, and what shall this man do?
3731	John21:22	Jesus saith unto him, If I will that he tarry till I come, what is that to thee? follow thou me.
3732	John21:23	Then went this saying abroad among the brethren, that that disciple should not die: yet Jesus said not unto him, He shall not die; but, If I will that he tarry till I come, what is that to thee?
3733	John21:24	This is the disciple which testifieth of these things, and wrote these things: and we know that his testimony is true.
3734	Matt28:16	Then the eleven disciples went away into Galilee, into a mountain where Jesus had appointed them.
3735	Matt28:18	And Jesus came and spake unto them, saying, All power is given unto me in heaven and in earth.
3736	Mark16:15	And he said unto them, Go ye into all the world, and preach the gospel to every creature.
3737	Mark16:16	He that believeth and is baptized shall be saved; but he that believeth not shall be damned.
3738	Mark16:17	And these signs shall follow them that believe; In my name shall they cast out devils; they shall speak with new tongues;

THE TREE OF LIFE

3739	Mark16:18	They shall take up serpents; and if they drink any deadly thing, it shall not hurt them; they shall lay hands on the sick, and they shall recover.
3740	Matt28:19	Go ye therefore, and teach all nations, baptizing them in the name of the Father, and of the Son, and of the Holy Ghost:
3741	Matt28:20	Teaching them to observe all things whatsoever I have commanded you: and, lo, I am with you alway, even unto the end of the world. Amen.
3742	Mark16:20	And they went forth, and preached every where, the Lord working with them, and confirming the word with signs following. Amen.
3743	Luke24:53	And were continually in the temple, praising and blessing God. Amen.
3744	John20:30	And many other signs truly did Jesus in the presence of his disciples, which are not written in this book:
3745	John20:31	But these are written, that ye might believe that Jesus is the Christ, the Son of God; and that believing ye might have life through his name.
3746	John21:25	And there are also many other things which Jesus did, the which, if they should be written every one, I suppose that even the world itself could not contain the books that should be written. Amen.
3747	Matt1:1	The book of the generation of Jesus Christ, the son of David, the son of Abraham.
3748	Matt1:2	Abraham begat Isaac; and Isaac begat Jacob; and Jacob begat Judas and his brethren;
3749	Matt1:3	And Judas begat Phares and Zara of Thamar; and Phares begat Esrom; and Esrom begat Aram;
3750	Matt1:4	And Aram begat Aminadab; and Aminadab begat Naasson; and Naasson begat Salmon;
3751	Matt1:5	And Salmon begat Booz of Rachab; and Booz begat Obed of Ruth; and Obed begat Jesse;
3752	Matt1:6	And Jesse begat David the king; and David the king begat Solomon of her that had been the wife of Urias;
3753	Matt1:7	And Solomon begat Roboam; and Roboam begat Abia; and Abia begat Asa;
3754	Matt1:8	And Asa begat Josaphat; and Josaphat begat Joram; and Joram begat Ozias;
3755	Matt1:9	And Ozias begat Joatham; and Joatham begat Achaz; and Achaz begat Ezekias;
3756	Matt1:10	And Ezekias begat Manasses; and Manasses begat Amon; and Amon begat Josias;
3757	Matt1:11	And Josias begat Jechonias and his brethren, about the time they were carried away to Babylon:
3758	Matt1:12	And after they were brought to Babylon, Jechonias begat Salathiel; and Salathiel begat Zorobabel;
3759	Matt1:13	And Zorobabel begat Abiud; and Abiud begat Eliakim; and Eliakim begat Azor;
3760	Matt1:14	And Azor begat Sadoc; and Sadoc begat Achim; and Achim begat Eliud;
3761	Matt1:15	And Eliud begat Eleazar; and Eleazar begat Matthan; and Matthan begat Jacob;
3762	Matt1:16	And Jacob begat Joseph the husband of Mary, of whom was born Jesus, who is called Christ.
3763	Matt1:17	So all the generations from Abraham to David are fourteen generations; and from David until the carrying away into Babylon are fourteen generations; and from the carrying away into Babylon unto Christ are fourteen generations.
3764	Luke3:23	And Jesus himself began to be about thirty years of age, being (as was supposed) the son of Joseph, which was the son of Heli,
3765	Luke3:24	Which was the son of Matthat, which was the son of Levi, which was the son of Melchi, which was the son of Janna, which was the son of Joseph,
3766	Luke3:25	Which was the son of Mattathias, which was the son of Amos, which was the son of Naum, which was the son of Esli, which was the son of Nagge,
3767	Luke3:26	Which was the son of Maath, which was the son of Mattathias, which was the son of Semei, which was the son of Joseph, which was the son of Juda,

THE TREE OF LIFE

3768	Luke3:27	Which was the son of Joanna, which was the son of Rhesa, which was the son of Zorobabel, which was the son of Salathiel, which was the son of Neri,
3769	Luke3:28	Which was the son of Melchi, which was the son of Addi, which was the son of Cosam, which was the son of Elmodam, which was the son of Er,
3770	Luke3:29	Which was the son of Jose, which was the son of Eliezer, which was the son of Jorim, which was the son of Matthat, which was the son of Levi,
3771	Luke3:30	Which was the son of Simeon, which was the son of Juda, which was the son of Joseph, which was the son of Jonan, which was the son of Eliakim,
3772	Luke3:31	Which was the son of Melea, which was the son of Menan, which was the son of Mattatha, which was the son of Nathan, which was the son of David,
3773	Luke3:32	Which was the son of Jesse, which was the son of Obed, which was the son of Booz, which was the son of Salmon, which was the son of Naasson,
3774	Luke3:33	Which was the son of Aminadab, which was the son of Aram, which was the son of Esrom, which was the son of Phares, which was the son of Juda,
3775	Luke3:34	Which was the son of Jacob, which was the son of Isaac, which was the son of Abraham, which was the son of Thara, which was the son of Nachor,
3776	Luke3:35	Which was the son of Saruch, which was the son of Ragau, which was the son of Phalec, which was the son of Heber, which was the son of Sala,
3777	Luke3:36	Which was the son of Cainan, which was the son of Arphaxad, which was the son of Sem, which was the son of Noe, which was the son of Lamech,
3778	Luke3:37	Which was the son of Mathusala, which was the son of Enoch, which was the son of Jared, which was the son of Maleleel, which was the son of Cainan,
3779	Luke3:38	Which was the son of Enos, which was the son of Seth, which was the son of Adam, which was the son of God.